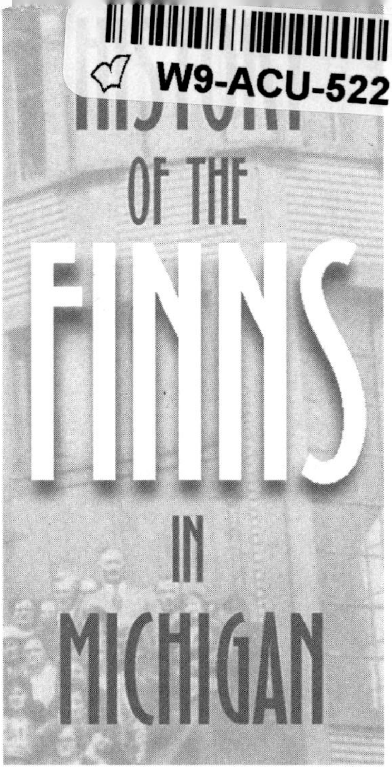
OF THE
FINNS
IN
MICHIGAN

Dr. Armas K. E. Holmio, archivist,
Suomi College.

HISTORY OF THE FINNS IN MICHIGAN

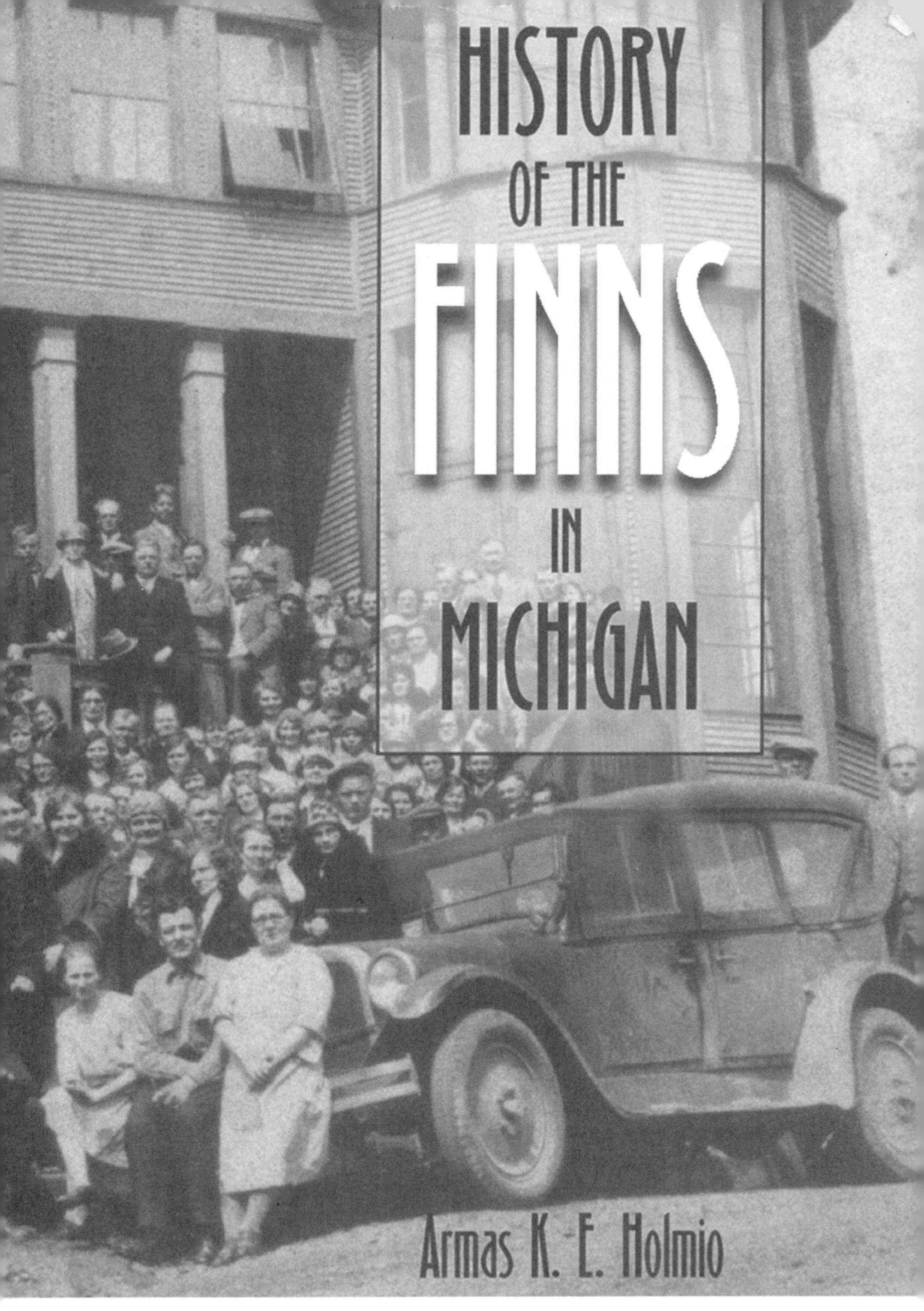

Armas K. E. Holmio

Translated by Ellen M. Ryynanen

ayne State University Press Detroit

GREAT LAKES BOOKS

A complete listing of the books in this series can be found at the back of this volume.

PHILIP P. MASON, Editor
Department of History, Wayne State University

DR. CHARLES K. HYDE, Associate Editor
Department of History, Wayne State University

Manufactured in the United States of America.
05 04 03 02 01 5 4 3 2 1

Library of Congress Cataloging-in-Publication Data

Holmio, Armas Kustaa Ensio, 1897–
History of the Finns in Michigan / by Armas K.E. Holmio ; translated by Ellen M. Ryynanen.
p. cm.—(Great Lakes books)
Includes bibliographical references.
ISBN 0-8143-2790-7 (cloth : alk. paper)—ISBN 0-8143-2974-8 (pbk. : alk. paper)
1. Finnish Americans—Michigan—History. I. Title. II. Series.
F575.F5 H65 2001
977.4'00494541—dc21 00-051330

Unless otherwise noted, all photographs are provided courtesy of the Finnish American Historical Archives, Finlandia University, Hancock, Michigan.

Published with the generous assistance of the Finlandia Foundation Trust

Contents

Foreword

After World War II Armas K. E. Holmio and other Finnish Americans began to explore their immigrant past. The immigrant generation was fast disappearing along with its organizations and newspapers. During the heyday of immigrant life before the war, few individuals had the resources or the time to preserve systematically evidence of the Finnish experience. Because the present demanded much from them in coping with the vicissitudes of living in a new land, it left immigrants little time to think how the future might view them. Within the two decades after the war, however, Holmio and others made a frantic effort to salvage the evidence needed to prepare historical accounts of their past.

In 1945 Suomi College in Hancock, Michigan (renamed Finlandia University in July 2000), renewed its erstwhile work of collecting Finnish American historical materials on the occasion of its fiftieth anniversary. The collecting had started in 1932, but the Great Depression stalled the work. The Suomi Synod, or Finnish American Evangelical Lutheran Church, which operated the college and its seminary, lacked resources to continue it. Soon after the war's end, however, the college reconsidered the matter and began to plan the establishment of the Finnish American Historical Archives.

Professor John I. Kolehmainen of Heidelberg College (Ohio) spent 1945–1946 at the college and assisted the planners of the archives. Kolehmainen, the leading American scholar of Finnish immigration, also surveyed the materials held by the college and prepared a bibliographical guide of immigrant publications. In 1947 the college published his guide under the title *The Finns in America.*[1] In 1950 the Finnish American Historical Archives finally acquired its own room, which was tended on a part-time basis by a college librarian.

Armas Holmio came on the scene in 1946 just after Kolehmainen completed his stay in Hancock. The college had invited him to become professor of history, particularly church history. Assuming responsibility as archivist of the Finnish American Historical Archives in 1954, Holmio also later served as a seminary dean. Born in Finland in 1897, he had studied at the Theological Department of the University of Helsinki and was ordained in 1921. Before coming to the United States in 1926, he began his professional career as literature director of the Finnish Missionary Society from 1921 to 1929 and then served as Finnish seamen's pastor in San Francisco from 1930 to 1933, and as pastor of Finnish congregations in Boston and Cape Cod, Massachusetts, from 1933 to 1943. During World War II he served the U.S. Army as a chaplain and worked also with its military intelligence branch. In addition, in 1940 he received a doctorate in theology from Boston University, writing a dissertation that was published as *The Lutheran Reformation and the Jews: The Birth of the Protestant Jewish Missions.*[2] Holmio died in 1977.

When Holmio arrived in America in the mid-1920s, the influx of immigrants from Finland had peaked. In 1920 the number of foreign-born Finns in the United States reached its highest level at 149,824. Thereafter their numbers declined as U.S. immigration policies, the Great Depression, and other factors slowed the influx to an infinitesimal level. By 1940 the immigrant generation numbered 117,210, and in 1950, 95,506; ten years later it was only 67,395, or less than half the total in 1920.

Although the immigrant generation managed to maintain its community activities—such as churches, labor halls, and newspapers—at a high level until the 1940s, it could no longer do so after World War II. Their community life lost much of its vitality because of declining numbers. U.S.–born Finnish Americans did not always embrace the cultural activities of their parents, and during the war they began dispersing from immigrant centers to seek work elsewhere. Finns reduced the level of their institutional life: labor halls were closed; the *Päivälehti* was the first of several major newspapers to suspend operations; the Suomi Synod merged in 1962 with the Lutheran Church in America; and the Central Cooperative Wholesale combined in 1963 with a non-Finnish organization. The immigrant era was fast closing.

Even before the immigrant era had reached its plateau, however, Finnish Americans were occasionally exploring their past. They did so not so much to preserve a golden age as to mark milestones in their lives. Their history began in the 1860s with the arrival of the earliest immigrants from the Russian Grand Duchy of Finland. Immigrant numbers peaked between 1899 and the eve of World War I partly because of political unrest and the lack of land and jobs in Finland. After the war Finland achieved independence and underwent a bitter civil war. While 20 percent or more of the immigrants returned to Finland, the others worked in such fields as mining, agriculture, and domestic service. They organized all kinds of competing societies and churches as well as newspapers in adapting to their new environment. Soon they were recording their organizational histories. In short, all were struggling to create Finnish-American history.

After working as an editor for the *Siirtolainen* (The immigrant) of Brooklyn, New York, in the 1890s, Akseli Järnefelt returned to Finland where he published a survey of Finnish American communities. Besides drawing on his own journalistic work, Järnefelt acknowledged ten editors and clergymen for furnishing him with information. Over two-thirds of his book is devoted to surveys of immigrant settlements in a tier of northern states from New England to the West Coast. Brief chapters focus on Finns in Alaska and Canada and the seventeenth-century New Sweden colony. Most chapters highlight the coming of Finns as well as their employment and institutional life in a chronological framework. In addition, one brief chapter discusses Swede Finns. The last fifth of the book reviews community life: churches, schools, temperance societies, the labor movement, women's activities, and newspapers. The author reassured his readers in Finland that, except for a few socialists and others who promoted class hatred, the community life was uplifting the immigrants and need not make the old homeland ashamed of them.[3]

In contrast, immigrant churchmen promoted the writing of histories that were inspirational in nature for the benefit of Finns staying in the United States. In 1911 the Reverend William Rautanen of the Suomi Synod completed a book reviewing forty years of competition between Finnish churches. Although he favored the Evangelical Lutherans for remaining closest to their mother church in Finland, Rautanen concluded that Finnish-American churches would ensure the survival of their faith after they lost their national identity through the "melting pot" in the United States.[4] Juho Nikander, who was the leading Suomi Synod founder, edited a volume on the twenty-fifth anniversary of his church and thanked God for its progress which gave renewed hope that it would continue to move forward.[5]

Likewise their socialist rivals turned to history. The socialist newspaper *Työmies*, for example, covered the history of its first ten years in an anniversary booklet in which an editor, Toivo Hiltunen, recounted the decade's experiences as paving the way for an even more powerful socialist movement in the future.[6] In 1925 the socialist editor Frans J. Syrjälä wrote an account of the Finnish-American labor movement that celebrated past accomplishments: workers had better economic opportunities and respect than before because of the participation of Finns in strikes and other struggles.[7]

But no immigrant was more diligent in pursuing the past than Solomon Ilmonen who was a graduate of the first seminary class in Hancock. In 1912 he wrote a book on the waxing and waning fortunes of the Finnish National Temperance Brotherhood. Despite demanding pastoral duties that took him to states from Massachusetts to California, he pursued historical inquiries in local libraries and contacted Finns for information about themselves and fellow immigrants. In particular, he collected biographical information for three volumes on early Finnish immigrants as well as those who arrived later; the third volume lists names of immigrants who arrived in various communities after the 1880s. His other historical writings include an account of the Finnish experience in New Sweden in Delaware during the 1600s. Furthermore, he tried unsuccessfully to establish a permanent Finnish American historical society.[8]

In 1930–31 Ilmonen completed his two-volume history with thirty-three chapters on Finnish-American culture. Three chapters survey immigrant settlements, notable events, and mine accidents. Eleven deal with organized religious and temperance activities, and one with the socialist movement. Another group covers schools, newspapers, athletics, literature, music, and benefit societies. Other chapters focus on the Finnish presence in business, agriculture, professions, and public life. Two discuss Finns in World War I and their wartime loyalty, and three highlight immigrant links with the old country: helping Finland, visiting there, and keeping other connections.[9]

Despite their catalogue of various competing organized activities, the volumes suggest that early immigrants arrived with a nationalist legacy of a cultural consensus rooted in the Lutheran faith of Finland, but they had difficulty recreating that consensus. This failure was due to the lack of resources and clergymen, religious rivalries, and influences of the dominant American secular culture. By the early 1890s, subsequently, the anticlerical movement and the socialists divided immigrant communities even more than before. Ilmonen attributed the spread of socialism and the rejection of the religious legacy of Finland to the influx of newer radical immigrants; they did not support the work of their predecessors who had established churches and temperance organizations in the United States. Nationalistic-minded Finns blamed socialists for endangering the reputations of all Finns as good workers and loyal Americans. These Finns reinforced the movement to establish a consensus by affirming a nationalistic religious-based legacy from Finland that they argued had worked to enrich the cultural life of the United States[10] In short, Ilmonen amplified Järnefelt's formula for historical writing that could not ignore the divisions within Finnish immigrant communities.

Finnish American scholars also between the two world wars explored the immigrant experience. Their professional writings reflected the influence of the new social sciences preoccupied with analyzing the extent of acculturation, or "Americanization," generally among immigrant groups. The first Finnish American scholar to do so was Clemens Niemi who in 1919 completed a master's thesis in sociology at the University of Chicago on the Americanization of Finns in Houghton County, Michigan. Niemi's conclusion was that the assimilation of the Finns was "so swift that he will not present any conflicting racial problem in the future." Even the less "thoughtful" Finnish workers (presumably the radicals) were assimilating because they copied both "good" and "bad" aspects of the American labor movement.[11]

The process of assimilation drew the attention of other scholars such as John Wargelin who was president of Suomi College. While working for a master's degree at the University of Michigan, Wargelin prepared a paper for a sociology course that became the main basis of his book, *The Americanization of the Finns.* He concluded that Finns were assimilating well because there were no "very radical differences between the social environment and the cultural status of the old country [Finland] and those of America."[12]

In 1931 Eino F. Laakso praised the educational and social advances of first- and second-generation Finnish Americans in Massachusetts that speeded their Americanization.[13] Non-Finnish scholars, most notably Eugene Van Cleef, agreed that Finns were adapting to the new country, and that their radicalism was disappearing in the process.[14]

Of the second-generation Finnish American scholars, only John I. Kolehmainen devoted his professional writing as a historian to the Finnish immigrant experience. In 1937 he completed a doctoral dissertation on Ohio's Finns which not only focused on such topics as employment and settlement, but also dealt with religious, socialist, and other organizational activities that were just as divisive as elsewhere. Kolehmainen concluded, however, that few Ohio Finns had been lured by the gospel of class struggle.[15] His research led by the end of World War II to prolific publishing of articles on a wide range of Finnish-related topics such as intermarriage, cooperatives, language patterns, Michigan newspapers, and the rural background of emigration from Finland.[16]

From 1945 to the 1960s new Finnish American scholars intensified their study of the disappearing immigrant past. Kolehmainen continued his explorations that produced, among others, an appreciative volume on the newspaper *Raivaaja* and another one on the farmers who struggled on northern Wisconsin's cutover lands and rejected both "an outworn immigrant garb" and "an inadequate working-class philosophy" in building cooperatives.[17] Walfrid Jokinen completed both a thesis and a dissertation on a sociological profile of Finns, emphasizing their adaptation to American society.[18] In 1957 A. William Hoglund wrote a dissertation emphasizing the influence of both the old homeland and the American environment in shaping the organizational life of Finns between 1880 and 1920.[19]

In Finland other scholars, notably at the University of Turku, probed the immigrant story. By 1974 the scholarly talent in various disciplines in the United States and abroad made possible the first international conference on the Finnish immigrant experience. More than five hundred scholars and lay persons attended the conference held at the University of Minnesota–Duluth.[20] The conference was followed by four others, the last one taking place in 1996.

Lay persons were even more numerous in this search for immigrant history. The Hiawatha Land Finnish American Historical Society in Crystal Falls, Michigan, began to collect immigrant-related materials which were eventually transferred to the Finnish American Historical Archives. Also the Crystal Falls society erected a granite marker to honor the first Finnish settlers in the area. In places such as Hibbing, Minnesota, Conneant, Ohio, and Rolla, North Dakota, Finns erected similar markers in the 1950s. In addition, Finnish Americans supported the Duluth conference in 1974 and contributed to the Finnish collection of the Immigration History Research Center which had opened at the University of Minnesota in 1965.

The most active historical nonacademic group was the Minnesota Finnish American Historical Society. Its founders included Alex Kyyhkynen of Duluth and other prominent participants in the tercentenary celebration of the arrival of Finns and Swedes in Delaware in 1638. In 1943 Kyyhkynen suggested that a painting of Finnish pioneer settlers should be commissioned for presentation to the state of Minnesota. When state officials agreed to accept such a painting, the project's sponsors established the Minnesota Finnish American Historical Society in 1943. The society's growth was somewhat slow until the celebration of Minnesota's centennial as a state in 1949 when it organized a special "Finnish day." The society also asked local chapters to raise money and collect materials for a book on the history of the state's Finns.

By 1953 the project was launched with a plan to prepare thematic chapters for a book on the state's Finns that reflected the influence of the scholar Walfrid Jokinen.[21] Its sponsors changed the plan, however, for a Finnish-language book with chapters focusing mainly on Finns in the state's major regions and providing short historical accounts of settlements and activities in particular communities: local interests prevailed in the volume that began with three chapters on the background of the Finnish people in Finland, Finnish immigration, and Minnesota's history. Jokinen was not retained to write the book, because as one historical society leader said, immigrant Finns rather than "Americans" should determine how to portray the historical record of themselves.[22] Hans R. Wasastjerna, a young scholar from Finland studying on a Fulbright scholarship at the University of Minnesota, prepared the volume. The book appeared in 1957, and subsequently Toivo Rosvall translated it into English.[23]

The Minnesota book inspired Michigan Finns to prepare a similar history of their state. In 1958 twenty-two Finns met at Suomi College to establish the Michigan Finnish Historical Society with the goal of producing a comparable book. The participants represented church, temperance, labor, and cooperative groups as well as the nationalist Kaleva fraternal order. They later designated Armas Holmio to prepare the volume as he was familiar with Finnish literary materials that he was collecting and organizing at the Finnish American Historical Archives. It took eight years to complete the book, partly because its author could not devote himself full time to its preparation.[24] The book appeared in 1967.[25]

The format of the 639-page book parallels somewhat that of its 780-page Minnesota counterpart. Both begin with initial chapters describing their respective states as well as two others which introduce the people of Finland and trace Finnish immigration; also the Michigan volume has a separate chapter on the Finns who settled in New Sweden. (The English translation of the Michigan book omits the initial chapter on the state.) The next group of chapters in each volume has sections on particular communities within each major county or region where Finns lived and worked. The Minnesota book devotes almost 90 percent of its space to this group, and the Michigan volume uses almost 25 percent and emphasizes early arrivals from Finland as well as employment conditions. While the former similarly discusses both first-comers and employment in the settlements, it also incorporates extensive discussions of organizational activities. In contrast, the Michigan book separates such activities into another group, devoting over 35 percent to separate chapters on churches, temperance societies, labor, cooperatives, and the Kaleva lodge. Its organizational section is followed by chapters on Swede Finns, cultural activities (such as newspaper publishing and Suomi College), parishes of origin in Finland, relationships between immigrants and Finland, and biographical sketches. Just like the Minnesota book, the Michigan one concludes with lists of bibliographies and reproductions of photographs.

Holmio's narrative history of Michigan's Finns is extensively documented. It makes a marked effort to demonstrate with footnotes and bibliographical references the sources of information about immigrant history that still aroused debate in the 1960s. Although Solomon Ilmonen had discussed many of the same matters that Holmio does, the former did not make any scholarly attempt to identify his sources. On the other hand, Holmio does not employ the academic approach to immigrants that Finnish American and other scholars were beginning to use after World War II.

He was perhaps closest to the pioneer Finnish American scholar John I. Kolehmainen who emphasized the narrative approach rather than new statistical and other social science methodologies.[26] So his book does not employ analytic concepts about such matters as gender, social class, ethnicity, and community; thus, its discussion on the parishes or origin is not connected with explanations of immigrant behavior. But just as the Minnesota book, Holmio's volume often places its state's experiences in the context of the evolution of Finnish communities generally in the United States; for example, the immigrant press served readers both in Michigan and in other states. In a sense, Holmio's state study is Finnish-American history writ large.

Holmio saw a synthetic thread of Finnish consensus, or cultural nationalism, in the immigrant experience. That consensus was mirrored in the multigroup sponsorship of the project that produced his book. Just as Ilmonen and Wasastjerna, Holmio dealt with ideological and organizational rivalries that once divided the Finns. He, too, did not ignore the rift over radicalism that developed before World War I. At the same time he recognized the later decline of the labor movement that had initially opposed nationalistic fellow immigrants. The Russo-Finnish War of 1939–40, Holmio emphasized, speeded up bringing together immigrants irrespective of political and religious differences.[27] Ex-radicals came to affirm their Finnishness particularly after World War II. Recalling that immigrants often had arrived embittered with a homeland that had condemned them for leaving, Holmio expressed pleasure that a healthy generic nationalist (Finnish) spirit had survived in the hearts of old immigrants.[28] The unstated corollary is appreciation for the decline of labor hostility to that spirit. In short,

Holmio's volume is a celebration of the coming together of Michigan Finns who wanted to read about their history in Finnish.

It is fortunate to have an English-language translation of the book. Few American readers have maintained the language skill to read it in the original. There are still relatively few English-language books and other publications on the history of Finnish immigrants. The exceptions include the English translation of the Minnesota volume and the writings of scholars such as Kolehmainen and Hoglund. In 1977 Kolehmainen completed a book on the basis of his doctoral dissertation that focuses on the Finns of Ohio, Pennsylvania, and West Virginia. Other notable publications are the proceedings of the first three international Finnforum conferences on Finnish immigrants and selected papers from the fifth conference in the *Journal of Finnish Studies* (December 1997). Still others include the annual issues of *Finnish Americana* edited by Michael G. Karni, the occasional booklets of the Finnish American Historical Society of the West, and the studies of Finland scholars such as Reino Kero, Keijo Virtanen, and Auvo Kostiainen. In translation, Holmio's book becomes an important addition to this still skimpy literature. The book not only records the history of Finns in Michigan but also relates it to the larger dimensions of the Finnish experience elsewhere in the United States.

A. William Hoglund
University of Connecticut

1 The Origin of the Finns

Helmi Warren, who was the daughter of a Finnish-American druggist and, in her own right, a well-known travel agent, has described the situation with regard to Finns during her early school days in Calumet, Michigan, in the 1890s. Most of the children in Helmi's grade were Finnish—flaxen-haired and blue-eyed. But according to American textbooks, the Finns were Mongolians. The teacher who, though kind, was unfamiliar with the secrets of history, attempted to soften the blow by explaining that the Finns were a mixed race, partly white and partly yellow. She told the children they should not be unhappy about it because "mixed races are always the most gifted." Helmi occasionally took a little neighbor home with her at lunchtime. One day she in turn was invited to her friend's home. She had barely reached the front porch when the friend's mother realized that her daughter's playmate was a Finn. Helmi was turned away immediately, and the daughter of the house was forbidden to associate with "that Mongolian."[1] John Wargelin, a pastor of the Evangelical Lutheran Church and a former president of Suomi College, also tells how, when he was a child in Crystal Falls some years earlier, he and his friends were ridiculed and stoned on their way to school. "Because of our strange language," he says, "we were considered an alien race who had no right to settle in this country."[2]

The Finns themselves were the chief offenders in supporting the Mongolian theory of their origin, which cannot be justified scientifically. Inspired by Hegel's philosophy of history, the schools of national history came into being. Guizot of France, Macaulay of England, Treitschke of Germany, Karamzin of Russia, and Graetz of the Jews each wrote a monumental history of his nation, in which his own country was portrayed as having had a glorious past. In this past were seen to be the supportive and directive forces of civilization. Even the smaller nations entered this race in which it appeared that nothing would be lost, but that national glory would be gained instead. Asia, *officina gentium* (cradle of nations) with its mystery and antiquity had a strong appeal to researchers as a the source of nations.[3] Körösi Csoma (1784–1842), a Hungarian, became a monk among the Tibetan lamas and developed the theory that Tibet was the original home of the Magyars. Soon the Finns, too, were in the race, tracing the roots of their family tree to the Far East and trying to prove that they, as a nation, were thousands of years older than any west European country.

The originator of the Mongolian theory of the origin of the Finns was a German anthropologist, Johann Friedrich Blumenbach (1752–1840). On the basis of comparative anatomy and cranial measurements he divided mankind into five races: Caucasian, or White: Mongolian, or Yellow; Malayan, or Brown; Negro, or Black; and American, or Red. He happened to classify the Finns as belonging to the Yellow race.

Independently of Blumenbach, M. A. Castrén (1813–1852), a brilliant Finnish linguist and ethnologist (who, while still a young man, collapsed under the strain of his Asian tours) made a study of Ural-Altaic philology and systematized it. He himself thought that as a by-product of this activity he had discovered the origin of the Finns. In November 1843, on reaching the village of Obdorsk beyond the Ural Mountains, he assumed that he was "among people who, whether near or distant in lineage, had descended from Mother Kaleva," and he rejoiced in being able "to breathe the air which had produced the first spark of life in the breasts of his forefathers." On September 9, 1849, in a lecture at the University of Helsinki, Castrén definitely located the original home of the Finnish peoples as having been in the Altai Mountains.[4] Thus, the theory of the Asian origin of the Finns received academic endorsement. For decades, even leading scientists held fast to the opinion that the Finns were related to Asian peoples.

This theory provided poets and other writers with exceptional subject matter. August Ahlquist, in his "fairy tale" tells of five Maidens—Tja, Erma, Unus, Kri, and Uometar—who left the shores of an Altaic mountain lake to travel far to the west in search of their friend, a youth by the name of Vapaus. Each maiden took a part of his name, attaching it to her own. Thus their names became Vatja, Perma, Aunus, Ukri, and Suometar. Eventually they became the ancestors of the new

Finnish peoples.[5] Juhani Aho, in his well-known short story, "Sauna," wrote as follows: "That old, dear sauna of mine, the true ideal of a Finnish sauna, the most lasting tradition from the times of our Altaic ancestors."

The theory of the Asiatic origin of the Finns appeared even in textbooks, first in Finland, then in other countries. Y. S. Yrjo-Koskinen (1830–1903) incorporated Castrén's theory into his history of the Finnish people, which was published in 1869–72. He classified the "nations which had performed on the stage of history" into Semitics, Aryans or Indo-Europeans, and Turanians or Ural-Altaics. He subdivided the last-named group into four: Tunguses, Mongols, Turks, and Finns. Supported by Yrjo-Koskinen's history, which was used for decades as an authority, the theory of the Asian origin of the Finns and of their kinship with the Mongols was undisputed. It is no wonder that in its uniqueness this theory found its way into German encyclopedias, and from them into Anglo-Saxon literature.[6]

The distinguishing characteristics of the Mongolian are a short, slender figure, small hands, yellowish skin, and black, straight hair. During the uncritical period, no one inquired as to where Finns of this description could be found. The Mongolian theory of the origin of the Finns disappeared generations ago from scientific works, and from Europe in general. In America, however, it has been kept alive by various means, mostly through some writers' ignorance of the facts, but sometimes deliberately as an imagined attack on the Finns.[7] The Finns themselves were instrumental in bringing the question of their Mongolianism to America, and it is they who have kept it alive to the present. Socialist Matti Kurikka, with his black hair streaming over his shoulders, and accompanying himself on the piano, sang in Finnish American labor halls at the turn of the century:

> Why did the Huguenots leave the beautiful country of France?
> Why did William Penn go to distant Pennsylvania?
> Why did ancient Abraham leave his home?
> Why did Vaino's people not stay beyond the Ural Mountains?
> Why can't Suomi, even now, keep her peninsula as her own?[8]

In Sointula, the Utopian settlement founded on Malcolm Island in British Columbia by Kurikka, the people of Kaleva (Finns) considered the Indians their kinsmen. Using verse of Finland as a model, J. W. Eloheimo wrote (freely translated):

When for her son, Ilmatar
Found a bride
Whose name was Suometar
From the Altaic tribes.[9]

An enthusiastic supporter of the Finnish cause, Pastor Evert Maattala, in speaking of *Kalevala* in his book *Why Do I Want to Be a Finn?* published in 1915, wrote, "That epic is like a deep, mysterious night in whose womb hundreds of generations of Finnish peoples on the mountain slopes of Asia were conceived, and dreamed of their future existence."[10] John Lauttamus, a blacksmith and a folk writer, in his 1922 publication, *Amerikan Tuulahduksia*, has his hero Vilho Veijola say, "It is not by mere chance that our ancestors migrated from the steppes of Asia to the Finnish peninsula and settled there."[11] In the same year, C. Rudolph Raattama wrote that the Finns as a race were a Scandinavian and Asian mixture.[12] Fresh impetus for flights of imagination was given by a Finnish artist and sculptor, Georg Sigurd Wettenhoff-Asp (1870–1946) who, under the name of Vettenhovi-Aspa, produced some strange philological ideas.[13] He attempted to prove that the Finnish language was the original language of mankind, and that the Finns were the torchbearers of civilization, ahead of all the rest of the world. To him, Gaurisankar, which was still considered the highest mountain peak in the world, was the *auringon sankari* (sun hero) of the Finns. According to him, the ancient name of Egypt was Kemi, the Finnish *kymi*, or mighty river, which was later called the Nile. Also, the island of Sumatra was called Suomaatar by the prehistoric Finns. China received its name from the Finnish word *kiinni*, meaning closed, because China was closed off by a solid wall. Palestine was originally Pallastienoo. These childish conclusions were accepted by the Finns of Finland with a tongue-in-cheek attitude. But among Finnish Americans the situation was different. For example, a writer using the pen name of E. A. Louhi, took them seriously and wrote in his introduction to *The Delaware Finns* how the Finns, seven and eight thousand years ago, populated the endless steppes reaching from Mongolia to the Danube, and how the cultures of the ancient Sumerians, Egyptians, and Babylonians had their origin in the Finnish civilization.[14] It is interesting to note how these completely erroneous conceptions, which have for ages been forgotten in Finland, have continued to thrive among Finnish Americans. Even as late as the 1950s, a Suomi College student who was deeply loyal to his nationality and its history tried to prove that the "Scourge of God," Attila, and his Huns were Finns. In 1961, *Työmies-Eteenpäin* newspaper gave space to a correspondent from Palmer, who discussed the Asiatic home of the Finns and the origin of the Finns from the Ainu of Japan.[15] In 1962, the newspaper *Työväen Osuustoimintalehti* gave space to an Ontario correspondent who, using an "English encyclopedia" as an authority, wrote that the Finnish people had originated in Asia.[16] *Siirtokansan Kalenteri* of 1962 contains an article, the writer of which in all seriousness says that the warning words on Belshazzar's palace walls "mene, mene, tekel ufarsin" remind him of the Finnish "mene, mene, tekeella vaara" (go, go, danger threatens).[17] He also believes that the Finns descended from one of the ten lost tribes of Israel. Similar types of stories appeared as "history" even in *Kalevainen* of 1962.[18]

At first glance, there are two reasons for this peculiar circumstance in which the misleading theories that developed during the last century should still crop up in American writings, generations after they had completely disappeared in Finland. The first is that most libraries of Finnish societies were established at the end of the 1800s and at the beginning of the 1900s and recent literature was seldom acquired. Insofar as any of these libraries still exist, they still do not offer their patrons the results of modern research. The same still holds true all down the line, even among the educated Finns who make use of Finnish writings: their home libraries very seldom include even the first *Tietosanakirja* (encyclopedia). The second reason is that up to the present no definite attempt has been made to rectify, in American publications, either false concepts of the origin of the Finns or misconceptions concerning the history of Finland.

A few illustrations will suffice to show that the "Mongolian question" has been a sort of thorn in the flesh to Finnish Americans for generations. For example, the Webster English dictionary, basic authority on thousands of questions to American school teachers, the first edition of which appeared in 1828, even in the 1948 edition says that the Finns are "of ancient Mongolian origin."[19] Another leading English dictionary, *Funk and Wagnalls*, whose first edition appeared in 1891–93, still states in the edition of 1956 that Finnish is a name for peoples belonging to ancient Mongolian stock.[20] From *Webster* and *Funk and Wagnalls*, this erroneous concept was transferred to encyclopedias and history and geography textbooks, and from them into American fiction.

At Suomi College in the spring of 1962, the students in a class studying the history of Finland found similar statements in about forty publications. The following examples were chosen from several prominent works and are given in chronological order. The *New Schaff-Herzog Encyclopedia* states that "the Finns, a branch of the Ural-Altaic race, originated on the banks of the Yenisei River or Lake Baikal in Asia."[21]

The *New Practical Reference Library* describes a typical Finn as having a short but strongly built body, a round head, a low, curving forehead, a flat face, high cheekbones, and slanting eyes.[22] The *World Book*, an encyclopedia much used in schools by children and young people, states in the edition of 1919, that outwardly Finns resemble Mongolians, to whom they are racially related.[23] Edna Ferber, in her novel *Come and Get It*, which is about life in the logging camps of northern Michigan and Wisconsin, writes that in the work area cooking camp "at the stove . . . presided the cook, a slant-eyed Finn."[24] In his lively descriptive work about Upper Michigan, *Call It North Country*, John Bartlow Martin writes of the Michigan Finns that "many changed their names, but they could not change their high cheekbones, their flat foreheads."[25] Most unexpected is the erroneous statement made by Professor William L. Langer of Harvard University in his book *An Encyclopedia of World History, Ancient, Medieval, Modern*, in which he writes, "The Bulgarians . . . were members of the Finno-Tatar race, probably related to the Huns."[26] *The New Funk & Wagnalls Encyclopedia* reports that "Finns are a people of possibly Mongolian origin."[27] On October 26, 1958, the *Milwaukee Sentinel*, a newspaper that is widely circulated in Michigan, carried an article by Huey Bracken about Russia's strained relations with Finland. It was up-to-date and favorable toward Finland, but toward the end of it there was a singular statement, apparently taken from some obsolete encyclopedia, to the effect that the original Finns were part of a huge Asiatic invasion and were related to the Hungarians, Turks, and Mongolians. A similar statement appears in the 1962 *World Almanac*, a publication of the *New York World Telegram* and the *Sun*. In August 1961 a well-known newspaper columnist, George E. Sokolsky, whose witty articles were read throughout the country, published an article on Mongolia. In this article, which appeared in hundreds of newspapers, there was a fanciful statement to the effect that the Chinese and Japanese are not Mongolians and that the Mongols are more closely related to the Turks, who are called Uigurs and who later appeared in Hungary and Finland.[28]

Among Finnish Americans, the best-known and almost classic example of a scientific blunder is the one by history professor Richard M. Dorson of the University of Michigan in his collection of the folklore of Upper Michigan, *Bloodstoppers and Bearwalkers*, published in 1952. He began his introduction to the folktales of Michigan Finns with these surprising words:

> The coming of the Finn has rocked the northwoods country. He is today what the red man was two centuries ago, the exotic stranger

> from another world. In many ways the popular myths surrounding the Indian and the Finn run parallel. Both derive from a shadowy Mongolian stock—"just look at their raised cheekbones and slanting eyes." Both live intimately with the fields and woods. Both possess supernatural stamina, strength, and tenacity. Both drink feverishly and fight barbarously. Both practice shamanistic magic and ritual, drawn from a deep well of folk belief. Both are secretive, clannish, inscrutable, and steadfast in their own peculiar social code. Even the Finnish and Indian epics are supposedly kin, for did not Longfellow model "The Song of Hiawatha" on the form of the *Kalevala?*[29]

These oddities reported by Dorson and published by the Harvard University Press are sometimes presented by Finnish Americans as burlesques for the pleasure of audiences at their festivities. Dorson's sources of information on Finns and their mythology were, among others, the works of the Italian, Domenico Comparetti, and the Englishman, John Abercromby, which were outdated by half a century.[30]

Finnish Americans, for the most part, have had a good-natured attitude toward the matter, or they have remained completely indifferent to it. Only occasionally have they roused to underscore their western racial heritage. The Reverand Antti Lepisto Sr. did just that by word and pen while studying at the University of Chicago in 1919.[31] Twice this has been done more forcefully, first in Minnesota, then in Michigan. The Minnesota case had for its background the immigration law of 1882, which forbade entry into the United States and the right of citizenship to anyone of the colored races excepting Africans. On January 4, 1908, a certain district prosecutor by the name of John E. Sweet attempted, on the basis of this law, to deny citizenship papers to John Svan and sixteen other Finns. Svan, according to Sweet, was a Mongol and, therefore, a colored person who had no legal right to become a United States citizen.

This case aroused an enormous amount of interest among the Finns. What would their children, neighbors, and friends say? If Sweet won, the legal decision would have far-reaching consequences. Svan had prepared himself competently for the Duluth circuit court session at which the case was presented and, with his supporters, proved that Sweet's statements were groundless. The district court judge, William A. Cant, gave his decision on January 17, affirming that the Finns belonged to the white race. Among those born overseas, who are applying for citizenship in these areas of the country, he said, there are none who are more fair-skinned than the Finns. The Finnish newspapers accepted the decision with great satisfaction, with the exception of the Socialist papers, which felt that "the proletariat do not have a native land," and that "nationalism is a bourgeois concept." A certain paper said, "Our sons do not much care whether they are Celts, Mongols, or Teutons as long as they can enjoy their rights and are treated like human beings."[32] This Minnesota Mongolian story attracted much attention, even in Finland, where the famous linguist and explorer, Gustaf John Ramstedt (1873–1950), together with Professor Joos. J. Mikkola, published an article titled "Are We Mongols?" in the *Kansanvalistusseuran Kalenteri*.[33] The part of the article written by Ramstedt was published in America in the *Kalenteri* of the Finland Steamship Company Agency in 1910.[34] The writers proved that the assumption that the Finns had originated in Asia was never anything but conjecture, and that it appeared at that time (1908) only in works of authors who either did not want, or were unable, to keep pace with modern scientific developments.

The most important dispute over the Mongolian question in Michigan had a somewhat unusual background. The Prohibition Law, which had become effective in 1919 in Finland, had become impossible to enforce and had been repealed in January 1932 at an extra session of the Diet. America, too, was in the process of repealing her Prohibition Law, which had come into force on January 16, 1920. When news of the fate of the Finnish prohibition law arrived, George A. Osborn, the editor and publisher of the *Sault Evening News* and a friend of the temperance movement, on January 11, 1932, published an editorial titled "America Is Not Finland." Apparently using uncritically some antiquated encyclopedia or encyclopedias, he wrote, among other things, the following:

> The result of the alcohol plebiscite in Finland has no bearing whatever upon the United States. It can be no reflection upon American citizens of Finnish birth or ancestry to state that that country is not in a class with this in anything. It is not as intellectual and not as moral and has a temperament so different as to make comparison unfair if not odious.
>
> There are ethnologists who say the Finns are Mongols. This makes little difference because there are many high grade tartars. Tamerlane was one and Genghis and Kublai khan and like as not Alaric and that scourge of death Attila. Even the Huns are thought by many to have been half Mongol or more.
>
> The Finns are brave and clean and phlegmatic and with a courage born of the aurora borealis have fought many things in addition to the most rigorous climate in the world. The best of the Finns seeking to improve their lot immigrated to America and thus escaped the Russian knout and despotism at the same time. They make as

> good citizens as the best and the third generation is always purely American of the highest standards.
>
> The Finns that remain in Finland are similar in a way to the Canadians that remain in Canada. They have not the initiative of those who left. This lack in constructiveness is a handicap also of vision and judgment in many instances. We are stating these things in general terms.
>
> Anyhow America is not following Finland. America is endeavoring to lead the entire world to finer and better things. If Finland or any other peoples wish to monkey with poison that may be their lookout but they do it in opposition to the example and the advice of this country.
>
> America takes its wisdom from the highest source it can be found. And Finland shall come back to sense when the better Finns awaken and lead their land.

Thus, the article was based on false assumptions: Finland was pictured as a Russian province where gendarmes raged, and from where only the strongest had succeeded in escaping to America, the weaker ones remaining in the difficult circumstances of their native land. Fallacies such as these could be endured. But the unwarranted mention of Mongols in connection with Finns outraged the Finns. Two men accepted the challenge and appeared in behalf of their countrymen. They were Oscar J. Larson, a former congressman, and Pastor John Wargelin.

Oscar John Larson was born in Oulu, May 20, 1871, and arrived in Calumet in 1875 with his parents. Having graduated from the University of Michigan as the first Finnish American lawyer, he was elected attorney for the village of Red Jacket; the prosecuting attorney of Keweenaw County in 1896; and, two years later, to the same position in Houghton County. In 1907 he moved to Duluth, opened a law office, and became active in the Republican party. In 1920 this political activity led Larson, who was known as an exceptionally effective speaker, to two terms in the United States Congress. In his activities there and in other areas, Larson invariably proved himself to be a true Finn and a defender of the interests of his countrymen and of his native land.[35]

Pastor John Wargelin was born in Isokyrö, September 26, 1881, and as a child came to Champion with his parents. His father had been born in Ylistaro as Isak Wargelin, and his mother in Isokyrö as Elisabet Uitto. John Wargelin was a member of the first group of students at Suomi College, completing the seven-year course in 1904. Two years later he graduated from the theological seminary of the college and was ordained in Hancock on June 6, 1906. He received his master's degree in education from the University of Michigan in 1923. According to a story preserved in the family, the ancestor of the Wargelins was a seaman named Wolf who had escaped from a British ship and settled in Koivulahti. The name may have been derived from the corresponding Swedish term *varg*, meaning "wolf." There were many clergymen in the family. John Wargelin's great, great grandfather, Isak Wargelin (1753–1813) was a pastor in Härmä, and before him his father, Anders Wargelin (1718–1804) had been a pastor in Lapua. During the "Mongol Skirmish" John Wargelin was the president of Suomi College.

Twenty-five years earlier Wargelin, as a newly ordained young pastor, had already courageously defended the Finns against the attacks of another Sault Ste. Marie newspaper, the *Soo Times*. Now, as president of Suomi College, he again considered it his duty to speak out. His reply to Osborn was printed in the January 21, 1932, issue of the *Daily Mining Gazette* of Houghton, and parts of it were published in Finnish translation in the *Amerikan Suometar* on January 23. The *Sault Evening News* published it on February 3.

On the prohibition issue, Wargelin agreed with Osborn, noting at the same time that some of the world's prominent scientists working on the alcoholism problem were Finns—Dr. Matti Helenius-Seppala and Professor Taavi Laitinen, for example. "Finland has not yet spoken her last word on this matter." But the major part of the reply was concerned with the Mongolian question:

> After passing this judgment as a moralist [on the repeal of the Finnish Prohibition Act] he [Osborn] makes use of the disproved Mongolian theory of the origin of the Finns, evidently building up foundation for his conclusion that such a nation can not reason soundly on great social and moral questions, and that the result of the alcohol plebiscite in Finland has no significance as far as other races are concerned. . . . Why appeal to racial prejudices? Does the writer offer any proofs of his generalizations? None whatever. A considerate person would not belittle his neighbor by calling to his attention, his inferiority, neither will a fair-minded citizen appeal to popular fallacies in his reasoning on social questions. . . . Reasoning on unsound premises and with an appeal to prejudice represents a fallacy known in logic as an "argument ad populum." The editorial in question is a good example of it.

Toward the end of his answer Wargelin says:

> In justice to Finland it is fair to admit that, for example, her architecture and music are conceded a leading place in their respective fields,

> popular and higher education in Finland rank very high, and in athletics she has gained the praise of all nations. What country can boast of records like those of Paavo Nurmi? And as to the morals of the Finns, it might be necessary for us Americans to remind ourselves that we live in a glass-house before throwing stones at others.

George A. Osborn's commentary on John Wargelin's letter in the same February 3 issue was polite and mildly apologetic, referring to his opponent as "a scholar," "a gentleman," and "a distinguished Finn." Osborn wrote:

> Reading his copious reply carefully, one may conclude that the thing that got under his skin was the reference to the Mongolian theory of the origin of the Finns. Dr. Wargelin is right. There is no proof for it, any more than there is that all darker people have Negro blood or that the Mediterranean races are pigmented from Africa.

Osborn's discussion of the repeal of the Finnish prohibition law was somewhat misleading: the prohibition law was passed when Finland was under Russian rule; independent Finland shows its independence even in that it repeals a law made at that time.

Two days later, on February 5, Osborn published Oscar J. Larson's lengthy comment (dated January 21 at Duluth) on Osborn's editorial. Dignified in tone but sharply worded, the article comprised eighteen paragraphs. The first thirteen pointed out proofs of the high level of Finnish culture and of the athletic achievements of the Finns. Larson compared Finland with Greece, which also was a small country but attained the highest level of culture in its day.

> With no intention of making any invidious comparisons may I call your attention to an appraisal of the education of the people of Finland, made not by a Finn, but by an Englishman, Ernest Young. In his book, "Finland, the Land of a Thousand Lakes," he says:
>
> "No one who knows anything about the Finns will deny that they are the best educated nation in the world. Neither Germany nor America can claim equality with them in this respect."
>
> Illiteracy in Finland is less than one per cent. It is practically nil. In our own country it is six per cent. In your state of Michigan it is three per cent.
>
> Mr. Editor, it will not help the prohibition cause for us to make comparisons. The facts are against us. The people of Finland are not seeped in ignorance. They are a well-educated people.

In the fourteenth and fifteenth paragraphs of his article, Larson touched lightly on the race question:

> You intimate in the editorial that the Finns are of a Mongolian origin. If that were true, what of it? But it is not true. That theory, which was based merely on philological grounds, has been discarded by the present day ethnologists and anthropologists. It would require too much space to discuss that interesting subject fully. Suffice it to quote briefly from an article in the Encyclopedia Americana written by Harry Elmer Barnes, erstwhile professor of historical sociology, Smith College. Speaking of this race, this is what he states therein:
>
> "From the racial standpoint Ripley, the leading authority on the racial distribution of Europe, holds that the Finns are a branch of the primordial Nordic stock which inhabited the region now known as Russia and from which have been differentiated the Teutonic, Letto-Lithuanian and Finnish types."[36]

Toward the end of his article Larson examined Osborn's strange statement that the better class of Finns had moved to America and that those who were helpless, inefficient, and without initiative had been left in the old homeland.

> No, Mr, Editor, the intellectual elite of Finland nor all the venturesome and courageous did not immigrate to this country. Most of them remained there to work out Finland's destiny. With some exceptions those of us who came here were the hewers of wood and the carriers of water, the manual workers, the socalled common people. We are glad we came to this wonderful land of opportunity where the gates are wide open to achieve success in the battle of life. Our immigration is comparatively recent. Our progress has been somewhat slow, but we hope some day even some of us may also occupy a few places of power and influence in the industrial, financial, political, professional, and educational life in the country.

Larson's article appeared in its entirety in *Amerikan Suometar* of February 9, translated into Finnish. John Manni of Kettle River, Minnesota, also sent in a reply to Osborn's editorial. It was published in the February 8 issue of the *Sault Evening News*, which received other protests from many quarters, "some unsigned and bitter in tone." The Finns of Michigan were on the alert and ready to strike back when necessary. George A. Osborn, editor and publisher of the *Evening News* ended the dialogue with an editorial titled "That Finland Editorial," lamenting the loss Michigan suffered when Oscar Larson moved to Duluth, and recalling how thirty years previously at a Republican rally in Grand Rapids, Larson had made a fine speech in which Osborn's father, Chase S. Osborn, had been named candidate for governor. He admitted that the editorial staff had learned many lessons and would be more careful about what they published in the future.

It is easier to answer the question of who the Finns are not than that of who they are. The common error which historians have made in speaking of the origin of the Finns has been the confusion of language with race. The language of a people may change in a relatively short time, but the race, with its distinctive characteristics, is less easily changed. The French are a classic example of this in Europe, and the African Americans in the United States. The French are basically Celts but speak a Latin language; the African Americans are not Anglo-Saxons despite the fact that they speak English. In northern Europe the Lapps have made the Finnish language their own from time immemorial although they are not racially related to the Finns.

The genealogical roots of the Finnish language go back thousands of years. In ancient times, a forest people whom philologists call the primitive Uralians, inhabited what is now eastern Russia. To the south were the early Indo-Europeans. Both are assumed to have descended from an even earlier parent race. The Uralians spread out over broader and broader areas, and peoples who had spoken the same language became differentiated into two groups, the Finno-Ugrian and the Samoyed.[37] This separation occurred about five thousand years ago, in approximately 3000 B.C. Philology calls these peoples the Finno-Ugric and the Samoyedic parent stock. In time, the majority of the Samoyed tribes wandered into Siberia, where scattered remnants still live. The Yurak-Samoyeds, remnants of which are still found in northern Russia on the tundra in the vicinity of Archangel, remained in Europe.[38]

About 2500 B.C., the Hungarian, Ostiak, and Vogul languages developed from the original Finno-Ugric and still form their own language groups. The wanderings of the Hungarian-speaking peoples ended about 900 A.D. on the Dacian plains, whereas the Ostiaks and Voguls eventually moved to Siberia. With the continued dispersion of tribes to areas distant from each other, the Syrjenian and the Votiak languages developed and are still spoken in eastern and northeastern areas of Russia. According to philologists, these languages originated about 1000 B.C.

Approximately five hundred years later, the breaking up of the Finno-Ugric ancestral language had reached the stage at which the Chermissian and Mordvinian languages came into being. Remnants of the scattered Mordvinian tribes still inhabit middle and eastern Russia, and Cheremissians are found in the Middle Volga area. Over a period of thousands of years, there had developed, from the Finno-Ugric parent language, what may be called a basic Finnish language, from which, during the last centuries of the pre-Christian era, developed the Baltic Finnish languages: Estonian, Livonian, Votiak, Karelian, Vepsic, and Finnish. In short, the language and the peoples speaking it had gradually moved to the west and northwest. Having come this far, the researcher begins at last to be justified in speaking of a language and a people as being one.

In the last chapter of *Germania*, the Roman historian Tacitus, who died about A.D. 117, gives a grim picture of a Fennia-named people, who are sometimes assumed to have been the ancient Finns:

> Nothing can compare with the fierceness or wildness of the Fenni, and nothing is so loathesome as their filthiness and poverty. Without weapons, without horses, without permanent dwellings, they lead a nomadic life; their food consists of herbs, and their only clothing is the hides of animals, and the bare ground is their bed.

This description, however, does not in any way fit even the earliest Finns, who were hunters and fishermen and tended reindeer herds, cultivated barley and wheat, dried and threshed their grain in buildings put up for that purpose. They knew how to build homes of logs and how to provide them with thresholds and with vents for smoke. Their women spun thread, wove cloth, and adorned themselves with brooches, buckles, and rings. It is known that words for these things were already in use among primitive Finns.

The peoples who spoke the Finno-Ugric languages had, in ancient times, been in contact with peoples who spoke an Indo-European tongue; certain Finnish words are permanent proof of this fact. After a long interruption, this contact was renewed when the primitive Finns arrived in the vicinity of the Baltic Sea and came into close relationship with the Baltic peoples, who spoke an Indo-European language. The Baltic language groups are formed from the ancient Prussian, Lithuanian, and Lettish. At about the time of Christ's birth, the early Finns also came into contact with Teutonic peoples, mainly the Goths. Both the Baltic peoples and the Teutons enriched the Finno-Baltic languages with numerous new words which have been preserved, especially in the Finnish language.

Of the primitive Finns, the Livonians, who are already becoming extinct, remained on the shores of the Gulf of Riga. Extinction seems also to be the fate of the Votyaks who settled in Ingria. The Vepsianes eventually moved to the banks of the Syväri river in eastern Karelia, and the Estonians remained to the south of the Gulf of

Finland. All the Finn-related peoples, including the Hungarians, have been under Russian control permanently or temporarily during various phases of their history. Only the Finns have retained their national identity.

The movement of the Finns from the Baltic regions into Finland began at the beginning of the Christian era and continued for about eight hundred years. They arrived in their permanent homeland in three tribes. The Hämäläiset, who are considered to be the direct descendants of the primitive Finns, were the first to come over the sea to western Finland, spreading from there to the east and north. The southwestern Finns, who gave their name to the country and the nation, stayed longer in the area south of the Gulf of Finland among the Estonians, being, quite possibly, of the same stock, until they sailed across the Gulf to Finland. The Karelians, about whose tribal origin there is much disagreement among researchers, took possession of the shores of Lake Ladoga, spreading to the west, north, and east. A fourth major tribe of Finland, the Savolainens, are considered by more recent scientific researchers to be a branch of the Karelian tribe with which Hämäläinen elements have merged.[39]

It is possible that in some Finnish families there flows a thin stream of blood from the unknown prehistoric peoples from which were born the Uralians and the Indo-Europeans of long ago. Even so, the frequently mentioned relationship of Finns and Hungarians is just as distant as, for example, the relationship of the English and the Persians. Thousands of years of contact of each nation with many other nations have blended all together, so that most European nations are, in a way, second cousins to one another.

2 Early Emigration from Finland

The "Forest Finns" of Central Sweden

Although emigration from Finland reached its peak between 1890 and 1930, that period of emigration was not the only such period in the long history of the country. According to many historians, Finns had moved to Sweden already in the early Christian centuries, and they may well have been the first to settle in some parts of that country. When, at the beginning of the thirteenth century, Finnish history and Swedish history began to merge, eventually leading to the formation of a single kingdom, the gradual movement of Finns across the Gulf of Bothnia continued, so that by the time of the reign of King Gustavus Vasa (1523–1560) there were Finnish settlements of considerable size in Sweden. Duke Charles of Södermanland, son of Gustavus Vasa, encouraged the Finns to move into his duchy, promising them many advantages, because it was important to Sweden to have the large forest areas of the interior settled so that the lands would be taxable. In Savo, especially in the large parish of Rautalammi, and in northern Häme, the invitation was accepted, and in the 1580s the flow of emigration from Finland to Sweden began, increasing noticeably upon the duke's ascension to the throne of Sweden-Finland as Charles IX (1599–1611). These "Forest Finns," as they were called, spread to 150 parishes of central Sweden, many of them going as far as Norway. The largest settlement was in Vermland, where, at the beginning of the nineteenth century, it has been estimated there were 14,000 Finns. At that time there are supposed to have been 40,000 Finns in all of central Scandinavia.

The Delaware Finns

The next development in the history of Finnish emigration was on a much smaller scale, but it was of great importance otherwise. In the wars of Charles IX and his famous son, Gustavus II Adolphus, Sweden-Finland had become the leading military power of the North, having won back ancient Finnish lands from Russia and Poland, gaining almost complete control of the Baltic Sea. During the Thirty Years' War, this new northern power took its place beside the other leading European powers. The best-known names of that period were those of Gustavus II Adolphus, who fell in the successful battle of Lützen in 1632, and his Finnish cavalrymen, the feared *Hakkapeliitat*, against whom the protection of Heaven was implored in an addition to the litany.

Already before the country had joined in the Thirty Years' War, the leading men of the kingdom had come to the conclusion that their new position as a military power presupposed overseas colonies, and commerce extending beyond European waters. The person who initiated action in the matter was Willem Usselinx, a Dutchman who had moved to Sweden. He convinced the king of the economic value of such an enterprise. In 1626, Gustavus II Adolphus signed a charter authorizing the South Company to carry on trade "in Asia, Africa, America, and Magellanica," and to establish colonies in areas which were not yet occupied by other powers. Shares were sold immediately in both Finland and Sweden. The king himself signed up for 450,000 thalers' worth (about 360,000 dollars), but did not pay for them. Because of a lack of funds, the company collapsed, and Usselinx returned to Holland in 1629. That same year, the Ship Company, which was formed to take the place of the South Company, inherited its assets and obligations. The clergy and nobility were compelled to buy shares in the new company under threat of imprisonment. This company, financed by force and directed by the government, managed the country's foreign trade during the difficult war years, with copper and iron as the most important exports paying its foreign debts.

But new markets were needed for Sweden's iron and copper. The merchants of Holland, of whom the most important was Peter Minuit, who had been in America as the governor of New Amsterdam, turned their attention to the Delaware River region. Axel Oxenstierna, who headed the government as chancellor after the king's death, saw the value of the idea. In 1637 he authorized the establishment of the New Sweden Company. The Finnish admiral, Klaus Fleming, became the motive force of the company. Fleming was born in Askainen in

1592, on the Louhisaari estate. He began his university studies in Wittenberg, famous from Luther's times, and continued them in other universities. On returning to his homeland he took on various responsibilities, finally rising to the rank of admiral and head of the Swedish-Finnish navy.

As the manager of the New Sweden Company, the dynamic admiral acted fast. Two ships, the *Kalmar Nyckel* and the *Fogel Grip*, were equipped for a voyage and sent on their way in November 1637. In March 1638, they anchored in the Delaware River. There were no immigrants on this expedition led by Peter Minuit, so the frequent mention of this date as the year in which colonization began is inaccurate. What actually took place was the purchase, from the Indians, of the land along the west side of the Delaware River, extending from present-day Wilmington to Philadelphia, a total of about 5,000 square miles. The purchase price was paid in gold and silver articles, copper kettles, and trinkets of various kinds. Thus New Sweden was born.

Before the homeward voyage, a fortress was built on the bank of the Christina River, which empties into the Delaware. It was a simple palisade with cannon positioned in its log tower. The fortress also served as a trading post. Mauno Kling, a Finn, was left in charge of it with a garrison of twenty-three men, about half of whom were Dutch.

After the ships had returned to Sweden and the accounts were settled, it became clear that the expedition had cost $23,000 and had returned furs and other goods worth only $10,000. Enthusiasm began to die down, but Klaus Fleming did not lose courage. He started on a second voyage with the *Kalmar Nyckel* in the fall of 1639, reaching his destination in the following April after a stormy and miserable voyage. Among the passengers were Peter Ridder, governor of New Sweden; Pastor Reerus Terkillus; and some colonists, of whom three were Finns, according to Ilmonen. They were seamen, Lars Anderson from Aland, and soldiers Maunu Anderson-the-Finn and Peter Rambo.

In the meantime, the South Company and the New Sweden Company had been combined. The Dutch had relinquished their part in the company by selling their shares. New Sweden was now a purely Swedish-Finnish colony, to the settlement of which Admiral Fleming began to give more attention, attempting to attract more Finns to it. He was quite successful in this attempt, but there were tragic circumstances in connection with it.

The peasants of Save and Häme had gone to Sweden as immigrants, depending on the assurance that they could freely clear land for crops by cutting and burning the wild surface growth of trees and brush. Such burned-over clearings produced good crops of rye in the first two years, sometimes up to fifty-fold and more, after which several crops of oats were successful. After the oat crops, the land became unproductive meadow. Those who practiced this type of farming were continually forced to destroy additional forests to obtain new land. As the Finnish forest farmers increased in number in Sweden, they were looked on with disfavor because of their farming methods, which not only destroyed forests, but also made it difficult to obtain charcoal for Sweden's expanding mining industry. The preparation of land for cultivation by forest burning was forbidden under threat of severe punishment. In many areas actual persecution began. The Finnish farmers' cottages were burned and the inhabitants were forced to leave. Many were even murdered. A large number returned to Finland, but the majority became accustomed to a new way of life. Some accepted the proposal of authorities that they emigrate across the Atlantic Ocean. That was the actual beginning of the immigration of Finns to America.

Because there were not enough persons willing to leave, Lieutenant Mauno Kling, who had returned from America, went to Finnish villages to urge them to go. "The Government of Sweden extended a helping hand in the search for emigrants" by ordering the governors of Vermland, Nerike, and Dalecarlia to arrest the wandering, homeless Finns and send them to Göteberg. In this way, over fifty emigrants were obtained, almost all of them Finns, whom the *Kalmar Nyckel* carried to Delaware, leaving in the fall of 1641 and arriving there at the beginning of the next year. Thus, in 1642 there was actually a Finnish settlement in Delaware.

The lists of passengers, written in Swedish, included many Finnish names in their Swedish forms, as did later church records. Ilmonen, however, claims to have verified the following as being names of Finns on the expedition: Peter Kekkinen, Martti Marttinen, Knut Marttinen, Soren Minkkinen, Olli Rasanen, and Anders Tossava from the forest areas of central Sweden. Matti Hansson, a servant of Klaus Fleming, was from Porvoo, Finland, and Johan Sprint was from Uusimaa. Many were accompanied by their families. According to the agreement—in so far as an agreement can be spoken of in connection with forced colonization—free men were to serve the company at least two years to cover their traveling expenses, and "criminals" a longer period, up to six years. Thus, land was not yet distributed among the colonists.

Admiral Fleming appears to have continued in his attempts to get as many Finns as possible to go to the colony. For this purpose, he took into the company's service Lieutenant Colonel Johan Printz, who had returned from the Thirty Years' War, and sent him to Finland to recruit settlers. Printz may have gotten a few men from Korsholm province and from northwest Finland. In addition, a few minor criminals consented to accept a change of their sentences to emigration as did bookkeeper Johan Fransson of Viipari. From Dalecarlia and Vermland came Kristian Boije, a Finnish nobleman, and Anders Hommanen, Walle Lohi, Israel Helminen, Matti Piipari, as well as many other Finns with Swedish names. The expedition, led by Johan Printz, who had been named governor of the colony of New Sweden, arrived at its destination in the spring of 1643.

A short period of inactivity followed in the affairs of the New Sweden Company when Sweden-Finland became involved in a war with Denmark. In that war, Klaus Fleming, the energetic leader of the colonization movement, lost his life on his flagship on July 16, 1644, but by the next year communication between Delaware and the mother country was again in order. Misfortune followed, however; a ship carrying colonists struck a coral reef to the north of Puerto Rico, and the hundred Swedes and Finns on it were captured by Spaniards. They were so harshly treated that after many perilous adventures only twenty were able to return to Sweden. As a consequence, interest in colonization began to wane.

From Delaware, however, there were good reports, and soon there were more applicants than the company could transport across the Atlantic. In the fall of 1653, the ship *Orn* set sail for Delaware with 230 colonists and 40 soldiers as passengers. Disease and miserable conditions took such a heavy toll, however, that a hundred were buried at sea before the ship reached its destination in May of the following year. The captain of another ship missed the mouth of the Delaware River and sailed to Long Island, where the governor of the Dutch colony seized the ship with its cargo. The passengers were permitted to go to Delaware, but some, like Mauno Staeck from Turku and John Tomminen, were pleased with New Amsterdam and decided to settle there.

In the meantime, the queen of Sweden-Finland, Christina, daughter of Gustavus II Adolphus, had abdicated in 1654, become a Catholic, and moved to Rome. Her cousin, Charles X Gustavus, had ascended the throne. The kingdom was at its peak, well able to defend itself against half of Europe in the war that broke out. The enterprising king also took an interest in the affairs of New Sweden. With the intention of importing tobacco from Virginia, in addition to carrying on the Delaware trade and transporting colonists, the name of the company was changed to the American Trading Company. Numerous shares in the new company were purchased in Finland also, the city of Viborg being among the new shareholders.

By the order of the king, the ship *Mercurius*, equipped with fourteen cannon, was readied for a voyage to America. Johan Papegoja, who had previously visited Delaware, was ordered to lead the expedition, and Henrik Olsson, a Finn who had also been in Delaware, was to be his interpreter and assistant. Many more applicants appeared to make the voyage than the ship could possibly carry. In addition to the officers, soldiers, servants, and seamen, the *Mercurius* could take only 110 passengers. Two hundred Finns, over a hundred of them from Vermland, had arrived in Göteborg. Papegoja wrote:

> It is both sad and embarrassing that they could not be taken along. Because these people, now deceived in their hopes, had sacrificed their property, used up their money on the long journey to the coast, and now had to take a beggar's staff to wander on unknown highways, such a great weeping and lamenting began as is seldom seen.

The passenger list of the *Mercurius*, which has been preserved, has the passengers classified as follows:

Officers and servants	9
Swedish wives	2
Swedish girls	2
Finnish men, old and young	33
Finnish wives	16
Finnish girls	11
Finnish children, 12 years and under	32
Total	105

This was the last official expedition to come from the old country to New Sweden. At about this time, New Sweden disappeared from the stage of history. The energetic Peter Stuyvesant of New Netherlands occupied it in September of 1655 without bloodshed, for the Swedish garrison was too small to officer resistance. The change from Swedish to Dutch rule did not bring any noticeable changes to the Finnish settlers. In letters to relatives, they continued to praise living conditions and their way of life. This kept interest in Delaware alive. In 1664, without the knowledge of the government, 140 Finnish men, women, and children went by way of Christiania to Amsterdam. Despite protests from Stockholm, the city of Amsterdam sent them to their destination in Delaware. That same year the British seized control of the Dutch colony in America.

The Delaware Swedish-Finnish colony bore the official impress of Sweden, for governors, other officials, clergy, and soldiers were, for the most part, Swedish. The great majority of colonists, however, were Finns. On the other hand, soldiers added to the total number of Swedes, for some of them remained as settlers after their terms of service were over. Comradeship in arms, a common culture, marriage, and the back-and-forth movement from one country to the other created families in Sweden-Finland that had rights of residence on both sides of the Gulf of Bothnia. In Delaware, too, there appear to have been instances of events which one researcher might list on the Finnish side, and another, on the Swedish, each with ample justification.

It is obvious, however, that the colony of New Sweden was more Finnish in nationality than Swedish. This fact has been an embarrasment to some Swedish historians. Amandus Johnson, born in Sweden in 1877, speaks of the Finns in his extensive study of the Delaware colony. But when his two-volume work, *The Swedish Settlements on the Delaware*, published in 1919, appeared in Swedish, it had been condensed to such an extent that almost all the parts pertaining to the Finns were omitted, even though there had not been many of them in the first place.[1] In his concise study of the Delaware Finns, Professor John H. Wuorinen states cautiously that "in 1656 at least one-half of the population of New Sweden was Finnish."[2] Pastor Salomon Ilmonen, in his works on Delaware, apparently puts the Finns in true historical perspective, but because he seldom mentions his sources or verifies his facts in any other way, he is of comparatively little value to researchers.[3] The same may be said of E. A. Louhi's *The Delaware Finns*. The Swedish writer, Richard Gothe, who has made extensive studies of the Finns in central Sweden, has reached the conclusion that the Finns in the Delaware colony may well have made up 75 percent of the population, as he declared in his lecture at the Delaware festival which was held at the University of Helsinki on May 23, 1938.[4] The definitive history of the Delaware Finns is still to be written by someone who would have access to archives and church records in Finland and Sweden to trace their origins.

The colony of New Sweden had its true beginnings during the governorship of Johan Printz, from 1643 to 1653. He was harsh and sometimes even cruel, but he got things done. Fur trading with the Indians was carried on, fields were cleared, the raising of corn and tobacco was begun, and farm after farm appeared on the landscape. One of the most important Finnish settlements was Finland, today called Marcus Hook, about ten miles up the Delaware River on the west bank. About ten miles west of Finland in the Schuylkill River valley there was another Finnish farming community, which extended to the northern parts of present-day Philadelphia. The third and the most extensive Finnish settlement was the village of Mulikkamäki, opposite the village of Finland, on the east bank of the Delaware, on what is now known as the New Jersey side. There were also Finns in Upland, a Swedish settlement on Brandywine Creek that became famous during the Revolutionary War, and the areas south of Wilmington up to the Maryland border, not to mention smaller settlements.

Among these Delaware Finns there were some very colorful personalities. Pastor Laurentius Lock, who is sometimes considered to have been a Swede, had many adventurous experiences. His wife ran away with another man, leaving him to take care of their many children. The pastor got a divorce and soon remarried. Because he was the only pastor in the settlement, he performed the wedding ceremony himself, thus running into difficulties with strict Dutch officials. He was fined, but Governor Stuyvesant revoked the sentence.

In 1669, an event known as the "Long Finn rebellion" took place. It has been, in fun, called the first attempt at an American war for independence. Behind the scheme were a certain Swedish adventurer and a Finn by the name of Coleman, who began to agitate among the Finnish, Swedish, and Dutch colonists to get them to rebel against the British. Coleman, who spoke a little of the Delaware Indian language, stated that he would rouse even the Indians to join them. Nothing happened, however, except that the British officials got wind of the plans. Coleman fled among the Indians, the Swede was flogged, and many settlers who had participated in the scheme were compelled to pay heavy fines.

The greatest change in the life of the Finnish settlers occurred when William Penn and his Quakers arrived in 1681. King Charles II had owed Penn £16,000 and reimbursed him by giving him rights of ownership to extensive areas in America. This marked the beginning of the Pennsylvania colony and of the city of Philadelphia. The first settlers were guaranteed their former rights to private property and lands, the freedom of religion, and self-government in church congregations. In discussions concerning these matters, the Finns were represented by Lars Cock and Peter Rambo. Cock's parents were Vermland Finns, but he was born in America. Because he spoke Swedish, Finnish, English, and Indian, Penn took him into his service as interpreter. Cock was present at the organization of the Pennsylvania government. The new colony became a haven for thousands of Quakers who had been persecuted for their religion in their homeland. Twenty-three shiploads arrived already during that first year, and the Finnish villages and other settlements were literally submerged in a British world.

The archbishop of Sweden, who was also the head of the bishops of Finland, had sent pastors to attend to the spiritual needs of immigrants. When England took possession of the colony, the pastors leaving their homeland often went by the way of London, sometimes even being ordained by the bishop of London who was the head of all the English congregations across the sea. Consequently, there was a close relationship between the Finnish-Swedish congregations of the Delaware colony and the Anglican church. They were so close that within a relatively short time they were absorbed by the Anglican church. Another, more practical reason for this was that, as a small minority, the Finns, Swedes, and the Dutch began, within a few generations, to use the English language even in their homes. This absorption would have taken place earlier had not greatly increased immigration from Germany in the 1750s strengthened the small, previously established Lutheran congregations. After the Revolutionary War no more pastors came from the old country, and with the demand of the younger generation for services in the English language, the problem resolved itself, as it were, when the congregations joined the Anglican church, whose rectors had already been ministering to them. Of the churches built by the Finns and Swedes, two were still in use in the 1960s: Holy Trinity Church, which had been built in Wilmington in 1699, and the Gloria Dei Church, a brick structure that had been built in Philadelphia the following year.

Two names connected with the history of the Finnish colony in Delaware are worthy of special mention. The first is Pietari Kalm, the famous Finnish naturalist and a professor at Turku University, who was born in Sweden in 1716 while his parents were there as war refugees. In 1748–51, Kalm made an exploratory expedition in North America, publishing the results of his studies in an extensive work which appeared in English, German, Swedish, Dutch, and French. Kalm was the first European to visit the Niagara Falls. He remained a long time among his countrymen in Delaware, even preaching in their churches.

The second prominent name is that of John Morton, a judge of the Pennsylvania Supreme Court and a representative of his colony in the Congress at the time of the American Revolution. On July 4, 1776, the majority of the representatives of twelve of the colonies had voted for independence. The last to vote were the five representatives of the large and populous colony of Pennsylvania. Two of them voted in favor of continuing as a British colony. Two, namely Benjamin Franklin and James Wilson, voted in favor of independence. The tension was great when John Morton, the last of all to vote, stepped up before the chairman. His vote would determine on which side Pennsylvania would stand and whether the colonies were in agreement on the subject of independence. Morton's resounding "Aye" decided the issue. His name is among the signers of the Declaration of Independence.

Morton's great, great-grandfather, Martti Marttinen, was born in Rautalampi in about 1606. He had first moved with other emigrants to central Sweden and later, voluntarily with his family, to Delaware. His son, also called Martti, had been born in about 1630 in Sweden.[5] The Marttinen family name appears in documents in many different forms, depending on the nationality and accuracy of the one who has made the notation. Among the variations are Martinsson, Martense, Martensson, and Martenen. The younger Martti Marttinen's son John began to use the form Morton. His son, also John Morton, was the signer of the Declaration of Independence. The Morton, or Marttinen, home still stands in Rautalampi, kept up as a museum by present kin.

The descendants of the Delaware Finns have long ago been absorbed by other nationalities, and the old Finnish family names have disappeared. In many cases, however, in Philadelphia and surrounding areas, they can still be traced back to their original forms, sometimes quite easily. Take, for example, the following: Helm from Helmi; Jockin from Jokinen; Cox, Cock, and Kuckow from Kukkonen; Turner from Turunen; and Parchon from Parkkonen.[6]

There were two additional important reasons for the movement of Finns to the forest areas of central Sweden, from where they eventually emigrated to Delaware. The first was the Peasants' War of 1597, when the Ostrobothnians rose up against their noble oppressors, with disastrous consequences. The other was the proximity of the Russian border and the uncertainty of conditions it caused. During the 800 years of Finnish history there had been 125 years of war, so it is easy to understand why the promise of free land to cultivate at a safe distance from their eastern oppressor was attractive. Since Swedish officials did not keep the promises that had been made, Delaware soon meant the opening of doors to a secure and peaceful life.

Emigration to Northern Scandinavia

Before permanent settlements were established, individual settlers had moved over the Tornio River to the wilderness areas of Sweden. When permanent settlements began to develop and church congregations were started on both sides of the border, regular immigration to northern Sweden began. It is thought to have started in the

1740s. The largest Finnish settlements in the Swedish northwest evolved into the following parishes and subordinate chapel parishes: Alatornio, Karunki, Hietaniemi, Ylitornio, Korpilompolo, Pajala, Täräntö, Muonionalusta, Junosuanto, Kaaresuanto, Jukkasjärvi, and Jällivaara, all of which were in the province of Norrbotten. In 1860 the Finnish population in northern Sweden was approximately 14,000; in 1880, about 16,500; in 1900, about 22,000; and in 1910, about 25,000. In reality, the Finnish population was greater than official statistics indicate.

The Norrbotten Finnish settlement is a direct continuation of the area of the Finnish side of the border, and reciprocal relations have always been very lively. Nor do the Finns living on the west side of the Tornio River consider themselves to be "immigrants." In many parishes they are the majority and, in a way, the Finnish language serves as the international language in all of northern Scandinavia. The Church of Sweden has made certain that the rectors and pastors of the country's northern congregations are bilingual and that the Finns have church books in their own language. The Swedish government, on the other hand, has attempted to follow the policy of nationalization.[7] Northern Sweden made a notable contribution to the immigration of Finns to America, especially to Michigan.

In his booklet *Suomalaisten siirtolaisuus Norjasta Amerikkaan* (Finnish emigration from Norway to America) John I. Kolehmainen gives a carefully researched report on Finnish emigration to Ruija, a remote area of northern Norway known to them by this name for hundreds of years.[8] The permanent Finnish settlement in northern Norway began during the Great Northern War (1700–1721), when many families fled there from northern Finland to escape Russian atrocities. In 1721, after the treaty of Uusikaupunki (Nystad) which ended the Great Northern War, the Russians departed, but hunger and poverty remained as the scourge of the far North. Traders and nomadic Lapps brought wonderful tales of the endless supplies of fish in the Arctic waters, and of the good wages to be earned in ceaselessly operating copper mines. In Ruija, they said, one did not have to eat bark bread; pure, unadulterated rye bread was the daily fare. Thus, the Ruija "fever" began.

Norwegian statistics of the eighteenth century do not distinguish between Finns and Lapps and thus accurate figures are not obtainable on the Finns in Norway. Some idea of the increase in Finnish immigration can be obtained, however, from the following figures: In 1756, according to the census, there were in Finmarken, the northernmost province of Norway, 389 Norwegian families and 642 Finnish and

Lapp families. In 1799, there were about 2,000 Norwegians and about 3,500 Finns and Lapps.

During the past century, Norwegian statistics began to distinguish between the *Finner* or Lapps and the *Kvaener* or Finns. Detailed information is also available from Finnish sources. In 1858, for example, a total of 393 persons moved from Utsjoki to Ruija. Other parishes of northern Finland from which emigrants went to Norway were Kemi, Alatornio, Karunki, Ylitornio, Turtola, Kolari, Tervola, Rovaniemi, Kuolajärvi, and Kuusamo. In addition, Swedish Finns from Norrbotten province also moved there. The Finmarken Finns received a considerable addition to their numbers when the years of severe famine (1866–68) in Finland drove people from their homes to other areas in search of relief from starvation.

The life of the northern Norwegian fishermen was extremely hard and material gain was usually small. The villagers shivering amidst the bare rocks suffered from scurvy because of a lack of vegetables. A few Finns, however, managed to dig small potato patches in the rocky soil and even keep a cow or two.

The living conditions of those who worked in the mines were somewhat better. The English had begun to mine copper in Kaafjord in 1826 and extended their activities to Kvaenangen. The Finns were in demand as miners. In 1855 there were 854 persons in the Kaafjord international settlement. Of them, 439 were Finns, 273 Norwegians, and the rest Swedish, English, etc. The English mine superintendents took rather good care of their men. The Finns lived in their own "village," and there was a small vegetable garden adjacent to each home. After the middle of the century, copper mining declined, and one after another, the miners moved away, before long to Michigan and Minnesota. Only ruins are left in Finmarken where the Finns once lived and worked.

The Norwegian Finns also had other troubles which, in time, helped to answer the question of whether to go to America or not. Fishing laws were irksome, denying, as they did, free fishing rights to foreigners. The only possibility of income for many was to work for the captain-owner of a fishing vessel, or for a local merchant, with the result that at the end of a poor season, the workers would be in debt for clothes, equipment, and supplies.

In general, relations between Norwegians and their Finnish neighbors were good, but the attitude of the government and officials often aroused suspicion toward the Finns. These suspicions were often intensified by the midcentury Fennomani of the Finns. The most important occurrence in this connection was the enactment in 1860 of a law which, in addition to making education compulsory, ruled that only the Norwegian language should be used in schools. In the larger Finnish settlements such as Kaafjord, Alten, Neiden, and Vadsö, where Finnish had been taught by Finnish teachers, the new school law was seen as a blow at their rights to use Finnish.

Religious matters also caused a cooling of official attitudes toward the Finns. The Laestadian revival movement, which began in northern Sweden, had spread among the Norwegian Lapps. It took a wild and brutal form, especially in the Kautokeino parish. For example, on November 8, 1852, after cruel torture, the Lapps, in a religious frenzy, murdered a Norwegian merchant and rural police chief who was a guest in his home. A Rector Hvoslef was flogged for hours "so that the Devil would leave him." "Unconverted" Lapps were cruelly mistreated until help came from a neighboring village to save these victims of frenzied religious fanatics.[9] The Norwegians believed the Finns had a share in these savageries, for Swedish Laestadianism had originated as a Finnish-language movement. To understand the situation, it is necessary to realize that the Norwegian church had just recently begun to attend to the spiritual needs of the Lapps in their own language. In Sweden and Finland, where the roots of missionary work among the Lapps were centuries old and where such work had been done for their enlightenment and civilization, such phenomena as those at Kautokeino did not occur. The tragic happenings in that parish must also be mentioned among the causes that explain the emigration of comparatively large numbers of Finns from Ruija to America.

Kolehmainen mentions yet another unusual situation that helped to create suspicion toward Finland and to cool relations. In Ruija the national borders had been indefinite, and part of the Arctic shore had been a so-called common territory. In 1826, a survey was made and this territory was divided among Norway, Russia, and Finland. The interests of Finland were so poorly attended to in this survey that she was left without access to the Arctic Ocean. In 1851, when Russia indicated that she wanted to get Varanger Fjord under her control, there was uneasy tension in Norway. When Aukusti Vilhelm Ervasti, in his travelogue *Suomaläiset Jäämeren rannalla* (The Finns on the shore of the Arctic), published in 1884, stated that Finmarken more logically belonged to Finland than to Norway, the Norwegians felt it was the last straw. Suspicions concerning the purpose of the Finnish settlements in Ruija were aroused. The far northern part of Norway was sparsely settled, and although the Finnish settlements were very small, Finns made up the majority of the population in several areas on the Arctic shore. This preponderance of Finns caused the Norwegian government to take vigorous action toward the restriction of Finnish immigration.

In 1900, the situation was as follows: The total population of Finmarken was approximately 64,100. Of this number, 17,200 were Lapps, about 6,700 were Finns, and 6,000 were a mixed group of Finnish-Lappish-Norwegian descent. Pure Norwegians made up only a little over half of the entire population. About half of all persons in the province spoke Finnish, for the Lapps, the mixed group, and most of the Norwegians were able to speak the language.[10]

The Finns in Alaska

The establishment of small Finnish settlements in Siberia and Amur were also part of the total Finnish emigration movement, but since it has not been proved to have had any connection with the flow of immigration to America, it has been disregarded in this presentation.[11] Mention of a small Alaskan Finnish settlement and its origin seems more appropriate.

Russians had begun the conquest of Siberia in 1574 during the time of Ivan the Terrible. In 1699, during the reign of Peter the Great, the Kamchatka peninsula finally came into their hands, and the Russians permanently settled on the shores of the Pacific Ocean. On an exploratory trip in 1728, a Danish navy officer, Vitus Bering, who was in the service of Russia, discovered at the far eastern edge of Siberia a strait that joins the Pacific and Arctic Oceans and now bears the name of its discoverer. He had been very close to the Alaskan coast, but because of the perpetual fog he had not seen it. On another expedition he reached the southern shore of Alaska on July 15, 1741. On that day the history of Alaska began.

The first Alaskan Finn known by name was Aleksander Kuparinen, a carpenter from Viipuri. He had arrived with the Russians in 1794. He died in Sitka in the early 1820s. It is possible that at that time there were other Finns in "Russian America," for men were being recruited in St. Petersburg and in surrounding areas where there were numerous Finnish carpenters and shipbuilders. Because of their skills they were much in demand.

The name of Arvid Adolf Etholen is directly connected with the history of the Finns in Alaska. Etholen was born in 1794 in Helsinki; in 1817 he entered the service of the Russian navy as an officer. His first command took him to Alaska. Up to 1832 he was a commander on ships of the Russian American Company, making extensive exploratory trips along the Alaskan coast and as far south as California, Chile, and the South Sea Islands. From 1832 to 1838 he was assistant to the chief administrator of Russia's North American colonies. Between 1838 and 1845 he was governor-general. He resigned from the service in 1847 with the rank of vice-admiral. He died at Elimaki in Finland in 1876.

Etholen's chief interest in Alaska was to study the possibility of colonization and later, when he had arrived at a favorable conclusion, to procure immigrants. The white population may have risen to 1,500 during Etholen's time. Among them were many Finns, but it is impossible to discover how many. There may have been about 300. In any event, there were Finns in positions of leadership. In addition to Etholen there were his chief assistant, Lieutenant Johan Bartram; the pastor of the congregation, Uno Cygnaeus (1810–88); the physician of the immigrant settlement, Reinhold Ferdinand Sahlberg (1811–74); and sea captains Gustaf Nybom and D. A. Gronberg, to mention only the most important. The most famous of the Finns of Alaska was Uno Cygnaeus, pastor to the Finnish, German, and Swedish Lutheran settlers from 1840 to 1845. His real life work, however, was done at home, as "the father of the public schools of Finland."

The centers of colonization in Alaska were Sitka, Kodiak, and Unalaska, the last-mentioned a trading post in the Aleutian Islands. Through the efforts of Cygnaeus and Etholen, a church was built in Sitka. This first Protestant church on the Pacific coast has since been razed, but a picture of it and the plan for it have been preserved. The organ used by Cygnaeus is also in the Sitka museum. After Cygnaeus, the pastors of the Alaska colony were the Finns, Gabriel Plathan and his successor, Georg Gustaf Winter.

Whale oil and furs became the most important products of the colony. Trade in them increased to such an extent that a new company was organized in Turku in 1849, the Russian-Finnish Whaling Company, which soon had six ships in service between the Gulf of Finland and Alaska. The Crimean War, which started in 1853, destroyed the greater part of the Finnish merchant fleet and also interrupted the Alaskan trade. In 1854, a squadron of the English-French navy sailed to the northern parts of the Pacific, burned the Russian military station and trading post at Petropavlovsk on the extreme southern tip of Kamchatka, and afterward visited Sitka. The enemy, however, did not destroy Sitka, probably for the reason that the British Hudson Bay Company and the Russian American Company had common interests. The ship *Aino* of the Russian-Finnish Whaling Company fleet happened to be in the vicinity of Alaska at the time of the visit of the

British-French navy, and it was burned. The crew managed to reach shore safely and many of the men decided to stay in the colony permanently.

The Russian American Company had so ruthlessly exploited the seal and the sea otter that catches were smaller and smaller each succeeding year. The company remained economically solvent only because of the tea trade with China, in which it had a monopoly. The Russian government was unwilling to invest funds in an unprofitable enterprise and refused to renew the company's charter. An additional reason for this refusal was that there was fear in St. Petersburg that England might occupy Alaska, which there was no possibility of defending. Russia offered to sell the territory to the United States and, after negotiations, William H. Seward agreed to buy it for $7,200,000 or about two cents per acre. The Senate ratified the agreement on May 28, 1867, and President Andrew Johnson signed it on June 30. On October 18 of that same year, a short ceremony was held, at which the Russian flag was taken down and the American flag, which at that time had thirty-seven stars, was raised. A few hundred Russian subjects returned to their homeland, and those who stayed in Alaska, among them almost all the Finns of the colony, became American citizens.

3 More Recent Emigration from Finland

When Finnish emigration was discussed in older Finnish writings up to the beginning of the twentieth century, it was, almost without exception, treated as a phenomenon that was not a credit to the country, nor to the tribe of Vaino. "Child of Finland, do not trade away your land so fair and sweet," was the sometimes soft-voiced, sometimes louder plea to youth in these writings. But when, in the second half of the nineteenth century, 25 million emigrants left Europe for America and, as large migrations also occurred from one country to another in other parts of the world, it was obvious that a universal phenomenon with its own set pattern of rules was in operation.

The wave of emigration which flowed from Europe starting about the middle of the century had its beginnings mainly in western and northern parts of the continent, from Germany, England, Ireland, Scandinavia, Holland, and Belgium. As the rapid development of industry in these countries began to create new opportunities for work, the pace of emigration leveled off and gradually subsided. In the 1890s the greatest numbers of emigrants left from eastern and southern Europe, especially from Italy, Austria-Hungary, and Poland.

Of the European countries from which emigration occurred, Sweden, Norway, Denmark, Holland, Switzerland, and Belgium may be compared with Finland in population, culture, and other features. Table 1 gives comparative statistics from 1871 through 1930.[1]

During this sixty-year period, emigration from Denmark was approximately the same as from Finland; from Norway it was twice as much; from Sweden, three times more. Emigration from Finland,

Table 1: Comparative Emigration from Scandinavia, 1871–1930

YEAR	FINLAND	SWEDEN	NORWAY	DENMARK	HOLLAND	SWITZER-LAND	BELGIUM
1871–80	500	102,500	95,400	38,600	43,000	35,700	7,800
1881–90	2,700	327,500	186,700	81,600	52,100	90,900	40,300
1891–1900	59,100	204,500	94,900	51,500	23,900	44,100	28,500
1901–10	158,800	224,000	190,900	73,400	28,000	49,100	30,600
1911–20	67,400	86,000	61,500	51,600	21,700	38,200	27,900
1921–30	56,100	106,000	86,600	59,000	32,300	53,200	27,600
	344,600	1,044,500	716,000	355,700	201,000	321,200	162,700

therefore, was average among the smaller civilized countries of Europe.[2]

The Rise and Decline of the Tar Industry

To understand Finnish emigration, it is necessary to remember how Finland adjusted itself to European trade and maritime commerce. During the Middle Ages when furs were fashionable in southern and central Europe, Finland became one of the most important fur suppliers. Then, too, with meat being prohibited on the numerous fast days of the church, more fish were needed than the western and southern European fishermen were able to supply. The rivers of Finland were so rich in salmon that servants often refused to be employed if the prospective master did not agree in writing that they would not have to eat salmon on more than three days a week. Because of their great abundance, salted salmon and dried codfish became important exports. After the discovery of America, the age of ocean navigation began. At the time, western European forests were producing the wood necessary for shipbuilding. Finland produced the tar, rising to the very top among the tar producers of the world.

Tar had been prepared for home use in Finland for eons, but in the seventeenth century it became the country's leading product in world trade and contributed especially to the development of Ostrobothnia. When the Great Northern War ended in 1721, and Karjala and Viipuri were ceded to Russia, the tar trade of the Saima chain of lakes ended, and Ostrobothnia became the most important tar-producing area in Sweden-Finland, so that by the end of the eighteenth century, 80 percent of the tar from the entire kingdom of Sweden-

Finland was exported from Ostrobothnia; it amounted to 95 percent from Finland proper. The Ostrobothnian foreign tar trade at that time amounted to 80,000 barrels annually, increasing to approximately 225,000 in the 1850s.

The Ostrobothnian tar industry makes an interesting chapter in the cultural history of Finland, and at the same time provides an unusual background for emigration. Distillation of tar was specialized work, and the charcoal pit expert was an important and respected man whose pay was two marks per day, or twice as much as that of an ordinary worker. The barrels of tar were taken along rivers to the coast in long tar boats that carried from twelve to fourteen barrels each. Three men were needed to manage a boat. If the forest was fairly near the coast, the tar was taken overland, in which case a horse and man could transport three or four barrels at the most at one time. When the "Tar Finns" arrived in a city with their loads, the merchants entertained them lavishly. Great banquets were prepared and included beer and liquor. The men were likely to stay in the city for several days enjoying the free entertainment, finally selling their tar to the tradesman making the highest offer. A considerable portion of the money received was left with the merchants of the city in payment for goods to take home, home-coming gifts, and liquor for the trip home. After farewell drinks, the return journey was often begun in a state of intoxication. Although tar brought wealth and increased economic well-being, at the same time it caused a slackening of morals and, especially, increased drunkenness.

The banquets for the "Tar Finns" resulted in so many complaints by the general public that the government strictly forbade them by a royal proclamation issued on December 7, 1771. But the order was disregarded, and the entertainments continued to the middle of the nineteenth century.

As a result of the tar trade, a prosperous shipbuilding industry sprang up in Ostrobothnian coastal cities. After the Napoleonic Wars there was a great increase in ocean commerce all over the world, even reaching Ostrobothnia. In 1815 there were 110 ships at coastal cities, but by 1838 the number had increased to 189. At the beginning of the century, Finnish ships sailed, especially to Holland and Spain, with tar and wood products, returning with salt, coffee, tobacco, and sugar. Soon northern brigs, barques, and frigates were sailing even as far as Brazil. Tar warehouses owned by big business concerns sprang up in coastal cities. Wealth spread even to interior parishes. Ilmajoki, especially, became so prosperous that the writer of its history is able to say that "the womenfolk wore six-inch silver buckles on their breasts and kerchiefs costing fifty six-dollars over their shoulders." The largest tar warehouses were in Vaasa and Oulu, but Raahe, Uusikaarlepyy, Kokkola, Pietarsaari, Kristiina, and Tornio also became important for trading in tar as well as for supplying ships. The largest individual shipowners were Carl Gustaf Wolff of Vaasa, who had twenty ships, and Lundberg and Company of Raahe.

"Money circulates, the standard of living rises, Ostrobothnia prospers," stated a Finnish historian of that period. This economic prosperity also meant general cultural progress. Students from Ostrobothnia began to make up an ever more important part of the student body of the Universities of Turku and Helsinki. Ostrobothnia contributed a large number of famous names to the modern history of Finland. Among them are Henrik Gabriel Porthan, Antti Chydenius, J. V. Snellman, J. L. Runeberg, Sakari Topelius, Yrjo Sakari Yrjo-Koskinen, and Gustaf Johansson.

Four severe blows in rapid succession cut short the prosperity of Ostrobothnia. The first was the Crimean War, 1853–56. Because the Finnish ships sailed under the Russian flag, the British and French navies treated them as enemies. They seized about 28,500 tons of shipping, and owners of the ships that were at foreign ports were forced to sell them for a mere pittance. Thus, the total loss to the Finnish merchant fleet was about 77,000 tons. Most of the ships lost were Ostrobothnian vessels.

In the spring of 1854, the British fleet commanded by Admiral Sir Charles Napier, and the French fleet commanded by vice-admiral Parseval-Deschernes—a total of eighty ships and forty-three thousand men—sailed into Finnish waters. The ships in the harbors of Raahe and Oulu, the shipyards, and the stocks of wood products and tar were set afire and destroyed. At Kokkola the enemy was driven back, badly beaten. The following summer, the British attempted to invade Vaasa, Kokkola, Pietarsaari, and Rauma but were repelled. Even so, some ships and warehouses were destroyed. This fighting was called the Åland War by the general public, because the event of most importance to the Finns took place in Åland. That was the capture of the small fortress of Bomarsund. The incident was the subject of a ballad:

That Åland War was terrible
When, with four hundred ships,
The Englishmen sailed to the shores of Suomi,
And the intention of the enemy was
To shoot the fortress to smithereens
And to capture its soldiers.

The effects of the war were most sorely felt by Ostrobothnia, which had lost almost all of its merchant fleet. She also experienced a serious interruption in her tar trade.

The second blow followed closely upon the first. It was the opening of the Saima Canal to navigation in 1856. This thirty-six-mile-long canal from Saima to Viipuri connected the whole of Savo and Karelia by way of Kuopio, Iisalmi, and Nurmes, with the sea, thus directing commerce away from Ostrobothnia, to Viipuri. The Ostrobothnians, however, struggled heroically to recover from these two blows. By 1865, the Ostrobothnian cities again had 182 ships ploughing the seas, and tar production, too, continued as formerly on a large scale.

The third disaster was the great famine of the 1860s. In 1865, the harvest was poor throughout the country, and endless rain and overflowing rivers and lakes destroyed the crops the following summer. In many areas, mobs of beggars wandered about, spreading disease. In 1867, winter continued far into spring. By fall there was hardly anything to harvest. Destitution and misery increased, and people traveled from northern and eastern Finland to areas which were reputed to be more prosperous. Starvation and diseases, of which typhoid fever was the most destructive, raised the mortality rate in 1868 in Finland to the hitherto unheard-of figure of almost 78 deaths per thousand. In many parishes the mortality rate was even greater. In Parkano, for example, one in four died; in Reisjärvi, more than one in five; and in Ruovesi, nearly one in five. Everywhere there were great numbers of the graves of unknown dead. During these years of famine, the population of Finland decreased by approximately 10 percent. Decades later, parents still had their children read Pietari Paivarinta's shocking book *Pikakuvia 1867 Katovuodesta ja Sen Seurauksista* (Glimpses of the famine year of 1867 and its consequences) so that they might see for themselves how true were the tales their parents had told them of those times of horror. Ostrobothnia and especially its northern areas suffered relatively more than many other parts of the country.

The fourth and most destructive blow to Ostrobothnia's prosperity was a development of international significance, namely, the use of steamships. This was not entirely unexpected, for steamboats had been experimentally used since James Watt had built the first steam engine in 1769. For decades these small boats were being used only by the wealthy or the more eccentric, not seeming to have any practical value. But the situation changed when steamships began to make trips between Europe and New York. In truth, the beginning of the use of steam for propelling ships was very modest. The American sailing vessel *Savannah* was equipped with a steam engine and paddle wheels and crossed the Atlantic in 1819 in 29 days and 11 hours. But during this celebrated trip, the engine had been used for only 80 hours.

Regular movement of ships between Liverpool and New York began in 1838 when the *Sirius* and the *Great Western* arrived in New York harbor within a few hours of each other, starting a continuing competition among shipping companies. Soon Atlantic traffic was in full swing as one great company after another joined the race.

In the meantime, steamships had also begun to take over the commerce on European waters. In 1833, Finland launched her first steamboat, *Ilmarinen*, a tugboat, on the Saima. Starting in 1836, the Turku steamships carried on commerce on a route from Turku to Helsinki, to Tallin, to St. Petersburg, to Stockholm, and back to Turku. Finland's fleet of steamships grew rapidly. In 1866 the country had 62 steamships; by 1882 their number had increased to 216.[3] The old sailing vessels continued to ply the seas for a long time, but new sailing vessels were seldom built anymore, either in Finland or in other countries.

The Ostrobothnian shipyards, which for technical and economic reasons were not able to build steel ships, stopped building ships altogether. Because steel ships do not require tar, the tar trade, which had been Ostrobothnia's main source of wealth, also came to an end. Many individuals tried stubbornly to keep up their hopes with the old saying that as long as the wind blows there will be sailing vessels. Others spoke scornfully of the modern day, when ships were of steel and men of wood, and idealized the past, when men were of steel and ships of wood. But the truth remained that the "Land of Ten Streams," which had been impoverished by war, the Saima canal, and famine, faced critical times. The solution to the problems of Ostrobothnia was emigration overseas. Since Ostrobothnia was by far the largest area from which emigration occurred, it is reasonable to study the causes of emigration mainly from the point of view of that area. Many of the reasons for emigration from there qualify as reasons for emigration from other parts of Finland.

Ostrobothnian emigration has been interestingly and competently described by Anna-Leena Toivonen of Seinäjoki. Her extensive dissertation *Etelä-Pohjanmaan Valtamerentakainen Siirtolaisuus 1867–1930* (Overseas emigration from southern Ostrobothnia) was published in 1963.[4] Because of its recent nature, it is natural that her work should have greatly influenced the following presentation.

Two forms of topsoil destruction had ruined the foundations of Ostrobothnian economy. The first was *kytöviljelys* (land-burning). Land that was to be prepared for cultivation by this method was covered with branches, twigs, and decayed logs already in winter. Later on, layers of topsoil and turf were laid over them. This accumulation was set afire and allowed to burn slowly until nothing but ashes was left. Land thus prepared produced one, or at the most, two good crops of rye or oats, after which it was for a long time almost worthless meadow and pasture land. "Kytöviljelys" was even more destructive than *kaskiviljelys* (forest-burning), which was discussed earlier. It destroyed the rich humus, whereas forest-burning ruined only the top layer of soil. In swamplands, however, there was some justification for this type of farming. The person responsible for starting land-burning in Ostrobothnia was Iisak Brenner (1603–70) of Isokyrö.

The other form of soil destruction was the previously discussed distillation of tar, which destroyed forests. It brought about a short period of prosperity, but left land from which even the last vestige of fertility was later drained by the land-burning process described above.

The Country Is Unable to Feed Her Children

With the slowing down of shipbuilding and the end of tar distilling, the productive life of the area collapsed. Finland's industrial development, which was progressing in the southern and central parts of the country because of good harbors, a network of railroads, canals, and raw materials, bypassed Ostrobothnia. Farming should have provided economic security for the province, but Ostrobothnian agriculture could not feed its growing numbers of inhabitants. With the increase in population, farmlands were divided into ever smaller portions, so that the cultivated land on many farms was under two hectares, or five American acres, in size. "This kind of farm can feed no kind of family, to say nothing of a large one." Besides, farming methods were very primitive. Because of the small size of the farms, farm work was available only in certain seasons. The Ostrobothnian representatives in the Diet complained that the state was trying to forget the province. The representative from Ilmajoki, Iisakki Hannuksela, was especially vigorous in his presentation of the problems of his province.[5]

The loss of farm jobs was partly compensated for by temporary work. Ostrobothnian men worked in southern cities of Finland, in factories and on railroad construction projects. They also worked in Sweden, in the harbors of the Gulf of Riga, and even as far away as the Black Sea. It was not unusual for them to go even to Ruija in northern Norway. In many parishes the development of home industries brought additional income. For example, in Vähäkyrö there appeared many tinsmiths whose earnings were so good that they often were able to purchase homes. The tinsmiths of Vähäkyrö frequently traveled far to sell their products. Because their most popular item was a child's toy called a "fyrry" the whole parish was nicknamed Fyrrykyröö.[6] In many communities, the women competed in the weaving of cloth and rugs. Some parishes became well known for the making of horse collars or hames.

Although the generally small size of the farmsteads was a great disadvantage, much more serious and unfortunate was the fact that the majority of the Finnish rural population owned no land at all. In 1870, 92.6 percent of the people of Finland lived in rural areas; in 1880, 91.6 percent; in 1890, 90.1 percent; and in 1900, 87.5 percent. The increase in urban population was due largely to the increase in the population of four cities, namely, Helsinki, Turku, Tampere, and Viipuri, none of which were in the area from which emigration occurred. Thus, most of

Table 2: Rural Occupations in Finland, 1870

	NUMBER	PERCENT
Landowners	83,030	13.0
Tenant farmers	11,561	1.8
Small tenant farmers	56,597	8.8
Hired workers	358,154	56.0
Landowners' sons and other assistants	41,660	6.5
Dependents, cottagers, and other landless	88,949	13.9
Total	639,951	100.0

the population was agricultural. Table 2 is an accounting of the people who earned their livelihood through agricultural pursuits at the beginning of emigration from Finland in 1870.[7]

If the landowners and their sons and assistants such as foremen, gardners, etc., are combined in a single group, the total number in this group in 1870 was 124,690 or 19.5 percent of the male agricultural population. Tenant farmers, or those who rented individual farmsteads, formed their own small group, whose insecure position is suggested by a proverb: "The tenant farmer's threshold is slippery." They were, however, very independent.

Throughout the year, a farm needed a fixed number of workers, the actual number depending on the size of the farmstead and on the living habits of the master and mistress. From spring to fall, many extra workers were needed, and to insure their availability, the landowners had, with the passage of time, developed a system of retaining small tenant farmers and cottagers on their lands. The small tenant-farmer group developed in two ways. First, because of the complicated laws concerning the distribution of land, it was customary to give small rental farms to younger children of a family as their inheritance. Secondly, the right to clear land and to build a cottage on it was given to almost any able-bodied man. The main purpose of lease contracts was to make sure that the landowner would have manpower when he needed it most, during the busy seasons. The lease had to be paid for almost entirely by day work. In addition, there was some overtime work with small compensation, as well as the obligation to make whatever equipment or tools were needed on the farm. Agreements were often oral, and because the law did not specify the duration of the lease, the cottager always lived in a nightmarish fear of eviction, especially when a change of landowners occurred. On the other hand, according to R. H. Oittinen, the historian of Finland's working class, the tenant farmers were a socially enlightened group, and their standard of living was, on the whole, quite satisfactory for those times.[8]

Among the farm population, hired workers amounted to 56 percent. In the eighteenth century, the state had taken action to insure labor for landowners by providing for a legal protective system and for compulsory labor. Persons without means, about whose ability to pay taxes or to fulfill other public obligations there was doubt, had to go to work for someone else. Thus they were no longer vagrants, for their masters gave them legal protection and agreed to pay their taxes. This system did not give much consideration to the rights of the hired laborer. According to the law, a person had to find work, but the landowner was not compelled to hire anyone. The search for more profitable places of employment was restricted, for on one's search one might be arrested for vagrancy. This arrangement guaranteed labor for the landowner and, at the same time, kept wages low. Not until 1879 was freedom of movement permitted hired workers. In the vagrancy law of 1883 a vagrant was defined as one who "does not have any money for his own livelihood and lives an immoral, depraved life." After the passage of these laws, honest workers could move from place to place as they pleased.

Maidservants and hired men acquired with the help of the compulsory labor law formed the largest group in the population. By 1870 their number had risen to 360,000 persons. They did not live in actual need, for they were provided with room and board as well as with some of their clothing. But cash wages were very small, working days unmercifully long, and treatment unkind. Early marriages took place, followed by many children, after which the men would try to become tenant farmers or even cottagers, or they would stay on with the landowner as hired hands, receiving part of their wages in provisions. The majority of emigrants came from this large group of hired men and maidservants.

The so-called landless population also contributed large numbers to emigration. To this group belonged day workers, and landowners' and tenant farmers' younger children who were not able to find a livelihood at home, as well as landowners who had lost their property. Some of them, especially in western Finland, were cottagers who had small rented habitations but not enough land to support their families. These landless workers at temporary jobs were sometimes called day laborers, but they had different names in different parts of the country. They were always a difficult problem in a community and often a burden to parish relief work. Some of them continued to live in these circumstances through lack of desire to seek permanent work, but others fell into this pattern of life because of the poor wages paid by employers, which compelled a man with a large family to depend on public assistance to the poor.[9]

In 1867–92, agricultural workers formed 90 percent of the emigrants from southern Ostrobothnia; only a scant 10 percent were from other occupational groups. During this same period, about sixteen thousand persons emigrated from southern Ostrobothnia and about fifteen thousand from all the rest of Finland.[10] The Ostrobothnian percentages of vocations approximate those of other parts of Finland.

In Finnish literature the difficult life on farms in Finland is frequently presented as the main cause of emigration. In Juhani Aho's short story "The Landlord and the Cottager," the cottager speaks thus:

> Here we have cut down forests, made meadows, cleared lands for cultivation, drained swamps and marshes. A cruel place was this when we came here with my late father, and years of wretched life were lived here. And now that the place has taken form and we are beginning to get grain in return for our labors, he [the landowner] plans to take it from us. And I don't suppose there is any hope for us. He has done the same thing to other cottagers, too.

In early Finnish-American literature, similar descriptions were quite common. For example, there is the story "Vieraalla Maalla" (In a foreign land) by Vaino Kataja in *Nuori Suomi IV*.[11] The hero, Juho Kavanto of northern Finland, had run his ailing father's farm and paid his debts and the interest on other obligations. The father died and creditors appeared. First, all personal property was taken, and then the farmstead was auctioned off. It was bought by the largest creditor, a wealthy neighbor. Juho hired himself out to another neighbor. While at work one day he saw the son of the new owner of his father's property plowing his best field. A great bitterness filled his heart. Without revealing his plans, without even collecting his last pay, and without saying farewell to anyone, he departed for America.

Even more bitter is the poem signed with the initials M. T. in *Amerikan Suomalaisten Osoitekalenteri* in 1903.[12] The poem is titled "Torpan Poika" (The cottager's son). It tells of the struggles of five sons beside their cottager father. When the home was finally in good condition and bread was more plentiful, they were stunned by the receipt of a notice of eviction. The father swore, and the mother became ill of a fever and died. The poet has the son say:

> Now I belong to the league of the poor; I follow its flag,
> That blood-red flag and its pure ideal.
> That ideal makes amends for everything.
> It can even conquer oppression.

In a poem titled "Suomi-aidille" (To Mother Finland), Kalle Koski says:

> Mother Finland, do not criticize those of your sons
> For whom your gifts are not enough to provide a livelihood.
> You do know, and understand—do you not—how we have
>   known hunger,
> How large a number of your children have been condemned
>   to poverty.
> But if there is anything to complain about
> In that your children move to foreign lands
> Because of poverty, complain about this,
> That (in Finland) the sharing of gifts is unequal and
>   unreasonable.
> Some of your children know nothing of want
> For, year after year, they eat the bread of hundreds.
> If you would demand even a small adjustment of these
>   inequities,
> The number leaving the land would be less by half.[13]

In an interview with Eino and Maria Keranen of Watton, Michigan, which appeared in the Oulu *Kaleva* in 1950 is the following statement: "They had left [Finland] to seek bread, and to our question as to whether they had found it, we got an affirmative answer. They said that in America the purchasing power of an hour's wages was three times that in Kainuu, from where they had come to America."

In conversing with former tenant farmers and cottagers who in their youth had exchanged the difficult circumstances of their homeland for the life of an immigrant in a foreign country, and who in their old age have had the opportunity to visit their old homeland, one often hears the following affirmation: Present-day Finland is no longer the same country from which they left. Progress has been just as great as in America, and one of the causes for emigration from Finland—the search for better living conditions—has completely disappeared.

Steamship Lines and Their Agents

Although overpopulation and the inability of Finland's agriculture to guarantee sufficient earnings for ever-increasing numbers of inhabitants were the most important causes of emigration, there were others that should be pointed out.

After the causes already given, the most important cause of the emigration of the 1860s, 1870s, and 1880s was the advertising done by steamship lines. The first big transatlantic shipping company was the Cunard Line, started in 1840 by Samuel Cunard of Halifax, who immediately put four ships into service: the *Britannia*, *Acadia*, *Caledonia*, and *Columbia*. The secret of the Cunard Line's success was an agreement with the English admiralty to carry mail, an arrangement that enabled Cunard, for the time being, to beat his competitors. One of the first of the competitor ships was the *Great Britain*, the first iron-hulled screw steamer. The *Great Britain*'s brilliant career ended in four years, however, because its owners were not able to get government aid. In an attempt to destroy Cunard's monopoly, some Americans established the Collins Line in 1850 with the aid of funds appropriated by Congress. The company launched four large and costly wooden ships. The *Atlantic* was destroyed in a collision, and the *Pacific* vanished without a trace on one of its crossings. The management of the company was accused of irregularities, Congress discontinued its appropriation, and the Collins Line ceased operations in 1858.

In 1850 another company, the Inman Line, was also activated. It was satisfied to operate with smaller ships at slower speeds. It was successful without a government subsidy. In 1856, the North German

Lloyd Line and the Hamburg America Line of Germany entered the competition. In 1871 came the White Star Line, whose *Oceanic* was the predecessor of modern transatlantic steamers in construction and in convenience. In 1871 Britain's Allan Line, which had a branch office in Haaparanta, was also in operation. A little later, additional competitors were the American Line, the Anchor Line, the State Line, the Dominion Line, the National Line, the Scandinavian-American Line, and the Canadian Pacific Railway Company. Agents of the Anchor Line are known to have traveled in Finland soliciting business for their company.

In order to get to the European ports of these transatlantic lines, Finnish emigrants crossed over the Gulf of Bothnia in their own boats to Sweden, and on to Hamburg and Bremen or to some port in England by way of Göteborg. From 1874 on it was possible to go to Swedish ports from Vaasa on ships of the Ångfartygs-Aktiebolaget Gustaf Wasa Company of Finland. In the same year, a direct route from Vaasa to Hull, England, was opened when the Wasa-Nordsjö Ångbåts Ab Company's steamship *Fennia* was put into service. Thus there were direct connections to the west from the Finnish provinces providing the greatest number of emigrants.

The Finnish Steamship Company, established in 1883, soon developed into the greatest transporter of emigrants from Finland to England. Its ice-breaking steamships, *Urania* and *Astraea*, were built expressly for the transportation of third-class passengers. From 1891 on, practically all emigrants sailed from Hanko to Hull on that company's ships. Because the company also represented the more important British, American, and Canadian lines, German steamship lines were bypassed and emigration from Finland to America flowed by way of England until Swedish and Norwegian lines, too, began to compete with the others for passengers.

In her dissertation on southern Ostrobothnian emigration, Toivonen expressed the opinion that the results of the emigration agents' work in Finland were negligible except at the beginning of the movement.[14] Neither she nor the author of this present work has ever met a person who had been influenced by a steamship company agent to leave Finland for America. However, Lauri Hyrske, who made a study of the matter, was of the opinion that after the 1870s there was a "golden age of the emigrant-runner." Warnings against these recruiters were published in newspapers and almanacs.[15]

Of greater importance than pressure from these traveling agents or salesmen were the advertisements of steamship lines. Their wording and their pictures of ships speeding over the ocean were intended to suggest to the reader the way to find adventure and a better life in distant lands. The effect of this kind of advertising was often strengthened by highly exaggerated reports from America. Someone who had become a saloonkeeper might write about owning a hotel. A former shepherd boy might tell of being a superintendent of a large lumber camp where he was, in reality, the janitor of the bunkhouse and the cook's helper.[16] The stories of those who had been in America often emphasized the bright side of life and remained silent on its negative aspects. Then, too, the money sent home by many an immigrant strengthened the belief that "the streets of America are paved with gold." Thus, when one saw an advertisement that said that the office of the steamship line or its local agent would take care of everything, even to obtaining passports, without trouble or complications, and when the agent happened to be the parish sheriff, or a merchant, or some other fully trusted person, it made deciding to go to America quite easy. It was quite another thing to discover at the end of the journey that the streets were not paved with gold—that they were, in fact, not paved at all—and that the immigrant must start to pave them himself. Relatively few persons, probably none with families, would have emigrated if the steamship companies had not taken them by the hand, as it were, and led them from the very gates of home.

Steamship companies and their agents were of considerable importance to emigration from Finland in their work even on the American side of the Atlantic. It is impossible to say how many emigrants left their homeland with a ticket bought by some relative in America in their pocket. In any case, they formed a large percentage of the total number of Finnish immigrants to America. There was an immigration agent in each of the more important Finnish settlements, selling tickets and acting as broker in sending money to Finland.

The earliest of these agents carried on their business in Hancock, advertising regularly in the *Sankarin Maine* (The hero's record), a newspaper published by Matt Fredd. Postmaster M. L. Cardell advertised that, starting in January 1879, he would sell tickets for the National Line, whose ships were the "largest, the fastest, and the most comfortable." At the same time, Isaac Peterson, representative of the Allan Line, who could be reached at Ryan's store, began to advertise. He recommended his line, saying that it "is the cheapest and the best. Good management, plenty of food, and clean surroundings." In addition to Postmaster Cardell, the National Line acquired a second agent in Hancock, Andrew Hendriksen, who began to advertise in June 1879. He declared that he was selling tickets "from here to Europe and from there here at a lower price than the agents of any other steamship company—

26 dollars across the ocean, or 32 dollars from Scandinavian ports to New York, and all the way to Hancock for 47 dollars." Hendriksen was available at the Jos. Vertin store. The postmaster dropped out of the race, and Peterson and Hendriksen added large pictures of ships to their advertisements to attract even more ticket buyers.

In January 1880, the Inman Line appeared on the scene, with the same Andrew Hendriksen as agent; the State Line also came into the picture. Their agent was Samuel Isaksen, who said in his advertisements that the State Line sold tickets "as cheaply as any other line." A year later, Hendriksen was also the representative of the North German Lloyd Line. The advertisement of this line was interesting in that it claimed that its passengers would not become seasick on the North Sea, and that they would not get lost in England:

> This Lloyd Line has advantages over other steamship lines in that it takes passengers from Stockholm and other cities just as far away directly by railroad through Denmark to Bremen, Germany, from where their ships leave for New York by way of the English Channel. The passengers on this line avoid the revolting conditions on the North Sea that passengers on other lines must put up with, and they also avoid wandering about in England and getting lost. The cost is no higher than on other steamship lines.

The agents of the steamship lines also acted as brokers between immigrants and their homeland or, as the agent of the National Line advertised in *Sankarin Maine*, "Drafts are sold at the lowest rate of exchange."[17]

Soon the same type of competition as in Hancock was practiced among steamship companies in other, larger Finnish centers in Michigan. This competition extended even to Finland. For example, the Scandinavian & Finland-American Emigrant Company, which had its main office in New York, also had a large office in Finland in Hanko, with branch offices in Vaasa, Seinäjoki, Hyvinkää, and Helsinki.[18]

It was advantageous to steamship lines and their agents to have as many passengers as possible. In Finland their advertising was less obvious and less aggressive because of the almost universal opposition to emigration. In America the situation was just the opposite. Recruitment of new immigrants was generally approved of as an activity that was of value to the nation. The best way to be successful in this endeavor was to work through immigrants who had already settled in America. In Ironwood, William Maki, a steamship agent, appealed to them in his advertisement thus: "Citizens, remember that when you need to bring your relatives or friends here from Finland, the best place to buy your tickets is from me because I am an agent for all the steamship lines."

The large number of these agents at Finnish centers all over America indicates that the advertising of the steamship lines and their agents is a factor to be considered in the study of emigration from Finland to America.

The experience of Michigan with the work of immigration agents in European countries other than Finland points in the same direction. For example, the state had an agent in Hamburg from 1869 to 1874 who, in addition to working in Germany, also traveled in Denmark and Austria distributing leaflets that described the state's attractive features. The results, however, did not justify the cost. The efforts of steamship lines and of mining and land companies in foreign countries to draw emigrants to America proved sufficient for that approach, so the state immigration agents were sent among Europeans already living in America to carry on their work.

The eloquent appeal of Governor David H. Jerome of Michigan, in his inaugural message to the legislature in 1881, to reestablish the offices of commissioner of immigration and assistant commissioner of immigration is suggestive of the value of immigrants to a state. He urged that

> to secure our share of the emigrants now landing upon the shores of the United States, we should make known our resources, so rich, numerous, and varied; our fertile lands now in market at moderate prices, our admirable school system, and the many attractions offered to the emigrant who desires not only good soil and a healthy climate, but good markets, good government, and pleasant social relations, which are assured by the general character and traditions of Michigan society.[19]

The offices were reestablished. Frederick Morley became the commissioner of immigration and Charles K. Backus the assistant commissioner. Pamphlets were printed in English, German, and Dutch, and a 144-page book titled *Michigan and Its Resources* was published.[20]

Patriotic Causes of Emigration

The most important cause of modern emigration from Finland, as discussed at the beginning of this chapter, was the economic conditions in some parts of the country: overpopulation, the large numbers of landless people, poor wages, and the uncertainty of employment. Another important cause was the advertising of steamship companies. Toward the end of the nineteenth century still another cause, new and different from the earlier ones, developed: patriotism (rightly or wrongly interpreted).

To understand this cause, a few words of explanation are needed. Throughout the centuries, Finland has been the battlefield in war between the East and West. Karelia, its easternmost province, was always the first to experience Russian attacks. The Karelian coat of arms, which was carried for the first time at the funeral of King Gustavus Vasa in 1560, shows two sinewy arms; one hand holds the curved Eastern scimitar and the other a straight Western sword. A few decades later, when Finland acquired its own official coat of arms, the swords of the Karelian coat of arms were pictured on it. The Finnish lion carries the straight Western sword in its paw and tramples under its feet the curved Eastern scimitar.

The last time these swords had clashed on Finnish soil was in 1808–9. The king of Sweden-Finland, Gustavus IV Adolphus, refused to honor Napoleon's continental blockade, meant to cut England off from trade with the European mainland. Instead, he continued friendly relations with Great Britain. Napoleon and Tsar Alexander I of Russia had agreed in Tilsit in 1807 that it was Russia's duty to persuade Sweden to comply. When diplomatic pressure failed, the Russian army marched into Finland in February 1808. Sweden left Finland to fight an overpowering enemy almost completely alone, and the war ended on September 17, 1809, with the treaty of Hamina, in which Sweden formally ceded Finland after centuries of continuous relationship as a single state. While the war was still in progress, in March 1809, at the Diet session held in Porvoo, at which Alexander I was present in person, an agreement between the tsar and the Finnish Diet was reached. The former acknowledged Finland to be an independent state, and the latter accepted the tsar as their grand duke.

After the peace treaty of Hamina, relations between Finland and Russia were generally satisfactory, even though the reign of Nicholas I (1825–55) was a time of reaction. On ascending the throne, the tsars swore to abide by the agreement made in the Porvoo Diet, and to support the constitution of Finland. There were forebodings of restrictions during the reign of Alexander III (1881–94). Fanatically nationalistic Russian newspapers published attacks against Finnish autonomy as well as demands that Finland be more closely united with the Russian empire.

With the ascension of the incompetent and unfriendly Nicholas II to the throne in 1894, the situation rapidly worsened. Although he took the oath and gave his sovereign promise to honor the constitutional government of Finland, he was so vacillating of temperament and so dependent on others that he soon surrendered to pan-Slavic elements among his advisers. To them, an autonomous, democratic, and Western-minded Finland had long been a thorn in the side. In 1898 the tsar sent General Nicholas Bobrikov to be his representative in Finland and to serve as governor-general of the country. Bobrikov's duty was to Russianize Finland and to destroy its privileged status as an independent state.

The so-called February Manifesto, published in February 1899 with Bobrikov's cooperation, allowed the tsar to promulgate such laws as were "common to Finland and Russia" without the concurrence of the Finnish Diet. Efforts of the senate and the Diet to revoke the manifesto were to no avail, and the emperor refused to grant an audience with representatives of the Diet. He also disregarded the "Great Address," which had been signed by over half a million citizens of Finland, demanding a retraction of the illegal manifesto. One illegal act followed another. In St. Petersburg a new military service act was promulgated. It could not be enforced, however, because in many areas the members of draft boards refused to work, and because the young men subject to military service refused to answer the call. The Finnish national army was disbanded. Russian was specified as the official language in higher administrative offices. Newspapers were forced to cease publication, and the governor-general was given the right to banish from the country anyone who was considered a hindrance to him in his work.

The outcome of all this was a wave of "patriotic emigration": departure from Finland to avoid illegally imposed Russian military service. It had already begun during the time of reaction in the reign of Alexander III. In 1891, Bishop Gustaf Johansson of Kuopio stated in the Diet that "during these past years many have left the country because of the unrest and apprehension caused by constant attacks in many Russian newspapers and by several changes in the law."[21] The February Manifesto ultimately caused a nationwide emigration movement. Ostrobothnia was still the leader in emigration, but people also began to leave parishes and towns from which none had gone to America previously.

On June 16, 1904, Eugen Schauman shot to death Governor-General Bobrikov in the Senate in Helsinki. His comrade in arms against Finland, Minister of the Interior Viatcheslav von Flehve, was assassinated in St. Petersburg six weeks later. Liberal and revolutionary factions began to spring up in Russia, and when the Russo-Japanese War ended in 1905 with the defeat of Russia, serious disturbances took place in the country. During the first days of November 1905 a general strike began in Finland in which all classes participated. The Russian government yielded. Nicholas II signed the so-called November manifesto, which countermanded the illegal dictates of previous years. Finland got a unicameral parliament the next year, and every citizen who had reached the age of twenty-four was given the right to vote, including women.

Wilho Leikas, a Calumet printer, distributed a four-page postcard in honor of Eugen Schauman; on one page were pictured two men who look more like Turks than Finns, carrying the Goddess of Liberty. On the pennant carried by the goddess is the date on which Nicholas II signed the November Manifesto. November 1, 1905, the date at the bottom of the picture, apparently stands for the beginning of the general strike. Another picture on the card shows Nicholas II on his knees beside his fallen throne.

The growth of the emigration movement was halted when some of its causes were eliminated. In some years, the numbers leaving the country were even below the usual average. Nevertheless, the generally suspicious attitude toward Russia was justified when in 1909 Lieutenant-General Frans Albert Seyn, a well-known enemy of Finland, was named governor-general of the country, and new political oppression began. The number of emigrants again rose rapidly.

Table 3 shows emigration from Finland to other countries from 1890 to the beginning of World War I. Because the province of Vaasa had the most emigrants, it is used for comparison to underscore the fact that under Russian oppression emigration increased, not only from limited areas but from all of Finland.

In her studies of emigration, Toivonen gave special attention to the effect of political oppression on emigration. She also provided many interesting details about happenings of those years.[22] Because of difficulties in regard to passports, men from the coastal parishes often sailed across the Gulf of Bothnia to Sweden in open boats. Men from the interior parishes were more dependent on passports if they were of age for military service. But passports were not absolutely impossible to obtain. In Hanko, a passport could be purchased "from the secret shop of the activists," steamship agents sold forged passports for five marks apiece, and there is thought to have been a "passport factory" in Seinäjoki. Since the real or fabricated reason for going to America was

Table 3: Emigration from Finland, 1890–1915

YEAR	EMIGRANTS FROM VAASA	EMIGRANTS FROM ALL OF FINLAND
1890	3,116	3,940
1891	2,053	2,809
1892	3,315	3,922
1893	5,714	9,117
1894	879	1,380
1895	3,083	4,020
1896	3,782	5,185
1897	1,359	1,916
1898	2,630	3,467
1899	8,658	12,075
1900	6,715	10,397
1901	7,316	12,561
1902	11,111	23,152
1903	6,977	16,964
1904	5,150	10,952
1905	8,453	17,427
1906	8,133	17,517
1907	7,375	16,296
1908	2,567	5,812
1909	8,300	19,144
1910	8,054	19,007
1911	3,819	9,372
1912	4,200	10,724
1913	7,490	20,057
1914	2,237	6,474
1915	2,353	4,041

avoidance of the military service illegally imposed by Russia, the matter bore the stamp of patriotism. "When even the sheriff shook hands in farewell, and the provost blessed the journey, using a falsified passport did not bother the conscience."

Many of those who fled to avoid military service traveled with passports that had been issued to someone else. The real owner of the passport sent it by mail, perhaps from England, to a friend and, later, to another. In this way one passport sometimes served many men before it expired.[23]

The career of Aleksander Larson, who came to America to avoid being called into military service, is an example of what sometimes happened.[24] Larson, a farmer's son, was born near Kokkola in 1861. The military service law of December 27, 1878, had created restlessness among the Finnish people even though it concerned service in their own army, for they feared they would be sent to defend Russia. On reaching age twenty-one, when he became eligible for military service, Alex, as he now called himself, went by boat across Merenkurkku to Sundsvall, from where he went by train to Göteborg. His journey continued from there on a ship of the National Steamship Line to New York, and from there to Detroit and on to Bay City, where the railroad ended. From there Alex was taken by paddle-wheel steamboat to Oscoda, where he found a cousin who had arrived previously. Eventually he found work in a large sawmill in East Tawas. There he married Mathilda Johanson, who had been born in Perko in 1859.

In 1888, with his wife and little daughter, he returned to Finland to his father's farm. A few months passed peacefully, but one day a policeman came to arrest him as a deserter. After a long wait in jail he was freed. He decided to go back to America, but there was no possibility of getting a passport. In the summer of 1890 he sent his wife (his daughter had died) by the regular route from Hanko to Liverpool. Alex himself hid in Vaasa harbor on a ship leaving for Sundsvall. In Liverpool he met his wife, who had arrived there three days earlier. Back in East Tawas, he returned to his old job in the sawmill.

The mass movement of Finnish Leftists to the United States and Canada after 1918 when they had lost the War of Independence and the Civil War, may also be considered emigration for political reasons, a fact that seems generally to be ignored by historians of Finnish emigration.

After the United States became involved in World War I, entry into the United States was stopped, and the flow of immigration ceased. In 1920 it again became possible to enter the country, and the numbers of immigrants from Finland increased rapidly. There were thousands among them who found the political situation in their homeland oppressive. Statistics of emigration from Finland during the final phases of the war and during the years following are shown in Table 4. The province of Vaasa is again used for the purpose of comparison.

Table 4: Emigration from Finland, 1918–25

YEAR	EMIGRANTS FROM VAASA	EMIGRANTS FROM ALL OF FINLAND
1918	897	1,900
1919	308	1,085
1920	2,425	5,595
1921	999	3,557
1922	1,872	5,715
1923	5,028	13,835
1924	2,037	5,108
1925	902	2,075

Other Causes of Emigration

The other causes of emigration were similar, in that they brought people to America with the thought that after staying in the country for a while they would return to their homeland. One of the most frequent causes for leaving Finland was to earn money to buy a house and to finance a marriage. Although the workday in America was shorter than that in Finland, wages were better, so that an unmarried man could quite easily save a sizeable amount in a relatively short time. A large number of immigrants saved so much money in a few years that when they returned to Finland they were financially independent.

At the beginning of the present century, this procedure to earn money for a home and marriage was a popular subject of Finnish-American literature.[25] It has been less frequently shown that more work had to be done in the shorter American workday than in the longer Finnish workday, and that the pace at which work was done was much more hurried than that to which most immigrants were accustomed. A carpenter recently arrived from Finland tells this story about his first morning on a big construction job:

> The boss told us to put hinges and locks on doors. I took a door and began to fit a hinge on it. The boss watched me for a while, shook his head, and said it was not done like that in America. I didn't understand what he meant so he asked me to help him. We raised eight doors side by side on their edges, and he took a yardstick and with one stroke of a marking pencil he drew a line across them all to indicate the placement of the hinges. "It's quicker this way," he said, and walked away. The following day he came to look at my work and said

> that by and by I would be a carpenter. And to think I had thought I already was one.[26]

Some of the Finns adapted themselves to the new methods of work and reached their goals, while others withdrew from the competition in disappointment. Some of them may have left on this temporary type of excursion because of a desire for adventure. The brilliant but often overlooked writer about Finnish emigration, Konni Zilliacus, presents this last-mentioned group in unvarnished words.

> Among the emigrants there are many elements that are not a great loss to their fatherland when they leave. There are the university students who have ruined their future in Helsinki; there are many kinds of youths who have been able to borrow money too easily, or who had dipped their fingers into poorly locked cash registers; clergy who have lived too wildly to be suited even for country pastorates; artisans or businessmen who have flown higher than their wings could bear them; and finally, a large number of indeterminate creatures who have gone to rack and ruin for no real reason, more through happy-go-lucky bungling than because of bad characteristics.[27]

It is probably through translating Zilliacus into Finnish that Juhani Aho found a theme for his story "A Leap into Another World," in which he tells how Matti Kariniemi, a university student, *civis aeternus* (eternal student), a drunkard and brawler, left Finland to seek adventure in America. "And so Matti Kariniemi went to America. And he became a man. According to recent reports, he is a pastor in America. And I have seen the returned emigrant whose child he baptized."

The fictional Matti Kariniemi is a representation of living personalities. For on settling in America permanently, many an adventurer of bad habits in his youth mended his ways as Matti did and became a respected citizen. There were other men, of course, who did not improve but returned to their homeland as prodigal sons.

Among the causes of emigration given in local literature about immigrants, mention is quite often made of "impatience with Finland's class society," which is compared unfavorably with the "classless" democracy of America. Nevertheless, the present writer, in his many contacts with Finnish immigrants, has never met anyone who left his homeland for that reason. If any immigrant to America ever had such a thought, he was soon disillusioned and realized that on this side of the Atlantic there were sharp class distinctions, and that the immigrant who was unable to speak English belonged to the lowest class. Behind the talk of class society in Finland was the memory of the earlier days of the Finnish four-chamber Diet in which, up to 1906, the leaders of the country were seated according to class as nobility, clergy, bourgeoisie, and peasants. More recently, in speaking of a class society in Finland, what is meant is that there, as in other European countries, it is customary to use titles in speaking to people, whereas in America even the president is addressed as "Mister."

In connection with the causes of emigration, it is well to mention that thousands of Finns who came to America with the firm resolve to return to the land of their birth as soon as they had accumulated enough money abandoned this idea after 1918. They had deposited their money in Finnish banks, and the postwar inflation, which also affected many other European countries, lowered the value of their savings to almost nothing. They did not have the courage to try again, or they were too old to begin anew.

4 The First Finn in Michigan

Until an older document is discovered in the hidden recesses of some archive or other, the story of the life and activities of Finns in Michigan must begin with the picture Fredrika Bremer gives of the few days she spent in Lower Michigan in mid-September 1850.[1]

There were many gifted individuals in the Finnish branch of the Bremer family. They distinguished themselves in mining or as authors and journalists. The one instrumental in bringing the greatest fame to the family was Fredrika Bremer, who was born on the Tuorla estate in Piikkiö on August 17, 1801, and died in Sweden on December 31, 1865. She was a writer and a zealous champion of liberalism. Her father was a wholesale merchant who moved his business and his family to Sweden in 1804. Of Fredrika Bremer's many travels abroad, her extensive journey in North America in 1849–51 is especially noteworthy. In Stockholm in 1853–54 she published a large, two-volume work titled *Hemmen i den Nya verlden, En dagbok i bref, skrifna under tvenne års resor i Norra Amerika och på Cuba* (Homes of the New World: A diary of two years of travel in North America and Cuba). The work appeared in English under the brief title *Homes of the New World*, and achieved a wide readership.[2] Because of the unusual interest of the subject matter, the complete report on her trip across Lower Michigan is included here:

> For me, however, the sail across Lake Erie was like a sunbright festival, in that magnificent steamer where even a piano was heard in the crowded saloon, and where a polite and most agreeable captain took charge of me in the kindest manner. My good old pioneer related to

me various incidents of his life, his religious conversion, his first love and his last, which was quite recent; the old gentleman declaring himself to be half in love with "that Yankee woman, Mrs. L.;" and I do not wonder at it. It convinced me that he had good taste. He declared himself to be "first and foremost a great ladies' man."[3]

At four o'clock in the afternoon—that is to say, of the day after we went on board, we reached Detroit, a city first founded by the French upon that narrow strait between the Lakes Erie and St. Clair, which separates Michigan from Canada. The shores, as seen from the vessel, appeared to be laid out in small farms consisting of regular allotments, surrounded by plantations. The land seemed to be low but fertile, undulating hill and valley. Detroit is, like Buffalo, a city where business life preponderates, yet still it looked to me pleasanter and more friendly than Buffalo. I saw at the hotel some tiresome catechisers, and also some very agreeable people, people whom one could talk well and frankly with, and whom one could like in all respects. Among these I remember, in particular, the Episcopal bishop of Michigan, a frank, excellent, and intellectual man; and a mother and her daughters. I was able to exchange a few cordial words with them, words out of the earnest depths of life, and such always do me good. The people of Detroit were, for the rest, pleased with their city and their way of life there, pleased with themselves, and with each other. And this seems to me to be the case in most of the places that I have been to here in the West.

The following evening we were at Anne Arbor, a pretty little rural city. Here also I received visitors, and was examined as usual. My good old pioneer did not approve of traveling *incognito*, but insisted upon it that people should be known by people, and could not comprehend how any one could be tired, and need a cessation of introductions and questions. In Anne Arbor, also, the people were much pleased with themselves, their city, its situation, and way of life. The city derived its name from the circumstance that when the first settlers came to the place they consisted principally of one family, and while the woods were felled and the land plowed, the laborers had no other dwelling than a tent-like shed of boughs and canvas, where the mother of the family, "Anne," prepared the food, and cared for the comfort of all. That was the domestic hearth; that was the calm haven where all the laborers found rest and refreshment under the protection of Mother Anne. Hence they called the tent Anne's Arbor or Bower, and the city, which by degrees sprung up around it, retained the name. And with its neat houses and gardens upon the green hills and slopes the little city looked, indeed, like a peaceful retreat from the unquiet of the world.

We remained over night at Anne Arbor. The following morning we set off by rail-road and traveled directly across the State of Michigan. Through the whole distance I saw small farms, with their well-built houses, surrounded by well-cultivated land; fields of wheat and maize, and orchards full of apple and peach trees. In the wilder districts the fields were brilliant with some beautiful kind of violet and blue flowers, which the rapidity of our journey prevented me from examining more closely, and with tall sunflowers, the heads of which were as large as young trees. It was splendid and beautiful. My old pioneer told me that he never had seen any where such an affluence of magnificent flowers as in Michigan, especially in the olden times before the wilderness was broken up into fields. Michigan is one of the youngest states of the Union, but has a rich soil, particularly calculated for the growth of wheat, and is greatly on the increase. The legislation is of the most liberal description, and it has abolished capital punishment in its penal code. Nevertheless, I heard of crime having been committed in this state which deserved death, or at least imprisonment for life, if any crime does deserve it. A young man of a respectable family in Detroit, during a hunt, had shot clandestinely and repeatedly at another young man, his best friend, merely to rob him of his pocket-book. He had been condemned for an attempt to murder, which he acknowledged, only to twenty years' imprisonment. And in prison he was visited by young ladies, who went to teach him French and to play on the guitar! One of these traveled with me on the rail-road. She spoke of the young prisoner's "agreeable demeanor!" there is a leniency toward crime and the criminal which is disgusting, and which proves a laxity of moral feeling.

The weather was glorious the whole day. The sun preceded us westward. We steered our course directly toward the sun; and the nearer it sank toward the earth, more brightly glowed the evening sky as with the most transcendent gold. The country, through the whole extent, was lowland, and monotonous. Here and there wound along a lovely little wooded stream. Here and there in the woods were small frame houses, and beside one and another of them wooden sheds, upon which a board was fastened, whereon might be read in white letters, half a yard high, the word "Grocery." The cultivated districts were in all cases divided regularly, scattered over with farm-houses resembling those of our better class of peasant farmers. The settlers in the West purchase allotments of from eighty to one hundred and sixty or two hundred acres, seldom less and seldom more. The land costs, in the first instance, what is called "government price," one dollar and a quarter per acre; and will, if well cultivated, produce abundant harvests within a few years. The farmers here work hard, live frugally, but well, and bring up strong, able families. The children, however, seldom follow the occupation of their fathers. They are sent to schools, and after that endeavor to raise themselves by political or public life. These small farms are the nurseries from which

> the Northwest States obtain their best officials and teachers, both male and female. A vigorous, pious, laborious race grows up here. I received much enlightenment on this subject from my good old pioneer, who, with his piety, his restless activity, his humanity, his great information, and his youthfully warm heart, even in advancing years, was a good type of the first cultivators of the wilderness in this country. He parted from me on the journey in order to reach his home in the little city of Niles.
>
> In company with an agreeable gentleman, Mr. H., and his agreeable sister-in-law, I went on board the steamer which crosses Lake Michigan. The sun had now sunk; but the evening sky glowed with the brightest crimson above the sea-like lake. We departed amid its splendor and in the light of the new moon. The water was calm as a mirror.
>
> On the morning of the 13th of September, I saw the sun shine over Chicago.[4]

Frederika Bremer wrote this entertaining narrative in Chicago on September 15, when impressions of her experience were still fresh in her mind. It shows how the young and growing state of Michigan looked to a cultured and widely traveled Finnish lady. Her mention of the diversions afforded a criminal in a Michigan prison was obviously based on an individual case, which seems to have disturbed the sensibilities of the authoress at the time.

It would have been interesting if, on her travels, Fredrika Bremer had chanced to meet Elise Waerenskjold, a gifted Norwegian writer who had been living in Texas since 1847. Elise Waerenskjold, too, was in many ways ahead of her times.[5]

5 The Copper Country

The more recent immigration to America from Finland has no definite starting date. A sailor here and a sailor there left his ship and settled in Boston, Brooklyn, Pensacola, or some other seaport. The California Gold Rush, which began in the spring of 1848, attracted a large number of seamen when they chanced to stop at San Francisco or some other West Coast port. During the Crimean War (1853–56), when Finnish ships were in danger of being captured by the British and French men-of-war, many of the vessels in American harbors at the time were sold. Sometimes entire crews were left ashore. At the beginning of the Civil War in 1861, there were, according to Ilmonen, approximately one thousand Finns in America, of whom about one hundred joined the Union forces, most of them being former seamen who went into the navy. However, no names of Michigan Finns can be found on army or navy rosters, for the first permanent Finnish settlers did not come to the state until toward the end of the war.[1]

The Copper Country, which includes Houghton, Baraga, Ontonagon, and Keweenaw Counties, became the home of the earliest Finnish settlers. "Kuparisaari," or Copper Island, as the Finns call it, actually means the part of the Keweenaw Peninsula which juts out into Lake Superior on the north side of Portage Lake. Its inhabitants often aver that they live outside the American mainland. In practical usage, however, the term includes towns such as Oskar, Atlantic, Baltic, South Range, Houghton, Dodgeville, and Hurontown, on the south side of Portage. Finns living in these areas consider themselves as being unquestionably "Copper Islanders."

Hancock

The U.S. Civil War was instrumental in bringing the first Finnish settlers to Michigan. For a time, the war caused a depression in the state's copper mining industry. Because young men were called to arms or moved to Canada to avoid conscription, the mines lost many of their best workmen. In the latter part of 1864, the Ontonagon mines had only half their normal labor force, and at the Cliff Mine manpower had fallen to one fourth of what it had been at the beginning of the war.[2] The Quincy Mining Company set about solving the problem in a hitherto untried way.

The company had been established in 1848 and had started mining on Quincy Hill north of Portage Lake. The mining town of Hancock sprang up between the lake and the mine. Officials were first elected on March 10, 1863. This date is considered the date of the founding of Hancock. The next mining company to appear on the scene was the Pewabic, which had found rich deposits of amygdaloid containing pure copper, and which became a competitor of the Quincy. To get more manpower and to free itself of competition, the Quincy Mining Company sent Christian Taftes, who was a member of their office force, to northern Norway in the spring of 1864 to recruit skilled labor. Taftes was especially suited for this task, having come from the Tornio river valley and speaking both Finnish and Swedish fluently.[3]

In the summer of the same year, over a hundred of Taftes's skilled workers arrived in Hancock. They were mostly Norwegians from the Kaafjord and Alten mines. Among them were a few Finns and Swedes, but their names are not known. In any case, the arrival of this expedition was the modest beginning of the first Finnish settlements in the Copper Country, especially in Hancock.[4]

Taftes's trip to the mines of Norway caused a stir among the Ruija Finns. To add to the excitement, there were letters from America that told of available work, of the possibility of acquiring free homestead lands, of the abundance of game and fish, and of the plenitude of food and other essentials of existence. To the people of the frozen north, accustomed to barely making a living, this called to mind the Old Testament writer's "As cold waters to a thirsty soul, so is good news from a far country."

On May 17, 1865, a sailing vessel left Trondhjem with a group of thirty Finns, their destination the Quincy Mine. Among them were Henrik Commes, Olli Danielson, Isak Eiby, Johan Karppanen, Johan Kihlanki, Antti Länkki, Aleksander Lintulahti, Matti Maikko, Johan Peter Noppa, Peter Lampa, Isak Podas, Olli Sutinen, Johan Svarvari, and Peter Christopher, a Norwegian Finn. Many of the men were accompanied by their families. The ship brought them to Quebec, where tickets were purchased for their destination. The ticket office attendant could not find a place named Quincy in Michigan. The situation looked bad until someone remembered that the Quincy mine was in Hancock. Hancock was found, and the journey continued by lake steamer to its destination.

It was June 23, the eve of St. John's Day, when the boat reached Hancock. The greater part of the area on which the present city stands was then covered with heavy forest. Parallel to the lakeshore ran Hancock and Quincy streets. They were cut across by deep gullies caused by thousands of years of heavy rain. There were wooden bridges across these ravines, which have since been filled with gravel from the hilltop and are now known as Tezcuco, Ravine, and Montezuma streets. In 1861 a stamp mill was built below Front and Reservation streets. That same year the first hardware store in Hancock was opened on the corner of Quincy and Reservation streets, where the Finnish Mutual Fire Insurance Company building now stands. M. J. McGurrin opened the town's first drugstore in 1865. In addition, there were a few small grocery stores and a shop where James Artman sold handmade harnesses. The population of the town may have been about four hundred in all, the great majority of miners living in small houses near their work in the immediate vicinity of the mines.[5]

When the Finns had disembarked with their meager possessions and stood on the dock, they were greeted by the townspeople, among whom were some Norwegians who took them to a Norwegian boarding house. The following day the Finns went to the Quincy mine to look for work, since June 24 was not a holiday in America as it was in Finland. One of the Finns, Peter Christopher, had with him a letter of recommendation from the English mining engineer at Kaafjord. It so happened that the Quincy mine captain knew him, having attended the same engineering school. The Finns thus received special consideration. Jobs were found for all of them, and several small log buildings in Swedetown were given them to live in. That summer a few more Finns from Kaafjord and Alten arrived with some Norwegians, so that by the end of 1865 there were fifty Finnish immigrants in Hancock.[6] During the following summers, single Finns and Finns with families came from other Finnish villages of Finmarken. From Hancock, the Finns spread to the little communities growing up near the mines owned by the Quincy Mining Company. They included Franklin, Boston, and Mesnard. A Quincy company mill was built in Ripley on the shore of Portage Lake to the east of Hancock, and many Finnish families soon moved there.

In 1866, Johan Karppanen, Kalle Herrala, and Matti Mauna, who had been working at the Quincy mine, decided to exchange copper mining for gold mining and left for the California gold fields. They did not reach their destination. With a number of other travellers they were ambushed and killed by Indians in Utah.[7]

On Sunday, April 11, 1869, a disaster struck Hancock. At a saloon on the spot where the post office is now located, the stovepipe of the potbellied stove exploded and soon the building was in flames. A strong west wind spread the fire from one building to another and across the wooden bridges over the ravines. In a short time three-fourths of Hancock lay in ruins. The Congregational Church, built in 1862, was destroyed, and almost all of the business places as well as most of the homes. St. Anne's Catholic Church, built in 1861, and the German St. Peter and St. Paul Lutheran Church, finished in 1867, were spared. It took two years to rebuild Hancock.

In the early years of the Copper Country mining industry, the first miners came from the silver, tin, and copper mines of the eastern states. Miners also arrived very early from England, Ireland, and Germany. Those from Cornwall soon became the core of mining personnel. Because they spoke English and were highly skilled and experienced miners they became foremen and captains.[8] But Finns were soon numerous as well.

Although the total emigration from Finland, according to too-low official estimates, was only 500 in the 1870s and 2,700 in the 1880s, and although many of those who came to America went to Minnesota, immigration to the Copper Country increased rapidly, for it was invariably the destination of Finns from the northern parts of Norway and Sweden.

During the summer of 1873 especially, the Finnish population of the Copper Country increased considerably. Many immigrants came from northwest parts, from Finmark, and from Oulu, where the emigration movement was spreading. In the beginning at least, there was disappointment for these newcomers because some of the iron mines in Ishpeming closed that fall, and large numbers of unemployed men came from there to the Copper Country to find work. With so much manpower available, the mining companies paid lower wages and used the ore obtained at smaller cost in competing with other copper mining companies. Because of poor wages and the uncertainty of work, many Finns moved further west, initiating a trend that continued for a long time. For example, on June 7, 1879, a boat left Hancock for Duluth with many passengers of many different nationalities, and half of them were Finns.[9]

In 1875, when Hancock was incorporated as a village, a school was built where the present high school stands. There is an indication of the small size of the village at that time in the statement about the school's being "far away in the western part and outside the village limits." In this small village, whose population included many different nationalities, the Finns were noticeably active. In 1876 they published their own newspaper, *Amerikan Suomalainen Lehti* (The Finnish American paper) which, however, expired the same year for lack of support and because of the weaknesses of the publisher. The weekly newspapers that followed, namely, the *Swen Tuuva* and its continuation *Sankarin Maine* (1878–81), published by Matti Fredd, lasted longer because of the support of local subscribers.

The only organized activity of Finns in the Copper Country during these early days was the work of church congregations. It was divided along the lines of regular Lutheranism and Laestadianism. The Laestadians did not announce their meetings in newspapers, but Pastor A. E. Backman of the regular Lutheran church always announced his services, which were held in the Finnish Norwegian church built in 1867 beyond the village, on Quincy Hill.

Among the advertisements in Fredd's newspaper there were at first no advertisements of Finnish business concerns. Offering their professional services to the Finns of the community there were the dentist, Dr. D. G. Grant; the "French" doctor, J. E. Scallon; a German physician by the name of C. Hafenreffer; and the law firm of Chandler and Grant. Among the business places soliciting Finnish patronage were the following: the D. T. Macdonald and the A. J. Scott drugstores; the Edward Ryan, P. Ruppe, and Jos. Vertin stores dealing in general merchandise; the Holland, Cardell and Company hardware store; Pete Wagner's "barbering and bathing" house; and G. Deimelin's jewelry store. The first advertisement of a Finnish concern to the Finns in Hancock and the surrounding areas was the following:

> This is to announce to the public that the undersigned will bring a large number of the best milk cows to Hancock and Calumet as soon as the shipping season opens.
>
> Franklin, Minn., 29 March 1879.
>
> Peter Lahti

Living conditions in the Copper Country in the early days explain the offer to sell cows to people living in town. When the shipping season closed in late fall, it was necessary to wait until spring for the arrival of boats with provisions, except for the supplies that were brought to L'Anse by train, and from there by horse teams to the Copper Country. Thus, it was necessary for a household to be as self-supporting as possible. An aid to self-sufficiency for a family was to keep at least one cow. The streets of the village were so arranged that between each two of them ran a narrow alley which separated the backs of the lots on which the homes stood facing the streets. Each resident had a barn with an attendant woodshed in his backyard verging on the alley, along which the cows would be taken to the common pastures of the village. In 1960 there were still some homes in West Hancock with cow barns in their backyards, although the cows had long since disappeared.

In his newspaper, Matti Fredd advertised that he also kept a bookstore; otherwise, Hancock remained without any Finnish business establishments until Peter Christopher started a Finnish restaurant on Tezcuco street, which he advertised in October 1879 as also having rooms and "everything required by the traveling man." Christopher's restaurant was in a convenient location, for the Mineral Range railroad station was on the shore of Portage Lake at the foot of Tezcuco Street. From there, trains made three round trips a day to Calumet. But railroad connections to the outside world were not available except from L'Anse, about thirty-five miles away. During the open season, the steamboat *Ivanhoe* left at 6:30 A.M. every day from the Hancock dock, crossed the lake to the Houghton side, and left from there at 7:00 for L'Anse. The train from L'Anse arrived in Chicago at 5:30 the next morning. Chicago was one of the gateways to the outside world from the Copper Country until flight service became possible from the area's own airport and brought about the end of railroad passenger service.

The figures in table 5 from histories of Michigan give some idea of the growth of population in the Copper Country.

Toward the end of the 1880s the population of the Copper Country began to grow rapidly. This growth was due to increase of activity in the mining industry and to an influx of immigrants. Accurate statistics are hard to find because censuses had not been exact in the first place; secondly, mining towns sprang up and died out in rapid succession; thirdly, a large number of miners and lumberjacks were transients. In 1899–1900, according to official figures, the population of Hancock was only 1,662, but the inhabitants of the surrounding small villages considered themselves as much residents of Hancock as the people living within the city. *Polk's Houghton County Directory* (1899–1900) listed names and addresses of 4,900 persons residing in

Table 5: Population Growth in the Copper Country, 1850–1900

YEAR	1850	1854	1860	1864
Total*	1,097	6,492	13,821	18,811

YEAR	1870	1880	1890	1900
Houghton County	13,882	22,473	35,389	66,063
Keweenaw County	4,206	4,270	2,805	3,217

*In statistics up to 1864 the numbers from Houghton, Ontonagon, and Keweenaw counties appear as a combined total.

the Hancock area.[10] Of these, 457 had unmistakably Finnish names, approximately one in ten; it is impossible to estimate how many of the Matsons, Johnsons, Larsons, and other non-Finnish names were actually the names of Finns. Obviously, the 4,900 did not include all of the residents of Hancock and surrounding areas. It was impossible for the publishers of the directory to find and list all the names. In the introduction of the directory, the publishers estimated that the actual population may have been about 9,000 in the Hancock area. Calumet and its surrounding areas may have had a population of 38,000.

By the turn of the century, cultural activities had begun among the Finns. Both the Laestadians and the young Suomi Synod had built churches, the temperance society had a fine hall, and the first Suomi College building had been built. Their choruses and bands attracted the notice of many besides Finns. Many Finns had become businessmen. Henry Haapapuro had a butcher shop on Minnesota Street, and Sam Junttila and John Wayrynen had a general store and bakery. On Elevation Street, William Koppanen had a grocery store. August Pelto had a tailor shop on Quincy Street, and William Hagerty and Matti Rauhala had one on Tezcuco Street. In the downtown area there was a jewelry store run by Charles Waara. Henry Sakari had a slaughterhouse, and Jacob Tolonen a blacksmith shop. Andrew Johnson and Isaac Tolonen were both in the lumber business. Jafet Nopola, William Anttila, Elias Hoskela, and John Kermu were proprietors of saloons, all of them on Tezcuco Street. Newspapers and periodicals, both religious and secular, were being published, and J. K. Nikander and Juho Heikki Jasberg had opened a Finnish bookstore. At this time, the only Finn among the city officials was Andrew Johnson, who was road commissioner.

Other businessmen of Hancock included Edward Waara, a watchmaker and goldsmith, who was born in Alkkula, Oulu, in 1855, arrived in Calumet in 1881, and went into the trade he had learned from his father. In 1885 he moved his business to Hancock where his son, Charles Waara, continued it until 1950. Henry Sakari was born in the church village of Matarenki, across from Aavasaksa, in 1863 and arrived in the Copper Country in 1887. His slaughtering business expanded in the early years of the twentieth century into a big enterprise of many departments, including a grocery store. Many of the later Finnish businessmen of the Copper Country got their first experience in business by working for Sakari. Frank Eilola was born in Merijärvi in 1864. After becoming acquainted with the New World through many activities, he started Frank Eilola and Company in 1906. Besides handling food and clothing, the company also sold lumber and charcoal and supplied the charcoal used by many Copper Country smelters. Eilola's two important business partners were John Olson, born in Kittilä in 1885, and Nels Erickson, born in Ylitornio, Sweden, in 1887.

William Johnson, son of Andrew Johnson, was born in Hancock in 1883, studied at Valparaiso University, and followed his father in the lumber business. Isak Lehto, born in Matarenki in 1860, and John Latva, born in Pulkkila in 1864, opened a general store together toward the end of the 1890s. The business prospered and expanded. Latva sold his share to Lehto and opened a store of his own. Oscar Nordstrom, born in Hietaniemi, Sweden, in 1883, had a grocery store on Summit Street for many years. Nestor Lepisto, born in Veteli in 1882, and Efraim Lohela, born in Pyhäjärvi in the province of Oulu in the same year, opened a grocery store together in 1911. Matti Mattson, born in Nurmo in 1881, started a soft drinks factory about 1910, a business that attracted many temperance-minded Finns. Charles A. Kukkonen, born in Muhos in 1889, arrived in Hancock in 1903, registering immediately at Suomi College. After learning the English language and acquiring skill in photography, he set up his own business in 1912. The name "Kukkonen Studio" appears on innumerable photographs of Copper Country Finns and their activities. The business was owned until the 1990s by Carl Kukkonen, son of the original owner.

Ever since the former seaman and student of pharmacology Oswald H. Beckman, the son of a clergyman of Jalasjärvi, became the first Finnish-American physician in 1884, local Finns have been interested in both medicine and pharmacology. The earliest known Finnish druggist in Hancock was Zachris Werner Nikander, who was working for Carl Printz by 1889 and who completed his pharmacological examinations in Lansing in 1891. While Nikander was away attending to his drugstores elsewhere, A. W. Lindholm opened the Hancockin Suomalainen Apteekki (Finnish Drugstore). It was bought by Andrew Bram, who was born in Pyhäjoki in 1869. Bram was an active businessman who served his community in many ways. He was county treasurer for a time and was appointed postmaster of Hancock in 1923. In 1912, Bram sold his drugstore to Werner Nikander, who had returned to Hancock and who, in turn, sold it to Axel Durchman, born in Viitasaari in 1881. Durchman had graduated from Ferris Institute. He died in 1926. The drugstore is no longer in Finnish hands. The other drugstore in Hancock was also owned by Finns, the last of them being Walter Mattson, who died in 1961.

A Finnish hospital was started in Hancock in the spring of 1917, "because the local Catholic institution did not meet the requirements of Protestants," as was stated in a leaflet put out by the board of directors of the new hospital. The president of the board was Oscar Nordstrom; the vice-president, Frank Olson; the treasurer, Matti Mattson. Werner Nikander served as manager and was, in many ways, the animating spirit of the institution.

The hospital was located in east Hancock on the hillside overlooking Portage Lake, from where there was a beautiful view of Houghton. It had twenty-five beds. The three Finnish doctors of the area, along with nine others, performed operations and cared for patients there. Dr. Holm came from Ishpeming twice a month until 1923, when he moved to Hancock and rented the hospital in his own name. Holm's fame as a surgeon drew patients to Hancock from as far away as Canada. But the sixteen-room hospital building with its twenty-five beds proved inadequate, and patients' fees, which often remained unpaid, did not meet expenses. When Holm moved to the West in 1931, the hospital had already closed its doors. Holm died in Encino, California, in 1960. Decades after the closing of the hospital, Copper Country Finns still remembered it and its Finnish personnel with nostalgia. Dr. Henry L. Sarvela and Victor E. Lepisto were two of the more recent Finnish physicians of Hancock. The latter, an opthalmologist, was well known for spending his summer vacations working among the poor people of India, donating his services.

Finnish tailors gave a special flair to Hancock. Many of them in their youth had belonged to the famous community of tailors in the Finnish colony in St. Petersburg. In addition to the previously mentioned Pelto and Rauhala, there were Laurell, Klemetti, and Honkanen, each of whom had a shop of his own. Theodor Laurell was born in Ylistaro and learned tailoring in Helsinki. Hugo Klemetti came from Sotkamo. He had a shop in South Range before moving to Hancock. Matti Honkanen was from Pielisjärvi. He had added to his professional knowledge and skill by studying in Germany on a grant from the government of Finland.

Toward the end of the 1880s the Finns of the area began to organize sickness and accident insurance associations. By the turn of the century they had about one hundred of these associations. Suomalainen Sairastus ja Loukkaus-Apuyhdistys (The Finnish sickness and accident aid association) was founded in 1892. At first, its field of activity was only Houghton County, but later it extended to Keweenaw, Baraga, and Ontonagon Counties. The association's constitution read, in part, "The purpose of this association is to aid and support, with our funds, those who through illness or accident have become unable to work; also, in case of death, to provide a proper burial." With 320 members in 1907, membership was at its highest. It leveled off to about 300 until 1913 when, because of the Copper Country strike and other circumstances, a mass movement of Finns to Detroit and elsewhere occurred. In 1930 the membership was still about 200, but by the 1960s there were only a few members. The membership fee was 50 cents per month. Medical assistance, which is called *kipuraha* (sick money) in the account books, was one dollar per day, in addition to which a nurse's salary was often paid. At the beginning of the century, burial aid was $75, going up to $150 later on. Burial aid for the wife of a member was $25. The amounts paid varied with the financial condition of the company. For a generation, the association paid out $2,000 per year, on the average, to members. Nestor Jauhiainen was the last of the officers and had served the company for a long time.[11]

The special character of three different Finnish institutions was impressed on Hancock at the beginning of the century. They were the Finnish labor movement, the churches, and, especially, Suomi College. Because of these, Hancock has sometimes been called the Athens of Finnish Americans.

In this connection there were two Finns of Hancock who were well known in their day. One of them was Lauri Moilanen, who, as Big Louis Moilanen, became famous as perhaps the biggest man in the world. He was born in Puolanka in 1885 and came to Hancock with his parents as a child. Full-grown, he was eight feet, four inches tall—as tall as the famous Taneli Cajanus of Paltamo (1703–49), who served for a time in the Potsdam Giants' Guard of King Fredrik Wilhelm I of Prussia. Louis Moilanen weighed four hundred pounds and wore size 18 shoes. Well-proportioned, handsome, and intelligent, he was admired wherever he went. He spent some time in the Ringling Brothers Circus, and ran a saloon for a time, where he could reach both ends of the bar at once, but he preferred to work on the family farm. In 1911 he was elected justice of the peace. He died about two years later, of tubular meningitis.[12]

The other outstanding personality was John Kiiskila, a well-known lawyer thought of as the "Grand Old Man of Hancock." His life story is typical in struggles, trials, perseverance, and achievements of many Finnish immigrants and immigrants of other nationalities who have achieved success in the face of great odds.

John Kiiskila was born in Heinäjärvi, Liminka, Finland, on April 1, 1871, the son of a poor tenant farmer. At six years of age he became a shepherd, and later learned the cobbler's trade from his father. When he came to America and arrived in Franklin, Minnesota, in 1890, he was unable to read or write, but he had a burning desire for an education. During his summer vacations and on weekends he worked on farms; the rest of the time he attended school. By the spring of 1894, he had completed his elementary and secondary school work. In the fall of that year he registered at the Northern Indiana Normal School, receiving his Bachelor of Science degree after three years. To earn his way he often worked from early evening to midnight repairing other students' shoes. From 1898 to 1901 he taught at Suomi College, saving enough money to continue his education. He enrolled at the University of Michigan to study law. Shoe repair and work in the university restaurant supplemented his small savings. By the time he received his law degree in the spring of 1904, his last dollar was gone. He set up a law office in Hancock and worked there for forty-two years. After 1946 he saw clients at his home, taking care of their business at the county courthouse even at the age of ninety. Finnish working people especially made use of his services. During the Copper Country Strike in 1913–14, he acted as attorney for hundreds of his countrymen. When he was eighty-four years old, the Copper Country Bar Association elected him president, a position he held for six years. When he was nearly ninety, Kiiskila represented his bar association in national meetings in Philadelphia and California. He was also one of the representatives of the American bar at the anniversary celebration of the bar of England in London in 1957. On the same trip he carried verbal and written greetings to Urho Kekkonen, president of Finland. As a young lawyer, he wrote the widely circulated pamphlet *Ohjeita Kansalaispaperin Hakijoille ja Sitä Koskevat Lait* (Instructions for those seeking citizenship and laws pertaining to it).[13] After the death of his first wife, German-born Louisa F. Gerstner, he was married in 1948 to Anna M. Danson, the granddaughter of the famous Finnish statesman, J. V. Snellman. Together they participated in local Finnish activities, especially in the Finnish Historical Society of Michigan. Kiiskila died on April 1, 1963.

Calumet

Twelve miles toward Keweenaw Point from Hancock is the village of Calumet, whose name in the Chippewa Indian language means peacepipe. The name is somewhat misleading.

To the north of the village of Laurium was Red Jacket with its post office, and beyond Red Jacket was Calumet with its post office, which served the small mining communities of the area. Calumet, however, was more than just a small post office. Near there, Edwin J. Hulbert had discovered a rich deposit of conglomerate copper ore and organized the Calumet Mining Company in 1861. Production was started in 1864, and two years later the nearby Hecla mine also began production. Through his poor management, Hulbert brought his company to the verge of bankruptcy. He was released from his duties, and the company chose the eminent zoologist Alexander Emanuel Agassiz (1835–1910), son of the famous Swiss naturalist Louis Agassiz, to take his place. Under his direction the Calumet and Hecla mines combined with several others and became the Calumet and Hecla Mining Company. In addition to the first two mines, the company soon had a number of other mines in operation.

As the industry developed, the copper mines began to use new methods and machinery. In the 1880s, men who had swung the sledgehammer were given pneumatic drills and more powerful explosives. The old hand winches and small steam engines gave way to new and more powerful steam-driven machinery, with which men were taken into the mines and ore was raised to the surface much faster than before. The crushing of ore for the smelters was also done more efficiently. Under Agassiz's direction, production of the Calumet and Hecla Company rose to hitherto unheard-of heights. Other Copper Country mining companies followed suit, and by 1880 copper production in Upper Michigan was about fifty million pounds. Up to 1887, when it was surpassed by Montana, Arizona, and other western states, Michigan was the leading copper-producing state. Even so, copper production in Michigan continued to increase. In 1887, for example, it was 76 million pounds; in 1900 it was about 156 million pounds; and in the peak year of 1916, it was 266 million pounds.[14]

Calumet became world famous, and its name appeared on maps in ever larger print in spite of the fact that Laurium and Red Jacket, whose borders soon had merged with Calumet's, were actually greater in population. As the largest copper mining center in America, Calumet attracted a growing number of Finns, so that at the beginning of the twentieth century it was sometimes called the "Finnish-American capital." It was entitled to the epithet because of the approximately eight thousand Finns who had established cultural societies, church congregations, and newspapers within its borders.[15] Because of the influence of Suomi College, however, Hancock later surpassed Calumet in educational and cultural endeavors.

The oldest known Finnish business enterprise in America was Henry Johnson and Co., which had a fine building on Pine Street. It was opened in 1875 by John Henrik Johnson, who was born in Norway in 1848 and died in Calumet in 1922. The business was later bought by Johan Peter Noppa and became J. P. Noppa and Co. Noppa was born in Norway in 1843 and died in 1903.

There were eventually many Finnish business places on Pine Street in Calumet, which the Finns called "Mäntykatu," and which non-Finns disparagingly called "Shoepack Avenue." The Finns were also often called "herring chokers," but because of their numbers and strength, as well as their honesty and industry, they emerged unscathed from the petty nationalistic battles of the mining town.

There were a number of Finnish businesses in the Calumet and Red Jacket areas. Examples of the oldest and best known are the following: Salomon J. Haarala, who was born in Kaatjard, Norway, in 1854. He came to Calumet as a youth and worked as a photographer and a groceryman among the miners. After trying his luck as president of the Finnish Gold Mining Company of Leadville, Colorado, he settled in New York Mills, Minnesota, in 1884, and in 1889 became the first Finnish postmaster in that state.[16] Other early photographers were John Stolt, Matti Matson, and William Nara. Nara's grandsons became doctors in the Copper Country. Robert O. Nara is a dentist in Houghton and John W. Nara is a veterinarian. Photographers were very busy in Finnish settlements, for the first thing many a man did, as soon as he was able, was to send to his home in Finland pictures in which he appeared with a heavy watch chain across his chest and a derby hat on his head.

Among the first tailors in Calumet was E. Lauren, whose shop was above the old post office. Already in 1901 it was advertised as being "old." There was also a tailor shop above the Peter Sauer house on Fifth Street. A tailor by the name of Michael Johnson was known as Tailor Mike.

On Pine Street, there were at least two well-known Finnish jewelry businesses. One belonged to Arvonen and Haapakoski. The owner of the other was Abram Vaananen, who was born in Pudasjärvi in 1847 and came to Calumet in 1879. In connection with his jewelry business he was also a steamship agent and broker, helping people send money to Finland. He moved to Detroit in 1920 and died there two years later. His children used the name Warren. August Warren, who at first was in business with his father, later established his own business on Fifth Street, moving to Detroit in 1919.

A large Finnish settlement always had its Finnish funeral directors, for especially when death occurred, the bereaved wished to be able to do business in their own language. This phenomenon has appeared among Finns in many states. The first Finnish undertaker in Calumet was William Kruka, who eventually moved to Painesdale. Other Calumet undertakers were Jacob Kallio and his wife, and John Wakevainen. One of the best known more recently was Oskar Peterson, who was born in Haaparanta in 1887 and came to America with his parents at the age of fifteen. He married Sigrid Heideman, a daughter of Pastor A. L. Heideman, and started his business in 1911. Peterson died in 1949. The business was taken over by his son, Gordon Peterson.

Proprietors of the earliest saunas were Salomon Lamppa and W. Murto. In a 1901 advertisement, Murto requested "that each one kindly bring his own towel." Some of the other businesses in town at the turn of the century were Oscar Keckonen's hardware store, Charles Ojala's shoe store, William Fredrickson's and Akseli Keskitalo's meat markets, Edward Keisu's bakery, and Mrs. M. E. Mikkola's candy store near the Bijou Theater.[17] Outside of town, not far from Calumet, fishermen carried on their trade on Lake Superior. One of the oldest and best known was Pekka Remali of the Calumet Waterworks area near the shoreline.

In each of the larger stores, regardless of the owner's nationality, there was at least one Finnish employee to serve Finnish customers. The Finns were able to buy on credit freely, for their honesty had become well known. The story is told about two lumberjacks who went to a certain Calumet store during the absence of the Finnish clerk. The owner sold them boots, mittens, and other apparel and gave each of the men his bill to sign. One wrote "Hyvä Tavara" (Nice goods) and the other "Maksa Velka" (Pay the bill). When the Finnish salesman returned, he immediately noticed the prank, but the owner of the store had unshakeable faith in the honesty of his customers. Nor was he mistaken, for a few weeks later the men returned to pay their bills.

As elsewhere, one form of Finnish American activity in Calumet was for many years the sickness and burial aid societies, already mentioned in connection with Hancock. Temperance societies and labor organizations offered this kind of service to their members in so far as members were willing to pay their monthly fees. Local aid societies were established toward the end of the 1880s, especially in the mining communities, where unhealthful work and frequent accidents caused much distress. The largest of these societies was Kalevan Sairastus ja Loukkausapuyhdistys (The Kaleva Sickness and Accident Insurance Company), founded in Calumet in 1888. Over a fifty-year period it paid out $50,000 to its members. Broadly speaking, social security and other protective insurance laws have to a great extent put an end to these private insurance associations.

There were many Finnish citizens in the Calumet area worthy of special mention. Space permits comment on only a few. One of them was Carl John Sorsen, who was born in Joensuu in 1870. He passed examinations in pharmacy in Finland and in Michigan. In 1898 he completed his medical education in Chicago and opened an office in Calumet. Shortly afterward he also opened a hospital of his own. While in Europe for his health, he died in London in 1907, a week after his wedding. His brother, Oscar Henrik Sorsen, who was born in Joensuu in 1872, was the first Finn to complete his dental studies in America. He was one of the leaders in the cultural life of the Finns in Calumet.

In the decade before the turn of the century and for a time afterward, the best-known Finnish woman, not only in Calumet but in the entire Copper Country, was Maggie Walz. Kreeta Kontra, or Maggie Walz, as she was commonly known, was born in Tervola. She came to America from Tornio in 1881 as a young girl, learned English quickly, and became an enterprising businesswoman. She and her friend Linda Mahlberg, an instructor at Suomi College, were enthusiastic supporters of women's rights and of the temperance movement, giving speeches even before non-Finnish groups. Maggie had the "voice of a sea captain," and her speeches were remembered long after her busy life had ended at the age of sixty-five.

As Hancock had in Louie Moilanen possibly the tallest man in the world, so Calumet had in Lydia Weidelman, who weighed 664 pounds, perhaps the world's heaviest woman. She was born in Heikkilänkylä in Kuusamo in 1888 and died in 1937. In America, the old family name of Weteläinen was changed to Weidelman. Lydia Weidelman was intelligent, had a good sense of humor, and carried her weight with dignity. Sometimes she appeared in Fourth of July parades in a horse-drawn carriage beside Big Louie Moilanen.

Other Communities North of Portage Lake

Between Hancock and Calumet, and around them, a number of communities sprang up, some of them purely Finnish in population.

Early in the history of the area, Quincy, which had taken its name from the mining company, merged with Hancock. The Finnish population and church congregation work were older there than in Hancock proper. Quincy Hill, with its high shafthouses and huge rock piles, could be seen for miles as one approached the Copper Country from the south. Mothers used to frighten their children into obedience with stories of the "Törmän Ukko" (Old Man of the Hill), whose wrath could not be doubted when explosions and air blasts deep in the mine shook the houses. Other nearby communities are Franklin, Coburntown, Arcadia, Concord City, Boston, and Frenchtown (the latter being originally a French Canadian settlement).

Boston, located on the railroad line between Hancock and Calumet, became the largest of these communities. It had been named after the local mine, on which livelihood in the area depended almost entirely. When the mine was closed between 1893 and 1895, the town was practically deserted, but by 1903 the Finnish population had reached 400.[18] By 1913 the population had increased to such an extent that in the ten-room elementary school some of the classes had to meet in the basement. The church and the Koitto Temperance Society led in ministering to the spiritual and intellectual needs of the Finns. They met in a jointly owned and maintained building. The situation was the same in Coburntown and Concord City. With the passage of years, some of the Finnish miners exchanged their pneumatic drills for plows and cleared extensive farms, on which, in addition to dairying, they raised potatoes and strawberries.

The boundary between Calumet and Laurium became indistinguishable as the villages expanded. Other communities sprang up here too, as in the Hancock area. Some of them are Osceola, Wolverine, Centennial Heights, Tamarack, Kearsarge, Ahmeek, Copper City, and Allouez. After a lull of some years, large new copper mines were opened in this area. A little farther from Calumet, in Keweenaw County, are the mining towns of Mohawk and Fulton, in which the Finnish population is estimated to have been about eight hundred in the first years of the twentieth century. Most of these Finns had been in America twenty-five years by that time. Because of their comparatively long residence here, their Americanization, as far as language goes, progressed further than in many other areas.

Twelve miles east of Mohawk on the shore of Lake Superior is the idyllic community of Gay, whose population has dwindled to fewer than one hundred persons, mainly Finns. A tall smokestack still stands there, all that is left of the former busy stamp mill. North of Gay, on the other side of the Tobacco River, Finnish fishermen lived at the mouth of the Betsy River. South of Gay, at the mouth of the Traverse River, is the Finnish fishing village of Big Traverse, and south of Big Traverse is Little Traverse, comprised mostly now of summer homes and camps. The only business in Little Traverse is the Gay Bar—a name which does not fit the establishment.

There were copper mines in Copper Harbor, Phoenix, Eagle River, and at Mt. Bohemia, but before the Finns arrived they had closed. During the busiest copper-mining years, Lac La Belle, a beautiful little lake at the foot of Mt. Bohemia near the tip of Keweenaw Peninsula, was the Finns' favorite vacation and recreation area. A railroad connected it with towns to the south. Finns have summer homes as well as businesses there.

Perhaps the best known, though the most humble, Lac La Belle Finn was Maria Keranen, better known as Keras-Mari or Loukusa-Maija, who had been born in Taivalkoski, Pudasjärvi.[19] After being widowed, she built herself a small shanty between the lake and the forest and made her living by trapping foxes and wolves and by hunting bears, whose skins brought a good price. Many a man hunting in the area stood frozen in his tracks when this strange apparition suddenly appeared before him in the depths of the wilderness. She wore mocassins; the cuffs of her pants were tucked inside home-knit stockings; a heavy sweater covered the upper part of her body; two long black braids hung from under a man's hat; under her arm she carried a gun. This was Keras-Mari in her everyday apparel. When she went to shop or to attend church in Calumet, she wore a dress. Her little home was neat, and she always had something to offer a guest. "Maija was one of those strong women who were formerly found in Finland," commented Bishop Koskimies of Finland, who visited her shanty in 1921, although Maija had died a few years earlier.[20]

One of the historical places in Copper Harbor, almost at the tip of the Keweenaw Peninsula, is the one-room schoolhouse, which also has a small apartment for the teacher. It is still in use after almost one hundred years. This most northerly of Michigan schools belongs in a history of Finns because of its winter activity, for many a teacher of Finnish background has taught there, surrounded by snow and solitude. The enrollment has sometimes been only one student, as it was in 1962–63 when the former Keweenaw County superintendent of schools K. Wilbert Kuopus became known as the teacher of just one boy, who also happened to be of Finnish extraction.

Locally famous, too, in his own way was the Hermit of Brockway Mountain, Bill Mattila, who lived his solitary life in the mountain hideaway from 1952 to 1985, when he was found dead, his only contact with the outside world through a friendly mailman.

Communities East of Hancock

Finns spread from Hancock eastward to little towns along the shore of Portage Lake. These towns owed their existence as well as their periods of prosperity and decline entirely to the Hancock and Calumet copper mines. Except for Dollar Bay, they follow the lakeshore in a west to east order. Eventually, homes were also built here and there on the steep hillside to the north of the lake, for the narrow valley along the shore, in which the Copper Range and Mineral Range railroads run, had been built in first. Nearest to Hancock and merging with it is Ripley. Along its four miles of shore were numerous white oil storage tanks and thousands of tons of black coal. On the steep hillside behind the village is the Mount Ripley Ski Hill, operated by and belonging to Michigan Technological University. Finnish miners have lived in Ripley almost from the time the Arcadian Mining Company began its operations in 1864. Later, many Finns worked at the Portage Coal and Dock Company, the Michigan Gas and Coke Company, and the Standard Oil Company, whose ships brought fuel to Ripley for the Copper Country's winter consumption. Although life in Ripley has become considerably quieter in recent years, there are still many beautiful homes on its hillsides.

About four miles east of Ripley is Dollar Bay. It was named after Captain Dollar and his lumber business, although some sources say it was named after its shape, which is round as a dollar. People began to settle near the bay in 1887 when mills were set up in the area. The oldest of these were a large sawmill and the Lake Superior Smelting Company, through whose smelters passed all the copper produced in the region, excepting that of the Calumet and Hecla. There were Finns in the Dollar Bay area from its very beginnings. Life there was unrestrained.[21]

The Onni (Fortune) Temperance Society was organized in 1890. Church services were held in this society's hall until 1940, when Finnish-language activities, excepting for a few meetings held in homes, began to decline as many Finns and Swedish-Finns joined the local church of the Augustana Synod. The hall which had belonged to the Onni Society was still standing in the 1960s and was being used as a warehouse. The Finnish labor movement never had a chapter in Dollar Bay.[22]

The Quincy Mining Company stamp mill is at Mason, a few miles east of Dollar Bay. There are several other stamp mills farther along—for example, the Ahmeek mill, which, during its busiest season, used up forty million gallons of water in twenty-four hours to wash out to the lake the sand from the crushed ore. In the 1960s a different process, seemingly the opposite of the one originally used, was introduced. The reddish stamp sand which was earlier discarded as residue is now mixed with water and pumped back into the mill, where, through modern reclamation methods, it still yields enough pure copper to make the procedure worthwhile. Finns have worked for years in these mills and smelters.

A short distance still farther east, the little Trap Rock River empties into a lake, which in turn opens into Portage Lake. French Canadians settled on the shore of this lake. In the dark of evening they saw gleams of light on the opposite shore, caused by Chippewa Indians moving about in their peacable activities, carrying torches. Because of this the French Canadians named the place Torch Lake. On the shore of Torch Lake are the Calumet and Hecla stamp mills and smelters, extending for about three miles along the shore, as well as the towns of Hubbell and Lake Linden. Most of the residents are of French descent, but among them there are some Finns.

Southeast of Lake Linden on the roads leading to Traverse, Rice Lake, and Rabbit Bay, there were fine farms with broad hayfields and potato and strawberry fields. Many of these farms were owned by Finns. Dreamland, an extensive community of summer homes, is situated where Torch Lake adjoins Portage Lake, and it extends many miles along the beautiful channel. Many Calumet and Hancock Finns now have summer cottages there in the "land of dreams," far from the reality of the outside world.

Directly south, at the end of a long wooded peninsula at the point where the east end of the Portage Ship Canal joins Lake Superior lies Jacobsville, a unique community, mostly Finnish. It was named after John Henry Jacobs who in 1884 founded the Jacobs Portage Redstone Company. The beautiful fine-grained red sandstone, which was easily quarried and cut, found favor with architects and building contractors in America. Soon there were five quarries operating full time, one of which was the Ruonavaara Redstone Company. There were many Finnish workmen in each of the quarries. Horses were used to move the heavy stones, some weighing tens of tons, to the dock, from which they were lifted by man- and horse-powered winches to large barges. Tugs towed the barges to Chicago, Detroit, and other destinations, wherever the demand was most urgent. Jacobsville sandstone was used as far away as New York, where the Waldorf-Astoria Hotel was built with Jacobsville sandstone. The industry was at its peak between 1890 and 1910, at which time the population of the village rose to 750 persons, the great majority of whom were Finns.

During Jacobsville's heydey there were many stores, barbershops, and saloons in the community, in addition to the temperance hall that was always a part of the Finnish American scene. The Nara brothers' store represented the Finnish nationality in business. It later belonged to Charles Marsy, and eventually to his daughter and son-in-law. The original Nara store building is at present the Apostolic Lutheran Church. Dominating the scene was the Suomi Synod Church. The tolling of its bell informed the community of the death of a Finn, and whatever Peter Pietila, the greatest storyteller of the region, was doing when the bell began its knell, he left immediately to perform his duties as gravedigger.

Jacobsville got a school of its own in 1899. A band was organized the same year. Some of its first Finnish members were Arnold Huuki, John Honkakoski, and Nick Sorvala. The older Finns in Jacobsville were mostly persons who had been born in Kemi and Oulu in Finland. They had come to Copper Country mining towns, but had moved away from them to live where they could breathe the invigorating air of Lake Superior. Their children, who continued their educations elsewhere after their elementary school days, are now scattered all over the country, from California to New York. This dispersion began after 1910, when cold gray concrete displaced the warm red sandstone of Jacobsville as a building material.

By 1963 the population of Jacobsville had fallen to seventy, and on December 30, 1964, Waino Sorvala carried the last mail over the frozen channel at Portage on the south side of Portage Lake to the Jacobsville post office, which closed its doors that very same day. Jean Tomlinson, who had inherited the duties of postmistress from her mother, the former Flossie Marsy, was transferred to the Houghton post office. But the small community continued its quiet existence. Former quarrymen turned to raising cattle and to growing strawberries. In the 1960s, well-known strawberry growers were Waino Palo, Waino Sorvala, A. V. Tuukkanen, Oscar Huhta, Verner Jutila, Edward Kauppi, and Waino Wittaniemi. A strawberry festival held each summer in the Copper Country draws large crowds of former residents and their children to the scenes of their childhood. To preserve memories of the bygone days, the Jacobsville Community Club was organized in 1950. In 1960 Waino Palo was the president; Tyyne Holman, vice-president; Ellen Ketola, treasurer; and Eunice Guy, secretary.[23]

Communities South of Portage Lake

The Houghton County seat is the village of Houghton, opposite Hancock on the south shore of Portage Lake. In 1876 a toll bridge was built to connect Houghton with Hancock and the Keweenaw Peninsula, north of Portage Lake. A swing bridge constructed in 1895 to replace the toll bridge was, in its turn, replaced in 1959 by one of the world's largest double-deck lift bridges. Even the great lake freighters of as much as twenty thousand tons' capacity can move under it when, in just a few minutes, the lift rises between its two supporting towers to its position 150 feet above the surface of the lake.

Houghton, for the most part, was to Finns just a gateway to the Copper Country. Comparatively few have chosen to live there. No Finnish church congregations were ever established there, nor were temperance societies or labor associations organized. There were a few Finnish businesses, however, such as a bakery, shoemaker shops, and barbershops. Finns of Houghton have belonged to Hancock churches, and they have taken part in other Finnish activities in the neighboring city. Even so, because of the well-known Michigan Technological University, Houghton is also of significance in the history of Michigan Finns. The school began its activity in 1886 as the Michigan Mining School, gradually expanding into a many-sided technical institution which was known for a time as the Michigan College of Mining and Technology. In 1964 it attained university status and became Michigan Technological University. In the 1960s its student enrollment reached three thousand, of which more than one-tenth were Finns in most years. In 1950, for example, among the six hundred receiving degrees, sixty had names that were obviously Finnish. How many of the others who had names like Anderson, Johnson, and other non-Finnish names were Finns is hard to estimate. The faculty, too, usually include a number of professors of Finnish descent.

In the Union Building of Michigan Technological University there was a room called the Finnish Room, which was often used for board and committee meetings, Finnish and otherwise. Its walls were hung with Finnish works of art. It owed its existence to the efforts of Professor Bert Heideman, Consul Tauno Tervo, and Finnish radio newsman Reino Suojanen, and to the gifts of Finnish donors.

At the top of the hill, going south, are two small communities in which many Finns have lived in past years, Hurontown and Dodgeville. The Finns from these towns worked in the mines of the Isle Royale Mining Company. Mountainlike heaps of residual ore from the mines gave the area a distinctive atmosphere. In Dodgeville, the Soihtu

Temperance Hall, set in a lovely grove of trees on the edge of the village, was still being used by the society in 1965.

Eight miles south of Houghton along Portage Lake is Chassell, which was named for John Chassell, who bought land there in 1867 for farming but sold it in 1881 to the Sturgeon River Lumber Company. The property was later bought by the Worcester Lumber Company, which ceased activity in 1928. In the logging and sawmill days great docks were located on the Sturgeon River and on the lake at Chassell. The cutover lands left by the lumber companies were sold cheap, and there were soon numerous Finnish "stump farmers" cultivating them. These settlers were church and temperance people from early immigration days. There were Suomi Synod and Laestadian Churches in the community, and a temperance society called Onnenkukka (Flower of Fortune). The Worcester Lumber Company sold lots in the area only on the condition that if liquor should be sold in buildings put up on lots purchased from them, the lots would immediately revert to the company. Thus, Chassell was born temperate and has remained that way. Even so, the temperance society had enough work to do fighting against liquor brought in from other parts of the Copper Country. Onnenkukka closed its doors a long time ago, but in the 1960s the Christian Temperance Society replaced it, remodelling an old church to use as a hall for a time.

At beautiful Leporanta (Restful Shore) near Chassell there are a great many summer cottages and year-round homes belonging to Finns. Some, with boats and fishing gear, are available to summer tourists. Many farms behind the town and in the Snake River, Sturgeon River, and Klingville areas have changed from dairy farming to the cultivation of strawberries. The annual summer strawberry festival in Chassell, with its parades and contests, has attracted wide notice, and people "come home" to Chassell during this weekend. In 1960, ten of the twenty-nine prizewinners were Finns. Girls of Finnish background once served as strawberry queens at these festivals, though now the contest is open to all candidates.

Otter Lake

East of Dollar Bay, between Torch and Portage Lakes at Point Mills, which the Finns call Balmanin Saari (Balman's Island) a rumor was going around during the summer of 1890 about a beautiful inland lake abounding in fish and surrounded by fertile land somewhere in the forests beyond Chassell. One Sunday morning two young men, Pekka

Tauriainen from Puolanka an Eenokki Pyykkonen, left by boat to cross Portage to the Sturgeon River. After rowing against the current all day and at times dragging their boat along the shore to avoid floating logs, they spent the night beside a campfire, wolves howling in the woods around them. The next morning they followed the river and found the lake. The lake was Otter Lake, the Finnish "Saukkojärvi." In size and beauty it exceeded the expectations of the two explorers. When they returned to Point Mills, five heads of families were inspired by their report to go to the Houghton County courthouse to apply for homesteads around the lake.

A thirty-five-foot boat was built, and on September 13, 1890, the adventurers left in two groups for their new life. One group went by water, while the other group went first to Chassell and then followed a rugged trail by foot along the Sturgeon River. The men and boys who made up this group had some livestock with them and carried as many portable goods as they were able. The boat and its passengers almost had an unfortunate end. There were nineteen women and children in the boat, which was steered by Antti Heikkinen and rowed by a few men who had agreed to escort them. In addition to the passengers, the boat carried household goods and supplies of food. While it was in the middle of Portage Lake, a storm came up suddenly. At the very last minute the boat got to the shore at Bootjack, opposite the mouth of the Sturgeon. It began to snow. Wet, chilled, and shivering with cold, the group spent the night around a campfire. The next morning was sunny and warm. Without further trouble, the little expedition got to Otter Lake, and the escorts went back home.

The persons who arrived on the shores of Otter Lake on September 14, 1890, were, in addition to the aforementioned Eenokki Pyykkonen and Pekka Tauriainen, John Sotaniemi, Antti Heikkinen, and Joseph Karki, all of whom had families, and Kalle and Pekka Keranen, bachelors. Eenokki Pyykkonen had been at his homestead earlier and had built a rough cabin, of which the roof was not yet finished. The women and children slept there the first night. Most of the men spent the night beside a campfire. A drenching rain made the night miserable for those trying to sleep indoors as well as for those outdoors.

Through cooperative effort a simple but sturdy log cabin was built near the lake for each family. The building of the first sauna illustrates the kind of energy and enthusiasm which characterized these pioneers. The work of cutting and shaping logs began in the dim light of dawn. By sunset the sauna was ready for use. Before winter set in, every family had a sauna, constructed cooperatively. This type of cooperation was characteristic of Otter Lake for many years, especially during hay-ing, grain harvesting, and potato picking time. While the men built houses, saunas, and barns, the women were busy too, cutting grass with sickles and drying it over pole racks for their cattle. When the lake was frozen, "many cut the thick horsetail grass which was then taken by sled to a shelter." The wilderness was alive with deer, and the lake yielded fish without much effort. Now and then the settlers caught a sturgeon and had a feast of caviar. There were many otter, after which the lake had been named. Their skins were made into bedcovers, caps, and mittens. Before snowfall, work was started on clearing land for cultivation.

The homesteads of these five families were on the eastern side of Otter Lake along the northern half, directly west of present-day Arnheim. The path leading to Arnheim led over swamps. These were crossed on logs set a step apart along the path. That is said to be the origin of the name Askel, which means step, for that community.

Word of the happy experience of these pioneers soon reached the ears of Copper Country miners. The following summer, the sound of axes was heard from the opposite shore of the lake, where Finnish families had come to clear homestead lands. The first one there was Pekka Hyypio with his family. Following him came Abraham Kangas, Jeremias Peterson, John Maliniemi, and Stephen Savela, all with families. With them came John Baumgartner, a German, who for years was the only non-Finn in the area. The new settlement was named Tapiola. There is some controversy as to who suggested the name. Whoever it was, he knew the ancient Finnish myth of Tapio, god of the forests. Tapiola also was the name of the first post office in the area. Malakias Maliniemi opened up the first local grocery store, in connection with his farm.

For ten years the children were taught at home. In the summer of 1901 a public meeting was held in the Stephen Savela home. Superintendent Griffith of the school district was present with an interpreter, for no one in the area was able to speak English. The outcome of the meeting was a decision to open a school the following fall in the Jeremias Peterson log cabin on the Tapiola side of the lake. The first teacher was William Niemi. After him came Helmi Warren. Both were from Calumet. They spent their free time working at everyday chores with the pioneer settlers, as well as in fishing and hunting with them, thus beginning the close cooperation between home and school that was always the characteristic of Otter Lake. Needless to say, school was difficult for the chidlren who spoke and understood only Finnish when they first started.

In the early years, school was alternately held at Tapiola and

Askel until each settlement had its own school. In Askel, school was held above the Antti Heikkinen home until a two-story school building was built in 1907, with a teachers' apartment on the upper floor. The list of persons who taught in Askel is almost exclusively Finnish: Minnie C. Ala, Amanda Hoyhtya, Fannie Skyttä, Sigrid Hakala, Ida Saari, Sophia Martti, Florence Liimatta, Ethelyn Tulppo, Lydia Kotilainen, Esther Savela, Milia Heikkinen, Elina Heikkinen. Some of them were local girls. The hiring of local people as teachers was common in many Finnish communities. It was also not unusual to see young men of the same age as their teacher, and even older, among the pupils.

On the west side of Otter River and southwest of Otter Lake is the farming community of Elo. The first Finn to arrive there on homestead land in the winter of 1894 was Lauri Moilanen, originally from Suomusalmu, with his wife and three children. A small log cabin that had been built by a previous adventurer was their home for the winter. At first, bears were a nuisance, with their attempts to get at the settlers' meager stores of food, but as the settlement grew and cultivated areas became more extensive, the forest and its wild creatures were no longer a problem.

The Copper Country strike of 1913–14 caused a migration of Finns to the Otter Lake region, for miner after miner left the mining towns to go wherever homestead lands were available. Population in these communities was at its peak about 1940, when there were thirty-five families in Askel, sixty in Elo, and two hundred in Tapiola. But even in the 1960s the population was comparatively large, for the fertile land had kept even the younger generation at home to continue in their fathers' footsteps in greater numbers than in less productive areas.

John A. Doelle, then superintendent of the Portage Township Schools, became interested in the Finns of Otter Lake. Admiring their tough pioneering spirit, he decided to help them as much as he could in their endeavors to get ahead. Because of his interest and initiative, a large two-story school was built in Tapiola by the State of Michigan. In his honor it was named the John A. Doelle Agricultural School. It developed into a typical American high school, differing only in that it offered a considerable number of agricultural courses and other courses of practical, as opposed to academic, value. In 1929 the school burned down, and a larger and better school was built to replace it. The school was the cultural center of the area, where the Finns and others were welcome to hold meetings, festivals, and the like. Demonstrating the cooperative spirit of the area, even as late as the 1960s a non-Finnish teacher had a welcome speech translated into Finnish and read it almost flawlessly, to the great delight of the audience.

Among the Finnish cultural enterprises was the Tapiola drama club organized and directed by Werner F. Savela in the 1930s. The club's greatest achievement was the presentation of *Seven Brothers*, Aleksis Kivi's masterpiece, which ran several times, each time to a capacity audience. *Seven Brothers* was followed by *Lea* and several other dramas that contributed to an understanding of the cultural values of the Finns among younger generation Finnish Americans and non-Finns alike.

Kyro and Nisula

One day the people of Elo heard the sound of a train whistle to the south, and a number of them went to find out what was going on beyond the woods. They discovered that a railroad had been built up to this point from Keweenaw Bay toward Mass. Finns had arrived in the area earlier, one of the first of them being Jacob Johnson from Kyrö. After his death in 1920 one of his friends wrote:

> A strong-looking Finn has just come with his tools and a lunch to the wilderness about ten miles north of Baraga. He has felled his first giant pine where his home will be built. The sun is setting in the west. The man sits on the fallen tree and glances about him. He sees nothing but forest—dense wilderness—all around him. He remembers the farms of Kyrö with their fields of waving grain and their flower-fragrant meadows. As his thoughts flew back there, a beautiful church—two of them—appeared in his mind's eye: an ancient one out of an old fairy tale and the other new and modern.[24]

Johnson and the other settlers decided to call the community Kyrö, after the place they came from in Finland. After the railroad was built through the cleared land, the name of the place changed to Kuro when the station was so named. Later it was called Pelkie, which Järnefelt-Rauanheimo thinks may have come from the name Pelkinen.[25] No one of that name, however, is known to have lived there.

The people of Pelkie have always been known for their devotion to church. Despite the smallness of the village, it has two Apostolic Lutheran churches in addition to an Evangelical Lutheran church. Finnish business enterprises included a cooperative store and a gas station. There were often teachers of Finnish background in the Pelkie Agricultural School. The postmaster from 1917 to 1954 was Matti H. Oja; his successor was Ralph Jokipii.[26]

About ten miles southwest of Pelkie was the Laird settlement, named after an early leading citizen. The first seven Finns there arrived from Baraga in 1894 to work their homestead lands. By the next year they had a log church, possibly the smallest that Finnish Americans have ever built. It was sixteen by twenty feet in size. The railroad which was being constructed from Keweenaw Bay to Mass to transport ore from the Mass area mines to a mill to be built on Lake Superior was within two miles of Laird in 1901. A depot and a post office were built there and named Alston after the postmaster, Joe Alston. This area also became a Finnish farming community after the forest had been felled.

The land between Alston and Laird is very hilly. Not until 1903 did the first train reach Laird. A post office was soon opened there. It was named Nisula after its first postmaster, August Nisula, who was also one of the leading Finns of the community, now called Nisula.

August Nisula was born in Reisjärvi in 1849. With his wife Gustava he was among the first Finns to come to Laird. He was an exceptionally big man and correspondingly strong, as if meant to be a pioneer. Nisula set up a sawmill with a shingle machine, which was a great help to the settlers in providing building materials for their homes. Several men started a flour mill in connection with the sawmill but it was unsuccessful. Nisula's daughter, Ida Maula, and her husband kept a general store. The fertile land gave rich returns for the labor of the pioneers, and Nisula became one of Michigan's most prosperous and beautiful Finnish communities. Aukusti Oravala, a well-known Finnish author and pastor, describes a visit he made there in 1925:

> The name of this place as well as that of the whole settlement and the congregation was Nisula. Here lived people from Suomussalmi, Puolanka, and Hyrynsalmi, with only a few from other parts of Finland. They came from Pettula (Land of Bark Bread) to Nisula (Land of Wheat), when they came from faraway lands of frost to this land of white bread. . . . Here one was surrounded by broad tilled fields, machinery and automobiles, and a fine yard with its silo and with apple trees red with fruit under one's window. The man never referred to these things; neither did he point them out nor puff out his chest in pride, but spoke the whole time about Suomussalmi, the Land of Bark Bread, with tears in his eyes and sorrow in his voice.[27]

For a time the Nisula Finns had a temperance society, but the hall burned down and activity ceased. The younger people organized a new temperance society, Selvä (Sober), which, too, with its hall has disappeared into the realms of memory. Many of the farms cultivated by the early pioneers have gone to grass, for some of the younger generation prefer to work in the mines or in the automobile industry. But, in many cases, the fields opened by grandfathers and fathers have been expanded with the help of modern farm machinery. The most outstanding memorial of the work of the older generation is the beautiful, high-steepled white church and the nearby cemetery in Nisula which are on the very rise of land on which the original little log church once stood.[28] The descendants of the Nisula pioneers are scattered all over America. The best known of them was Dr. Jacob Heikkinen, a professor of theology at the Gettysburg Theological Seminary and a Suomi Synod pastor.

The Keweenaw Bay Area

In the early years of the twentieth century, extensive lumbering was carried on in Arnheim, south of Chassell, where the largest camps were those of Fred Wilson of Calumet. From Arnheim southward, the area is a sparsely settled Finnish farming country that extends up to the little community of Keweenaw Bay. The bay itself, a twenty-mile long southward extension of Lake Superior with its mouth between Portage Entry and Pt. Abbaye, has many Finnish communities on its shores.

Finns had begun to arrive in the community of Keweenaw Bay during the last years of the nineteenth century. Among the first were Aaprami Maola and Salli Nisula. From Suomussalmi there were Isak Moilanen and his wife Liina Juntunen; from Rautalammi there was Heikki Korhonen; from Virrat, Matti Honkala; from Piippola, Robert Kaarlela and his wife. In the mid-1960s Anselm Wiideman, who had been born in Keuru in 1880, was still there, a veteran of church and temperance work.

Historic Baraga is to the south of the community of Keweenaw Bay, on the shore of Lake Superior. The region was known to French explorers who were the first to travel on Lake Superior. The community was named after Father Frederic Baraga, who established an Indian mission there in 1843, directing it until 1853 when he was made the first Catholic bishop of Upper Michigan. His successor for the next quarter of a century was the energetic Father G. Terhaust. Since then, Baraga has been mainly a Catholic community to which Finns and Swedes have made their contribution of Lutheranism.

The Finns came to Baraga to work in the sawmills, which began their operations in 1883, the year in which the Duluth, South Shore, and Atlantic Railroad extended its rails to the town. By 1892, so many Finns had arrived that they had their own temperance society and church congregation. The centers of cultural activity in Baraga for decades were the home of Seth Heikkinen and his wife, Elina Heusa, and that of John Maki and his wife, Minnie Perttula-Maki, a teacher at Suomi College. As the older generation gradually passed away, Finnish-language cultural activities also died out. The last to cease functioning was the Lutheran congregation, in 1963. There have regularly been Finnish-American teachers in Baraga schools, among them E. E. Erickson, superintendent of schools for a number of years. In 1961 there were five Finns on the seven-member school board.

The county seat of Baraga County is L'Anse, on the innermost curve of Keweenaw Bay. Its history dates back to 1660 when the French priest Rene Mesnard attempted missionary work among the Indians of the area. In the 1830s and 1840s the Methodists established missions under the leadership of John Clark and John H. Pitezel. The actual date of the founding of L'Anse was 1871, when a train of the Marquette, Houghton and Ontonagon Railroad Company arrived there for the first time. Peter Crebassa, a French-Canadian fur trader, is considered the founding father of L'Anse. He named it after the early trading post of the American Fur Company.

Finns came to L'Anse quite early, but their numbers were never great. They worked at the Smith Lumber Company sawmill that was destroyed by the fire of 1896, which also destroyed half the town. There was work at the sawmills of the Marshall Butters Lumber Company and the Ford Company as well as on the railroads. More recently they worked for the Celotex Corporation and Pettibone Corporation. As long as logging was done in the area, there were Finns in the lumber camps. Their hometown, in a way, was L'Anse. In a corner of the L'Anse cemetery there was a potter's field where unknown immigrants were buried. All immigrants, no matter what their nationality, were called bohunks.[29] There were a few marriages between immigrants and Indians. The children of Finnish and Indian parentage are called Findians.

The earliest known Finns in the L'Anse area were Henry Pajari, born in Tervola in 1855, who worked on railroad construction jobs; Theodor John Johnson, born in Ylistaro in 1897; and Henry Kotila. The greatest numbers of Finns arrived in L'Anse from 1923 to 1925, at the peak of the sawmill industry, and also in 1958 when the Celotex factory began to operate. They came mostly from the Finnish communities of Pequaming, Aura, Watton, Baraga, Arnheim, Pelkie, and Champion. They established the St. John's Lutheran church, later merged with the United Lutheran Church.

In the 1870s the peninsula extending northeastward from

L'Anse between Keweenaw Bay and Huron Bay was still the property of the Chippewa Indians. They had long appreciated the advantages this forest-covered peninsula, isolated by swamps, offered them in shelter, secure harbors, and waters abounding in fish. In 1877 the Hebard and Thurberg Lumber Company leased the peninsula from their chief, David King, and built a huge steam sawmill there the following year. The Indians had a village there known as Pe-qua-qua-wa-ming, which now is Pequaming. The annual production of the mill soon rose to 25 million feet of lumber. The company employed 650 men, including the men in the woods. After the death of King, his heirs sold the entire peninsula to Charles Hebard and his company, which then had full legal rights to the peninsula including its great oak forests. The land and sawmill were later owned by Detroit car manufacturer Henry Ford. There was also a quarry there worked by the Traverse Bay Red Stone Company.

Finns came to the area in the early years of the 1880s to work in the lumber camps and the sawmill. By 1886 they had their own little church built of materials denoted by the company. They also had a temperance society. There were about twenty Finnish families in the community. When the Ford Company closed its sawmill, the Finns moved away. The new owner of the property donated the deserted church to a Catholic mission which moved it to the Zeba Indian Reservation near L'Anse and named it St. Catherine's Mission Church.

Toward the end of the Copper Country strike in 1914, Charles Hebard began to sell cutover lands in the middle of the peninsula. Many jobless Finnish miners moved there with their families to farm these stump-covered areas. The first new settlers in 1914 were Tobias Hiltunen and his family. They arrived on June 20, having bought Hebard Thurberg's Camp Number 3 which still had buildings in habitable condition. In July, Andrew Lehto moved there. Louis Waisanen, who had been born in Suomussalmi, and his family came also in July, living first in the cookhouse of the Number 5 camp. John Lahti, Erik Sillanpaa, and Frank Aho and their families arrived later that summer. All of these arrivals of 1914 had experienced the struggles and discomforts of the strike and rejoiced in the change to the peace of country life. They named their new home Aura (Plow) because someone had found an old plow on his land, apparently left there by loggers. The clay soil produced good crops of potatoes, oats, and barley, and Aura, though small, became a flourishing agricultural community.

More Finns arrived after the closing of the sawmill in Pequaming. The temperance society, the cooperative store, the church, and a public hall became the centers of activity in the community. The fiftieth anniversary celebration was held toward the end of July in 1964. The featured item on the program was a play titled *The Realization of a Miner's Dream* by former resident Elsie Lehto Collins. It portrayed the hard life of the copper miner and the move to a peaceful, idyllic life in Aura. Two of the descendants of Aura pioneers are Dean Carl Waisanen of Suomi College and Fred Waisanen, a professor of sociology at Michigan State University.

A Swedish sea captain, Walfred Been, arrived in Keweenaw Bay with his vessel in the 1860s and, after staying for some time in Baraga, settled on the west shore of Huron Bay. He named the place Skåne after his home community in Sweden. It later became Skanee. Other Swedes also settled there, some to cultivate homestead lands, others to become fishermen. There were also a few Finns in the vicinity. Because of its beautiful location and because of the proximity of the Huron Mountains, Skanee has become a well-known tourist center. At the mouth of Huron Bay, a little to the southwest of Point Abbaye, was Finlander Bay, but the name no longer appears on more recent maps. It was a favorite haunt of Finnish fishermen.

Herman

One day in January 1901, two men left the train at the Summit depot, continuing by foot along the railroad to L'Anse. The men were Herman Keranen and Matti Anderson from Trout Creek. They had heard that forest land was available at a low price in this area, and they had come to investigate. Two months later they were followed by Kusti Kontio, Josef Pekkala, and Erik Kayramo. All of them bought land from the Duluth, South Shore, and Atlantic Railroad Company. It was sold to them by Nels Majhannu, a fellow Finn. They built makeshift cabins and began to cut logs, which were in great demand. Their plan was to cut and sell the valuable timber and then abandon the land, but the land appeared to be fertile and the locality was pleasant, so they decided to stay on as farmers. The new settlement was named Herman, after Herman Keranen.

Potatoes were planted among the stumps, the cabins were enlarged, barns were built and cattle bought, and the men's families were brought to their new homes. The men sold lumber for a living until the farms began to produce. In 1903 a post office was opened with Edward Hehkonen as postmaster. The same year saw the opening of a school. A non-Finn set up a saloon, and the Finns organized a temperance society to counteract its influence. Its work sometimes took a very practical turn. One night, for example, a hole was drilled up through the saloon floor under the whiskey barrel. The drill was allowed to go on through the bottom of the barrel. Shortly after this incident, the saloon keeper left the community.

The young men of Herman started an athletic club called the Pyrkijä (The Striver). They had building bees to put up a hall where the socialist organization and the drama club also held meetings. The cooperative store found quarters in the large basement of the hall. It expanded so that by 1927 it had a branch store in Aura. The hall burned with the store in 1931 but was soon rebuilt. A Finnish cooperative flour mill did not succeed, but the mill building was used for other purposes. For example, in 1934 during the Upper Michigan lumber strike, it became the strike headquarters. Later it became the post office and the postmaster's living quarters. The church-minded people of the community belonged to many different denominations, each of which was too small to build a church. Visiting preachers used the public hall for religious services. At its highest, the population numbered 350, but by 1961 it had fallen to 103. Charles Dantes, who has written about the history of Herman, describes the situation thus: "The farmers have given up their homes because of the weariness of old age or for other reasons. Houses with their accompanying buildings are deserted. Cowbells are no longer heard. A large number of young people have left for industrial centers to make their living by easier work."[30]

In many ways, Charles T. Dantes has been the outstanding citizen of Herman. He is a Finn from Northern Sweden who was born in Haaparanta and came to America in 1907, living almost exclusively in Herman. In 1908 he was married to Anna Pekkala in a wedding at the Herman school. After working for eleven years on the railroad, Dantes started a general store, but sold it later to the cooperative organization, staying on as manager. For a while he worked as manager of cooperative stores in Ishpeming and Detroit, but returned to his hometown, where he served as postmaster; he was sheriff of Baraga County from 1926 to 1930. He also served in a supervisory capacity on state and county highways.

Communities West of Portage Lake

One day early in May 1875, three young men started northward from Hancock in a sailboat. About six miles from the city they went ashore at the mouth of Coles Creek and walked west along the stream. The men were Jaakko Ojanpera, Oskar Eliasson, and Sakari

Hendrikson. About a mile from the mouth of the little river, they marked a homesite for Ojanpera, and a little farther on, one for each of the other men. From sunrise to sunset they worked at building their houses. They slept in the boat until one of the houses was liveable. When all three were near enough to completion to be lived in, the men got their wives from town.

The region was covered with dense forest. Each of the pioneers bought a few acres of woodland, and starting at the lakeshore, began to make logs, railroad ties, and cordwood. For hauling the wood they had a team of horses and an ox. The wood and logs were taken to Lake Linden by steamboat. From there they were sent to the mines by train. Since the steam boilers in the mines were fueled with wood, there was an almost endless demand for cordwood. More woodland was bought and more manpower acquired. New houses were built and new farmland cleared. The settlement was called Ojanpera after its leader.

Mail was fetched once a week from Houghton. Because this method was inconvenient, the settlers requested a post office of their own. Ojanpera, who was busy with other affairs, sent Eliasson to the Houghton post office to attend to details. When the postmaster there asked what name the Finns had given their community, Eliasson told them it was Ojanpera but he was unable to spell it in English. The postmaster then asked him what his own given name was, and upon being told that it was Oskar, he wrote it in the official papers as the name of the new post office. Eliasson, at the same time, became the postmaster of the newly named community.

After about eight years, Ojanpera sold his house and his share of the business to Eliasson and moved to Cokato, Minnesota.[31] Hendrikson had already left some time before. Oskar Eliasson eventually became the biggest lumberman in a wide area, sometimes working as many as a hundred men and sixty horses at a time. When lumbering was at its height in 1890–95, Eliasson and other lumbermen sometimes had as many as five hundred men working for them. A railroad was constructed from the forest to a dock on the lakeshore. A horse named Tomi started the cars moving, after which they rolled down the incline by force of gravity. Horses pulled the cars back up the incline. In time, the horses were replaced by a small steam locomotive. Eliasson eventually had his own lake schooner to transport the cordwood to Lake Linden, but coal eventually replaced wood as fuel in the mills and smelters. This led to the building of a sawmilll in Oskar. The mill produced dressed, as well as rough, lumber.

In 1881 Oskar was able to get a teacher for the children of the community. The following year a schoolhouse was built, and J. Salven was its first teacher. The school also became a place for church services and secular activities. When the population of the area warranted it, the enterprising Eliasson opened up a general store that carried everything from salt fish to pocket watches. The community also had a small tannery, a couple of shoemakers, a brickyard, and a public sauna.

A time of misfortune and a period of depression began in 1896 when a great forest fire aided by a strong west wind destroyed almost the entire community. In 1900 the sawmill and lumberyard burned with all of its stocks of lumber and its appurtenances. To compete with coal, Eliasson now started a charcoal kiln but it was not successful. The fires and other misfortunes led to bankruptcy in 1901. Eliasson moved to Minnesota and died in Cokato in 1931.

One of the problems that always came up in connection with expanding settlements was that of a cemetery. From Oskar, the bodies of the deceased were at first taken to Hancock for burial. Later they were interred on "Kusti Olson's land near the Canal School." The present cemetery was dedicated in 1897 by Pastor Eloheimo, and the addition to it in 1950 by Rev. P. A. Heideman. "It was a rainy day and the heavens wept during the sacred ceremony," says the historian of Oskar. There are many sad life dramas hidden in the cemeteries of the Finnish immigrants. For example, the first person to be buried in the Oskar cemetery was Nikolai Matson, born in Kuortane, who was killed in the woods by a falling tree. Another was "Pikku Heikki," or Little Henry, who was buried under a landslide while digging a well, where his wife found him too late. The third was John Karppa, a transient worker who never told anyone what was troubling him. He hanged himself from the seat of a road roller. The fourth was Antti Honkala, who was not at all sure-footed and fell into a brush fire he had started. His cries for help were answered too late. The place where this tragedy occurred is still known as Honkala's Gully.

Without a thought of conserving forests for future generations, the settlers cut down the woods farther and farther from the shore of Portage Lake, until at last it did not pay to haul logs to the water for shipment. Many Finnish families moved away. But others stayed on in the temporary log cabins in which they had already lived for years, and bought themselves from forty to eighty acres of cutover land. They hoed the earth around the stumps and planted potatoes, oats, and wheat. The stumps slowly decayed, and little by little the cultivated areas grew larger and larger. Thus, on Eliasson's former forest land were born the communities of Oskar, Liminga, Onnela, Heinola, Rauhala, North Superior, Redridge, and North Canal, where there still were Finnish dairy and strawberry farms in the 1960s.[32]

The best known of these communities is Liminga, where the first permanent settler was Matti Jaakkola, who was born in Kuusamo in 1868. He was one of the first woodsmen to begin cutting forests in that area. Jaakkola stayed where the first log cabin was built and the first well dug. Saving practically every dollar he earned, he soon had enough to buy tickets for his wife and children, his father and his two sisters. On their arrival, he instantaneously had a family of ten members. His wife, Greeta Johanna Tavela, was from Taivalkoski. Jaakkola's farm was eventually the largest in Liminga. He died in 1949. Other early settlers were Lassi Manninen, who was born in Taivalkoski in 1854; his wife, Anna Kurtti, from Pudasjärvi; and Jacob Alanen, who was born in Vimpeli. Alanen and his family lived on the outskirts of the community, above the shore of Lake Superior. He died in 1958 at age ninety-four.

In addition, there were three other men of considerable importance. Frank Eilola, a businessman, was born in Merijärvi in 1868. He got his business experience when he worked for Eliasson delivering groceries to lumber camps. In 1907 he bought Eliasson's farm, where he was still living when he died in 1950. Emil Tikkanen, born in Oulu in 1878, was one of the well-known building contractors of the Upper Peninsula. He died in 1958. Jacob Ruohonen, born in Vähäkyrö in 1882, wrote an extensive memoir of Oskar and of the early life of the Finns in the community.

There were very few people in the Oskar area in the 1960s, but a school picture of 1910 shows forty-two children, of whom thirty-two had Finnish names. Most of the ten with non-Finnish names were also probably Finnish.

Finnish settlements spread from Oskar along the Lake Superior shore to Redridge. In 1892 the Atlantic Mining Company built a wooden dam near the mouth of the Salmon Trout River to regulate the flow of water to its stamp mill. Ten years later the same company, in cooperation with the Baltic Mining Company, built a reinforced concrete dam below the wooden one. At 475 feet long and 75 feet high, it was said to be the largest dam of its kind in the world. Five hundred tons of steel and eight thousand cubic feet of concrete were used in building it. A billion and a quarter gallons of water accumulated behind it. This amount of water was sufficient for taking care of five thousand tons of ore every day of the year, not counting Sundays. This industrial community set in a rough wilderness attracted a large number of Finns. Although Redridge did not have a saloon, drunkenness and wild living prevailed, especially among the young people. The nondrinking Finns organized a temperance society to combat these evils, naming it the

Nuorison Kaunistus (Beauty of Youth), reflecting their own noble thoughts.

A small Suomi Synod church stands empty in Redridge as a memorial to the Finns. The concrete dam does not collect water any more, but there is a small lake behind the old wooden dam. About four miles southwest of Redridge there is the small community of Freda, which was built on the shore of Lake Superior by the Copper Range Company around the Champion stamp mill. Many of the Finns, however, have moved away, though some have come back to resettle the area.

Communities between Atlantic Mine and Painesdale

Along the road leading from Houghton to Duluth, there are several Finnish communities. The first of these is Atlantic Mine, five miles south of Hancock on M-26. It was named after the Atlantic Mining Company, which was organized in 1872 and later built a stamp mill near the abundant waters of Redridge, to which it was connected by a nine-mile-long railroad. The mine prospered until 1906. Atlantic Mine had an opera house, a hospital, and Finnish Lutheran, Catholic, and Methodist churches, all dependent on the mining industry, which produced nearly six million pounds of copper per year. The Jerome Bezotte hotel became locally known as the gathering place for wealthy businessmen and financiers. The fires and explosions of 1904–1906 brought about the closing of the mines, however, and although production started again in 1908, former prosperity did not return, for in the intervening period the Baltic and South Range mines had surpassed them.

Finns had come to Atlantic Mines as early as 1872, but their settlement did not begin to grow noticeably until the 1880s. Among the older Finns were Kalle Keiski, born in Lohtaja in 1851, and his wife, Kaisa Rinkari, born in Kemi in 1855; Joonas and Valpuri Keranen, born in Hyrynsalmi in 1854; and Matti Hiltunen, born in Puolanka in 1846, and his wife, Elsa Maria Kinnunen, also of Puolanka. Also among them were Andrew and Sofia Kallio, born in Isokyrö, whose daughter Tyyne was the wife of the late Edward J. Isaac, president of Suomi College from 1952 to 1954. When Finns first arrived in Atlantic Mine, they worked as woodsmen, clearing away the dense forest around the mine and the village. They also built the homes provided by the mining company for their employees. Soon, however, the Finns were attracted to the mines:

> And as the Finns are capable miners they were well liked by the foremen and so settled in the community, increasing in time to hundreds,

> so that it could be called a Finnish center. . . . Because there were saloons, their effect was felt among Finns as well as among non-Finns, for most of our fellow countrymen spent their leisure time in saloons, which were meeting places and newsrooms.

Thus the secretary of the Aura Temperance Society describes the situation in the minutes of the society. It was typical of the times that if a community had one general store and two meat markets, there were possibly twice as many saloons. Two of those in Atlantic Mine were owned by Finns, namely, Peter Lahti and Olli Turkki. The church and temperance societies were moral and cultural forces in the lives of the Finns. In 1886 the temperance-minded Finns organized the above-mentioned Aura (Plow) temperance society, its name symbolizing the opening of a wilderness for spiritual cultivation.[33] Four years later, a Suomi Synod congregation was organized. Its membership soon grew to nearly six hundred. The Laestadian congregation also grew appreciably. But the numbers of Finns decreased as mining activity lessened. At the turn of the century the Copper Range Railroad was built between Atlantic Mine and Houghton, making it easy for the Finns to participate in the many cultural activities enjoyed by the Finns of Hancock.

A few miles southwest of Atlantic Mine are the adjoining little towns of Baltic and South Range, and yet a few miles farther are Trimountain and Painesdale. During the latter part of the 1890s the region was still a virgin wilderness. The finding of rich copper deposits resulted in the organization of the Baltic Mining Company in 1897; the Copper Range Railroad Company in 1899; the Copper Range Consolidated Company in 1901; the Trimountain Mining Company in 1902; and the Champion Copper Company. Of these, the Copper Range Company became the greatest, with capital of $40 million. Its main headquarters was in Boston, Massachusetts, a city that has controlled the copper mining industry in Michigan. Its local administrative office was in Painesdale, named after William Paine, of "Boston dollars."

At first, the majority of workmen lived in Atlantic Mine, from where they were able to travel quickly to the new mines via the recently built railroad. The above-mentioned flourishing towns soon sprang up around these mines, however, and working men, mostly Finns, moved to them as houses were built. South Range, with such Finnish businesses as M. Kivi and Company and the Uitti Brothers, which were the oldest of them, and drugstores, restaurants, and cafes, became the business center of the area. The Knights of Kaleva put up a fine brick building in the middle of the business district. The Auran Kukka (Cornflower) Temperance Society also had a hall, as did the Finnish socialist organization. The Suomi Synod and Laestadian congregations had their own large churches. Baltic-South Range, or South Range, as it is generally called, is still an important business center despite the closing of the mines. Trimountain and Painesdale also had Finnish halls and churches.

Among the early Finnish settlers of Painsdale were Aksel Sydanmaa, born in Kuorevesi in 1891, and his wife, Liisa Amanda Larson, born in Lapua in 1893, as well as her parents, Matti Larson, born in Lapua in 1860, and his wife, Amanda Sofia Vanhamaki, born in Lehtimäki in 1865; Johan Fredrik Ollila, born in Kuusamo in 1881, and his wife, Susanna Vilhelmiina Kylmala; Aleksanteri Pohja, born in Viro in 1864; and Elias Storhok, born in Karstula in 1873.

Finns first settled in Trimountain in 1898. Within five years there were more than seventy families, a total of about five hundred persons. The men worked in nearby copper mines. By 1905 they had built an attractive church, "which must be paid for under very difficult circumstances."[34] Some of the older Finns were Paavo Luukkonen and his wife, Anna Leena Keranen, and their ten children; Matti and Ida Kovanen, with four children; and Kalle Arvid Ervast and his wife, Jenny Maria Kropsu.

Toivola

Times were tense in the Copper Country in 1893. Many of the men were unemployed, and even those who were employed, if they were family men, were hard-pressed to make a livelihood, for wages were low. For a workday beginning at 7 A.M. and ending at 6 P.M. a laborer received only $1.45. The Quincy Mining Company paid $49.60 per month, and Calumet and Hecla a little more. Many Finns, among them Daniel Eevonen, made plans to move elsewhere. Eevonen had heard that government homestead land was available about thirty miles west of Houghton along the road to Ontonagon, and he interested others in the matter.

Deep into the forest they went to seek home sites and, in the fall of 1893, Daniel Eevonen, John Aho, Elias Johnson, and Albert Laurila received their homestead papers. The first building completed was Eevonen's sauna, which served temporarily as a dwelling. John Aho and Matti Perala built a log cabin of huge round logs. One November evening when wet snow began to fall, the men took pity on a horse for which there was as yet no shelter, and brought it into the cabin. During the night the horse got loose, knocked over the stove, and otherwise, too, made the night "historic," as Aho later recalled.

It was spring before the men brought their families to their new home. On April 29, 1894, a small group left the Atlantic Mine area. It included John Aho and Elias Johnson and their families, and Albert Laurila, a bachelor. Each family had two children. There were also two cows in the procession, led by the children. The travelers spent two nights in the woods, for progress through the forest was slow. In many places the men had to open up a road for the horse and the wagon, which was loaded with tools and a small supply of food. The rivers were flooding so the food had to be carried across them to prevent its becoming wet. The group arrived at their destination on May 1, cold and wet. Until fall, they all lived together in the log cabin that Aho had built. Johnson and Laurila had their houses and barns ready before winter. They made hay around the beaver dams. They got flour, cattle feed, and other necessary items from Hancock by boat. Because the shortest route from the Lake Superior shore to their habitations was three miles through pathless forest, it took a man a whole day to carry the load of provisions home. Through cooperative effort, a road, poor but better than none at all, was opened to the highway, and it was possible to order goods from merchants in Hancock. However, the cost of transportation was sometimes more than the price of the goods.

When Pastor A. L. Heideman went to the community to baptize the first children born there, it did not yet have a name. Heideman thought Urhola (Place of Heroes) would be appropriate, since only heroes would dare to live in such a wilderness. On many a baptismal certificate, Urhola was given as the child's place of birth. The hardships of the early pioneers and the name of nearby Misery Bay suggested Kurjala (Place of Misery) as a suitable name. Nevertheless, when the railroad was completed in 1901 and the community got its own station, it was called Toivola (Place of Hope), which as been the official name since then.

The first temperance society of Toivola, the Toivola Soihtu (Toivola Torch) was active from 1908 to 1920, ceasing activity, as did others, when the prohibition law went into effect. Yet, temperance work was still needed. In 1937 the Soihtu society was reactivated. Since dancing was forbidden in the temperance hall, the young people of the area built themselves a hall in 1919. This hall burned on July 20, 1952, but was rebuilt on another site. It was used for many purposes.

Especially interesting in the history of Toivola is the eight-year struggle of the area farmers to get electricity to their homes, their efforts being constantly blocked by a certain company. On February 7, 1948, however, electric lights began to shine on Toivola farms. The leader in this struggle was Walter H. Salmi.

In the fall of 1936 the Workers' Alliance was formed. Its 117 members were laborers from the Toivola and Winona areas. The purpose of the alliance was to combat unemployment and to assist those in need. Representatives were sent to state and Upper Peninsula meetings of the unemployed held at Lansing, Escanaba, and Bessemer. The association stopped functioning because of internal dissension and because of the lessening of unemployment due to the increase in the production of war equipment and supplies. World War II also had another effect on life in Toivola. Seventy-six young men and women from Toivola homes served on the battlefronts of the war. Two of them died serving their country. On July 4, 1946, a memorial tablet honoring the veterans of the war was unveiled at Toivola beside the main highway.[35]

A few miles west of Toivola there is an indentation in the Lake Superior shoreline which has been called Misery Bay from very early times, apparently memorializing the sufferings endured by early white visitors to these regions. In the language of the older generation of Finns it is "Misuri Pei," and the lands along its shores were known to them as a good hunting area. Near the mouth of the Misery River is beautiful Agate Beach, where the people of Toivola have built a large, useful hall for summer activities. In July 1964 the seventieth anniversary celebration of Toivola and the annual meeting of the Michigan Finnish Historical Society had a combined festival there. People from as far away as Wisconsin and Minnesota were in attendance.

Mentioned earlier were Elias Johnson from Kuusjärvi and his wife, Anna Halsten, from Alajärvi, two of the first Finns to settle in Toivola. Their daughter Laura was the first child born in Toivola. Their third daughter was married to Walter H. Salmi. They were for many years the leading citizens of the community.

Other Finns who arrived before 1902 were Matti and Simon Eevonen, Daniel Lamberg, Samuel Suksi, Esais Trasti, Richard Jurmu, Emil Rahko, Erik Heikkinen, John Kallioinen, August Alaniva, William Rauvala, Benjamin Naasko, Anselm and Eino Wiideman, Sam and William Mattila, Matti Perala, August Kemppainen, John Kujala, Andrew Lindgren, Paavo and Daniel Marsi, Heikki Pohjola, John Maki, Erik Wiitala, and Mike Taskila.

In 1940 there were seventy dairy farms in Toivola, but the number had fallen to seven by 1961. This development is typical of many Finnish farming areas, from which young people have gone to big cities to seek employment in factories.

Mass and Surrounding Communities

Southwest of Toivola along the M-26 highway to Duluth, and beyond the Donken sawmill and lumberyard, is the small community of Twin Lakes and the beautiful state park of the same name, near which many Finns have their summer cottages. About forty miles from Houghton on this same highway is Mass City. It is the Finnish center of the area, not because of its size, which is small, but because of its central location in Ontonagon County.

Copper mining began on a high ridge on the north side of Mass City in 1850. Because the copper was of good quality and contained silver as well, there were soon three mines in operation: the Ridge, the Mass, and the Ogima. The Mineral Range railroad and the Chicago, Milwaukee and St. Paul railroad both had stations there. The Mass mine stamp mill was forty-eight miles away on the north side of Baraga on Keweenaw Bay. Its ruins could still be seen in the 1960s.

Finns began to move to the Mass area toward the end of the 1890s. Life there was harsh and crude, as it was in other mining towns. People of other nationalities had their churches and their hotels, but saloons were open to only the Finns. There is an amusing story that the Finns of Mass City had only one necktie amongst them. When someone wanted to go to the city—that is, Ontonagon—he had to find out who had used the tie last and presumably still had it in his possession. The Viheriá Ruusu (Green Rose) Temperance Society was started early and built a hall in which a church congregation also began to function. Later arrivals were the cooperative stores, of which Mass City eventually had two. One was owned by socialists; the other was nonpartisan. In the 1950s one could still find the store owned by Kalle, Edward, and Iisakki Nara, who had come from Alatornio; Victor Koskela's tannery; Y. J. Marttinen's grocery and general store; Charles Uotila's clothing store; and the Marttinen Auto Shop.

A short distance north of Mass City is Greenland, where the Adventure Mine was opened in some ancient mine pits in 1859. More important from the Finnish viewpoint was Rockland, a few miles southwest of Mass City and twelve miles southeast of Ontonagon, and dating back to the 1840s.

Rockland is where the fabulously rich Minesota Mining Company opened its first mines in 1847. Its Minesota mine alone distributed millions of dollars in dividends to stockholders in its eighteen years of activity. It is there that the largest mass of pure copper in Michigan is said to have been found. The name of the company and the mine was actually Minnesota, but a clerical error resulted in its being officially known in its misspelled form. At the turn of the century, when mining activity was renewed there, the mine was renamed the Michigan.

It was at this time that the Finns began to move to the locality, remaining, however, a minority among the predominantly Irish and

English population, who resented their coming on the scene. There are differences of opinion as to the reason for this resentment. The most objective and dependable was the explanation of Alfred Laakso, who lived in Rockland at that time. The Finns were mostly young men who had recently come from their homeland and were unable to speak English. After work they withdrew to their own activities. They had a Suomi Synod congregation, the Valkoruusu (White Rose) Temperance Society, and the Mehilainen (Bee) Band, directed by Alfred Laakso, who was also well known in the Finnish-American temperance movement. Only a few Finns visited the saloons, which were all owned by people of other nationalities. The aloofness of the Finns and their withdrawal into their own cultural activities, to counterbalance which the other nationalities had only saloons in addition to a couple of small churches, inspired jealousy and bitterness among these nationalities.[36] The situation soon became explosive. The trouble had actually begun as a labor struggle but changed immediately into a conflict of nationalities. For that reason it will be described here rather than in the discussion of the Finnish-American labor movement in a later chapter.

The Valkoruusu society had planned a big outdoor festival for July 4, 1906. The Mehilainen Band played cheery tunes as well as nostalgic ones that inspired a deep longing for the homeland in many Finnish hearts. The Western Federation of Miners had sent a Finnish-speaking organizer to the celebration. He asked to be allowed to speak and was granted permission. However, instead of giving a talk in keeping with the patriotic character of the festival, he agitated violently for a strike. The conditions were ripe for a strike, for wages were low and working conditions unsatisfactory. The strike began toward the end of July. Of the 300 men working at the Michigan mine (formerly the Minesota) 280 struck, most of them Finns.

The sheriff equipped a number of men with rifles and shotguns to protect those who tried to go to work. This act of caution was unnecessary, for the strikers had shown no signs of intending violence. On July 31, when a rather large crowd of strikers went to see who was going to work and to try to get them to join the strike, their way was blocked by the sheriff and his men. There was some pushing and shoving, but in the lawsuit that followed no one was able to testify that the strikers had used arms. The sheriff's men began to shoot without warning. The Finns thought this move was a bluff to frighten them, but when the shots zipped about their ears they fled. Ludvig Ojala, a member of the temperance society, was shot through the neck, and his body lay where it fell until noon the next day. Oskari Ohtonen, who was standing slightly to one side, watching the proceedings, was shot in the abdomen and thigh. He died the next day. August Huuskonen was the only Finn who had a gun. At the first shot, he fled, trying to load his weapon as he ran. When a shot hit him in the thigh he turned to aim, but another shot hit him in the same place. Huuskonen fell without being able to use his weapon.

A general persecution of Finns now began. During the evening and the early hours of the night, armed deputies broke into the homes of strikers and took 110 Finns to the upstairs area of the fire station, where "they had to lie on the hard floor without bedding; the food was unfit to eat; and the prisoners had to eat it from the dirty floor with their hands." Friends and relatives came with bedding and food, which were denied to the prisoners. A related incident concerned a Finn who had disappeared from the community at the time of the fracas. The night after the shooting, when the Finns heard a casket being taken to the cemetery, they thought a third Finn had been killed. Despite the protests of their wives, Antti Maki and his brother-in-law went to investigate. They discovered that the burial was that of a child who had died of a contagious disease. The Finn who had vanished reappeared in due time, alive and well. He had been in Ontonagon, where he had sought refuge.

The jailed men needed a lawyer. Possible choices were Oscar Larson of Calumet and John Kiiskila of Hancock. The majority favored Kiiskila because Larson was thought "to be on the companies' side." Kiiskila came to Rockland and immediately got better treatment and better food for the prisoners. At the preliminary hearing, most of the men were freed, but some were still held on the charge of "disturbing the peace," until many of them, disgusted with the filth of their place of imprisonment, paid twenty-dollar fines and were released. Thirteen Finns were accused of the murder of Ojala and Ohtonen, but not one of the sheriff's men.

This occurrence in Rockland attracted unusual attention, not only in Michigan newspapers but also in Finnish American newspapers all over the country. Public meetings were held and collections taken for lawyers' fees and to aid those who were in need. There were many false rumors that grew in the telling, among them one to the effect that the Russian consul general from Chicago, accompanied by eight lawyers, had come to Rockland by special train with the result that all the jailed Finns were released without delay.[37]

The case came up before the Ontonagon district court in March 1907. Oscar J. Larson of Calumet was called in to serve as prosecuting attorney. In this capacity he had a greater possibility of aiding his countrymen effectively than if he had been the attorney for the defense. The defense attorneys were Patrick O'Brien and his assistant, the Finnish lawyer Victor H. Gran from Duluth. The accused men were August Huuskonen, Matti Mayrynen, Jaakko Uusimaki, Jaakko Lindgren, Elias Maki, August Nyysti, Isak Siljander, Leander Johnson, Isak Kopila, Heikki Niiranen, and Fred Jaakkola.

On March 30, a verdict was reached on Huuskonen and Mayrynen, who were considered the chief offenders. They were freed. The following day the rest of the accused were also freed without further interrogation.[38] The Finnish newspapers, which had kept their readers in a state of constant tension for eight months, were jubilant. But the Finnish settlers of Rockland, who had won the battle for justice but lost the strike, gradually moved away. The congregation, the temperance society, and the band ceased activity because of a lack of members, but Rockland remains a permanent part of Finnish American history. Laakso ends his story about the happenings in Rockland with the following words:

> In Rockland I left a sauna, in connection with which I sold candy and soft drinks. Last summer [1960] I visited Rockland with my youngest son. I remembered well the place where I had built my sauna. But it had been torn down and not a sign of it was left. The Michigan mine, above which the tragedy occurred, has been idle for decades, and the whole community of Rockland has become a ghost town.

About fifteen miles toward Houghton from Mass City and a short distance north of highway M-26 is the small community of Winona, situated among huge piles of rock. Between 1895 and 1920 it was a lively mining town. The Winona Copper Company and the King Phillip Copper Company had seven miles there producing exceptionally rich ore. Production was at its peak during the last years of World War I. Lumbering and sawmills developed at the same time as the mines, continuing to prosper until about 1928.

Finns began to settle in Winona in the early years of the twentieth century to work at mining and lumbering. One of the earliest Finnish settlers was Abraham Laakso from Sievi, who arrived in America in 1888 and died in a mining accident in 1903. There were also Antti Kayrakangas, born in Paavola in 1865, and his wife Maria, born in Piippola in 1877. Others were Henrikki Erkinpoika Mustonen, born in Muhos in 1875; Johannes Nikodemuksenpoika Myllymaki, born in Töysä in 1877; and Anton Korkeamaki, born in Noormarkku in 1851.

In connection with mining, a story was still being told toward the end of the 1950s about the elderly widow of a Finnish farmer by the name of Riippa. She had a vein of copper running up to the surface on her land. She loosened the ore with a pickaxe and brought it to her yard in a wheelbarrow. As soon as she had a truckload, a mining company would buy the product of her labors.

The Elo (Life) Temperance Society was organized in the first years of the century. A church congregation followed in 1908. Temperance work gradually slowed down and eventually ceased after the Finns began to move away in 1917. The congregation continued its existence and, as late as 1959, built a small attractive church. Wilbert Poyhonen, a local businessman, was a leader in this project.[39]

A few miles from Mass City is the farming community of Wainola, which was first settled by Germans. The Finns began to arrive there in the first decade of the twentieth century, participating for a time in church and other activities at Mass City. The construction of the Wainola Hall in 1915 gave them their own meeting place. Their church was completed in 1935. Some of the first Finns there were Gust Kaarto, Nick Lahti, John Malila, John Ollila, Benjamin Martin, John Krekala, Henry Knuutila, Oscar Kemppainen, and Hannu Luttinen.

Woodspur, another farming area, lies along the highway between Rockland and Ontonagon. The Finns there have their own charming little church. The big White Pine copper mine where Finns as well as others come to work (from even as far as sixty miles away) is about twenty-three miles to the west. The town of Green, which used to be almost isolated in winter, lies halfway between Ontonagon and Silver City on Lake Superior. It is an active tourist center in the summer. Finns began to arrive there in 1903 to farm. Among the first were Samuel Siljander, Aaro Savola, Joonas Ruuttila, Henry Store, Emil Laitiainen, Antti Kirjavainen, Antti Kekki, August Niska, and Matti Fiskaali. In addition to farming they worked at the White Pine mines and at the Ontonagon paper factory. By the 1960s most of the older people had died, and their children had moved away.[40] Many Finnish schoolteachers, however, have remained in the area. Elmer Rautio, the superintendent of schools at White Pine, is one of them.

The county seat of Ontonagon County has the same name as the county. It is situated at the mouth of the Ontonagon River. On maps drawn by the Jesuits toward the end of the seventeenth century, the name of the river is given as Nantonagon, which meant "bowl" in the Indian language. The mouth of the river is a broad stretch of quiet water shaped like a wide bowl. There are many evidences in the area of the previously mentioned prehistoric pits where copper had been mined by unknown primitive miners. The village sprang up at the beginning of the copper boom. The harbor offered a suitable place for shipping ore as well as lumber products to distant markets. The village was almost completely destroyed by a fire on August 25, 1896, when the town's most important manufacturing plant, the Diamond Match Company, also went up in smoke. In two or three years, however, life in the community was back to normal.

The first Finn in Ontonagon, as far as is known, was Antti Maatta. He was born in Kuusamo, and arrived in the Ontonagon area in 1873.[41] There was no settlement there, however, until the turn of the century, and what was there never grew to sizable proportions. Many Finns worked in the local paper mills. But because official and unofficial trips were made to Ontonagon from other Finnish communities of the country, a few Finnish restaurants and cafeterias were opened, as well as saunas and saloons, which often had rooms for travelers.[42] A branch of the cooperative store in Mass City was opened in Ontonagon in 1917 to serve the Finns of the area.

The Ontonagon telephone directory of 1937 gives an indication of how much the Finnish population of the area had decreased since earlier days. Of 282 telephone subscribers, there were only two with Finnish names, in addition to the cooperative stores (which were Finnish businesses); in comparison, ten of the twenty-six subscribers in the Mass City area were Finns.

For decades the moving spirit of the Ontonagon County Historical Society was Charles Willman, a local probate judge of Finnish extraction who made extensive studies of the part played by conscripts and volunteers from Ontonagon County in the Civil War.

From Ewen to Three Lakes

Near the boundaries of the Copper Country, in the southern parts of Ontonagon, Houghton, and Baraga Counties in an almost straight line from west to east on Highway 28 is a series of small Finnish communities. The westernmost towns are all located in the valley of the Ontonagon River and its branches. When areas around the copper mines of Mass City, Rockland, White Pine, and others had been cleared of forests, lumber companies turned their attention to this valley. The demand for lumber at the copper mines had become smaller, but new markets had become available, for, once the logs were in a tributary of the Ontonagon River, water transportation was available all the way to Chicago. The Ontonagon Lumber Company, which was owned by wealthy Chicagoans, was the first to begin cutting the forests of the area. It began its work there in 1881. The next year, the Sisson and

Lilley Lumber Company came. The activities of the Diamond Match Company eventually became the most extensive.

The larger centers of lumbering activity developed into villages and small towns. Ewen, the farthest west, is on the South Branch of the Ontonagon River. With its theaters and saloons it became a gathering place for lumberjacks and was famous for riotous living. Five miles east of Ewen is Bruce Crossing, a railroad crossing named after a saloon- and hotelkeeper. Bruce Crossing is on the old Military Road which led from Green Bay to Ontonagon and which intersects Highway 28 at that point. The name Military Road is misleading, for the road was used as a post road, never for military purposes.

One day toward the end of summer in 1893, huge clouds of smoke were seen billowing toward Ewen from the direction of Matchwood to the west. Driven by a strong wind, the fire advanced so rapidly in woods dried up by many weeks of rainless weather that many persons at lumber camps barely escaped with their lives. Trains took people from Ewen to Bruce Crossing. After the fire, tens of thousands of acres of forest, dozens of logging camps, and millions of feet of cut timber lay in ashes. This fire marked the beginning of the end of lumbering in the area. By the first years of the twentieth century, the forests had been destroyed and life had become more placid.[43]

In 1913 the Copper Country strike, which dealt a severe blow to life in Finnish communities of the Copper Country, brought into existence with one blow, as it were, the Finnish settlements at Ewen, Bruce Crossing, and North Bruce, four miles north on the Military Road. There had been transient Finnish workers at area logging camps, but the first permanent farmer in the Ewen-Bruce Crossing area was Matti Hannuksela, who was born in Oulainen in 1885 and died in 1961. Among the first arrivals were Adam Mykkanen, born in Kaavi in 1880, and Antti Niemela, born in Tyrnävä in 1873.

Finns arrived in Ewen, Bruce Crossing, and North Bruce in 1913–14, according to Suomi Synod church records, numbering eighty-two from Calumet, fifty-six from Hancock, and twenty from South Range, Atlantic, Hubbell, Lake Linden, and other communities affected by the Copper strike. If to these were added the Laestadians, who did not usually keep records, and those with no church affiliation, it would be obvious that the majority of Finns in the area had come from the Copper Country.[44] Very few arrived after the time of the strike (1913).

Because of its central location, Bruce Crossing became one of the most prosperous cooperative centers in the Upper Peninsula, with its grocery and general merchandise stores, its dairies, and its oil and gas businesses.[45] An important individual business was the manufacture of sauna stoves by Leo Nippa and his son. During past decades their stoves have been sold by the thousands, some of them going even to Alaska and Hawaii. In the 1960s there were many Finnish motels, restaurants, cafeterias, auto shops, insurance offices, hardware stores, and other stores in Ewen and Bruce Crossing. The postmistress in Ewen was Signe Kangas. The Knights of Kaleva were no longer active, but the Laestadian and Evangelical Lutheran congregations were still functioning.

A few miles east of Bruce Crossing is Paynesville, which was named after an early settler. The forest here consisted of small pines that did not attract lumber companies as did the forests of the Ontonagon valley to the west. The area was suitable for farming, and the first Finnish homesteaders arrived there before the end of the nineteenth century. Among the first to come there was Oskar Arvid Hirvela, born in Ylivieska in 1866, who, according to the Paynesville church records, arrived in Bruce Crossing in 1888, moving to Paynesville from there. Other early arrivals were Nikolai Murtonen, born in Virrat in 1857; Jaakko Keranen, born in Hyrynsalmi in 1851; Matti Hautala, born in Nivala in 1860; and Matti Kosonen, born in Pieksämäki in 1854. Records also mention Edward Juusola, born in Kemi in 1873, and Andrew Wierimaa, born in Ylivieska in 1881, who was for many years justice of the peace in the second decade of this century. A Lutheran church was built on his land. In the 1960s the more important Finnish businesses of this quiet farming community were a cooperative store and two motels. The postmistress was Lula Murto.

A beautiful pine forest extends from Paynesville to Trout Creek. It attracted Finns in search of homestead lands. In the 1930s they still made up 80 percent of the population.[46] The settlement followed the railroad lines which were constructed through the wilderness for the use of lumber companies. The Duluth, South Shore, and Atlantic was built from Nestoria toward Duluth, and when the trains began to come to Trout Creek, Finns also soon appeared.

By the 1890s there were so many of them in these areas that they had a temperance hall in Agate, which was a center of Finnish activities for a long time. Later a "people's hall" replaced the temperance hall. Both halls were used for many kinds of gatherings, from dances to church services. The Paynesville people also participated in the Agate hall activities until the 1920s when they had their own social life. In the 1930s, Trout Creek began to be the center of the area. The people's hall at Agate was deserted and eventually given to the Lutheran congregation of Trout Creek who dismantled it for the lumber and built a church in 1925. This church was located halfway between Agate and Trout Creek.

Some of the first Finns in Agate and Trout Creek were Sulo Hayrynen, Matti Ojala, John Niemi, John Ollila, Herman Hautala, and Johan Edward Helin, all family men. The largest Finnish farm at the beginning of the century was that of John Eric Anderson upon whose recommendation many Finns came to the area. At the beginning of the 1960s, the Finns of Trout Creek could be classified according to occupation as follows: lumbering and sawmills, 23 percent; White Pine Copper Mine, 21 percent; farming, 20 percent; business, 11 percent; construction work, 7 percent; other occupations, 18 percent.[47]

In the 1960s the Finns had a cooperative store, a cafeteria, and a gas station in Trout Creek. There have been a large number of Finnish-American teachers in the communities between Ewen and Trout Creek. Many Finns have also held public office in these areas.

In Kenton, a few miles to the east, there were fairly large numbers of Finns at the turn of the century working as farmers and lumberjacks and taking part in church activities. The Finnish farms have for the most part disappeared, but in the 1960s there were still a Finnish gas station and a motel. The postmaster was Tom Haarala, a Finn.

To the east of Kenton is Sidnaw, which has remained virtually untouched by Finns. On the other hand, just a little farther east, Watton and Covington are almost completely Finnish. These settlements also developed as a result of the construction of the Duluth, South Shore, and Atlantic Railroad. A few French and Swedish families had come there first. The aim of the Finns was to acquire farms of their own. Around their homes they planted ever larger potato, corn, wheat, and hay fields. Until 1960, lumbering was also a part of the farmers' regular routine, for the big lumber companies had not cleared out the timber here as thoroughly as they had in many other areas.

There is an indication of the greater economic activity of the area at the beginning of the twentieth century in the fact that even between Covington and Watton, which are only a few miles apart, there was a railroad stop that was known as Leo Siding. In 1899 the Onnen Satama (Happy Harbor) Temperance Society was activated. The hall, which was known in its time as "pölypaksi" (dust box), is now being used by the township. The temperance society was followed soon after by Suomi Synod, Laestadian, and National congregations, and a little later still, by an athletic club, the Ponnistus (Effort).

The Bethany Church, which formerly belonged to the Suomi Synod, is worth seeing. Elmer A. Forsberg of the Chicago Art Institute, a professor from Helsinki, was in Covington in 1932, directing a summer school for artists when the men of the congregation were engaged in repairing the church. He offered to make the planning of the interior a project of the Art Institute without charge. In addition to Forsberg, architects Edward Westervelt and Theodore Hofmeester, Jr., also had a part in the planning. The Bethany Church became a sanctuary of unusual artistic merit when the products of the artists' planning—the triptych portraying the Last Supper, the altar itself with its railing, the statues of Saints Peter and Paul, the other woodwork, and the hammered steel candelabra and ceiling lights—were set in place the following summer. In 1936 the church received the gift of stained-glass windows from the Schuyler family of Chicago. The windows depict the various occupations of the people of Covington.

The first Finns to come to Watton and Covington came from Cooks near Rapid River after logging had ended there. A large number also came from Newberry and Ishpeming. So many had originally come from Karvia, Finland, that a certain part of Watton was called Karvia Corner. Another neighborhood was called Jurva's Corner. August Huttula, born in Simo in 1863, was an important figure in the settling of the area. Arriving in Covington in 1899, he cleared almost three hundred acres for cultivation. At the same time, he was a land agent. In the 1960s the main building on his farm was used as an old people's rest home. His son, Charles Hutula, is a furniture dealer in L'Anse.

Among other early arrivals were Erkki Eskeli, born in Lappajärvi in 1846 and died in 1918; Mikko Visuri, born in Ylivieska in 1877; Antti Salomon Seppala, born in Nurmo in 1850; Eino Makela, born in Ii in 1886; Nikodemus Salliluoma, born in Karvia in 1860; Johan Jakob Lehtiniemi, born in Jalasjärvi in 1863; Juha Hellberg, born in Alahärmä in 1877; Kalle Niemi, born in Ullava in 1860; and August and Anselm Godell. The children and grandchildren of these early settlers now live on their farms. Names have been changed in some instances. For example, Salliluoma has become Salli, and Lehtiniemi has become Leaf. (Lehti is "leaf" in Finnish.)

One of the most prominent leaders among the older generation was John Kustaa Kytölä, born in Teuva in 1867 and died in 1945. After serving for some time in the Hämeenlinna battalion of sharpshooters and working as a policeman in Helsinki, he came to America in 1900. In addition to being a farmer, he was also a well-known temperance speaker. His memoirs, which tell of his own experiences in the time of Nikolai Bobrikoff, governor general for the tsar in Finland, for example, and in the time of the great European Delegation, were published in the *Minnesotan Uutiset* (Minnesota News) in August 1950.

In addition to cooperative stores, there were in Watton and

Covington in the 1960s a Finnish cooperative dairy, grocery stores, gas stations, and auto repair businesses. Finnish teachers have been employed in the schools. Finns also have held community government offices. Verner Godell of Watton and Alma Hill of Covington have been postmasters.

For fifty years, from 1915 to 1965, the Finnish population remained approximately the same. Some of the younger generation moved south to work in industrial centers, but enough of them remained in their home area to keep the general atmosphere of Watton and Covington basically Finnish.[48]

Fifteen miles east of Covington is the important railroad station of Nestoria, in the vicinity of which there are some Finnish farms. The Finns of this area gave to American literature Robert Travers's lively and refreshing picture of old Jacob Niskanen, who, when brought to court on false charges, silenced the prosecuting attorney as well as the witnesses with his murderous wit.[49]

Near the eastern border of the Copper Country, a short distance from the Marquette County line, is the beautiful little community of Three Lakes. Around the three lakes—Ruth, George, and Beaufort—are many Finnish summer cottages, among them the fine Kaleva Pirtti, the summer meeting place of the Knights and Ladies of the Kaleva organization.[50]

6 Gogebic County

Gogebic County is in the extreme western part of the Upper Peninsula, bounded on the east by Ontonagon and Iron counties. Originally it was a part of Ontonagon County. However, because roads to the county seat at the mouth of the Ontonagon River were sometimes impassable, especially in the winter months, the question of setting up the western part of the area as a separate county was put to a vote on June 4, 1886. There was only one vote against the proposal. Consequently, Gogebic County began its independent existence on February 2, 1887. Its name came from Agogebic, the Indian name of the area.

The economic backbone of the region has been the bed of iron ore, twenty miles long and, at the most, three miles wide, that begins at the Castile mine east of Wakefield and ends at the Atlantic mine in Wisconsin. In 1881 J. Lansier Norrie of New York started mining where the Ashland mine was opened a little later in the vicinity of present-day Ironwood. Not satisfied with production there, Norrie started mining in a place subsequently known as the Norrie mine and found a rich vein of iron ore at a depth of sixteen feet. The Ashland mine became the property of the Cleveland-Cliffs Company, while the Norrie, East Norrie, and Aurora mines to the east belonged to the Oliver Mining Company, which also acquired the Pabst mine opened by Fred Pabst, a Milwaukee brewer. For a long time, the combined production of these mines amounted to more than a million tons of iron ore annually. A short distance outside of Ironwood, the Newport mine was opened in 1886. It became the largest and deepest in the area.

Railroad companies soon began to compete for the transportation of the ore from Ironwood. The first to appear on the scene was the Milwaukee, Lake Shore, and Western railroad, in the fall of 1884. It was purchased later by the Chicago and North Western. Soon there were also the Wisconsin Central and the Duluth, South Shore, and Atlantic. Thus, there were trains of three railroad companies coming to this small mining town deep in the forest wilderness.

Around the Colby, Yale, Tilden, Mikado, Brotherton, and Sunday Lake mines to the east of Ironwood the town of Bessemer sprang up, becoming the county seat of Gogebic County, with a courthouse, hotels, and business establishments.

Sunday Lake, which was so named by the first white explorers, who reached it on a Sunday, is a few miles east of Bessemer. Small communities developed on the south shore of the lake, and when the Chicago and North Western reached the area with its railroad, the depot was called "Siding." During the winter of 1885–86, a surveyor by the name of G. M. Wakefield was in the vicinity mapping the area, and the name "Siding" was changed to Wakefield in his honor. In addition to iron mining, logging was important to the economic development of the community.[1]

In 1888 the first mining inspector was chosen for Gogebic County. From then on, there are accurate records on ore production and also on lives lost in the mines. The highest annual yield of iron ore was 7.3 million tons in 1919. Production fell off steadily after that, until, by the 1960s, it had ceased almost entirely.

There were Finns in the Ironwood area almost from the beginning, and by 1885 there was a permanent Finnish settlement. The strongest representation of Finns was from Jalasjärvi, but there were also a great many from Ilmajoki, Kortesjärvi, Lehtimäki, and Kauhajoki. The first to come from Jalasjärvi were John Kangas, Iisakki Korpela, Isak Laitamaki, Henry Luoma, John Mikkola, Oskar Moisia, and Iisakki Seppala. From Ilmajoki there were Antti Hakala, Matti Laakso, Iisakki Neva, and Salomon Ylivarvi. From Kortesjärvi came Erik Luoma, Kusti Olli, and Erik Vähakangas, and from Lehtimaki, Oskar and Jacob Hintsa, John Pohjoisaho, Nikolai Suokonaho, and Nikolai Suni. Later records indicate that all of Ostrobothnia was represented.

There were churches, a temperance society, workingmen's organizations, printing presses, and newspapers comparatively early. The oldest Finnish businesses were Oskar Nordling's drugstore, Jacob Olli's photography studio, John P. Bekola's clothing store, Heikkila and Maunus's tailor shop, Anderson and Sillberg's general store, John G. Helli's butcher shop, John Svard's shoemaker shop, etc. Businesses that came later were Charley Auvinen's grocery, Isaac Aili's store, Nestor Hautala's and Jacob Kilponen's oil businesses, and many others. The leading clothing stores, especially, were for a long time owned by Finns.[2]

Most of the Finnish men worked in the mines, experiencing the joys and sorrows of their vocation. In the last column of early church records, there often appear the words "Died in a mining accident." The fate of a miner's family of Ironwood in the following story could have been the fate of a miner's family in the Copper Country, Ishpeming, or any other mining community.

Eenokki and Matleena came to America in the 1880s, and Eenokki found work in a mine. After some time, there was an accident, and he and many other Finns were buried under a slide of rock deep in the mine. There was no law to protect the widow or minor children. The company, however, accepted Eenokki's sons, thirteen-year-old Lasse and fourteen-year-old Joope, to work as errand boys whose duties consisted of all kinds of small tasks such as carrying water and tools to workmen. Their working hours and the dangers they were exposed to were the same as those of the adult workers. Lasse was so small that the bottom of the dinner pail he carried scraped the ground. Because of the boys' small wages, Matleena had to take in full-time boarders to help support herself and her little daughter, Loviisa. The men who worked the night shift slept in the daytime, and the men who worked the daytime shift slept at night in the beds just vacated by the night shift men. For the money they paid Matleena for room and board, she had to wash their clothes too. Years passed, and Lasse and Joope grew to be full-fledged miners known as Patience and Perseverance, for no one could pronounce their family name. When the power drill came into use, wages were better in contract work, and Matleena's life was brighter. But just at this time another accident occurred. The "skip" with which the men were lowered into the mine broke loose from its cable. Joope was crushed to death and Lasse was crippled for life. When Loviisa was sixteen, she died as a result of an appendectomy. Matleena married a bigamist who had left a family in Finland. He soon drank up her savings and left her to struggle along alone in the hard life of an immigrant.[3]

Sometimes a mining mishap had an ending that was brighter than its beginning. For example, on Friday, September 24, 1926, three electricians were plunged to the depths of the Pabst mine when their defective lift went out of control. The accident imprisoned forty-three men on the eighth level. Among them were twelve Finns, five of them unmarried and seven with families. Alfred Maki descended into the dark tunnels with a flashlight tied to his wrist and returned with the news that he had heard signals. The rescue crew began the long and dangerous task of opening a tunnel to the trapped men. On Wednesday afternoon they got the reassurance that the men were alive. They had air and water, but their only nourishment was "tea," which they made by boiling birch bark pulled from timbers over the flames of their carbide lamps. Late that afternoon the men came to the surface. The first of them was Samuel F. Synkelma, walking briskly and in good spirits. All the whistles in Ironwood began to blow. It is estimated that there were seven thousand persons at the mine to greet the men.[4]

There were hundreds of Finnish families in Ironwood worthy of mention. One was Tuomas Nyman of Ylistaro who had come to America so early that he did logging in the area where Aurora and Suffolk streets were later laid out. John Hakkinen of Töysä arrived in Ironwood about 1890. His daughter Lydia and Nyman's son Jacob W. arrived there at the beginning of the century and were married in 1902. The following year a son, Theodore Thomas, was born to them. Jacob worked in the Norrie mine for some time but moved later to the Ontario Gold Rock gold mine, hoping to get better wages. He died there in a mining accident in 1909. The widow and her four children returned to Ironwood to live with her parents, working as a seamstress to support her family. While still hardly more than a child, Theodore went to work in the mines. In time he married another miner's daughter, Aina Maki, born in Kurikka. Theodore Nyman took part in all worthwhile Finnish activities. He became the inspector of mines in Gogebic County. Until his death he was active in the local branch of the Michigan Finnish Historical Society. Jacob Kilponen and Karl Wirtanen were also especially active in this organization. Over the decades at least a hundred Finns have held city and township offices in Ironwood.

Older Finns of the area enjoy talking about what happened on May 15, 1921. It was a warm Whitsunday afternoon, and hundreds of people lined the sides of the road leading from Ironwood to Bessemer. The cause of this was a bet made by William Jalonen, a painter from the parish of Lappi, with Emil Rova. Jalonen bet Rova $300 that he could carry one thousand silver dollars from Ironwood to Bessemer without stopping to rest. Rova promised to give Jalonen $1,000 if he should succeed. Jalonen won the bet, but he was a very tired man when he reached his destination.

So many Finns moved into Bessemer that by 1887 they had a temperance society called the Kaiku (Echo), which in the absence of a Finnish central organization, joined the Good Templars with other early temperance societies, thus coming under Swedish leadership for a time. Somewhat later the Finns of Bessemer also had churches and a socialist organization.

Some of the early Finns of the area were John Morris and Kustaa

Mursu from Pudasjärvi, Elias Blumberg from Lappi, Nikolai Laitila and John Pessi from Kauhava, John Unkuri from Ylihärmä, Antti Kleimola from Kälviä, and Kasper Vahala from Halsua.

An exceptionally large number of Finns have held county and township offices. Among them were Thomas Koski, sheriff of Gogebic County from 1919 to 1922; Axel E. Tenlen, deputy sheriff from 1945 to 1956 and sheriff from 1956 on; Oscar Ketola, county treasurer from 1906 to 1909 and from 1914 to 1915; and Harry K. Bay, judge of probate and circuit court judge from 1925 until his death. Others who served the public in one way or another in the 1960s were school principals Carlo Heikkinen and Mae Ross; teachers William Carrell, Francis J. Tallio, and Mrs. Wayne Salonen; and city council members Reino M. Koski and Ina M. Hauta.

When the mines began to close down in the 1960s, many Finnish families moved away.[5] The closing of the Geneva mine in 1961, for example, resulted in unemployment for 280 men.

In Wakefield, a few miles east of Bessemer, a kind of thing happened which altogether too often causes difficulty to researchers in Finnish American history. Alfred Laakso, well known in the cooperative and temperance movements, wrote about it as follows:

> As you know, the old minute books have not been sent there to the Historical Archives. Since material for a history of the Finns of Michigan is being gathered, Wakefield should also be doing its share. An irrecoverable loss has occurred, for a great many books of minutes have vanished completely. Just last night I heard what had happened. The books are supposed to have been stored in the attic of the hall, and it is assumed that when a group of women did the spring cleaning, the minutes were all burned with the rubbish, becoming a total loss. Such things happen when something has become everybody's business and is, in the end, nobody's business.[6]

That is what actually had happened, with this exception, however, that some records had been retrieved earlier from the old archives of the temperance hall.

There have been Finns in Wakefield since 1886. Some of the first to come from Lapua were Anton Jaakonpoika Teppo, August Kaara, Kustaa Sippola, Isak Ulvina, and John Saarikoski. From Kuusamo there were Antti Karvonen, Antti Teeriniemi, and Johan Peter Jaakkola. From Isokyrö came John Pikka, Herman Liimakka, and Valentin Haukkala. There were also Matti Iisakinpoika Lohinen and Juho Torkko from Kurikka. Many parishes of Finland were represented in Wakefield.

The Finns of Wakefield organized a temperance society called Toivo (Hope) in 1889. This was followed by church congregations and other groups and organizations. There have also been many Finnish businesses over the years. According to an informant from Wakefield, the following Finns were still in business there in the 1960s: Victor Lepisto, banker, born in Ishpeming in 1892: William Kuivinen, insurance man, born in Wakefield in 1895 of parents who had come from Vähäkyrö; Elmer Hill, mayor; Tauno Jarvinen, a city official; and Wilbert J. Junttila, Alvin Kumpula, John A. Ronn, businessmen.

There have been numerous small communities around Bessemer, Ironwood, and Wakefield with Finns making up a part of their population. The most important of these was Jessieville, which had a Finnish church and a temperance hall at the beginning of the century. Leading Finns were Nikolai Anderson from Soini and Heikki Haavisto from Alavus. A little community called Kantoniemi was named after a Victor Kantoniemi. North Ironwood was called Pohjoiskylä by the Finns. The leading Finns there at the beginning of the century were Johan Saari from Nurmo and Samuel Jokipii from Jalasjärvi.

7 Marquette, Dickinson, and Iron Counties

In 1843, when the Upper Peninsula of Michigan was divided into six counties—Marquette, Delta, Chippewa, Mackinac, Schoolcraft, and Ontonagon—parts of the present Iron and Dickinson counties belonged to Marquette County. Iron County was organized in 1885 and Dickinson in 1891, and Marquette County shrank to its present size. After the Copper Country, Marquette County is the oldest and most extensive area in Michigan with a large Finnish population. Here they were not the first pioneers as they were in many parts of the Copper Country, for before them had come many Americans from the New England states, Germans, French Canadians, Swedes, and Irish, to work in the rich iron mines near Teal Lake. Marquette is the oldest city of the area, Negaunee, started about 1846, is the second oldest, and Ishpeming, founded in 1856, is the third.

The Jackson Mining Company was the first iron mining company to come to the region. It was followed by the Marquette Iron Company in 1848, and the Cleveland Iron Mining Company a little later. Rich new beds of ore were found in Forsythe, Champion, Humboldt, and Michigamme. New railroad companies were organized to build railways to the new mines to transport iron ore to Marquette, which became the largest ore shipping port in the Upper Peninsula; from there a continuous stream of ore boats carried raw material for the endless needs of the growing American steel industry. A railroad was built across the Upper Peninsula to Escanaba, which also became an important iron ore export center.

Whereas copper was mined in the depths of the earth, iron was first obtained from open pits. The miners made holes ten to twelve feet deep in the rock, using a drill and a heavy sledge hammer powered by their own muscles. The holes were filled with black gunpowder which broke the rock into chunks of various sizes when it exploded. From thirty-five to sixty cents a foot was paid for the drilling of the holes, depending on the quality of the rock. The ore was loaded into cars which were drawn by mules or horses to the railroad. In some places the ground sloped toward the railway, and the heavy cars ran down by gravity, their speed controlled by men at the brakes. The mules or horses pulled the empty cars back up the incline. Accidents often occurred when the brakes failed and the cars hurtled with ever-increasing speed to their destruction. Frequent accidents were also caused by the premature explosion of the gunpowder and by flying rocks. When a death occurred in these iron mines, it was customary for each miner to donate half of one day's wages to the widow. The mining company also usually allowed the family of the deceased to live one month in the company house. In winter, it also might provide a half ton of coal.

Ishpeming was the largest mining community in this area. Before 1880, the Cleveland, New York, Superior, Marquette, Lake Angeline, Barnum, Foster, Salisbury, and National mines were in operation. If life was raw in the Copper Country, it was even more so in iron-mining towns. The majority of the men lived in rooming houses which were also called "flop houses," and the only gathering places were saloons. John Bartlow Martin gives a vivid picture of life in iron-mining communities in *Call It North Country.*

The first Finns came into this background in the 1870s. One of the earliest to come was Mikko Mantonen, or Kantola, born in 1840 in Kannus, who came to Ishpeming with his wife toward the end of the 1860s. Others were Nels Majhannu, born in Haaparanda in 1848, who was a businessman until his death in 1919; Matti Soderbacka, born in Alajärvi in 1840; Abram Hirvaskari, born in Siikajoki in 1850, who later dropped the "kari" from his name. There were also Adam Kangas, born in Pulkkila in 1858, and his wife, Erika Ylitalo, from Ii. Kustaa Adolf Ruona, a storekeeper, born in Kuortane in 1869, and his wife Sanna Maria Ekola, born in Alahärmä, had eleven children who, like their parents, accomplished much for the cultural life of Finnish Americans. Older records also mention Matti Skytta, born in Kurikka in 1872 and died in Ishpeming in 1918, who was known for his interest in the enlightenment of the masses.[1] Because the Finnish population of Ishpeming had reached 2,000 by 1903 and was still growing, it is obvious that only a few persons can be mentioned by name.

The first Finnish businesses, probably founded as early as the 1880s, were several "Finlanders' saloons" along Pearl Street.[2] By the turn of the century there were other Finnish business establishments such as a mercantile company, a furniture store, a funeral parlor, E. Ristikangas's jewelry store, and J. Vanhala's candy store. Somewhat later there were the J. Koski Mercantile Company, A. Kettunen and Son tailoring business, Elson's Bottling Works, the Ruusi-Vivian Oil Company, and many others. The Finns who have held city and township offices are too numerous to mention. The people of Ishpeming have taken part in the work of the Michigan Finnish Historical Society enthusiastically from the beginning.

About three miles from Ishpeming, the little community of Winthrop developed around the National mine. Finnish families began to come there toward the end of the 1890s. Leading citizens were Emil Havelin, Kusti Kulju, and August Annala. North Lake, a small community three miles to the west of Ishpeming, grew up around the Moods mine. Many Finns began their life as immigrants there, living in men's boardinghouses.[3]

In the 1870s and 1880s gold was found in the Silver Lake region to the north of Ishpeming, in the sands of Dead River, and on the slopes of the Huron Mountains. Julius Ropes, postmaster in Ishpeming, opened a gold mine in 1881. Because it did not produce enough gold to make operations worthwhile, it closed in 1897. There were many Fins among the workmen at the Ropes Mine.

According to the statistics compiled in April 1907 by an anonymous writer, there were in Ishpeming at that time 2,958 Finns, including 1,804 men and 1,154 women. Among the men there were 908 miners, 62 artisans, 45 businessmen, 30 farmers, 49 temporary workers, 7 white-collar workers, and 18 saloon keepers and assistants. One hundred fifty-six Finns owned their own homes, and 42 owned farms. Two hundred seventy-eight had received their citizenship papers.[4]

Negaunee is between Marquette and Ishpeming, very close to the latter. The saloons and churches there symbolized the conflict between good and evil. The streets were covered every spring with earth that was red from its iron ore content. The red dust settled everywhere, so that church pews and tables in saloons alike were red. There were complaints from the church that many persons were spending their time in saloons and at the dances held in them, and that even temperance men were living a wild life and belittling the Word of God. A certain group was accused of spreading discord and encouraging the ridiculing of church services.[5]

An occurrence in Negaunee was different from usual developments in a mining town. The veins of iron ore ran under the city, so the Cleveland Cliffs Company moved eighty buildings, including a Finnish church, to another location, where their security would not be threatened by the mining going on under them.

Among the first Finns in Negaunee were Juho and Amanda Noponen, Konsta Vertanen, Matti Krook, Elias Ritanen, Erkki Kivikangas, Hermanni Rantala, Salomon Hyyppa, Mikko Annala, Matti Gortz and his wife Hedvig Ulrika, Henrik Heinonen, Matti Huhtela, Abraham Boulsam, Viktor Grejus, and Aaprami Humalalampi. Their descendants and the descendants of other early settlers of Negaunee were fourth-generation Finnish Americans.

The people of Negaunee have willingly given of their services to the Michigan Finnish Historical Society, especially the members of the Knights of Kaleva and the temperance society. Two of the foremost men were Nestor Erkkila and Victor Mäkelä, who were also directors of the Michigan Finnish Historical Society.

Among the scores of Finnish enterprises that have existed in Negaunee during the past several generations, the theaters of Jafet Rytkonen may well be mentioned because of the rarity of Finnish theater owners. He built two movie theaters in Negaunee, the Star and the Vista, and he also owned the two theaters in Ishpeming for a time.

A unique community interest of the Negaunee Finns was the "Kansan Koti," (People's Home), the purpose of which was to bring the Finns together in "one big family" and to develop "the self-assurance of the Negaunee Finns and to further cultural interests in a spirit of Christian morality." Dances and all immoral pastimes were forbidden, as were church services and devotions.[6]

The Negaunee Finns have shared in the good and bad times experienced by their city. A result of one of the bad times, the strike of 1905, was the formation of a chorus. At the time of the strike of 1905, a number of men went fishing on Silver Lake to find food for themselves and their families. Since it happened that most of them were good singers or were able to play musical instruments, they organized the chorus, which was called the Negaunee Fish Union. Their musical numbers were original, composed by members. The chorus was in existence for a long time after its inception at Silver Lake. Its first director was Kaarle Pelto. After his death, John Kujala, his son-in-law, succeeded him. Concerts were given outside of Negaunee as well as in the community. After the chorus had earned enough money to pay for a monument for Kaarle Pelto's grave and for a fence and a cement walk around the temperance hall, they often sang to help out other worthy projects. Frequently they sang a certain song about Negaunee as their first number. It was a nonsense song in "Finnglish," a mongrel mixture of

"Finnified" English words used with Finnish. After each verse it made use of the following refrain, which has been popular with Finnish Americans:

Sun tuutima lullan tuutima lullan lei,
Sun tuutima lullan luikkis ja tuutima lullan lei.[7]

The verses included such forms as "safti" for "shaft," "paasi" for "boss," "soveli" for "shovel." But because it is impossible to retain the spirit of "Finnglish" in translation, the verses will not be translated here.

On the edge of Negaunee there was a sawmill called the Eagle Mill, where many Finns were employed. The Finns called the area "Iikelmilli" (the Finnish form of Eagle Mill spelled phonetically). Palmer, a small mining town a few miles from Negaunee, has a history dating back to 1865. Ninety percent of its inhabitants were Finns. Community officials, teachers, firemen, police, and businesses have been mostly Finnish. William Riekki was the postmaster for a long time. The Lutheran church has been their most important community interest.[8]

Some of the older Finns in Palmer were Pietari Moilanen, Olli Aittola, Paavali Seppanen, John Riekki, Matti Lassila, Sakari Kurtti, Antti Lampinen, Matti Kokko, and Juho Pietila. Near Negaunee, too, is the small farming community of Uusi Suomi (New Finland). For decades the people of Uusi Suomi have taken part in the cultural activities of Negaunee. Some of the older residents there were August Tenhunen, born in Kiuruvesi in 1866, and his family.

Marquette was developing into an important port for shipping iron ore when on June 11, 1868, a fire which had started in the Marquette, Houghton, and Ontonagon Company railroad yards destroyed a large part of the town with its business buildings and docks. Rebuilding, however, progressed rapidly, and by 1870, only two years later, 856,000 tons of ore, the greatest amount to this time, were shipped from Marquette. The quantity shipped out increased year by year. By 1910 it was 5 million tons.

Two other factors contributed to the development of Marquette into the "Queen City of Lake Superior." The first was the completion in 1881 of the Marquette and Mackinac railroad which opened up quick transportation to Detroit from all of the Upper Peninsula. The other was the establishment, in 1899, of the normal school which became Northern Michigan University in the 1960s.

Marquette has attracted many Finns because it is a port and railroad center providing employment. The fact that it had a teacher's college was also important, for teaching has long been favored as a profession by Upper Michigan Finns, especially as a vocation for women, and hundreds of them have completed their studies at Marquette. There have also been Finns among the professors at the college. In the 1960s some of them were Kauko A. Wahtera, Taisto Niemi, Allan Niemi, and Henry Heimonen. The professors and students of the university have given a special character to Finnish clubs and congregations in the Marquette area.

Some of the first Finns in Marquette were Josef Vanhala, born in Tyrnävä in 1835; August Hyytinen, born in Jyväskylä in 1858; Nikolai Johnson, born in Kauhajoki in 1869; Samuel Pohjonen, born in Kurikka in 1852; Jaakko Sippola, born in Isokyrö in 1856; Jaakko Miilunpohja, born in Ylihärmä in 1866; and Antti Vuorenmaa, born in Kauhava in 1866. All were men with families. One of the many persons in Marquette who gave of their time and services to the Michigan Finnish Historical Society was Toivo Pelto, who was born in Jurva in 1887 and died in 1962. With John Lammi, John Key, and Gust Pakkala, he was also a member of the Kamasaksa Kvartetti (Peddlers' Quartet), an independent group that appeared in many concerts and programs during the first years of the century.

To the west of Ishpeming are the Finnish communities of Humboldt, Champion, and Michigamme, and south of them is Republic. All of them are part of the Marquette County iron region. Champion dates back to 1863, Humboldt to 1864, and Michigamme to 1872. Champion, where the Champion Iron Company started mining in 1867, became the center of the area, with hotels, boardinghouses, saloons, and churches. Humboldt developed around the mines of the Washington Iron Company. At Michigamme, which is situated at the west end of a beautiful lake of the same name, mining was begun by Jacob Houghton in 1872. The following year a fire destroyed the town, which was by then pretty well established. It was soon rebuilt, however. The shores of Lake Michigamme have been much used for summer weekend recreation by Finns of Negaunee, Ishpeming, and Marquette.

Finns first came to Humboldt, Champion, and Michigamme in the 1870s. By 1880 there were so many Finns in the area that they had a church and a temperance hall in Champion. Among the first Finns in the area were John Beldo, John Chalenius, and Oskar Hietikko from Teuva; Erik Kohtala and Tapani Lehto from Nivala; Kalle Tauriainen from Suomussalmi; John Lappalainen from Iisalmi; Matti Merila from Muhos; and Matti Heilala from Vihanti. All of them lived at the Beacon Location.[9]

One of the best-known Finns of Humboldt was Matti Autio,

who had lost an arm in a mining accident. The French Canadians, of whom there were a great many doing logging in the area, used to call him "Finlander," a term which many Finns resented because of the derisive way it was used. One day when Autio went into a saloon, someone punched him in the ribs and the others there laughed. Autio grabbed a nearby chair with his one hand and swung it around vigorously. In a few moments the saloon was empty. The next morning people who met him on the street addressed him respectfully as Mr. Autio.[10]

Among the first Finns to arrive in Michigamme in 1872 were Olli Pajari, born in Tervola in 1852, who later as a businessman in Minnesota used the name Olaf Pary; his brother Henrik Pajari; and Anna Halvari, born in Rovaniemi.

In 1912, activity in these communities began to slow down. Mines closed, one after another, and people moved away. Some Finns, however, have stayed on, earning their livelihood as farmers, motel owners, or storekeepers.

In the spring of 1869 a rich bed of iron was discovered on the banks of the Michigamme River, about ten miles south of Champion. This led to the organization of the Republic Iron Company in 1870 and to the beginnings of the town of Republic, which was first known as Iron City. The mine began to produce ore two years later. The water of the Michigamme River was used for the stamp mill. In addition to the original Republic mine, the West Republic mine was also opened nearby.

At the beginning of this mining enterprise, most of the people in Republic were Frenchmen, who were soon followed by Irishmen and Swedes. There were also a few Finns among the first residents, two of whom were the brothers Alex and Anton Laxstrom from Turku, who arrived in 1872. Shortly afterward came Isak Wickman, Petter Kerttu, Jacob Aho, Asarias Autio, and Isak and Johan Sammeli. Olli Kivilahti of Kemijärvi came in 1873, and August and Matti Miettunen, cousins, came in 1880. Hundreds of Finns arrived in the early years of the 1880s. Vihtori Laine described life in the Finnish settlement at that time. "Our people had fallen deep into the slavery of drunkenness, from which it was difficult for them to free themselves. Wagon loads of beer were almost continuously in front of their houses, from where it was carried inside. Drinking went on as long as there was money to pay for liquor. Quarrels and fights resulted."

This picture, however, is not to be accepted without reservations, for a vigorous cultural life also developed among the Finns. The first project was the band started by August Miettunen. In 1883 and 1884 Pekka Vesterinen, cantor-organist from Temmes, conducted a school for children, serving at the same time as director of Finnish and Swedish choruses. In 1885 the temperance society Onnen Aika (Happy Era) was organized, and Evangelical and Apostolic Lutheran churches appeared soon after. Suomalainen Kansallis-Raittius Veljeysseura (the Finnish National-Temperance Brotherhood), which has been an influence for good among Finnish Americans, was also started in Republic. In 1912 a gymnastic and athletic club, in existence for a long time, was organized. Between 1895 and 1913 many Finns became farmers around the town.

In addition to cooperatives, there have been many other Finnish businesses in Republic. Among the oldest were Herman Nikula's leather and shoemaker shop and Sillberg's store. Isak Sillberg, born in Oulu in 1857 and died in 1913, was one of the leading Finns of the community. His abilities were much used in connection with church and temperance activities. The Sarepta Old People's Home was established by Pastor K. V. Mykkanen in Republic. For decades, the home cared for hundreds of elderly Finns in their sunset years. When Pastor Mykkanen moved to Florida to manage a similar home, which he had started in Sanford, his son and daughter-in-law, Benjamin and Ruth Mykkanen, took over the management of the Sarepta.[11]

In the southwest corner of Dickinson County, in the curve of the Menominee River and surrounded by Wisconsin on three sides, are the towns of Iron Mountain and Kingsford, whose borders have merged. The first buildings were constructed in the forest wilderness in 1879. The first iron mines were owned by the Chapin Mining Company, the Hamilton Ore Company, and the Pewabic Company. Lumbering also provided work for hundreds of persons. Iron Mountain became the county seat.

The Finnish settlement is young, having been started in 1922 to 1925, when many of the iron range mines were shut down. The local Ford factory provided employment. Most of the people came from Ishpeming; some came from Kipling, Republic, and Negaunee, as well as from Hibbing, Minnesota. Among them were Joseph Lammi, born in Teuva in 1875; William Nestor Kangas, born in Merikarvia in 1887; Joseph Heiskala, born in Ikaalinen in 1896; Otto Romo, born in Oulainen in 1874; August Hill, born in Jalasjärvi in 1873; Emil Jacob Tuomela, born in Ishpeming in 1892; Charles Fredrik Lindell, born in Lavia in 1888. All were family men, some of them with grown children. They immediately organized a church congregation and planned the usual activities. Finns of Iron Mountain and Kingsford have been in business, including insurance, as well as in professions, such as teaching, for example. Many have been employed in various departments of the veterans' hospital which was built there in the 1950s.[12]

The oldest Finnish community, although it was never large, is Foster City, about twenty-five miles northeast of Iron Mountain. In the 1910s there were perhaps ten Finnish farmers there, who worked in the local sawmill for extra income. By the 1950s, the number of Finnish families had fallen to four, but one of the officials of the township was still a Finn.[13]

Iron County is to the west of Marquette and Dickinson Counties. The Finnish population is centered around Crystal Falls, Amasa, Iron River, and Stambaugh. White men became interested in this Indian-occupied region after August 1851, when Harvey Mellon, a government surveyor, found iron ore on a hillside in the Stambaugh region. The great pine forests of the area also attracted their interest. It is said that there were thirty logging camps operating in the Crystal Falls area at one time.

Permanent settlement began in the latter part of the 1870s, when mining companies began their operations. The first in the area was the Metropolitan Iron Company with a mine in Iron River. The Nanaimo mine, owned by the MacKinnon Brothers Company, was also there. The Crystal Falls Iron Company started mining in 1880. Soon after, when the Chicago and Northwestern Railroad laid its lines there, the mining and logging communities grew rapidly. Crystal Falls, situated in an exceptionally beautiful region, was incorporated and became the county seat.

In addition to becoming the county seat, Crystal Falls became the largest Finnish community in Iron County. Transient miners had lived there earlier, but permanent Finnish settlement did not begin until 1887. It is then that Matti Hurja, born in Evijärvi in 1863, came to the area. In spite of the fact that his life was a continuous struggle with such things as injury at work and failure at business, Matti Hurja was the guiding spirit of national and temperance movements until his death in 1931. His son, Emil Hurja, became known throughout the country as a "political mathematician," whose predictions and estimates of votes were exceptionally accurate.

Matti Syvajarvi from Kortesjärvi and Matti Anderson from Evijärvi arrived in Crystal Falls in the same year as Matti Hurja. Anderson was the first Finn to build a home near the falls for which the town was named. The first Finnish business venture was the shoemaker shop of Andrew Sund, who had been born in Evijärvi. This was followed by Anderson's restaurant, Hurja's store and steamship ticket agency, J. A. Nummis's photography studio, Osterberg and Company grocery store,

Nikki Maki's softdrink factory, as well as many others in more recent years.

Mining was not the only occupation available to Finns of this area. Many were employed in the logging industry, and those who aspired to an economically more independent life became farmers. Finnish farms were scattered all about the area, but most of them were along the highway leading to Iron River. Along this road were the farms of John Kaski, Maurits Harju, Alex Ekola, Hjalmar Makila, and John Harmanmaa, as well as that of John A. Pietilä, which in its day was the largest Finnish farmstead in Iron County. Among the farmers along the road to Amasa were Iisakki Hulkko, John Vierikko, Alex Aho, and Samuel Maki, as well as many others. Many of these farmers raised potatoes on a large scale. In the 1960s, some of the farms were being managed by third-generation Finnish Americans.

The Finns of Crystal Falls have always been known for cultural activities to which they have attracted people of other Finnish communities. In addition to the churches, the formerly very active temperance society Toivola (Land of Hope), the Finnish socialist organization, and the Finnish Historical Society of Hiawathaland, there were the Virkistys (Recreation) mixed chorus, active at the beginning of the twentieth century, and the Suomi College Alumni Club, whose members came from throughout Iron County. In a prominent place in front of the courthouse there is a stately monument to the early local Finnish pioneers. Some of the leaders in Finnish cultural enterprises have been Johanna Harmanmaa, Hjalmar Makila, and Lempi Auvinen.

The "Crystal Falls Song" composed by John Salmi in 1904 was often sung by choruses in programs in which numbers in a light vein were suitable.[14] It is similar in tone to the previously mentioned Negaunee song and made use of the same "Tuutima lullan" refrain.[15]

The first mines in Stambaugh and Iron River were followed by the Beta, Sheridan, Hiawatha, Caspian, and Dober mines, as well as many others. The production of iron remained very small, however, because the ore was not of good quality; furthermore, it was hidden under heavy deposits of morainal drift.

Settlements here, too, sprang up around the mines. The first Finns to arrive in Stambaugh and Iron River came in 1895. But permanent settlement did not take place until after 1899, when the families of Antti Siikaniva, Ananias Vilen, Jack Koski, and Isak Rova are known to have come. They were followed a few years later by Henrik A. Aalto, Frank Erickson, Ville Maki, and John Santala from Merikarvia; Herman Henrickson, Matti Kniivila, and Aleksi and Yrjo Mattson from Evijarvi;

and Matti Koski, Erland Saarijarvi, Kusti Anderson, Kalle Borsbacka, L. E. Hertzen, and Martin Kivela from other areas of Finland.

Both communities had active social groups and church congregations. The temperance people had a society called the Yrittäjä (Striver). The labor movement, with its women's clubs, attracted many Finns. Participation in the work of the Finnish historical organizations has been especially good, outstanding participants being Edith Aspholm, Dr. Konstant Koski, and Alex Wattuaho. For decades, Finns have been well represented in business enterprises, especially in grocery and restaurant businesses. Local government offices have often been held by Finns. Ainer Hendrickson, for example, was the mayor of Stambaugh for a time.

A short distance south of Stambaugh is the small town of Caspian, where there were a great many Finns some years ago. In the 1930s the county school system arranged to hold night school classes in Americanization for immigrants. Jenny Salmi was the first teacher. Augusta Lahti and Edith Aspholm succeeded her. Finns also lived in the village of Beechwood, a few miles northwest of Iron River. Their outstanding institution was the Finnish National Church.

The Finnish children of Iron River and Stambaugh had a good reputation as students. An anonymous historian regretfully points out that only too often the children of Finnish immigrants were anxious to forget their ancestry. When mining activity ceased, many Finns became farmers.[16] Here, as elsewhere, many Finns served in public offices.

Amasa, a small town in a farming region, is about twelve miles north of Crystal Falls on the highway to Covington. Iron ore was found there in 1888, and the Hemlock River Iron Company started mining operations shortly after. Finns were among the first settlers, many of them coming from Crystal Falls. A Lutheran congregation and a temperance society were started in 1896, to be followed by a band in 1900, a Finnish National congregation in 1903, and a workingmen's association in 1907. The local union of the Western Federation of Miners was also established in 1907, earlier than in most other mining towns. About 25 percent of the Amasa Finns were Swedish Finns.

8 The Eastern Counties of the Upper Peninsula

There are no Finnish settlements in the extensive eastern part of the Upper Peninsula as large as those in its central and western parts. The Finnish communities are scattered over wide areas and are at great distances from one another. The southernmost county, Menominee, which thrusts itself like a wedge between Wisconsin and Green Bay, has been almost completely bypassed by the Finns.

Delta County

Delta County, which is northeast of Menominee County and borders on Lake Michigan and Green Bay, has several important rivers that empty into the northern extensions of Green Bay called Little Bay De Noc and Big Bay De Noc. Between these bays there is a peninsula almost twenty miles long. In the imagination of the first white settlers, the mouths of the rivers and their banks were like the famous delta of the Nile River, so they gave the peninsula its unusual name. The county was officially organized in 1843, but lively activity did not begin there until twenty years later, after the Chicago and North Western Railroad Company had built a railroad through the wilderness to Negaunee. Soon after its completion early in 1865, loads of iron ore began to arrive in Escanaba, which became an important port and business center.

The first Finnish settlement in Delta County was at Kipling, which is north of Gladstone on the shore of Little Bay De Noc. The Cleveland Cliffs Company moved its smelter there around 1895. Finns moved there to work in the smelter or at charcoal kilns. For two or three years they had a temperance society as well as a church congregation. When the smelter closed down in 1923, the forty-three Finnish families there moved away. In the 1960s, only a few Finns were living in Kipling.

Maple Ridge, in the northwest corner of the county, developed into the largest Finnish community of Delta County. Its name was changed to Rock in 1917. The first Finn to settle there was Thomas Kaminen, who came in 1904 but later returned to Finland. In the fall of the same year, E. Ahola arrived from Negaunee and built himself a log cabin in the depths of the wilderness. He worked in the Negaunee iron mines but devoted his spare time to his homestead in Maple Ridge until he was able, in 1906, to bring his family to their new home. In his memoir Ahola writes thus:

> All the heavy work such as roadbuilding was done cooperatively. Even the women shared in the work by being at hand to make coffee. Nor did they hesitate to pick up an axe to cut down trees and brush beside their men. Forests were felled and homes were built. Everyone had to saw his own boards. So there was a sawhorse by every house. Summer evenings were often spent sitting around smudge fires which were used as protection against insects. Even at twilight a neighbor's saw could be heard biting into the wood, and someone could be heard tapping a wedge.[1]

In addition to Ahola, other early settlers were Vihtori Alanko, John and Oskari Kaminen, John Lauri, Jacob Ahola, Jacob Kaukola, and Wester Rajala. The first Finnish child born there was Jacob Kaukola's son, George.

When government homestead lands were no longer available, it became necessary to resort to land agents. The most important of these were the Jewish Kurz brothers of Escanaba. At first the price of land ranged from $400 to $500 for forty acres, rising considerably at the end of World War I, when large numbers of industrial workers began to move to farming areas. Some of the Finnish would-be landowners had unfortunate experiences. Although it is true that the lumber buyers provided money for the downpayment as well as for the purchase of a horse and tools, to be paid back later, they kept the price of lumber so low that, after struggling for two or three years to make a living from selling the lumber off the land he was clearing, the settler would give up and move away, leaving everything he had worked for. The only thing left to him would be unhappy memories of his and his family's sufferings. Other settlers were more fortunate, especially if they had at least a little capital of their own.

The first group activity of the Finns at Maple Ridge was the establishment of a Lutheran congregation in 1911. A socialist cell was started the next year. In 1913, the Copper Country strike motivated large numbers of Finnish miners and their families to replace the turmoil of a mining town with the peacefulness of country life. Those who came to Maple Ridge started a cooperative store and a temperance society. They also increased the membership of the congregation and the socialist organization. The cooperative store was of great economic value to the farmers, and its value to them increased significantly when it began to handle their lumber, forcing independent agents to raise the prices they would pay. Eventually the bitter experiences of earlier settlers passed into history.[2]

Churches and halls were built in the first years of settlement. Social life was centered around the church, the cooperative, and the socialist hall. For a time choruses, a forty-member orchestra, and a gymnastic and athletic club enriched the community. These kinds of activity were at their peak while Arvo Rivers was the manager of the cooperative store, partly because of his interest in them. The population of Rock, which was 653 in 1900, was 1,300 sixty years later, with Finns predominating. In addition to their own activities, general community activities have also interested the Finns. Large numbers have participated in the American Legion, the parent-teacher association, the volunteer fire department, and 4-H clubs. They have been regularly represented on school faculties and in public offices. One of them, John Jokela, served as mailman for decades, having started his career when the only means of transportation in winter was a sleigh drawn by a team of horses.[3]

Among the early settlers of Rock there were many persons worthy of special mention. One of them was Arvid Mustonen, born in Ruokolahti in 1891, who came to America in 1910. After studying commercial subjects for a few months at the Smithville Workingmen's College, he went out West, experiencing bad times as well as the good times associated with the war industry. While there he married Ida Maria Heija, who had come from Imatra. After serving as the advertising manager of *Industrialisti* in Duluth for about two years, he was made manager of the Rock Farmers Mutual Fire Insurance Company early in 1923.

Here he accomplished his lifework. The insurance company had been organized in 1915. It had sold only a few policies, and the debt incurred through initial expenditures was large. Mustonen managed the company until 1948. Under his management it became a strong firm with total insurance sold amounting to $10 million. He was also a member of the board of directors of the cooperative association and its credit union and was frequently a delegate to the meetings of the Central Cooperative Society. In 1950 and 1958 he represented the Central Cooperative Society at the annual meetings of the SOK (a Finnish cooperative organization) at Tampere and Helsinki respectively. In 1948, because of his interest in local history, he was chosen to be a member of the board of the Delta County Historical Society, which has a museum and archives with large collections of material in Escanaba. He served as its president in 1959–60.

The Stonington Peninsula, which lies between Little Bay De Noc and Big Bay De Noc, was settled by Scandinavians toward the end of the last century. In 1922, a Finnish university student by the name of Cook, who was working as an agent for a land company, got about ten Finnish families of Negaunee interested in buying land near Martin Bay on the east side of the peninsula. Most of the men were miners, but there were a grocery delivery man and a bartender among them. They got started by felling trees and selling lumber; farming brought only small returns. Since most of them had large families, they had to mortgage their farms and buildings. During the Great Depression, some lost their farms, but others managed to struggle on. Of those who had arrived in 1922, there were several still alive in 1961. They were John H. Fallstrom, born in Ylistaro in 1876, Nestori Ojala, and a few others. At that time the Kolli and Siitari families were second generation Finnish Americans.[4]

Cooks and Seney

Schoolcraft County, named for Henry R. Schoolcraft, an important personage in the history of Michigan, lies to the east of Delta County. The county seat is Manistique at the mouth of the Monistique River. The town was supposed to have been called Monistique, after the river, but a clerical error substituted an "a" for the "o" of Monistique. The county was covered with great forests which were for a long time a source of wealth to the county. Leading lumber companies were the Chicago Lumbering Company, started in 1863, and the Weston Lumber Company, founded twenty years later. Their combined production rose to 80 million feet a year. Ships of the Tonwanda Barge Line transported the lumber to New York.

The Cleveland Cliffs Mining Company started extensive lumbering operations in the southwest part of the county early in the 1890s. Trees were cut into cordwood which was taken to Kipling to be made into charcoal. Trains made stops at Cooks Mills depot, which had been named for mills owned by brothers whose name was Cook. It was later shortened to Cooks. The woodsmen were mostly Finns. In the spring of 1896 there were enough of them to start a temperance society called Kullervo after a hero of Finnish mythology. By fall they had a church congregation. Among the Finns living in Cooks at the turn of the century were the following: Matti Friberg from Lapua; Ismael Wiljanen, Viktor Niemi, and Adolf Rilli from Isojoki; Kalle Niemi and the cantor Heikki Laasasenaho from Soini; Ananias Lind from Kyläkarvia; Johan Jakob Lehtiniemi from Jalasjärvi; and Erkki Eskeli from Lappajärvi.

Pastor J. J. Hoikka wrote about the Cooks lumber camps, saying that some people had an aversion to lumber camps in general, "for which there may sometimes have been a reason."

> For nearly ten years now . . . the writer of this has been in many parts of Northern Michigan, preaching and performing other ministerial duties at Finnish lumber camps, and nowhere has he slept more soundly or eaten with greater relish than in these very lumber camps. May this be a tribute to the cleanliness of Finnish loggers and their wives in their camp housekeeping.[5]

Jacob Havunen from Kauhajoki built a cabin where he and his wife provided board and lodging for fifty unmarried men. Contrary to the usual custom, the Cooks area had no mess hall or cook camp provided by the company. Family men built their own small wooden shacks covered with tar paper. They were light in weight and were easily moved as the work progressed further into the forest. In addition to Finns, there were many French Canadians who usually worked as drivers. They had their own hall, where Catholic mass was sometimes held. When dances were held in the hall, the altar was turned against the wall. The bicycle was the most common mode of transportation at Cooks.

The death rate in the Cooks area was high. Common causes of death were tuberculosis, typhoid fever, and pneumonia. Now and then a man was "killed by a falling tree." Soon after 1905 the forests were depleted, and the people moved away. Many Finns went to Covington, Watton, Trenary, Eben, and Kaleva, and to Owen, Wisconsin. Only a few Finns elected to stay there as stump farmers. The last of them was John Aho, who died in 1958.[6]

A few Finns moved to Manistique at the beginning of the century. There was, for example, John Pakka, who died in a railroad accident in 1900. In the 1960s there were still a few Finnish farmsteads outside the city. One of them was that of Otto W. Johnson.

The small, quiet town of Seney is near the eastern border of Schoolcraft County, at the junction of Highways #28 and #77 on beautiful Fox River. Its present idyllic peacefulness contrasts sharply with the atmosphere of earlier days. A few large lumber companies started lumbering in this area in the 1880s. When the Duluth, South Shore, and Atlantic Railroad Company laid their tracks there, the depot was called Seney after a certain contractor whose camps happened to be nearby. The railroad made Seney the center of a wide area. Many company offices appeared there as well as hotels, stores, restaurants, and saloons, in addition to monotonous rows of simply constructed homes for workmen and their families.

In addition to Slavs, Frenchmen, and Scandinavians, there were many Finnish loggers and wood cutters in Seney. Up to the present time, no records have been found of their intellectual interests. They built neither churches nor temperance halls, nor did ministers apparently ever stop there to preach. The Finns, along with those of other nationalities, sank into the corruption and wildness of logging camp life. An incident that occurred in the very first days of the village's existence, gave a glimpse of what was to come. When the first trainload of lumberjacks arrived from southern Michigan, they kicked in and smashed all the windows of the train to show what life there was going to be like.

The Finns were clannish and always associated with other Finns, speaking Finnish among themselves even if they knew English. There was no question of inferiority complexes. An old story tells how the Finns, in playing cards with non-Finns, gave hints and information in Finnish to each other, thus winning money from those who did not understand their language. There are many other stories—almost legends—about Finns here as well as elsewhere, especially about their drinking, their physical strength, and their fighting ability when thoroughly aroused. Here are two of them:

One Saturday evening a Finnish woodcutter went into a saloon and ordered drinks. When he paid for them, the others there saw his bundle of bills. When he left the place, a non-Finn started after him. The saloonkeeper warned him: "Don't follow him, he's a Finn!" But the other paid no heed. Half an hour later there was a weak knock at the saloon door, and in crawled the would-be thief covered with blood. The Finn had had pity on his assailant and had spared his life but, to remind him of the transitoriness of life, he had given him dozens of small knife wounds.

The other tale is less bloody. A Finnish lumberjack had his own little shack outside the village and beyond the cemetery. One Saturday night, after the usual "good time," he staggered homeward by way of a shortcut through the cemetery. In the dim moonlight he fell into a freshly dug grave and could not get out. Some time later he heard footsteps and called for help. The newcomer, too, was a Finn in a state of inebriation as bad as that of the man in the grave. "What do you want?" he asked when he heard the cry for help. "It's cold down here," answered the other. "Of course it's cold. You've kicked away all the nice warm sand they covered you with when you were buried."[7]

The influence of the famous Lithuanian anarchist, Emma Goldman (1869–1940), reached even to Seney without, however, having much effect. Whenever a socialist agitator appeared at a logging camp, he usually left in a hurry, for everyone appeared to be satisfied with conditions as they were. The owners and managers of lumber camps made money, and the workmen had good times, in keeping with their small requirements.

Seney became nationally, though unhappily, known through Leon Czolgosz, a Pole who was born in Chicago. He had come under the influence of Emma Goldman and came to Seney following trouble with the police in Detroit. Because of dissension caused by his agitating, he was compelled to leave Seney. A few years later, on September 6, 1901, this Polish anarchist shot President William McKinley in Buffalo, New York.

The death rate was high among those working in the forests. Because they often had to work in swamps and their feet were often continuously wet, they became victims of pneumonia and typhoid. The forests, however, were soon depleted and people moved away, leaving only 200 in the town that had once had a population of 3,500. The Finnish settlement was completely gone. The Seney swamps and former forest areas have since then become a national wildlife refuge, where great numbers of birds, especially waterfowl, come to nest.

Alger County

Alger County, which has about eighty miles of Lake Superior shoreline, is to the north of Delta and Schoolcraft Counties. It was a part of Schoolcraft County until 1885, when it was organized as an independent county with Au Train as the county seat. The history of the area actually began in 1850 when the Munising Company acquired land along Lake Superior and built a good road across the peninsula from Munising to Little Bay De Noc. Because of a lack of funds, all their plans did not materialize. The property was eventually acquired by the well-known Marquette businessman, Peter White, who built the Old Munising smelter there in 1867. Later it was purchased by the Munising Iron Company. At Onota, a few miles west on the Superior shore, there was another iron smelter. Onota had been for a short time the county seat of the original, more inclusive, Schoolcraft County.

The prosperity of the area came to an end in 1877 when the Munising Iron Company went into bankruptcy, and Onota, with the surrounding forests, was destroyed by a great fire. Activity was not renewed there until the fall of 1895, when Timothy Nester began to build the present Munising, which soon reached the ruins of Old Munising. Within a year, there were 3,000 persons living in the town and earning their livelihood in the woodworking industry which developed rapidly at that time and was still flourishing in the 1960s.

Permanent Finnish settlement began in Munising in 1895. Among the first to arrive were Kalle Backman, born in Pieksämäki in 1855, and his wife, born in Rautu; John Riihimaa, born in Parkano; Matti Lampinen, born in Karstula. John N. Korpela, a banker, who was born in Teuva, was for decades a leader in Finnish activities, and served as the city treasurer for over forty years. The oldest of Finnish organizations were the workingmen's club, a Lutheran congregation, and a twenty-two-member band. One of the Finnish businessmen there in the 1960s was Waino Knuuttila. Cliff Camp, five miles southwest of Munising, attracted so many Finns because of extensive lumbering there, that it was considered the headquarters of the Taimen Oksa (Trout Branch) Temperance Society of the Munising area.

In the early fall of 1900 a number of Finnish woodsmen moved north from Cooks into the southern part of Alger County where the cutting of cordwood had begun at Cliff Spur near Trenary along the banks of a little river that ran through beautiful maple forests. Workmen came there from various places, including French Canadians from Canada. Soon there were hundreds of men at Cliff Spur. Later that fall there was an epidemic of typhoid fever caused by contaminated drinking water. It continued through the winter. "Many lost their hair, and teeth became loose. Many began to eat too heavily after recovering and died of that. A total of twenty-seven died." The Finns had their own cemetery in the woods, where about ten typhoid victims were buried. The cemetery was dedicated on June 4, 1901, by Pastor J. J. Hoikka.[8]

Leading Finnish citizens of Cliff Spur were Jaakko and Juho Koukkari and Vihtori Johnson. Most of the men were unmarried and lived with families as boarders at a time when a straw bed and three meals a day cost $15 a month. Cutting cordwood was contract work. A strong man could earn up to $3 a day, but daily earnings often were only about $2. After two or three years, forest work was no longer available and the Finns moved to the Trenary area, most of them to become farmers, without having started any of their usual group activities at Cliff Spur.[9]

Kiva, about ten miles northwest of the Trenary on U.S. Highway 41, is a Finnish farming community which had its beginnings in 1913. Its first pioneer was Antti Peterson from Ylivieska. Other early settlers were Henry Tuuri, Emil Vierikko, and Henry Lampi from Alavus, and Leander Peterson from Ylivieska.

The first settlers of Chatham and Eben on Highway M-94, about twelve miles south of Lake Superior, came from Wisconsin and Canada to work in the forests. Finns first came in 1902, also to work at lumbering, for the whole region was still a logging area. The largest camps in Rock River Township were Rumely, Dorsey, Sundell, Loud Spur, and Cold Springs. The first Finns came from Cooks, among them Evert Holm, August Norgi, Kustaa, Lintala, Matti Pantti, and many others. Families soon came from the mining villages of the Copper Country and from the Marquette County iron mining towns. As forest work became unavailable, the Finns, who comprised about three fourths of the population, began to look for farm lands. Among the pioneer farmers of Rumely were Johan Vastamaki, Evert Niemi, and Otto Laine. In Chatham, pioneers were John Kamppila, Kalle Johnson, Samuel Leppamaki, Edward Luoma, and many others.[10]

The high percentage of Finns in these areas is shown by the fact that in 1951 there were 38 telephone subscribers in Eben, of whom 26 had Finnish names; of the 110 subscribers at Chatham, 34 had Finnish names.[11] Schoolteachers and township officers have been Finns for the most part.

Since the 1890s Finns have lived in the farming area of Deerton in the extreme western part of Alger County, a short distance from Lake Superior. Some of the best known Finns of this quiet countryside were Heikki Pihlainen, born in Karstula in 1873; Albanus Maki, born in Karstula in 1882; Herman August Alanko, born in Ilmajoki in 1870; Severi Tuominen, born in Jyväskylä in 1875; and Isak Karvonen, born in Kuusamo in 1887. Eugene Sinervo, an artist, was a leading citizen of the community. He was a member of the Board of Directors of the Central Cooperative Wholesale and was also on the staff of WLUC-TV, Marquette. A Lutheran congregation and a cooperative store have been active in the area. Many Finnish businessmen of the Upper Peninsula have summer cottages on the shore of Lake Superior near Deerton.

Grand Marais, also on Lake Superior but on the eastern border of Alger County, was given this name, meaning large swamp, by French fur traders. Beautiful Sable Lake, which has been called a jewel of the wilderness, is nearby. After the Civil War, logging companies were attracted to the area's mighty pine forests. Until the building of a railroad to Seney, the lumber from two sawmills was loaded on steamboats in the sheltered harbor of Grand Marais to be transported elsewhere.

The first Finns there, about twenty persons, came to Grand Marais in 1893 from East Tawas in the Lower Peninsula, where lumbering activities were nearly at an end. Among them were Matti Setala from Ylihärmä and Aleksi Abrahamson from Himanka. The group activities of the Finns were a Lutheran congregation and a temperance society called Askel (Step), most activity being centered around the latter in the early years. In 1905 a church and a temperance hall were built side by side at the same time, in competition as it were. Grand Marais was one of those rare places where neither socialism nor non-Lutheran denominations ever got a foothold. The Finnish population was always quite small, being only 100–200 in the first decade of the century when the town was flourishing and the total population was over 3,000. By 1910 the forests had been destroyed and the railroad was soon torn up. It looked as though Grand Marais was about to become a ghost town. In some instances, farms and buildings brought only enough money to pay the price of tickets for a family to move to Detroit, where most of the Finns went to find work.

Grand Marais did not, however, succumb. In 1917, work was started on Highway M-77, which connected Grand Marais with Seney, twenty-five miles away, and led from there to other parts of the country. The highway attracted tourists and the tourist industry to this beautiful part of the state, providing employment for many Finns as well as others. But a few Finns still earned their livelihood by fishing, even as late as the 1960s.[12]

Luce County

Luce County, originally a part of Chippewa County, became an independent unit in 1887, and Newberry, in an area which five years before had been untouched forest, became the county seat. The industry around which the city developed was the Vulcan Furnace, founded in 1882 as a charcoal kiln and iron furnace later known as the Newberry Lumber and Chemical Company. Lumbering and the cutting of cordwood also contributed to the development of the city.

These industries attracted to the area the two nationalities that were the most numerous there during the early days of the community, namely the French Canadians and the Finns. The former arrived first and looked askance at the Finns who came after them, especially when they deprived them of their jobs. Bitterness developed because the companies favored the physically powerful Finns as loaders and drivers, leaving the Frenchmen to the saw and the axe. Johan Henrik Kauramaki, who was born in Honkajoki in 1859, told his son, V. K. Kauramaki, that when he came straight to Newberry from Finland at the age of twenty-one and stepped off the train, his greeting was a blow in the face delivered by a Frenchman. "I wanted to turn around and go back home," he said, "but since I had come on borrowed money, I was forced to stay." At another time, a large number of French Canadians went to a certain logging camp to thrash the Finns, who were, however, prepared. In the fight that followed, one of the assailants lost his life; the others escaped. After that the Finns were not disturbed.

There were two hundred Finns in Newberry in 1888, when they organized a church congregation and a temperance society. Indicative of the character of the times was the fact that the temperance society, Onnen Aarre (Treasure of Happiness), was established in the logging camps and was active in them. The same persons were usually leaders in both the congregation and the temperance society. Some of them were John Pakka, Matti Hakala, John Filppus Erickson, Isak Hakola, and David Riberg. The previously mentioned Johan Henrik Kauramaki, or Papa Kauramaki, as he was known, was one of the honored elders of the area until his death in 1927. Later organizations were a socialist group (the doors of the hall closed in 1937) and a cooperative store. Many Finns have served as city officials and especially as employees in the school system. During past decades there have been a number of Finnish proprietors of public saunas, restaurants, rooming houses, and grocery stores.[13]

Newberry is widely known for its state-owned mental institution. The nine-hundred-acre area with its rows of buildings, its lawns, and its parklike groves is, after the Soo Locks and the Mackinac Bridge, a place well worth seeing. It was opened on November 1, 1895. Its first patients were Upper Peninsula people who had been hospitalized in a similar institution in Traverse City. Innumerable sad life stories have been hidden behind its walls over the years, including those of hundreds of Finns. In his memoirs, Professor Antti J. Pietila, who visited some of the Finns there in the summer of 1925, wrote as follows:

> I visited the state mental hospital at Newberry, which had about 1,200 patients. I was told that more than half were Finns. This is shocking. So many Finnish people in one state who are mentally ill! There must

> be special reasons for this. Many have been depressed by strange, adverse conditions, feelings of insecurity, and homesickness. Some have suffered head injuries. But there are also many of those whose becoming mentally disturbed to the point of illness cannot be explained excepting by a wicked, sinful life. When once a Finn has fallen into sin, he is a violent and completely unrestrained drunkard and debauchee.[14]

Although the estimate given to Pietila may have been somewhat exaggerated, the Finns did make up the greatest number of patients at the institution at that time. This fact receives support from a statement written in 1917: "At a certain period in the history of Michigan and Minnesota, there was a proportionately greater number of Finns than of any other nationality in prisons and mental institutions."[15]

But the situation with regard to the Newberry hospital changed completely in the next forty years. According to statistics of 1960, in which all patients were classified according to church affiliation into Lutherans, Catholics, and "others," there were 2,012 patients. Of them, 612 were Lutherans, 800 were Catholics, and 600 "others." All the Finns were classified as Lutherans. There were 158 of them, or 7.85 percent of the total number of patients. The Finns were further divided into Apostolic Lutherans, or Laestadians, of whom there were 19, and into Evangelical Lutherans, which included all the rest of the Finns. There were 139 of them. A larger number of the Finnish inmates were elderly people whose mental imbalance had been caused by the inability to speak the English language and by loneliness—in other words, by having been abandoned by children and other relatives.[16]

In the extreme southwest corner of Luce County, on the shore of beautiful Manistique Lake, there was a Bible camp with the Indian name of Manakiki. It was sponsored by the Suomi Synod and was much used by members until the merger of the Synod with the Lutheran Church in America, when it became the property of the larger body and was sold for business reasons. Many Finns still have summer cottages in the vicinity, and there are a few widely scattered Finnish farms in the area.

Sault Ste. Marie, Sugar Island, and Rudyard

When Chippewa County was organized in 1825, it extended from Lake Huron to the Mississippi River, but as the states of Minnesota, Wisconsin, and Michigan entered the Union it was reduced in size piece by piece until all that remained under that name was the extreme northeast portion in Michigan bounded by Luce and Mackinac counties and Lakes Superior and Huron.

When Charles T. Harvey constructed the canal at Sault Ste. Marie in 1853–55, there may well have been Finns among his workmen, for recruiters were sent to Boston and New York with explicit orders to bring back workers of north European background.[17] According to another story preserved in the "Soo" area, the first Finns did not arrive until 1864.[18] Ilmonen claimed that they came in 1870 although he had not been able to find Finnish names to prove it.[19]

The expansion of the canal and the addition of locks continued for decades. It has become the world's busiest waterway, which, in the 1960s, handled tonnage greater than the combined tonnage of the Panama and Suez Canals.

The canal attracted temporary Finnish workers, some of whom became permanent residents of the area. The Finnish settlement at the Soo has never been large, probably never over two hundred, if only the Finns born in Finland are taken into consideration. Some of the early Finns about whom detailed information is available are the following: Matti August Mattson, born in Rovaniemi in 1867, and his wife, Kreeta Sofie, born in Isokyrö, who bore him seven children; Tuomas Finnila, born in Laihia in 1867, and his wife, Maria Nurmilaakso, also the mother of seven children; Johan Hill, born in Ylistaro in 1871, and his wife, Ida Sofia Ketola, from Kalajoki, who too had seven children; Joonas Maki, born in Jyväskylä in 1873, and his wife, Justiina, from Kauhava, also with seven children; Oscar Muntter and his wife, Anna Eliina Finnila, from Laihia, had five children born at the Soo; and Tuomas Ranta, born in Nurmo in 1882, and his wife, Maria, from Kauhava, who had eight children, one of whom, Lilja Sanelma, married Edward J. Welch. One of the oldest and best known Finns of the Sault Ste. Marie area was Herman Haapala.

The first organization of the Soo Finns was a temperance society called Turva (Security). When it closed its doors for a time, its members attended meetings of the Pelastuksen Sankari (Hero of Salvation) society across the canal at Sault Ste. Marie in Ontario, Canada, until their own society was reactivated at the beginning of the century. An independent church congregation was started in 1900 by Erik Johanson, a Swedish Finn who had been ordained by Pastor Eloheimo. This congregation joined the Suomi Synod in 1907. Its first regular pastor was John Wargelin. During his pastorate the socialists of the area called a public meeting for the purpose of establishing a Finnish lending library and suggested that some "good literature" should be acquired for the edification of the people. Wargelin, who had just completed a seminary course in apologetics, inquired what they meant by good literature. It came to light that the works of Karl Kautsky, Robert Ingersoll, and James Allman were meant. A decision was made in favor of establishing a library and setting it up in a building owned by the congregation. The pastor was chosen to be the librarian. The books of Allman, Ingersoll, and Kautsky were not acquired. Neither the socialists nor the Knights of Kaleva ever got a foothold in the area. The Finnish cooperative store and the Lutheran congregation were in existence until the 1960s, when they joined American groups.

Brimley, twelve miles to the southwest of Sault Ste. Marie on a bay of Lake Superior, had its beginnings in 1873 as a logging area that had Bay Mills as its center. A short distance away, however, the terrain was more favorable, so one winter the church and the dwellings were moved across the ice to the new location which was first called Superior but later became Brimley. After 1904 some Finnish farmers came to the area. Among the best known were John Koskitalo and Antti Anttonen originally from Temmes, Henry Ojala from Alavieska, and Johan Knuuttila from Piippola. The Brimley Finns came from the Copper Country. They were always so few in number that they never had a church congregation or other organizations.

Below the locks, the St. Mary's River divides into two branches between which there are several large islands. The most northerly of these is Sugar Island, the Finnish "Sokerisaari," sixteen miles long and eight miles wide at its northern end. The Indian name for it was "Sisibakmatominis," meaning maple sugar island. At the time that the United Nations was organized in 1945, Sugar Island was considered as a possibility for its headquarters.

The Finnish settlement on Sugar Island had its beginnings in 1916, when Frank Adolf Aaltonen, having left his work as organizer for the Western Federation of Miners, arrived there as a land agent for a railroad company.[20] He bought land cheaply from the Indians and was publicly criticized for it. Aaltonen traveled in Canada and in the Copper Country, where he had been one of the leaders of the strike, and encouraged the Finns to move to Sugar Island to farm. Fifty-three families and a number of single men decided to do so. Forceful in personality and proficient in English, Aaltonen managed to procure a motor ferry to carry traffic between the island and the mainland, and to have a road built from one end of the island to the other. A few years later, he moved to the eastern states to accept employment in cooperatives. The Finns of Sugar Island were to be found mostly in the towns of Baie de Wasai, Payment, and Willwalk.

Leading Finns were Victor Wiik, Frank Kuusisto, and Jack

Koivisto. Through their efforts and the combined efforts of many others, a hall was built for social activities which included a band and drama clubs. The activities were mostly socialistic in spirit, but the hall was open to pastors who sometimes came from Sault Ste. Marie and Newberry to preach there. In 1960, after a long period of disuse, the hall was sold, and the $200 received for it was donated to the *Työmies-Eteenpäin* (Workingman-forward) and *Naisten Viiri* (Women's pennant) publications. By that time, almost all of the pioneers of the older generation were deceased, but their children still lived there, some of them in the homes built by their parents. But they were not farmers as their parents had been. Most of them were office workers, laborers, and teachers, who worked in Sault Ste. Marie. Post offices, too, had been discontinued, and mail was brought in from the Soo to individual mail boxes on the roadside. In the mid 1960s every other name on these boxes was Finnish. The best-known Finnish business was Niemela's Tourist Center.[21]

For a long time there have been scattered Finnish farming areas south of Sault Ste. Marie, especially around Dafter and Kinross. Pioneers at Kinross were Johan Maki from Siikainen, Nikolai Pylvainen from Kangasniemi, Elias Tulppo from Piippola, and Matti Luostari from Kauhava. However, the largest Finnish community is Rudyard which appeared on maps in the 1880s. Finns first came there at the turn of the century. The earliest known reference to them is in Pastor Johan Bäck's travelogue of 1904:

> Leaving Hancock at 10:15 on the night train, I arrived in Rudyard the following day about 1:30 P.M. There is a small Finnish farming community near the station. I was met by Leander Maki, who had come here from Marquette County a few years ago with his family. Almost all the Finns here are from Marquette and Houghton counties. . . . The Finnish farms nearest to the depot are not even a mile away. The farthest ones are about ten miles distant. . . . The land is as flat here as the surface of a lake; the soil is clay covered by a fertile layer of clayey humus. The best trees were cut down a long time ago, leaving only those of poor quality, in addition to which there is some new undergrowth. It is a difficult task, therefore, to prepare the soil for cultivation. However, stumps are more easily removed here than from sandy soil in which roots grow deeper.

Then Pastor Bäck, who was familiar with farming, says that with good irrigation Rudyard could become a valuable farming area, but that funds would be needed. He also said that "the land company had already donated forty acres of land for a church and parsonage and for the support of a minister and his family."[22]

Some of the first Finns in the Rudyard area were Henry, Kaarlo, and Kustaa Halonen from Paltamo; Matti Steikari from Lapua, Matti Kompsi from Laihia, and Antti Nasi and Antti Soderman from Evijärvi. As cultivated lands increased and swamps were drained, income became more satisfactory and life became more comfortable. The most important products were potatoes, oats, and hay, which were sold by the trainload.

The aforementioned Pastor Erik Johanson, who was working among the Swedish Finns in Cedarville on the shore of Lake Huron at this time, had started church activities in Rudyard toward the end of the 1890s. The spacious stone church of the St. James Finnish Lutheran Congregation, which was organized in 1902, was the social center for Finns still in the 1960s.[23] The Finnish cooperative store was the largest business in the area for a long time. Hans P. Lankinen, a storekeeper, was one of the leading Finns until his death early in the 1960s. Strongville was for a time also a farming community—actually a southern extension of the large Rudyard farming area.

Drummond Island and St. Ignace

Twenty-mile-long Drummond Island at the mouth of the St. Mary's River was important in the early history of both Canada and Michigan. The history of the Finnish settlement there is somewhat unusual. The first Finn to arrive was Victor Hiltunen, or Hilden, the son of a large landowner in Parkano. He came in 1894 or 1896. He was a single man whose occupations were lumbering and fishing, and who built himself a house on state-owned land at the edge of the village of Maxton.

The founder of the permanent Finnish settlement on Drummond Island was Maggie Walz, or Kreeta (Margareeta) Kontra, mentioned earlier in connection with the history of the Calumet Finns as one of the best known and most individualistic of them. She came to America in 1881 at the age of twelve. In Finland before she left for America, she had been warned against Indians and their tomahawks. On her very first evening staying with relatives in Wolverine she had an experience that was frightening in light of the warnings she had had. She was sent out to get some water. On the way to the well she met a squaw and froze with fear. But the squaw only muttered a greeting and went on her way. After attending school for a few years, Maggie Walz became housekeeper for Jaakko Ojanpera in Oskar, where she served until she started her own business enterprises with headquarters in Calumet.

In 1902 Maggie Walz went to Drummond Island as a government land agent and established a second home there. She began immediately to plan a Finnish settlement. When her plans were ready and an old building in Scammon Cove had been prepared as a home for new arrivals, she began to travel to Finnish communities of the Upper Peninsula to recruit settlers. The first of them to arrive on the island was Kristian Salmonson, who came by water from Hancock with his family in 1905. For decades people remembered the great supply of household goods he brought with him, including a cow. His homestead was soon well established. Seven other families and three single men came later that year. The family men were Karl Palmroos; Karl Heinonen, Kalle Toivonen, and Antti Toivola from Kellokoski; Jacob Heikkinen from Ylivieska; and Salomon Ruohomaki from Virrat. One of the unmarried men was August Wirtanen from Kellokoski. A Laestadian preacher, Joel Sikkila of Kyrö, arrived in 1906, as did John Laakso from Luvia, Otto Korpi from Honkajoki, and Albert Koskela from Parkano. Antti Komulainen, Joel Kemppainen, and Kalle Holman of Kuhmoniemi came in 1907. The last Finns arrived in 1913, when there were estimated to be about 300 Finns on the island, most of them from the Copper Country.

The first Finnish community was named Kreetan for the original first name of its founder, Maggie Walz. There were a school and a post office there, with Maggie Walz herself serving as postmaster. This first town of Kreetan was deserted when the Finns moved to Scammon Cove, whose name was now changed to Kreetan and later to Johnswood. The local sawmill provided employment for the Finns, Irishmen, and Frenchmen of the area. Johnswood disappeared from the map in 1925, when the sawmill ceased operations and the settlers dismantled their homes to rebuild them in more fertile parts of the island.

The farms the Finns acquired usually consisted of land that had been ravaged by forest fires. They were often far beyond stretches of pathless wilderness and the soil was poor. Many a settler's family suffered great hardships before the land began to produce a livelihood. The boards for the first log cabins were sawed by hand. Roofs were shingled with chips and birch bark. Stumps were pried out with heavy wooden poles. Hay for their cattle came from swamps, where it was piled to await the fall freeze, when it was brought home by sled. Two or three trips a year were made by boat to the village of De Tour on the mainland to purchase necessities and to make arrangements with lumber buyers. Logs were brought to a predetermined place on the shore in winter. From there a steam tug would tow them away in the spring. Sometimes, through very rarely, it happened that a ship would run aground in the shallow water of the strait, and its cargo would be tossed into the water to make it possible to free the vessel. If the settlers managed to get to the place soon enough with their boats, they might take home a considerable amount of valuable goods.

For about thirty years there was much activity among the Drummond Island Finns. There was a Suomi Synod congregation started in 1908 by Pastor Jacob Manta. Church services were also held in private homes as were those of Joel Sikkila, the Laestadian preacher. A farmers' association was organized the same year, with Karl Palmroos and Antti Toivola among its leaders. By 1913 they were able, by the use of volunteer labor, to build themselves a large hall with a dining room and a stage. In addition to the socialist farmers' association, other groups using the hall were a youth league, a women's club, and the theater and gymnastics clubs. Aku Rissanen, a socialist leader who spent his summers on Drummond Island, taught a socialist "Sunday School" there for a time. The hall also had a fairly large lending library. A fire late on Halloween night in 1928 completely destroyed the hall. It had not been insured and it was never rebuilt. Group activity among the Finns ceased altogether in 1936. Upon attaining adulthood, the children moved away to seek an easier living, and the lands cleared by their parents were abandoned. When the socialists became numerous on the island, Maggie Walz, who was a Laestadian, left the area to continue her business enterprises elsewhere.

Although many Finns left the island, many remained. Most of the men who stayed worked in the limestone quarry, which is claimed to be one of the world's largest, with a peak annual production of two million tons. Others earned their livelihood by serving summer tourists, hunters, and sports fishermen. In 1961 there were 600 people living on the island. Of them fifty-three were Finnish.[24] Some of the Finns were active in the island's historical society.

Lakes Huron and Michigan are connected by the Straits of Mackinac, with St. Ignace on the north shore and Mackinaw City on the south shore. Both towns played an important part in French and English history. After the era of fur trading had passed, the source of income for St. Ignace was its seven sawmills. The lumber and sawmill industries attracted some Finns there as temporary residents who sponsored church activity for a short time but left no permanent memorial. In the 1920s there were still a few Finnish families there, namely, those of Onni and Kalle Siren from Pihtiputaas, Matti Anttile from Pyhäjoki, and August Holm from Marttila.

9 Lower Michigan

The total population of Lower Michigan is thirty times greater than that of the Upper Peninsula. But the ratio of Finns to non-Finns in these two areas was just the reverse for a long time. However, at the height of the lumbering activity of the 1870s and 1880s there were Finns in Lower Michigan by the thousands. When lumbering ended they went to the lumber camps and the copper and iron mines of the Upper Peninsula as well as to northern Minnesota. Some of the Finns stayed in the Lower Peninsula as farmers because they were able to get satisfactory land at a low price, and some stayed to work in factories. When Reverend Salomon Ilmonen traveled in Lower Michigan in the early 1920s, he found many small Finnish communities from which the Finns have since disappeared, having either left or become absorbed into American life.

At the time of Ilmonen's visit there were still some Finnish farmers in the vicinity of Grayling, eighty miles directly south of Mackinaw City. Among them were Pekka Kiiski from Kurkijoki; Adam Hyotylainen, Jonas Virtanen, Kalle Tahvonen, and Jonas Pynnonen from Toivakka; and Nestor Vallas from Joutsa. In the Lewiston area, near Grayling, the Finnish farmers were August Valden from Tampere, Henry Halberg from Lapua, Asarias Turppa from Isokyrö, and Johan Kuivinen from Ylistaro. The leading Finns in Jennings, near Lake City, were August Hannila and August Erickson from Kalajoki, and Henry Forsman and August Lampela from Isojoki.

As early as 1868 there were Finns in Muskegon, which was one of the great centers of the sawmill industry of Michigan in the nineteenth century. The first of them was Jacob Haikola from Kalajoki.

Later arrivals were Matti Vickstrom and Matti Mattila from Kokkola. Inland from Muskegon in the Ravenna area, there were some Finnish farmers from 1890 on, among them Tuomas and Emil Pietila from Alavus and Sylvester Kantola from Teuva. In such centers of industry, government, and culture as Lansing, Grand Rapids, Ann Arbor, Pontiac, and Flint there were smaller Finnish colonies.[1] The largest Finnish communities in Lower Michigan have been and still were in the 1960s in Kaleva, Lake City, East Tawas, and Detroit. Each has a history differing greatly from that of other areas.

Kaleva

In 1888 there was an unusual railroad building contest in Lower Michigan. The Chicago and West Michigan Railroad Company was laying tracks northward, and the Manistee and Northeastern Company was pushing northeastward through great forests. The companies had agreed that the second to arrive at the prearranged intersection, about twenty miles from Manistee, was to install necessary special rails and switches and build and maintain the depot. The Chicago and West Michigan Company won the contest, and the Manistee and Northeastern was obliged to foot the bill for the installations.[2]

The railroad companies cut down the forests and, toward the end of the 1890s, the area with its endless stumps and brush piles was, according to stories told by older Finns, a veritable wasteland and a vale of sorrows. The New York National Land Association became interested in the region, however, and sent a Finnish agent, Jacob E. Saari, who was born in Kälviä, to look it over. He saw its possibilities and took immediate action. He changed the name of the station from Manistee Crossing to Kaleva, and in 1899 began to advertise it in Finnish publications, describing it as a fine agricultural area with land available at $5 an acre. Inquiries came literally from all directions, and from the spring of 1900 on, Saari, or "Settler Jack," as he was widely known, had an office in Manistee.

There were about twenty families in the area when the Finns arrived. Some of them were families of Civil War veterans who had received government lands, and others were leftovers from the days of lumbering. John White's little place of business, which was also the post office, was the only store. Real activity began with the coming of the Finns. The first to arrive with Saari was John Haaksiluoto, originally from Raahe, with his wife, from Jersey City in April 1900. This began such a migration as has occurred at no other time in the history of

Finnish-American farming communities. The largest numbers of Finns came from the Copper Country, Marquette County, Detroit, and the state of Wyoming. Smaller numbers came from Massachusetts, California, and Ontario, Canada. This influx was the result of Saari's effective advertising, the most important carrier of which was the newspaper *Siirtolainen* (the immigrant).

Almost all of the Finns who came to Kaleva were family men. A good idea of the states of origin can be obtained from the carefully kept church records of the Lutheran congregation from 1902 to 1927. The families that joined the congregation during that period had a total of 441 children, born in the states and Canada (see table 6).

Table 6: Birthplaces of Second-Generation Finnish Immigrant Children, Kaleva, Michigan, 1902–27

Michigan	219	Illinois	15	Oregon	4
Wyoming	46	North Dakota	13	Wisconsin	3
Ohio	29	Minnesota	13	New Jersey	3
Montana	18	South Dakota	8	California	2
Pennsylvania	18	Washington	7	Kentucky	1
Massachusetts	17	Ontario, Can.	5		
New York	15	Indiana	5		

The Ontario Finns came from Port Arthur; the Wyoming Finns from Rock Springs, Hanna, and Carbon. The Massachusetts Finns were all from Cape Ann. Those who came from Pennsylvania were from Nanty Glo, and those from Illinois were from Chicago.

All the villages and little communities of the extensive Kaleva area have naturally had Finnish names. For example, Ylistaro got its name from Ylistaro, Finland, the birthplace of its first pioneer Jaakko Lemponen. The town of Wiitala was named for Johan Wiitala who came from Alavus, and the village of Lappi for Tobias Lappi, the first to build a home there. Puustinen was named for Otto Puustinen from Nilsiä, and Kanniainen for Kustaa Kanniainen from Oulu.

Through Saari's efforts, *Siirtolainen* was moved from Brooklyn to Kaleva in the fall of 1901. Edited and published by Saari and Antero Riippa, it was of great importance in the success of the new settlement. Nothing more completely Finnish had ever before been offered to settlers in America than what was being offered in Kaleva, where street names even had a familiar Finnish sound: Wuoksi, Osmo, Panu, Tapio,

Walta. In addition to publishing *Siirtolainen*, the Finnish American Publishing Company opened a general store with which the John White business merged.

Jacob Saari is said to have returned to Finland a wealthy man. Gradually the Kaleva settlement too became prosperous. But life was hard in the early days because summers were dry and the soil was not as rich as it had been advertised to be. In addition to the usual farming and cattle raising, the cultivation of cucumbers and pole beans, to which the soil was well suited, provided income. The cucumbers were salted and sent by the trainload to the pickle factories of Pittsburgh.

In 1902 the temperance society Kalevatar and a Lutheran congregation were organized and held their meetings in a jointly owned hall. In 1913 the congregation built a church which for a long time was reputed to be the most imposing Finnish American country church, although the story that it had a seating capacity of 750 was exaggerated. Since the congregation did not have funds for building a parsonage, the enterprising Pastor Antti Kononen had one built at his own expense, later selling it to the congregation. The Finnish church and the parsonage dominated the landscape. Up to 1940 the chief language used in the area was Finnish even though the children learned English at school. Marriage between Finns and non-Finns was still unknown. It was not until 1950 that Kaleva became Americanized in language and in the acceptance of marriage between Finns and non-Finns.

Over the decades the Finns of Kaleva have been in many kinds of businesses. The oldest of these was the Union Store Company. The Cooperative Mercantile and Produce Company was organized a little later to compete with it. It was not, however, a typical cooperative as the name would indicate. John Makinen, who had come from Kurikka, started a soft drinks company, also in 1907, with Alex Ketonen from Kauhava as his partner. The business became an exceptionally large one. Because of the dust storms of the 1920s, which caused considerable damage to crops, the farmers turned their attention to raising dairy cattle with such success that in 1928 the Golden Cooperative Creamery Company was organized by 150 Finnish farmers. The weekly output of butter amounted to as much as 2,000 pounds. In 1944 the dairy became the property of a private owner, but dairying increased the value of the land and became the chief source of income. The biggest businesses owned by Finns have been the Kaskinen Motor Company established in 1924 by Ferdinand Kaskinen, the oil and machinery business of Johan and Emil Rengo, and the Makinen Tackle Company established by William Makinen.[3]

Jennings and Lake City

In Missaukee County, about forty-five miles directly east of Kaleva, there is a lake also called Missaukee, around which a number of Finns settled as early as 1886, first to work in the lumber industry, and later to cultivate homestead lands. At first the center of the settlement was the west side of the lake, where the village of Jennings with its large sawmills developed. Ilmonen mentions August Hannila and August Erickson of Kalajoki, Mikko Vaihkola from Joutsa, and Henry Forsman and August Lampela from Isojoki as having been among the first Finns to come there. Other early settlers were August Ripatti from Hirvensalmi and his wife, Wilhelmiina Mesiainen, from Joutsa; Frans O. Perahannu, and Veikko and Tauno Kaipiainen from Jyväskylä and the latter's wife, Rosa Mesiainen, from Joutsa; and Hugo Valenius and Frans Salmi from Eurajoki. By 1909 they were able to start a Lutheran congregation. In 1921 they bought a church building, which was, however, in the wrong location, for the Finnish population was then centered around Lake City on the east side of Lake Missaukee. In 1923 the church was moved there. It was the center of Finnish activity for decades.[4]

East Tawas

Tawas City and East Tawas are across the state from Kaleva on the shore of Lake Huron at the mouth of Saginaw Bay. Starting in 1877, East Tawas and nearby Oscoda, which were surrounded by great forests, attracted large numbers of Finns. In the 1880s and early 1890s the Finnish population rose to several hundred. Wages in the lumbering and sawmill industries were better than average. It is said that in some years more money was sent to Finland from this area than from any other Finnish community of comparable size. Those who were able to save money soon acquired a small fortune, but with ruthless cutting the forests were soon destroyed. Saloons and their accompaniment of evils flourished. Pastor Kaarlo Huotari, who visited there in 1894, wrote as follows about the area after the days of prosperity had passed:

> Now things are different. Only a few sawmills are operating, even those only in the summertime. Most of the lumber for them is brought from Canada. There are many vacant houses. . . . Au Sable on the right bank of the Au Sable River . . . is almost completely deserted, so that costly houses stand vacant, and would not bring a penny on the market. The people have had to move elsewhere be-

> cause of the lack of income. Because there are no farming areas around Oscoda and East Tawas it is necessary for residents to leave the area. Last spring there were 160 adult Finns in East Tawas and 60 in Oscoda; now there are 100 and 30 respectively.[5]

However, fishing and employment in the sugar factories and saltworks of the area saved the situation, and many Finns who had left returned. The Raivaaja (Pioneer) temperance society was organized in 1893, and in 1894, a Lutheran congregation was started under the leadership of Pastor Kaarlo Huotari. These became the centers of group activity among the Finns. Their choral group and bank were directed by a Finnish-speaking Swedish merchant from Skane. Cooperative activity continued under the leadership of Pastors J. J. Hoikka (1895–1900) and Antero Riippa, who followed him, both of them serving the Augustana Swedish and the Suomi Synod Finnish congregations concurrently.

The Finnish settlement, however, thinned out. Some of the people moved to Alabaster, a few miles south of East Tawas on the shore of Lake Huron. The Finns there had an active congregation from 1914 to 1929. The East Tawas congregation was removed from the Suomi Synod roster in 1956, but it had already ceased activity some time before.

In his book about the history of Finnish Americans, Ilmonen mentions twenty of the earliest settlers in the East Tawas area.[6] To this comment should be added the highlights of the lives of several exceptional shoemakers. One was Jaakko H. Kniivila who was born in Evijärvi in 1855 and came to East Tawas in 1884. In partnership with Jaakko Lofman from Kaustinen, he made high-top waterproof boots. The reputation of these boots was such that it brought him orders from as far away as Louisiana. Kniivila died in 1916. His son, Werner Ahonen, born in Ikaalinen, was one of the active oldsters of East Tawas at the age of eighty years.[7]

Another shoemaker was a former farmhand, Aapo Koivukoski, who opened a shoemaker shop in East Tawas. On February 24, 1897, he wrote a letter to U.S. president William McKinley, asking him if he would accept a gift of Finnish slippers. An affirmative answer came with the request that the slippers be size 7½. Koivukoski made the slippers and sent them to the president, whose secretary, John Addison Porter, wrote the official note of appreciation: "The President has asked me to convey his gratitude to you for your friendly gesture toward him." Professor John I. Kolehmainen, who tells of this incident, avers that no one asked Aapo why he had taken it upon himself to supply the president with slippers; everyone seemed to know that he was just paying his own debt of gratitude to America.[8]

Detroit

It may well be that as early as the 1850s some Finnish seaman sailing on the Great Lakes considered Detroit his hometown. Alex Lampi is mentioned as having lived there in 1852, working first in the shipyards, and later as a carpenter until his death in about 1880. The city directory of 1890 lists nine families with the name of Korte, all of whom lived in the eastern part of the city. Jeweller Frank Korte, who was employed in the Kaiser Jewelry Shop, is listed as early as 1855. Alfred Korte, who is listed as a jeweller from 1880 on, may have been his son. A Benhard Korte worked in a carriage or harness shop from 1867 until he started his own eventually prosperous business ten years later. Starting in 1871 there is a millinery business listed under the name of Katherine Korte. There was even a Korte Avenue in the eastern part of the city, indicating that persons belonging to this family were highly respected citizens.[9]

The Finns of Detroit have worked at many vocations. They have been seamen and sailors, carpenters, businessmen, engineers, and specialists of various kinds. Because of the size of the city, they were not often aware of one another's existence. They did not begin to increase in number until the first decade of the twentieth century, and not until the second decade was this increase rapid. There were two important reasons for this rise in Finnish population after 1910. The first was the birth of the automobile industry, which offered employment. The other was the labor troubles which closed many iron and copper mines in the Upper Peninsula about the same time. This increase continued for decades. In 1900 there were only a few Finns in Detroit; in 1914 there were 1,500; in 1917 there were 3,000; in 1938 the number was 15,000; in the 1960s the estimate was 40,000 persons of Finnish descent. Because the thousands of Finns who first came to Detroit had either been born in Finland and had lived in the Upper Peninsula for some time or were the children of Finnish-born citizens, they were recognized by their Finnish accent and by the outspokenness of the miners. They often heard themselves called "Northern Hillbillies." In their turn they made fun of the fact that Detroiters knew nothing about the Upper Peninsula except that Sault Ste. Marie was important because of its locks, and that Marquette had some connection with early Jesuit missionaries.

Finns, of course, came to Detroit from other parts of the United States as well as from the Upper Peninsula of Michigan. One of the most interesting of those who did was Alexander Hamlin, whose name in Finland had been Hamalainen. He was born in Koivisto in 1878, went to sea as a fifteen-year-old, worked as a harbor pilot in Viipuri, came to America, and was employed in auto body plants in Springfield and Amesbury, Massachusetts. He moved to Detroit in 1910 with other Finns who worked in these factories. One of them was a coppersmith, Otto Lindstrom, from Helsinki. He brought with him "a piano, a dog as big as a small horse, and a family." Lindstrom, Hamlin, and Yrjo Lahteenmaki, a tinsmith from Tampere, taught other Finns, and sometimes Poles, the secrets of manufacturing auto bodies. Because the work was done on contract, skilled workers were able to make good money. By the following year Hamlin had a two-story house which he had worked on in the evenings. It was the first house built in Detroit by a Finn of this generation. In his memoirs Hamlin often refers to Henry Ford, whose house in Dearborn he helped to build. The Fords often employed Finnish servants and the crew of their yacht were Finns. Sometimes Ford would come to inspect his yacht while the men were having a meal. He would sit down to chat with them and to partake of their Finnish meal of potatoes boiled in their jackets and salt-pork gravy. The high wages offered in the automobile industry caused all the Finns who were working in the salt mines of Detroit to leave them for work in the factories.[10]

The history of the Detroit Finns is also the history of their clubs, societies, and congregations, for whoever did not belong into one or more of them was, in a way, outside the Finnish community. The oldest organized group activity was church work, which began when the St. John's Lutheran congregation was organized in 1914. The church has been served by such well-known pastors as Lauri R. Ahlman, Salomon Ilmonen, and Emil J. Paananen. Between two and three hundred members left this church and established the Bethlehem congregation in 1937. Its pastors have been Dr. Jacob W. Heikkinen and Eino Tuori. Both of these congregations experienced the phenomenon that occurs in many large American cities, namely that of the black population's becoming dominant in a so-called white area. Both congregations sold their churches and rebuilt in new areas where the members of the congregations had already moved. A third church of the Suomi Synod, the Northwest Emmanuel, was dedicated in 1957.

The Apostolic Lutheran congregation of Detroit was also organized in 1914 and church services were held in private homes. Arthur and Paul Heideman, father and son, preached there until 1920, when

Jacob Halvary was called to be the resident minister. He was followed by John M. Nelson, who was succeeded by Raymond H. Tulkki. Pastors of the Finnish National Church stopped there to hold services whenever they passed through Detroit after 1919. Their Salem congregation was organized in 1921 by Pastor A. Hassel. In 1943, R. W. Heikkinen became its pastor. The most recently established Finnish church there is a Finnish Congregational Church established in 1940 by Pastor Niilo Tuomenoksa.

An important gathering place for Detroit Finns was the Kaleva Home of the Ladies of Kaleva on the corner of Indiandale and Montville Place (now the Finnish Center Association), where in addition to the Aura Knights of Kaleva and the Auratar Ladies of Kaleva which were organized in 1917, many other groups and committees met. One of them was the Suomi College Alumni Association, in whose activities hundreds of former Suomi College students living in the Detroit area have participated since 1925. Einar W. Laine was its president for many years.

Detroit is an international city, not only because of its early history when its French and British phases merged into the American, but also because of the composition of its present population. The Cosmopolitan Women's Club has forty national subdivisions. In the early 1920s, Helmi Warren became its first Finnish member. Now there are no more than seventeen, for membership is restricted. For decades, Finnish members have held all possible offices, including the presidency. They have been instrumental in planning Finnish programs and events for their organization as well as for the general public.

The relations between the Finns and the Estonians in Detroit have been especially warm and friendly. Finns have regularly attended the memorial celebrations of Eesti Vabariigi (Republic of Estonia) and have sometimes participated in the flag ceremony which is traditional at the beginning of a program. The Estonian Men's Chorus of Detroit often sang at Finnish programs under the direction of Professor A. Kasemets.

Over the years the Finns of Detroit have sponsored many activities and enterprises, among them the Finnish Businessmen's Club which was organized in 1928. Its name was later changed to Finnish American Club of Detroit. The club built a good sauna on Walnut Lake on the outskirts of the city, with facilities for swimming and boating. The most important Finnish political organization is the Finnish Democratic League. Among the many businesses owned by Finns, an outstanding one was the world-famous tackle factory established by Charles Helin. It sold millions of the lures he had invented and developed. The numerous Finnish doctors and merchants as well as the many persons employed in schools, post offices, police departments, and elsewhere indicate that Finns have become a vital part of the active life of the great metropolis.

Two special occasions brought the Finns into public notice. The first was Detroit's 250th anniversary celebration in 1951, in which the Finns were represented in the great festival parade by a beautiful float designed by architect Eero Waskinen, and in which they also appeared in choruses and folk dances. The second occasion was the three-day visit of President and Mrs. Urho K. Kekkonen of the Republic of Finland to Detroit in October 1961, when the Finnish community honored them with special church services and banquets. A person who served on the Finnish committees for both of these occasions was Dr. George W. Sippola, the president of the Michigan Finnish American Historical Society.[11]

10 Churches

The oldest influence for unity among the Finns is the church with its congregations. In the Delaware colony every subject of the kingdom of Sweden was a member of the state church and belonged to the local congregation. Broadly speaking, this was also true in Alaska, where the Finnish governors working for Russia invited and attracted other Finns, making the colony largely Finnish Lutheran in church affiliation.

A political and religious development that began in Finland affected the spiritual life of Finnish Americans. At the time when Finland became a part of the Russian Empire in 1809 and Viipuri with its Lutheran and Greek Orthodox population became a part of the Finnish political state, Finland had two state churches: the Evangelical Lutheran Church of the majority and the Greek Orthodox Church of the Minority.

The position of the Finnish Lutheran Church as a state church was being steadily weakened by great revivals—Pietism, Evangelism, and the prayer movement as well as Laestadianism, which had originated in Sweden. The state church was in existence officially until the first years of the twentieth century, but in practice the situation had already changed by the 1860s, when modern emigration from Finland began. By virtue of their citizenship all the emigrants were members of the Evangelical Lutheran state church, but those who belonged to revivalist groups felt a strong spiritual bond with other members of their own groups. Among the Finns who came to America there were comparatively large numbers of Laestadians because most of the earliest immigrants of this period came from the northern areas of Scandinavia where the Laestadian movement had begun.

The Laestadians or Apostolic Lutherans

Lars Levi Laestadius (1800–1861) was an internationally known botanist who left his scientific vocation to study for the ministry and made serving the parish of Pajala in Sweden as its rector his lifework. An exceptional linguist and a gifted preacher, he became the spiritual leader of Finns, Swedes, and Lapps in extensive areas. When he experienced a profound spiritual awakening in 1844, the religious movement which was already centered around him became a powerful revival that spread rapidly over national boundaries from Sweden into Finland and Norway.

Laestadianism spread mainly through lay preachers sent out by the founder of the movement. The best known of these were Juhani Raattamaa (d. 1899), Erkki Antti Juhonpieti (d. 1900), and Heikki Parkajoki (d. 1895). In the simple but powerful language of the common people, they taught the fundamentals of the way of salvation to ignorant and immoral people. With impassioned sermons on the law, with spiritual condemnation of those who were not members of the movement, and by portrayal of the eternal bliss of "Christians"—those who belonged to it—attempts were made to bring listeners to the "narrow gate," which meant repentance and the confession of sins before a meeting of believers. Raattamaa "found" and put into use "the keys of the Kingdom of Heaven," which meant the forgiveness of sins by the assemblage or congregation. The happy cries and the jumping for joy of those who experienced salvation led to the application of the derisive name of "Holy Hoppers" to the group by nonmembers.

After the death of Laestadius, when the movement was left almost entirely to the leadership of uneducated lay preachers, great narrow-mindedness and bias appeared in its life and doctrine. Only the word of God as preached among themselves was the living Word of God; the confession of sins before the congregation was the only way to salvation—the sanctification of life was forgotten; their attitude toward the Lutheran church as well as toward other churches was condemnatory. According to them, Christianity had apparently dawned only in Lapland.

Nevertheless, the more evangelistic and broad-minded ideas of Laestadius remained alive beside this self-righteousness, advocated especially by Juhani Raattamaa, the preserver of the Laestadian tradition and a Christian personality greatly respected even outside the movement. After the dissolution of 1896, this trend continued as a "new revival" which was joined by a considerable number of Finnish clergymen and many enlightened laymen. Members of this new revival movement emphasized the authority of the Bible, the need for prayer and for a consecrated life, the obligation to participate in missionary work, and the reading of the Bible and the works of Luther in addition to the sermons of Laestadius. Thus, they are closer in spirit to Lutheranism in general than are the conservatives. Finnish American Laestadianism differs from the Laestadianism of Finland chiefly in that its leadership has remained for the most part in the hands of lay preachers, and in that it has carefully isolated itself from other Lutheran denominations, whereas the Finnish Laestadians, as members of the Evangelical Lutheran Church of Finland, have remained in contact not only with other Lutheran churches but with all of Christianity as well.

The Norwegians and the Swedes in America were considerably ahead of the Finns in their religious life because they had come to this country earlier. The Swedish Augustana Synod and the Norwegian Hauge Synod had been established by 1860. As a result of their initiative a meeting of local Swedes, Finns, and Norwegians was held in Hancock on June 16, 1867. There was no serious language barrier, for most of the Swedes and Norwegians were familiar with Finnish, which was used as the "international" language in northern Scandinavia, from where most of these immigrants had come. Furthermore, many Finns were familiar with Swedish or Norwegian. The meeting was conducted by Pastor A. E. Fridrichsen.[1] He assured the gathering of his competence by announcing that he was "a theological candidate from the University of Christiania in Norway and had been ordained as an Evangelical Lutheran pastor."[2]

The "Norske, Quaener, og Svenske," as the minutes in Norwegian have it, meaning Norwegians, Finns, and Swedes, decided to organize a Scandinavian Evangelical Lutheran congregation.[3] This name was apparently used for the church by the Swedes and Finns; among the Norwegians it was known as the Norwegian congregation.[4] They had a right to call it that, for the pastors were Norwegians and the language used most of the time was Norwegian. The Finns were soon in the majority in the congregation, which belonged to the Augustana Synod. A small, unpretentious church was built on Quincy Hill north of Hancock. The first pastor was A. E. Fridrichsen, who served from 1867 to 1871, preaching to the Finns through an interpreter, a Norwegian Finn by the name of Amund Hagen. Fridrichsen was followed by H. Roernaes, also a Norwegian, who served from 1871 to 1876.

Finnish immigration was gradually increasing. Large numbers of Finns joined the congregation, including many Laestadians. Antti Vitikka, or Vitikkohuhta, born near Haaparanda, who arrived from Hammerfest in 1870, was a leading Laestadian. He was once seen weeping, and when friends asked him what the cause of his sorrow was, he told them that he was unhappy about the lack of concern among the people of the locality for God and His Word. He was asked to speak at worship services, and many Finns came to hear his simple testimony. These services, apparently held in 1870, were probably the first Laestadian worship services to be held in the New World.[5]

These church meetings soon brought the Laestadians into open conflict with Pastor Roernaes, who had a fair knowledge of the Finnish language. He had already become familiar with the distinctive outward characteristics of this group. All finery in dress was considered sinful. This idea was carried so far as to deny even plain straw hats to women and neckties and watch chains to men. At funerals the hearse and floral wreaths were forbidden. Altar paintings, pulpits, and church bells were condemned as devices used by Satan against Christianity. When the Laestadians began to hold their own worship services and even became so aggressive as to approach the pastor in his own parsonage to advise him about "the way of salvation according to the Bible," it was too much for Roernaes. In a public church announcement made some time in 1872 he forbade them the sacraments, even the right to serve as sponsors at a baptism and the right to Christian burial. This clumsy act struck such a serious blow to the relations between Laestadians and other Lutherans that even after the passage of a hundred years the would had not yet healed.

Thus excommunicated, the Laestadians were now compelled to attend to their own religious needs. At the request of the modest and humble Antti Vitikka, and at his expense, a former cantor, Salomon Kortetniemi, had come to America from Akkula the year before to be Vitikka's "assistant in the Lord." Kortetniemi rose from the position of assistant to that of leader. A congregation was organized on December 21, 1872, with Kortetniemi as pastor. It was registered on January 11, 1873, as the Salomon Kortetniemi Lutheran Society. The origin of this unusual name for a congregation is uncertain. Two explanations have been given. One is that the Finns, because of their poor command of English, were not able to explain their purpose to the county clerk, who came to the conclusion that they had organized a society in honor of a national hero just as the Irish had organized societies honoring St.

Patrick. The other is that the name reflects Kortetniemi's own ambition: "He strove cleverly and unscrupulously to become lord and master on the basis of work pioneered by another."[6]

A church was built on Pine Street in Calumet in 1873. The local mining company donated a lot and $500 toward construction costs. Kortetniemi, who had no talent for preaching, wrote his sermons and read them at worship services. The liturgical portions of the services were better than the sermons, for Kortetniemi followed the handbook of the Church of Finland. When Pastor Roernaes heard of this, he had Kortetniemi summoned to court for illegal performance of ministerial duties. Naturally, in this land of religious freedom, Roernaes's position was not upheld.

Kortetniemi began to feel resistance and opposition, especially since new preachers who considered themselves to be representatives of a purer Laestadianism were arriving from the old country. The Congregation of the Firstborn in Lapland sent representatives to Michigan to serve as mediators. Since they were not able to bring about the desired result, Raattamaa sent Johan Takkinen of Kuusamo to the Copper Country in 1877. Takkinen was a former violinist who on experiencing a spiritual awakening had flung his violin "after the Devil" and had begun to preach repentance with all the ardor of his nature.

After the arrival of Takkinen, those who objected to Kortetniemi came into conflict with him in an attempt to replace him with Takkinen as the head of the congregation in Calumet, which was becoming the headquarters of Laestadianism in America. David Castren, the first schoolteacher among the Finnish Americans and friend of Kortetniemi, also turned against him. He brought the dispute into the columns of the secular newspaper, *Swen Tuuva*, of Hancock, publishing articles attacking his former friend. In 1878, when Takkinen, who was visiting in Sweden, received the blessing of the Congregation of the Firstborn in Lapland, the Calumet congregation installed him as their pastor.

Equipped with this Laestadian "Apostolic succession," Takkinen went to work. His first act was to change the peculiar name of the congregation to The Finnish Apostolic Lutheran Church of Calumet, which is supposed to have been suggested by Castren. The decision to accept the name was made on April 22, 1879. The reason for approval of the word "Apostolic" in the name was that it was meant to differentiate this group clearly from the Evangelical Lutheran Church, which was also beginning to be represented by congregations in the Copper Country. Apparently no one in the group knew the actual canonical meaning of the word, but ever since that time the term "Apostolic Lutheran" has been used to refer to the American Laestadians.

Takkinen was a devoted friend of children. He published a primer for them titled *Ameriikan Suomalainen Aapinen*, which involved him in a theological conflict because he had added the word "Gethsemane" to the Creed, which was included in it, making the controversial statement: "In Gethsemane, He descended into Hell." He took a firm stand against church formalities, eliminating the singing of chants, kneeling for the Confession of Sins, standing for the recitation of the Creed, taking oaths, exorcising, making the sign of the cross at baptism, and the churching of women after childbirth, all of which he considered to be superstitions. Raattamaa, who required the observance of church law in Sweden and Finland because Laestadianism in these countries was a revival movement within the state churches, condoned Takkinen's measures in free America. "In Takkinen's time the American Laestadian Church became what it has been ever since."[7]

By this time dissension and separatism had affected Laestadianism in Sweden and Finland and were brought to Michigan and Minnesota by new immigrants. Takkinen began to examine recent arrivals to find out how thorough their conversion had been, whether they truly loved the elders of Lapland, etc. Three men rose to the leadership of the freer evangelical Laestadianism in Michigan. They were Pekka Strolberg; Pekka Berg, a painter from Oulu; and Johan Mullo from Kalajoki. Salomon Kortetniemi, now known as Korteukko (Old Man Korte) because of his age, joined them as did a large number of others who objected to Takkinen's strictness. This group began to hold worship services in the Calumet Kansanvalistusseura (Society for the Enlightenment of the People) Hall. For this reason they were called the "Haalilaiset." (Hall People).

There was dissension in Takkinen's group, too, originating mostly in the uncompromising attitudes of their leader, and opposition to him began to grow. When, two days before Christmas 1888, the congregation met for the annual election of a pastor, they were so excited and noisy that after the chairman, Emil Vesterinen, had tried unsuccessfully to call the meeting to order, he announced that it was postponed to some indefinite future time. But at two o'clock in the afternoon a large number of church members, mostly opponents of Takkinen, met in the church to continue the meeting. This afternoon meeting had actually been proposed at the morning session, but the chairman had either not paid attention to the proposal or had not heard it because of the confusion. Johan Peter Noppa was elected chairman. There were eighty-one qualified voters present. Johan Takkinen and

Roanpaa were the candidates. The latter was a preacher who had had charge of the congregation while Takkinen was on his trip to Sweden. Roanpaa received sixty-seven votes and was named pastor. According to certain information, the total number of the congregation entitled to vote at that time was 135. Thus, the two factions were equal in size. Nor did Roanpaa and Takkinen have any doctrinal differences of opinion. Both followed the tenets of Raattamaa's Congregation of the Firstborn in Lapland.

Takkinen's supporters considered the afternoon extension of the meeting illegal and, calling it a "rush election," took the matter of retaining the church building to court. After two years of lawsuits which cost an amount equal to the price of the church in question, the state supreme court declared the meeting and its decision legal because the chairman of the morning meeting had not set a time for the continuation of the meeting, and it assigned the church and the parsonage to the faction supporting Roanpaa. These years and those which followed were the saddest, most quarrelsome period in the history of the Calumet Finns. The dissension did not, however, affect negatively the spread of Laestadianism to any noticeable degree.

Having lost their church, the Takkinen faction built a smaller church across the street, not far from the other. They called themselves the "older persuasion," claiming to be a direct continuation of the congregation established by Kortetniemi in 1867, and they are known as the Old Apostolic Lutheran Church. The other faction was more recent, having been born in the rush election of 1888. Doctrinal differences at first were minimal. Contemporaries, however, thought that in Takkinen's church sermons on the Law and on the demands of a moral life were emphasized whereas in Roanpaa's church a more evangelical spirit prevailed.

The rivalry between these two main factions of American Laestadianism led to a kind of church-building contest. Wherever one group built a church, the other built one too. Thus, the community of Wolverine, two miles north of Calumet, acquired two churches; two miles north, Allouez also got two, and yet two miles north of that, Mohawk also acquired two. At Boston, however, halfway between Calumet and Hancock, only one church was built. Most of these small churches were simple, unadorned wooden structures that did not have a steeple, a sacristy, or even a cross to indicate their spiritual purpose. Each had a janitor to attend to the cleaning and the heating. Each also had a strong-voiced cantor to lead in the singing of hymns, and a lay preacher elected annually from among the older men of the small congregation. Two larger churches, next in size to the churches on Pine Street in

Calumet, were eventually built on Franklin Street and Pine Street in Hancock. They belong to the Apostolic Lutheran Church and the First Apostolic Lutheran Church, respectively.

The elders of the Church of the Firstborn in Lapland were in a difficult position because both of the American Laestadian congregations acknowledged their leadership and appealed to them in difficulties as to a higher court of justice. Nevertheless, they still called Takkinen "Brother Takkinen" and were inclined to use the terms "separatists" and "new-born sect" about the Roanpaa congregation. The situation became even more complicated when David Castren wrote to Aatu Laitinen, the rector of Enontekiö, inviting him to become a pastor in the Roanpaa congregation. Laitinen declined the offer but referred it to Pastor Arthur Leopold Heideman, who wrote to Calumet expressing his willingness to accept the pastorate if he should be invited. An invitation was sent to him with his fare.[8] Heideman arrived in Calumet on Midsummer's Eve of 1890. Thus, into the Finnish-American scene stepped a man who became an outstanding leader among his fellow Finns in this country.

Arthur Leopold Heideman, whose family name was originally Hyvarinen, was born in Oulu on March 8, 1862. He graduated from the Swedish lyceum in Oulu in 1882 and went to study philosophy at the University of Helsinki. While working as a tutor in the parish of Sodankylä, he became acquainted with the Laestadians, at first ridiculing their faith. Later he was strongly affected by their witnessing, experienced a powerful awakening, and began to study for the ministry. He was ordained in Porvoo in 1885. After serving as an assistant or acting pastor in various congregations, sometimes persecuted for his new faith, he was sent to Kivijärvi as an assistant to Provost Frans Petter Krank. In his sermons there Heideman said that "the Christianity of Kivijärvi is only on the roof of the church"—he became famous for his sharp aphorisms—and that the Cross must come down into the heart. Provost Krank and his family were his first converts, and Krank's daughter Lempi became Heideman's wife. With the spread of the Laestadian revival in Kivijärvi, the provost and his son-in-law were summoned to court for heresy. The Vaasa court of appeals rejected the accusation as groundless. This minor unpleasantness helped him to decide to go to America. Because of his independence of spirit as a man and a Finn he did not ask permission from the Swedish Church of the Firstborn to leave. He did, however, visit Raattamaa to bid him farewell.

Heideman's congregation in Calumet grew rapidly, for some of Takkinen's followers also joined it. Reconciliation was attempted a number of times, but there were always two obstacles: First, the Heideman faction demanded that the Takkinen faction join their congregation. Second, the Takkinen faction demanded that the "rush election" be confessed as a sin and that forgiveness for it be asked. In the meantime, Takkinen died on a preaching tour in Finland in the winter of 1892. Roanpaa and another preacher, Aapo Hietanen, died in Boston in the spring of 1896. They were on their way to Cape Cod to visit Laestadians there and stopped for a night at a hotel. When they went to bed they blew out the gaslight and were asphyxiated. The original leaders of the opposed factions were now gone but the struggle continued.

One of the several attempts at reconciliation was made at a meeting held in the fall of 1893. It was decided there that the "Big Church" and the "Little Church" should be used alternately for combined worship services. This effort at unity did not, however, produce the desired result, even though the leaders of Laestadianism in Sweden brought pressure to bear in favor of it. The situation became even more difficult when the Laestadianism of the Old Country split in two upon Raattamaa's death in 1899. The Gellivaara area of Swedish Lapland became the center of "Western Laestadianism," or the "Firstborn," and the Tornio River valley in Sweden and Finland became the center of "Eastern," or "Conservative," Laestadianism. This example was followed in America by a deepening and widening of the already existing breach. Although the large number of such names of factions as Takkislainens, Kortetniemilainens, Laanavaaralainens, Gellivaaralainens, Haalilainens, and Raattamaalainens indicates the extent of fragmentation in early Laestadianism in America, there is also an indication of even more fragmentation in later names such as Heidemanians, Pollarites, Firstborn, Little Firstborn, Big Meeting group, and Newly Awakened.

In 1908 the mainstream of American Laestadianism began to divide into two branches, one of which was the Conservative, or Heidemanian, faction. The other, which had many lay preachers among its leaders, was called the Big Meeting group. However, as long as Heideman was in full vigor, his personality kept the two groups loosely united.

Heideman died on November 7, 1928. Shortly before his death the two main trends in American Laestadianism had definitely turned into separate channels. The Big Meeting group organized a church called the Finnish Apostolic Lutheran Church of America ("Finnish" was later omitted from the name). Its bylaws were tentatively approved on September 9, 1928, at a meeting of delegates from congregations of the church held in Ironwood, and were ratified at a meeting held in Pendleton, Oregon, in 1929, which is considered the official year of organization. Johan Daniel Oberg, born in Rautalammi in 1862, was elected president. He had come to America in 1892 and had served as a preacher in Cokato, Minnesota, and in Laurium. Because of failing health he resigned from the presidency in 1942 and died in 1946. Members of the first board of directors were Evert Maattala and Frank Eilola, vice presidents; Jacob Uitti, secretary; and Henry Sakari and August Huttula, treasurers.

After Oberg's resignation, Pastor Andrew Mickelsen became the head of the Apostolic Lutheran Church, which is usually called the "Kirkkokunta" (the Church). He had been born into Laestadianism, for his grandfather, Mikko Jokela, was the brother of the well-known preachers Pietari Hanhivaara and Fredrik Paksuniemi of Kittilä. Mikko Jokela's son, Matti Jokela, moved to Vesisaari, Norway, where he married Emma Tiberg, a Norwegian. On August 4, 1897, a son, Andreas, was born to them. The family name was changed to its Norwegian form, Mickelsen, and two years later, when the family moved to Minnesota, the name Andreas was changed to Andrew.

Already as a young man Andrew Mickelsen was asked to speak at Laestadian services. In order to acquire a deeper understanding of the Bible and to perfect himself in the art of preaching, he studied at the Moody Bible Institute in Chicago from 1922 to 1925. While attending the Institute, he organized a congregation of Laestadians in the vicinity. He married Mary Bikki on September 3, 1924.[9] In 1937 he became the pastor of the Hancock congregation and vice president of the Apostolic Lutheran Church. He was elected president of the church in 1942. In addition to the presidency of the church and the pastorate of the Hancock congregation, he sometimes had charge of as many as twenty congregations at one time, in a broad area extending from Bruce Crossing to Eben Junction.

After the death of Heideman in 1928, the leadership of the Heideman church—officially known as the First Apostolic Lutheran Church—fell to his son, Paul Arthur Heideman. Paul Heideman was born in Calumet on August 1, 1890, completed his studies at the University of Helsinki in 1916, and was ordained in Porvoo the same year. He returned to America to serve as his father's assistant, traveling to Laestadian communities all over the country, from the New England states to Oregon and Washington. In 1934 he married Eva Maria Kankkonen of Astoria, and in 1954 he received the title of provost from the Church of Finland in recognition of his work among Finnish Americans.

Table 7 shows the number of congregations and preaching places of the First Apostolic Lutheran Church and the Apostolic Lutheran Church of America in Michigan, the United States, and Canada in the 1960s.

In addition to the congregation of these two main groups of Laestadians, there were at this time twelve congregations of the Firstborn, two of them in Michigan—namely in Calumet and Detroit. There were also sixteen evangelical Laestadian groups, three of them in Michigan—at Eben Junction-Chatham, Ishpeming, and Negaunee. There was also a small congregation of Newly Awakened in North Ironwood with Lars Levi Aaltonen, who had studied at the school of the Missionary Society of Finland, serving as their pastor.

Nine Laestadian congregations shared a church with some other Laestadian group, and four of them shared a church with a Suomi Synod congregation in their community. Many Laestadians who lived in communities that had no Laestadian church belonged to local synod congregations. It also happened comparatively often that a Laestadian preacher from Finland was able to speak in a synod church after he had been refused permission to preach in a local Laestadian church that belonged to a faction different from the one to which he belonged. It is just this narrow-minded attitude toward Christians of other persuasions that has been an obstacle throughout the years to the spread of the revival movement started by the Prophet of Lapland. Nevertheless, the thousands of Finnish American families belonging to these congregations are both morally and nationalistically in the forefront among the Finnish immigrants. The strength of the national and religious spirit among Laestadians is seen in the fact that when other leading Finnish churches merged with American churches in the early 1960s, the Laestadian churches remained independent and retained their identity.

One characteristic of Laestadianism is that the congregations do not usually keep records of their membership, nor do their bylaws give clear specifications as to who are considered members and who are not. The total lack of statistics opens the way for possible exaggeration when figures are needed. The estimates of the membership of Laestadian groups in the United States and Canada in 1965, shown in Table 8, are probably close to the truth.[10]

For a time the Laestadians had two newspapers, both published in Calumet. The first was *Valvoja* (Guardian), the common newspaper of most of the Apostolic Lutheran groups, but taken over by the Apostolic Lutheran Church of America as a general Apostolic Lutheran paper in 1931 when the First Apostolic Lutheran Church began to publish

Table 7: Laestadian Congregations in the U.S. and Canada

	FIRST APOSTOLIC LUTHERAN CHURCH (HEIDEMAN)	APOSTOLIC LUTHERAN CHURCH OF AMERICA (MICKELSEN)
Michigan	Ann Arbor	Agate
	Atlantic	Alston
	Baraga	Atlantic
	Boston	Boston
	Calumet	Bruce Crossing
	Covington	Champion
	Detroit	Crystal Falls
	Dollar Bay	Detroit
	Eben Junction-Chatham	Eben Junction-Chatham
	Ewen	Elo
	Fulton	Greenland
	Hancock	Hancock
	Herman	Herman
	Humboldt	Ironwood
	Iron River	Jacobsville
	Ishpeming	Laurium
	Jacobsville	Mass
	L'Anse	Negaunee
	Liminga	Oskar
	Mass	Pelkie
	Muskegon	Republic
	Negaunee	Rudyard
	Oskar	South Range
	Palmer	Tapiola
	Paynesville	Toivola
	Pelkie	Watton
	Pequaming	Woodspur
	Redridge-Beacon Hill	Wakefield
	South Range	
	Woodspur	
	30	28
Arizona	1	
California	1	2

Table 7: Laestadian Congregations in the U.S. and Canada *(continued)*

	FIRST APOSTOLIC LUTHERAN CHURCH (HEIDEMAN)	APOSTOLIC LUTHERAN CHURCH OF AMERICA (MICKELSEN)
Idaho		1
Illinois	1	
Massachusetts	3	1
Minnesota	12	15
New Hampshire		1
New York		1
North Dakota	1	2
Oregon	2	5
South Dakota	1	2
Washington	2	5
Wisconsin		2
Canada	5	1
Totals	59	66

Table 8: Laestadian Churches in America, 1965

Apostolic Lutheran Church of America	10,000
First Apostolic Lutheran Church	9,000
Firstborn	1,000
Evangelicals	1,500
Newly Awakened	250
Total	21,750

its own newspaper, *Opas* (Guide). There were also other publications. *Kristillinen Kuukauslehti* (Christian monthly) was published from 1915 to 1962, in its later years under the sponsorship of the Apostolic Lutheran Church. *Rauhan Tervehdys* (Greetings of peace) has been published by the First Apostolic Lutheran Church from 1922 to the present. The minutes of the summer meetings of the Big Meeting group and of the Apostolic Lutheran Church, which it became, were published annually starting in 1908. For the First Apostolic Lutheran Church Paul Heideman has edited Finnish and English songbooks with the church handbook for ministers included. Mary B. Mickelsen edited

Hymns and Songs of Zion with four-part music for the Apostolic Lutheran Church.[11] Uuras Saarnivaara has published a number of historical works of which the most extensive is the Finnish version of the *History of the Laestadian or Apostolic-Lutheran Movement in America.*[12] Many printings of Swebilius's *Catechism* and of Leinberg's *Bible History* have been made for Sunday school use. Since the nineteenth century many "missionary letters" from the elders of Lapland have been published in pamphlet form. The Firstborn (Old Apostolic Lutheran Church) published an English translation of Laestadius's *Postilla.*[13]

The greatest service to the scholarly study of Laestadius and the revival movement named for him was made by Finnish Americans when they saved the original manuscript of his *Dårhushjonet* (Inhabitant of a mental institution). In some unknown way it had come temporarily into the possession of Heikki Koller, a Norwegian Finn who was born in 1859. He had a reading knowledge of several languages and was an exceptionally well informed, self-educated preacher who practically lived in the Calumet library and who collected his master's manuscripts as though they were sacred relics. Before he died he revealed their hiding place to his friend, Pastor A. V. Tuukkanen, who eventually sent them to the Society of Finnish Church History in Helsinki.[14]

The Suomi Synod

Although the Laestadians left the Scandinavian Evangelical Lutheran congregation which had been established in 1867, the other Finns continued their affiliation with it. Finns, Norwegians, and Swedes had moved to the Calumet area in such large numbers that soon the question of building a church there came up. In 1876 a church was built on Schoolcraft Street. It was called the Trinity Church. The name did not refer to the Holy Trinity, but to the three nationalities, each of which had a one-third interest in the property. The congregation belonged to the Norwegian Hauge Synod. The Swedes left the church and formed their own congregation. Pastor H. Roernaes, who had banished the Laestadians from the combined congregation, moved to Iowa, and the Finns were expected to supply a new pastor. They wrote to K. J. G. Sirelius (1818–88), the head of the Finnish Missionary Society, requesting his aid. The result was a call to Pastor A. E. Backman.

Alfred Elieser Backman was born in the factory community of Kurimo in Oulu Province on September 18, 1844. He began to study law in 1867 at Helsinki but transferred to the department of theology. He was ordained to the ministry in 1875. He arrived in Calumet on

September 10, 1876. His first official act was to dedicate the recently completed church with the Norwegian Pastor Ostedahl. This first pioneer in the history of the Finnish American Evangelical Lutheran Church preached in Finnish to his own countrymen and in Swedish to the Norwegians and Swedes in his congregation. He established congregations in Calumet, Quincy, and Allouez, and made preaching tours among the Finns of the Marquette area and even in Minnesota and Ohio. The parsonage was built in Hancock. The crude life of the immigrants, most of whom were young men, the opposition of the Laestadians, and poor health influenced him to return to Finland in 1883.[15] Before returning to his native country, Backman taught Rev. Philip Wambsgans, the German Lutheran pastor, enough Finnish so that he was able to read the church handbook with reasonable fluency and to perform ministerial duties for the Finns who were left without a pastor of their own.

At the request of C. O. Olander, pastor of the Swedish congregation of Calumet, the Augustana Synod sent a former missionary, Pastor Aleksander Malmstrom, who knew enough Finnish to get along, to the Copper Country. Without being invited by the congregation to do so, he established himself in the Finnish parsonage and began to hold church services. The congregation was satisfied with the situation and decided to let Malmstrom serve until a pastor from Finland was available. Malmstrom soon had an unusual rival. A tailor, Heikki Turunen, from Kuusjärvi, appeared in Hancock and began to give sermons. The Trinity congregation of Calumet were pleased with his free-flowing style of speech and elected him their temporary pastor. It is said he made a two-week trip to Minneapolis and returned from there with a certificate given to him by some Norwegian professor, verifying that he had been ordained. Malmstrom, however, refused to surrender the church records to the tailor.

Back in Finland, Pastor Backman placed an advertisement concerning the vacancy in the Copper Country in a newspaper, hoping to find a young pastor who would go there to continue the work he had started. J. K. Nikander, acting rector of Ruskeala, saw the advertisement and applied. Juho Kustaa Nikander was born in Lami on September 3, 1855. Struggling with poverty, he studied at the lyceum of Jyväskylä and graduated in 1874. He was ordained in Porvoo in 1879. While he was attending the University of Helsinki, he lived in the home of Karl Gustaf Totterman, director of the Finnish Missionary Society, earning his room and board by tutoring the children of the family. At that time he became well acquainted with all aspects of the missionary ideal that was beginning to permeate the Church of Finland. This acquaintance continued in his first official position, that of assistant to Rector Sirelius of Mikkeli, who had previously been the director of the Missionary Society.

While waiting for a reply to his application, Nikander, who felt himself to be spiritually ready to serve as a pastor to the immigrants, took the pastoral examination which qualified him for a permanent position. The call from America finally came, and with his younger sister, Wilhelmina, he left Finland in the fall of 1884, arriving in Hancock on Saturday, January 3, 1885. A special program to welcome him had been planned at the Quincy church for that evening. After the travel-weary Nikander had given his first sermon, Turunen, the tailor-preacher, went into the pulpit and gave a pompous speech which ended with the words: "Now you have heard what gifts each of us has!" With this experience Nikander began his lifework in America, which to this day has not been surpassed by any other Finnish American.

Nikander was, above all, an organizer of congregations. When he arrived in America, he inherited Backman's three congregations in the Copper Country. When he died in 1919, the church had increased to 145 congregations in a huge area extending from Canada to the Gulf of Mexico and from the Atlantic Ocean to the Pacific. His basic principle was that if there is first in existence a living congregation, in time a church will follow. During his first years in Copper Country, he established preaching places in Dollar Bay, Franklin, Boston, the Huron and Atlantic mines, and Jacobsville. In the year of his arrival he also got church work started in Ishpeming.

By the time Nikander came to the Copper Country, the Norwegian element had also left the church that had been organized as the Scandinavian Evangelical Lutheran Congregation, and it was becoming the Finnish American Evangelical Lutheran Church. In the work of the church Nikander soon had three colleagues whose accomplishments were to leave a deep impression on this church and on Finnish American life in general. Of these three, Jacob Hoikka and Johan Eloheimo were fighting spirits, but Kaarle Tolonen, like Nikander, was simply a hard worker, quiet and persevering.

Jakob Juhonpoika Hoikka was born in Rovaniemi on July 8, 1854, and came to America as an immigrant in 1873. After working for a short time as a seaman on Lake Superior, he went to Minnesota to work on Finnish farms, intending to become a farmer himself. After meeting N. J. Brink, a pastor of the Augustana Synod, Hoikka, who had been brought up in a Christian home, felt a desire to become a minister. On Pastor Brink's recommendation he was accepted as a student at Augustana College in Rock Island, Illinois, in the fall of 1875. When he had completed his college work, he registered in the seminary and was ordained in 1883. He served for two years in Astoria, Oregon, where he started a congregation. In 1885 he came to Republic, Michigan, to serve as pastor of a Swedish congregation, but at the same time he worked among his fellow countrymen, setting up preaching places in Champion, Newberry, and Negaunee, in addition to serving the congregation he had organized in Ishpeming.

John Wilhelm Eloheimo, who had changed his name from the Swedish Lindquist to Eloheimo, had been called to serve the congregation in Astoria. Eloheimo was born in Sahalahti in 1845. He was ordained in 1874 and served for a time as a pastor in Helsinki and Porvoo as well as elsewhere. When he arrived in Astoria in 1888, he immediately began to plan a church patterned after the state church of Finland. This project was, however, postponed when he received a call from the Calumet congregation. Because of its growing membership, this congregation had decided to leave the Quincy Scandinavian congregation, as had the Hancock Finns, who had sold their share in the church to the Norwegians and were building a large new church on Reservation Street in Hancock. When Eloheimo came to serve the Calumet church, Nikander stayed on as pastor of the Hancock congregation. Until the church was completed in 1889, worship services were held in the Pohjantähti (North Star) Temperance Hall. In the balcony of the new church, which was the most imposing one owned by Finnish Americans of that time, there was a large pipe organ, and in the tower there was a huge bell on which were inscribed the words "O earth, earth, hear the word of the Lord" (Jer. 22:29).

The third man who appeared on the Finnish Evangelical Lutheran scene in Michigan at this time was K. L. Tolonen. Kaarle Leonard Tolonen, a tailor's son, was born in Kajaani on October 27, 1845. He studied at the Finnish Missionary Society School and worked in Amboland, Africa, as a missionary of the Church of Finland. When he returned to his homeland he worked as an itinerant preacher and as a teacher in the missionary school. When Niilo Majhannu, president of the Ishpeming congregation, was traveling in Finland, he met Tolonen. On his recommendation Tolonen was invited to become pastor of the Ishpeming church. He accepted the call and arrived in 1888 to serve not only the Ishpeming congregation but the Champion and Negaunee congregations as well.

The Finnish American Evangelical Lutherans now had four pastors, all in the prime of life. They often had joint "mission festivals" in their congregations. At the conclusion of each of these festivals the four pastors would hold a conference. At these pastoral meetings plans were made for combining the congregations into an organized church. Possible names for it were considered, as were guiding principles for its constitution. The first practical outcome of these sessions was the decision to publish *Paimen-Sanomia* (Shepherd's tidings), a religious weekly that appeared for the first time in January 1889. Other results were the recommendation of "Suomi Synod" as the name for the church, and a proposal for its constitution.

In a research paper, Henry R. Kangas states that Hoikka, who was a member of the Augustana Synod until 1904, when he joined the Suomi Synod, proposed that the Finnish church join the Augustana Synod.[16] Gustaf Johansson, Bishop of Kuopio, recommended the union as a temporary measure until the Finnish church should be strong enough to stand on its own feet.[17] Nikander, Finnish-minded always, did not publish this part of the letter from Johansson in *Paimen-Sanomia*, only the part in which the bishop wished them success in their plan and gave them his blessing.[18]

A bitter newspaper quarrel about the Suomi Synod broke out even before it was organized. The two newspapers involved were starting publication in Calumet at this time. They were *Kansan Lehti* (People's paper), edited by Johan Ekman, and *Kalevan Kaiku* (Echo of Kaleva), edited by H. Hela. The editors first became involved in a furious competition for subscribers. Pastor Eloheimo had no connection with the matter, but in keeping with his temperament he joined in the struggle and took a stand on the side of the *Kalevan Kaiku*. In a short time the newspaper articles deteriorated to personal libel. The matter was taken to court, where the verdict was in favor of Ekman, who was an effective speaker. The dispute became centered on the synod, which was still in the planning stage. Ekman managed to get possession of the manuscript of the constitution prepared by Eloheimo, in which Eloheimo outlined a plan for a church controlled by the clergy as he had done earlier in Astoria. Eloheimo's recommendation was never published excepting in Ekman's articles because it was edited by Nikander and Tolonen before it was presented at the church convention. But *Kansan Lehti*'s accusations of high-church attitudes and of a nondemocratic spirit in the projected synod remained alive for a long time.

The organizational meeting of the new synod was held in the Trinity Church in Calumet on Tuesday, March 25, 1890. There were sixteen delegates, sent by nine congregations, and four pastors attending ex officio. The lay representatives were the following: Alex Leinonen, A. A. Bajari, N. A. Lempeä, Olli Rousu, and E. W. Wenberg from Calumet; Carl A. Silfven, Andrew Johnson, and Thomas Suni from Hancock; Joseph Salmu from Jacobsville; Carl Silberg from Republic;

John H. Jasberg and Niilo Majhannu from Ishpeming; John F. Erickson from Newberry; E. W. Lund from Ironwood; Henrik Heinonen from Negaunee; and Henry Sarvela from Savo, South Dakota. The pastors were Hoikka from Newberry, Eloheimo from Calumet, Tolonen from Ishpeming, and Nikander from Hancock.

Eloheimo was the chairman of the meeting, and Nikander was the secretary. "Suomi Synod" was approved as the name of the newly organized church and, with minor changes, the seventy-two-paragraph constitution was also approved. A consistory of four clergymen was set up to be the governing body. This complete bypassing of laymen as participants in the administration of the church was hardly justifiable even at that time, and later on it became even less justifiable. Bishop Johansson, among others, was critical of it. When it came to electing the president of the new synod, three ballots were necessary. Nikander was finally elected. Eloheimo received the second-highest number of votes and was made secretary to compensate for not having won the presidency. Tolonen was made treasurer and Hoikka became notary. Far-reaching in their effects were the decisions made then to call a "missionary pastor" from Finland to work among the immigrants, and to accept *Paimen-Sanomia* as the official organ of the synod. The clergy and the other delegates signed the constitution and the minutes of the meeting.

A cold north wind was blowing snow into drifts across the roads when the weary members of this historic convention left for their lodgings late that night. The early years of the synod, too, were stormy. Difficulties arose in the consistory itself. Earlier in the year, Hoikka had already been corresponding with the Church of Sweden about the possibility of a pastorate, and he moved to Sweden soon after the meeting in Calumet. He became a Swedish citizen on September 1, 1890, and the very next day was assigned to various duties in the Finnish parishes of the Diocese of Hernösand. He sent articles to the *Työmies* newspaper published in Ishpeming by F. Karinen, criticizing and counseling the recently organized Suomi Synod, with whose constitution he, too, was dissatisfied. Hoikka was trying to be helpful, but his comments were misunderstood and only added to the difficulties of the synod. Nikander replied sharply to Hoikka in *Työmies*, and together with Tolonen and Eloheimo, sent a complaint against Hoikka, dated November 12, 1890 in Ishpeming, to the Bishop of Hernösand. The disagreement eventually ended in a cordial correspondence between Hoikka and Nikander, and to Hoikka's return to his first congregation in Astoria in the fall of 1893.

From the very beginning there had been strong opposition to

the Suomi Synod in Ishpeming, where F. Karinen attacked Tolonen in his newspaper. He called a meeting for the purpose of discharging Tolonen from his ministerial duties. This effort failed, however, because not many members of the congregation were present and because intoxicated persons in the assemblage made it impossible to continue the meeting.

Eloheimo, however, caused the most trouble to the church leadership. Johan Ekman and *Kansan Lehti* had seen to it that the majority of the Calumet congregation were against joining the synod. At a meeting held to decide the issue Eloheimo, who had called the police to stand guard at the church doors, demanded that the congregation join. Some of the more aggressive opponents of the synod announced their resignation from the congregation, and others followed their example. Apparently unperturbed, Eloheimo crossed out names from the church records until only 200 were left of the original 700. The 200 voted in favor of joining the synod. Those who left the congregation went in a body to the Calumet Opera House and organized a "Kansallisseurakunta" (National Congregation). Their purpose had been to organize a "Kansan Seurakunta" (People's Congregation) as opposed to a clergy-controlled church, but in the rush there was a confusion of terms and "kansallis" was used instead of "kansan." The group attempted to get possession of the church building through a lawsuit, but because they were the ones who had left the congregation they were unsuccessful.

The synod congregation in Calumet had now become so small that it could not pay the pastor's salary. Consequently, Eloheimo moved to Ironwood early in 1891 to serve as pastor there. The congregations of neighboring Wakefield and Bessemer were also members of the Suomi Synod. All went well at first, Eloheimo working conscientiously as pastor and as secretary of the Consistory. Soon, however, there were complaints to the effect that he was neglecting his duties, even the worship services, and secluding himself in his office. This mysterious behavior was explained in an unexpected way at the end of the year. The Consistory, in which Kaarlo Huotari, the missionary pastor from Finland, took Hoikka's place, sent a letter to Eloheimo from a meeting held in Negaunee on December 3. It began thus:

> The members of the Suomi Synod Consistory have read the pamphlet you have published, titled "Proclamation of the Universal Kingdom During the Chiliad to Come" and have found it to be a false and offensive work in which, among other things, the name of our Holy God and of our Precious Savior, as well as their sacred words, are

> obviously mixed with lies and wrongly used in a most terrible way, and the divine promises of the Kingdom of God are turned to the service of egotistical whims.

The Consistory demanded that Eloheimo let them know within thirty days whether he was the original author of the booklet, why he had translated it into English, why he was distributing it, and who was the "Minister William" mentioned in it. An arrogant reply came immediately from Eloheimo: He was resigning from the Suomi Synod and from his official duties in it.

Because of its peculiar nature, the pamphlet attracted notice even as far away as Finland.[19] Its form and content can be described as follows: The "two witnesses" of the Book of Revelations (11:3–7) had traveled in Europe and America and had left a sealed document in the care of "Minister William" in America before they lost their lives in Russia. That "Proclamation" was this document. Like the books of the Bible, it is divided into chapters, of which there are twenty-four, and the chapters are divided into verses. The book prophesies the speedy coming of the millennium and outlines the main features of its government, with its council, state chancellor, army, eight-hour workday, etc. In it, as God's representative, is the pious William of the Elohid tribe who, like Moses, at first wished humbly to be excused from the responsibility but then bowed to the will of the "Supreme Majesty."

"William Elohid" was of course William Eloheimo himself, who, already in Finland, had been known as a great dreamer. The Consistory released him from his ministerial duties, informing the congregation of this action by circular letter. Eloheimo recanted and announced that he would rejoin the synod. But the Consistory refused to take him back. At the church convention held in Ishpeming in 1892, where Eloheimo had appealed the case, a decision was made in favor of the Consistory. The question of the ownership of the Ironwood church was taken to court, where the case ended in a victory for Eloheimo. The courts did not accept as valid the synod's rule that in case of the discontinuance of a congregation its property should go to the synod, but maintained that the congregation should decide what to do about its property. There were, however, so many persons dissatisfied with Eloheimo that they formed the "Finnish Evangelical Lutheran St. Paul's Church of Ironwood," which joined the synod.

Eloheimo then organized his own church, the "Fenno-American Church," which was episcopal in form, with Eloheimo, of course, as bishop. In Michigan the church had congregations in Ironwood, Bessemer, Wakefield, and Ishpeming. There were also a few congregations in the states of Montana, Massachusetts, and Maine. Eloheimo ordained nine ministers for his church. They were Gustaf Pauruus, a tanner from Härmä; John Henrik Kampi, a circuit-school teacher from Isojoki; John Nissila, a baker from Vähäkyrö; Iisakki Reinila, a university student from Kurikka; and Mikko Kivinen, a painter. As a bond between congregations there was *Kirkkokunnan Lehti*, published in Ironwood by Eloheimo. It had about six hundred subscribers. As the official badge of his episcopacy, Bishop Eloheimo wore over his Finnish clerical garb a leather belt with a sword hanging from it, the uses of which he explained with verses from the Bible.

In the minutes of the sixth convention of the Suomi Synod, which was held in June 1905 in Ironwood, there is an item to the effect that at the beginning of the meeting a delegation led by J. W. Lähde arrived with a written proposal from Eloheimo. The proposal suggested a merger of the churches on condition that certain changes be made in the constitution of the synod, and that the pastors ordained by Eloheimo be accepted as pastors of the merged church. At the end of the minutes there is a brief notation saying that "the aforementioned written proposal gave the church convention no grounds for action."

Eloheimo wrote to the Senate of Finland, applying for a position as rector in some imperial parish.[20] The Senate's reply stated that his application was lacking in information concerning his conduct in America and his relations with the Suomi Synod and in samples of religious works he had published in America. It advised him to turn to the chapter of the diocese in which he had formerly served. In 1895, when material support in Ironwood decreased to a minimum, Eloheimo transferred the church to his own name in a way that proved valid in the eyes of the law. Finally, all support ceased. Within a few years the Fenno-American Church was nothing but a memory.

The Suomi Synod survived these struggles and even succeeded in making progress. At the organizational meeting in 1890 there had been four pastors and the representatives of only nine congregations, of which eight were in Michigan. At the end of 1895 there were thirty-eight congregations, of which nineteen were in Michigan. After the historic organizational meeting the following congregations were established and became members of the synod: Allouez-Ahmeek, Baraga, Bessemer, Champion, Copper Falls and Central Mine, Crystal Falls, East Tawas, Michigamme, Palmer, Pequaming, and Wakefield. Although there had been only one delegate from a state other than Michigan at the organizational meeting, the doctrine of the Evangelical Lutheran Church had spread so that there were now nineteen congregations outside the state: six in Minnesota, four in South Dakota, two in Wyoming, two in Wisconsin, and one each in Illinois, Ohio, Massachusetts, Oregon, and Canada. The number of pastors had increased in five years from four to twelve. Seven of them had been ordained in Finland, five in America. Of these five, one had a master's degree from the University of Helsinki, another was an ordained minister of the Church of Sweden, and one had studied theology at the University of Helsinki. Only two were borderline cases, for whom the Consistory had approved ordination because of the shortage of pastors. In general the level of competence among these synod pastors was comparatively high, a fact that contributed to the rapid growth of the synod. There were also in this group a number of pastors who, in addition to being well trained, were men of deep spirituality.[21]

The Suomi Synod, 1896–1906

In the ten-year period extending from the founding of Suomi College to the appearance of the church scene of the first pastors trained in Suomi Synod's own seminary, church activity centered around the college and seminary.

During this period a change took place in the leadership of the synod. In 1898 Nikander resigned from the presidency to devote all his time to his duties as president of, and instructor at, Suomi College. Tolonen was elected president of the synod and served in that capacity until his death in the church parsonage at Ishpeming on April 4, 1902. In June of that year, the convention held at Crystal Falls had difficulty in electing a new president. The two candidates, Pastor Johan Bäck of the Hancock congregation and Pastor Pekka Airaksinen of the Calumet church, each received approximately the same number of votes in several attempts. Both withdrew from candidacy, and the convention begged Nikander to be a candidate again. He consented and was unanimously elected.

The years 1896–1906 were years of growth. In Michigan, twenty-one new congregations joined the synod; fifty-three churches in other states joined. The new congregations of Michigan communities came into the Synod in the following order: Laird-Nisula, Trout Creek, Grand Marais, Marquette, Atlantic Mine, Trimountain, Metsistö-Cooks Mills, Mass City, Stambaugh, Rudyard, Kaleva, Amasa, Chatham (known as Karjala at that time), Rockland, Eben, Princeton-Gwinn, Deerton, Kyrö, Painesdale, Sault Ste. Marie, and Baltic-South Range. Outside Michigan the greatest growth occurred in Minnesota, where sixteen new congregations were organized. Pennsylvania had nine new synod churches; Ohio had seven; and Massachusetts had five. New states on the Suomi Synod map were New York, Pennsylvania, Indiana, Mississippi, Montana, and Washington. The membership, which was about 7,500 in 1895, rose to 23,500 at the end of 1906. It was the greatest increase in such a short time in the history of the Suomi Synod. In addition to congregations, there were twenty-two preaching places where contact was made with thousands of additional Finns. There were also 107 Sunday schools. Thirty-two congregations conducted summer schools for children. In addition to their religious purpose, these summer schools were an effort to preserve the Finnish language and culture among young Finnish Americans. The Finnish language was used exclusively in these schools.

By the end of 1906 there were twenty-two pastors serving the synod, five of them being graduates from the seminary that year. The number of pastors, even with this welcome addition from the seminary, did not answer the needs of increased membership. All the more significant is the principle still followed by the Consistory that the educational level of synod pastors should be the highest possible. Because of this standard, many applicants were refused consideration. They included a large number from Finland—catechists, university students, public schoolteachers, colporteurs, newspaper editors, and others—who hoped to become pastors in America without further education or special qualifications, thus to attain a position among immigrants at a level they were unable to reach in Finland.

Important accomplishments of this period were the completion of the Suomi College building, the establishment of the Finnish Lutheran Book Concern with its newspapers and calendars, and the opening of the theological seminary, all of which were facilities for the expansion of the work of the synod.[22]

The Suomi Synod, 1907–1922

The Suomi Synod continued to grow during the next sixteen years. In that period, nineteen new congregations in Michigan joined it. Fifty-eight congregations in other states and Canada also joined. The Michigan congregations were established in the following order: Covington, Mohawk, Winona, Paynesville, Diorite, Maple Ridge-Rock, Paavola, Chassell, Houghton, Askel-Arnheim, Oskar, Uusi Suomi, Alabaster, Wainola, Keweenaw Bay, Toivola, Detroit, St. Ignace, and Trenary. Outside the home state the growth of the synod was again greatest in Minnesota, where twenty new congregations were born;

California was second with six new congregations; and Washington was third. States not previously represented were West Virginia, New Hampshire, and North Dakota. Canada's contribution to the synod was the congregation organized in Cobalt, to the north of North Bay in Ontario. Total membership reached a new high—36,269 baptized members—in 1922.

While Hoikka was with the Augustana Synod, he became familiar with its form of organization and was in favor of following it in the Suomi Synod. He promoted the division of the synod into districts or conferences. His proposal was approved at the church convention held in Eveleth, Minnesota, in 1909. In time Michigan, Minnesota, Eastern, Ohio-Pennsylvania, and Western conferences were formed, the last-named soon dividing into California and Columbia conferences. The Illinois Conference was established later. This subdivision led to annual meetings of individual conferences, including young people's conventions and Sunday school festivals with official meetings, and to various publications, all of which helped to made the overall work of the synod more effective.

One of the most notable happenings of 1914–16 was the holding of conferences with the Finnish National Church to consider a merger. The plan, however, collapsed because of the unwillingness of either side to make concessions with far-reaching consequences. During this period, too, the Michigan congregations became involved in a struggle with socialism and its atheistic attitudes, which were spreading rapidly, and which reached a climax in the Copper Country strike of 1913–14. The most important single event of this period was the twenty-fifty anniversary celebration of the synod, which was held in connection with the annual church convention in Hancock in 1915. Just as the Church of Finland at its seven-hundredth anniversary festival in 1857 had organized the Finnish Missionary Society, so the Suomi Synod at the celebration marking its quarter-century of history decided to become active in missionary work in China.

During this period important changes occurred in the leadership of the synod. Hoikka, whose mother church was the Augustana Synod, had become a member of the Suomi Synod in 1904. In it he worked even more zealously than before for the spiritual welfare of his countrymen. In recognition of his work, the 1915 synod convention bestowed on him the honorary title of doctor of theology. Hoikka died two years later, on July 14, 1917.[23]

Nikander had received the honorary degree of doctor of theology from Augustana College in 1906. However, he appears to have liked better the title of "Juho Setä" (Uncle John), under which he wrote for Finnish American children in the papers he published for them from 1892 to his death in 1919. His own major interests were classical languages and Hebrew, which he taught in the seminary, and literary activities. For decades he edited *Kirkollinen Kalenteri* (Church calendar) and Suomi College publications. He also wrote a history of the church, but it was never published. His real lifework was accomplished as president of Suomi College and president of the Suomi Synod. Under his leadership the synod developed into a vital immigrant church, and Suomi College struggled ever onward under a burden of debt, which never succeeded in shaking Nikander's faith in God's guidance. A cerebral stroke ended his busy life on January 13, 1919.

At the church convention the following summer, Pastor Alvar Rautalahti of Ishpeming was elected president of the synod. Rautalahti was born in Honkilahti on May 21, 1882. He was ordained in the Turku Cathedral in 1907 and came to America the following year to serve as pastor of the Brooklyn congregation. The care of an extensive parish and the travel required of the president weakened his health so that at the convention of 1922 he asked to be relieved of his duties as president. During Rautalahti's term of office the synod had continued to grow, and Augustana had bestowed on him the honorary title of doctor of theology.

The Suomi Synod, 1923–54

At the church convention held in Negaunee in 1922, Alfred Haapanen (known as Haapaniemi in Finland), pastor of the Hancock congregation, was elected president of the synod. Haapanen was born in Karvia on October 19, 1874, into a family who belonged to the prayer revival movement. He came to America as an immigrant in 1893, first living in Montana. In 1906, after eight years of study at Suomi College and Theological Seminary, he was ordained. In 1936 the Norwegian Lutheran Theological Seminary of St. Paul bestowed on him the honorary title of doctor of theology. The presidency of the Suomi Synod was separated from the work of a pastor in 1924. At the same time Hancock was chosen to be the headquarters of the synod. Haapanen was president of the synod for twenty-eight years, from 1922 to 1950. Haapanen—industrious, quiet, and humble "servus servorum Dei" (servant of God's servants) as Professor Pietilä characterized him—was head of the synod throughout its most difficult decades. Perhaps it was at least partly due to his patience and forbearance that the synod was able to survive these years.

In 1923 a period of retrogression began for the Suomi Synod. Membership decreased rapidly, falling from 36,000 to 23,000, hitting "the bottom of the poor years" in 1936. In reality the membership was even less than the figures show, for it was customary to include baptized and confirmed persons who had no connection with a synod congregation, as well as those who had moved away from the area, in addition to indefinite numbers of persons who had been "subject to influence," meaning those whose only contact with the church had been, perhaps, attendance at a baptism or a funeral.

A number of reasons have been given for this decline in membership. First, the new immigration laws of the United States had lowered the quota for Finland to a few hundred a year. Second, the spirit of the times was inimical to the church—materialistic and evil. Third, the attacks of Finnish leftist newspapers against Christianity were relentless. Fourth, church activities were conducted almost entirely in Finnish despite the fact that a generation or two of younger Finns had been born in America and were using the English language, in some cases exclusively, in preference to Finnish.

The last-mentioned reason is the most valid. Even activities of the seminary were conducted for a long time entirely in Finnish with the result that some of the pastors graduating from there were unable to use the English language effectively in their work. It was not until the 1930s that this situation was remedied. Sunday schools, too, in many congregations were conducted entirely in Finnish for ten, perhaps even twenty, years too long. The same was true also of worship services; English services were not instituted as soon as they might have been. The result was a "lost generation" as far as the synod was concerned, for many young people joined American churches where services were held in English.

The decline in immigration and the anti-church spirit of the times were not valid reasons, for at this time America in general was experiencing a period of vigorous growth in church membership. For example, in the Swedish Augustana Synod, which was just as dependent on immigration as the Suomi Synod, membership increased 75 percent between 1920 and 1954. It is true that some local congregations, especially in the Copper Country, lost many members because of the closing of the mines. Nevertheless, since most of them moved to other Finnish communities in Michigan, especially to Detroit, this loss had only a minimal effect on the total Suomi Synod membership in the state.

There were other losses in addition to the loss of members. It became necessary, for example, to give up the San Francisco Seamen's

Mission, and to surrender the Canadian congregations to the United Lutheran Church. It is left for a writer of Finnish American church history to discuss reasons other than the wrong policy with regard to language for this phenomenon of retrogression, which was also experienced by other Finnish American churches at this time. In any case it appears that some of the reasons were related to the fact that church leadership had not fostered the right church spirit in members. Antti J. Pietila, a keen-eyed observer, saw this greatest threat to Finnish-American Christianity and wrote about it thus:

> Unless there are some spiritually awakened Christians in your congregations, or unless you are fortunate enough to have a spiritually alive pastor, there is danger that you will fall into some kind of nominal Christianity. Your congregation will then be a business enterprise beside other business enterprises, and your church service will be the kind of group activity or educational session that temperance and masonic meetings are; they will not be the worshiping of God in Spirit and in Truth. The pastor attends to his ministerial duties and then busies himself with his own affairs, and the congregation believe they have done all that is necessary when they have paid their dues and attended church services now and then.[24]

On the other hand there is much to be said on the positive side for the Suomi Synod during this period. A number of new congregations were established. In Michigan there were the Bethlehem and Northwest Emmanual congregations in Detroit, and those at Dafter, Daggett, L'Anse, Montreal, Munising, North Bruce, North Ironwood, Winthrop, and Woodlawn. Numerous new churches were built and many older ones were repaired. Church property increased to many times what it had been. At the time of the Finno-Russian wars (1939–45) the congregations of the synod engaged in extensive relief work for Finland, at the same time taking part in the activities of the American Red Cross. The Suomi Synod was the only Finnish American church with chaplains in the United States Army and Navy. In 1950 the synod began missionary work in Japan, sending three missionaries there, one of whom was Mrs. Florence Elson from Eben, Michigan. Later, Eino J. Vehanen, pastor of the Hancock congregation, also went to Japan. He was the son of a missionary who had worked in Africa for the Finnish Missionary Society. His wife Aune was the daughter of a missionary to Japan.[25]

Having survived the Great Depression of the 1930s, the synod began to grow until its membership reached 30,000 in 1945, remaining at about that figure for approximately ten years. When Haapanen retired in 1950, John Wargelin, who had been a fellow student at Suomi College and Seminary, was elected president. Wargelin had accomplished much in the service of the synod as a pastor and as president of Suomi College. In 1925 he had received the honorary degree of doctor of theology from Wittenberg College. For the first time, the synod had a president who spoke English fluently and could take part in discussions between churchmen of non-Finnish denominations without being handicapped by a language barrier. The most impressive event of these years was the bestowal of the Bishop's Cross on the president of the synod by the Church of Finland. The cross was presented to Wargelin, president at the time, by Bishop Elis Gulin of Tampere in the Evangelical Lutheran church of Hancock. During this period, too, the ministers' pension fund was organized in such a way that each congregation included a certain amount in its dues for the pension fund. Disabled and retired pastors received $600 per year from the fund.

The Last Years of the Suomi Synod, 1955–62

After the church convention of 1955, seventy-four-year-old John Wargelin retired from the presidency of the synod, and his son Raymond succeeded him. Raymond Wargelin was born in Republic on June 25, 1911, and was the first American-born president of the synod. He was ordained from the Suomi Theological Seminary in 1936 and served the synod as pastor, holding various positions of responsibility in the church. He received the honorary title of doctor of theology from St. Paul Lutheran Seminary in 1956.

During Raymond Wargelin's term of office, the Suomi Synod again achieved the membership which it had had at the time of Nikander's death and during the presidency of Alvar Rautalahti, about forty years before. In 1958 the 37,000 mark was passed. That year also saw the beginning of the dissolution of the synod in the merger of the seminary with the Maywood Seminary and its removal to Maywood, Illinois.

The most important happening of this period was the series of discussions carried on for many years by the United Lutheran Church, the Augustana Synod, the Danish Church, and the Suomi Synod about a merger. By this time the synod had become convinced that because English was the chief language of the church, because the era of immigration was past, because the majority of church members were American born, and because the synod had taken its place among the other Lutheran churches of America, it was no longer practical or justifiable to retain and emphasize the Finnish nationality of the church through remaining independent. Unexpectedly few objections to the proposed merger appeared in newspapers. In the negotiations the Finnish-speaking congregations and pastors were guaranteed the right to form their own Suomi Conference, which would look after the rights of the rapidly departing older generation to services and spiritual care in their own language. From Michigan the members on the interchurch standing committee were Raymond Wargelin, Armas Holmio, and Ralph Jalkanen.

The Suomi Synod congregations throughout the country voted on the merger in February 1961. Of the 10,577 members who used their right to vote, 8,217 were in favor of the merger, and 2,360, or 22 percent, were against it. In Michigan, 2,455 were in favor of it, and 912, or 27 percent, against it, whereas in Minnesota nearly one-third voted against it. In casting their votes against the merger, the older generation were showing their love for the Suomi Synod, which was to them the church of their fathers. There were very few older persons present at the church convention in Fairport Harbor, Ohio, on June 26, 1961, when the question was voted on, for representation was in the hands of the younger generation. The final decisive vote was 215 votes in favor of the merger and 21 against.

The last convention of the synod was held at Cobo Hall in Detroit the following year. When the assemblage adjourned on Wednesday, June 27, the seventy-two-year-old history of the Suomi Synod ended. The representatives stood up to sing "Sun haltuus, rakas Isäni" (Into Thy Hands, Dear Heavenly Father) and Martin Rinkart's "Now Thank We All Our God." The founding meeting of the Lutheran Church in America opened the following day with thirty-six delegates from the Suomi Synod in attendance. Those from Michigan were Pastors Raymond Wargelin, Ralph Jalkanen, Armas Holmio, and Ahti Karjala, and laymen Edwin Perttunen, Clarence Bjork, and Mrs. George Lelvis from Marquette; John Ansama and Mrs. Elma Krym from Detroit; and Frank Kaarto from Mass.

On Sunday, July 1, the Suomi Conference was organized in Detroit. It was joined by 78 pastors, 25 of them from Michigan, and 107 congregations of which 33 were in Michigan and 10 in Canada. The conference was divided into districts: California, Columbia, Eastern, Illinois, Lake Erie, Michigan, Minnesota, and Canada. Each of them had its own board of directors. Toward the end of 1962 the conference began to publish *Suomalainen* (The Finn), edited and printed in Hancock. The activity of the conference, however, soon became limited to annual district meetings and the general annual meeting, and to calling a minister annually from Finland to visit some of the congregations.

Suomalainen ceased publication within two years. The Canadian congregations reactivated it in Toronto under the name *Isien Usko* (Faith of our fathers). The principal task of the conference, which was to see to it that Finns of the older generation would be able to hear sermons in the Finnish language and to have spiritual guidance in their own tongue, had not been satisfactorily accomplished up to 1971. In Michigan, for example, one Finnish pastor served eleven congregations, and several bilingual congregations were completely, or almost completely, without services in the Finnish language.

The Finnish Lutheran Book Concern

The beginnings of Suomi Synod publication go back as far as 1884, six years before the synod was organized. In that year Pastors J. W. Lahde and J. J. Hoikka began to publish *Valvoja*, a religious monthly printed in Ashtabula Harbor, Ohio. Nikander joined the partnership later. The publication was discontinued in 1886. Nikander, Hoikka, and Tolonen decided to make another attempt at publication and started *Paimen-Sanomia*, which appeared for the first time in January 1889. Nikander was editor-in-chief and Hoikka and Tolonen served as assistant editors. The publication was printed on a hand press in Nikander's parsonage on Quincy Hill. When the Suomi Synod, which was organized the following year, approved the paper as its official organ, the number of subscribers increased rapidly. A small building was erected on the parsonage lot and a steam-powered press purchased. Additional publications soon appeared. One was *Lehtiä Lapsille ja Kuviakin*, whose name was changed soon after to *Lasten Lehti* (Children's paper), and *Joulu-Lehti* (Christmas paper), which became *Suomi Opiston Joululehti* (Suomi College Christmas paper).

In 1896 Nikander, Tolonen, and J. H. Jasberg, a businessman, opened the Finnish Book Store. On February 28, 1899, Pastors Nikander, Tolonen, J. Bäck, and R. Ylönen and laymen Alex Leinonen, Isak Sillberg, and Jacob Holmlund formed the Amerikan Suometar Publishing Company. Its purpose was "to publish a newspaper called the *Amerikan Suometar* in Hancock and to do other printing." That same year a building was constructed behind Suomi College to become for sixty-five years the most important workshop in Finnish-American church life. The first issue of *Amerikan Suometar* came out in September. Of the many applicants for the position of editor, N. J. Ahlman from Hämeenlinna had been selected.

In ten years the new Suomi Synod, which had succeeded in

Table 9: Suomi Synod Congregations in Michigan

COMMUNITY	ORGANIZED	JOINED SUOMI SYNOD	CEASED ACTIVITY	MEMBERSHIP 1920	1940	1960
Alabaster		1914	1929	108		
Allouez-Ahmeek	9/15/1890	1891		108		
Amasa	1896			324	202	198
Askel-Arnheim		1912	1951*	44	33	
Atlantic	1899	1899		360	160	155
Baltic-South Range		1906		556	300	251
Baraga	1892	1892	1963†	84	57	38
Bessemer	1888	1891		178	90	118
Calumet	1876	1890		990	290	429
Champion	1889	1890		89	98	99
Chassell	1912	1912		109	155	249
Chatham	12/12/1903	1904	?			
Copper Falls and Central Mine	3/27/1891	1891	?			
Covington		1900		265	203	141
Crystal Falls	3/18/1891	1891		645	400	437
Dafter		1938	1962‡		18	53
Daggett		1924	1960§		25	10
Deerton	2/27/1905	1905		78	42	34
Detroit, St. John's	1914	1917		190	325	490
Detroit, Bethlehem	1937	1937			825	846
Detroit, NW Emmanuel	1953	1953				972
Diorite		1911	1926	31		
East Branch	3/25/1919	1919	1934	38		
East Tawas	5/3/1894	1894	1956	30	15	
Eben	10/26/1904	1905		211	100	210
Elo	1913	1913		90	146	119
Ewen	1915	1915		36	84	210
Grand Marais	10/7/1898	1898		136	55	43
Hancock	1867	1890		2,289	1,240	1,027
Houghton		1912‖				
Iron Mountain-Kingsford	1924	1925				
Ironwood	9/3/1888	1890		1,140	646	733
Ishpeming	2/1/1887	1890		1,518	1,033	1,758

Table 9: Suomi Synod Congregations in Michigan *(continued)*

COMMUNITY	ORGANIZED	JOINED SUOMI SYNOD	CEASED ACTIVITY	MEMBERSHIP 1920	1940	1960
Jacobsville	2/16/1890	1890	1951	76	16	
Jennings-Lake City	1912	1912		105	40	63
Kaleva	1/12/1902	1902		676	370	492
Keweenaw Bay	1915	1916		94	70	34
Kyro-Pelkie	4/21/1905	1905		173	211	123
Laird-Nisula	1896	1896		485	259	139
L'Anse	1924				39	117
Maple Ridge-Rock	8/3/1911	1912		232	122	57
Marquette		1899#			31	300
Mass	10/10/1901	1902		220	301	278
Metsistö	1898	1902				
Michigamme	3/30/1894	1894	1912			
Mohawk	10/4/1908	1909		360	158	125
Montreal-North Ironwood	1920	1920		90	92	69
National Mine-Winthrop	3/26/1905	1905				207
Negaunee	1887	1890		836	333	944
Newberry	1888	1890		306	259	240
North Bruce	1931	1932			59	49
Oskar		1912	1953	69	15	
Paavola		1911**				
Painesdale	4/19/1905	1905		139	224	70
Palmer	1889	1891		336	114	229
Paynesville	9/16/1907	1909		208	188	144
Pequaming-Aura	6/14/1894	1894	1952	32	42	
Princeton-Gwinn	11/15/1904	1905		434	173	186
Redridge-Beacon Hill	7/16/1905	1905	1959	108	60	
Rudyard	7/15/1902	1902		421	180	178
Republic	1886	1890		719	504	604
Rockland	5/22/1904	1904	1908?			
St. Ignace	9/24/1918	1919	1948	27	8	
Sault Ste. Marie	2/3/1906	1906		217	132	210
Stambaugh	7/28/1902	1902		173	79	246
Toivola	1917	1917		105	79	32

COMMUNITY	ORGANIZED	JOINED SUOMI SYNOD	CEASED ACTIVITY	MEMBERSHIP 1920	1940	1960
Trenary	10/27/1919	1919		100	35	93
Trimountain	1/26/1902	1902	1953	76	42	
Trout Creek	1897	1897		95	141	245
Uusi Suomi	1910	1913		132	20	107
Wainola	1/4/1914	1914		135	109	79
Wakefield	1890	1891		1,031	928	881
Winona	8/23/1909	1909	1951	81	27	
Winthrop		1911	1951	269	109	
Woodlawn	1905	1924	1959		28	
Membership of Michigan Congregations				18,208	12,345	17,078
Total Suomi Synod Membership				36,226	25,537	35,589

Note: Information, which is not always consistent, has been obrtained from annual reports of presidents, minutes of the Consistory meetings, and statistics in *Kirkollinen Kalenteri.*
*Joined the Elo congregation on January 21, 1951.
†Joined the Swedish congregation of Baraga.
‡Joined the Sault Ste. Marie congregation.
§The membership fell to three, and the congregation ceased activity.
‖Had been a part of the Hancock congregation and after a short period of independent existence rejoined it.
#Had long periods of inactivity.
**Had belonged to the Hancock congregation and rejoined it.

overcoming its early difficulties, had grown to be a church with fifty-three congregations and thirty preaching places that could seriously consider establishing its own publishing house to serve its expanding activities. The question of acquiring a publishing house was brought up at the church convention held in Calumet early in June 1900. As a result the Finnish Lutheran Book Concern was organized at that time. It purchased from their owners the three business enterprises mentioned above, paying $6,200 for *Paimen-Sanomia*, *Lasten Lehti*, and the printing press and buildings; $1,186.19 for *Amerikan Suometar;* and $2,455 for the Finnish Book Store with its stock and supplies, for a total of $9,841.19. Money was not used in the transaction because the purchaser had none. The debt was to be paid at the rate of $500 per year.[26] The final payment was made in 1919.

Over the years the managers of the Book Concern were J. H. Jasberg, 1900–1905; C. F. Asiala, 1905–10; Jacob Wirsula, 1910–14; Emil Pesonen, 1914–37; E. M. Laitala, 1937–44; Ray Olson, 1944–52;

John Heikkinen, 1952–54; and E. M. Laitala, 1954–62. Mathew Kangas also served as manager for a time, in about 1916–17.

There were several events in the history of the Hancock Book Concern, as it was generally known, that almost proved fatal. The first concerned the branch business, the Western Book Concern, established in Astoria in 1922. Its newspaper, *Lännen Suometar*, had been issued for only a few months when a fire on December 8, 1922, destroyed the business section of the city and with it the Western Book Concern with its press and all, causing a $15,000 loss to the synod. New blows came at the end of the decade when two of Astoria's largest banks closed, crippling the businesses of the area for a long time. The Hancock Book Concern was forced to cover the losses of the western enterprise, which amounted to about $65,000. When these difficulties had been overcome, a book and office supply store was opened in Hancock. This swallowed up the profits made by the printing press and put the business even deeper into debt. By 1958 the Book Concern was again free of debt, with annual business amounting to $150,000. The enterprise was on a sound basis at the time of the merger with the Lutheran Church in America. During the periods of restoration to solvency the managers were Emil Pesonen and E. M. Laitala, who were responsible for the Book Concern's remaining, in spite of all setbacks, able to serve the synod.

The greatest service of the Book Concern to the synod was the publication of church literature without material support from the synod. During the last years of their existence *Amerikan Suometar* and *Paimen-Sanomia* caused considerable losses for the Book Concern as the Finnish readership became smaller and smaller. The publications continued in existence, however, until December 1962, or to the end of the Suomi Synod as an independent institution. Established in 1889, *Paimen-Sanomia* had by far the longest life among Finnish American publications. *Amerikan Suometar*, established in 1899, was second in length of existence at the time it ceased publication. After that time, however, *Työmies*, established in 1903 and published until July 1998, superseded them. Another publication of long duration was *Kirkollinen Kalenteri* (Church calendar), which appeared for the first time in 1903 and was published in 1996. Edited by the presidents of the Suomi Synod, it is a first-rate source for the study of Finnish American history. After the merger of the churches it was published by the Suomi Conference. Still other long-lived publications were *Lasten Lehti* and *Nuorten Ystävä* (Young people's friend), the latter becoming the English-language *Lutheran Counselor* in 1938 after overcoming many objections to the change.

The most outstanding of these publications was *Amerikan Suometar*, which appeared three times a week for most of its lifetime. It had many editors worthy of mention, among them the following: N. J. Ahlman, K. V. Arminen, Pastor Adolph Riippa, A. M. Heikinheimo, J. L. Ollila, Emil Saastamoinen, John Rantamaki, Heikki Karhu, Pastor Hugo M. Hillila, and Pastor Yrjo F. Joki. *Amerikan Suometar* represented peaceful national, moral, and religious attitudes in the frequently stormy seas of Finnish-American newspaper publishing.

The other publishing done by the Finnish Lutheran Book Concern was extensive, consisting of frequent new editions of the *Aapinen* (A-B-C Book), the *Catechism*, *Songs of Zion*, Sunday school songbooks, hymnals, Bible histories, and other necessities of congregational work, as well as a large selection of other literature for Finns all over America. Among Finnish American businesses, the Book Concern was also one of the largest agencies handling books published in Finland.[27]

The Finnish National Church

Following the example of the National congregation organized in Calumet in 1890, many other groups that were dissatisfied with the Suomi Synod organized congregations of the same name in various parts of the country. Some of them came into contact with persons associated with the Finnish Lutheran Gospel Association of Finland. The first of these Gospel Association men was William Kontio, known as Williamson in America. He had experienced an evangelical awakening in Helsinki and had preached in the meeting house of the Gospel Association. He came to Oregon with his family in 1881 and met Pastor Hoikka, who encouraged him to become a preacher. Ordained by the Hauge Synod, he preached evangelical Christianity in a wide area. He was present at the conferences preceding the organization of the Suomi Synod, but he was not in agreement with the Beckian doctrines of its founders concerning the Bible.

Another evangelically oriented man was Mikael Kivi, who had come from evangelical circles in Finland. He was ordained by Eloheimo and served as a minister in Eloheimo's episcopal congregations in Ishpeming, Negaunee, and Calumet, also holding gospel meetings in Hancock. After the dissolution of Eloheimo's church the evangelical influence continued in opposition to the synod in the independent Lutheran congregations that had not joined it.

The first actual clash between the synod and the National Church occurred in the Illinois congregations. It was caused by Pastor

Karl Aksel Adheimer Koski, formerly Renfors, who had been in difficulties in both Ingria and Finland. He applied for a position in the Suomi Synod, but the Consistory, knowing about his past, did not approve his application. In 1895 Koski became pastor of an independent congregation in Chicago and managed to draw the majority of the members of the synod congregation there into his church. All the Waukegan congregation left the synod and invited Koski to be their pastor. He organized a congregation in De Kalb as well. In the summer of 1897 Koski left Chicago, visited Astoria, and settled in Wyoming to serve the Hanna and Rock Springs Finnish National congregations. At the same time he published articles attacking the Suomi Synod in *Amerikan Uutiset* newspaper of Calumet.

After the dissolution of Eloheimo's episcopal church, Kalle Haapakoski, the editor of *Amerikan Uutiset*, had often expressed the opinion that a new church, more democratic than the synod, should be organized. Pastor Koski began to work at putting this idea into effect. On May 10, 1898, in the name of the Rock Springs Finnish Evangelical Lutheran congregation, he invited all the Finnish National congregations to send their pastors and lay representatives to Rock Springs for a meeting to be held on June 26 for the purpose of organizing a new church.

The invitation was accepted by seven Finnish National congregations: Rock Springs, Hanna, and North Kemmerer congregations in Wyoming; Astoria in Oregon; Chavre Lake in Minnesota; and Calumet and Ishpeming congregations in Michigan. Kalle Haapakoski represented the Michigan congregations. As the only pastor present, Koski directed the three-day conference. It was decided that the new church would be called the Finnish American Evangelical National Lutheran Church. Bylaws were also formulated for it.

There was some difficulty in finding a president for the newly organized church. Pastor Koski refused to accept the position because of the recency of his arrival in America. He suggested Eloheimo, who was then the pastor of the Calumet Finnish National church. Haapakoski, whom Eloheimo had dropped from the congregation because he had opposed joining the synod, spoke of him now as a "friend and advocate" of the Finnish National Lutheran Church. A telegram was sent to Eloheimo asking if he would accept the office of president. An affirmative reply arrived the next day. Pastor Koski was elected vice-president; Charles Orth of Hanna, secretary; and Henrik Erickson-Nulu, treasurer.

It was decided that the next year's church convention would be held in Calumet. Eloheimo, however, did not show any interest in the newly organized church, whose views did not correspond with his own, so he failed to issue a call for the convention. In the winter of 1900 he moved to Wyoming to be the pastor of independent congregations, and in 1902 he moved from there to Laird, Idaho, where he established the Finnish community of Elo, organized a congregation, and built a church. He died there on December 8, 1913.

Eloheimo's only act as president of the Finnish American National Lutheran Church was to ordain colporteur Erik Johanson. Johanson became pastor of the Sault Ste. Marie congregation and served it until 1904. He also organized a congregation in Chatham. Later, Johanson resigned from pastoral work and died about 1925 in Alberta, Canada. During the early phases of its existence, the Finnish American National Church was actually under the leadership of Pastor Koski, who traveled about, organizing congregations.

The Calumet congregation, which was without a pastor after Eloheimo's departure, sent a call to Rector Wilhelm Adrian Mandellof of Säkylä, Finland, who accepted and became the real organizer of the Finnish American National Lutheran Church. The son of a pastor, he was born on January 31, 1848, in Kankaanpää, matriculated at the University of Helsinki in 1867, was ordained in Kuopio in 1873, and came to Calumet in October 1899. He was a pious, broad-minded man who supported Suomi College and advocated joining the Suomi Synod. At first he also had the confidence of the Laestadians, for as a pastor in Paltamo, Finland, he had found peace of conscience through private confession and absolution, for which reason those unfamiliar with the facts thought he was a Laestadian.

Having become familiar with the situation, he asked Eloheimo to arrange for a church convention to be held in Ironwood early in October 1900. Mandellof was elected president of the church, and Pastor Mikael Kivi vice president. The constitution was studied and amended. The Confession of the Church of Finland was approved for the National Church, omitting mention of the Church of Finland, and the United States and Canada were specified as its field of activity. Apparently through Mandellof's influence, it was stated that one of the purposes or aims of the Finnish National Lutheran Church was "to insure participation in the spiritual fellowship of Christianity to Finnish immigrants and their descendants." Church government was to be in the hands of a board composed, in its early phases, of two pastors and three laymen. Later, only the treasurer was a layman.

A period of lively activity followed the Ironwood convention. Juho Heikki Heimonen, assistant at the San Francisco Seamen's Mission, born in Nilsiä in 1865, and John Hjalmar Varmanen, assistant at the Brooklyn Seamen's Mission, born in Taivassalo, were ordained by Mandellof. Heimonen struggled for many years in pioneer work in the area around Port Arthur, Canada, after which he moved to Marquette, where he died in 1946. Varmanen went over to the Augustana Synod. Mandellof devoted himself especially to finding pastors for his growing church. Scholastic requirements were low, but a devout heart and a clear understanding of evangelical doctrine were absolutely necessary. Mandellof based his attitude on the words of St. Paul in Ephesians 4:11, according to which Christ sent out the first servants of the church without formal education or examinations. The Finnish National Church followed this principle for a long time, but eventually abandoned it to begin educating their pastors in Missouri Synod seminaries.

In the meanwhile, through the efforts of Pastor Williamson, the Evangelical Lutheran Free National Church had been organized in Ohio in February 1900. It was joined by the Ashtabula Harbor, Conneaut, Fairport, Ohio, and Erie, Pennsylvania congregations. On September 1, 1901, this Free National Church with its four congregations and their pastors joined the Finnish National Church. At the beginning of the same year, Mandellof had begun to publish the monthly *Todistusten Joukko* (A cloud of witnesses), the official church organ, of which Mikael Kivi became editor in 1902. The support given this publication encouraged the church to purchase a printing press in Ironwood and to publish a weekly newspaper, *Kansan Lehti* (People's paper). This enterprise was unsuccessful and *Kansan Lehti* went into bankruptcy at the beginning of 1903, taking *Todistusten Joukko* along with it.

By this time Mandellof had moved to Rock Springs, and from there he moved to Ely in 1903. At all times he endeavored to be a truly good shepherd to his congregations. If during a pastoral visit he found the mother of a family in tears because the husband was spending his time and money in taverns, he would pray with her and then go out to search for the drunkard. It usually happened that as he stepped into the saloon, all noise and swearing stopped, for Mandellof's personality immediately commanded respect, and the guilty person, more often than not, humbly left the place to be led home by Mandellof. The pioneering work he was doing under the difficult conditions of immigrant life became hard for Mandellof, who was approaching the age of sixty. The loss of the publications had also affected him. After a little less than six years in America—a short time, but one rich in returns—Mandellof went back to Finland in 1905, dying on January 13, 1916, while he was rector of Asikkala.

The example of the Suomi Synod publishing company and its publications kept alive in the Finnish National Church the desire to have their own church organ, but the failure of their first attempt made them cautious about trying again. The issue was decided by Pastor Pietari Vuori, formerly Bergenstrom, who was born in Rääkkylä in 1869. He was orphaned as a child, acquired his religious convictions in the evangelical movement, and came to America in 1893. When Suomi College opened in the fall of 1896, Vuori registered as a student. After receiving a reminder about attending services of the Finnish National Church, he left Suomi College in 1899 and moved to Calumet to continue his studies privately as Mandellof's student. He was ordained in 1901.

Vapaa Sana (Free word) newspaper owned and edited by Otto Massinen, brother-in-law of Eloheimo, was being published in Ironwood. Vuori purchased the paper early in 1906 and began to publish it as a weekly titled *Auttaja* (The helper). The name came from 2 Corinthians 1:24: "but are helpers of your joy." At the church convention held in Wakefield the next summer, *Auttaja* was approved as the official voice of the church, and the church board was ordered to take responsibility for its content. Soon after, Vuori donated his paper to the church, which in 1909 purchased the press on which it had been printed, naming the business the Finnish Printing Company. *Auttaja* was issued as a newspaper and devotional publication until 1964. Early in 1965 the Missouri Synod began to publish it in St. Louis as a religious monthly. The paper's longtime editor, Dr. J. E. Nopola, moved with the paper to the Missouri Synod headquarters.

Before returning to Finland, Mandellof was present at the organization of his own educational institution. His purpose was to found a school which would serve all immigrants, not just those belonging to one church, so it was named the People's College. The school opened in rented rooms in Minneapolis in September 1903. Pastor E. W. Saaranen from Heinola, Finland, was called to be its president. Others on the faculty were Eetu Aaltio and Miss Aina Williamson. A theological seminary was to be established later on in connection with the school. Already at the beginning of the spring term in the first part of January 1904, the school occupied large new quarters in Smithville, a suburb of Duluth on the shore of Lake Superior.

In planning the People's College, however, a fateful error was made in keeping the school separate from the church, with a supporting organization of its own and its own board. Anyone could become a member of the supporting organization by paying an annual fee of one dollar. Before long there were so many socialists in the organization that when, at the annual meeting of 1906, an attempt was made to transfer the People's College to the control of the church, the proposition was voted down. The socialists now put members of their party on the board. The board discharged E. Virkki, who had served as chairman of the board after Saaranen left to serve the Suomi Synod, and chose L. Haataja in his place. The name of the school was changed to Workingmen's College, and its curriculum was changed to serve the ideals of the growing labor movement.

The church presidents who followed Mandellof—William Williamson (1906–08) and Karl Gustaf Rissanen (1908–13)—tried to the best of their ability to remedy the effects of this blow to the Finnish National Church. The situation was, however, made even more difficult by certain moral indiscretions committed by Williamson and another clergyman, and also by doctrinal bickering. To make matters worse, church membership fell off. It is not surprising that in his first annual report Rissanen stated that the future of the church looked gloomy. He also stated that church statistics had been exaggerated.

By "exaggerated" figures Rissanen meant especially the totals in Williamson's annual report, which Pastor Antti Kononen had published in *Kansalliskirkkokunnan Kalenteri Karkausvuodelle 1908* (National church calendar for leap year 1908). According to these statistics the congregations of the Finnish National Church in Michigan were those in Calumet, Bessemer, Ironwood, Stambaugh, Wakefield, Paynesville, Chatham, and Rockland, with a total membership of 2,918. Outside Michigan the church had twenty-three congregations with a total membership of 3,716, making a grand total of 6,634. In most cases the membership had been reported in round numbers, a practice that almost always led to exaggeration.

Another interesting practice, also of long standing, was that of including in the total membership of the church the membership of independent congregations served by pastors of the National Church. The statistics in the church calendar of 1908 included fifty-six such congregations, almost twice as many as actually belonged to the National Church. There were ten such independent congregations in Michigan: Rumley, Amasa, Mass City, Winona, Laird, Tamarack City, Coalwood, Marquette, Montreal, and Marengo. The membership of these independent congregations was 6,927, making a total of 13,611 the membership of the National Church. This method of figuring out totals brings to mind the practice mentioned earlier in connection with the Suomi Synod—that of including in the membership those who had been "subject to influence."

During Pietari Vuori's term of office as president, 1913–18, among the more important events were the discussions about a merger with the Suomi Synod held in Hancock in the winter of 1913–14. The pastors' conferences progressed so smoothly that a merger appeared to be inevitable. Bylaws for the united church were even prepared, but the proposal was not accepted by the general church conventions. A proposal to establish a theological seminary in Ironwood, presented at the church convention held in Calumet in 1917, was favorably received. The seminary opened its doors in January of the following year with Pastor Arne Vasunta from Nurmijärvi as president. When he was elected president of the church in 1918, he chose Pastor K. E. Salonen to succeed him.

Kaarlo Erkki Salonen was born in Teisko in 1883. He was ordained in Porvoo in 1911. After serving as a missionary in Japan he joined the clergy of the Suomi Synod. He was president of the National Church Theological Seminary from 1918 to 1923. He was also the editor of *Auttaja* at the same time. The first graduates of the seminary—Gustaf Axel Aho, Axel Edwin Kokkonen, and Lauri Nikolai Wilenius—were ordained at the church convention held in Ironwood in 1921. The day of the ordination was a day of celebration for the National Church. When Salonen became involved in serving the Ironwood congregation as pastor in addition to his other work, however, he did not have enough time to do justice to the seminary. By 1923 there were no seminary students either.

Confronted with this critical situation, the National Church made an attempt to join the Missouri Synod. The first conferences about the possibility of joining were held in February 1923 and discussions were continued that summer at the Ironwood church convention, at which Dr. F. Pfotenhauer, president of the Missouri Synod, was also present. Unity in faith was confirmed, but on the question of women's right to speak at meetings and to vote in congregational elections there was a difference of opinion. In the National Church, women had the same rights as men, whereas in the Missouri Synod they did not. K. E. Salonen, who was preparing to return to missionary work in Japan, wrote strong protests against the merger. Opinion within the National Church was divided and caused violent clashes which were aggravated by M. N. Westerback's pamphlet *Erimielisyydet Kansalliskirkossa: Niitten Syyt ja Seuraukset* (Disagreements in the National Church: Their causes and consequences).[28]

During these years of crisis from 1923 to 1931, the president of the National Church was Matti Wiskari, born in Jääski in 1887, a graduate of Finland's school for cantors and organists and a preacher of the Gospel Association. It was largely due to his calm and impartial leadership that the National Church remained intact. G. A. Aho, who became the president in 1931, was born on October 9, 1897 in Minnesota and was the first president of the National Church who had not previously been a pastor in Michigan. He came into office at the time of the Great Depression, which seriously affected churches as well as other institutions and the general economy of the country. During Aho's term of office, young men of the church who wanted to become ministers studied at the Missouri Synod's Concordia Seminary in Springfield, Illinois. In time, this solved the problem of the shortage of clergy which was threatening the future of the National Church.

The year 1934 was a critical year in the life of the church, with many problems to be solved. One problem was the dearth of would-be pastors; there were only two Finnish students at the Springfield seminary. Another was the loss of subscribers to *Auttaja* because of a public dispute concerning temperance. Still another was that renewed negotiations for a merger with the Suomi Synod only deepened the gulf between the churches.

The question of theological training, which had been a burning issue for decades, was settled in the fall of 1938 when a Finnish department was established at the Concordia Seminary, with Alexander Monto as its head. Monto was born in Jääski in 1890 and came to America as a young man. He earned a master's degree at the University of Chicago and, among other things, was in the service of the United States government for seven years as an inspector of secondary schools in the Philippines. In the seminary he taught Finnish, psychology, and economics. His home was a gathering place for the Finnish students, of whom there were sometimes close to twenty.

When the fiftieth anniversary celebration of the National Church was held during the church convention of 1948 in Calumet, the Finnish Printing Company, which had changed its name to National Publishing Company and whose property had increased considerably in value, was free of debt, and the church was otherwise also financially secure. Sunday school work was carried on entirely in English, and the majority of congregations were bilingual. That year the National Church also started work among the Finnish immigrants in North Queensland, Australia. G. A. Aho, president of the church, had received the honorary title of doctor of theology the previous year from the Concordia Seminary.

Pastor J. E. Nopola was elected president of the National Church in 1953. Jalo Elias Nopola was born in Covington on July 10, 1907. He graduated from the Concordia Seminary and was ordained in 1931. In 1943, after having served eleven years in Canadian congregations, he became editor of *Auttaja*. Nopola was the first president of the church who was a pastor of the National Church trained in the Missouri Synod seminary. Most of the other pastors of the church were also graduates of Concordia. A merger with the Missouri Synod seemed inevitable. It was only a matter of time. Nopola received the honorary title of doctor of theology from the seminary, but was forced to leave his position as president of the church because of a critical illness. At the end of 1958 Pastor Emil A. Heino succeeded him.

Heino was born in Ashtabula in 1903. He studied law for a time but soon registered at Concordia Seminary and was ordained in 1934. His congregational work was done in Minnesota. At the 1960 church convention Heino brought up the question of a merger with the Missouri Synod, but the majority of the representatives were not interested in discussing the matter. Within a year, however, a complete change of attitude occurred, so that in 1961, at the Ely church convention, 112 voted for the merger and only 59 opposed it.

The last convention of the National Church was held in Esko, Minnesota, in June 1963. The final arrangements for the merger with the Missouri Synod were approved. The agreement guaranteed the rights of the Finnish-speaking members of bilingual congregations. A committee of eight, four from the National Church and four from the Missouri Synod, was to see to it that the seminary would train Finnish-speaking pastors as long as they were needed, that religious publications in the Finnish language would be continued, and that former pastors of the National Church and representatives of congregations might meet whenever necessary to discuss Finnish-language activities. Other provisions of the agreement concerned the publishing company in Ironwood and other business matters.[29] The merger took place officially on January 1, 1964. *Auttaja* was transferred to the Concordia Publishing House, which continued publishing it as a religious weekly.[30]

Other Churches

In comparison with Lutheran churches, other churches have played a very small part in the history of the spiritual life of the Finns. There were several of some importance however.

In addition to training ministers for service in its own congregations, the American Congregational Church also trained pastors in its theological seminary in Chicago for work among immigrants. Because their work had the character of missionary work they were known as missionary pastors, and the congregations established by them were known as mission congregations. It is in this way that the Suomalainen Lähetyskirkko (Finnish Congregational Church), which in Finland is

Table 10: The Finnish National Lutheran Church Congregations in Michigan, 1948 and 1960

COMMUNITY	ORGANIZED	1948 CONFIRMED MEMBERS	1948 TOTAL MEMBERSHIP	1960 CONFIRMED MEMBERS
Amasa	1903	?	75	61
Beechwood	1904	?	50	60
Bessemer	1888	45	60	68
Calumet	1890	117	161	151
Covington	1908	120	175	141
Detroit	1921	123	197	249
Ironwood	1898	710	980	237
Marquette	1898	220	298	225
Mass	1900	?	26	17
Wakefield	1890	80	115	106
			2,205	1,386

Table 11: Total Statistics of the Finnish National Lutheran Church, 1948 and 1960

STATE	CONGREGATIONS	1948 TOTAL MEMBERSHIP	1960 CONFIRMED MEMBERS
Michigan	11	2,205	1,386
Wisconsin	12	346	489
Minnesota	21	1,533	1,891
North Dakota	3	341	282
South Dakota	1	?	?
Montana	1	?	?
Ohio	6	859	909
New Jersey	1	54	37
New York	2	183	104
Massachusetts	5	813	374
New Hampshire	3	98	90
Canada	5	731	653
	71	7,163	6,215

known as the Free Church, originated. Its first ministers in America were trained in the Swedish department of the Chicago seminary until the Finns acquired their own school, the Finnish Training School, in connection with the seminary. Despite the location of the seminary, the activity of the Congregational Church was not directed toward the Midwest, but mostly toward the New England states and New York, where they also had small schools for preachers.

The first attempts of this church to extend its influence to Michigan were not successful. In 1898 Frans Karl Lehtinen, a preacher from Ashtabula, traveled about in the Ishpeming area in the hope of organizing congregations, and in the summer of 1901, Pastors Andrew Groop and K. A. Lindroos, who had been ordained from the Chicago seminary, traveled more widely in the Upper Peninsula. Proficient in the Swedish language, they also visited among the Swedish Free Church, or Waldenstromian, congregations. Finnish congregations, however, were not organized. The Finns of Michigan did not have a Congregational Church congregation until 1940, when Pastor Niilo Tuomenoksa organized one in Detroit which met in homes of members.[31]

The Methodist Church began to function among the Finns of Michigan in 1900, when Pastor G. A. Hiden came from Finland to acquaint himself with the possibilities. The following year he settled permanently in Negaunee, whence his influence spread to eleven preaching places, the most important of which were Ishpeming, Marquette, and Princeton, Michigan. Such activity was made possible at the conference of the American Methodist Church held in Albany, New York, in the fall of 1902. At this conference the church consented to provide a generous amount of support for missionary work among the Finns of Michigan.[32] Important men in this activity, which emanated from Ishpeming, were Pastor A. V. Tuukkanen, and Kaarlo Ruotsalainen, who arrived from Finland in 1927 and worked in Michigan until his death in 1953. Both of these men distinguished themselves in the temperance movement and in relief work for Finland. Some of the other Methodist ministers who served congregations that later joined Lutheran churches in Ishpeming, Ironwood, Calumet, Laurium, and Rudyard were Peter Talikka, Matti Pitkanen, Viljo Heiman, Aleksi Poobus, Hjalmar Salmi, and Pietari Pennanen.

The doctrinal kinship of the Methodist Church with the Lutheran Church led many of the well-trained Methodist ministers to churches in Finland, the United States, and Canada, to labor in them for long periods of time as pastors and as writers. Among them were Pastor Toivo Rajalinna, Niilo Tuomenoksa, Viljo Heiman, and Johannes Virtanen. The Methodist hymnal, *Rauhan Sointuja*, was frequently used in Lutheran church programs.[33]

Of other denominations, the Baptist Church also had a following, though a small one, in Michigan. Their first representative among the Finns was an uneducated man from Kortesjärvi, who tried to spread his faith in Michigan in 1891. In the same year he also appeared in Massachusetts, where he attempted to publish a newspaper, *Lanesvillen Sanomat* (Lanesville tidings) which, according to his advertisement, was printed in two languages, "Finnish and Enges (English) so that one could learn to read Enges."[34] The next attempt at spreading the Baptist faith in Michigan was made by some laymen from Swedish parishes of Southern Ostrobothnia, where the Baptists had a foothold. M. Esselstrom of this group started a small congregation in Negaunee in 1902. A. Laurikainen, who used the label "Baptisti Lähetys Saarnaaja" (Baptist Missionary Preacher), under his name is known to have been working in Hancock in 1904. The few Finnish Baptists of Michigan have been members of American Baptist congregations.

11 The Rise and Decline of the Temperance Movement

The festive drink of the ancient Finns was ale, the "home-brewed beer of the Kalevainens." Just as the Greek and Roman poets praised wine and the beauty of vineyards, so did the Finns of early times praise ale and the cultivation of barley and hops. In pagan Finnish homes, verses on the origin of ale were recited, and magic incantations on brewing it were chanted before the housewife began to make the beverage. To stimulate fermentation and to give more potency to the ale, honey or mead was added to it. The result was that

Peerless drink for pious people
Charmed the women into laughter,
Made the men feel gay and frisky,
Set the sober folk rejoicing,
Set the simple folk a-dancing.

Already before the age of Christianity, however, the folk poetry of Finland was pointing out and deploring the negative aspects of ale. Its intoxicating character was due to hops. The Finnish form of the word, "humala," came to mean drunkenness. Hops were condemned in this line of a poem: "Humala, Son of Boisterous, was sown in the earth as vipers." The boisterousness caused by ale was also pictured in another poem, which stated that ale robbed men of their wits and boys of half their wits, and that it made men riot without their hats and women dance without their veils. The poet of the *Kanteletar* considered it a terrible fate for a young woman to become the wife of a drunkard. He wrote

Preserve,
O Great Creator,
This tender maid
From the ale-crazed drunkard
And his bed.

In the introduction to his Finnish translation of the *Psalter* published in 1551, Mikael Agricola, the religious reformer of Finland, describes how the pagans worshipped Ukko, the god of rain and thunder. This worship was at its height in early summer when rains at the right time would insure the success of the annual harvest. The Ukko festivals often became noisy drinking bouts, of which Agricola speaks thus in his versified introduction:

When spring sowing was in progress,
Ukko's toast was drunk
From Ukko's bushel measure.
Maid and woman became tipsy,
And many shameful things were done
That were seen and heard.

By Agricola's time four hundred years had passed since Christianity had been introduced in Finland, but pagan customs had been preserved in outlying areas and were still in evidence even in the following century.

During the Middle Ages there were in the towns of Finland professional orders or guilds which, in addition to accomplishing much good, also served as private drinking clubs. In many guilds, every Tuesday night was "souls' night," when every member and his wife were required to be in attendance under threat of fines. When smoke from the incense burner had filled the hall and holy water had been sprinkled about, nine memorial toasts to souls were drunk. They were drunk from a large horn, participants standing before the guild fire and singing between toasts. The toasts were divided into groups of three, between each two of which the members sat and chatted while waiting for new thirst. The first drink in the first group was a toast "in memory of our Lord," the next to the Virgin Mary, and the third to St. George. The second series was drunk to the Holy Cross, to St. Erik, and to St. Olaf. The first toast of the third group was dedicated to St. Gertrude, the second to St. Benedict, and the third to all the saints. These soul toasts were all drunk in ale, which also flowed freely at regular guild meetings. The character of these meetings is suggested by the proverb:

"Running to the guild, crawling home." Imported wines did not reach Finland until the end of the Middle Ages, and even then, because of their cost, they were used only by the higher nobility, the wealthier merchants, and the top-ranking clergy.

The excessive use of ale and the resultant moral corruption did not pass unnoticed by the Catholic clergy of the Middle Ages. The priests ordered the painting of pictures on the walls of their churches to illustrate the demoralization caused by ale-drinking, and just as they did with other paintings that decorated their churches, they explained their meaning in sermons. A painting of this kind has been preserved in the church in Lohja, Finland. It shows some of the nobility at a drinking party, where demons have found a situation favorable to their work: One is urging guests to drink more; another is offering someone the apple of the Fall; and a third is drawing a drinking man and woman closer together. Drinking in general and the endless toasts to souls were condemned in sermons. But the toasts to Our Lord and to the Virgin Mary were not condemned, possibly because of the established opinion that the drinking of these toasts was a serious religious matter.[1] From the point of view of the national economy, however, the making of ale was important, for Finnish ale, known for its excellence, was exported in great quantities.

The ale problem of the Middle Ages in Finland changed at the beginning of the modern period into a liquor problem that gradually swelled into an exceptionally difficult social problem, perhaps more serious in Finland and other northern countries than elsewhere.

Liquor is a general term applied to the beverages containing a large percentage of alcohol and produced by distillation. It may have become known in Europe through the Arabs, for chemistry was one of the sciences that especially interested them. In addition to saltpeter, sulphuric acid, nitric acid, and other chemical products, they are thought to have produced alcoholic drinks stronger than wine. Liquor was considered a panacea which would give the human body strength to combat all disorders, ailments, and diseases. This characteristic is reflected in its scientific Latin names: *aqua vitae* (water of life) and *spiritus frumenti* (spirit or life of grain). In their natural form, grain and wine nourished, but in their "refined" form, or as liquor, it was thought they also cured. The use of spirits for medicinal purposes is described in a Danish cookbook of 1625:

> The aches and pains in feet, back, etc, cease when they are rubbed with strong liquor. If the voice is hoarse, rub the neck with spirits and drink some every morning for three days without partaking of food.

> If the hearing is poor, put a drop of liquor in the ear and hearing will return. Whoever drinks a small spoonful of spirits each morning will seldom be ill, for liquor destoys the mucous fluid which produces illnesses. If a little liquor is drunk every morning, worms will die whether they are in the heart, the lungs, or the liver. If a person loses the power of speech just before his death, liquor should be poured into his mouth and he will speak again.

Wars, famines, and plagues in the sixteenth, seventeenth, and eighteenth centuries in Finland gave more than enough reason for the use of this miracle medicine. King John III, a former duke of Finland, wrote two pamphlets in which he advised the use of spirits against the plague. Clergymen carried liquor with them as medicine for weakened patients. Generals gave it to their men before battle. Mothers administered it with milk to their infants to protect them from illness. The belief in spirits as a general miracle medicine disappeared gradually as higher cultural standards developed, but its use for pleasure continued at a fearful rate. Even Luther, when appealed to, said, "If God can forgive me for having annoyed and bored Him for twenty years by saying Masses, He will not be offended if I take a drink now and then and, in all honesty, rejoice with good people and give glory to God, let the world say what it will." After such a statement it was easy to forget that Luther had also said that the original maker of ale was the "Plague of Germany," and that a life of drunkenness was a pig's life.

Ale had been prepared for home use in almost every household. Hard liquor, too, was soon being produced at home. When some of the kings of Sweden-Finland attempted to restrict distillation of spirits, the nobility were the first to oppose any limitation because distillation, which was not yet common among the lower classes, was a source of considerable income for them. In the Diet of 1660 the rights of the clergy were protected by a statement assuring the clergy that they had an unchallengeable right to "refine" their grain into liquor as well as into bread. The king best known for his interest in temperance was Charles XII, himself a total abstainer, who in 1709 prohibited all distilling in Sweden and Finland. When the plague began to rage in the kingdom, however, it was blamed on the lack of liquor, and in the king's absence on a military campaign the kingdom's first prohibition law was repealed, having been in force for two days less than a year. After the horrors of the Great Terror, during which the population of Finland decreased by one-half, distillation again became general, and intoxication increased to a hitherto unheard-of degree. In the reign of King Gustavus III (1771–92) the production of liquor was declared the sole right of the crown. Eleven government distilleries were built in Finland, namely in Turku, Helsinki, Tampere, Pori, Hämeenlinna, Vaasa, Lovisa, Kuopio, Joensuu, Uusi Kaarlepyy, and Oulu. The king had been warned that he could concern himself with everything excepting religion and the distillation of spirits. The costly product of the government distilleries did not sell, the courts were overflowing with violation cases, and prisons were full of those who had been sentenced for illegal distilling. The people were given back their right to make liquor. In a decree passed in 1800, distillation was equated with the ownership of land, the argument being that liquor was a side product of agriculture. Every landowner had to pay a distillation tax which actually forced him into distilling. One-fifth of the country's grain supply was used in the production of liquor, a circumstance that caused the price of grain to rise, the raising of cattle to be neglected, and the cost of living to climb, hurting the landless population especially. The stores of grain were eventually exhausted. This depletion of vital grain caused bitter suffering, especially during the great famine years of 1812–13 and 1867–68.

The consumption of liquor increased each year during the period of free distillation for home use so that it was at least thirteen liters per person per year, in addition to quantities of ale and wine. Liquor and the enjoyment of it had become such a part of the life of the people that it was like "bone of its bone and flesh of its flesh." Fathers and mothers used it, and servants sometimes received part of their wages in grain from which they made liquor in the family still. Liquor was sometimes added to infants' milk to make them sleep better. Moral decay inevitably followed. This moral deterioration was not only in Finland but everywhere in the western world.

Early Phases of the Temperance Movement

Eventually there was a reaction to the unrestricted and unrestrained use of liquor. It began in England and America, the latter becoming the cradle of the modern temperance movement. Lord Lonsdale, in 1743, made a speech in the British House of Lords urging the government to consider the liquor problem. Benjamin Franklin (1706–90), the most popular famous person in the history of the United States, observed complete abstinence all his life. As a youth he was ridiculed by his fellow workers because of his temperance. Once he picked up a heavy crowbar and held it straight out with arms extended and challenged the drinkers to do the same. No one attempted the feat. Thomas Jefferson, the author of the Declaration of Independence and the third president of the United States, was also in favor of temperance.

The father of the modern temperance movement was Dr. Benjamin Rush, a contemporary of Franklin and Jefferson who was born in Byberry near Philadelphia on Christmas Eve 1745. He was one of the signers of the Declaration of Independence and during the Revolution served as a doctor in the army and the navy. In 1785 he published a scientific work on the effects of strong liquor. Rush's reputation as a great patriot and his work as a chemist caused his book to be widely read and to be translated into several languages. The Quakers and the Methodists had already accepted temperance as a matter to be considered in their programs, and Rush recommended that all churches join in working for a prohibition law. His book brought about the organization of a temperance society in Connecticut in 1789—the first in America—and of the first temperance society in the state of New York in 1808. However, these two societies died out when the first wave of enthusiasm had passed. Influenced by Rush's book, Lyman Beecher (1775–1863), the famous Congregational minister and theologian, became interested in temperance, organized a new temperance society in Connecticut in 1813, and effected the passage of laws restricting the sale of liquor. When another political party came into power, however, these laws were repealed and the friends of temperance were disheartened. But with the ever-increasing stream of immigrants who headed for the growing industrial cities, drunkenness and moral laxity also increased.

The situation demanded action. At a meeting in Boston on February 13, 1826, the American Society for the Promotion of Temperance was founded and its bylaws were approved. The whole United States became its field of activity, and Dr. Justin Edwards, who, as "the world's first professional temperance worker," devoted all his time to directing the work, became its secretary. Unusual methods were sometimes used to obtain funds. For example, the title of honorary vice president could be purchased for $250. The work expanded rapidly so that by the end of 1828 there were 220 local organizations with a total membership of over 100,000. There were also eleven paid temperance speakers, and hundreds of clergymen and patriotic citizens gave of their time to the cause as speakers and writers. After the society had been active for six years, 2,000 distilleries had ceased production, 5,000 retail liquor stores had closed, and 5,000 drunkards had been rehabilitated for useful citizenship. At first the society's struggle was only against distilled liquor. But at a convention of temperance societies of the United States held in Saratoga, New York, in 1836, war was declared against wine and beer as well. Thus a stand for total abstinence was taken nationally as had already been done locally by some societies. In 1851 a secret society called the Independent Order of Good Templars was organized in Utica, New York, to further the cause of temperance. It was to play an important part in the development of the Finnish American temperance movement.

During its formative years the American temperance movement had a number of powerful personalities in its ranks. One such personality was John Bartholomew Gough (1817–86), who was born in England and came to America at the age of eleven. On reaching manhood he became an incurable drunkard. Even the death of his wife and children from hunger and misery did not reform him, but there came a day when a certain Quaker saved him from suicide. In 1842 Gough took the pledge of temperance and dedicated his life thereafter to being a temperance speaker in his new homeland as well as in the land of his birth. It is said that he influenced 200,000 persons to become teetotalers. On February 15, 1886, in the midst of a powerful lecture he was giving in Frankfort, Pennsylvania, this "world's greatest temperance speaker" suffered a stroke. He died three days later.

Another temperance crusade similar to Gough's was the "Washington Movement," in which reformed drunkards were leading speakers at great gatherings. The director of the movement was John Hawkins, himself a former drunkard, who had been influenced by his little daughter to become an abstainer.[2] Neal Dow (1804–97), a member of an old Quaker family, came into contact with saloonkeepers in his hometown of Portland, Maine, when he was trying to save a friend who had fallen into drunkenness. He familiarized himself with temperance literature, dedicated himself to temperance work, and traveled throughout Maine as a temperance speaker. His work was well rewarded when on June 2, 1851, the Maine Prohibition Law—the famous "Maine Law"—which Dow himself had written and pushed through, went into effect. In the American Civil War, Dow served as a colonel and a brigadier general. He was also the temperance candidate in the presidential election of 1880. The American temperance movement received an exceptionally powerful boost when Ireland's great apostle of temperance, the Catholic priest Theobald Mathew, traveled here in 1849–51, lecturing and organizing numerous Father Mathew Total Abstinence Societies.

In Finland, too, a national temperance movement had begun. Its roots reached back to the period of freedom and enlightenment when the clergy had considered it their duty to give many kinds of practical advice to the people. They preached about the cultivation of potatoes and the draining of swamps, on vaccination for smallpox, and on the importance of temperance. Thus, Juhana Wegelius the Younger, principal of a Tornio school, who published a great book of sermons in 1747–49, based his sermon for the Second Sunday in Advent on Luke 21:25–35, stressing verse 34, which reads in part: "And take heed to yourselves, lest at any time your hearts be overcharged with surfeiting and drunkenness." The following excerpt serves as an example of the thoughts expressed in this powerful temperance sermon:

> Many say that drunkenness is not forbidden or even mentioned in God's Law, or the Ten Commandments. But, dear Soul, the entire Bible is a powerful explanation of God's Law and shows how all sins, even those which are not mentioned specifically in the Ten Commandments, such as greed, drunkenness, anger, pride, and others of the kind, are contrary to the Law of God, and how judgment has been declared upon them; even without this I say everyone can easily see that excessive drinking and eating are against every commandment in the Decalogue.

Wegelius then takes the commandments one by one, finding in each a thought supporting temperance and condemning drunkenness.[3]

The first step toward an organized temperance movement in Finland was taken in 1817, when the government urged governors and clergy to do everything in their power to get people to become temperate. In some congregations, organizations against "drunkenness, immorality, and the desire for ostentation" were started. Pentti Jaakko Ignatius, rector of Halikko and composer of hymns, especially was active in the work. The Evangelical Society of Finland, which had been established in 1817 at the time of the three-hundredth anniversary of the Reformation, published two temperance tracts, one in 1821 and the other in 1825: *Varoitus Juopumusta Vastaan* (Warning against drunkenness) and *Muutamat Varoitussanat Tapain Puhtaudesta* (A few words of advice concerning clean habits), of which 33,000 copies were distributed free of charge at parish catechetical meetings. In 1833 the Finnish temperance workers came unexpectedly into contact with the American temperance movement. The American temperance society organized in 1826 had decided to spread its concepts around the world and had sent a representative to St. Petersburg. As a result of his efforts a small tract about drinking was translated into Finnish, Estonian, and Russian. The Finnish title was *Juopumuxen Erinomaiset Edut* (The special benefits of drunkenness), of which about 5,000 copies were distributed in Finland.

Finnish newspapers also published articles about temperance work in America.[4] This over-the-sea influence continued even in the next decade, when at the request of Tsar Nicholas I, Robert Baird's work about temperance societies of the United States was translated into Finnish under the title *Pohjos-Amerikan Yhdys-Waltakuntien Kohtuullisuuden Seurat.*

The greatest triumph of the American temperance ideal in Finland was Henrik Renqvist (1789–1866), known as "Kukkos-pastori" after his father, Henrik Kukkonen, a farmer of Ilomantsi. During the war between Russia and Finland he earned money as a traveling salesman, selling liquor and other commodities to the Russian soldiers. After his ordination in 1817, the Prayer Revival movement developed around him. One of its requirements was total abstinence. Renqvist wrote temperance tracts and was the most influential pioneer of temperance in his day.[5] His best-known writing on temperance is the eighty-six-page *Viinan Kauhistus* (The horror of liquor), in which he revealed his knowledge of temperance tracts published in Sweden as well as his familiarity with the principles of the American temperance movement. He also revealed his knowledge of the latter's motto, that states that it is only a step from so-called moderate drinking to excessive use of liquor.

Because of Renqvist's influence, men of the rising Finnish nationalistic movement also became interested in temperance. Elias Lönnrot, compiler of the *Kalevala* poems, organized the first temperance society in Kajaani in 1834. It was in existence only a short time, but he later wrote a few folk stories about it. Of them, "Three Days in the Village of Sairio" became the best known. J. V. Snellman published news about the temperance societies of Sweden, England, and Ireland in *Maamiehen Ystävä* (Farmer's friend), which he edited. Several temperance societies were organized in Finland. Two examples are the ones that were established in Jämsä and Jyväskylä in 1846. Liquor did much harm especially in Lapland until 1838, when the government forbade the sending of hard liquor to the region, expanding this "Lapp Prohibition Law" in 1842 to include all alcoholic beverages. Influenced by the Laestadian revival, a temperance society was organized in Lapland in 1844. Through the initiative of J. V. Snellman and Professor Stefan Baranovski, a society called Friends of Moderation was established in Helsinki in 1859. Its bylaws were approved by the tsar the following year. The society, however, was barely able to keep going. In 1866 a law was passed forbidding the distilling of liquor for home use. A ballad of the day reported it thus:

In 1866
There was a new law in Finland.
Distillation of liquor was forbidden;
Merrymaking was not allowed.

The law of 1866 lowered the consumption of liquor in Finland from thirteen liters to three liters per person per year. On the other hand, the use of beer increased tenfold, awakening the temperance people to the realization that new and vigorous work must begin, stressing total abstinence, not just moderation. Pioneers of this new movement in Finland were the author Minna Canth in Kuopio; Hilda Hellman in Vaasa; a missionary, Emil Hedenstrom, and a teacher, Kaarle Verkko, in Turku; and Kaarle Heino in Helsinki. Their initiative and leadership led to the organization of societies for the promotion of total abstinence. The most important of these were organized in Vaasa in 1877, in Turku in 1881, and in Helsinki in 1882. As early as 1873, men working in the Helsinki Gasworks, the Töölö Sugar Refinery, and the Stenberg Machine Shop had organized temperance societies to serve their own needs. Temperance work in Finland received a tremendous boost when a licentiate of medicine, Aksel August Granfelt (1846–1919), secretary of the Society for the Enlightenment of the People, joined the Friends of Temperance. During his long secretaryship, from 1878 to 1907, he put the society, whose work was carried on all over the country, into the service of temperance as well as enlightenment. Dr. Granfelt was a man of action. In 1883 he joined the Friends of Moderation, which had been inactive for seven years, bringing into it such people as Kaarle Heino, Matti Tarkkanen, Kaarle Krohn, Kustavi Grotenfelt, and others who in time were to become part of the cultural history of Finland. They selected a new board of directors, formulated new rules and bylaws, and changed the name of the organization to Friends of Temperance. The government approved the bylaws the next year. In its twenty-three years of existence the Friends of Moderation had not organized a single local society. The Friends of Temperance considered the establishment of local groups their most important task. The first to be organized were the Koitto and the Eos of Helsinki. By February 1885 the society had thirty-seven local organizations with a total of 234 members. At the general temperance meeting held in Helsinki in 1888, the Friends of Temperance Society was accepted as the central organization of the temperance societies throughout the country. The temperance workers of Finland had thus finally become organized and had created for themselves a powerful organ of administration and accomplishment.[6]

Norwegian-Finnish-Swedish Church, Quincy Hill, Michigan. Early 1880s.

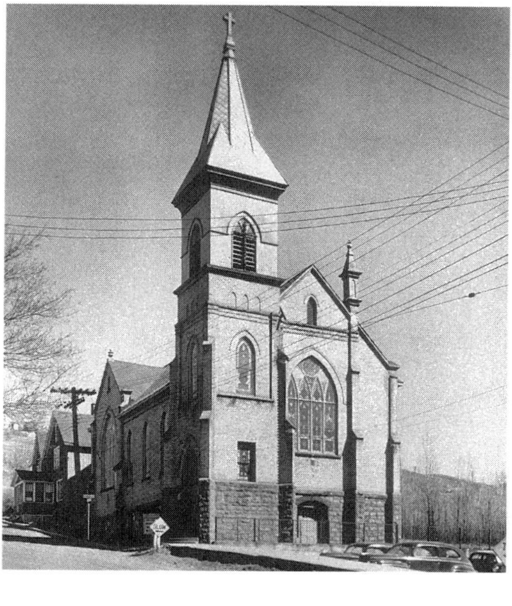

Finnish Evangelical
Lutheran Church,
Hancock, Michigan.

Bethlehem Lutheran Church, Calumet, Michigan.

Evangelical Lutheran Church, Kaleva, Michigan.

Finnish National Lutheran Church, Calumet, Michigan, 1890s.

Confirmation class, 1906. Finnish Evangelical Lutheran Church, Hancock, Michigan.

Finnish Evangelical
Lutheran Church,
Republic, Michigan.

Finnish National Temperance Brotherhood Office, Negaunee, Michigan, 1898.

Bethlehem Lutheran Church, Newberry, Michigan.

Kaleva Temperance Hall, Kearsarge, Michigan (ca. 1905).

Finnish National Brothers Temperance Association, 25th Annual Convention, July 1912, Hancock, Michigan.

Negaunee Labor Temple, Negaunee, Michigan.

Labor play, "Death Church," 1912. Liberty Finn Hall, Marquette, Michigan.

Western Federation of Miners Union Office, Hancock, Michigan, 1913.
Courtesy Jack Deo, Superior View Historical Photography.

Finnish Cooperative Store, Mass, Michigan.

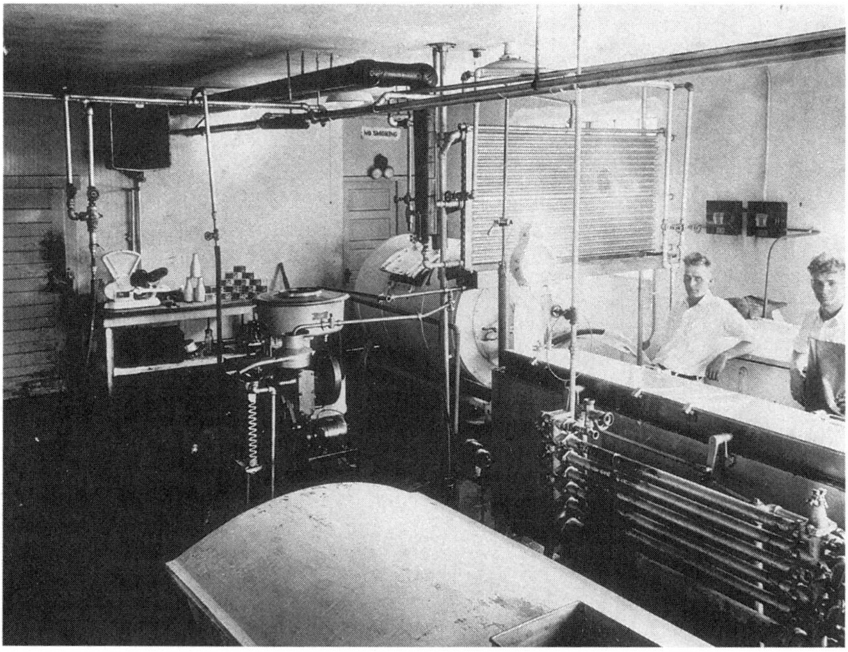

Marquette Dairy Co-op.

Kangas and Kyllonen Market, Mass City, Michigan (ca. 1900).

Jacobsville Sandstone Quarry before 1900, Jacobsville, Michigan.

Finnish Lutheran Book Concern, Hancock, Michigan.

Interior of Finnish Lutheran Book Concern, Hancock, Michigan, 1916–17.

Staff of Finnish Lutheran Book Concern, Hancock, Michigan, 1915.

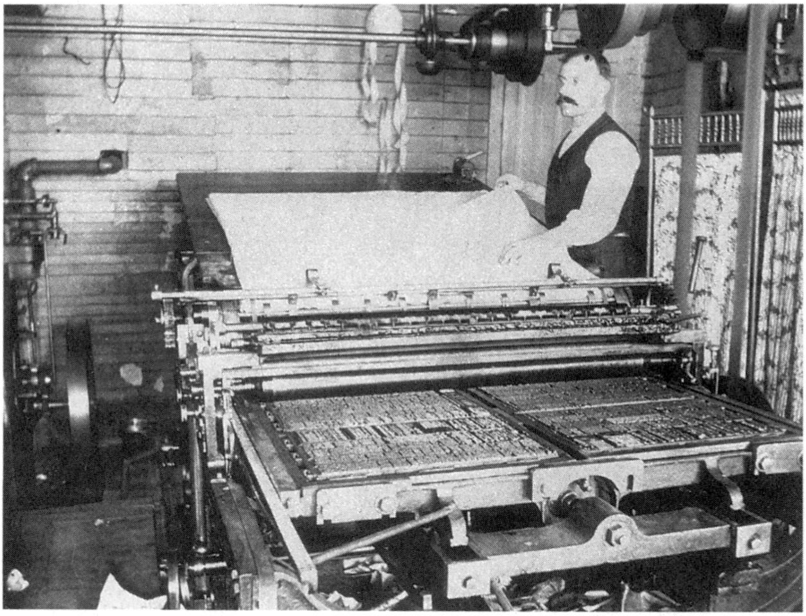

Printing press of *Amerikan Suomalainen*, Hancock, Michigan (ca. 1898).

Juha Kustaa Nikander, founder of Suomi College and Theological Seminary and president of Suomi College from 1896 to 1919.

Suomi College "Old Main" (1890s). Courtesy Jack Deo, Superior View Historical Photography.

Americanization classes, Caspian, Michigan, 1938. Edith Aspholm, Americanization teacher.

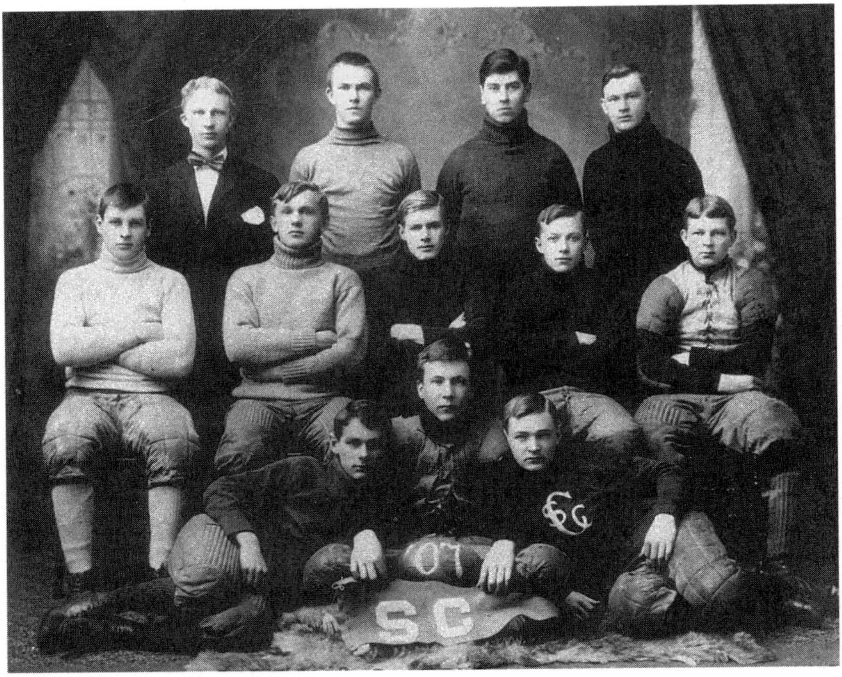

Suomi College football team, 1907.

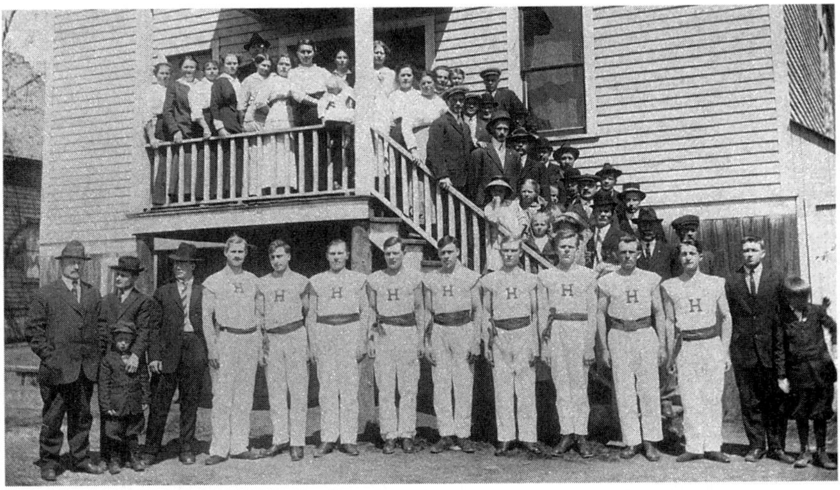

Members of the athletic society "Huima" at South Range, Michigan. Photograph taken at the Copper Country Temperance Societies' Meeting at the South Range Hall (1909). Temperance representatives are on the stairs; "Huima" athletes are in white uniforms.

Liberty Band, 1913. Liberty Finn Hall, Marquette, Michigan.

Finnish Band, Princeton, Michigan, 1909. Courtesy Forsyth Township Historical Society.

Marquette Finnish Band, Marquette, Michigan, 1907.

The finest Copper Country wrestler—Karlo Lehto.

Loading docks, Jacobsville, Michigan. Sandstone was shipped to lake ports from Duluth to Buffalo. The red sandstone buildings in lake port towns are of Jacobsville stone (prior to 1900).

Calumet to Wolverine via streetcar.

Peoples Auto Company, Calumet, Michigan.

Ordination ceremony of Suomi Synod (five students) showing pastors officiating, 1958. Left to right: Dr. Armas K. E. Holmio, Dr. Douglas Ollila, Sr., Dr. Raymond Wargelin, and Dr. Bernhard Hillila.

The Laestadians (c. 1920).

Suomi Synod pastors' wives (c. 1940).

AMERIKAN
Suomalainen Lehti.

PRINTED AT THE OFFICE OF THE "NORTHWESTERN MINING JOURNAL," HANCOCK.

N:o. 6. PERJANTAINA 2 PÄIWÄNÄ KESÄKUUTA 1876. KAKSI DOLLARIA WUODELTA.

Amerikan
Suomalainen Lehti.
A. J. MUIKKU, toimittaja.

"Amerikan Suomalainen Lehti."
(The American-Finnish Journal.)
The first, and only, Finnish Newspaper published in the United States.
ISSUED EVERY FRIDAY BY
A. JOHN MUIKKU,
Editor and Proprietor.
Office, in the NORTHWESTERN MINING JOURNAL Building, Hancock, L. S. Mich
SUBSCRIPTION:
$2.00 PER YEAR, IN ADVANCE.
All Kinds of Job Printing
in the Finnish, German and Scandinavian languages will be done with promptness.

kunnalliset olot uusien yritysten ja ansio-paikkojen suhteen owat kowin muukosten alaiset ja sillä on meidän tarkastaminen ainoastansa niitä etuja ja waston sia, jotka luonto ja asema owat kullekin tienoolle pysywäisesti osaksi määränneet.

Minnesota. „L'Etoile du Nort" (Pohjan tähti) nähdään mielilauseena Minnesotan waakunassa ja tätä nimeänsä se ei ole aiwan suotta omistanutkaan, sillä Minnesota on monin puolin merkillisin kaikista pohjois waltioista. Asemansa suhteen se on melkein Pohjois-Amerikan mannermaan keskustana, ollen täältä melkein sama matka Atlantiin mereen ja Tyyneen mereen, kuin myöskin Mexicolahteen ja Hudson Bayhin. Täällä owat myöskin kahden Amerikan suurimman wesijokien, Mississippin ja St. Lawrence wirran lähteet. Tämä on myöskin wesirikkain kaikista länsi-waltioista, joka sille antaa luotettawan he-

likkun, usein unhottaa olewansa Pohjois Amerikan takasaloissa ja hän uneksii sa... Pohjois Suomen sydänmaissa, kunnes hän repii weriin katensa ja kaswonsa noissa pahan juonisissa piikkisissä ...ensaissa ja huomaa suuren erhetyksensä. Näissä metsissä on meidänkin maanmiestemme tunnettu Cokaton siirtokunta ja toiwottawaa olisi että useammat maanmiehistämme, jotka huoletointa omaa kotia uneksiwat, asettuisiwat tänne ...ansalaistensa naapureiksi, ennen kuin maan arwo on liian korkealle kohounut, aikka kaikki maa luiskahtanut muukalaisten käsiin. Jatketaan.

St. James, Minnesota. Yöllä 14 ja 15 päiwän wälillä toukokuussa tapahtui onnetoin tapaus. Ukkosen ilman jyristessä löi salama alas ja tappoi kaksi norjalaista lasta, toinen 10 wuoden wanha ja toinen taas 5 wuotias. Lasin

Jumalan palwelus
pidetään ensi sunnuntaina, helluntai päiwänä, kello 7 iltasella Quincyn koulukuoneessa. Pastori H. Roernaes pitää tösaarnan.—Hän muuttaa parin wiikkauden perästä Jowan waltioon.—Kaikki owat terwe-tulleet.

Suomesta.

Uudenmaan hewois-ystäwäinyhdistyksen kokouksessa toispäiwänä keskusteltiin hewoisseppäkoulujen perustamisesta, jonka tarpeellisuudesta kaikki oliwat yksimieliset.

Kultakanta Suomessa. Tähän asti on Suomessa rahan arwon perusteena ollut hopea, mutta nyt kuin tuota metallia löydetään niin yltäkyllin, niin sen arwokin halwentuu, joten Suomen raha on joutunut takapajulle. Mutta nyt säätyjen pankki-edusmiesten

First Finnish-language paper in America, Hancock, Michigan, 1876.

Suomi College choir directed by Arthur Hill, Hancock, Michigan.

Finnish Evangelical Lutheran Church, Hancock, Michigan, 1948 (Reverend Onni A. Koski).

Liquor and the First Finnish Immigrants

In 1905 a serious-minded man of the people wrote in his memoirs about liquor and the early immigrants:

> It makes me shudder to recall the terrible unscrupulousness with which those who had just arrived in the country were lured into saloons. After a week or two, the morally clean boys and girls from backwoods areas were quite at home in these dens of iniquity. This is where the term "free country" was explained to them in a way that still charms those with mistaken ideas. This is where young people were taught attitudes of disrespect toward their elders. Here our young maidens were "cleansed" of their innocence—ideals of purity supposedly became freer in this "free country. . . ." In the old homeland, families had worshiped together, and in the spring they had listened together to the call of the cuckoo; here, there was brawling, swearing, and the enjoyment of the "cuckooing" of the beer barrel. The previously quiet Finnish wife was not shy any more, nor was the clean-cut youth from Finland. Neither did the young girl recently arrived from Finland blush any more as she carried beer to her lodgings.[7]

In those days it was a characteristic of high-minded Finnish nationalism to view the life of the immigrant in this poor light, and against this gloomy background to paint an idealistic picture of Finland, where people's habits were clean, and life was lived in a Christian way.

In *Siirtolaisen Opas* (Immigrant's guide) for 1910, Pastor M. I. Kuusi wrote as follows:

> Dancing, playing cards, swearing, and making merry, the immigrants come across the ocean. Upon reaching the shores of America, they become scattered all over the new homeland. But the effect of their wicked life together and the seeds of false ideas of freedom remain in their hearts. They have drunk a toast to freedom of the flesh and are as if intoxicated. Onward they go in a state of stupefaction. . . . Arriving in their new home areas they find employment. During the day they work; in the evening and even at night they sit in saloons and other places of amusement. They are now in the land of freedom. . . . And soon they are so far gone that modesty, morality, and conscience are as if they had been torn to shreds.[8]

Actually, it was not always true that immigration and America had ruined the temperate man and maiden from Finland. Often the immigrant contributed to the wickedness of life. In the latter half of the nineteenth century, during the most important period in the history of emigration from Finland, drunkenness and low morality were prevalent there to a frightening degree. Here are two random examples. Matthew Putkonen writes about living conditions among the common people in the 1860s, giving this realistic description of people traveling in a third-class railroad coach:

> But in order to become convinced of how shameless and immoral strong liquor makes those who use it, let us drop into a third-class railroad coach and ride a few times between the cities they connect. We will surely see many of our fellow citizens who are badly intoxicated already at the beginning of their journey. Protruding from the men's pockets we see the necks of bottles containing firewater, which the men handle with the utmost care as if they were cherished idols. But that isn't all. After short intervals the hard tips the bottle to the lips and pours the fiery, lusty liquid into the already burning throat. Then the man offers the bottle to one and another of his friends, encouraging them generously with: You taste this too. . . . Now, would you like to approach these surfeited men of the world and start a conversation with them? Of course not. If nothing else would keep you from it, you would be prevented by the stink that flows from their mouths and sickens anyone who is not accustomed to such a nauseating smell.[9]

Putkonen pictured life among country people. Those who worked in factories and at construction jobs in cities were even more in the grip of beer and liquor. In his book on the Finnish labor movement, in which he strictly avoids all exaggeration, R. H. Oittinen gives the following colorful description of the situation.

> Outdoor workers, especially construction workers, drank constantly. In summer, beer was brought continually to construction sites so that sometimes all the money a man had earned went for his beer debt at the end of the week. Those who wanted to drink in the factories often found some cause for celebration and would let some "hero of the day" pay the check. Young boys often carried drinks to the older men and were given a drink to show that they were becoming men. Upon becoming craftsmen themselves they were already experienced drinkers and were obliged to plan a drinking party for their fellow workers to celebrate the occasion. Whereas beer was drunk copiously during the week, the weekend drink was liquor. It was as though drinking was the only way they knew to use their leisure time. Liquor had to be taken along on island trips; it had to be available on name days, at baptisms, and at funerals, etc. The widespread use of intoxicating

drinks greatly slowed down the spiritual and material progress of the working people.[10]

The first generations of Finnish immigrants came to Michigan, as well as to America as a whole, mostly from conditions similar to those described. At first the majority of even the educated persons among them were not temperance-minded. Thus it was natural for life and customs to continue in America much as they had been in the old country and for evenings and weekends to be spent, as in Finland, in drinking. The drinking that took place among the Finnish immigrants in mining areas of Michigan cannot be blamed on the American way of life, for drinking was about the same among the Finns even in mining towns which were almost completely Finnish in population. Despite the evidence of heavy drinking, it is also to be remembered, however, that the dangers of alcohol were known, perhaps instinctively. Its use was not defended; it was something to be ashamed of. Because of this attitude and because there were among the immigrants many temperate persons, including church people and members of revival groups as well as others, there was a good foundation for the development of the temperance movement.

The Good Templar Period

At first the work of American temperance societies was concentrated mostly in the industrial cities of the eastern states, and it was carried on entirely in the English language. Great numbers of immigrants, insofar as they came from other than Anglo-Saxon countries, were left untouched by it. The small churches, too, that sprang up in the mining areas of Michigan were established for their own members who had come from elsewhere, and they did not generally pay any attention to those who spoke a different language. Before the coming of the Finns, John H. Pitezel, a Methodist minister called Yellow Beard by the Indians, had been a missionary among the Indians of the Copper Country and had preached about temperance.[11] But his mission field and the mission fields of other itinerant preachers like him included only Indians in addition to English-speaking persons.

The situation changed when the Independent Order of Good Templars, which was more or less international, became interested in the Scandinavian immigrants and established a special branch for temperance work and cultural activity among them. From 1882 on, the central office of the Good Templars' Scandinavian branch was in New York. It organized Good Templar groups among the Norwegians of the

Copper Country and among the Swedes of Marquette and Gogebic Counties. The Finns, who had come to America later than the Swedes and Norwegians and were not yet involved in similar activities of their own, were happy to be invited to the Scandinavians' meetings, for the same faith, hundreds of years of shared destiny, and similar customs drew them closer to their north European neighbors than to other nationalities. Since perhaps a third of the early Finnish immigrants had come from Norway, and many others had come from northern Sweden, there were among them considerable numbers of those who understood the Scandinavian languages.[12] It is true that in Finland Snellman had already pronounced the death sentence on Scandinavianism, but the immigrants had hardly been touched by the national-political aspects of Scandinavian-Finnish relations.

The earliest contact between the Finnish immigrants and the Scandinavian Good Templars may have occurred in the mining community of Allouez, a short distance north of Calumet. The Norwegians there had a Good Templar society called the Tornea. In 1883 about half of its members were Finnish, and programs and socials were conducted bilingually. In Calumet a number of Finns belonged to the Norwegian Nora Society. In Ironwood, too, Finns belonged to the Swedish society. In Hancock so many Finns joined the Norwegian Good Templars that to preserve their own identity they urged the Finns to organize a society of their own.

This step had been considered by the Finns for some time, and on February 22, 1885, a small number of them gathered in the Norwegian church on Quincy Hill to organize a temperance society. This first Finnish temperance society in America, which joined the Scandinavian branch of the Good Templar organization, was given the beautiful name of Pohjantahti (North Star). The society's old minutes have disappeared, complained Ilmonen already in 1910, but he was able to report that the following persons were among the first members: Kalle Silfven, Antti Kumlin, Kontra Niiranen, Olli Halonen, Erkki Alamaa, Kustaa Allen, Matti Kakela, Tiitus Lammi, Joonas Koski, Matti Liisanantti, Antti Saaranen, Matti Mikkola, and Juho Ollanketo. Their first concern was to build a more conveniently located hall, for the Norwegians' meeting place was too far away. Land for the project was received as a gift; basket socials and gifts of money provided funds for the purchase of materials. Much of the labor was also donated, and in the summer of 1886 a large hall was completed. This first hall of Pohjantahti was on Quincy Hill, some distance from the center of town.[13]

The second Finnish temperance society was organized in Republic. On a Sunday afternoon in June 1885, a number of Finns were enjoying themselves at a lakeshore when the question of whether it wasn't time to stop drinking and to get into worthwhile activities was brought up. A certain young man got up on a stump and gave an inspiring talk promoting the establishment of a temperance society. A society named the Onnen Aika (Time of Happiness) was organized. Since there was a Swedish Good Templar society, the Klippan, in the area, it was decided to join it for the time being. Seventeen men joined. The Klippan Society had planned a big temperance festival for July and asked the Finns to find a Finnish speaker for the occasion. They invited a young pastor from Hancock, J. K. Nikander, but because he was unable to be present, he sent a copy of his lecture to be read at the festival. An epidemic of a contagious disease spread to Republic, however, and the festival had to be postponed. In the meantime, the Onnen Aika had been accepted as a member of the Good Templar organization. Its first official meeting was held in the Swedish Hall on August 2. Nikander's speech was read on this occasion. "It is doubtful that there has ever been another speech as welcome as the one read at this meeting, where there were not many who had ever heard a temperance lecture," wrote Isak Sillberg, who had attended the meeting. In September a glee club was organized, and a weekly school for little children was started. In November, women began to join the society. On Christmas Day a lottery was held; proceeds went to the temperance society, the children's school, and foreign missions. Those who would have liked to dance at this program were refused permission.[14] The first minutes of the Onnen Aika, which were written on loose sheets of paper, have been lost. Minutes preserved in bound volumes start with November 1888. Inside the cover of the oldest of these is the legend: Minutes of the Scandinavian Finnish Temperance Society Onnen Aika No. 2.

In January 1885, six Finns joined the Norwegian Nora Society of Calumet. They were William Kitti, David Castren, Arvid Rautiola, Alex Alatalo, Heikki Hirvela, and August Toppila. However, they soon came to the conclusion that the Finns of the area should have a society of their own, and so they called an organizational meeting to be held on September 6 in the Temple of Honor Hall. Thirteen men joined this third temperance society organized by Finnish Americans. The name selected for it was Hyvä Toivo (Good Hope). When the Finnish Hall was completed the following spring, the Hyvä Toivo rented it for its meetings at $100 per year. The first meeting was held there on Easter Day, April 25, 1886. Fifty persons, accompanied by a band, marched through the city to the meeting.[15]

At about the same time that the Calumet Hyvä Toivo was organized, a temperance society of the same name was also organized in

Ashtabula Harbor, Ohio. It became the object of the saloonkeepers' wrath and soon ceased activity. The next four societies were organized in Michigan, which may well be called the cradle of the Finnish American temperance movement.

Of the temperance societies organized in 1886 the first was started in Ishpeming. Conditions were such that the reputation of the Finns as a nationality was in danger:

> They were ne'er-do-wells and wasted their precious time packed in saloons, some playing cards, others brawling and swearing, some looking for a fight. Still others sat with arms around each other, drinking toasts to friendship without caring in the least how their families fared. . . . But at long last a shining ray of light burned in the hearts of those who recognized the danger to us as a nationality. . . . That ray of light was the ideal of temperance. When that ideal became clear to our countrymen, several of them met to discuss the future happiness of our people. They came to the unanimous decision that they would sacrifice all their free time to saving our national reputation and our youth. To accomplish this they organized a temperance society and promised each other that they would be total abstainers. Thus the temperance society was the first guardian of our national reputation here in Ishpeming.[16]

The Ishpeming temperance society was organized on January 25 and named Väinö.[17] Fourteen persons became charter members. The first officers are not known, for the earliest records have disappeared. In 1888 the officers were Kaarlo Lahti, William Perttula, Henry Juntunen, and Emil Anttila.[18]

David Castren, the president of the Pohjantähti Temperance Society of Hancock, went to the new Finnish settlement in Atlantic Mine with several other members to organize a temperance society there. A report on the meeting is given in the 221-page history of the Aura Society:

> On May 16, 1886, our countrymen came to carry out the plan they had been considering for some time, that of organizing a temperance society to protect our national reputation and to keep individuals from becoming slaves of liquor. . . . "Aura" was chosen to be its name. Taking into consideration the living conditions of those times, the name was well chosen. For the area was still in its original natural state rather than ready for sowing. The same may be said about the majority of the people there. This Aura [Plow] was created to turn under, the weeds growing in the Finnish nationality and to prepare space for the planting of a fruitful morality.

The Aura Society became number 73 in the Scandinavian division of the Good Templars. John Setig was elected president and I. W. Rovainen, secretary. Meetings were to be held at the home of Olof J. Halonen, and Halonen was to procure special collars to be worn at meetings. These collars and the Good Templars' caps appear to have looked strange to the miners of Atlantic. Apparently spending time in saloons was not disapproved, evidently because there was no other place for people to gather. The only condition mentioned in the history is that "they must not join in card or billiard playing or buy intoxicating drinks for others." The majority, however, decided that card playing was permissible, except in saloons. But a firm stand was taken against the use of liquor, and violators were expelled from the society "without further discussion." The first woman to join the Aura Society was Anna Valpuri Halonen.

According to the minutes of the Valo (Light) Temperance Society of Ironwood, the society was organized at the home of Erick Norman on November 21, 1886, by Herman Helander, a Finnish jeweler who was the Good Templars' representative in the Copper Country.[19] There were sixteen charter members. Among the first officers were John P. Dickley, John Nieminen, Viktor Sandberg, and John Reini.[20]

A temperance society called Kaiku (Echo) was organized in Bessemer on June 26, 1887, but its minutes have not been found. From the ledgers of 1893–1905 it is evident that in 1893 there was only one of the charter members left. He was Elias Eliasson, who returned to Finland around 1900. The Tornea Society at the Allouez mine soon had so many Finns in it that it was listed as a Finnish society in the Good Templars' roster of member societies.[21]

During this period, temperance work had also made good progress in Minnesota, where Pohjan Leimu (Northern Lights) was organized in Tower in 1886. Other societies organized in 1886 were Toivon Tähti (Star of Hope) in Duluth and Kilpi (Shield) in New York Mills. Temperance societies were also organized in the West. In 1886 Ilta Hetki (Eventide) was organized in Lead, South Dakota, and in 1887 Kansan Onni (People's Happiness) in Perry in the same state. There was also one for a short time in Noyon Hill, California, and also one called Lännen Rusko (Western Glow) at the Carbon Coal Mine in Wyoming. Temperance societies organized in the East were Armon Lähde (Fountain of Grace) in Tarrytown, New York, and Hyvä Tahto (Good Will) in Ashtabula Harbor, the latter replacing the defunct Hyvä Toivo.

Of these first eighteen Finnish-American temperance societies, fourteen belonged to the Good Templar organization; the rest were independent. A Finnish translation of the Good Templars' handbook titled *Käsikirja Suomalaisille Temppeleille* was provided, and meetings were conducted according to the form and order outlined in it. Because the Independent Order of Good Templers was a secret society, the Finns, too, had to learn to conduct meetings behind closed doors and to wear insignia of rank and bright-colored badges around their necks or on their breasts. They also had to learn to address one another with peculiar-sounding titles such as Chief Templar for their president, and Titular Templar for the vice president, Chaplain, Marshal, Assistant Marshal, Outside Guard, Inside Guard, etc. The meeting room had a stage for the high officials and a small altar at which the chaplain read a dignified prayer from the handbook, praising God for the protection he gave members of the society and for the opportunity provided them to promote temperance. The sick and needy, especially drunkards and their families, were committed to God's care. The guards at their stations kept outsiders from coming in.

Those who wanted to join the society sat in a waiting room during the opening activities. From there, the marshal brought them into the meeting and introduced them. After a few questions, the rules were read to them and they took the vow of temperance. This was followed by a prayer and a rather lengthy speech about the responsibilities of membership, after which there was a general round of handshaking, and the new members took their place among the older members as equals.

The question of violators, meaning those who had slipped back into using liquor, was frequently an important item at meetings. Occasionally it happened that some honest soul would stand up, confess his error, and beg forgiveness, but usually offenses were revealed by "informers" in person or by letter to the Chief Templar. Sometimes members would report them at meetings. The violator was reprimanded and his violation was recorded in the minutes. After several violations he lost his membership. A record was also kept of members who were ill; they were given aid from a common fund. Toward the end of each meeting there was usually a brief program which included short talks, music, recitations, and group singing. The meeting always closed with a prayer. Open meetings or public socials were also held, which provided an opportunity to present programs about temperance and recruit new members.

According to Ilmonen's estimates, the membership of Finnish-American temperance societies at the end of 1887 was about 700.[22] The Finns, however, did not feel quite at home in the Good Templar organization. One reason was that the main branch in New York was controlled by Swedes, and correspondence was carried on in English or

Swedish, creating difficulties for persons not familiar with those languages as means of formal communication. There were only a few individuals among the Finnish immigrants who were familiar with formal English or Swedish, and these educated persons were seldom members of temperance societies. The Finns born in Norway and Sweden remained in Scandinavian "temples." Another reason was that the custom of meeting behind closed doors was alien to the Finns, especially at first, for they felt there was nothing to hide in temperance work. Quite the contrary. On the other hand, the exemplary organization of the Templars and the ceremonial procedures at meetings inspired confidence. The Finns eventually became accustomed to these things, and they became the heritage of the independent Finnish American temperance movement. Thus, the factors to which the Finns found it impossible to adjust were the foreign leadership and the language barrier.

The Finnish National Temperance Brotherhood

Separation of the Finns from the Good Templars occurred first in Republic. The Onnen Aika Society had received the Finnish translation of the handbook from the Good Templar headquarters in New York but not the bylaws. To remedy this lack, the Finns of Republic translated the bylaws themselves and had them printed. They also sold them to other Finnish temperance societies. The Good Templar organization did not approve this and claimed ownership rights to the Finnish translation of the bylaws. This in turn created dissatisfaction among the temperance people of Republic, who now began to consider establishing a central organization of their own. The same conclusion had been reached by other temperance societies for another reason, namely, the example of Finland where a large central organization, Raittiuden Ystävät, had recently been organized. In 1887 there had also been articles in favor of withdrawal from Swedish leadership in the Finnish newspaper *Uusi Kotimaa* (New homeland), which was published in New York Mills. Onnen Aika of Republic took a decisive step by initiating correspondence about the matter with other societies. Pohjantähti of Hancock, Väinö of Ishpeming, Aura of Atlantic Mine, and Kaiku of Bessemer all agreed that a Finnish national temperance league should be organized and urged Onnen Aika to call a meeting for that purpose. When it was certain that these five societies were in unanimous agreement on withdrawal from the Good Templars, Onnen Aika invited their official representatives to a meeting in Republic on January 19, 1888.[23]

Representatives of Onnen Aika, Väinö, and Pohjantähti attended the meeting. Valo of Ironwood and Aura of Atlantic Mine sent greetings and indicated that they would join later. The thirteen delegates in attendance elected Isak Sillberg chairman and Jafet Lukkarila secretary. The second paragraph of the tersely worded minutes reads. The name suggested by the committee selected by the Onnen Aika Society, Suomalainen Kansallis Raittius Weljeys Seura (The Finnish National Temperance Brotherhood) of North America was approved. (The initials of the Finnish form of the name, SKRV, are commonly used for the organization and will be used in this English translation. It was also commonly called the Brotherhood.) No mention is made in the minutes of the actual formalities of organization. With the approval of the name the organization itself was also approved. With those few words and a minimum of formality, one of the most meaningful decisions in Finnish American history was made, a decision of importance to Finnish immigrants for decades. On the day following its organization the new society was registered and legalized at the office of the local justice of the peace, with the signing of papers to be sent to the offices of the State of Michigan. Pohjantähti Society was entrusted with the task of selecting a seven-member board to serve until the first annual meeting should be held. The members were to be chosen from the Hancock society. A requirement was that they should be true temperance men. This temporary board of directors was to get work started on rules and handbooks with the help of committees chosen by the Onnen Aika and Väinö societies.

The newly organized Brotherhood, as it was first called, began its activities immediately. Pohjantähti held its first meeting on Sunday, January 22, just three days after the Republic meeting and selected the following men for the temporary board: Kalle Silfven, Erik Alamaa, Antti Kumlin, Joonas Koski, Matti Matson, Alfred Liisanantti, and Johan Ollanketo. The newly selected board elected officers immediately, making Kalle Silfven president, Antti Kumlin secretary, and Erik Alamaa treasurer. Simple machinery was thus set up for the work of the Brotherhood. At a meeting held on February 4, the board decided to enter the societies joining the Brotherhood in their books in chronological order, the number assigned becoming in each case a part of the name of the society. This simple device was of great practical value, for it made identification of a particular society in correspondence, records, accounts, etc., very easy. Under this new system of identification the local societies of the Brotherhood were numbered as follows: Pohjantähti no. 1, Onnen Aika no. 2, Väinö no. 3, Valo no. 4, Aura no. 5, and Kaiku no. 6.

After the Republic meeting, the first temperance society organized was Aamurusko (Morning Glow) in Negaunee. The organizational meeting was held in the Finnish church on Sunday, March 11. After a lecture by O. Riikonen, twenty-one men became charter members of the new society, which immediately joined the Brotherhood. Jacob Salo was elected president; Johan Tolonen, vice president and treasurer; A. L. Sorsen, delegate and secretary; Abram Peitso, secretary-treasurer; John Sahlson, reader; John Mursu, custodian; Leander Salo, inside guard; Matti Seikkula, outside guard. The Good Templar bylaws were followed so literally that a "former president" was also elected, and Isak Iivari was chosen for that questionable office. Additional officers elected at an April meeting were a vice-marshal, a "right-hand assistant to the president," and a "left-hand assistant to the president." Meetings were held frequently and new members joined at every one of them so that by June the total membership was seventy-two. Sometimes, at Sunday evening programs, O. Riikonen entertained the audience with a "mechanical picture show," meaning a magic lantern show. Although the society was given the use of the church free of charge, it was not considered suitable for meetings, so the Anthony Hall was rented. The financial condition of the society was poor, for despite good attendance, collections were small, sometimes as little as 49, 35, or even 14 cents. In the initial rush of activity, the formalities of joining the Brotherhood and the payment of membership fees were forgotten, but shortly afterwards the society joined the SKRV as Aamurusko no. 7, and was even represented at the first annual meeting of the Brotherhood, though in a way unofficially.[24]

This first annual meeting was held in Hancock on June 21–23, 1888, and was hosted by Pohjantähti. Sixteen delegates were present, all from Michigan. This group, though small, was capable, as well as knowledgeable about its goals, and it made decisions which became traditions in the Finnish American temperance movement. The bylaws, adapted from the Good Templars' bylaws so as to be better suited to conditions prevailing among the Finns, were approved with the following provision: "Temperance societies must not plan amusements, parades, etc., for Sundays or church holidays." There was a difference of opinion about dancing, for some members were in favor of it as a means of attracting young people. A large majority were against it and approved the following addition to the bylaws: "Dancing is absolutely forbidden, in the name of the temperance society." The handbook prepared by the board was approved. Its rules were familiar for the most part, for they were similar to those known from previous association with the Good Templars. The practice of paying $50 as burial aid to the family of a member when he died was also started at this time. Each local society was to pay a quarterly fee of 20 cents per member to the Brotherhood, which was to pay out the burial aid money from funds thus acquired. For the other expenses of the Brotherhood every local organization was required to pay an annual fee of $10. In the first regular election of the board, the following persons were elected: Isak Sillberg, president; Josef Kuivas, vice president; Jafet Lukkarila, secretary; J. H. Jasberg, treasurer. All of these men were from Republic. Other members elected were Johan Tolonen of Negaunee, and Kalle Lahti and Leander Aho of Ishpeming. Republic became the headquarters of the Brotherhood because all the officers were men of that community. Before the end of the meeting another notable decision was made: The board was to order temperance tracts from Finland to be sold by local societies.[25]

The meeting was followed by a big temperance festival on Midsummers Day, starting a custom which has been practiced for seventy-five years. This first public Finnish American outdoor temperance festival was held on the shore of Portage Lake. The trip from Hancock was made by passenger boat. The public was not yet accustomed to the idea of a serious, idealistic temperance festival but regarded it as an occasion for entertainment, including dancing. Chairs and benches were used as obstacles on the deck of the boat when the young people attempted to dance on the way to the picnic grounds. Later, too, the dance question created many problems for the Brotherhood. Nevertheless, the program presented in a grove of white birches was a complete success. The band played and inspiring talks were given. Tears filled many an eye, for hearts were warmed and moved by the ideal of temperance and by the spirit of nationalism. The surroundings, too, contributed to a feeling of nostalgia, for they reminded many a person of the land of his birth.

When word spread that the Michigan temperance societies had established a central organization, the previously mentioned Iltahetki and Kansan Onni of South Dakota and Pohjan Leimu and Toivon Tähti of Minnesota, as well as Savotar (Lady of Savo), which had been organized on April 9 in Frederick, South Dakota, joined the SKRV before the end of 1888. Toward the end of this year, two more societies were organized in Michigan, both joining the Brotherhood immediately. The first of these was Onnen Aarre (Treasure of Happiness) no. 13 in Newberry on December 16. Among its first officers were Emil Leppäluoto, John Erickson, and Jacob Pukkila.[26]

On December 23, Koitto (Dawn) no. 14 was organized at the Peninsular Mine to the north of Hancock. It was to have a long and eventful history. The community soon became known as Boston and the temperance society was better known as the Boston Temperance Society. The old records have disappeared, but according to the SKRV roster, some of the first officers were John Rautio, Antti Palola, Jacob Erkkila, Matti Kinnunen, and Matti Immonen.[27] Thus, by the end of 1888, its year of organization, the Brotherhood had fourteen member societies, of which nine were in Michigan, three in South Dakota, and two in Minnesota.

On New Year's Day 1889, the temperance society Toivo (Hope) no. 15 was organized in Wakefield through the initiative of Louis Anderson, who had previously been a member of the Valo Society of Ironwood. Sixteen persons joined as charter members. By the next year they had a hall of their own, unpretentious though it was.[28] In addition to Toivo of Wakefield, four other societies were organized in the state in 1889. Turva (Security) of Sault Ste. Marie began on February 10, with Andrew Vesa and John Stolt as two of its officers. The society, however, ceased activity already in December of the same year when members moved away from the area. It was reactivated almost ten years later. On May 6 Kointähti (Morning Star) no. 18 was organized in Champion. On Sunday, May 12, Taimi (Seedling) was organized in Palmer, and a week later the Kaleva no. 20 was started in Kearsarge. Societies of other states joining the Brotherhood in 1889 were Pohjolan Lempi (Sweetheart of the North), which was organized in Brainerd, Minnesota, on February 4; Valpas (Alert) of Seward, South Dakota, organized on June 24; and Aamun Koitto (Daybreak) of Fitchburg, Massachusetts, organized on September 20. Thus, in less than two years, twenty-five temperance societies had joined the Brotherhood, seventeen of them in Michigan. The beginning looked promising. A bright future was also indicated by the second annual meeting, which was held in Ishpeming in June 1889 with twenty-four delegates from seventeen societies in attendance. Because five of these societies were represented by proxy, the number of delegates was actually nineteen, which was considered quite satisfactory. The subject discussed most extensively was the starting of a newspaper to be the voice of temperance and of the SKRV. Fredrik Karinen of Ishpeming volunteered to edit it, on condition that the Brotherhood establish a printing company and procure the necessary machinery. This of course would have been overwhelmingly expensive. As a workable alternative, the SKRV offered Karinen $150 per year to promote temperance through his own newspaper and to publish temperance news in it. The burial aid fund, which had been started by the board, was officially approved. On the death of a member who had kept up his payments, $50 would be paid from the common fund as burial aid, the fund to be accumulated by the collection of 20 cents per quarter from every member. This arrangement was in effect permanently. Onnen Aika suggested setting up a life insurance plan. Although support was cordial, the Brotherhood did not dare to undertake one at the time. With the approval of the Brotherhood such an insurance did materialize later on with its own operative machinery. The publishing of *Raittiuskalenteri* (Temperance calendar) was also considered but did not become a reality until many years later. At the temperance festival that followed the meeting the speaker was Pastor K. L. Tolonen, a former president of the Helsinki Koitto Temperance Society, who had just arrived from Finland. This was the first personal contact between the temperance movement of Finland and the Finnish American temperance movement.

The Friends of Temperance Organization

Differences of opinion which at first appeared to be extremely serious developed among the temperance people. Hyvä Toivo Society was organized in Calumet in 1885 and approved as no. 21 of the Brotherhood on June 2, 1889.[29] In the annual meeting of the SKRV held in Ishpeming on July 18–19, the representatives of Hyvä Toivo recommended that the handbook of the Brotherhood be revised and that the twelfth section of the bylaws be deleted. This paragraph read as follows:

> Let not the board of the Brotherhood or any local society sponsor, in the name of the society, public outdoor amusements such as parades or other similar activities on Sundays or holidays, excepting socials or other activities like them, which contribute to the development of temperance and temperance societies. These latter are permissible even on Sundays, and all friends of temperance are encouraged to plan them and to take part in them.

This implies that the question was one of allowing greater freedom in the planning of programs by local societies. A proposal was also made to remove from the handbook the regulation prohibiting dancing and the one about compulsory prayer. The representatives of the Hyvä Toivo Society did not receive any support, just the assurance that they had the right to bring their recommendation for a new handbook to the next annual meeting. Hyvä Toivo went on the warpath and began to publish articles in *Työmies* and *Amerikan Suometar* newspapers against the tyranny of the Brotherhood and its board of directors. At a meeting held in Ishpeming on November 28, 1889, the board of directors presented an ultimatum to the Calumet society: either prove the truth of the accusations or beg forgiveness for them, or be ousted from the SKRV. Since repentance was not forthcoming, the board expelled Hyvä Toivo from the Brotherhood on December 27.[30] The separation was so definitely final that no. 27, Hyvä Toivo's number, was assigned to another society, Vartija (Guardian), also of Calumet. The desire for more freedom for local societies was not the only reason for the crisis which had developed, perhaps not even the basic one. Another was that in both of the annual meetings held thus far, the Copper Country societies had been ignored in the election of members for the Brotherhood's board of directors. It was thought that a new organization might remedy this situation. Adopting the name of the Finnish Friends of Temperance (Raittiuden Ystävät) for the new organization also pointed to nationalistic influences.

The organizational meeting was held in 1890, on January 19, or St. Henry's Day, which commemorates the martyrdom of the patron saint of Finland. Most of the first board members were from Calumet. None of the recommended radical changes were made in the rules of the new central organization. Prayers were not eliminated, but a less restrictive attitude was taken toward young people's amusements and toward Sunday entertainments.[31] The establishment of this second central organization was expected to lead to continued open conflict in the divided temperance movement, but such was not the case. The ideal of temperance produced such a powerful spirit of brotherhood in temperance people that those who belonged to different societies in the same community felt that they were fighting together for the same cause and the same goal. Neighborly relations were good, members visited each other's society meetings, and during annual meetings the customary friendly greetings by telegram were exchanged. In addition, competition between the two groups may well have promoted the cause of temperance.[32] By the end of the century, thirty-three local societies had joined the Friends of Temperance organization, which followed the custom of the Brotherhood in assigning numbers to the societies according to the order of their joining.

Seventeen of these societies were in Michigan (see table 12). There were six societies in Minnesota that belonged to the Friends of Temperance organization, three in Wyoming, two in Wisconsin, and one each in Montana, Washington, Massachusetts, and Canada.[33]

Despite the fairly large number of societies that belonged to it, the Friends of Temperance organization was weak in comparison with the SKRV. It was able to finance the publication of *Raittiuden Ystäväin Kalenteri* (Friends of temperance calendar) for only two years, 1900 and

Table 12: Friends of Temperance Societies in Michigan

NAME	COMMUNITY	DATE OF JOINING
Hyvä Toivo no. 1	Calumet	January 9, 1890*
Huvi-Leima no. 3	Jacobsville	March 23, 1890
Onni no. 5	Dollar Bay	November 30, 1890
Toivola no. 6	Crystal Falls	November 27, 1890
Pohjantähti no. 7	Hancock	December 28, 1890
Kansan Hyvä no. 8	Allouez	November 1, 1891
Valon Säde	Hancock	November 1, 1891
Toivon Ruusu no. 11	Halfway, Jacobsville	March, 1892
Längelmä no. 12	Copper Falls	April, 1893
Raivaaja no. 13	East Tawas	August 13, 1893
Riento no. 15	Ishpeming	July 16, 1894
Elon Tähti no. 16	Allouez	July, 1894
Saaren Kukka no. 17	Kearsarge	July, 1894
Koitto no. 23	Ironwood	September 22, 1895
Sovinto no. 26	Bessemer	March 12, 1896
Suoja no. 30	Bessemer	February 19, 1898
Valon Alku no. 33	Arcadian Mine	November 20, 1898

* Joseph Gaberson, *RYK*, 1900, p. 7f., from which this list is taken, gives this date, which is the date on which the Friends of Temperance organization was established. January 19 was the date given by Ilmonen.

1901. At the turn of the century the organization had only ten active societies; the others had become defunct or had joined the SKRV, from which only a few had come into the Friends organization. The following cases throw some light on the situation. Pohjantähti of Hancock, which had many members, belonged to the Friends of Temperance for only a short while, for the decision to join the Friends had been made during a blizzard, when only a few people had come to the decisive meeting. The decision was rescinded at the following meeting, which was held in nice weather with more persons in attendance. Elon Tähti (Star of Life) of Allouez, organized in 1894, ceased activity already the next year, when its members joined the Saaren Kukka (Island Flower) of Kearsarge. This Saaren Kukka was one of the strongest members of the Friends of Temperance organization, building a hall the very first year of its existence and paying for it in a very short time.[34] Huvi-Leima (Sign of Pleasure) of Jacobsville built a small hall "where dancing was about the most important thing on the program." Two members of the society are said never to have broken their vow of temperance. In 1899 the society had six active members.[35] In Ishpeming some of the persons who had left the Väinö Society, organized a new one called Orpo (Orphan) on January 26, 1892. Its name was changed to Riento (Endeavor) when it joined the Friends of Temperance. Its membership was about 130. There were difficulties with regard to a meeting place, until the hall above the Finnish Cooperative Store on Division Street became available to them. The lively competition between Väinö and Riento redounded to the advantage of the temperance movement.

Onni Temperance Society of Dollar Bay, which was organized in 1890, was exceptionally active. Its membership was usually about fifty. At first it included Swedish Finns, who organized their own society in 1899. In 1898 Onni Society acquired its own large hall, in which dancing was forbidden and in which both Swedish and Finnish Lutheran pastors conducted worship services regularly. An unknown writer gives recognition to the achievements of temperance work in Dollar Bay in the following words:

> The names of many family men who formerly amused themselves in saloons are now on the roster of the Friends of Temperance. They have become the real support and security of their homes. Tears of sorrow have changed to tears of joy. Thus, the scythe of temperance has cut away misery and poverty from the drunkard's home, in which peace and love now reign.[36]

In Bessemer, the activity of the Kaiku Society slowed down considerably. The somewhat obscure ledgers of the society indicate that at the end of 1897 the membership was about thirty-five at the most. There would have been plenty of room for others in the society. But the usual discontent caused by the narrow-mindedness of the Brotherhood prevailed, and so, on February 20, 1898, a meeting was held for the purpose of organizing another temperance society. The society, which immediately joined the Friends of Temperance, was called Suoja (Shelter). Its large hall was completed in the summer of 1900. In Bessemer, too, the organization of another society created new enthusiasm for temperance work. The Kaiku, which had been half dormant, tripled its membership within two years. The Suoja's membership increased to over a hundred. There was such harmony between the two societies that programs were always planned for different times so that members of each could attend the programs of the other and even take part in them.[37]

The Brotherhood, 1890–1902: 146 New Temperance Societies

The thirteen years following the organization of the Friends of Temperance were a period of great growth in the SKRV and in Finnish American temperance work in general. Immigration from Finland was increasing rapidly. The Finnish settlements already established saw the numbers of their countrymen double and triple. New settlements also sprang up in twenty states and in Canada. The temperance movement was sufficiently flexible and the temperance workers had sufficient initiative to cope with the ever more demanding situation. Proof of this is in the 146 temperance societies which were organized in these years and joined the Brotherhood. For a clear picture of the situation they are all listed here. The number after the name of each society is its number in the SKRV, and the date before each name is the date on which the society joined the Brotherhood. When the date of organization is different, separate mention is made of it in parentheses.

1890

2/2 Valon Leimu no. 26, Rockport, Mass. (July 1884)
5/5 Lannen Rusko no. 27, Nanaimo, British Columbia
2/16 Valo Nuorempi no. 28, Rocklin, Calif.
4/9 Ilmarinen no. 29, Cloquet, Minn.
4/5 Sovittaja no. 30, Worcester, Mass.
5/30 Huvitus no. 31, Baraga, Mich.
5/11 Kalevan Miekka no. 32, Montreal, Wis.
5/29 Kannel no. 33, West Superior, Wis.
6/15 Valon Säde no. 34, Jesseville, Mich.
8/4 Vuoriston Ruusu no. 35, Hanna, Wyo.
8/25 Valon Toivo no. 36, Tacoma, Wash.
8/25 Tyyni Valo no. 37, Portland, Ore.
9/20 Laakson Kukka no. 38, Red Lodge, Mont.
9/27 Onni no. 39, Carbonado, Wash.
10/8 Rauhan Toivo no. 40, Brooklyn, N.Y.
12/14 Uljas Koitto no. 41, Quincy, Mass.

1891

3/30 Onnen Koitto no. 42, Port Arthur, Ont.
4/5 Jalo no. 43, Dana, Wyo.
5/7 Pelastaja no. 44, Lanesville, Mass.
9/20 Niemen Neiti no. 45, Dollar Bay, Mich.

10/26 Erämaan Tähti no. 46, Mezaba, Minn.
11/4 Voiton Kilpi no. 47, Niantic, Conn.
12/12 Kultala no. 48, West Gardner, Mass.

1892

1/25 Miekka no. 49, New York Mills (Nov. 1886)
2/28 Toivon Taimi no. 50, Pequaming, Mich.
3/27 Urho no. 51, Hurley, Wis.
6/19 Lännen Toivo no. 52, Fort Bragg, Calif.
8/28 Vellamo no. 53, Mansfield Mine, Mich.
9/11 Sivistys no. 54, Dunn Mine, Mich.
9/18 Toivola no. 55, Crystal Falls, Mich. (Nov. 27, 1890)
10/31 Ilmiö no. 56, Biwabik, Minn.
12/1 Ilon Ääni no. 57, Sand Coulee, Mont.
12/13 Erämaan Tähti Nuorempi no. 58, Glen Rock, Wyo.

1893

1/21 Rauhan Satama no. 59, Long Cove, Me.
2/25 Lännen Lilja no. 60, Burnett, Wash.
3/12 Valon Tuote no. 61, Virginia, Minn.
3/26 Onnen Kukka no. 62, Chassell, Mich.
4/23 Toivon Leimu no. 63, Vinal Haven, Me.
7/2 Rauhan Koti no. 64, Marfield, Minn.
9/13 Murtaja no. 65, San Francisco, Calif.
10/15 Siirtola no. 66, Chicago, Ill.
10/15 Sulo no. 67, Jacksonville, Ohio.
12/17 Pelastuksen Sankari no. 68, Sault Ste. Marie, Ont.

1894

2/4 Kasvi no. 69, Fairport Harbor, Ohio
4/3 Elo no. 70, Ontonagon, Mich.
4/12 Kannan Kukka no. 71, Belt, Mont.
6/10 Kuringon Säde no. 72, Rock Springs, Wyo.
6/17 Kaivajain Kuisto no. 73, Leadville, Colo.
8/5 Ahti no. 74, Waukegan, Ill.
8/5 Into no. 75, Clarks Island, Me.
8/12 Ilo-huuto no. 76, Cambria, Wyo.
10/7 Oras no. 77, New York, N.Y.
11/4 Uusi Kasvi no. 78, West Gardner, Mass.
10/28 Aamunkoitto no. 79, Brooklyn, N.Y. (Jan. 16, 1887)

11/18 Oikeuden Ohje no. 80, Copper Cliff, Ont.
11/25 Sampo no. 81, Pigeon Cove, Mass.
12/2 Suoja no. 82, Anita, Pa.

1895

1/31 Toivon Säde no. 83, Whiting, Ind.
3/17 Alku no. 84, Maynard, Mass.
4/21 Hedelmä no. 85, Warren, Ohio
5/12 Kilpi no. 86, Conneaut, Ohio
6/30 Iltarusko no. 87, Trout Creek, Mich.
7/5 Lännen Tähti no. 88, Eureka, Calif.
7/21 Valon Kipene no. 89, Iron Belt, Wis.
7/21 Valon Lähde no. 90, Eveleth, Minn.
8/11 Tapio no. 91, Hibbing, Minn.[38]
11/8 Askel no. 92, Grand Marais, Mich.
12/15 Taistelia no. 93, Salem, Mass.
12/12 Uusi Toivo no. 94, New Castle, Pa.

1896

1/5 Toivon Alku no. 95, Girard, Ohio
1/2 Boston Koti no. 96, Brighton, Mass.
1/26 Onnela no. 97, Iron Mountain, Mich.
2/9 Ilon Säde no. 98, Opechee, Mich.
2/9 Vilpas no. 99, Estelline, So. Dak.
3/22 Kylvö no. 100, DeKalb, Ill.
3/15 Korven Kukka no. 101, Amasa, Mich.
3/23 Idän Tähti no. 102, Marlborough, N.H.
5/3 Kullervo no. 103, Cooks, Mich.
5/31 Väinötär no. 104, National Mine, Mich.
6/22 Virran Lapsi no. 105, Bonner, Mont.
7/24 Kipinä no. 106, Bessemer, Pa.
9/13 Vilpas Kokelas no. 107, East Jaffery, N.Y.
10/12 Toivon Uutinen no. 108, Clinton, Ind.

1897

1/3 Järven Kukka no. 109, Sparta, Minn.
2/10 Sorretun Alku no. 110, West Quincy, Mass.
8/10 Onnen Aamu no. 111, Mullan, Idaho
11/20 Uusi Vartija no. 112, Calumet, Mich.

1898

1/30	Morgon Stjernan no. 113, Ironwood, Mich.
2/20	Vuoriston Tähti no. 114, Scofield, Utah
3/13	Alku no. 115, Jersey City and Hoboken, N.Y.
4/24	Nord no. 116, Bessemer, Mich.
5/1	Aalto no. 117, Marquette, Mich.
6/18	Österbotten no. 118, Negaunee, Mich.
7/17	Runeberg no. 119, Eveleth, Minn.
7/17	Tyyni no. 120, Erie, Pa.
11/6	Onnen Toivo no. 121, Burton, Ohio
11/17	Valon Nousu no. 122, Iron Belt, Wis.
12/11	Kanerva no. 123, Diamondville, Wyo.
?	Ilon Toivo no. 124, Stockett, Mont. (April 10, 1898)

1899

2/5	Onnen Tuki no. 125, French Lake, Minn.
2/6	Liljan i Dalen no. 126, Amasa, Mich.
3/14	Onnen Ääni no. 127, Floodwood, Minn.
3/26	Vuoriston Ruusu no. 128, Troy, N.H.
4/16	Stjernan i Hemmet no. 129, Crystal Falls, Mich.
4/30	Topelius no. 130, Iron Mountain, Mich.
5/14	Söner af Vasa no. 131, Gladstone, Mich.
5/21	Klippan no. 132, Ludington, Mich.
7/9	Viheriä Ruusu no. 133, Greenland, Mich.
9/10	Otava no. 134, Fulton, Mich.
11/19	Skogens Ljus no. 135, Parginton, Mich.
11/28	Onnen Satama no. 136, Covington, Mich.
12/17	Yrittäjä no. 137, Stambaugh, Mich.
12/17	Nouse no. 138, Arcadian Mine, Mich.
12/17	Metsän Opas no. 139, Welch, Mich.

1900

1/20	Vasa no. 140, Butte, Mont.
2/18	Sakari Topelius no. 141, Princeton, Mich.
4/29	Helmi no. 142, Elba Mine, McKinley, Minn.
4/19	Norden no. 143, Eureka, Utah
5/20	Ahto no. 144, Aberdeen, Wash.
5/27	Raivaaja no. 145, Michigamme, Mich.
6/16	Erämaan Tähti no. 146, Clear Creek, Utah
6/24	Taisto no. 147, Holmes City, Minn.

9/16 Enighet no. 148, Dollar Bay, Mich.
10/21 Liljan pä Fjellen no. 149, Metropolitan, Mich.
10/28 Kyntäjä no. 150, Copper Range Mine, Mich.
12/9 Auran Kukka no. 151, Baltic Mine, Mich.

1901

1/5 Libanon no. 152, Norwood, Mass.
3/3 Suomi no. 153, East Cambridge, Mass.
7/21 Taimen Oksa no. 154, Munising, Mich.
9/19 Muisto no. 155, Chisholm, Minn.
10/6 Pellervo no. 156, Rapid River, Mich.
10/13 Voiton Tähti no. 157, Hurontown, Mich.
10/13 Hoppet no. 158, Ashland, Wis.

1902

1/5 Murtimon Toivo no. 159, Lyons, Colo.
1/12 Kalevatar no. 160, Kaleva, Mich.
1/12 Nurmen Kukka no. 161, Amasa, Mich.
2/2 Onnen Alku no. 162, Neihant, Mont. (Dec. 10, 1899)
3/23 Niemen Ruusu no. 163, Waino, Wis.
6/1 Hem i Enighet no. 164, Escanaba, Mich.
6/16 Morgon Rodnan no. 165, Telluride, Colo.
7/20 Stjernan af Finland no. 166, Bingham, Utah
7/20 Onni no. 167, Stevenson Mine, Minn.
10/5 Lännen Koitto no. 168, Everett, Wash.
10/12 Sjöman af Suomi no. 169, Marshfield, Ore.
10/19 Vesa no. 170, Glassport, Pa.
11/2 Koivula no. 171, Romley, Mich.

The names of many of these societies suggest the conditions under which they were formed or the hopes and expectations of their founders that the societies would bring about changes for the better. "Hope," "Light," and "Happiness," which are names of conditions that were grievously lacking in many homes, were frequently used. Temperance work was literally a struggle to rescue men from the saloons and to find peace and happiness for their families. Nationalistic names such as Suomi, Runeberg, Topelius, Kalevan Miekka, Kalevatar, Stjernan af Finland (Star of Finland), Söner of Vasa (Sons of Vaasa), and Ilmarinen make up a small minority. Not until temperance work had begun to bear fruit and the level of morality among the Finns had been raised was attention focused on national and other cultural matters.

Of the 171 temperance societies which joined the SKRV from 1885 to 1902, 63 were in Michigan. The Finnish and Swedish Finnish temperance societies outside Michigan were distributed as follows: Minnesota 20, Massachusetts 14; Wisconsin and Montana seven each; Ohio and Wyoming six each; Pennsylvania, New York, South Dakota, and Washington five each; California and Canada four each; Maine, Illinois, Utah, and Colorado three each; New Hampshire, Indiana, and Oregon two each; and Connecticut and Idaho one each. Thus, Michigan was still in the vanguard of the Finnish-American temperance movement.

The following brief survey of the temperance societies organized in Michigan between 1890 and 1902 gives some idea of the situation with regard to temperance work all over the country.

A week before the organization of the Friends of Temperance in Calumet on January 19, 1890, a temperance society called Pohjola (North) no. 25 was organized at the Allouez Mine, but it left the SKRV already in April of the following year. The next society organized in Michigan was Huvitus no. 31, in Baraga, on May 30, 1890. It also ceased activity the following year. The direct cause of the failure of this society was drinking, which reduced the ranks of temperance people so much that meetings could not be held. Huvitus recovered, however, and became active again in the fall of the following year. Membership increased and a hall was planned. There was only $15 in the treasury, but gifts of money and the aid of sister societies made it possible for the Huvitus to meet under its own roof by March 1892.[39] From the very beginning the temperance hall in Baraga was used as the Lutheran church and it continued to be so used for decades.

A temperance society was organized in Jessieville, near Ironwood, on June 15, 1890. In honor of Valo (Light) Society of Ironwood it was name Valon Säde (Ray of Light) and became number 34.[40] The next society in Michigan was not organized until September 20, 1891, when the Finns of Dollar Bay organized Niemen Neiti no. 45, which was not active long. It apparently ceased activity early because the vigorous Onni Society, which has already been mentioned as having been organized some time before, was sufficient for local needs.

The first society organized in 1892 in connection with the Brotherhood was the Toivon Taimi (Seedling of Hope) no. 50, in Pequaming on the forested shore of Lake Superior, on February 28. By the time of its fifth anniversary celebration, 148 persons had taken the pledge. Membership varied from 20 to 50, and the spirit of the society was praised as being serious and idealistic. Because of a decrease in the Finnish population, 1901–2 was the last year of activity for the Toivon Taimi.[41]

On August 28, 1892, Vellamo no. 53 was organized at the Mansfield Mine in Iron County with fourteen charter members. At first, meetings were held at the homes of Isak Williams and August Mattila at a rental of one dollar per month. The society made money by selling soft drinks and cigars at meetings and by sponsoring socials. The membership was young, and illness is seldom mentioned in the minutes, but violations of the pledge were discussed at almost every meeting. In the fall of 1893 a serious accident occurred in the Mansfield Mine and work stopped. When the Finns moved elsewhere to seek employment, the Vellamo ceased activity. It was reactivated two years later when the mine was put into operation again. The first meeting after reactivation was held on Easter Sunday, April 14, 1895. Work continued regularly, but it was limited in scope.[42] On September 11, 1892, a society was also organized at the Dunn Mine in Iron County and named Sivistys (Culture) no. 54, but with the closing of the mine the following year the Sivistys also ceased activity.[43]

On November 27, 1890, Toivola (Place of Hope) Temperance Society was organized in Crystal Falls and immediately joined the Friends of Temperance as number 6. There were seventy-one charter members, and activity began with unusual momentum. By spring the society already had a spacious hall, which was made considerably larger at the end of the century. Toivola did not, however, stay on as a member of the Friends of Temperance but on September 18, 1892, joined the SKRV as number 55.[44] The names most often mentioned in the old minutes are those of Herman Hendrickson and Matti Hurja, the latter as having, among other things, borrowed money to pay the debt on the hall. Toivola was one of the first temperance societies to place crosses on the graves of departed members. As far as the practical work of a temperance society outside its own membership goes, Toivola was in the forefront. Although many of the Finnish American societies limited their work to their own nationality, Toivola was concerned about the liquor situation in general. For example, in 1895 and 1901, committees were selected to see that liquor regulations were followed in the saloons of Crystal Falls. Another project was the publication of a handwritten paper titled *Raittiuden Kehitys* (Progress of temperance) for the enrichment of temperance programs. It started publication on September 30, 1894, with Herman Hendrickson as editor. From 1900 on, the paper was called simply *Kehitys.* Gust Kangas was the editor. In 1894 a choral group was started and soon after, an organ was acquired. A year later a four-man committee was selected to get a women's sewing club started. This unusual occurrence was frequently referred to in later programs. A lending library was established in 1893, and in 1894 a "sickness aid company" was organized in connection with the society. After much discussion, a drama club was also organized. It gave its first performance on July 1, 1894, but the name of the play has been forgotten. The pioneers and leaders of the dramatic activity were Elias Puotinen and Herman Hendrickson. On September 15, 1895, a "speakers' club" was organized to help members in the art of appearing before the public. Evening socials were planned for the good of the church, and as early as the spring of 1895 a program was planned for the benefit of Suomi College. Interest in Suomi College continued, and on September 29, 1901, an association whose purpose was to help support Suomi College was organized.[45]

No additional societies in Michigan joined the SKRV until six months after the Toivola of Crystal Falls had joined, a relatively long time for this period of rapid growth in the temperance movement. The next society to join was Onnen Kukka (Flower of Happiness) no. 62, organized in Chassell on March 26, 1893. This society ceased activity in the summer of 1897 but was reactivated on March 27, 1898. Even after this second attempt, it was not of long duration. After Onnen Kukka, almost a year passed before another temperance society was organized in the state, this one in Ontonagon. On April 3, 1894, Elämän Lanka (Thread of Life) no. 70 was organized, receiving the name Elo (Life) soon after. After the great fire destroyed the city of Ontonagon in the summer of 1896, Elo ceased activity for seven years.

In 1895 two new societies in Michigan joined the SKRV. The first was Iltarusko (Evening Glow) no. 87, organized in Trout Creek on June 30 by Alex Pantti, who had been sent there by the Brotherhood. Eighteen members registered at the time. By September of the next year so much progress had been made that it was decided to build a hall to be used for cultural purposes. The hall was ready in time for the Christmas program. Temperance work was carried on diligently and discipline was good, judging by the fact that violators of the pledge were expelled at almost every meeting. It was the responsibility of the president to announce the names of violators at the meetings, a custom which was generally followed in temperance societies. Once when the chairman of the Iltarusko did not make the expected announcement the secretary, Henry Mämmi, commented rather sharply in the minutes: "The chairman knew absolutely nothing about charges [of violation]." The Finnish population gradually became very small, and Iltarusko's last meeting was held in Trout Creek on October 21, 1900. The society was reactivated a few years later in Herman.[46] The other society organized in 1895 was Urhoolinen Askel (Courageous Step) no. 92, in Grand Marais on November 8. It died at its birth but was reactivated on May 16, 1897, with its name shortened to Askel.

In 1896 five new societies were organized in Michigan and joined the Brotherhood. The first one was Kilpailija (Competitor) no. 97 of Iron Mountain, on January 26, but it ceased activity after six months. It was reactivated on March 5, 1899, when twenty-two persons joined. Its name was changed at that time to Onnela (Place of Happiness). The reactivation was the accomplishment of Matti Hurja, who gave a powerful temperance speech on the occasion. Closed meetings were the rule, but on Good Friday an open meeting was held, and all were welcome. The room in which they met and which they called a hall was rented from the president of the society for 50 cents per session. Onnela Society, too, was short-lived because the Finns moved away from the area. The last meeting was held in April 1900. The only property left was nineteen songbooks.[47]

On February 9, Ilon Säde (Gleam of Joy) no. 98 was organized at the Opechee Mine in Osceola near Calumet with twenty-two members. It withdrew from the Brotherhood on January 20, 1902, because of the "strictness of the rules." The secretary of the Brotherhood, however, noted in the minutes that the separation of Ilon Säde from the SKRV was due to "the very light-minded attitude" of the members of the society.[48] On March 15 Korven Kukka (Flower of the Wilderness) no. 101 was organized in Amasa. The society had a humble beginning and endured the hardships of the early settlers, especially during the first four years, when the members had to be satisfied to meet in inconvenient places. That matter was taken care of and activity got new impetus when a two-story hall was completed in 1900. The meetings of Korven Kukka were held upstairs and the congregation held worship services in the downstairs area, which was furnished as a church from the very beginning. The cooperation between the temperance society and the congregation worked to the advantage of both. The minutes of the society indicate the serious moral attitudes of the majority of members: spiritually rich material was favored for programs, violators were handled with firmness, and a combined effort was made with Swedish and American temperance societies to see that liquor laws were observed in saloons.[49]

Kullervo no. 103, organized in Cooks in Schoolcraft County on May 3, 1896, was in a class by itself. It was the lumberjacks' temperance society, its members being men who worked in the great forests north of Rapid River. Just after the turn of the century the president of the society was Samuel Krankkala, who later became a pastor of the National Church. John Wiljanen, who had arrived from Finland in 1899, was secretary at the time, and his brother Victor was vice president. The Kullervo built a small hall, which was moved from place to place as lumbering progressed and the location of the men's bunkhouses was changed. The congregation used the hall free of charge.[50] Women were important in the activity of the Kullervo Society. Sources mention Amanda Lovisa Kulju, born in Töysä in 1852, who died of tuberculosis in Cooks on November 4, 1899, leaving her husband and two children. They also mention Hilda Johanna Heinonen, born in Alavus, who died at the birth of her first child on June 13, 1900, at only twenty-five years of age. The fate of these women gives some idea of the hard conditions under which the wives of the lumberjacks lived. One of the leading men was Tapani Heikkila, born in Pudasjärvi in 1860, who was often a delegate at SKRV annual meetings.[51] When the transient workers left because employment in the lumbering business had become less available and the jobs that were available were in the hands of nondrinking family men, Kullervo considered its work finished and ceased activity, leaving its hall to the congregation of Metsistö.

On May 31, 1896, a temperance society named Väinötär no. 104 was organized at National Mine, near Ishpeming, with twenty-one charter members. So many Finns from Kuortane lived in the area that they comprised almost half the membership of Väinötär. Because of the employment situation, so many Finns moved away from the community that the society was forced to suspend its activities in the summer of 1899.[52] It was reactivated on February 16, 1902, under the new name of Elon Tähti (Star of Life).[53]

In 1897 only one new temperance society of Michigan joined the Brotherhood. It was Uusi Vartija (New Guard), which began activity in Calumet with ten members on November 20. Of the Calumet temperance societies, Hyvä Toivo had joined the Friends of Temperance some time before, and Vartija had left the SKRV in 1896. Uusi Vartija gave the Brotherhood a new foothold in this important center of Finnish population. The meetings were held in the Kansanvalistusseura Hall. The membership was only about seventy despite the large Finnish population of the area. Uusi Vartija followed the custom of free admission to their meetings, even of those who did not belong to the society. Visitors were always welcomed as guests of honor.[54]

In 1898 the Swedish Finns in America began to participate in temperance work through societies of their own, which will be discussed later. This year, only one Finnish-language society in Michigan joined the SKRV. It was Aalto (Wave) no. 117 of Marquette, organized on May 1 with eleven charter members. The Finnish population of Marquette at this time was small and life in general was primitive and wild. Many of those who were trying to create and establish a new way of life were swept back into old habits, and violations were common. All the more worthy of respect is the work of those men and women who stood courageously at their posts until a better day arrived.[55]

In 1899 six new Finnish temperance societies in Michigan joined the Brotherhood. The first of them was Viheriä Ruusu (Green Rose) no. 133, organized in Greenland on July 9. In the fall of 1901, when Mass had become the center of Finnish population in the area, Viheriä Ruusu moved there and built a hall. The following winter, members who were indifferent to the idea of temperance were the majority and voted to leave the SKRV and changed the name of the hall to Kansan Koti (People's Home). The minority fought this action and, with the assistance of the board of directors of the SKRV and the attorney Oscar Larson, succeeded in getting the situation back to normal, if only temporarily.[56] The second society organized in 1899 was Otava (Big Dipper) no. 134 of Fulton, near Mohawk, on September 10. The hall was built in Mohawk, which became the home of the society. The minutes of the first years have disappeared and with them all information about the early activities of the society.[57]

On November 28, 1899, Onnen Satama (Port of Happiness) no. 136 was organized in Covington with Annie Wooke representing the Brotherhood. A former lumber company mess camp behind Hutula's farm was purchased for $100 and remodeled into a spacious hall. The first social held there enabled Onnen Satama to pay half the price of the hall. At the same time, its membership increased from eighteen to thirty-six. Sometime in 1909, malicious-minded persons broke into the hall and destroyed the oldest minutes and other records of the society.[58] In spite of its small size the Covington society was extremely active because of the energetic and skillful temperance worker John K. Kytölä, who had moved there from Calumet. He was born in Teuva on June 29, 1867, arrived in America in 1900, and died on December 14, 1945. Kytölä was a good speaker and illustrated his lectures with lantern slides. The magic lantern was new to listeners and attracted capacity audiences to temperance halls wherever Kytölä appeared on his lecture tours. His wife, Aurora Lönnquist Kytölä, worked for temperance beside her husband.[59]

On December 17, 1899, three temperance societies were organized in Michigan. This may well be the record number for one day in the history of the Finnish American temperance movement. They were

Yrittäjä (Striver) no. 137 of Stambaugh, Nouse (Arise) no. 138 of Arcadian Mine, and Metsän Opas (Forest Guide) no. 139 of Welch. Yrittäjä was organized by members of the Toivola Temperance Society of Crystal Falls at the request of the Brotherhood.[60] Members of Pohjantähti of Hancock went to Concord City at Arcadian Mine to organize Nouse, which twenty-one members joined. Meetings were first held upstairs of the home of Matt Johnson, the president of the society, but when it became inconvenient to meet there, they were held in the Swedish Hall. When the Arcadian Mine closed down, the temperance society of Paavola, as the Finns called the community, slowed down considerably.[61] John Filippus Erickson of Newberry was the representative of the Brotherhood at the organizational meeting of the third society organized on December 17. It was Metsän Opas at Welch in Mackinac County. When lumbering ended in the area, the activity of the society also ceased, and the small capital of $4.50 and a few songbooks were sent to the central organization.[62]

In 1900 four new temperance societies joined the SKRV in Michigan. The first of them was organized at the Swanzey Mine in Princeton. There was no church activity among the Finns there at this time. Alex Pantti reports that the saloon was called a church, the saloon keeper a minister, and the bartender an assistant minister. Women as well as men spent Sundays in the saloon, drinking and playing cards. It was estimated that the small Finnish population spent $600 per month in the saloon. Henry Tavajarvi of Negaunee went there as a representative of the Brotherhood and called a meeting for Sunday, February 18. The result of his visit was the organization of a temperance society called Sakari Topelius no. 141. Within three weeks the society had twenty-eight members, about half the Finnish population of Princeton. Life among the Finns began to change immediately. The leading men of the community had joined the society and their influence was felt even outside the Sakari Topelius Society. A Sunday school was started, and plans for calling a pastor to conduct worship services were discussed.[63]

On May 27, Raivaaja (Pioneer) no. 145 was organized in Michigamme. When employment was no longer available, the Finns moved elsewhere, mostly to Ishpeming, where the members of the Raivaaja joined the Väinö Society. In Negaunee they joined the Aamurusko Society. When most of the Finns left Michigamme, the Finnish saloon keeper, Matti Lind, moved his business to Ishpeming. The Raivaaja ceased activity in the fall of 1901 but was reactivated in October of the following year when work again became available.[64] On October 28, Kyntäjä (Plowman) no. 150 was organized at the Copper Range Mine in Painesdale with twenty-one members, some of whom were from neighboring Trimountain. Leaders of the meeting were J. H. Jasberg and H. Haapapuro from Hancock. Kyntäjä got off to a good start. Meetings always ended with a program of solos, speeches, recitations, etc. A fine hall was built in the wooded area between Painesdale and Trimountain. The first meeting in it was held on February 24, 1901. Differences of opinion apparently developed between Kyntäjä and the Brotherhood. Although the reasons for them are not clear even in the minutes, there is brief mention in the minutes of September 28, 1902, of the fact that Hemming Siikala had brought up the question of the society's becoming independent.[65] "After long and careful deliberation," a vote was taken on October 12. Only five members wished to remain in the Brotherhood; 63 voted for independence. Separation from the SKRV followed.[66]

On December 9, 1900, the home of Jaakko Kuitula in Baltic was filled with men and women who had come to hear what John Jarvenpaa of Atlantic Mine, representative of the SKRV, had to say. After his speech, Auran Kukka (Cornflower) no. 151 was organized with thirty-one members. Jarvenpaa heard their temperance pledges and announced that the society was an accomplished fact. Because of the rapid increase in membership Kuitula's house was soon too small for meetings, and construction was started on a hall which was completed at the end of the following summer. With the acquisition of their own hall, the society became even more active than it had already been. In addition to meetings and socials, a speaking club met up to three times a week for the practice of diction and public speaking. Night school classes were also sponsored.[67]

In 1901 three temperance societies were organized in Michigan and joined the SKRV. The first one had its beginnings in the office of Tapani Heikkila's lumber camp in the deep forest about five miles southwest of Munising. The meeting was held on Sunday, July 21, and was conducted by Alex Pantti. It began with a prayer and a short speech by Pantti, after which Pantti and Tapani Heikkila presented "The Dialogue of Master Aholin and Kuvala," which was about temperance. Because many former members of Taimi Society of Palmer joined it, the new society was called Taimen Oksa (Sprig of a Seedling) no. 154. Thirty-four persons joined; nineteen of them were veterans of Taimi. These experienced temperance workers enabled the society to become very active immediately. Socials were held and support was given to Suomi College. In planning socials it was customary to select a "beggars' committee" by which was meant a committee of persons whose duty it was to solicit contributions for the socials.[68]

The Kullervo Society of Cooks had ceased activity, but members who had moved to the neighboring community of Rapid River, where lumbering was still being done, saw the need for temperance work there, too. At a meeting held on October 6, 1901, and led by Matti Kamppinen, Pellervo no. 156 was organized. Fourteen persons joined and Kamppinen became president. When lumbering ended in Rapid River, temperance activity moved to Cliff Spur and from there, before the end of the year, to Chatham, where most of the members of Pellervo had gone to become farmers.[69] A temperance society called Voiton Tähti (Star of Victory) no. 157 was organized in Hurontown, south of Houghton, on October 13 of the same year, when K. A. Staudinger, a representative of the Brotherhood, went there for that purpose. Twenty-nine persons joined. Their meetings were held upstairs of a private home. Because of a lack of funds they were not able to consider a hall of their own, so they turned to the local mining company, which gave them the use of an old workshop. By repairing it and lining it with boards, the society acquired a neat and adequate hall into which they moved in June 1902. "Finnish songs, poems, lectures and speeches, rang out clearly against the walls of the new hall." But hardly two months had passed before the mining company lessened its labor force. Unmarried men were the first to leave the community, followed later by the family men. Before long there were only four men left in Voiton Tähti, which ceased activity. The hall was returned to the mining company.[70]

Two new temperance societies in Michigan, both organized on Sunday, January 12, joined the Brotherhood in 1902. The date was an important one in the history of the farming community of Kaleva, for it was the birthday of their Lutheran congregation as well as the temperance society. The atmosphere at the founding of the society was described thus by editor Antero Riippa of *Siirtolainen*, who became the society's first correspondent:

> The men who gathered in the office of the *Siirtolainen*—there was as yet no other suitable meeting place in the community—to lay the foundation for idealistic work in the new farming area were full of enthusiasm. Men had come even from distant lumber camps to be founders of and assistants in the work which we Finns especially have learned to consider a blessing to our immigrants. . . . It is doubtful if the memory will ever be erased from the mind of this writer, of that moment when filled with feelings of warmth and brotherhood we organized the society, which was named the Kalevatar in honor of the community.[71]

The construction of a hall was undertaken immediately. The local land company donated a lot, and American non-Finnish businessmen of Manistee, as well as others, made contributions of money. Lumber was cut at working bees in the forest. The congregation lent the society money, and the hall, which was sixty feet long and thirty feet wide, was dedicated before Christmas.

The other society organized on the same day was Nurmen Kukka (Meadow Flower) no. 161 in the Amasa farming area. It had a quiet existence about which not much information is available.

Between 1890 and 1902 was the period of greatest growth in the Finnish American temperance movement. At the end of that period there were 165 active temperance societies altogether. Of these, 95 belonged to the SKRV, 18 to the Friends of Temperance, 19 to the Eastern Finnish Temperance League, and 6 to the Western Temperance League. The remaining societies were independent. Total membership went up to 10,000. Michigan was still the leading state in the Finnish American temperance movement.

In addition to the organization of the Friends of Temperance at the beginning of this period, another outstanding happening was the thirteenth annual meeting and festival of the SKRV held in Hancock in the summer of 1900. Attendance was larger than it had ever been before. Meetings were held in the recently completed Suomi College building, a circumstance which in itself helped to bring the temperance movement into closer contact with other Finnish cultural activities. A sign of this was the decision made at this meeting to eliminate the use of passwords and the holding of secret meetings with all their formalities, all of which had been inherited from the Good Templars and had now become a hindrance to Finnish temperance work. Pastor J. Bäck was called to be the editor of *Raittiuslehti* (Temperance paper), another circumstance which helped to unify Finnish American cultural forces. The number of copies issued at a time increased to four thousand.

This closer contact with other aspects of Finnish American cultural life produced results already in the following annual meeting, which was held in Duluth. The candidate of the progressive faction, Jacob Kaminen of Ishpeming, won the presidency of the SKRV by a great majority, defeating the incumbent Isak Sillberg, the less aggressive and more cautious candidate of the older generation. Mikko Skytta, who was also of the more progressive faction, continued as vice president.

The victory of the progressives did not bring about any great changes in activities within the local societies. Dances were still forbidden, and the former strict attitude still prevailed against alcoholic patent medicines, the use of which had become more general. A new aim was to broaden the scope of temperance work by bringing it out of the Finnish temperance halls and into contact with the life of the communities around them. Some societies succeeded well in this new endeavor and began to take part in the rising struggle for prohibition; others still remained isolated and withdrawn from general activity.

From 1903 to Prohibition

The Finnish American temperance movement between 1903 and 1919 is most effectively considered against the background of the struggle for prohibition in the United States. By 1906, eighteen states had voted for prohibition, but it had been repealed in fifteen, leaving only Maine, Kansas, and North Dakota dry states. Temperance people had to start their work anew, practically from the beginning, making most progress in the South and the West. In many states saloons were closed on Sundays, and the sale of liquor was forbidden on holidays and election days. It was also forbidden in the District of Columbia and on Indian reservations. The Prohibition party, which had been organized in 1867 through the initiative of John Russel, a Methodist minister from Michigan, grew so large that in the presidential election its candidate received over 200,000 votes.

The efforts of many counties and states to enforce prohibition were almost pointless because liquor was easily available from neighboring counties or states. The Webb-Kenyon Act, approved by Congress in 1913, forbade the transportation of liquor into dry states, but supervision was practically impossible. To the great satisfaction of temperance people, on November 21, 1918, Congress approved the Wartime Prohibition Act, which was to be in effect from the following June 30th to the end of demobilization. On October 28, 1919, Congress overrode the president's veto despite his protests and passed the Volstead Prohibition Enforcement Act, which all the states excepting Connecticut and Rhode Island ratified. At this point, the majority of the Finnish American temperance societies considered their work finished.

During the time between 1903 and 1919, the following temperance societies were organized and joined the SKRV. The first date is the date of admission into the Brotherhood. If the date of organization is different, it is given in parentheses.[72]

1903

1/18 Onnen Opas no. 172, Newberry Camps, Mich.
Mustanmäen Kukka no. 173, Terry, So. Dak.
Valon Alku no. 174, Mikardo Mine, Wakefield, Mich.

3/7 Selvä no. 175, Nisula, Mich.
9/13 Kylväjä no. 176, Trimountain, Mich.
9/27 Elo no. 177, Winona, Mich.
11/15 Valkoruusu no. 178, Rockland, Mich.
Pyrintö no. 179, Coal Centre, Pa.
Kuusen Humina no. 180, Nanty Glo, Pa.
Laaksonruusu no. 181, Ansonville, Pa.
Santakiven Kukka no. 182, Sandstone, Minn.

1904

2/28 Voitonlippu no. 183, Monessen, Pa. Its branch:
Rauhan Alku, Coal Centre, Pa. (Jan. 26, 1908)
4/27 Rauhan Lilja no. 184, Brownsville, Pa.
5/24 Kupariruusu no. 185, Calumet, Mich.
Laakson Lilja no. 186, Berry County, O.
Etelän Ruusu no. 187, Swantworth, Miss.
Urhojen Liitto no. 188, Vintondale, Pa.
10/2 Rannan Ruusu no. 189, Oskar, Mich.
Etelän Avain no. 190, South Range, Mich.
Taiston Alku no. 191, Finlayson, Minn.
Nuorison Kaunistus no. 192, Redridge, Mich.
12/11 Yritys no. 193, Granite, Mont.

1905

1/22 Suomen Ruusu no. 194, Cleveland, O.
Metsän Kukka no. 195, Uusi Suomi, Mich.
3/2 Valotar no. 196, Montreal, Mich.
Lahja no. 197, Tower, Minn.
Toivon Sankari no. 198, Youngstown, O.
8/13 Hyökkäys no. 199, Aurora, Minn.
10/15 Elon Toivo no. 200, Onnela, Mich.
12/31 Uuden Vuoden Lahja no. 201, Lowelville, O.
Tuomi no. 202, Richmond, N.Y.

1906

3/18 Vellamo no. 203, Laurium, Mich.
Pyrintö no. 204, Cobalt, Ontario
12/9 Voiton Seppele no. 205, Sugar Creek, O.

1907

1/28 Toivolan Valo, no. 206, Toivola, Minn.
10/3 Säde no. 207, Hancock, Mich. (Jan. 7, 1904)

3/24	Palon Riento no. 208, Palo, Minn.
4/7	Virginian Tähti no. 209, Clarksburg, W. Va. (May 6, 1906)
5/23	Kevään Kukka no. 210, Victoria Mine, Mich.
12/15	Jouluruusu no. 211, Janow, Manitoba
12/29	Soihtu no. 212, Brainerd, Minn.

1908

1/1	Riento no. 213, Monson, Me.
3/30	Apilan Kukka no. 214, Rudyard, Mich.
4/12	Vuoren Säde no. 215, Belt, Mont.
6/18	Hyvä Toivo no. 216, Sandstone, Minn.
10/11	Toivolan Soihtu no. 217, Toivola, Mich.
10/19	Elo no. 218, Van Buskirk, Wis.
11/22	Toivon Alku no. 219, Ramsay, Mich.

1909

1/3	Kosken Kukka no. 220, West Ishpeming, Mich.
1/3	Lehti no. 221, Bovey, Minn.
5/9	Valon Opas no. 222, Pegla, Minn.
5/9	Aallotar no. 223, Winton, Minn.
5/11	Isien Toivo no. 224, Redgranite, Wis.
5/9	Kukoistus no. 225, Fall River, Mass.
8/15	Vuokko no. 226, Maynard, Mass.
8/8	Uskallus no. 227, Joliet, Ill.
9/19	Saima no. 228, Diorite, Mich.
11/7	Männikön Kukka no. 229, Gwinn, Mich.

1911

4/23	Tarmo no. 230, Turtle Lake, Wis.
5/14	Touvon Oras no. 231, Victoria Mine, Ontario
12/31	Soihtu no. 232, Dodgeville, Mich.

1912

4/14	Salonkukka no. 233, ? (Feb. 24, 1910)
12/15	Urpa no. 234, Hubbell, Mich.

1913

10/7	Lemminkukka no. 235, Wright, Minn.
10/27	Ponnistus no. 236, Brackett, N. Dak.

11/7 Eteenpäin no. 237, Wing, N. Dak.
11/9 Aavikon Kukka no. 238, Braddock, N. Dak.

1914

1/12 Virkistys no. 239, Chisholm, Minn.
2/8 Pohjanvalo no. 240, Moose Lake, Minn.
9/27 Apilankukka no. 241, Angora, Minn.
9/27 Valon Aura no. 242, Alavus, Minn.
Uusi Yritys no. 243, Biwabik, Minn. (1906)

1916

10/22 Onnen Askel no. 244, Askel, Mich.

Thus, during this period, twenty-five temperance societies were organized in Michigan and joined the Brotherhood; seventeen in Minnesota, seven in Pennsylvania; five in Ohio; three each in North Dakota, Wisconsin, and Canada; two each in Massachusetts and Montana; and one each in South Dakota, Mississippi, New York, West Virginia, Maine, and Illinois. There is also one listed without a place name, making a total of seventy-four on the continent. A total of fifteen new societies joined the Friends of Temperance and the Western and Eastern leagues.

Several of the new societies organized in Michigan are worthy of special mention. Onnen Opas (Guide to Happiness) was organized in the lumbering area outside Newberry because Onnen Aarre in the town was too far away for the workmen to attend. The reading room and library especially were much used during the long weekends. The work of Onnen Opas ceased when lumbering ended in the late summer of 1906.[73] The Selvä (Sober) Society of Nisula survived the departure of members who left to form a rival independent society. They also survived the fire which struck two years later and destroyed their new hall. The society ceased activity for the duration of World War I because of a lack of members, but when the men returned from the war the society was reactivated.[74]

With a small majority of its members in favor of the Brotherhood and the rest desiring more freedom, the Kylväjä (Sower) Society of Trimountain had a stormy existence.[75] After being dormant for two years, activity was renewed in 1915. The Elo Society of Ontonagon, which had ceased to function after the disastrous fire of 1896, was re-established in Winona, where many Ontonagon Finns had gone because of the growing mining activity there. The work of the society was carried on as long as the mines remained active.

The Valkoruusu (White Rose) Society of Rockland had an exceptionally good start. Members included, for example, Fabian Tolonen, Hans P. Lankinen, and Alfred Laakso, all of whom participated in many cultural activities in the following decades. The Rockland Strike, which developed into a struggle between the Finns and the other nationalities of the area, delivered a severe blow to the temperance society. After employment became unavailable, the society ceased activity in 1911.[76] Another society, Kupariruusu (Copper Rose) was organized by miners of Centennial Heights, near Calumet, who combined their society with Uusi Vartija of Calumet in 1909.

The Rannan Ruusu (Rose of the Shore) Society began its activities as Laakson Ruusu (Rose of the Valley) in Oskar, south of Portage Lake, but its name was changed in 1904, the year it was organized. Socialists joined Rannan Ruusu in large numbers, but because they did not succeed in their efforts to gain control of the society, they soon left it. The last meeting of the society was held in September 1930.[77]

A temperance society was started in South Range in the fall of 1904. Because the Finns pronounced the name of the community "Saut Renssi," the "renssi" part became confused with the word "wrench," which in Finnglish was also pronounced "renssi." Since a wrench is a "ruuviavain" in Finnish, the latter part meaning key, the new society was named Etelän Avain (Southern Key). In March 1906 Etelän Avain joined Auran Kukka of neighboring Baltic, even relinquishing its hall to it.[78] A society called Valotar was organized at the Montreal Mine in Gogebic County for the benefit of miners' families. It ceased activity in 1917.

Elon Toivo (Hope of Life) was a temperance society in the community of Onnela, between Atlantic Mine and Redridge. (Its home, in some sources, is mistakenly given as Atlantic Mine.) The society even survived the slump in temperance work caused by the Prohibition Law.[79] On the north side of Portage Lake, so many members of the Pohjantähti Society of Hancock lived in the nearby mining community of Franklin, that a branch society named Säde (Ray) was organized there in 1904. It became an independent society after three years.[80] Apilankukka (Clover Blossom) of Rudyard, organized by Alfred Laakso, was active from 1908 to 1910.[81] At the time of the prohibition struggle in 1917 the society was reactivated and worked hard for its ideals.

In Laurium, which adjoins Calumet, there were thirty saloons, some of them owned by Finns. To counterbalance their effect, the Vellamo Society was organized in 1906. At first their meetings were held in a hall above the post office, but at the beginning of the following year, meetings were held in their own establishment, a church building purchased from the Baptists for $4,200. The price proved too high for the small membership of the Vellamo, and the society soon ceased activity.[82]

The Toivon Alku (Beginning of Hope) Society, founded in Ramsay in 1908, was in existence for only two years. Kosken Kukka (Flower of the Rapids), organized in West Ishpeming in 1909, was active for three years, and Saima, organized at the Diorite Mine in the same year, lasted four years. Alma Hinkkanen, a speaker traveling for the SKRV, visited Gwinn in 1909 and organized a society named Männikön Kukka (Flower of the Pine Grove) after the stately pines of the area. The Sakari Topelius Society of neighboring Princeton joined Männikön Kukka in 1911, selling their hall for $600 to some Italians who remodeled it into a dwelling.[83] Toivolan Soihtu (Torch) of Toivola and Soihtu of Dodgeville remained in existence for many years, Soihtu of Dodgeville until the 1970s.

The Urpa (Bud) Society of Hubbell, which had belonged to the Friends of Temperance, joined the Brotherhood in 1912, but it was not long-lived. In their enthusiasm for the cause of prohibition, the Finns of the small community of Askel in the Otter Lake region, organized the Onnen Askel (Happy Step) Temperance Society. When the battle for prohibition had been won, the society ceased activity.

There were so many temperance societies in the central and western parts of the Upper Peninsula that it was natural for them to become organized by area. The first league to be thus organized was Kuparialueen Raittius Liitto (the Copper Country Temperance League) in 1906. Because the earliest minutes have disappeared, no more definite date of organization can be found.[84] The next was the Iron County Temperance League, organized on April 12, 1907, at a meeting held in the Toivola Hall in Crystal Falls.[85] On April 28 the Marquette County Temperance League was organized in Ishpeming. August 30, 1908, marked the beginning of the Gogebic Area Temperance League at a meeting in Ironwood.[86] These leagues added to the efficiency of temperance work in these areas where individual societies were widely scattered.

By this time the Finnish American temperance movement was beginning to feel the need for a new central organization that would include all local temperance societies and absorb the four existing central organizations—the SKRV, the Friends of Temperance, and the Eastern and Western temperance leagues. The first joint "peace meeting" was held in DeKalb, Illinois, early in January 1908. The delegates proposed that the new central organization be called the Finnish American Temperance League. They also prepared a draft of a constitution.[87] These proposals failed to get the necessary support. In the SKRV especially there was displeasure at the attempt to eliminate its name.

The next conference was held in Sault Ste. Marie toward the end of August of the same year. At this meeting, only the Brotherhood and the Friends of Temperance were represented. The plan to unite was considered a failure. There were many reasons for the failure. The Eastern and Western leagues were too far away; the Brotherhood had carried the burden of the expenses of the negotiations almost alone; the leading societies were accustomed to their own procedures and regulations and were unwilling to make changes.

Not until decades later was union achieved. When it came, it came in a different and more practical way when a general convention of Finnish American temperance people was held in Waukegan in June 1944 in connection with the annual meeting and festival of the SKRV, with Alfred Erickson, president of the Eastern Finnish National Temperance League, as chairman. The establishment of the United Finnish Temperance Council was unanimously approved. Its members were to be representatives from the Eastern, Ohio-Pennsylvania, Illinois, Minnesota, Michigan, and Wisconsin leagues. This new central organization began immediately to arrange for combined nationwide summer festivals, participation made ever more possible by the increase in travel among the Finns because of convenient means of transportation.

During this period, the purposes and ideals of the temperance movement were made known by old as well as by newer methods. Speakers from Finland were invited, including, for example, the teachers K. Hyttinen, Vilho Reima, and Alma Hinkkanen. Courses in temperance work were started in 1904; lecturers were capable men like Pastors Heikki Anias, V. Rautanen, M. I. Kuusi, and J. K. Lammi, as well as Dr. K. Sorsen and John Kiiskila, the well-known lawyer. Activity among children was also carried on in the form of "hope leagues." Essay contests were held, and participants included many persons from as far away as Finland.

At the beginning of the period under consideration, a newspaper debate took place between a few of the clergy and some of the temperance people. Some temperance societies demanded that clergymen become members. They even interfered with church matters; for example, by giving orders against the use of wine at Holy Communion. The temperance paper also willingly made space available for critical articles about the clergy. Pastor J. J. Hoikka, in his plainspoken way, began to fight against the authoritarian demands of the temperance societies and against their interference in the affairs of the church, whose responsibility included, as he emphasized, the fostering of the Christian's freedom of choice. In *Paimen-Sanomat* and *Amerikan Suometar* he exposed the "spiritual intemperance" frequently evidenced at temperance meetings by contempt for church services and the Word of God and by light-minded behavior. The attacks of leaders in the temperance movement against the Suomi Synod caused strained relations between the church and the movement for decades. The clergy of the synod had supported Finnish American temperance work from the very beginning. They had appeared as speakers at innumerable meetings and had continuously helped out temperance publications by writing articles for them. One of the pastors who worked with the temperance movement in this manner was Heikki Anias, who was born in Alavieska, and who was pastor in Ely, Minnesota, at this time. The clergy of other Finnish churches were spared the difficulties experienced by the pastors of the synod because they did not usually participate in temperance work.

This period, from 1903 to 1919, ended in a victory for prohibition throughout the United States. In some of the counties of the Upper Peninsula of Michigan the work of the temperance societies was a deciding factor in the final outcome. Enthusiasm for prohibition was so great in some Finnish communities that on election day women were standing in line two hours before the doors of voting places were opened, for it was women and children who had suffered most from the saloon business.

Michigan would have been the fifth state to accept prohibition if a procedural error had not been made in the House of Representatives on January 23, 1918, in the handling of the matter. As it was, the question did not come up again until January 2, 1919, when Michigan became the sixteenth state to approve the Prohibition Law.

The Decline of the Temperance Movement

The first direct result of the Prohibition Law was a surprise to temperance workers. With the enactment of the law, large numbers of members of temperance societies considered their work done and left the movement. As early as 1922, *Raittiuskalenteri* carried articles about Michigan societies, reporting the following kinds of facts: Membership, which at one time was 125, has "fallen off so much that now there are only 20 members." "Lately the membership has become so small that activity has also slackened." Four years later an old veteran of temperance work wrote as follows: "Feeling sad and disheartened I wrote on this question: Will the Brotherhood reach its fiftieth anniversary? When we remember the founding of the Brotherhood and its early progress to its highest point of development, who of us would then have believed that we would one day slip downward at such a pace as we are going now?"[88]

This downward trend can be seen in the fact that in 1903 there were 95 active societies in the Brotherhood, with a total membership of 5,675.[89] Twenty-three years later—in 1926—there were only 35 societies in it, with a total of 817 members.[90] Heikki Karhu, who at this time was writing the annual reports for *Raittiuskalenteri*, expressed his feelings the following year in the words of Lieutenant Ziden in the "Tales of Ensign Stal": "Hurrah! What a clever trick. Now we can die like gentlemen!" The presidents' annual reports for the following years say nothing at all about membership. Outside the Brotherhood, the decline was even more pronounced.

Misconceptions concerning the significance of the Prohibition Law were not the only reasons for this development. Another reason was that the socialists, especially in the West, had succeeded in getting control of many temperance societies and their halls and other property. Throughout the country still another reason existed: The older generation were keeping younger members from the governing boards of the temperance societies. They were also persistently conducting meetings in the Finnish language, a circumstance which was as great a mistake as was the too-long-continued use of only Finnish in the church.[91] The consequence was that the younger generation, as a rule, did not follow in their parents' footsteps as temperance workers. The effect of this was felt more and more as the older generation began to die off ever more rapidly. At the same time, the increased rate of death among older members created financial difficulties for the central organization because of the $50 burial aid that had been guaranteed for each paying member.[92] These funeral bills were a perpetual cause of anxiety for the SKRV board. There was also frequent criticism even within the temperance societies to the effect that they did temperance work only among those already temperate and had no effect on life outside their halls.

The board of the SKRV, however, could not be criticized for inactivity. Meetings were held frequently, and itinerant speakers were sent on their rounds every year. Among the lecturers were Finnish Americans of great ability, including Mrs. Thyra Rautalahti, Mrs. Minnie Perttula-Maki, Onni K. Syrjaniemi, Henry Moilanen, and Pastors Salomon Ilmonen, V. Rautanen, and John Wargelin. *Raittiuskansan*

Kalenteri (Temperance people's calendar) was published regularly, although issues became smaller, falling from the previous thousands to only 1,200 in 1928. Even so, with profits from the sale of these calendars it was possible to pay other bills.

In Finland many changes were made in the Prohibition Law over the years, but its enforcement became impossible because of public opposition to it. In a general election held at the end of 1931, in which 45 percent of eligible voters participated, 72 percent voted in favor of repealing the Prohibition Law. A new liquor law was passed on February 9, 1932. It went into effect on April 5, restoring regulated liquor traffic in the country. With regard to prohibition, the experience of the United States was similar to that of Finland. By December 5, 1933, thirty-six states had voted against prohibition. On that date, with the majority vote against it, the American Prohibition Law was repealed.

By 1933 the Finnish American temperance movement had become so weak that it could no longer afford to publish its calendar. Three societies, all of them in Minnesota, promised to provide financial assistance, but the board could not risk publication with such meager support. Carl H. Salminen, editor of *Päivälehti*, a newspaper published in Duluth, partially remedied the situation by allotting ample space for temperance news in his *Siirtokansan Kalenteri* (Immigrants' calendar). Shortly before, Esa Torkko, president of the SKRV for many years, had written as follows: "Thus, the SKRV is unable to do temperance work as before. The temperance leagues are also doomed. The four leagues left are too weak to accomplish much of importance."[93]

The repeal of the Prohibition Law roused the temperance societies to activity again and checked the rate of decline for a time. *Raittiuskansan Kalenteri* was published again and activity in many societies was lively. Table 13 shows how the number of temperance societies decreased from 1928 to 1965.[94]

The temperance societies of Michigan got a welcome addition to their thinning ranks on September 2, 1962, when the Finnish Christian Temperance Society was organized at the Saralampi summer cottage at Agate Beach. Charter members were John and Anna Kiiskila, Wilhard and Naimi Riutta, Emil and Annikki Saralampi, Matti and Elvi Ruoho, and Jenny Johnson. The society purchased an unused church building on the main street of Chassell. With a moderate amount of repair work, they acquired a practical meeting place that included a kitchen and a dining room.

In addition to the Finnish Christian Temperance Society, active temperance societies in Michigan in 1966 were Yksimielisyyden

Table 13: Finnish American Temperance Societies, 1928–65

YEAR	SKRV MICHIGAN	SKRV OTHER STATES	OTHER TEMPERANCE LEAGUES	INDEPENDENT SOCIETIES
1928	20	17	?	16
1934	16	17	?	16
1935	15	17	?	13
1945	8	11	26	?
		Total of Other States, Other Temperance Leagues, and Independent Societies		
1965	5		13	

Aalto (Wave of Harmony) in Marquette, Soihtu in Dodgeville, Toivolan Soihtu in Toivola, and Roihu (Flame) in Coburntown. In 1898 a society called Aalto (Wave) had been organized in Marquette and joined the SKRV, and the following year a society called Yksimielisyys had been organized and had joined the Eastern Finnish Temperance League. In 1900 these societies separated from their parent societies and merged under the name Yksimielisyyden Aalto. They remained independent but worked closely with various central organizations in their common activities.[95] Soihtu of Dodgeville, which was organized on December 31, 1911, has survived over a half-century of struggle; in 1966 it had the largest membership of all the Finnish temperance societies in Michigan.[96] Toivolan Soihtu was three years older, having been organized in 1908. When the Prohibition Law went into effect, the society considered its work finished, but it was reorganized sometime after the law was repealed. The organizer was Onni K. Syrjaniemi. Albin Lahikainen became president, and Mayme Salmi was the secretary.[97] Roihu was organized in Coburntown in 1934. The local Sunday school building, which belonged to the Hancock congregation, was used for meetings. The programs were of high quality, for talent available from Suomi College was frequently used.[98]

In a period of thirty years, from the 1880s to the 1910s, the Finnish American temperance movement did valuable work in raising the level of morality among Finnish immigrants. Since then it has gradually become less active. In the 1960s, the few old veterans in the remaining five small temperance societies of Michigan were a respected reminder of the former days of vigorous activity and great accomplishment. Their work and the work of their fathers was a valuable aid to the church in raising the level of life among the pioneer generations.

In the 1960s

From the 1930s on, it has been obvious that as far as active temperance work is concerned, the Finnish American temperance movement is past history. At last even the cooperatives, which had always kept "King Alcohol" off their shelves, following this practice to the end of their independent existence, upon merging with the American cooperative movement brought beer and wine into their stores. From 1950 on, practical temperance work has been left entirely to the police, the courts of justice, and the Michigan Liquor Control Commission. Participation of the Finns of Upper Michigan in the ownership of licensed liquor businesses has always been small. The statistics of

Table 14: Finnish Americans in Michigan in the Liquor Business, 1960

COUNTY	WHOLESALE AND RETAIL BUSINESSES	NUMBER OF BUSINESSES OWNED BY FINNS
Keweenaw	23	5
Houghton	174	36
Baraga	39	12
Marquette	284	22
Alger	95	11
Chippewa	120	6
Luce	36	1
Iron	135	5
Ontonogan	50	19
Gogebic	118	6
Delta	262	0
Mackinac	66	0
	1,402	123

the Liquor Control Commission for February 1960 in table 14 show ownership of wholesale and retail businesses in counties of the Upper Peninsula.

It is probably because of the temperance movement that the participation of Finns in the liquor business, as compared with other nationalities, has been proportionately much smaller than the number of Finns in the Upper Peninsula.

12 The Rise and Decline of the Labor Movement

The Labor Movement in Finland to 1903

Because of the geographical location and the historical development of Finland, the economic and political movements of Central and Western Europe arrived there considerably later than elsewhere. When fast-growing industrialism and expanding overseas commerce were already revolutionizing social conditions in England and in many other European countries, life in Finland was still characterized by quiet, unhurried home industry. But eventually industrialism reached Finland too. Table 15 shows how rapidly it expanded.

Table 15: Industrial Growth in Finland, 1869–1909

DATE	NUMBER OF FACTORIES	NUMBER OF WORKERS
1869	339	10,114
1879	436	12,892
1889	1,123	39,200
1899	1,757	75,900
1909	2,007	86,374

This rapid development of industry in a capital-poor country was the result of an abundance of cheap raw material, namely lumber; an abundance of cheap energy in the form of waterfalls and firewood; and the availability of cheap, though usually unskilled, labor. The rapidly growing labor force alone created new and temporarily unsolvable problems. There were even greater numbers of workers in agriculture, which in 1870 employed 358,154 hired hands in addition to 88,949 tenants, cottagers, and others without land of their own, making a total of 447,103 persons.[1] The landless population did not increase much during the following decades. For example, in 1930 it was only 120,000 greater than it had been sixty years before, even though the population of the country had doubled. There were many reasons for this development. One reason was the freedom of choice of occupation realized in 1879, which gave tens of thousands of persons the opportunity to make use of their initiative and enterprise. Other reasons were emigration overseas, migration to cities, mechanization of agriculture, and the creation of new independent farms.

Nevertheless, there were still in Finland half a million laborers whose workdays were extremely long, whose wages were far from satisfactory, whose living conditions, especially in rural areas, were miserable. Up to 1906 they had no political rights. In addition to everything else, the use of liquor was so heavy, especially among factory workers, that the week's wages were often used to pay the liquor bill. Thus, when the international labor movement reached Finland, the background for its development was ready.

The first labor organizations in Finland were started and directed by manufacturers and tradesmen as societies for educational work among laborers, but they remained passive. The most important of these were Helsingin Työväenyhdistys (Helsinki Workingmen's Association) and Vaasan Suomalainen Työväenyhdistys (Finnish Workingmen's Association of Vaasa). The founder and president of the Helsinki organization was Viktor Julius von Wright, the manager of a small furniture business, after whom this phase of the Finnish labor movement is called Wrightism. One of its purposes was to improve living conditions; another was to prevent the socialist labor movement from getting a foothold in Finland. It followed closely the pattern of the idealistic German labor movement, to which militant and revolutionary ideas were completely foreign.

Toward the end of the 1880s, however, the workers in Finland began to break away from this kind of guardianship by establishing trade unions, which were followed by proletarian labor associations in which the new socialistic ideas from Germany soon took root. In 1895 *Työmies* (Workingman) was started. Its editor from 1896 to 1899 was Matti Kurikka, who was soon afterward well known in America for arousing class-consciousness, for advocating the workers' right to strike, and for demanding safer working conditions, higher wages, and shorter hours. At a meeting of delegates from labor associations held in Turku in 1899, the Finnish Labor Party was organized. At a party convention in Forsa in 1903 it was named the Social Democratic party of Finland. The party followed the so-called Erfurt Program that the German Socialist party had followed since 1891.[2]

Early Phases in America

The rise of the labor movement among the Finns in America must be studied against this background of developments in Finland. Since 1876 there had been in the United States a labor party called the Socialist Labor party, but because of the language barrier, it was able no more than were other socialist organizations to reach Finnish Americans. The first independent attempt at organization was made by the Finns in the spirit of Wrightism in Brooklyn in 1891 with the establishment of Työväenyhdistys Imatra (Imatra Labor Association), which was active for many decades.[3] A sister society in Michigan, Suomiseura (Finnish Society) of Calumet, however, was in existence only a short time although its membership reached 200. It succumbed to the "party division between white-collar workers and laborers." It was followed by the more vigorous Saima Labor Association of Fitchburg, Massachusetts, and the Jousi Society of Hancock.

The Jousi Society was organized in 1901 by persons who had left the Pohjantähti Temperance Society, the first of them being actors who demanded more freedom than the more serious-minded religious leaders allowed them. Thus, Jousi (BoW) began as a temperance society, but the temperance idea fell by the wayside and the society became a labor organization. Leaders were N. J. Ahlman, Oskar Tanner, and Isak Lundberg. Meetings were held in the Germania Hall in Hancock. The Kerredge Theater was rented for their more important plays. These plays were often quite demanding. They included such dramas as *Regina von Emmeritz*, *Daniel Hjort*, *Tukkijoella*, *Nummisuutarit*, and *Elinan Surma*. As one of the early leaders, Ahlman worked with skill and enthusiasm for the idealistic and nationalistic labor movement, in which everyone could participate, for 95 percent of the Finnish immigrants belonged to the working class. The situation was such that a person could be, at the same time, a member and even an office holder in a church congregation, the temperance society, and the labor association. However, the situation soon changed.

In the early days of their existence, the labor associations worked as independent units completely separate from one another. Their first joint meeting was held in Gardner, Massachusetts, in 1903.

At this meeting Amerikan Suomalainen Työväenliitto Imatra (Finnish American Workingmen's League Imatra)—known in briefer form as the Imatra League—was organized. Thirty-two labor associations joined the league, with a total membership of 1,500. The leading groups in this project were the idealistic Imatra of Brooklyn and Jousi of Hancock.

In the meantime, the Finnish American labor movement had acquired a newspaper of its own. In 1899, Antero Ferdinand Tanner—natural scientist, free-thinker, and advocate of free love—had arrived from Finland. In 1900 he started the socialist paper, *Amerikan Työmies* (American workingman) in Harlem. The associate editor was J. W. Lähde, a former pastor who had joined the socialists; assistants were Martin Hendrickson and Alex Halonen. Because of disagreements among the editors, the enterprise failed after a few months. Tanner went to Minneapolis to continue the study of medicine. At the same time, the satirical paper *Ampiainen* (Wasp), published in connection with *Amerikan Työmies*, also ceased publication. The work of *Amerikan Työmies* was continued by *Amerikan Suomalainen Työmies* (Finnish American Workingman), published in Worcester, Massachusetts. The first number came out on July 20, 1903. The manager and editor was Vihtori Kosonen. Its purpose was stated thus:

> It is our dearest wish to solve the labor problem. We will apply the unshakeable principles of the international labor movement to the solution of this important social problem. . . . We demand human dignity and justice for the oppressed! To attain our goal, we are peaceably seeking through our representatives, a way to exert social and political influence. . . . With regard to religion we are broad-minded, and we try to develop in our readers a proper understanding of the doctrines of Jesus of Nazareth and to encourage them to apply these teachings to everyday life.

Even with this comparatively cautious program, the publication was opposed by the Imatra League as well as by nationalistic Finnish American newspapers. Kosonen made a trip to Michigan and Minnesota to solicit subscriptions, but it was unsuccessful. One man could still carry the entire issue of the weekly to the post office in a sack on his back. In the summer of 1904 the paper moved to Hancock, Michigan. The first number of the paper, renamed simply *Työmies*, came out on August 16.

"Imatraism" had gotten a foothold in Michigan also, especially in Ironwood, where the Rauha (Peace) Labor Society was active. The

Minnesota and Michigan societies that belonged to the Imatra League organized Amerikan Suomalainen Työväen Liitto (Finnish American Working People's League) which was also intended to be nationwide in scope. The idea had originated in Ironwood, but the central office was set up in Duluth. On August 11 and 12 in 1904, a few days before *Työmies* began publication in Hancock, an official meeting attended by representatives of the Jousi Society of Hancock and the Suomi Society of Calumet was held in Duluth. The former was represented by Oskar E. Tanner, E. Nieminen, and Isak Lundberg, the latter by John A. Harpet. Lively debate took place between the "Bread Socialists," who were in favor of joining the American Socialist party, and the idealists who supported the Imatra League in its advocacy of an independent Finnish American stand. The men from the Jousi Society managed to tip the scales in favor of the latter by a one-vote majority.

The Cleveland Meeting

The recently arrived socialists who had become familiar with political thought and activity in labor organizations in Finland were not satisfied with the views of the Imatra League, which *Työmies* had also begun to oppose. Through their efforts, a meeting of representatives of Finnish-American labor organizations was held in Cleveland from October 3 to 6 in 1904. Among the delegates from Michigan were Vihtori Kosonen, who had come to Hancock with *Työmies*, and E. Nieminen. The group reached the conclusion that "only by joining the Socialist party can our labor movement gain recognition and have some effect on the development of socialism in this country." Another important result of the meeting was the establishment of the newspaper *Raivaaja* as the official organ of the party in the Eastern states. Its first editor was Taavi Tainio (1874–1929), recently arrived from Finland, who, however, returned to his homeland in the fall of 1905 to become editor-in-chief of *Sosialisti* in Turku.

The decision reached at the Cleveland meeting to join the Socialist party signified, first of all, the end of the Imatra League, for with the exception of the original founding society of Brooklyn, all the labor associations which were members of the league gradually went over to Marxian socialism. In this changeover they lost many members, but the losses were made up in a few years when radical labor groups grew so rapidly that nothing like it had ever before been seen in the Finnish American labor movement.

There were many reasons for this rapid growth. First of all, immigration was at its peak, each year bringing to America great numbers of members of Finland's labor organizations. Experienced in these organizations, they had firsthand knowledge about the development of the labor situation in Finland. Some had been in the groups that had gathered around the Helsinki Diet on the night of April 14–15, 1905, when violence seemed inevitable because the Diet had refused to approve the new franchise law. Many had participated in the general strike that occurred the following November, and in 1906 they had celebrated the act which, with one blow, changed the structure of the Diet from the most antiquated in Europe to the most modern.[4] A second reason was that the bitterness which followed the strike of the tenant farmers on the Laukko estate and their consequent eviction also spread to Finnish American laborers. This bitterness was increased by the irresponsibility of mining companies toward their workmen and by frequent mining accidents, most of which were caused by faulty equipment, during the strike that began in July 1907 among the iron miners in Minnesota. In the Finnish calendars of this period there are many obituaries of Finns who had died in mining accidents. The organizers for the Western Federation of Miners, among whom were many Finns, including John Valimaki, who was in the forefront among them, used these happenings to their advantage, promising to remedy the situation quickly through trade unions. The unions worked hand in hand with local socialist groups. It was at this time that the labor organizations began to be labeled socialistic. There was also the agitating practiced by the socialist papers *Työmies* and *Raivaaja*, as well as *Toveri*, which had been started in Astoria in 1907. The result was the rapid growth of the SSJ, or Suomalainen Socialistijärjestö (Finnish Socialist Organization), in which the number of local divisions grew comparatively much faster than their membership (see table 16).[5]

In 1917, Michigan, with its 20 groups, ranked third in number

Table 16: SSJ Membership, 1906–17

YEAR	LOCAL DIVISIONS	MEMBERSHIP	YEAR	LOCAL DIVISIONS	MEMBERSHIP
1906	53	2,000	1912	248	11,536
1907	133	2,928	1913	260	12,651
1908	150	3,960	1914	227	11,657
1909	160	5,384	1915	212	8,859
1910	173	7,767	1916	224	9,396
1911	217	9,139	1917	219	10,089

of divisions. Massachusetts was second, with 26; and Minnesota was first, with 33. Of the labor organizations in Michigan, the Suomalainen Socialistijärjestö (Finnish Socialist Organization—SSJ) in Hancock was the most important. In 1904 it had become the leader of the Finnish American labor movement, a position it held for ten years. The reason for this development was that *Työmies*, the most important organ of the movement, with its editorial staff, was located in Hancock during the eleven-year period beginning in 1904.

Työmies, 1904–14

During the eleven years that *Työmies* was published in Hancock, this Finnish center was also the center of the Finnish American labor movement in the midwestern states. When the Työmies Publishing Company was established, N. J. Ahlman, editor of *Päivälehti*, became the manager. There was friction between the editor-in-chief, Vihtori Kosonen, and Ahlman from the very first. Neither one emerged victorious. Ahlman was compelled to resign. Kosonen was relieved of his duties as editor while he was on an agitating tour. He was replaced by Kaapo Murros, who had worked as an editor in Finland as well as in America, where he had been on the editorial staff of *Siirtolainen*.

By the end of 1904 *Työmies* had 1,000 subscribers. At first it was printed in the basement of a certain building, but in 1905 the paper was moved to a new building put up for it in West Hancock by Matt Fredd. Murros's editorship ended when he was fined $3,000 for a libelous statement about a Finnish physician and thought it best to return to Finland. The new editors were Toivo Hiltunen, who had come from *Toveri* (Comrade) newspaper in Astoria, and W. W. Korhonen, a young pharmacy student who was called the "Pill Peddler" by his enemies. In 1904 the paper became a triweekly, which meant that its linotype machine was in operation twenty-four hours a day.

The year 1904 also brought two men from Finland to the editorial staff of *Työmies*. They were men who were connected with the Finnish American labor movement for a long time afterward. One of them was Aku Rissanen, born in Viipuri in 1881, who had done editorial work on socialist newspapers and, because of his participation in Finland's general strike and in the Viaporin Rebellion, had been forced to leave the country. He was made editor-in-chief of *Työmies*. The other newcomer from Finland was Leo Laukki, previously known as Lindqvist (b. 1880, Helsinki), who had been a lieutenant in the Russian Imperial Cavalry. He, like Rissanen, had been compelled to leave Finland after participating in the Viaporin Rebellion. He became the assistant editor of the paper.

These men, "who had come from the maelstrom of revolution," as was exaggeratedly said, gave new impetus to the radicalism which *Työmies* had already been advocating for several years. In the preceding fall the Finnish socialists of Hancock had appeared in the trade unions' Labor Day parade carrying a red flag. After that incident, the city council made a ruling forbidding the display of a red flag at public affairs. The law was tested on Sunday, July 28, 1907, when the Finnish socialists held their summer festival. Their parade passed along the main street of the city with the American flag and the red flag of revolution at its head. When the procession reached the town hall, where the police department was housed, the police confiscated the red flag and the pennants of the labor organizations. They also arrested their bearers and the organizers of the parade, a total of thirteen persons. Among those arrested were Leo Laukki, Toivo Hiltunen, and Frank Aaltonen, all of whom were released the same day. The justice of the peace judged them guilty of violation of the flag ordinance and of disturbing the peace. The district court confirmed the verdict, but when the case was appealed to the State Supreme Court, it was forgotten there. The incident created tension between the socialists and other residents of the city. Relations were strained to the breaking point six years later, at the time of the miners' strike.

Rissanen moved to Astoria to edit *Toveri*, and Laukki became an instructor at the Workingmen's College near Duluth. Vieno Severi Alanne, a chemical engineer who was born in Hämeenlinna in 1879, took their place as editor of *Työmies*. Carefully and impartially he tried to raise the standards of the paper and to settle the endless disputes that occurred among the editorial staff and in the board. The paper, edited with more propriety and polish, did not please the majority of the labor organizations, which saw bourgeois influence in the editor's efforts. Alanne was asked to leave, only to be called back to become editor-in-chief. He was released again. At this time he began to compile his *Finnish-English Dictionary*. Later, he devoted himself to the cooperative movement, publishing works about it which received international notice.

The editors of *Työmies* continued to change frequently. Some of them were men of ability; others came to the task straight from the mines. Other Finnish American newspapers scoffed at the editorial staff of *Työmies*, calling it the "jätkästaapi" (hobo headquarters), a name the staff attempted to use as a title of honor. In spite of these difficulties, subscriptions increased from year to year, rising to 10,000 in 1911. By then the paper appeared six times a week and acquired larger quarters in the recently built three-story Kansankoti (People's Home). Rissanen and Laukki were again on the editorial staff, in addition to Eemeli Parras, a capable new man. *Työmies* ceased publication in Hancock in the summer of 1914.[6]

The Labor Movement and the Church

In the publication of the Finnish Labor Organization titled *40 Vuotta* (Forty years), which appeared in 1946, Hilja Frilund reminisced that

> There probably was never in any other community such a nest of cultural and educational activity as we had in Hancock. The editorial staff of *Työmies* and all its personnel were a part of the active element in the Jousi [organization]. The smoking room of the Jousi became a clubroom where intelligent men debated about many subjects, sometimes of real import, sometimes manufactured for the occasion. This is where world happenings were discussed critically. And with what great enthusiasm![7]

Much of the enthusiasm and energy in the Finnish American labor movement in the early part of the century was aimed directly or indirectly at the church and Christianity. This attitude of opposition to the church had been inherited from Finland where, at the time of the birth of the labor movement, there had been two lines of thought about it among the clergy. The representatives of the activist groups, such as Professor A. F. Granfelt (1815–92), Dean Elis Bergroth (1854–1906), and Professor Martti Ruuth (1870–1962) considered it necessary for the clergy to participate in the movement. The representatives of the passivists, whose leader was Gustaf Johansson (1844–1930), the bishop of Kuopio who later became archbishop of Finland, took a firm stand against the participation of the clergy in the labor movement. Excepting for a small minority of activists, the clergy followed the lead of their archbishop.

Two happenings at the end of the century widened the gulf between the clergy and the working class. First, the bishop of Porvoo, Herman Rabergh, made a speech in 1896 in which he characterized the Finnish labor movement as merely an imitation of foreign developments. Second, the church convention of 1898 decided that the amount of property owned should still affect the right to vote in church elections, and the maximum number of votes allowed remained at twenty-five. Rabergh's statement and the decision of the church convention embittered the working people, one of the results being that radicals Matti Kurikka, A. B. Makela, and N. F. af Ursin were better able than before to impress their views on the labor movement.[8]

Thus the labor movement came into Finnish American life with attitudes of suspicion and even of hostility toward the church. In Fitchburg and Astoria, but especially in Hancock, the publishing business, which had grown rapidly in connection with leftist papers, began from the very first to serve anti-church attitudes. Books on socialism, economics, and social policies written from the point of view of materialism and the class struggle were especially popular. They were widely distributed.[9]

It was strange that during the early phases of the labor struggle, the church—above all the Suomi Synod, which had its own clergy and its own publishing house—did not officially take a stand against materialism and for the Christian way of life, nor even clearly define its attitude toward the labor question. It was even stranger in light of the fact that the great majority of people in Finnish American congregations belonged to the working class. The matter of involvement was left to the discretion of individual pastors. Some of them condemned socialism and the labor movement in the severest terms, thus widening the gulf, while most of them remained neutral.[10] There were, however, some pastors who took an active part in discussions about the question.

One of them was Pastor Iisakki Katajamaa, who was born in Alatornio in 1876 and died in Alston, Michigan, in 1911. Because of his early death he did not have time to prepare and publish an extensive study, but in his lectures at Suomi College and in his calendar articles he defined his position. "Society is the product of historical development, and its renewal in new forms must be based on whatever has been acceptable in the past, always keeping in mind the fact that the fundamental condition for the reorganization of society is the inward renewal of its members." Katajamaa was unreservedly in favor of the workers' right to improve their economic situation. At the same time, he severely criticized materialism and claimed that religion should not be allowed to enter into discussions about social problems.[11]

Another pastor who had an understanding of labor problems and participated in this type of discussion on the affirmative side was Pastor Viljami Rautanen, who was born in Helsinki in 1882 and died in Cleveland, Ohio, in 1960. In articles published in *Amerikan Suometar*, and in his short treatise titled *Kirkko ja Sosiaaliset Kysymykset* (The church and social questions) he reiterated his ideas.

> If the church doesn't include social problems in its program and strive for their solution, others will do so, and what is even worse, they may do so in the wrong spirit or use a one-sided approach. . . . Insofar as it is possible, the church should become more than ever involved in social problems. Such are, for example, the care of the needy, labor movements, and trade unions.[12]

Most Finnish Americans, however, came into contact with socialism not through more or less scholarly works, but through blasphemy and crude attacks against Christianity in atheistic speeches and writings. In the period between 1905 and 1907 alone at least seventeen pamphlets by the well-known agnostic Robert G. Ingersoll (1833–99) were translated into Finnish and printed on *Työmies*'s press. They included, for example, *Some Mistakes of Moses*, *Christmas Sermon*, *About the Holy Bible*, and *What Is Religion?* An expression of anti-church sentiment appeared in an annual publication of *Työmies* for 1913, titled *Uuden Ajan Soihtu I* (New era beacon). In it John Korpi declared a relentless war against the church that "wields the sceptre of ignorance and slavery." Blasphemy appeared in its crudest form in the songbooks used at socialist meetings, such as *Työväen Laulukirja* (Workers' songbook) and *Veikeitä Kupletteja* (Clever couplets).[13] This mockery of religion also included ridiculing and treating rudely the clergy who, when traveling, stayed at public rooming houses.

At a meeting of representatives of the SSJ held in Hibbing, Minnesota, in the early part of August 1906, much time was devoted to the question of religion. On the basis of three reports, the discussions ended with several resolutions, of which the following were the most important:

> All religions which in one way or another oppose the economic equality of all people and deny class struggle as a means of attaining economic equality, must be resisted by the Social Democratic Party of America. . . . Agitators must study church religions in the light of historical and scientific truth and demonstrate their class character.[14]

These resolutions gave added impetus to the struggle against religion, which was in actual practice directed more against the church and the clergy than toward Christianity in general.

With regard to reactions of individuals to the question, there was another side to it. Mikko Wastila, editor of the communist paper *Työmies-Eteenpäin*, in an article published on April 28, 1961, wrote that for many persons it was as if lightning had struck from the heavens when they heard their first program against religion, for often these programs offended even some of the party members, who still retained, as a heritage from their past, an attitude of outward respect at least for the Christian religion.

The reply of the church to such abuse was sometimes given in a funeral sermon when the members of a labor organization were all present at the burial service of a comrade. This required more than average tact from a pastor. If tact was lacking, the talk had a negative effect.[15] The pulpit during regular services was a better place for the presentation of counterattacks, and it was frequently used for that purpose in many communities. The most effective countermeasure, however, was the printed work, which the church finally began to use, as the socialist attacks, instead of proclaiming a materialistic philosophy in a general way, began to attack Christianity more directly. The publishing house of the Finnish Congregational Church in Fitchburg, Massachusetts, in 1904–1905, published two pertinent works by Thomas deWitt Talmage (1832–1902).[16] L. A. Lambert's *Notes on Ingersoll*, translated into Finnish by J. Jarvi, was published in Ironwood in 1908. Viljami Rautanen of the Suomi Synod wrote articles defending Christianity for *Amerikan Suometar* and for Suomi College publications.

Within the labor movement, Christianity was declared to be a proletarian socialist religion, and Jesus was construed to be a revolutionary leader. Books written by Kautsky, White, Ricker, and Crooker in this vein were widely distributed.[17] The Finnish church in Michigan did not do much to defend its own historical religious views, except by selling devotional and Sunday school literature imported from Finland.[18]

In more recent times there have been complaints from both the church and the labor movement that neither side ever made any effort to establish personal contact with the opponent although published material would have offered points of departure for discussions between knowledgeable individuals. In the 1920s, however, attacks against the church began to subside gradually for three reasons. First, on January 1, 1922, the religious freedom law went into effect in Finland, eliminating the reasons for the anti-church movement. Its effect was felt in America as well as in Finland in the socialist press. Secondly, the intermarriage of children belonging to different churches brought religious-minded relatives into leftist families. Third, the leftist families as a rule did not teach the Finnish language to their children, with the result that propaganda in the Finnish language was not read by the younger generation. This circumstance led to the cessation of the publication of such propaganda excepting in newspapers.[19]

The Copper Country Strike, 1913–14

The Copper Country miners had organized the Copper Country Trade Union, which belonged to the Western Federation of Miners as no. 16. It had local branches at various mines. On July 14, 1913, this trade union sent a letter to eighteen copper mining companies in the area extending from Mohawk to Winona. The letter stated that the miners were "dissatisfied with wages, work hours, and other conditions"; that they had referred this matter to the union for negotiation; that their representatives were ready to discuss it with representatives of the companies at a place to be specified by the companies not later than July 28; and that Trade Union no. 16 had given their leaders the right to call a strike unless the companies replied by July 21. The letter was signed by the secretary of the union, C. R. Hietala, and the president, Dan Sullivan.

The most important cause of discontent was the length of the working day, which varied from nine to ten and a half hours. The time was figured from the moment of arrival at the shaft opening to the time of return to the surface. The time it took to descend into the mine and return to the surface varied from twenty minutes to an hour and forty minutes, depending on the mine and its depth. The actual working day, therefore, varied considerably in length, being the most variable in the conglomerate mines, where the blasting had to be done at the end of the workday. In the mines of Butte, Montana, which are often compared with the mines of the Copper Country, the workday was eight hours. It was figured from the time the miner arrived underground at his place of work to the time of arrival at the surface after work.

The wages paid in Copper Country mines were for the most part somewhat lower—in some instances considerably lower—than in the Butte-area mines. On the other hand, the cost of food and other necessities in Butte averaged 30–33 percent higher than in the Copper Country. The daily wages of the Copper Country miners—the men who did the drilling—varied from $2.54 to $5.13 per day in the first half of 1913, the average wage being about $3.20. The pay of trammers, who shoveled the ore into cars and ran them to the skip, varied from $2.24 to $3.14, averaging about $2.63 per day. In connection with wages, housing must be mentioned also. The eighteen copper mining companies had built 278 log houses and 2,767 frame houses for workmen and their families. These homes had from three to ten rooms, the usual number being five. The rent paid to the companies ranged from 50 cents to $7.50 per month, averaging 80 cents per room per month. Most of these homes had water piped into them. In addition, 1,721 miners had their own homes on land leased from the companies. The annual rent for lots ranged from $1 at Winona to $10, the average being $5 per year.

In addition to complaints about wages there were complaints about the one-man drill, which had recently been put into use, and about the treatment the workmen received from subordinate bosses. The latter was an especially sensitive issue to recently arrived immigrants, who were often pushed around and who, because of difficulties with the English language, often hesitated to complain to higher officials. There were thousands of men, both Finns and non-Finns, who belonged to this group.

Worker opinion concerning the one-man drill was divided. Some considered it better than the two-man drill previously used. Others were better satisfied with the 290-pound drill operated by two men. The new 150-pound drill had been designed for operation by one man and was considered more efficient than the older, heavier machine. The companies refused to consider going back to the old drill and would not even discuss the possibility. Among the other causes of dissatisfaction there were none that could not have been eliminated through discussions between workers and company officials. The higher officials admitted frankly that there was room for improvement in the behavior of subordinate bosses toward workmen. They also recognized the fact that the eight-hour day had already begun its successful career in American industry. In the Copper Country the eight-hour day went into effect on January 1, 1914. As for the demand for higher wages, the miners were reasonable. They wanted a minimum daily wage of $3.50 for miners and $3.00 for trammers.

The core of the trouble between the miners and the mining companies was actually a difference of opinion about recognizing the Western Federation of Miners as the legal representative of the Copper Country miners. This federation, which was later replaced by the International Union of Mine, Mill, and Smelter Workers, was at that time the most powerful member of the American Labor Union. The American Labor Union, which gave birth in 1905 to the IWW—Industrial Workers of the World—was still closely affiliated with the American Socialist party in 1913. The mining companies of the Copper Country considered the Western Federation of Miners an outside organization that had nothing to do with activities in Michigan and refused to negotiate with it since most of the workmen did not belong to it.

Table 17 shows the distribution of miners in Copper Country mines on July 22, 1913. Most of the miners were Finns, up to 80 percent in some of the smaller mines. There was also a good representation

Table 17: Distribution of Miners in Copper Country Mines, July 22, 1913

Mohawk Mining Co.	851
Ahmeek Mining Co.	830
Allouez Mining Co.	308
Osceola Consolidated Mining Co.	1,143
Wolverine Copper Mining Co.	387
Centennial Copper Mining Co.	118
Calumet & Hecla Mining Co.	4,107
Tamarack Mining Co.	610
Laurium Mining Co.	25
La Salle Mining Co.	43
Oneco Copper Co.	25
Franklin Mining Co.	322
Quincy Mining Co.	1,483
Hancock Consolidated Mining Co.	161
Isle Royale Copper Co.	709
Superior Copper Co.	162
Copper Range Consolidated Co.	2,716
Winona Copper Co.	300
Total	14,300

of English, Italians, and Croatians. It is no longer possible to find out how many workmen belonged to the local union and through it to the Western Federation of Miners. The statement by Sulkanen that "at the beginning of the strike, over 13,000 men were members of the organization, increasing to 16,000 during the strike" is erroneous.[20] For example, a vote taken before the start of the strike revealed that only 171 men out of the 2,495 participating in the vote at the mines of the Copper Range Consolidated Company belonged to the union. At the end of the strike the total number of miners in the Copper Country mines was still less than 16,000.

Since not one of the mining companies replied to the ultimatum of July 14, the leaders of the union—more accurately, the representatives sent by the Western Federation of Miners to the Copper Country—announced that the strike would begin on Wednesday, July 23. By Friday, all work underground had ceased, though not for long.

Gradually the number of those who wanted to work increased, so that by October 8, for example, 5,445 men had returned to work, 2,079 of them being underground workers.

Relations between strikers and nonstrikers were bitter from the very beginning and led to violence. The strikers arranged to hold their demonstration parades at such times and at such places that they would be sure to meet the men going to or coming from work. The small police forces of the mining towns had neither the means nor the ability, in many cases, to enforce the law and maintain order. The Houghton County sheriff hired fifty-two men from the Waddell-Mahon Detective Agency to guard the banks, the newspapers, and the mines. This action, however, did not produce the expected results. Instead, it made the situation worse. On September 20 the district court issued an injunction forbidding members of the Western Federation of Miners to take part in demonstrations near the mines or against workers elsewhere. After nine days, however, the injunction was revoked and disturbances recurred. The worst of them were the stoning of and shooting at the train running between Calumet and Ahmeek to take men to and from work, and the blowing up of a house. In many cases of violence it was impossible to find out which side was responsible. The sheriff of Houghton County was unable to uphold law and order and asked for aid from the governor of Michigan, who responded by sending National Guard troops to the Copper Country. Order was satisfactorily maintained from then on.

The headquarters of the strikers were at the Kansankoti, which had just been built by the Finnish labor organization of Hancock. There, in the printing shop of *Työmies*, *Miners' Bulletin*, which occasionally included an Italian section titled *Bollettino dei Minatori*, was also published, twice weekly.

To counterbalance the Western Federation of Miners, the Citizens' Alliance was established early in November. It published a paper titled *Truth*. This paper, whose front page was in English and whose back page was sometimes in Finnish, was printed on the presses of the Book Concern, the Suomi Synod's publishing house. According to the second issue of *Truth*, which appeared on November 29, there were already 6,132 members in the Citizens' Alliance, somewhat more than in the local union of the Western Federation of Miners. The Citizens' Alliance also included working miners who did not approve of the socialistic, anti-church spirit of the union, for it sometimes happened that, as a condition for getting his strike pay from the union, a striking miner had to leave his church.[21]

Nor was the church by any means innocent of blame for the

worsening of conditions. When *Miners' Bulletin* and the *Hancock Journal* suggested that the churches, too, should express themselves on the matter, the Rev. W. E. Marvin, on July 16, 1913, wrote an open letter to the *Miners' Bulletin* on behalf of the Copper Country Methodist Ministerial Association, condemning the strikers in no uncertain terms. The Suomi Synod was more cautious. It apparently feared the possibility that the leading mining companies might close their mines and move to Montana and Arizona, causing overwhelming difficulties for its still struggling Suomi College.[22] Only Pastor Viljami Rautanen of the synod wrote articles, in *Amerikan Suometar*, expressing the opinion that the workers had the right to organize and to act through representatives chosen by them. The Catholic Church sent Father Peter E. Dietz, editor of the diocesan publication *Michigan Catholic*, to appraise the situation. In a long and courageous statement published in the *Miners' Bulletin* in its entirety, he explained the philosophy of his church and the position of Pope Leo XIII on socialism, concluding that just as the stockholders of the mines had organized and were expressing themselves through the directors of their companies, so the workers, too, had the right to organize and, without interference from the outside, to select whomever they wished as their spokesman.[23] In other words, Father Dietz was demanding recognition of the Western Federation of Miners as the representative of the workmen.

At about five o'clock on Christmas Eve in Calumet a tragedy occurred, the effects of which were felt for decades. A program for the families of striking miners was being held at the Italian Hall. When the children were marching to the stage to receive their Christmas gifts, someone in the hall shouted "fire!" Panic ensued, and children and adults began to run down the steep stairs which led to the street. Because the doors at the foot of the stairs opened inward, it was impossible to open them as the mass of humanity pressed against them. At least seventy-three persons were smothered or trampled to death, most of them Finnish children and their mothers, with a few elderly persons among them. Thousands of persons lined the streets of Calumet the next Sunday when the two-mile-long funeral procession wound its way to the cemetery in silence. Scores of persons lay injured in hospitals. There is some disagreement as to how many perished.

On Christmas Day—the day after a tragedy that need not have occurred, for "there was no fire"—there was a public meeting which was attended by people of all classes and nationalities. The Catholic and Presbyterian churches were officially represented. A twelve-member committee, on which Oscar Kekkonen represented the Finns, was named to aid the unfortunate families, widows, and orphans. In two days the committee collected $20,000.

A meeting of leaders of the Finnish labor movement was held in Duluth concerning the tragedy already in the evening of that December 24. Aku Rissanen, Leo Laukki, John Viita, John Korpi, and Martin Hendrickson met at the latter's home to discuss action to be taken. "We decided to make full use immediately of the strength of our organization and our party." That very night Rissanen was sent on his way to Hancock.[24] At his direction, the incident was labeled a deliberate attack on the strikers. Rumors were spread that the man who had shouted "fire" had been wearing a Citizens' Alliance button and that deputy sheriffs had prevented women and children from getting out into the street. At the official investigation, witnesses who had been in the hall were unable to prove that they had heard and seen a man wearing Citizens' Alliance identification yelling "fire." They had definitely heard the shout, and they said it had come from the rear of the hall. According to all eyewitnesses, the behavior of the deputy sheriffs and the police on the scene had been exactly the opposite of what the *Miners' Bulletin* claimed. Who had given the false alarm, either thoughtlessly or deliberately, has never, to this day, been discovered.

The strike continued into 1914 but gradually weakened. Finns began to move away from the Copper Country in large numbers, to Bruce Crossing, Rock, and Rudyard in the Upper Peninsula, and to Kaleva and Detroit in Lower Michigan, as well as westward to Minnesota, and eastward to the Atlantic, especially to the Cape Ann granite quarries and the Cape Cod cranberry bogs. At some of the smaller mines the strike gradually became one in name rather than in fact, for miners returned to work practically in full force. The Western Federation of Miners began to run out of funds, and in meetings held from April 8 to 11, the local union notified the strikers at various mines that they would have to be satisfied with less strike pay or return to work on company terms. The strike, which had lasted 265 days, had brought great financial difficulties, even destitution, especially to men with families.

On Easter Day, April 12, voting took place on ending or continuing the strike. Several different reports on the results of the voting were published. *Amerikan Suometar* of April 14 stated that according to information received, 5,997 men had voted, of whom 4,560 had voted to end the strike and 1,437 to continue it. The *Miners' Bulletin* gave no figures; it merely announced that most of the workers had voted to return to work. C. R. Hietala, secretary of the local union, reported that a total of 4,740 had voted, of whom 3,104 were in favor of ending the strike and 1,636 in favor of continuing it, and that local figures would not be revealed. Table 18 shows the figures published on April 14, by the *Daily Mining Gazette.*

Table 18: Copper Country Strike Vote, 1914

	AGAINST CONTINUING STRIKE	FOR CONTINUING STRIKE
South Range	495	93
Calumet	281	391
Ahmeek	600	72
Hancock	365	255
Mass	121	56
Totals	1,862	867

At some mines a vote had not been necessary because workers had already been on their jobs for a long time. Strikers returned to work on Wednesday, April 15. The companies had already agreed to demands made the previous summer concerning working hours and wages. The condition for acceptance for work was relinquishment of the Western Federation of Miners membership card. Thus, the strikers had both won and lost.[25]

Results of the Strike

The almost nine-month-long strike, with its tensions and disturbances, changed the face of the Copper Country considerably. So many people moved away that church membership and membership in other Finnish organizations fell to low levels. The Citizens' Alliance considered its work finished and ceased activity. On April 9, 1914, however, some of its more active members organized the Finnish Anti-socialistic League in Hancock. At about the same time a corresponding organization was started in Calumet. The purpose of the league was to work against un-American and anti-religious socialism as well as to indicate to the American public that most Finns were not socialists. By June 23, 246 persons had joined the Finnish Anti-socialistic League of Hancock.[26]

One of the most noticeable results of the strike was the moving of *Työmies* paper away from Michigan to Wisconsin. The causes for its moving were, in addition to the failure of the strike, the loss of advertising in the paper due to the activities of the Anti-socialistic League, and the strife within the Finnish American labor movement itself. The paper admitted with some bitterness that even after a ten-year struggle it still had to leave the Copper Country in the hands of church people. In October 1914 *Työmies* moved to Superior, Wisconsin, to become a neighbor of its rival and enemy, *Sosialisti*, which had started publication early in June. The Anti-socialistic League ceased activity a year later.

Labor Organizations

In 1917, the Finnish American Socialist Organization had 11,302 members (see table 19).[27] These memberships were all "paid in full." With regard to dues, organizational discipline was absolute. The average membership of the various local divisions was fifty. An interesting fact concerning membership is that in Hancock alone, for example, the number of adults in the Suomi Synod congregation was almost as great as the total membership of the twenty socialist divisions in the entire state of Michigan. In 1917 the membership of Suomi Synod congregations in the state as a whole was 7,397 adults, nearly six times greater than the total membership of all the socialist groups in Michigan. Because of their tight organization and other factors, however, the socialists were much more powerful in their communities than might have been expected considering their small membership.

During the years 1904–14, when *Työmies* was being published in Hancock, Jousi, the local socialist organization, was the leading Finnish organization in the state. The cultural socialism advocated by J. N. Ahlman was voted out, and from 1907 on, Jousi belonged to the Socialist party. A workingmen's organization was started in Calumet in 1904; the most notable of its leaders was Wilho Leikas. This organization became inactive immediately after the strike. A Finnish socialist organization was also started in Bessemer in 1904 or 1905. Its first meetings were held in the hall belonging to the Suoja (Shelter) Temperance Society. Soon, however, it took over the society and the hall, naming the hall the Kansantalo (People's Hall). Of special interest is the fact that there were disagreements with the Finnish ministers and preachers over funeral sermons, with the result that the socialists stopped having the clergy officiate at their funerals and weddings. They even refused to have their children baptized. The hall with all the records kept there burned down in the fall of 1922. A new hall was built the following spring. When membership fell off in 1946, the hall was sold. All activity of the group ceased in 1953, and its property was donated to *Industrialisti*.[28]

Table 19: Membership in Amerikan Suomalainen Sosialistijärjestö (Finnish American Socialist Organization), 1917

STATE	DIVISIONS	MEMBERS	FINNISH POPULATION	PERCENTAGE OF SOCIALISTS
Arizona	1	39	699	5
California	9	440	8,995	4
Colorado	2	62	1,857	3
Connecticut	6	159	1,231	12
Idaho	5	151	954	15
Illinois	4	428	3,182	13
Indiana	2	61	315	19
Maine	4	67	1,214	5
Maryland	1	30	?	?
Massachusetts	26	2,552	16,170	15
Michigan	20	1,269	55,548	2
Minnesota	33	1,122	44,463	2
Montana	7	167	6,623	2
Nevada	2	57	233	24
New Hampshire	10	210	1,214	17
New Jersey	6	205	2,259	9
New York	7	1,069	11,506	9
North Dakota	3	54	2,610	2
Ohio	9	518	7,201	7
Oregon	4	382	7,711	4
Pennsylvania	9	483	3,688	13
Rhode Island	2	26	462	5
South Dakota	1	63	3,075	2
Utah	3	80	1,535	5
Vermont	5	118	467	25
Washington	18	717	13,258	5
West Virginia	2	83	?	?
Wisconsin	10	236	9,696	3
Wyoming	8	353	2,154	16
29 states	219	11,201	208,320	5

In 1905 the socialist organizations of Negaunee and Ishpeming appeared on the scene and were for a short time the most powerful in Michigan. Among those present at the organization of the Negaunee division were Matti Kurikka, Taavi Tainio, and Frank Aaltonen. The meeting was held on May 21, 1905. For several years the group met and worked under unfavorable conditions in the Nokihaali (Soot Hall). In 1910, the splendid Työntemppeli (Labor Temple) was completed. Matti Tenhunen wrote: "It is a building which the bourgeoisie and their stooges view in a cold sweat." Activity began with the presentation of the play *Daniel Hjort*, and continued in full vigor for a number of years. Lawsuits, and disagreements within the organization, however, caused it to be dissolved, and the Labor Temple went to the county for delinquent taxes. The Ishpeming society was organized on July 12, 1905, and was active about ten years, after which it too succumbed to the effects of communism, which caused the dissolution of the Finnish American labor movement.

A socialist division was organized in Marquette in 1906, and on Labor Day of 1912 they dedicated Liberty Hall. The organization barely managed to stay in existence and finally ceased activity in 1938. In Ironwood the Rauha (Peace) labor organization was active in 1900, but it was soon dissolved. It was reactivated as a socialist division in 1906. Within two years it had a large hall called the Palace, which was unusually well equipped for dramatic presentations, musical programs, and gymnastic performances. Eventually the organization lost most of its members because of internal dissension. The Palace was torn down in 1940.

Detroit's first Finnish socialist division was organized in 1906 by socialists from Cleveland. In 1914 they acquired their first hall, and in 1923 they built a combination hall and office building, which cost $100,000. A few years later the group purchased a large place on Loon Lake for summer vacations and festivals. The Detroit division was for some time one of the strongest Finnish American socialist organizations, until it too collapsed in the dissolution caused by the growth of communism, losing even its hall.[29]

The Finnish socialist division organized in Rock, Michigan, in 1912 gathered into it Finnish leftists from wide areas outside the town. Of all the labor organizations in Michigan, Rock had the greatest amount of theatrical activity, the number of performances totaling over 250. Later, interest turned to the cooperative movement. In Munising, because of the comparative isolation of the community, the activity of the socialist organization was concentrated mostly on serving its own membership. In addition to the usual activities, which included a speaking society, a women's group, and a band, it also operated a rooming house for unmarried men, a cooperative restaurant called Pyrintö (Aspiration), and a small cooperative store. In 1926 this organization was named the Finnish Club.[30]

In addition to the socialist organizations already mentioned, there were others in the following communities that included many Finns in their population: Grand Rapids, Grayling, Pontiac, Kaleva, Drummond Island, Sault Ste. Marie, Daggett, Newberry, Eben Junction, Covington, Kenton, Michigamme, Herman, Amasa, Iron River, Crystal Falls, Mass, Paynesville, Wainola, Bruce Crossing, Wakefield, Ontonagon, South Range, Atlantic Mine, Trimountain, Ahmeek, and Allouez.

The Socialist Party of America was always small, appealing mostly to immigrants. In 1918, for example, its total membership was only 82,000, of which 34,000 belonged to non-English divisions, the Finns being the largest group, with 11,000 members. Following them came the Germans, the Jews, and the Lithuanians.[31]

The Dissolution Caused by Communism

On March 18, 1918, the leaders of the Russian Bolshevik Revolution accepted "Russian Communist Party" as the name of their political group, thus revealing their complete separation from the socialists. Revolutionary elements in various other countries followed the example of their Russian counterparts, and so there were soon scores of communist parties around the world. Communism took hold in the Finnish American labor movement with relative ease because radical elements were already powerfully represented in it. These elements included paid agitators; *Köyhälistön Nuija* (Hammer of the proletariat), published in Hancock from 1906 to 1912; *Työmies;* and numerous special publications.

In this trend toward communism, an especially big part was played by the Workingmen's College, which was wrested from the Finnish National Church in the summer of 1906, and which, in addition to satisfying the cultural needs of the working people, taught Marxist socialism and the philosophy of materialism. Teachers and administrative personnel in the college were radicals known in America and Finland, such as Kalle Leonard Haataja, Leo Laukki, Aku Rissanen, Yrjo Sirola, and the Latvian J. G. Ohsol. On special occasions a red flag was flown above the college beside the Stars and Stripes, and the annual publication started in 1908 was called *Vallankumous* (Revolution).

After the Cleveland meeting discussed earlier, which laid the foundation for the trend still further to the left in the Finnish American labor movement, there were manifestations of this trend in the national meetings of representatives of socialist organizations. The meeting of 1906, in which some of the delegates from Michigan were Gust Anttila from Trimountain, Kusti Korhonen from Mass, Albin Vauhkonen from Ishpeming, Oskar Maki and Vilho Leikas from Calumet, and V. S. Holmsten, Kaapo Murros, and Toivo Salonen from Hancock, was held in Hibbing at the time of the Viaporin Rebellion. The following cablegram was sent to the participants in the uprising: "Socialist Executive Committee, Helsinki, Finland: The convention of the Finnish Socialists greets its comrades in revolution. May the red flag wave for sacred freedom!—Representatives of the Socialists."

In a meeting held in Hancock at the end of August 1909, the majority rejected the industrial unionism of the Industrial Workers of the World (IWW), but all were in agreement on the resolution that "we consider the red flag to be the symbol of freedom, brotherhood, and equality for all." Evidence presented at a meeting held at the Workingmen's College in June 1912 confirmed the fact that this was apparently the heyday of the Finnish American labor movement: There were 189 organizations with a total of 13,667 members, of whom 8,474 had "paid in full." At this meeting, too, sabotage was condemned. This was just the calm before the storm.

The strikes of 1912–14—in the textile mills of the east, in the copper mines of Michigan, and in the rubber industry of Pennsylvania—brought up the question of policy and tactics. Was not syndicalism with its trade unions too passive? It made use only of the boycott, sabotage, and strike, from which the more wealthy classes always seemed to emerge victorious, while the working class was condemned beforehand to failure, poverty, and misery.[32] The Finns who had joined the IWW had an answer: The struggle between capital and labor must continue until the proletariat of the world has taken over land and production and eliminated the wage system. People from the Workingmen's College were leaders among the advocates of this "new direction."

The struggle started from disagreements over small matters in the socialist organization of Negaunee, which split into two factions, one supporting Frank Aaltonen and the other supporting William Risto. The conflict spread to include the entire Finnish American labor movement, with Leo Laukki as leader of the radicals. It continued in the district meetings held in the East, in the West, and in Hancock. The final break came at the annual meeting of the Työmies Publishing Company in the summer of 1914. The radicals left the Hancock meeting and established a rival newspaper titled *Sosialisti* in Duluth. Its name was soon changed to *Teollisuustyöläinen* (Industrial worker) and later to *Industrialisti*. *Sosialisti* had an auspicious beginning as a daily with over 4,000 subscribers, but it ceased publication in 1916. At the fourth convention of representatives of the Finnish Socialist Organization in Chicago toward the end of November in 1914, losses caused by communism were confirmed.

The entry of the United States into World War I on April 6, 1917, created a wave of patriotism that was fraught with consequences for socialism. It was a historical coincidence that the meeting of the American Socialist party, at which Santeri Nuorteva was the leader of the Finnish delegation, had been called for April 7 in St. Louis. Morris Hillquit, the chairman, gave a long anti-war speech which the convention approved. The newspapers of the country took hold of the matter, making an issue of the fact that foreign-speaking immigrants formed a large part of the Socialist party. Many socialist papers lost their postal franchise, socialist halls were destroyed or damaged, and socialist leaders were sent to prison. In the West, the Finnish American labor movement, led by *Toveri* of Astoria, was especially hard pressed. Throughout the country, Finnish socialist organizations lost many members.

The war for independence in Finland in 1918, which was accompanied by a regrettable civil war, was not a struggle between the laboring class and the bourgeoisie, for the White Army too was largely made up of laborers. It was fundamentally the country's struggle to free itself of Russian control. The leadership of the Finnish American labor movement, with its newspapers and writers, gave its wholehearted support to the Finnish Red Guard and Russia.[33] It is well to remember, however, that in 1918–21, Finnish American leftists sent great amounts of food and clothing to refugee families in prison camps. But the procommunist stand taken by the leaders of the Finnish American labor movement on the happenings in Finland caused many members whose relatives were on the White side to withdraw from the movement. There was, however, some compensation to the labor movement temporarily in the Red Guardists who came to America after World War I.

The Communist Party of America was organized at a stormy meeting in Chicago in the summer of 1919. The Communist Labor Party, or CLP, and the Communist Party of America, or CP, were established. These two organizations became one at a secret meeting held in May of the following year in Bridgeman, Michigan, with a representative of the Moscow Comintern in attendance.[34]

The conflict between the Finnish American socialists and the communists continued in the fifth representative congress of the socialist organization, held in Chicago in 1919, and in the sixth and last, which was held in Waukegan beginning on Christmas Day in 1920. The final separation of the labor movement from the Socialist party took place here, and union with the Communist party followed. Several socialist organizations declared themselves to be independent. There were some socialist organizations left in Massachusetts, centered around the *Raivaaja* newspaper. The few societies left in Michigan moved into the industrial workers' unionist camp.

In 1921 the communist newspaper *Eteenpäin* (Forward) was established in New York. In 1950 it was moved to Superior, Wisconsin, where it merged with *Työmies* and became *Työmies Eteenpäin.* At a convention in Chicago in January 1927, the Finnish Labor Organization of the United States was established as a subsidiary of the Communist Party of America. Forty delegates from the United States and one from Canada attended this convention. There were ten persons representing the central states: John Orasmaa, O. E. Toivonen, Herman Kortesoja, Paul Voimala, Helmi Ronkkonen, John Kokko, Emil Juntunen, John Kiiskila, John Rukkila, and Jack Steele.[35] Two years later this organization attempted to get control of the Finnish American cooperatives.[36] Between 1927 and 1930 it was gradually "bolshevized" to the status of a satellite to which orders came through higher levels of command. That marked the end of independent local organizations. However, this Finnish American organization which was a subdivision of the Ameri and Communist Party had the unusual distinction of sometimes being permitted to make direct contact with communist headquarters in Moscow.

The Karelian Venture

The Finnish Labor Organization, soon after its establishment, was given the task of building up the Karelian Autonomous Soviet Socialist Republic, which had been set up in 1923, and whose rich forests were of great importance to the economy of the Soviet Union. The Soviet Union was recruiting engineers and skilled laborers from many countries at the time, and it was thought that the Finnish American leftists would be able to serve the cause of revolution especially well in the ancient lands of Kalevala. To prepare the Finnish Americans for this, Molotov's extensive lecture on the economic program of the Soviet Union, which he delivered at the plenary session of the Executive Committee of the Communist International (Comintern) in Moscow on February 25, 1930, was translated into Finnish.[37] It was distributed through cells of the Labor Organization in America. An office of technical aid to Soviet Karelia was opened in New York.[38] Its function was to find laborers, machinery, tools, and equipment, and transportation for them, to Karelia.

When the machinery for accomplishing this was in order, Matti Tenhunen and Martin Hendrickson were sent on a recruiting mission throughout the United States and Canada. The timing for this project was exactly right, for the United States was experiencing an economic depression, a situation which led many people to listen with interest to colorful stories about Russian freedom and the glorious future of Karelia. Those who decided to go there were not all communists by any means. Among them were persons motivated by high ideals, even a few who were inspired by a spirit of nationalism. The basic principle behind the recruiting had nothing to do with a man's enthusiasm for communism; it had everything to do with his possibilities as "technical aid" to Karelia, meaning specifically his automobile, his tractor, his tools, and above all, his money—all things that he was expected to take to Karelia with him.

The figures on the number of Finns who went to Karelia between 1930 and 1933 vary from two thousand to ten thousand and include the Canadian Finns. When the fact that most of the families who participated in this venture were young and had many children is taken into consideration, a figure of six thousand to seven thousand is probably a reasonable estimate. It is not clear how many of the number were from Michigan, but reasoning from the knowledge that from one small farming community, fifteen adults and seventeen children went, it becomes obvious that hundreds must have gone from the state as a whole. It was a carpenter from a Michigan town who reminisced thus about his adventure in Karelia:

> I traveled with my wife and two children on a ship of the Swedish-American Line to Tallinn. Accomodations were luxurious. But upon crossing the Russian border on an Estonian train, everything changed. The food was such that as Americans we were in desperate straits. In one way or another the *kasha*, or buckwheat porridge, which we ate with olive oil because there was no milk, went down. At the logging camp we lived with several other families in a pigpen that had been converted into a barracks. Our American housewives got it into satisfactory condition, considering the situation.
>
> Because I was a carpenter I got better wages than many of the others, who had no special trade. As long as the clothes and tools we had brought from America lasted, we were able to manage somehow. We were not permitted to build houses for ourselves. We were

> there on temporary permits which had to be renewed every six months. For the children's sake we tried to keep a cow, but the tax on it was so high that we could not afford it. The situation affected our nerves, and when the Americans began to quarrel, a Finnish party man, later called a politruk, was put in charge. He sold us government bonds for dollars, but he kept the dollars for himself, reporting them as rubles; he was seized and liquidated. But the Americans and Canadians put the Karelian lumber industry on its feet, setting up loading and unloading equipment such as had never before been seen in Karelia, and repairing the circular saws so that they were useable.
>
> Once, wages were not received for a long time. The Finns had a meeting and sent in a protest. Russian party bosses appeared on the scene and announced that party actions must not be criticized and demanded that the protest be revoked. When, after two years, the choice had to be made as to whether to become a citizen of the Soviet Union or leave the country, we returned to America by way of Finland. Those who had not succeeded in hiding their money were compelled to stay in Karelia because they were unable to pay for transportation.

Stalin, who became the Soviet dictator after the death of Lenin in 1924, had gradually changed his views on domestic policy and become more pan-Slavic and anti-foreign. Liquidation of Finns began among those who had arrived in Russia after the revolution of 1918. They were accused of a variety of crimes and imprisoned or taken away to labor camps where they disappeared. The general housecleaning which began in 1937, the political background of which, including Reinhard Heyrich's part in it and the liquidation of the leadership of the Red Army, does not belong in this discussion, also brought the adventure of the American and Canadian Finns in Karelia to a painful end. They were accused of being saboteurs and anti-revolutionary agents of capitalist governments. The high hopes with which many Michigan Finns had started on their journey to Karelia ended unhappily and even tragically in the ski factory of Petroskoi and the limestone quarries of Hiilisuo, Kontupohja, and Olenia. Leo Laukki, Matti Tenhunen, Martin Hendrickson, Oscar Corgan, and many other men connected with the labor movement in Michigan ended their days in one of these places or in some unknown prison.[39]

The year 1938 has gone down in history as the "Karelian Finns' year of terror," when Matushenko, Moscow's commissioner of Karelian Internal Affairs, was in authority. Persecution was directed even against the dead. Santeri Nuorteva, who had died while still in the good graces of the government, had been buried in a place of honor in the center of Petroskoi. He was declared an enemy of the people, and his burial site was leveled so that its location could no longer be ascertained. The liquidation of Finnish Americans was directed mostly at the middle aged and elderly. The younger generation, whose way of thinking there was some possibility of Russifying, were spared. In the fighting in East Karelia in 1941, the Russians made use of Finnish American soldiers. They clad them in uniforms of the Finnish Army and had them serve as patrols. They also parachuted them behind the lines, causing some confusion at first. Because these men spoke American "Finnglish," however, they were soon discovered and captured.[40]

Karelian Soviet literature printed in Petroskoi and Leningrad was carefully silent about the work and the fate of the Finnish Canadians and Finnish Americans, although in East Karelia their work was of sufficient importance to have been mentioned at least. Kuprijanov's work on this period in the history of Karelia does not give any information about the happenings of 1930–40. it gives only statistics on Soviet medals of honor bestowed during the war and exaggerated figures on destroyed industrial plants.[41] However, information is available from other sources.[42]

The End of the Finnish American Labor Movement

The establishment of the Finnish Labor Organization of the United States in 1927 as a subdivision of the American Communist Party started a series of events which eventually brought about the end of the Finnish American labor movement. Total dissolution of many local divisions occurred, often because the majority of members refused to submit to the dictates of the all-powerful Executive Committee and to the payment of fees which had been raised from already high levels. The economic depression of the 1930s caused others to leave the movement. The departure of the thousands of members who had succumbed to the "Karelia Fever" resulted in great financial loss, for they were the ones who were well off and able to pay their dues.

Many of the persons who had gone to Karelia were fortunate in being able to return to their old homes. With typical Finnish caution they had, though breaking all ties with the capitalistic world, left savings in banks in the United States and Canada. Because of these savings they were able to return—it was possible to do so up to 1933—and to begin life anew in the New World. These persons never again joined Communist organizations. Consequently the Communists considered them traitors to the party.

When the Finnish American communists, under the direction of Kullervo Manner, who had been sent from Moscow, attempted to take over the Central Cooperative Wholesale and failed, only three of the many cooperatives in Michigan—those in Mass, Ironwood, and Eben—were left under communist control.[43] In Minnesota there were four, and in Wisconsin, two. There were none left in other states. Most of the businesses controlled by the communists were small and lasted only a short time.

A setback was also experienced in Astoria where *Toveri* was rapidly losing subscribers. The explanation given for the consequent demise of the paper was that the presses were needed in Petroskoi to serve the Finnish Karelian Republic. However, the presses were apparently left in Leningrad at the *Pravda* printing plant, which began to issue propaganda in the Finnish language at that time.[44]

Aversion to communism gradually became so strong that in some communities public opinion compelled the Finnish communists to close their halls. In many places communist divisions became so small that they sold their halls, and the "cells" met in private homes, which were able to accommodate their shrunken membership.

In 1930 the Finnish organization comprised eight districts: Massachusetts, New York, Ohio, Illinois, Minnesota-Wisconsin, Upper Michigan, Rocky Mountain states, and Pacific states. Oskar Rahkonen of Ironwood was the secretary of the Upper Michigan District for a long time.

Because of the fact that the United States and Canada were allies of the Soviet Union in World War II, there was a temporary renewal of enthusiasm in the communist parties of these countries. There was also increased activity in Finnish American communist cells. For example, the leftists of Sugar Island published, in the Sault Ste. Marie *Evening News*, an attack against Finland signed by fifty-two persons. In December 1959 Gus Hall, a Finn, became secretary of the American Communist party. He currently serves as the national chair of this organization. Hall was born as Arvo Mikko Halberg to parents who had been born in Lapua, came to Minnesota at the beginning of the century, and lived in Virginia, Alavus, and Cherry. This Finnish leadership in the party did not increase communist activity among the Finns of Upper Michigan.

Just before the establishment of the Finnish communist organization and the resulting dissolution of the socialist labor movement, there were 197 Finnish labor organizations in the United States, or 22 fewer than in 1917. Twenty-four of them were in Michigan. At the beginning of the 1960s, or thirty-five years later, among the communists of Michigan there was activity worth mentioning only in fewer than ten localities which, arranged according to the extent of activity, were Detroit, Rock, Covington-Watton, Mass, Eben, Ironwood, Negaunee, South Range, and Baraga. By 1962 the Upper Michigan district had become the smallest of the Finnish districts.

Starting in 1952, summer get-togethers called old timers' festivals were held by the older people. They were first held in Bruce Crossing and later at the Ponnistus Hall in Covington. After 1955 the Rock organization was usually the host. People from many states attended these festivals and programs. It was customary to donate a part of the proceeds to *Industrialisti.* The Committee of the Upper Michigan District of the Finnish Communist party had a separate festival. It was first held at Lake Gogebic, and from 1964 on in Mass. Those who attended these festivals did not use the name of their party in connection with them. They called themselves representatives of educational societies, cultural clubs, farmers' associations, or Finnish progressive organizations.

13 The Knights and Ladies of Kaleva

The strongest expression of loyalty to their Finnish heritage among the Finnish Americans has been the activity of the Knights and Ladies of Kaleva. The founder of the Kaleva society was John Stone, who was born in Oulu on September 13, 1865, and attended school there. He came to America in 1887 and settled in the small sawmill town of Tower, Minnesota, with his young wife, Sofia, whose maiden name was Kraftenberg. From Tower he moved to Belt, Montana, where he entered business, having become financially secure. He also lived for a time in the Copper Country of Michigan, where, with David Kuona as partner, he established a coffee roastery. He died in Virginia, Minnesota, on March 13, 1946, and was buried in South Range.

John Stone was a Finnish-minded man of high ideals. His tender heart was moved by the low level of life among the Finns working in the mines of Montana. He was troubled even more by the fact that the elements serving as spiritual and intellectual leaders of the Finns wasted their energies in bickering among themselves. These elements included newspapers, temperance societies, and churches. The newspapers quarreled among themselves; some of them attacked the church and the temperance movement; there was dissension among the temperance people and within the churches; and there was tension between the clergy and the temperance societies.

Stone and several of his friends considered ways of remedying the situation. They came to the conclusion that a society should be established to foster "tieto ja taito"—knowledge and accomplishment—in its members, help them appreciate the higher values of life, and open their eyes to the originality and power of Finnish culture.

Based on Christianity but neutral in all political matters, this kind of society would be able to draw Finns from various groups and to settle differences between conflicting elements.[1] It was thought that an organization patterned after American secret societies would produce the best results. With his friends, Stone formulated bylaws and rules of procedure. Stone himself often worked through the night, destroyed the results of his labors, and started again from the beginning. After three years of deliberation he felt that he had finally worked out a satisfactory plan.

On a certain Sunday in January 1898, the organizational meeting of the Knights of Kaleva was held in the Finnish church in Belt. In addition to Stone, persons present included acquaintances whom he had invited in addition to his trusted friends, Jussi Jaaskelainen, Daniel Kuona, Matti Rautio, and Jacob Talso, who later studied medicine and moved to Ishpeming. There were possibly others, but their names are not known. Since Stone was probably not a member of any American secret society, some other charter member must have had a thorough knowledge of their internal operations, for the new Finnish society followed their rituals and procedures closely. The name chosen was Kalevan Ritarit (Knights of Kaleva), which suggests the high nationalistic ideals that inspired the founders. The guiding principles and the aims of the Knights of Kaleva were also determined at this meeting. Majority rule was adopted. The requirements of membership were stressed: Applicants and candidates were to be of the best element among the Finns—men who would always be willing to devote themselves in various ways to the welfare of their immigrant countrymen and to the nurturing of a spirit of kinship among them. All work was to be a voluntary labor of love. Church membership was taken for granted. A local member organization belonging to the Knights of Kaleva was to be called a "maja" (lodge).[2]

It is obvious that John Stone and his friends were influenced by the romantic Finnish nationalism which, during the 1890s, absorbed ideas from the *Kalevala* poems. The works of its leading writers and poets, such as Juhani Aho, Ilmari Kianto, Larin-Kyosti, and many others, were available in all the libraries of the Finnish American temperance societies. But when this romanticism in Finland began to serve the forces of active resistance to Russian oppression, it shifted among the Finns in America to the appreciation of the ancient culture of their nationality.

Naturally, the first local lodge of the Knights of Kaleva was organized in Belt, Montana, where the society was born. It was organized on July 30, 1898, and given the name Pellervoinen Maja no. 1.

From the very beginning Stone had thought that women should have an organization of their own, corresponding to the Knights of Kaleva. After he had experience in the activities of the men's organization, he set about establishing a women's society. He formulated rules and prepared a handbook for it. He called an organizational meeting in Red Lodge, Montana, for May 2, 1904. Thus was born Mielikki Tupa no. 1. From that time on, the women's local group has been called a "tupa." Their activity has been similar to that of the men's lodges. The titles of their officers are the feminine versions of the titles of the men's officers.

With the spread of the Kaleva movement and the increase in the number of lodges, central organizations became necessary. The central organization of the Knights of Kaleva came to be called Ylimaja (Supreme Lodge) and its head officer is known as the Y.E.V.J. or Ylin Ensimmainen Vertaistensa Joukossa (Supreme First among His Equals); the vice president is called the Y.T.V.J., standing for Supreme Second among His Equals. The reader of the devotions is called Y.P. or Ylin Pappi (High Priest). The central organization of the Ladies of Kaleva was named Ylitupa, and its officers' titles are Y.E. or Ylin Emäntä (Supreme Matron), etc. The headquarters of Ylimaja and Ylitupa are wherever the Y.E.V.J. and the Y.E. happen to be living at the time of their presidency.

The Kaleva Lodges in Michigan

Soon after the establishment of the Pellervoinen Lodge, the Ilmarinen Lodge no. 2 was started in Butte, Montana. Before the end of 1898, Jussi Jaaskelainen moved to Hancock and told his friends there about the Finnish movement that had started in Montana. When Jacob Talso and Daniel Kuona also moved from Belt to the Copper Country, they and Jaaskelainen called a meeting of trusted friends. It was held in Hancock on August 5, 1899. On that occasion the Nyyrikki Lodge no. 3 was organized; seventeen men joined it in addition to the three who had called the meeting. Thus the Kaleva organization got a firm foothold in Michigan.

The Nyyrikki Lodge held its last meeting in Hancock on December 17, 1904. Early the next year it moved to South Range, where it was active for many decades. The activity of the Nyyrikki has at times been very lively, and many other lodges have been organized as a result of encouragement given to others by its members, the most distant one being the Panu Lodge no. 24 in Fitchburg. Over a period of 65 years,

178 new members joined the Nyyrikki, and 36 transferred to it from other lodges. During the same period, 35 members transferred to other lodges, 6 returned to Finland, 7 were expelled, 1 resigned, 34 died, and 103 left for other reasons, making the membership 28 in 1964.

After the move to South Range, the meetings of the Nyyrikki Lodge were at first held in the Saima Hall, which was owned by the Auran Kukka Temperance Society. The members wanted to have a meeting place of their own and soon they were able to have one. A certain saloon company had begun to construct a large stone building but because of a lack of funds, left it unfinished. The local bank sold the lot and the unfinished building to the Nyyrikki Lodge for $6,000. Charles Heusa became construction foreman, and the building was completed in 1910. For a long time the meeting hall on the second floor was reputed to be the finest one belonging to Finns in Michigan. Because of the huge debt which resulted from the purchase, a fund drive was organized among Kaleva lodges throughout America. Membership increased rapidly until 1913, but during the Copper Country Strike, which began that year, "the economic and idealistic ideas of many members became confused, and they left the Knights of Kaleva."[3]

The Nyyrikki Lodge acquired a welcome auxiliary on September 28, 1906, when the Ladies of Kaleva Etelätär Lodge no. 9 was organized in South Range. Assisting in the organization were representatives of the Tuulikki Lodge of Calumet—Lydia Leselius and Lotta Hiltunen. Meetings have been held regularly twice a month. "We are still fortunate in that the only language we use in our meetings is our mother tongue, even though in our membership there are many who were born in America." An interesting and unusual fact is that at one time seven women of the John Jarvenpaa family belonged to the Etelätär Lodge. They were John Jarvenpaa's wife Maria and their six daughters.[4]

After the organization of Nyyrikki Lodge no. 3 the next ones were the Lemminkäinen Lodge no. 4 in Sand Coulee, Montana, and the Kalevainen Lodge no. 5 in Red Lodge. The sixth one was the Ahti Lodge organized just after the turn of the century by Jussi Jaaskelainen in Calumet, "where there were already more Finns than in Hämeenlinna [Finland]," according to a writer on the subject.[5] Jaaskelainen was the animating spirit of the lodge. In September 1903 he married Maria Petaja, who was born in Lumijärvi. She also became interested in the ideals of the Kaleva order and was present when the first lodge of the Ladies of Kaleva in Calumet, the Tuulikki no. 5, was organized. The Knights and Ladies of Kaleva built a large hall in Calumet for their activities. The Ahti Lodge grew so fast that by 1904 it was able to host the second annual meeting of the Knights of Kaleva. In 1909 the Ladies of Kaleva attended the annual meeting at Calumet as guests of the Tuulikki Lodge. This meeting was noteworthy because it rejected as "unnecessary" the suggestion made by members, who also belonged to temperance societies, that total abstinence should be included in the bylaws of the Ladies of Kaleva as a requirement for membership.

Hardly anything is said about the Ahti Lodge in the literature of the Knights of Kaleva. It gradually died out, largely because of internal dissension caused by the Copper Country Strike. The Ahti Lodge was certainly not the only organization hurt by this bitter labor struggle of 1913–14. The Finnish temperance societies and congregations also experienced dissension, for they also had members on both sides of the conflict. In time, the women's Tuulikki Lodge also ceased activity for the same reasons.

In chronological order, the next lodge organized in Michigan was the Osmo Lodge no. 11 of Ironwood. The organizational meeting was held on November 26, 1905, in a hall owned by a Finnish young people's club. There were fourteen charter members. Matti Koski, one of that group, was a member of the lodge for almost sixty years.[6]

The women's Kyllikki Lodge no. 7 was organized by representatives of the Vellamo Lodge of Ely, Minnesota, on February 2, 1906, to companion the men's Osmo Lodge. Many of the members were wives of members of the Osmo Lodge.

The Knights and Ladies of Kaleva in Ironwood held their meetings in the Valo Temperance Hall for a long time. When the Valo ceased activity in 1927, the Osmo Lodge bought the hall for $18,000. In ten years the hall was free of debt. This Kaleva hall has been remodeled frequently. On the ground floor it has space for two stores; on the second floor there are a large assembly room and a kitchen; on the third floor there is a fine meeting room used by the lodge. The Ironwood organization also has a summer cottage on Crystal Lake in Wisconsin, about twenty-three miles from Ironwood. The lodge is also a partner in the Kaleva Pirtti at Three Lakes.

The Osmo and Kyllikki lodges have been exceptionally active. Osmo meetings are held regularly every Wednesday evening, excepting in the summer months, when they are held every other Wednesday. The Kyllikki meetings are held twice a month excepting during a short time in the summer. The membership of the Osmo has averaged about fifty; in 1965 it was eighty. The membership of the Kyllikki has been about the same; in 1954 it was ninety. Of special interest among the activities of the Ironwood Kalevainens are the summer camps planned regularly for young people. The chief subjects studied at these educational sessions have been the Finnish language and the cultural history of Finland. The annual conventions of the Knights and Ladies of Kaleva were held in Ironwood in 1914 and 1932.[7]

The Knights of Kaleva began their activity anew in Hancock by organizing the Sotka Lodge no. 15 on November 3, 1906.[8] On September 19, 1907, the women's lodge, Kalevatar no. 14, was organized. Both lodges were very active. On special occasions programs of various kinds were provided by Suomi College. Visitors at Suomi College from Finland, such as Akseli Gallen-Kallela, Rafael Engelberg, Heikki Varis, and Elsa Heporauta, lectured frequently at meetings of the Kaleva lodges. The biggest event in the history of the Hancock Kaleva lodges was hosting the annual convention held in the Hibernia Hall in the summer of 1924. At this meeting the constitution was revised. The guests also visited Suomi College.

The Hancock Kalevainens had no hall of their own but rented a meeting room on the third floor of the old Kauth Building, which burned in 1944. In *Kalevainen* which appeared the next year, Victor Watia described the occurrence:

> The Sotka Lodge has been in existence almost a generation. . . . Its activity has been as smooth and steady as the life of a pious person—without criticism or commendation. There is nothing special to be said about it, except concerning the loss experienced last August. At that time, the building which housed the office of our lodge burned to the ground. All the Sotka Lodge's furnishings, records, and account books burned to ashes. It is no longer possible to write a chronological report based on them. So this memoir is like an indefinite end to the past activity of the lodge. The spirit of our lodge, however, is like the deathless soul in the ancient folk riddle: "It will not burn in fire, nor drown in water, and it does not fit into a crevice of the earth." The Sotka Lodge has resumed regular activity. New quarters have been rented. New furnishings and equipment have been purchased. We are rich in hope, and we face the future confidently.

Even so, the fire was a blow from which the Sotka Lodge never recovered completely. It ceased activity in the beginning of 1955, and the members remaining joined the Nyyrikki Lodge of South Range.

The women's Kalevatar continued its activity in Hancock, but when member after member died or became unable because of the infirmities of age to attend meetings, it ceased activity in the spring of 1964.[9]

The Kullervo Lodge no. 14 was organized in Mass on October 1, 1906, and the women's Aino Lodge no. 13 of Mass on August 28,

1907. Activity was at its peak and membership at its highest between 1910 and 1914. When work stoppages compelled large numbers of people to move away, membership in the Kaleva lodges fell so much that the Aino Lodge ceased activity in the spring of 1917, to become reactivated in the fall of 1921.

The men's lodge did not have to close its doors. The Kullervo Lodge built a hall and with the assistance of the Aino Lodge, even put up a summer cottage in the Twin Lakes area. One of the projects of the Aino Lodge was supplying the local high school library with books about Finland.[10]

The Virokannas Lodge no. 17 was active in Painesdale until 1918 at least. Its name and number were inherited by a lodge organized later on in Bruce Crossing. There was also a women's lodge, the Virotar no. 16, in Painesdale around 1910. Apparently the only indication left of its having been in existence is a group picture in *Kalevainen* in 1913. There is also no information available about the women's Suvetar Lodge of Crystal Falls.

On an evening in May 1907, a small group of interested persons gathered in the Ishpeming office of Jacob Kaminen, secretary of the Finnish National Temperance Brotherhood (SKRV), to discuss matters pertaining to their Finnish nationality. Two members of Kaleva lodges were present to explain the work of the Knights of Kaleva in upholding the values of the Finnish people. As a result of this meeting, the Taatto Lodge no. 18 was organized on May 30. It was joined on November 2, 1907 by the women's lodge, Sammotar.

At first the Kaleva lodges of Ishpeming met in rented quarters, but in 1911 they purchased a large old stone building which had been a livery stable. It was remodeled to become the Kaleva Hall. The building included a large meeting room, a kitchen, and a dining room. On the first floor were William Jackson's hardware and furniture store and funeral parlor, later an automobile repair shop. The Kaleva Hall was used by the lodge for over forty years, until it was sold in 1954. After that the lodge met in rented quarters on Cleveland Avenue.

Up to 1960, 210 persons had joined the Taatto Lodge, of whom 90 had died and 97 had either moved away or dropped out for other reasons, so that by 1960 there were only 23 members left. The women's Sammotar Lodge had 65 members in 1954. In the 1960s the membership was smaller, for persons of the older generation were passing away faster than new members were coming in from the younger generation. The annual conventions of the Knights of Kaleva of 1911 and 1952 were hosted by the Taatto Lodge, and the annual conventions of the Ladies of Kaleva by Sammotar in 1910 and 1952.[11]

The Kaukomieli Lodge no. 32, organized in Amasa in 1908 or 1909, has not left many evidences of its existence. In *Kalevainen* in 1929, Jack V. Koski reported that members of the Kaukomieli Lodge came from all parts of Iron County and that even those who lived further away were represented at lodge meetings. In 1954 there were only eleven members, of whom three were from Amasa, five from Crystal Falls, two from Kalamazoo, where they had moved, and one from Iron River. The auxiliary women's organization, Pihlajatar Lodge no. 28, was organized on November 19, 1909. The Pihlajatar was inactive for several years, but resumed activity again on July 20, 1927. By 1954 all activity had ceased.[12]

The Ahtolainen Lodge no. 33 of Negaunee was organized at meetings held in Ishpeming at the Taatto Lodge on May 15–17 and May 22, 1909. During the first fifty years of activity, 218 persons joined the lodge, of whom 51 have died and 108 left for one reason or another, the membership at the beginning of 1960 being 59.

Shortly before the organization of the Ahtolainen Lodge, a women's lodge had been organized in the area—on April 5, 1909 to be exact—in the presence of representatives of the Sammotar and Kyllikki lodges. Negaunee residents who had belonged to the Ishpeming organizations now joined the lodges in their own community.

The annual conventions of both the Knights and the Ladies of Kaleva were held in Negaunee in 1920 and included a fine parade along the streets of the city. Meetings were held in the Baulson Hall until 1913, after which the Odd Fellows Hall was rented. After 1918, meetings were held in the People's Home owned by the Aamurusko Temperance Society, which was purchased by the Ahtolainen Lodge in 1933 and renamed Kaleva House. With remodeling, it became a practical and dignified meeting place for Finns interested in their background and culture. The Knights and Ladies of Kaleva of Negaunee have worked closely together, holding a joint meeting once a month for planning their activities. An unusual public event was the program presented on channel 6, WLUC-TV, Marquette, by the Allitar Lodge to celebrate Finnish Independence Day in 1962. The program was seen and heard throughout Michigan and Wisconsin, and even in Canada.[13]

The Saarelainen Lodge of Knights was organized around 1910 in Mohawk and the Ladies of Kaleva Melatar Lodge no. 39 in January 1911. Activity, which had started at a lively pace, was brought to a stop by the Copper Country Strike. It was renewed after the strike, but with fewer members. Between 1911 and 1944, forty-three women joined Melatar; in the same period three members died and forty members moved from the community or left the society for some other reason.

The experience of the men's Saarelainen Lodge paralleled that of the Melatar.

In 1929 the Kalevainens of Mohawk purchased a summer cottage in a grove of birches in Gay, Michigan, on the shore of Lake Superior. With repair and remodeling, it became the attractive Kaleva Pirtti (Pirtti log cabin), which had the atmosphere of ancient Karelia about it. Because of small membership, activity ceased toward the end of the 1950s and the cottage was sold. But as long as the Kaleva Pirtti belonged to the Finns, Kalevainens came there in the summertime even from hundreds of miles away to visit under its rooftree and to enjoy the beauty of the Lake Superior shore.[14]

Kaleva lodge activity began in Wakefield on August 23, 1911, when the Knights of Kaleva Suomalainen Lodge no. 35 was organized with fifteen members of the Osmo Lodge of Ironwood present. Two years later, on August 2, 1913, the Ladies of Kaleva Laaksotar Lodge no. 10 was organized with the help of a loan from the men's lodge. Both organizations got off to a good start, for some of the members were familiar with the work of the Kalevainens from participation in the activities of the Ironwood lodges. By 1929 they had a building of their own.

The depression of the 1930s caused many families to move away from the community, and so the Knights and Ladies of Kaleva lost many of their members. "They did not, however, take with them the debt on our hall," a member pointed out wryly. Only seven members were left in the women's group. "Some were getting to rocking chair age," wrote a member of the Suomalainen Lodge. In 1960 the Laaksotar Lodge of the Ladies had twenty members; there were even fewer members in the men's Suomalainen Lodge.[15]

When large numbers of Finns moved from Upper Michigan, and especially from the Copper Country to Detroit, it was natural for them to join congregations and organizations in the area and to establish new ones. It was in this way that the Knights and Ladies of Kaleva organizations got started there. The Aura Lodge no. 44 of the Knights was organized at the home of Henry Hopponen on January 18, 1917. On April 16 of the same year the Auratar Lodge no. 49 of the Ladies was organized.[16]

For about ten years, meetings were held in the Danish Brotherhood Hall. In 1929 the St. John's Finnish Lutheran Church at 13211 Montville Place was purchased. Ten years after that, the building was completely remodeled because of expanded activity. For nearly thirty years this Kaleva Home was the center for gatherings of Finnish Americans interested in their Finnish background. Innumerable concerts, plays, and programs of various kinds were presented there. One of the more important programs arranged by the Detroit Kalevainens was a race in which Paavo Nurmi, the Flying Finn, participated to demonstrate his running ability. On that occasion, some of the Polish people are said to have called out, "Me Finn too!" On another occasion, the plans of the Kalevainens were interrupted by a race disturbance. Members of the Kaleva organization of Waukegan, Illinois, were coming to Detroit one beautiful Sunday in the early summer of 1943 to present a play titled *Pohjalaisia* (Ostrobothnians). A large hall in downtown Detroit, the Diamond Temple, had been rented. Everything was ready, from the reception committee to the "coffee cooks," in the kitchen, when without apparent reason a race riot started and was not brought under control until the next day. Because the Diamond Temple was in the riot area the play was not presented.

By 1929 the area around the Kaleva Home had become an integrated neighborhood and the building was sold to a black congregation for a church. The Kalevainens bought a new hall at 14023 Puritan Avenue. Lively activity continued. In 1937 a summer place on Cass Lake was purchased from James Vehkola. After his death it was called Vehkola Park. The swampy shore of the lake was filled in with thousands of loads of earth and made into a pleasant area for festivals and leisure activities. The most conspicuous summer event there was the bonfire on Midsummer Eve, in keeping with a custom brought from Finland. The name of the park was later changed to Kaleva Park.

The annual convention of the Knights and Ladies of Kaleva was held in Detroit in 1935. Through the efforts of the Detroit Kalevainens a Kaleva Knights lodge was organized in Helsinki in 1962 by Andrew I. Brask who went there for the purpose. It was named the Suomi Lodge no. 53.[17]

Around 1918 there was a Knights' lodge in Sault Ste. Marie called Arjala no. 46, about which there is no other information available excepting that Matti Hirvonen served as its delegate at the annual convention held in Waukegan in 1918.

Members of the Nyyrikki Lodge of South Range used to visit friends in Alston, telling them, at the same time, about the aspirations of the Kaleva order. The men of Alston became interested in joining the order. A meeting was held on April 28, 1935, to organize a lodge. Twenty-five members of the Nyyrikki Lodge and twelve local men were present. The charter members named the new lodge Elias Lodge no. 49 in honor of Elias Lonnrot. Meetings were held at the Pelkie school at first, but later on, a small house was bought in Alston and remodeled into a hall, which was soon sold however, because it was too small.

Since then, meetings have been held in the Nyyrikki Hall in South Range.

The women's Kanerva Lodge no. 12 was organized on November 8–9, 1935. Minnie Perttula-Maki, a former instructor and acting president of Suomi College, was one of the leading members of the Ladies of Kaleva and often went on lecture tours for them. After the meeting place of the Elias Lodge was sold, the Kaleva Ladies of the Kanerva Lodge met in their own homes.[18]

Around 1940, the Virokannas Lodge no. 17 of the Knights of Kaleva was organized in Bruce Crossing, and on December 3, 1941, the Kaiutar Lodge no. 34 of the Ladies of Kaleva had its beginnings. Meetings were first held in homes of members; then a local cooperative hall was rented for a time. In 1943 a meeting place in the second story of the town hall was rented and used up to December 22, 1953. On that day, the hall was being heated for the schoolchildren's Christmas program when fire broke out in the basement, near the furnace. In a couple of hours everything was completely destroyed. The Kalevainens lost all their furnishings and records. For some time after the fire, meetings were held in private homes.

In 1954, the Virokannas Lodge purchased a building which was remodeled for use as a hall, but membership fell off. People died, moved away from the area, or lost interest. In January 1959, when there were only twelve members left, a decision to sell the building was made, and meetings were again held in private homes. After the Knights of Kaleva Virokannas Lodge and the Ladies of Kaleva Kaiutar Lodge, there were no new Kaleva lodges established in Michigan for some time.[19]

During this period, when there were great changes in churches and in the cooperative and labor movements, the Kalevainens remained fundamentally unchanged. Although there was no great variation in the total membership of the Kaleva Knights and Ladies for decades, whatever growth there was, was greatest in areas where people had kept in touch with Finland. San Francisco, New York, and Ashtabula and Fairport Harbor in Ohio, as well as Port Arthur in Ontario are examples of such areas. The many members of the Kaleva order in Florida are people who have moved to the South from older Finnish communities in the North. Membership has decreased in areas where other Finnish organizations have also shrunk because the younger generation have moved to industrial centers. Experience has also shown that the Kaleva ideal as understood by Finnish Americans has not taken root in Finland. It is as if the hills of Karelia must be seen in the blue of distance and the "kantele" (harp) of Väinö heard across the ocean before they can inspire such high ideals of and feelings about nationality as are characteristic of the Kaleva spirit in America.

Emphasis on the Finnish Heritage

Stone knew that in Finland nationalistic ideals had developed in connection with the church, and he wanted his organization to bear the stamp of Christianity. Over the decades, the Kaleva groups have clung to this ideal. Every meeting begins and ends with a prayer. An examination of membership lists has shown that 75 percent of the members at the time of the survey belonged to Suomi Synod congregations. Most of the remaining members also belonged to Christian denominations, either to some other Finnish Lutheran church or, in a few cases, to some non-Lutheran Protestant congregation. Members of Kaleva lodges were often leaders and officers in their church congregations. About ten Suomi Synod pastors were sons of members of the Knights of Kaleva.

When members died, the black-edged notices sent out contained, for a long time, such well-established phrases as "gone to a higher dwelling place," "moved to a higher lodge of knights," "another candle on our tree of membership has gone out," but a Christian thought or symbol almost always accompanied them.

The main emphasis of the Kaleva program has always been on things pertaining to Finnish nationality. On the one hand it stressed all things Finnish and on the other, efforts to gather Finnish-minded Finnish Americans together and into group activity. One of the most noticeable manifestations of this nationalistic interest is the names of the lodges. Some of them come from ancient Finnish mythology, as does Ukko, but they are taken mostly from heroic epics, as are the names Vainamoinen, Vaino, Ilmarinen, Kaukomieli, Sampo, Sammotar, Kullervo, Lemminkainen. Other names come from nature or poetry, like Aallotar from "aalto" (wave), Paivatar from "paiva" (day), Valotar from "valo" (light), Metsola from "metsa" (woodland), etc. Some of them, like Virokannas, Virotar, and Vepsa, pertain to lineage or kinship. Less frequently, names have some connection with their location in America; for example, Etelatar in South Range, from "etela" (south); Saarelainen in Mohawk, from "Kupari Saari" (Copper Island); Tyynetar in Astoria, from "Tyyni Meri" (Pacific Ocean); and Kultaportti (Golden Gate) in San Francisco. The names of Finnish American temperance societies cover a wider range.

Every member of a Kaleva lodge was expected to be familiar

with *Kalevala*, the national epic of Finland. It was studied at meetings, lectures were given about it, and articles about it were published in *Kalevainen*, the official voice of the Knights and Ladies of Kaleva. At the suggestion of the Virokannas Lodge of Painesdale, the convention held in Waukegan in 1918 decided that a copy of *Kalevala* would be presented to every Knight who had gone beyond the third degree. When, during World War I, the supply of copies was sold out in American bookstores, Carl H. Salminen, who was a leader in the Kaleva organization, published a new edition in 1917 at his press in Duluth. In all modesty, the name of the publisher was omitted. Nor was the fact that the book was printed in America mentioned. During World War II, when copies were again unavailable, a second American edition was published. This was sponsored by the Knights and Ladies of Kaleva and printed by the Finnish Lutheran Book Concern in Hancock.

Finnish Americans themselves often did not have up-to-date information. In light of this fact it is understandable why the Chaldeans, the Altaics, the Sumerians—and even the Egyptian pyramids—crept into their explanations in the manner of Vettenhovi-Aspa's flights of fancy. Finnish Americans were eventually free of these fanciful concepts, and the Kalevainens became interested in studying the true history of Finland. It is amazing how much good Finnish literature, especially history, there is in the homes of Knights and Ladies of Kaleva. They extended this interest in Finnish culture to making frequent gifts of books about Finland in the English language to local high school libraries. Nor was it unusual for Kalevainens to send corrections to newspapers if articles in them about the Finns or Finland were incorrect or misleading. Their most effective expression of attachment to their fatherland was in widespread Finnish relief work, in which the Kalevainens were always in the forefront.

This interest in the history of the Finnish people expanded to include the history of the Finns in America. Already in the conventions of the Kaleva organization in the 1910s, the collection of historical materials was considered. "There was a lively discussion, in which it became clear that the task was considered important." This statement appears in the minutes of a Knights of Kaleva convention held in Ironwood in 1914, in instructions to the sixth degree Knights of the Ahjo Lodge, who were entrusted with the task. When the Finnish American Historical Archives was established at Suomi College, the Kalevainens were among the first to send materials there. They have also been in the front ranks in the work of the Finnish Historical Society of Michigan. This interest in the history of their own nationality is in the spirit of romantic nationalism characteristic of Topelius and Runeberg, which is still alive in Finland too.

At the convention of the Ladies of Kaleva held in Hancock in 1924, the Kyllikki Lodge of Ironwood initiated a discussion about the preservation of Finnish family names. "The proposal received support, and the expectation was that Kaleva lodge members would preserve their own family names in their original form."[20] The Ladies of Kaleva have been especially interested in the national costumes of Finland. It is not unusual for them to appear at programs celebrating Finnish Independence Day or Kalevala Day in the thousand-year-old costumes of Tuukkala in Savo or in that pride of Finland proper, the ancient costume of Perniö, to say nothing of the more common costumes of recent centuries, such as those of the parishes of Iitti, Oulu, Kokkola, Ilmajoki, Kurikka, or Härmä. On a wall of some homes of Kaleva Knights and Ladies may be seen a colorful display of postcards picturing Finnish national costumes, which for non-Finnish guests serves as a good introduction to ancient Finnish culture. One of the many projects of the Kaleva lodges has been the planning of group flights to Finland.

The language problem has been the downfall of many Finnish American organizations. It has been of advantage to very few. As of 1964 the Kalevainens were in the midst of a consideration of the question. "It is certain that the lovely Finnish language will disappear last from Kaleva meetings." Thus wrote Akseli Rauanheimo in 1928.[21] His prophecy has come true, for of the leading Finnish American organizations the Kaleva order has most successfully preserved the use of the Finnish language. As early as 1918 the question of using the English language was brought up among the Kalevainens of Detroit, although only a few of them knew what the issue really was.[22] An attempt was made to solve the problem by teaching Finnish to children of members of the Kaleva organization. But the demand for English as a second official language became more and more insistent. In 1947 Heikki Karhu revealed his understanding of the problems of the younger generation in the following questions addressed to the older generation:

> Do we realize that because we are citizens of it, this country is our children's fatherland as well as the land of their birth? Do we also realize that our children's native land is as dear to them as the land of our birth is to us who were born in Finland? Do we understand that the spirit of Americanism based on history and instilled in our children at school is more meaningful than anything we have been able to portray for them of the life and history of the land of our fathers? . . . And then, in our enthusiasm for preserving the Finnish language,

> have we (not) tried in every way to oppose the use of the English language by the children who have joined our group—the language that is easier for them to use and understand because they have become accustomed to it in school and feel shy about using the Finnish language because they speak it poorly?[23]

Some of the older members of the Kaleva organization felt, for a long time, that being Finnish and preserving Finnish culture in America were inseparable from the Finnish language. At first it was hard for them to understand that the Finnish Americans had reached a transition period in their history, during which, on the gradual departure of the older generation, new generations were taking their place, with their own language and customs. Among the Knights of Kaleva there were, however, enlightened leaders, fully bilingual, who understood the situation and handled the language question satisfactorily during this transition period. Andrew I. Brask, secretary of the Supreme Lodge, wrote thus in the lead article of *Kalevainen* of 1949:

> A new way of doing things has begun for us, and a new era. A new way in that we are gradually moving toward the use of the English language in our work, and a new era in that we are at the beginning of a second fifty-year period. The cover picture depicts the forging of the *Sampo.* We have been forging a *sampo* for 50 years. The makers have been very skillful. There is evidence of this in the fact that in this melting pot we are still Finnish. Whether we will still be Finns in spirit after the passage of another 50 years, even though we may not be using the Finnish language, depends on how we work at making the *sampo* from now on. The possibilities are limited. For no one is coming from Finland to take our places; we must look to our young people, who have been born in this country. But they are already being melded in the melting pot. Unless we "hammer" now, we will have no future.

In the English-language introduction to *Kalevainen* of 1950, Brask affirms that there is a great task before the Kaleva lodges: to preserve the Finnish heritage during this period of transition and to transfer it to Americans of Finnish background. Already for a long time the supreme lodges have published their rules and handbooks in English. Lodge after lodge of both Knights and Ladies has become bilingual. In the history of the women's Allitar Lodge of Negaunee, Alli Hepola wrote: "In our meetings we still use the Finnish language but, in keeping with the official decision, we are prepared to use the English language also whenever our younger members wish. Up to now they have wanted to use Finnish in order to learn to speak it better."

Around 1962, about half the Knights and Ladies of Kaleva had been born in Finland. Membership rosters also indicate that the Kaleva order was a family interest. The father and sons belonged to the Knights, and the mother and daughters to the Ladies. An example is the Richard Wirtanen family of Ironwood. Men of three generations have been members of the Osmo Lodge.[24]

Young people's work has been an important part of Kaleva activity. It was discussed already in 1912 in the convention held in Ashtabula, in which the possibility of working with the Kansallismielisen Nuorisoliitto (National Youth League) was considered. At the annual meeting held in Ironwood in 1914 it was confirmed that interest in this possibility had died out. A decision was made to keep youth work within the lodges. Matti Erkkila, delegate from the Kalevainen Lodge of Red Lodge, Montana, had prepared plans for an organization of active children's groups, called the Nuorten Ystävyysliitto (Young People's Friendship League). With a few small changes, the plans were approved, and a committee was selected to formulate plans for a similar organization for young adults.[25] In some of the large lodges the children's and young people's groups, known as the Junior Kalevas, were successful.

Summer camps became the most important form of youth activity. The first "young people's courses," as summer camps were then called, were held in the Upper Peninsula in 1934. Organizers were the Kullervo Lodge of Knights and the Aino Lodge of Ladies in Mass City, and the meeting place was their spacious summer house on the shore of Lake Roland in Houghton County. The camp opened on St. John's Day with twenty-three boys and the same number of girls between fifteen and eighteen years of age. The director of the camp was Nels Johnson, and lecturers were Alma Van Slyke, Hilma Hamina, Martta Nisonen, Professor Martti Nisonen, Pastor A. V. Tuukkanen, Kalle Tuomela, and Lauri Tuomela. Subjects regularly offered were the Finnish language, Finnish history and geography, Finnish American history, and elocution. In addition there were lectures on the following subjects: *Kalevala* and *Hiawatha* compared, the Kalevala epic, Finnish authors and their works, Finnish sports, the temperances movement in Finland, and Finnish music. Folk dances, sports, and swimming took up whatever time was left of the tight schedule. The closing exercises on July 2 turned out to be a big Finnish festival, with Seminarian Jacob Heikkinen as the main speaker.[26]

The next summer camp was planned by the Ironwood and Wakefield lodges for their summer place on the shore of Crystal Lake. There were ninety participants, and the courses in the main were the same as those offered the preceding summer. Nels Johnson affirmed that everyone knew Finnish sufficiently well to follow lectures in that language without difficulty. The teaching of Finnish was limited to the explanation and correction of errors made by the students. Young people who did not come from homes connected with the Kaleva organization were also in attendance.[27]

Summer camps were also sponsored by the Ishpeming, Marquette, and Negaunee Lodges. They had an advantage in that on October 2, 1933, a Junior Kaleva Club had been organized. It started with a large membership and lively activity, including Halloween and Christmas programs, dances, plays in the Finnish language, and lectures in English. The club took part in Fourth of July parades and performed Finnish folk dances in local schools.[28] The Negaunee club also was active in planning summer camps, but had a problem in that they had no summer cottage of their own. Participation in summer camp activity had become so extensive that rented facilities were no longer adequate.

The possibility of buying a summer camp was first discussed officially at a meeting of the Ahtolainen Lodge of Negaunee on August 24, 1937. At about the same time the matter was also being considered by the Taatto Lodge of Ishpeming. It was known that Emil Railo and Jafet Rytkönen had seventeen acres on lakeshore property at Three Lakes for sale. At a meeting held on September 14, the Ahtolainen Lodge selected five men for a committee to inspect the property, and two days later the Taatto Lodge selected three men for it. The committee reported that the location was beautiful, that it was near U.S. Highway 41, and that it had a good bathing beach that would accommodate groups of about a hundred. The price was a reasonable $700. The formalities of the transaction took some time, but the deed was finally signed in May 1938. The first trustees were Jacob P. Niemi and Nestor Eckloff from the Taatto Lodge and John J. Beldo and Nestor Wehmanen from the Ahtolainen Lodge.

In keeping with Finnish tradition, the sauna for the new summer place was built first. After its completion, a program was held on Sunday, September 18, 1938. Herman Maki, well known as a humorist, pronounced "magic" words over the sauna. The lowest bid, $4,473.05, for the construction of the 40 by 80 foot log cabin was made by Kielinen and Son. They completed the building in February 1939. The opening celebration was held on June 4. There were over a thousand guests, some from as far away as Minnesota. The speaker at the worship service was Dr. John Wargelin, who emphasized the importance of tolerance and harmony in Finnish activities. The main speaker of the afternoon was Hilma Hamina who, referring to the *Kalevala*, compared this new pirtti (lodge) to the great pirtti of Pohjola and the celebration they were having to the great wedding of Pohjola. Thus the Finns of the Upper Peninsula acquired a practical summer home modeled after the old homes of Finland.[29]

On January 12, 1943, the Kaleva Pirtti was incorporated as the Upper Peninsula Kaleva Pirtti. Its legal owners were the Knights and Ladies of the Kaleva lodges of the Upper Peninsula. The members of the men's organizations pay 50 cents a year and the Ladies 25 cents a year into the Pirtti fund. The members of the board of directors are selected at the annual meeting of the Knights and Ladies of Kaleva in September.[30]

With their own spacious summer home, it was easier to plan children's and young people's camp sessions. World War II, however, brought difficulties. Many of the young adults were called into service, and many others went to work in war industries and other areas of service. For this reason the summer camp activity became centered around children, and the age limit was lowered to ten years. This custom was continued after the war. Summer camps were usually conducted over a two-week period. The English language was used. But, in keeping with the Kaleva program, everyone was taught Finnish, and in a few days, participants learned to sing Finnish songs and to say grace in unison in Finnish.[31] There were many cases in which the seed of interest in the Finnish nationality and in the background and culture of the Finns planted at these Kaleva summer camps sprouted and grew into a permanent interest that brought young people to Suomi College after graduation from high school. It also influenced young people to continue their studies at universities of Finland.[32]

The most noticeable act of the Kaleva organization and the one that attracted the most interest was the sending of a greeting to the 100-Year Jubilee of the *Kalevala*, which was held in the Messu Hall in Helsinki on February 28, 1935. The festive cover of the booklet, which pictured a slender Finnish spruce and an American skyscraper with the harp of Vainamoinen and the smoke of wilderness bonfires between them, was designed by Paul Sjoblom. The greeting in the booklet read as follows:

> The American and Canadian Finns and friends of Finland send their most respectful greetings and dedicate this message with gratitude to the Fatherland and to the guardian of the spiritual heritage we have received from our forefathers—the Kalevala Seura (Society).
>
> Whoever took from it a twig
> Found happiness forever;

Whoever took its lofty crown
Found everlasting magic.

The first signatures on the greeting were those of President and Mrs. Franklin D. Roosevelt, Governor Herbert H. Lehman of New York, Mayor Fiorello La Guardia of New York City, the president of Columbia University, and other well-known Americans. There were over 10,000 Finnish American signatures and over 1,000 Finnish Canadian signatures. Of the states, Michigan, with 1,748, had the largest number. The Louhetar Lodge of the Ladies of Kaleva in New York City attended to the details of business connected with the greeting. The reading and presentation of the message in the Helsinki Messu Hall was one of the high points of the festival. The mention of the president of the United States as the first signer was followed by enthusiastic applause.[33]

In the late winter of 1939, Elsa Heporauta, an author from Helsinki, was a guest of the Kalevainens, serving at the same time as the representative of the wife of Kyosti Kallio, the then president of Finland. In a letter greeting the Ladies of Kaleva, Rouva (Mrs.) Kaisa Kallio wrote as follows:

> National feeling and a sense of kinship get their strength in the home and in the family circle, where the woman of Finland has always raised her children in the fear of God and in the love of the Fatherland. The fact that even across the ocean the same spirit of kinship is still strong, proves that there, too, the Finnish mother has been able to keep sacred the traditions of our ancestors.[34]

Publications

The lodges of the Knights and Ladies of Kaleva were as a rule in communities so far from one another that neighborly visits were out of the question. As a connecting link, the Kalevainens in Red Lodge began to print a paper titled *Perhepakinoita* (Family chatter) on a hand press. It was edited by Matti Erkkila. Copies of the paper were sent to Kaleva lodges all over the country, to all of their membership. The only remuneration requested was for mailing expenses, "if *Perhepakinoita* was worth it." The women's lodges became interested in the matter and took care of the postage. Gradually the idea developed that there should be a publication that would appear regularly and serve to keep Kaleva groups in touch and to spread interest in Finnish culture, even among outsiders. At the suggestion of J. A. Harpet, the publication was named

Kalevainen. It was decided to make it an annual which would always come out on Kalevala Day. The resolution was in effect continuously until 1997.[35]

The first number of *Kalevainen* appeared in 1913, edited by Matti Erkkila. His motto was the Finnish proverb "The beginning is always hard, but diligence brings results." He wrote as follows:

> *Kalevainen* . . . is starting off modestly on its journey around the world. It comes into your homes, bringing only homemade provisions. Its kindling wood has grown on land we have cleared. Its light comes from a flaming Finnish pine torch, which can light up only a Kaleva cabin. It feels itself a stranger in any other place. It knows no one there and no one there knows it. *Kalevainen* offers a simple Finnish greeting to the Finnish woman and the Finnish man.

In the earlier issues of *Kalevainen* the editor, in all modesty, has not included his name. After Erkkila, John A. Harpet of the Duluth Vuoksi Lodge was the editor for about ten years. From 1927 to 1956 *Kalevainen* was a Michigan publication, in that its editors for that thirty-year period were all Michigan people: 1927–35, Toivo Aartila of Marquette, a member of the Negaunee Ahtola Lodge; 1936–46, George Hepola, also a member of Ahtola Lodge; 1947, Andrew I. Brask, of the Aura Lodge of Detroit; 1948, Abel Kauranen, also of the Aura Lodge; 1949–56, again Andrew I. Brask with Minnie Perttula-Maki of Baraga as co-editor. In 1957–62 the editor was Alfons A. Ukkonen of Brooklyn and from 1963–65, Paavo Honka of Waukegan, Illinois. From 1966–68, Kerttu Arra, of Brooklyn, New York, served as editor, from 1969–70, Tauno Laakkonen, from 1971–78, Folke W. Sandstrom, from Virginia, Minnesota, from 1979–80, Tauno Numi, of New York, and from 1990–97, Aarne and Rose Aaltonen. During these decades *Kalevainen* became a large publication of fine typography.

In addition to the necessary rule books, handbooks, and minutes, the Kalevainens published a songbook in Hancock in 1914 titled *Kalevaisten Laulukirja* (Kalevainens' songbook) for use at their meetings. It was also sold without restriction to nonmembers.

In Duluth, between 1931 and 1933, Heikki Karhu published a monthly titled *Kalevan Kansa* (People of Kaleva) in the hope that it would become the official voice of the Kaleva order. His hope was not realized. Another publication sponsored by the Kaleva organization was S. C. Olin's brief history of the Finnish people, titled *Finlandia: The Racial Composition, the Language, and a Brief History of the Finnish People*, published by the Finnish Lutheran Book Concern in 1957.[36]

The early publishing activities of the Kalevainens brought them many vexations and raised opposition to them in church circles. They themselves were not always aware of the reason for the opposition. One problem was that a small number of theosophists, whose beliefs include elements of neo-Platonism and the ancient religions of India, had found their way into Kaleva lodges. As they understood it, *Kalevala* opened up a religious-mystical world to them, which, especially among the Finns, would take the place of historical Christianity. Through uninhibited flights of imagination *Kalevala* was upheld as the Book of Books, even above the Bible. It appears that the early editors of *Kalevainen* were serious, Finnish-minded men completely unfamiliar with the problems of editing a paper. To them, all articles were welcome as long as they had something to say about *Kalevala* or the Finns. Thus, the theosophists got writings published which regularly included attacks against the doctrines of the church.

Already in the first issue of *Kalevainen*, which appeared in 1913, Tiera (a pseudonym) said that "the flow of thought from ancient knowledge" will save the world, for "Christianity has been groping in the dark for salvation for almost 2,000 years," and that the letters INRI on the cross stood for Jam, Nur, Ruah, Jabestah, four metaphorical terms for the basic elements water, fire, air, and earth, which the church in its mistaken way interpreted to mean Jesus of Nazareth, King of the Jews. The situation was not improved when in the next year's issue the editor made the mistake of saying that "*Kalevainen* is the official interpreter of the spirit of the Knights and Ladies of Kaleva." The editor of the number published in 1915 hastened to correct Matti Erkkila's obvious error but went to the opposite extreme by saying that *Kalevainen* was so liberal that it had no special viewpoint:

> In this publication every author is responsible for the ideas he discusses. The editorial staff of *Kalevainen* does not consider itself justified in supporting any special idea in order to attack other ideas. The church-minded as well as the liberal-minded appear on their personal responsibility. Those who believe in idealistic socialism and the ancient wisdom of the *Kalevala* are equally entitled to be heard.

Kalevainen was thus open to theosophical propaganda. The theosophist attacks against the church reached their peak in the issue of 1918. M. S. (pen name) wrote under the heading "Is *Kalevala* Suitable As a Religious Book for the Finns?" He not only gave an affirmative answer to his question but using Pekka Ervast, the Finnish theosophical author as his authority, claimed that the Finnish people would soon have to make a choice between Christianity and the ancient heathenism of *Kalevala* or, alternatively, select the best from both. According to the author, "the Hebrew Bible . . . is exclusively about the life and history of a foreign land." In his conclusion he repeated his question and answered it:

> Must we look indefinitely to Palestine, Egypt, and Babylonia for inspiration and for the foundations of our moral teachings? No! For we have our own closer to us. Is it of help to us if other peoples hold their own poems and songs in esteem? No! As long as we do not become like them, esteeming our own. . . . Is *Kalevala*, therefore, suitable as a religious book for the Finns? It is suitable indeed![37]

Opposition to the Kaleva Order

It was of disadvantage to the church as well as to the Kaleva organization that the leaders of the church, who should have been knowledgeable about the visionary character of occult sciences and theosophy, did not get together with the leaders of the Kaleva organization, who, faced with the actual facts, would presumably have wanted to correct the mistakes of the editors of *Kalevainen*. The matter was left in the hands of equally incompetent church leaders. Some of the pastors—and there were some in all the Finnish churches—condemned the entire Kaleva organization as being non-Christian, unaware that *Kalevainen* included writings friendly to the church, and that many persons in Kaleva lodges were staunch members of congregations. In addition to public condemnation from the pulpit, the pastor would sometimes bypass a Kaleva lodge member of his congregation at Communion, saying, "This is not for you." Characteristic of the stand taken by a large number of the clergy in the 1910s and the 1920s is the statement of Pastor K. E. Salonen, president of the seminary of the National Church, in his evaluation of the spiritual status of some Finnish Americans:

> A large number of our kindred have gathered around a banner whose flaunting legend reads: The *Kalevala* is our Bible.
>
> The spiritual condition of this group is probably best described by the following appraisal: false erudition, smiling silence with regard to Christianity, imagined assurance of a higher light presumably attained by only a few, putting on an outward appearance of good, and self-complacancy.[38]

The National Church was the only organized Finnish American church that took an official stand against secret societies. In the

Suomi Synod and in the Laestadian groups the matter was left to the judgment of individual pastors or preachers, excepting that it has always been made clear that a pastor must not be or become a member of any secret society. The attitude of the National Church was expressed as follows:

> We oppose and condemn secret societies because they deny the basic truths of Christianity and because they blaspheme against God with their oaths and vows. The Word of God obligates us to take this stand, for the First and Second Commandments forbid the worship of false Gods and the taking of the name of the Lord in vain; throughout, it warns against participation in wrong religious activities.[39]

The claim sometimes made in writings against the church, that the Suomi Synod had declared war on all secret societies, does not, as has just been pointed out, hold true. The following excerpt from the novel *Elämää Ikuisessa Yössä* gives an untrue picture of the situation:

> The objects of the relentless animosity of the clergy were especially the members of secret societies, for the Suomi Synod had officially declared secret societies to be ungodly and denied members their congregational rights, the blessing of the church, and the sacraments, unless they indicated that they had truly repented. Other Finnish churches also followed unofficially the example of their older brother.[40]

In some Michigan towns the tense situation between the Kaleva organization and the local Finnish pastor continued to the early 1950s. But that sort of thing has become history. In the 1960s, pastors were often speakers on Kaleva programs, and Kalevainens were accepted, active members of congregations.

Attitudes of individuals toward the labor movement and toward leftist political affiliation among Finnish Americans sometimes created difficult situations in the meetings of lodges. During the strike of 1913–14, some of the Kaleva lodges had to close their doors. The stand taken on the war for independence in Finland also created tension in some lodges, for members had relatives on both sides. In general the attitude toward the situation in Finland at that fateful time was expressed by Jacob P. Niemi of the Taatto Lodge of Ishpeming: "With forgiveness in our hearts we want to remember the Reds, too, in their undecorated graves."[41] Relations between socialists and Kalevainens were always cold because idealistically they were so different that there was no possibility of harmony between them. On one side was internationalism; on the other, the spirit of Finnish nationalism.

Almost from the beginning, many Finns were inclined to distrust the Kaleva order simply because it was a secret society. Every now and then, church papers published articles condemning secret societies in general. Very often criticism was aimed directly at the Masons, but its real purpose was to strike indirectly at the Kaleva order. It was not often remembered that secret societies had long been a form of activity generally approved in America. The Good Templar temperance societies were secret societies with passwords and a system of guards to protect their private character, and the first Finnish temperance societies were patterned after them. The Kalevainens tried to defend themselves by explaining that they were not a secret society in the sense of an underground society, because everyone always knew when and where they were meeting, but rather in the sense of a closed club to whose meeetings outsiders had no more business coming than they had going to meetings of a church council or a temperance society board.[42]

As has been suggested, opposition to the Kaleva organization was often due to its secret character—not knowing what went on behind the closed doors. In his book *Amerikan Tuulahduksia* (Breezes from America) John Lauttamus has included a story apparently based on a true happening. The title of it is "Pekka Poonalasta" (About Pekka Poonola). It is about a man who hated all secret societies, but especially the Knights of Kaleva. He decided once and for all to expose their dark secrets.

Poonala bribed the janitor of the Kaleva lodge's rented quarters and hid himself in a dark closet just before a meeting. But the Knights of Kaleva had gotten wind of his plan and held a fake meeting in which a "candidate" was examined in such a hullabaloo that screaming with pretended terror he fled from his "tormenters" to the closet in which Poonala was hiding. The supposed candidate's pursuers seized Poonala instead of the other, gagged him, and put a sack over his head so that he was not able to explain that in the dark he had been mistaken for the man they wanted. He was put through frightening experiences, until at last he was declared to be unworthy of membership and was thrown out of the back door to the street because the "venipuncture" had shown him to have "prosaic" blood.[43]

Life within the Lodges

Because the Knights and Ladies of Kaleva are secret societies, we shall have to content ourselves by touching lightly on life and activity within the lodges. Of all the Finnish American organizations, including the churches, the Kalevainens have best retained their inner integrity and sense of unity. This is understandable in light of the fact that the candidates for membership are carefully screened. In 1914–18, however, there were signs of discord, which were obvious even to outsiders, among some of the leading men. The situation was as follows: Stone, the founder of the Kaleva order, considered himself to be the authority on all questions concerning the organization and lodge meetings because he had translated into Finnish a booklet on parliamentary law and procedures.[44] He examined very closely the minutes and decisions of the Supreme Lodge, as well as the things officers had done or not done and wrote corrections so that his beloved society would in all ways conform to the law. It is thus that he came into conflict with such powerful men as Carl H. Salminen and Matti Erkkila, to whom the work itself was sometimes more important than the letter of the law. Some of the controversies were even taken to court.

Usually the more serious disagreements within the lodges are settled according to the criminal code given in the general rules. The most important wrongs of which a member may be accused are "the breaking of the oath, unknightly behavior, and breaking the laws" of the United States. Accusations touching on the whole organization were examined and settled by the Committee on Legal Affairs.

There are some advantages to belonging to the Kaleva order, for example, in getting employment, for members are generally respected as trusted citizens, as are members of congregations and temperance societies. They also have a mutual life insurance fund to which each member pays a prescribed amount every month. The Kalevainens are also known for helping each other in times of trouble. Especially before social security went into effect, such help was of real importance to members.

To the members of the Kaleva organization the ideals of Finnish nationality and culture are something sacred and something not to be relinquished, but their attitude is in no way in conflict with their American citizenship. The latter means loyalty to the government of America, good proof of which is in the number of Gold Star mothers and in the names on memorial tablets listing our fallen soldiers. The former is to them the call of blood and a feeling of union with a people who for thousands of years has defied the East and struggled to retain its freedom and its culture. Aino Lilja Halkola expressed the harmony of these two loyalties in a poem she wrote for the fiftieth anniversary celebration held in Ely, Minnesota, in the summer of 1948. She used the blue and white flag of "our Finland" and "our Star Spangled Banner" waving together in a breeze to symbolize that harmony.

14 The Cooperative Movement

The Cooperative Movement in Finland

Cooperative activity for the purpose of obtaining economic advantages and achieving security is probably as old as mankind itself. Even present-day cooperatives have roots reaching back hundreds of years. Literature about Swedish and French cooperatives tells of very early cooperative dairies and cheese factories in the Alps region. German historians write about the economic group projects of the ancient Teutons. The earliest real cooperative activity in Finland was the community mill. Jointly owned mills were common in southern Finland already in the fifteenth century, and by the beginning of the nineteenth, there were four thousand water mills scattered throughout the country, of which the majority were cooperative mills. To become a partner in the ownership of a mill, all that was necessary was to help with the construction and expenses. Thus, leaseholders and tenant farmers as well as landowners had the privilege of becoming participants.

Fishing cooperatives which constructed salmon weirs in rivers also originated in the Middle Ages. In addition, there were on the lakes crews of seine fishermen, all of whom had equal rights. Later the right of seine fishing depended on ownership of both land and water, seine fishing thus becoming the special right of the larger landowners. Around 1650, cooperative sawmills became common in Finland. Cooperative hunting and seal-catching groups are known to have existed centuries ago. On the group hunting expeditions, nights were spent beside a common campfire; in the mornings each hunter went his own way, returning in the evenings to divide his game with the other members of his group.

This simple kind of cooperative activity extended even to a means of transportation to church. In the lake areas in the interior of Finland, trips to church were made in extremely long, specially built "church boats." Often as many as seven families went in one boat, which raced with other boats carrying other groups of families. The boats and boathouses were jointly owned by the families using them. The basis for shares in the church boat was the number of oarsmen provided by the participant. A large farm might have as many as six oarsmen. One of the pleasantest forms of cooperation in many areas of Finland formerly was the custom of heating only one sauna in a community on bath nights in the wintertime. Members of a sauna group would take turns heating their saunas to provide baths for the entire community. The serving of "sauna coffee" or some other kind of refreshment was included in the practice.[1]

All of the above-mentioned activities were in one way or another producers' cooperatives. The concept of consumers' cooperatives began in England, France, and Germany in the early years of the nineteenth century in connection with the growth of industrialism. A factor that contributed to its development was the desire of the increasing industrial population for economic security.

The modern consumer cooperative movement is considered to have originated in England in the utopian-socialist movement in which manufacturer Robert Owen (1771–1858) and Dr. William King were active. Starting in 1825, numerous cooperative businesses were established, and King's paper *The Co-operator* inspired enthusiasm for the movement. Cooperative congresses were held, and by 1834 there were nearly 500 cooperative stores in England. But cooperative activity soon began to fall off rapidly and the cooperatives disappeared, having, however, proved that consumer cooperatives were practicable. The first permanent success in the cooperative movement was experienced by a small group of textile workers, mostly flannel weavers, in the town of Rochdale. On August 15, 1844, they established the world's first modern cooperative association, the Rochdale Society of Equitable Pioneers.

The basic principles of the Rochdale Pioneers have been used continuously in the cooperative movement everywhere: Membership is open, not depending on church or political affiliation; goods are sold at the day's average price; the consumer receives dividends in proportion to his purchases; each shareholder has only one vote; purchases are made in cash; the cooperative idea is spread through education. The most important of these was the return of surplus funds to the purchaser in the form of dividends. Charles Howarth, one of the Rochdale Pioneers, is credited with having developed this principle.

The Industrial and Provident Societies Act passed by Parliament in 1852 and the supplementary act of 1862 facilitated the establishment of cooperative associations and opened the way to cooperative activity all over the country. They also led to the organization of the Co-operative Wholesale Society in 1863 and the Co-operative Union of Great Britain and Ireland a few years later.

The success of the Rochdale Pioneers attracted attention all over the world. In France, however, interest centered on laborers' production cooperatives, which were not successful with the exception of the agricultural syndicates that acted as marketing and purchasing agents for farmers. In Belgium and Germany there were a number of closed cooperative businesses which sold only to members, most of whom were tradesmen and craftsmen. The most important cooperatives were loan associations and people's banks. The reason why the cooperative movement did not yet succeed in Germany was that Ferdinand Lassalle (1825–64), father of German socialism, did not consider it worthwhile.

The Scandinavian countries, where the Industrial Revolution occurred generations later, were far behind other continental countries and the United Kingdom in this important economic development. Consequently, the cooperative movement, a concomitant of the Revolution, also reached Finland, and Scandinavia in general, much later. Without taking into account earlier scattered brief articles, the newspapers began in 1860 to publish articles about the cooperative movements of England, Germany, and France. The first promoters of the cooperative concept in Finland were Dr. Rietrikki Polen, who invented the term "osuuskunta" for "cooperative" in Finnish; Gustaf Tornudd, an engineer from Viipuri, who wrote about the Rochdale weavers; and Yrjo Koskinen, who saw in cooperatives a way for the laborer to become free of the "guardianship" of the employer.

The first practical attempts at the establishment of cooperatives in Finland were made in 1870, but they came to nothing. The first successful cooperative store was Viipurin Työläisten Ravintoaineiden Kauppayhtiö (Viipuri Laborers' Grocery Company)—Polen's term "osuuskunta" was not yet in general use. Gustaf Tornudd may well have been present when the business was established, for its rules followed closely the rules of the Rochdale cooperative, with which Tornudd was familiar.

The founders were the workmen at the Viipuri Machine Shop. The workmen at the railroad machine shop at Viipuri organized their own cooperative the following year, and a laborers' cooperative store was established in Tampere. Difficulties encountered by these early cooperative businesses were caused by credit sales, the sale of liquor, and the indifference of shareholders. But the groundwork for the movement had been laid, and small cooperative stores sprang up here and there. The Helsingin Yleinen Ravintoyhdistys (Helsinki General Grocery Company), established in 1889, which was exceptionally successful, became a model for others. Within a period of ten years it had four stores and 800 members. Returns to members sometimes amounted to as much as 12 percent.[2] Cooperative dairies were first started in the 1880s. Dr. Hannes Gebhard (1864–1933) became the father of the Finnish cooperative movement and its capable leader, who was frequently called to other countries because of his expertise. His book *Suomen Osuustoiminta Pääpiirteissaan* (The main features of the Finnish cooperative movement), published in 1914, was translated into English, French, German, Swedish, Russian, Estonian, and Latvian. In 1899 he started the Pellervo-Seura to promote the cooperative concept especially among farmers. In 1901, as a result of his work Finland passed the Cooperative Law.[3] By 1905 Finland had 187 cooperative businesses with a membership of 29,000.

Socialism and the cooperative movement arrived in Finland about the same time. Because of rising socialism, there had been conflict over policy very early in the West European cooperative movement. In France the conflict was between two factions, the socialists and the nonpartisans; in Belgium among three, namely, socialists, Catholics, and nonpartisans. The socialist cooperatives were expelled from the central organization in 1902. From the very beginning the socialists in Finland tried to get control of the cooperatives. In the first party meeting in 1901 the cooperatives were requested to contribute 10 percent of their annual earnings to support the labor movement. The conflict continued to get worse and worse until 1917, when the final separation between the socialists and the non-partisan cooperatives occurred.[4]

The Beginnings of the Finnish American Cooperative Movement

Immigrants—perhaps the Finns were the first to do so—brought their distinctive "company" stores to America. The Swedish Finns started a store of this kind, called the Finlanders Grocery Union, in Worcester, Massachusetts, in 1891.[5] A similar general store was set up by the Finnish farmers of New York Mills, Minnesota, in 1893 or 1894.[6] For about ten years, from 1895 to 1905, these stores were very popular among Finnish Americans, especially in Michigan. They were not, however, typical cooperatives as they have been thought to be, but limited enterprises owned by small groups of men. Most of them were short-lived, run as they were by persons completely unfamiliar with business life, bringing great financial loss to shareholders.[7] In 1895, the Cornish miners, following the example of the Finns, established similar stores in Calumet and Allouez. The Germans established one in Fitchburg, Massachusetts, the same year.[8]

Finnish immigrants are among the first to have introduced consumers' cooperatives in America. Bertram B. Fowler writes almost too flatteringly about them:

> America is greatly indebted to the Finns who came to America toward the end of the nineteenth century, for it was the Finns who brought to America a clearer understanding of economic democracy. According to these Finns, consumer cooperatives were the only possible economic system for a true democracy. Through this, the Finns did an inestimable service to American democracy.[9]

The Finns were so well known for their cooperative activity that in certain areas if two Finns were seen walking together on a Saturday night, it was said that they were on their way either to take a sauna bath or to form a new cooperative. Many persons thought the cooperatives to be socialistic enterprises. To many others they were the brunt of jokes until the depression of the early 1930s revealed the value of cooperatives, and these Finnish businesses began to draw an ever-growing number of members from outside their own nationality. In spite of bad times the cooperative store remained open and was able to help its members, whereas many other businesses had to close their doors.

It has been said that the first form of cooperative activity among Finns was "passing the hat from one to another" to collect funds in cases of misfortune to some fellow worker. "Poikatalot" (men's rooming houses) were sometimes owned by groups of single men and, as such, they were the earliest form of cooperative activity among Finnish Americans. The next oldest cooperative business activity was the fire insurance business: The Finnish Mutual Fire Insurance Company began its activities in Calumet in 1890. The oldest Finnish American cooperative dairy is the one organized in New York Mills, Minnesota, in 1901. The first Finnish American cooperative stores were opened in Minnesota. The pioneer was the Sampo of Menahga, whose charter was signed by thirteen men on November 28, 1903. The beginning was small and the going difficult. In his memoirs, Severi Alanne says that once some mice gnawed a tunnel through a watermelon on display in a window. In addition to such difficulties, the owners of the store experienced enmity and open hostility. Members had more enthusiasm for their enterprise than they had aptitude for organizing or developing their business.[10] When the Farmers' cooperative Sampo celebrated its fiftieth anniversary in 1953, however, it had a fine modern supermarket. It received congratulatory messages from President Dwight D. Eisenhower and from leading cooperatives all over the world.[11] The Finns of Massachusetts were the next with cooperative businesses. Quincy had a cooperative store in 1904, Fitchburg in 1905, and Maynard in 1906, the last mentioned having been organized in a sauna.[12] The Maynard and Fitchburg stores have developed into million-dollar businesses. The Finns in Illinois started their first cooperative store in Waukegan in 1911.

Finnish American Cooperatives in Michigan, 1907–17

The first Finnish cooperative store in Michigan was established in Republic in 1907 and named the Finnish Workmen's Association, pointing to its having originated through the initiative of the local labor organization. Shares were $5 each and the most one person could buy was twenty. Later the price was raised to $10. No matter how many shares a shareholder had, however, he was permitted only one vote. The first manager of the business was Matti Arola, who held the position for two years. He was followed by Walter Ericson, who managed the business for about ten years of steady growth. During his managership the store was given a new and more suitable name: Republic Finnish Co-operative Store.[13] The next to be established was the Crystal Falls Co-operative Society which was started in Crystal Falls in 1908. The activity of these two pioneer ventures remained small for a time.

Several more years went by before cooperatives became more firmly established in Michigan. In the mining towns there were many stores run by Finns and by people of other nationalities. Their prices were reasonable because of the competition among them, even lower than in many other areas of Finnish population. Table 20 shows the prices in 1913. On paying his weekly or monthly bill the customer received a discount of 2 to 3 percent on the above-mentioned prices. In comparison, at the mining areas of Montana, where thousands of Finns

Table 20: Prices, Finnish Co-operative Store, Republic, Michigan, 1913

1 lb. hamburger	.20
1 lb. roast	.24
1 bushel potatoes	.75
100 lbs. flour	3.00
100 lbs. sugar	5.40
1 gal. syrup	.45
1 lb. raisins or prunes	.10
5 lbs. oatmeal	.25

were employed, the price of groceries averaged 35 percent higher than in the Upper Peninsula.[14] In addition, copper production in Michigan from 1905 to 1912 was greater than ever before, or about 22.5 million pounds per year on the average, so that unemployment was not a problem in the Copper Country, nor was the establishment of cooperative stores felt to be necessary yet as was the case in some other states.

The cooperative movement among the Finns of Michigan got into full swing in 1913 when cooperative stores were started in Ironwood, Mass, Rock, and Rudyard. In Rock and Mass at least, the reason for the establishment of cooperative stores was undoubtedly the Copper Country strike that began on July 23, 1915. Accurate information is available about the establishment of the Rock cooperative store and about the early phases of its existence. Because the store's problems were typical of the birth pangs and early struggles of most cooperatives they will be described in some detail.

Immediately after the strike broke out, Rock received an addition to its small population in a large number of families from the Copper Country, who brought with them more hunger than dollars. But the heads of many of these families who had "fled from capitalism into the arms of Nature" had had experience in organized group activity in unions, congregations, temperance societies, or labor organizations, and all of them were sorely in need of economic security for their families. The sure, direct way to it was seen to be in a cooperative.

The organizational meeting of the Rock cooperative store was held on the farm of Elias Ahola on August 16, 1913, less than a month after the start of the strike. The minutes of the meeting do not mention the number of persons in attendance. Bylaws were formulated and a clause was added to the effect "that only the Finnish language will be used in meetings for the time being." An unpretentious store was built with labor contributed by members, and it was ready for use by November 11. The first load of lumber was brought to the location by Elias Ahola, who was living in Spencer, New York, twenty-five years later. He reminisced thus:

> The memory has remained unforgettably in my mind of how I got the first load of building supplies from 12 miles away for the Rock cooperative store. The future of our enterprise looked very uncertain when we take into consideration the state of affairs prevailing then and the pressures directed against us. . . . When I arrived in the village with my load of lumber, there were all kinds of idlers and loiterers gathered on the steps of the Rock saloon to sneer at us. They shouted taunts and gibes at me. But it was not surprising, for the crowds were all favorable to and supporters of the local storekeeper, among them some Finns. While I was unloading, someone came there too to stare. He asked me if I was going to build a store. I answered "Not I, but WE." My interrogator reflected that such an enterprise was a waste of time.

The secretary of the board of directors was Klaus Ruotsala, who called the cooperative a "store company" in the minutes. For their banking, or as Ruotsala says in the minutes, "their business partner in financial matters," they decided to use the First National Bank of Escanaba. For the time being, however, there was nothing to deposit in the bank. The first business manager was August Haanpaa, who knew nothing at all about business matters and was consequently fired a month later. Ruotsala ends the paragraph about this matter in his minutes with the words "Oscar Niemi and Walter Selin were chosen to denounce Haanpaa in the newspapers."

Before the end of the year John Vaara of Hancock was the new manager. John Maki, the manager of the Ishpeming office of *Työmies*, was called in to balance the books after about a month and a half of activity. According to his report, $700 worth of $10 shares had been sold; accounts receivable amounted to $1,100 because of sales for credit; and so-called friendly loans amounted to over $1,300. John Vaara left after a few months and William Marttila was selected to take his place.

At the end of the first year of business, on December 31, 1914, accounts receivable amounted to $8,870 and debts to $10,686. Paid capital amounted to only $1,163, or one-ninth of the debt. The business remained operative because a number of its founders had transferred to the cooperative store a successful lumber company which sold mostly firewood and pulpwood. In time the business became known as the Maple Ridge Farmer's Co-operative Store Company.

Marttila resigned from the managership in the winter of 1916. His successor was Alfred Vainio from Butte, Montana, who left after a few months. The new manager, Otto Lahtinen, had the thankless task of straightening out the ever more difficult financial situation in which the business found itself and other complications that had continued during the time Marttila was manager. Board meetings were held in rapid succession, often lasting till 2:30 in the morning. The complaint that members bought from independent storekeepers for cash and from the cooperative store on credit was frequently heard. At the time of the establishment of the Central Cooperative Wholesale in 1917 the stormy and difficult early phase of the cooperative store in Rock came to an end. The board had learned from its mistakes and Otto Lahtinen proved to be a capable manager who gradually got the situation straightened out.[15]

The organization of the Rock cooperative also set the wheels in motion for the organization in the same year, 1913, of the cooperative stores in Mass City, Rudyard, and Ironwood. The Mass cooperative was started at the time of the big Copper Country strike, when a large number of miners moved to the community with their families. When the independent storekeepers refused to sell to them on credit, they started their own cooperative store.[16] However, it was said soon afterward that "the miners participated hardly at all in efforts to develop the business."[17]

Early difficulties were great and managers changed so often that by the end of 1915 the reins were in the hands of the fifth manager, and the store was operating in the red. V. S. Alanne's portrayal of the situation in some cooperative stores he had seen applies to the Mass cooperative:

> In many stores complete confusion reigns, not so much because of a lack of space, but because of poor organization. Merchandise is scattered about, helter-skelter: women's stockings, horoshoes, saws, and trousers are all in one heap, and the clerks don't know anything about prices—they sell the merchandise by guesswork.[18]

In 1916, however, when Jack Vainionpaa became manager, things began to look brighter. Under the vigorous leadership of "Iso Jaakko" (Big Jack), they were able to accumulate capital, to get better organized, and to increase sales so that in 1916 they made $21,061.26. That year they even made a profit of $1,161.86, and in 1917 they built a store of their own.[19]

In Rudyard the Finnish cooperative store opened for business toward the end of 1913. The first manager was Toivo Niemo. Their start was very modest, for which reason those who opposed it gave it six months, but at the end of this period the monthly sales amounted to about $2,000.[20]

Ironwood was also in the process of establishing a cooperative store in 1913, and the following year the Finnish Cooperative Trading Company began to operate with capital of $1,500. But credit sales brought difficulties. This unhappy experience with credit sales, typical of the early phases of cooperative activity, caused Adolf Wirkkula, the manager of the cooperative store in Iron River, Wisconsin, to write a sharply worded article "Velkakauppapaholaisesta" (The credit sale demon).[21] Soon after its establishment the Ironwood store suffered a considerable loss through fire, but by 1915 it was so successful that sales for the year were over $65,000. The name was changed to National Cooperative Company. Some of the early managers were Theodore Leppala, Jack Vainionpaa, and Alfred Kaartinen. In 1917 the membership was 327 and sales amounted to $44,000.

In Sault Ste. Marie the Finnish Co-operative Merchants began activity in 1914. The following year, capital stock amounted to $2,075 and the profit for 1915 was $739. This was not the actual situation, however, for at the annual meeting held on March 16, 1916, it was reported that because of credit sales, accounts receivable amounted to $7,340.39. A decision was now made to collect 10 percent interest annually on unpaid accounts. The next year the auditor severely criticized the store's muddled bookkeeping and the board took action on the matter.[22] The chairman of the board at the beginning was Severi Rantanen; the manager was Fred Tuomisto.[23]

In Houghton County, especially Hancock, interest in cooperatives was evident immediately after the Copper Country strike. The first cooperative to be established was the Finnish Farmers' Association of Houghton County in 1914 to handle farmers' sales and purchases. There were 300 members when the business was established. The office was in Hancock.[24]

The first consumer cooperative was the Farmers' Co-operative Trading Company established in Hancock in 1914. Some planning for it had been done during the strike when many independent merchants refused to sell to strikers on credit. A store was opened immediately after the end of the strike with only $360 capital.[25] The business was incorporated on January 16, 1915. The store was on Franklin Street; V. Brander was made manager. When Brander left a few months later, John D. Nummivuori succeeded him. When the Hancock cooperative store was running satisfactorily, a branch store was opened in Calumet on Pine Street, which was well known among the Finns. Christian Niva was the manager. In South Range there were a number of persons who were interested in cooperatives. They began to send orders for merchandise to the Hancock store. For their convenience a store was opened in South Range also. Henry Koski, who had served as a union secretary during the Copper Country strike, was made manager in the summer of 1917.[26] A third branch store was opened in Arnheim in October 1916, but because it did not receive adequate support from the area farmers, it was closed in 1920.

Nummivuori, the general manager, was an enterprising man of action. On October 15, 1916, he spoke at a meeting held at the Paynesville young people's hall. It was decided there that a farmers' cooperative would be established and that a store would be opened as soon as $1,500 in capital had been collected. Nummivuori's travel expenses amounted to $5.29. To pay them, every man present contributed 24 cents. Apparently there were 22 men at the meeting, all of whom signed up as members of the new cooperative.[27]

From the minutes it is not clear if the store, which was opened a few months later, was a branch of the Hancock cooperative, as was the one in Bruce Crossing which was opened on May 1, 1917, with $750 capital.[28] Independent storekeepers posted notices in their display windows that they were no longer selling on credit, meaning to those who were buying also from the cooperative store. This move was a mistake which worked so greatly to the advantage of the cooperative store that after a short time, 140 of the 209 Bruce Crossing families were members of the cooperative.[29]

In Hancock, the cooperative had difficulty finding capital at first because the many bankrupt "store companies" had left unpleasant memories of their failure, and the public thought the cooperative movement was an attempt to reactivate these unsuccessful companies. This misunderstanding is reflected in the slow accumulation of capital: At the end of 1915 it amounted to $813, and a year later, to $1,571. It is also shown in the relatively small sales of the first two years: $74,955 in 1915 and $74,367 in 1916, including the proceeds from the branch stores.[30] The meat department was soon the best managed one in the business. Slaughter animals were purchased from farmers at higher prices than were paid by other stores, and the cooperative was still able to sell meat for less than the others.[31] By the end of 1917, the Hancock cooperative with its branches had a total of 600 members, and sales amounted to $250,000. Enthusiasm for cooperative activity and for supporting their own business was manifested through family socials which were held for their benefit. On one such occasion in Hancock in the spring of 1916, 300 participants were estimated to have been present. The early hardships were over.

The Covington cooperative also had its beginnings in 1914. At Suomi Synod church services, Pastor John Wargelin announced that a meeting to organize a "store company" would be held at the local temperance hall. The bylaws of the Rock cooperative store were read and approved, just as they were, for the new cooperative. A decision to sell two thousand shares at the nominal price of $5 per share was also made. Despite hard times, enough shares were sold so that the new group was able to build a small, unpretentious store on Otto Tarvainen's land at Leo Siding, about one and a half miles west of Covington.

Since wholesale dealers objected to selling merchandise on credit, the new cooperative approached the Hancock cooperative, which made a condition that all the money on hand should be turned over to it as advance payment for merchandise and that it would provide a manager for the new store, but the board turned down the proposition and decided to go ahead without outside help. With the board members as security they obtained a loan of $500 from the L'Anse bank, and with Julius Johnson as manager they got started. In 1916 Joseph Jurmu from Daggett became manager and a year later, Alfred Cayanus. The business was now moved to Covington, where the cooperative was able to rent store space cheaply from Dick Howe and Pat Tracy's saloon. In 1918 the business came to an end because of lack of support.[32]

In the history of cooperative activity in the Upper Peninsula, the year 1916 was a productive one. In addition to Arnheim and Paynesville, Eben Junction and Negaunee also acquired cooperative stores. Meetings had been held about the matter in Eben already in 1915 and a little more than $400 worth of shares had been sold. The money went into the construction of a small store building, which was opened the following summer as the Eben Farmers' Cooperative Store. William I. Niemi and Toivo A. Samanen were among the first business managers. In 1917 William Konno from Kauhajoki became manager. In Finland he had had practical experience with cooperative activity. He was assisted by his wife Tyyne, born in Sysmä, who was enthusiastically active in the Finns' three main interests—the church, temperance work, and cooperatives. Under the leadership of the Konnos the Eben cooperative store made rapid progress.[33] The first important change was the changeover from credit sales to cash sales entirely.

The meeting to establish the People's Co-operative Company in Negaunee was held in the Labor Temple on May 13, 1916, and a store was opened on Iron Street, where it still is. This first effort, however, ended in bankruptcy, but the business was started anew immediately. The first manager was J. A. Pelto, who was followed by Hjalmar Dantes. Before the end of 1917 the manager was Aku Rissanan, a newspaperman and lecturer. Credit sales had quickly consumed the capital of $1,500, and there were financial difficulties until toward the end of 1917, when the changeover to cash sales was made and the books were finally balanced.[34]

The uniting link between the first Finnish American cooperative stores was the frequently mentioned *Pelto ja Koti*, a monthly publication William Marttila had begun to edit in Winlock, Washington, in 1911. It was moved to the Työmies Publishing Company in Hancock the following year, with Marttila still as editor and John Kiiskila attending to the legal aspects of publication. In it Charles O. Knuutti of Milwaukee answered readers' questions about farm machinery. In 1914, when the Työmies Publishing Company moved to Superior with its publications, *Pelto ja Koti* achieved a readership of 6,000. The publication was well edited and included many subjects, but urban readers complained that most of the content was directed toward farmers, and readers with leftist inclinations wanted more politics in its pages. The paper ceased publication in 1921, when its last numbers were headed by a picture of the hammer and sickle.

The Establishment of the Central Cooperative Wholesale

It was natural for people in cooperatives, and especially the managers, to feel the need for a central organization to which they could turn for answers to questions on bookkeeping, auditing, the function of the cooperative, and many other related matters. A single cooperative store sometimes had difficulty with wholesalers who, because of the pressures exerted by independent store owners, were cool to the new Finnish enterprise. The first conference about the matter was held in Duluth in 1914. The meeting, which was attended by twenty store managers and other interested persons, decided to establish an organization called the Finnish American Cooperative Union and elected John D. Nummivuori as secretary. But there the plan ended because of a lack of funds. In writing about the situation in *Pelto ja Koti*, Marttila ended his article with these words: "The clamor about this matter in this paper will not cease until we have established a powerful cooperative organization."[35]

Another attempt at organizing was made at a meeting in Superior, Wisconsin, on July 1–2, 1916. Only two delegates from Michigan were present. They were Jack Vainionpaa, representing the Mass cooperative store, and John Okkonen, representing the Hancock store. Five cooperatives in Minnesota were represented, two in Wisconsin, one in Illinois, and five in Massachusetts. W. Boman from Massachusetts and Karl Helander from Illinois were elected chairmen, and John D. Nummivuori, who had moved to Superior, was elected secretary.

Boman and Marttila had prepared extensive reports and plans. The most lively discussion was about policy. The delegates from Michigan maintained that political neutrality was the only basis on which success would be assured in their state, especially in the Copper Country. The majority were in favor of socialism and of joint activity with organized labor. No one supported "radicalism." The delegates were unanimously agreed that, with regard to the procurement of capital, the minimum invested in the business by each member should be $50, and in case of bankruptcy, another $50, according to the law in several states. *Pelto ja Koti* was approved as the official voice of the organization, although its content was severely criticized. With an eye to convenient travel connections, Waukegan, Illinois, was selected as the location for the home office. The delegates from the eastern states, A. J. Partanen and W. Boman, were selected to draft the bylaws.[36] They worked fast and published their proposal as the constitution of the Finnish American Cooperative Union already in the September number of *Pelto ja Koti*.[37] According to the constitution, matters pertaining to the union were to be decided by the meetings of delegates and, in the intervals between meetings, by the administrative council and a committee of the union.

The statement of policy in the constitution was more radical than the discussion at the Superior meeting seemed to indicate it would be. Its beginning reads as follows:

> The Finnish American Cooperative Union accepts the principles of the international cooperative movement and agrees to abide by them. But at the same time, the Union declares that cooperatives, as a proletarian movement, are a part of the class struggle of organized labor against capitalism, and the Union maintains that cooperative activity, to be profitable to the laborer-consumer, must be allied with the class struggle.

In the meantime, the board of the Waukegan cooperative store had selected a five-man temporary union committee from its membership.[38] But the situation did not improve, even though a permanent union committee and an administrative council were selected soon after.[39] When the United States broke off diplomatic relations with the Central Powers on February 3, 1917, at the time of World War I, and declared war against them two months later, there was an exceptionally strong wave of patriotism in the country, which did not look with favor on activities carried on in a foreign language. Even the small Finnish cooperatives soon experienced antagonism and found themselves in more financial difficulties. The cooperative union provided neither relief nor financial security.

Already in 1906, J. C. Grey, president of the Cooperative Union in England, presented a plan for a union of individual cooperatives stores which would be distributors for a large central organization, functioning in much the same way as the powerful chain stores in America, with outlets all over the country. Cooperative buying and prices based on an average for each item would enable them to compete and help them to become financially secure.

The original impetus for the creation of this kind of organ to serve the Finnish American cooperative movement came from the Hancock cooperative when it published an invitation in *Pelto ja Koti* on August 1, 1917, to the cooperatives stores of Northern Michigan, Wisconsin, and Minnesota, to send their store managers and two or three of their board members to a meeting in Superior, Wisconsin. "Let us pool all our purchases together and let us make one of our stores a wholesale through which we will buy for all stores the merchandise which each business feels able to buy," read the invitation. The cooperative store in Iron River, Wisconsin, also joined in the invitation.[40]

The meeting was held on Sunday and Monday, July 29–30. Seventeen cooperative stores from four states were represented: Illinois, one; Minnesota, three; Wisconsin, five; and Michigan, eight. The delegates from the Michigan cooperatives were John Nummivuori, Oscar Komula, and John Okkonen from Hancock; Richard Wirtanen and Alfred Kaartinen from Ironwood; Jacob Vainionpaa from Mass; Otto Lahtinen from Rock; Elis Freeman from Marquette; Aku Rissanen and Kalle A. Nurmi from Negaunee; John Wierikko from Amasa; and Matti Kokkonen from Rudyard. Kalle Helander from Waukegan and John Nummivuori from Hancock were elected chairmen of the meeting, and Rissanen and Nurmi from Negaunee were made secretaries. The group was unanimously in favor of cooperative buying. The sixteenth paragraph of the minutes is interesting: "At the beginning of the afternoon session we listened to representatives of certain wholesalers and we asked them questions, Turppa serving as interpreter." E. E. Turppa was the delegate from Waukegan.

The representatives of the wholesale companies were not able to sway the delegates from their purpose. The next day they decided unanimously to organize "a central organization of cooperative stores and a bakery called the Cooperative Central Exchange," known briefly as the CCE. In Finnish it was known as Keskusosuuskunta. Superior was chosen for its headquarters. It was decided that an effort should be made to acquire $20,000 in capital, divided into 200 one-hundred-dollar shares "which the cooperatives may purchase . . . according to their estimated needs." Members elected to the board were from Superior, Cloquet, and Iron River, Wisconsin.[41] A collection, amounting to $15.50, was taken from those in attendance. It is highly improbable that any other wholesale had ever started with so little capital.

The Cooperative Central Exchange was incorporated according to the Wisconsin cooperative law on August 31, 1917.[42] The word "exchange" in the name implied the intention of handling farm products. This branch business, however, brought losses to both the farmers and the CCE; consequently, it was dropped and emphasis was placed on supplying cooperative stores with merchandise. In keeping with this emphasis, the name was changed to the Central Cooperative Wholesale (CCW). But it brought about no change in the pertinent and practical form of the name in use among the Finns. John D. Nummivuori was chosen to be the first general manager. He served in that capacity until 1922. By the middle of October, fifteen cooperative stores had joined the CCW, and the organization was well on its way.

Although the CCW had been established, its early phases of existence were beset with obstacles. For one thing the boards of small local cooperatives hesitated to join because they were afraid that the managership of their businesses would slip into the hands of the men in Superior and that the CCW would then become too powerful.[43] In a few years, however, there was a change for the better in the Finnish American cooperative movement and it began to grow rapidly. This growth was first seen in an increase in the number of cooperatives. At the time of the establishment of the CCW in 1917, fifteen cooperative stores in all had joined the organization, but two years later Michigan alone had fifteen member stores in it, in addition to which six other Michigan cooperatives used its services. Table 21 shows sales of the CCW to Finnish Cooperatives in Michigan and the amount of money they had in the CCW compared with cooperatives in other states gives a picture of the situation.

Thus, in addition to the fifteen Michigan cooperatives that

Table 21: Sales of CCW to Finnish Cooperatives, 1919

MEMBERS OF CCW		AMOUNT PD. FOR SHARES IN CCW 1919	PURCHASES FROM CCW 1919
Amasa Co-op Society		$ 100.00	$ 11,163.70
Drummond Co-op Club, Johnswood		100.00	—
Farmers Co-op Ass'n, Herman		100.00	6,775.67
Farmers Co-op Trading Co., Hancock		700.00	29,596.60
Finnish Co-op Trading Co., Ironwood		700.00	12,812.29
Ishpeming Consumers Co-op Ass'n		100.00	10,878.19
Mass Co-op Co.		200.00	7,652.63
Munising Co-op Ass'n		100.00	201.36
Newberry Co-op Ass'n		100.00	4,062.93
Peoples Co-op Store Co., Negaunee		25.00	6,313.01
Rock Co-op Co.		10.00	561.58
Settlers Co-op Trading Co., Bruce Crossing		100.00	16,226.96
Toivola Co-op Consumers Ass'n		100.00	1,292.81
Twin City Co-op Society, Iron River		100.00	2,987.04
Workers Co-op Society, Marquette		30.00	2,851.35
		$2,565.00	$111,376.12
NON-MEMBER BUSINESSES			
Crystal Falls Co-op Society			60.38
Eben Farmers Co-op Ass'n			109.80
Farmers Co-op Trading Co., Pelkie			1,127.74
Railway Employees Co-op Society, Escanaba			28.80
Soo Co-op Merchants Ass'n			111.36
Trenary Co-op Store			243.44
			$1,681.52
Totals for Michigan		$2,565.00	$113,057.64
OTHER STATES	NUMBER OF COOPERATIVES		
Minnesota	43 (18 in CCW)	$2,465.00	$119,668.64
Wisconsin	10 (5 in CCW)	1,660.00	51,499.92
Illinois	1 (CCW)	100.00	1,401.63
North Dakota	1 (CCW)	50.00	312.85
Masssachusetts	3		3,082.81
New York	1		30.00

Table 21: Sales of CCW to Finnish Cooperatives, 1919 *(continued)*

MEMBERS OF CCW	NUMBER OF COOPERATIVES	AMOUNT PD. FOR SHARES IN CCW 1919	PURCHASES FROM CCW 1919
Montana	1		12.75
Oregon	1		4,313.62
Washington	1		34.00
		$4,275.00	$180,356.22

were members of the CCW in 1919, there were twenty-five from other states, or a total of forty.[44] In 1929, when the second period in the history of the Finnish American cooperative movement in the Midwest ended, there were almost four times as many member stores in the CCW.

From 1917 to 1929

To the extent to which information has been available about the early history of the twenty-nine Michigan cooperative stores that were in existence before the establishment of the CCW, they have already been discussed. Between 1917 and 1929, cooperative stores were started in the following communities: Marquette, Herman, Amasa, and Iron River in 1917; Chatham in 1918; Ishpeming, Trenary, and Newberry in 1919; and Watton in 1921.

In Marquette, meetings had been held as early as 1915 to consider getting cooperative activity started. The next year, a decision was made to establish the Workers Co-operative Society, and the task of collecting money for shares from those who had expressed interest was undertaken. In the spring of 1917 a grocery store on Washington Street across from the town hall was purchased from John Lammi. Elis Freeman was the first manager.

Toivo Pelto wrote about the beginnings of the Marquette cooperative as follows:

> Our financial resources were not great, but our enthusiasm was all the greater. Because of our small capital, the early days were very difficult, and because we gave credit to our customers, the manager was forced to get emergency loans from shareholders. But we went forward anyhow. A meat market was opened in connection with the store, and in 1920 a branch store was opened in North Marquette. After a few years, the whole business was moved there to 1636 Presque Isle Ave-

> nue. . . . Managers and board members have changed, but special credit is due Jalmar Lehto for his 30 years of service on the board, settling differences and solving problems.[45]

For a number of years the store was completely independent, joining the Central Cooperative Wholesale in 1926.

The organizational meeting of the Amasa Co-operative Society was held on April 15, 1917, and the store was opened early that summer, when capital of over $3,000 had been collected through the sale of shares.[46] Ida Kuure reminisced about the early efforts of the Amasa cooperative in the following words:

> When we began to work at starting a cooperative store in Amasa, my husband Emil and I immediately bought ten shares. We women-folk certainly were very busy in connection with it. We held coffee socials, each in her home, and summer festivals; and we presented some long plays even, including *Naisorja*, *Tukkijoella*, *Hallin Janne*, *Murtovarkaus*, and *Murtuneita*, as well as many shorter ones, always to large audiences. The money received was turned over to the cooperative; I remember that once we donated a hundred dollars at one time.[47]

But even the initiative and enthusiasm of the women was not able to save the poorly managed business, which had only eighty members and only about $1,500 worth of sales per month. After three years of struggle, the business was bankrupt, but it was re-established. Credit of $2.80 was given for each $10 of the old $10 shares to those who bought shares in the re-established business. In 1922 the cooperative bought its own store building where it carried on business for a long time. In 1924 a fire destroyed the warehouse and some of the merchandise, but insurance paid for the losses suffered. The cooperative was a member of the CCW but because of difficulties caused by the fire, the membership was allowed to lapse; it was later renewed.[48]

A cooperative store called the Twin City Co-operative Society was started in 1917 in Iron River with $1,800 capital. Swedish Finns participated with enthusiasm. The beginning was promising; about a hundred members joined, and the business was opened in rented quarters in Riverside, from where it was moved in the fall of 1918 to larger quarters in the center of town. The cooperative joined the CCW at the same time. They had no experience, however; too much of their merchandise was sold on credit, and wholesale dealers refused to sell to them on credit. In 1919 the business went into bankruptcy.[49]

Among the cooperative businesses started in 1917 there was also the Farmers Co-operative Association of Herman; it had a unique background. The population of this village a few miles south of L'Anse had grown so much that a certain John Stickney decided that a store selling general merchandise, including groceries, would succeed there. However, he sold his business to two Finns, Haveri and Keranen, from whom it went to the railroad station agent, L. P. Perston. The next owner was again a Finn, the town's postmaster, Charles T. Dantes.

Before settling in Herman, some of the Finns had become familiar with cooperatives, Dantes among them, and got others interested in them. Meetings were held, a decision to start a cooperative store was made, and house-to-house solicitation for buyers of shares was done, and $800 was collected. It was obvious that there was not enough business in such a small community for two stores; thus everything depended on Dantes's attitude. He was in favor of the cooperative, sold his merchandise and store furnishings to it, and became its first manager in the spring of 1917. The Herman cooperative had the rare advantage of becoming the owner and operator of an already established business.

The Herman Farmers Co-operative Association joined the Central Cooperative with a $100 share soon after its organization. In 1922 the store was moved to the basement hall belonging to the Pyrkijä Athletic Society. It was centrally located though otherwise inconvenient. The low rent, however, was important in that the business made more profit than it would have in a more expensive place. This enabled it to open a branch store in nearby Aura in 1927.[50] Before this, the membership was 160, rising to over 200 with the addition of members from Aura. The Finns' enthusiasm for their cooperative store was great. Meetings were held frequently and the work of the board was evaluated, resulting in frequent changes of board members. The work of the CCW was also closely followed and delegates were sent to annual meetings.[51]

Members of the Finnish socialist organization in Ishpeming had formed a simple purchasing pool among themselves, providing members of the group with some of their groceries. This pool developed into the Ishpeming Consumers' Co-operative Association, which opened its store in 1919, joining the CCW at the same time. Its origin is clearly indicated in the motto it used during its early years: "A laborers' store, run by laborers for laborers."[52] By 1925 the membership was 198, and the business was making steady progress. In the statistical reports of the CCW the Ishpeming cooperative was sometimes listed as being first in sales, in itself a notable achievement, which indicates that the board had known how to select capable managers. Of them, Karl Lindewall was the best known during the early years of the cooperative's existence.

The establishment of a cooperative in Chatham was being considered already in the fall of 1915, when William Marttila, who was then the manager of the Rock cooperative store, went there to speak to interested persons about the matter. Later on, that same year, a committee selected by the farmers of the Chatham area visited a meeting of the Rock cooperative to learn about cooperatives firsthand.[53] In 1918 a cooperative store was opened, as a branch of the Eben cooperative temporarily, and "we were able to buy familiar [Finnish] foods from our own store in our own language." In the same year the Finnish farmers of Pelkie, who already had a dairy, also opened a cooperative store. The Finns of Drummond Island also organized a consumers' group centered in Johnswood. It joined the CCW immediately. The last Finnish American cooperative store started in 1918 was the Newberry Cooperative Association, which joined the CCW and bought shares in it even before it opened its store.[54] By 1925 the membership had reached 103. Sales that year amounted to $48,540.

The Farmers' Co-operative Store of Trenary was started in 1919. It became a member of the CCW two years later. By 1925 the membership was 142, and sales that year amounted to $61,000.

In the same year a consumers' ring, or purchasing club, called the Toivola Co-operative Consumers' Association, was started. In this sparsely populated area in Houghton County there was not much possibility for growth. By 1925 fourteen families had joined. In that year $897 worth of merchandise was purchased from the CCW and $861 worth was sold.[55]

In 1921, consumers' groups were organized in Palmer and Deerton and called cooperative associations. They joined the CCW in 1923. The Deerton Cooperative was, for the time being, only a listed name. In 1925, the Palmer group had eighteen members, and its purchases from the CCW amounted to $1,084.

As has been said earlier, the first cooperative venture of the Covington Finns failed, but in 1922 a new consumer organization was started with Bert Aalto as manager. In the very beginning they joined the CCW, from which they purchased $3,500 worth of merchandise the first year. Aalto was paid $20 per month for his efforts. A branch was started in Watton in 1923 with Joseph Trappu as manager.

In 1925, when they had progressed so far that their consumer ring had ninety-three families, they decided to open a cooperative store in Watton the next year. The consumer ring turned over its funds, about $500, to the store. The first manager was Otto Lahtinen, who served until 1931. When Nels Koski of Covington gave up his general store in 1928, the cooperative first rented and, in the following year, purchased his business building for a store to serve as a branch of the Watton cooperative. This was done at an opportune time, for a fire completely destroyed the Watton cooperative store on April 29, 1929, but the business was able to continue without interruption in the Covington store. The great interest of the community in the cooperative idea is evidenced also by the fact that coffee socials were held in homes, and outdoor festivals, which included programs and athletic competition, were planned to help support the cooperative.[56]

Among the consumer groups established in Upper Michigan there was one called the Railway Employees' Co-operative Society in Escanaba, organized by Finnish railroad men around 1918.

Several things worth mentioning happened between 1917 and 1929 among the cooperative stores that had been started before the organization of the CCW. The Finnish Co-operative Association, which was also called the Republic Farmers' Cooperative Association, was not really a cooperative business in the regular sense of the word, but rather a joint stock company which was using a misleading name. In 1929 the business came into the hands of cooperative-minded persons who selected Severi Petman to be the business manager. The store now joined the CCW and began to prosper. Sales, which had been \$27,000 in 1928, rose to \$48,500 in 1929, and went over \$50,000 in 1930 in spite of the Depression, which had just started. In 1929 the store started a small sausage factory which bought 15,400 pounds of meat from farmer members the very first year. By the end of 1930 there were 122 members, and assets amounted to \$11,465.[57] The Crystal Falls cooperative was still outside the CCW although it made use of some of its services to its advantage.

The cooperative store in Rock became the biggest business in its community. While sales had been \$28,000 in 1916, in 1920 they were four times greater, amounting to \$140,000. During the same period the cooperative's sale of lumber, which it still continued, increased to fifteen times greater, from \$13,000 to \$202,000. Otto Lahtinen, who was largely responsible for this increase, left the managership in the summer of 1921 when the board, fearing a business depression, lowered his salary. Membership was over 300. The next manager was Herman Kohtala, who served until the end of 1925, returning later to Finland as the head of International Harvester Company sales there. He was succeeded by Arvo N. Rivers, who was born in Kiikka, Finland, in 1895, and after his basic education in Finland, continued his studies at the Smithville Workingmen's College. He began his career in cooperatives as bookkeeper in the Rock store in 1916, in time becoming one of the best-known Finnish Americans in the cooperative movement, both in

Finnish American and non-Finnish American cooperative activity. Having worked at his bookkeeping for over eight years, he was now the manager and proceeded to work energetically for the store's progress. In 1930 the Rock cooperative, including the lumber business, achieved total sales of $453,000.[58]

The Mass cooperative store grew at a steady pace. The most critical period for it was the time of the changeover from credit sales to cash sales only. In fear of losing customers, a discount of 3 percent was given customers at first and 5 percent later, during the transition period.[59] A branch store was opened in Ontonagon in 1919. The membership, which in 1917 was 194, was 471 in 1925, including the Ontonagon store, and in 1927 it was 522. Sales, which in 1917 were $66,000, were $115,000 in 1925 and $146,000 in 1927, making the Mass cooperative the seventh in sales in the CCW at this time. The most colorful of the managers of this period was Maurice Raeburn, who had worked in cooperatives in Finland before coming to America in 1906. He then worked in the Philippines and in China at various jobs, and after his return to America he served as manager of cooperative stores in Minnesota before moving to Mass.[60]

The Rudyard cooperative experienced periods of progress after the managership was given to William Konno, who was experienced in cooperative work. The cooperative joined the CCW at that time. Business increased to $45,000 in 1926, and to $58,000 in 1927. Membership at this time was 200. A new building was acquired in 1930.

The Ironwood National Co-operative Company opened a branch store at Junet Siding on the Duluth, South Shore railroad in 1922 and another a little later on in North Bessemer. Despite these additions, the membership fell to a fraction of its former strength so that in 1924 it was only forty-five. But after 1924 it began to increase again. The sales thereafter were relatively high: $62,000 in 1924, $66,000 in 1924, and $71,000 in 1927.

The Farmers' Co-operative Trading Company of Hancock continued its steady growth. Its five branch stores were located in Calumet, Herman, South Range, Bruce Crossing, and Arnheim. The Finnish farmers of the Agate Siding area also wanted to organize a cooperative as a branch of the Hancock business but when Hancock asked for $3,000 capital in advance the plan was apparently dropped. Adolf Wirkkula, the general manager, left in 1923 to be manager of the large Finnish Co-operative Trading Company in Brooklyn, New York.[61] His successor in Hancock was Oscar Corgan, who served until 1926. Corgan was succeeded by John Jalmar Polkky, who held the position until 1934, serving also as a member of the board of the CCW until 1929. The economic development of the Hancock organization and its branches from 1917 to 1929 can be seen in the totals given in table 22.[62]

Table 22: Sales Figures, Finnish Cooperative, Hancock, Michigan 1917–29

1917	$245,497.00	1924	$123,932.09
1918	$264,110.14	1925	$146,194.70
1919	$229,192.76	1926	$154,312.83
1920	$192,214.70	1927	$136,091.26
1921	$134,486.40	1928	$145,121.40
1922	$123,394.91	1929	$182,434.05
1923	$102,639.67		

There were two reasons for the downward trend in sales starting in 1919. One was that the Bruce Crossing store in Ontonagon County left the mother store and continued as an independent cooperative, and the Arnheim store in Houghton County was closed because it was not profitable. The second reason was that after World War I there was a smaller demand for copper, resulting in the closing of some Copper Country mines or in less production, which forced hundreds and maybe thousands of families to move elsewhere to find employment. In addition, many people who had lived on credit left their debts unpaid so that when Oscar Corgan became the general manager of the Hancock cooperative in 1923 the amount due the store was about $23,000. This demonstrates a phenomenon that sometimes occurred elsewhere too: In a difficult situation Finns would do everything in their power to pay their debts to non-Finns because of national pride, but they were not so particular about debts owed their own countrymen. The downward trend in sales hit bottom in 1923, after which the situation improved considerably.

The members and the board of the Settlers' Co-operative Trading Company in Bruce Crossing became dissatisfied with the main store in Hancock. The first reason for dissatisfaction was the distance between the stores. As a bird flies, it was only sixty miles, but because the railroad was the only mode of transportation being used, the distance was about a hundred miles because it was necessary to go by way of Nestoria, which was considerably out of the way. But a more important reason was the question of how the profits should be used. The Bruce Crossing farmers maintained that profits from their business were being used to cover the losses incurred by other stores of the Hancock cooperative. In a special meeting held at the beginning of 1919 "the storm reached its peak, and in that meeting the Bruce Crossing cooperative decided to leave the Hancock store."[63] The sale of shares, which had been slow thus far, increased, for the consumer area was divided into districts, one of which each member of the board was responsible for visiting to sell shares to the farmers living in it.[64] The membership, which had been comparatively large from the very beginning considering local conditions, began to grow even larger, rising to 240 in 1925 and 368 in 1929.

Soon Paynesville joined the Bruce Crossing cooperative as a branch store, and a small outlet was also set up in Trout Creek. Even so, life as an independent business did not start off as free of difficulties as in the first wave of enthusiasm it had been thought it might. The depression which followed World War I brought with its debts, for the payment of which the board members had to "mortgage all their property that was not already mortgaged." "That included everything excepting wives and children" said a certain pioneer, reminiscing about those times. In 1925 a Ku Klux Klan group patterned after the Ku Klux Klan of the South and started by opponents of the Finnish cooperative movement appeared on the scene. However, there was no violence. Only a few harmless cross burnings took place.[65] Annual sales increased steadily: to $64,000 in 1924, $83,000 in 1925, $117,000 in 1926, $132,000 in 1927, $150,000 in 1929. The Bruce Crossing cooperative was the fourth largest cooperative in Michigan, following Eben Junction, Rock, and Hancock; and it was the tenth among the seventy-four member stores of the CCW.[66]

The Eben cooperative, which had grown to be one of the largest Finnish cooperative business of this period, experienced internal conflicts of which the most disturbing was the struggle between the "conservatives" and the "progressives." The conservatives, who had a secure majority on the board, considered the CCW too socialistic and refused to join it, while the more progressive faction, who admitted openly to being socialist-minded, demanded union with it. The spokesman for the conservatives was Chairman of the Board Jauhianen, and for the progressives the spokesman was Saul Mattson. William Marttila of Rock tried to serve as mediator and succeeded only in bringing the wrath of both groups on himself.[67] The progressive group eventually was victorious, and the cooperative joined the CCW in 1925. Branches were soon opened in Gwinn, Munising, and Chatham.

When John D. Nummivuori left his position as manager of the CCW in 1922, he was followed by Eskel Ronn, who served until 1931.

By 1929 the total number of member stores was ninety, of which one was in Canada. In addition, according to statistics, there were fifty-six stores that were not members of the CCW but which carried on business with them; three of them were in Canada. The sphere of activity of the CCW included seventy-five stores in Minnesota, twenty-nine in Michigan, twenty-one in Wisconsin, four in New York and in North Dakota, two in Illinois and in Pennsylvania, and one each in South Dakota, Washington, Oregon, and Ohio.[68] Thus, 51 percent of the stores were in Minnesota, 20 percent in Michigan, 15 percent in Wisconsin, and 14 percent in the rest of the states and Canada. Purchases from the CCW give a somewhat different picture: 60 percent made by Minnesota cooperatives, 25 percent by Michigan stores, 15 percent by Wisconsin stores, and 2 percent by the stores in the rest of the states.

Table 23 shows the sales of the CCW Finnish cooperative stores of Michigan, Minnesota, Wisconsin, and other states in 1929, as well as the amounts invested in the CCW.[69] The sales of the CCW in 1919 amounted to $310,322.16.[70] In ten years they had increased nearly sixfold. Its sales to Michigan cooperatives had increased nearly fourfold, to Wisconsin stores over fourfold, and to Minnesota stores over eightfold.

Communist Attempts to Control the CCW

As soon as the cooperative stores had passed through the early financial struggles and were firmly established, they became objects of interest to the leftists. The cooperative movement could be a weapon in the class struggle, and their annual profits could be used to promote socialist—and a little later—communist propaganda. One of the first attempts at control had been made at a Finnish American Socialist Organization meeting in Smithville in 1912 in the form of a resolution reading: "The meeting makes it an obligation of members of this organization to be active in cooperatives so that their annual profits may be used by local socialist divisions for educational work on socialism and the cooperative movement." These demands became more insistent each year as the struggle against the non-partisan cooperative activity promoted by Severi Alanne and George Halonen increased in intensity. The meeting of the Socialist Organization in Chicago in 1919 demanded that every local cooperative support the Communist Third International, and a meeting of delegates in 1925 decided "to concentrate even more on the intellectual guidance of cooperatives and through this means induce the movement itself to serve the class struggle of revolutionary labor."[71]

Table 23: Finnish Cooperative Sales, 1929

MICHIGAN MEMBER BUSINESSES	AMOUNT IN SHARES	PURCHASES FROM CCW 1929
Amasa Co-op Society	$ 159.35	$ 852.36
Deerton Co-op Ass'n	128.94	—
Drummond Co-op Club	124.86	745.50
Eben Farmers' Co-op Store Co.	1,400.00	47,485.92
Farmers' Co-op Ass'n, Herman	1,448.03	22,551.24
Farmers' Co-op Store, Nisula	191.82	12,612.02
Farmers' Co-op Trading Co., Hancock	3,820.64	54,898.59
Farmers' Co-op Trading Co., Pelkie	371.08	23,215.22
Finnish Co-op Merc. Co., Wakefield	166.19	12,252.52
Ishpeming Consumers' Co-op Ass'n	185.65	6,654.41
Mass Co-op Co.	3,712.83	58,030.68
National Co-op Co., Ironwood	2,448.42	26,132.75
Newberry Co-op Ass'n	852.95	9,682.49
Palmer Co-op Ass'n	186.21	871.09
Rock Co-op Co.	914.78	38,080.31
Rudyard Co-op Co.	433.71	10,353.79
Settlers' Co-op Trading Co., Bruce Crossing	2,839.57	49,132.11
Toivola Co-op Ass'n	236.49	669.80
Trenary Farmers' Co-op Store	632.68	19,604.38
Watton Co-op Store	586.08	20,014.88
Workers' Co-op Society, Marquette	2,855.58	8,481.12
	$23,695.86	$422,321.18
NON-MEMBER BUSINESSES		
Consumers' Co-op. Exchange, Detroit	35.56	5,328.36
Co-op. Toivo Co., Detroit	3.36	133.48
Crystal Falls Co-op. Society	16.14	181.48
Delta Milk Producers' Ass'n, Escanaba	—	1,141.50
Independent Club, Detroit	4.30	—
Republic Farmers' Co-op. Ass'n	66.29	14,159.25
Republic Finnish Farmers' Co-op. Ass'n	1.79	—
Soo Co-op. Merc. Ass'n	.83	832.37
	128.27	21,776.44
Member Businesses	23,695.86	422,321.18
Totals, Michigan	$23,824.13	$ 444,097.62

Table 23: Finnish Cooperative Sales, 1929 *(continued)*

	AMOUNT IN SHARES	PURCHASES FROM CCW 1929
Totals, Minnesota	45,493.43	1,022,361.53
Totals, Wisconsin	13,536.99	234,913.71
Totals of other states	2,126.71	36,597.40
Sales of CCW to independent stores in 1929		17,656.58
CCW Capital and Sales in 1929	$84,981.26	$1,755,626.84

The main attack began in the summer of 1929, soon after Stalin had given a speech in May to American communists attending a meeting of the Comintern and told them that the time was ripe for revolutionary action in their homeland and that all resources were to be put into use without delay to strengthen the American Communist party. Although the dispute raged mostly in Superior, Wisconsin, the Michigan cooperatives were well represented, and since the results affected the Finns of Michigan, a discussion of the matter is within the scope of this present work. The progress of events was briefly as follows: the American Communist Party sent a letter dated June 25, 1929, to the CCW, in which it demanded a "loan" of $5,000. The decision had been made by the secretariat of the Communist Party, and the CCW was expected to approve it as it stood. The executive committee of the board, which included Matti Tenhunen, Oscar Corgan, and Jack Vainionpaa, rejected the demand. Then, in a letter dated July 10, 1929, the secretary of the Finnish Socialist Organization and member of the executive committee of the Communist Party of America, Henry Puro (the former John Viita) demanded $1,000 from the CCW for the expenses of a certain Communist congress.[72]

In the fall, John Minor, representing the secretariat of the Communist party, came to Superior from New York, demanding that a certain percent of monthly sales receipts, for example, 1 percent, should be given to the Communist party. To check potential opposition, Minor advised the CCW to engage nominally a lawyer in New York to represent it and to earmark the percentage for the salary of this nonexistent lawyer. Since the total annual sales of the CCW in 1930 amounted to $1,767,000, complying with the demand would have meant a donation of $17,000 to the party in that year alone. Another demand presented by Minor was that Walter Harju, sales representative of the CCW who had worked as a secret agent in the CCW, should become a party organizer but still remain on the payroll of the CCW.

Minor returned to New York without having achieved success. Since the CCW board, including its communist members Corgan, Tenhunen, and Vainionpaa, had unanimously rejected the demands of the Party, the Party began to work through *Työmies.*

Karl Reeve was sent to the Superior area as a representative of the Communist party. With the editor of *Työmies*, Taavi Heino, he started the battle in the October 31, 1929, number of the paper by publishing an editorial titled "The Struggle Against Conservatism in the Cooperative Movement." The attacks against the CCW continued in issue after issue. Reeve also wrote about the Third Era, which would come with the Third International, and demanded that the cooperative movement submit to serving the ideology and the financial needs of the Communist party. The attacks were aimed especially at George Halonen, whose separation from his position as adviser in the CCW was demanded.

When the CCW was no longer permitted to publish articles in its own defense in *Työmies*, it began to publish its own paper titled *Keskusosuuskunnan Tiedonantaja* (Central cooperative informer) on December 12. Four large issues appeared until the beginning of January 1930, when its name changed to *Työvaen Osuustoimintalehti* (Workers' cooperative newspaper). Under that title it was published until 1965. Publication of a paper of their own was not a new venture, for the English-language monthly, the *Cooperative Pyramid Builder*, which was printed at *Työmies* press, had been appearing since 1926. In November 1929, the party set up a special commission in Superior, of which the aforementioned Reeve and Puro were members, in addition to a man using the name Peterson, who was sent from New York and was a representative of the Third International in Moscow, which suggests how important it was to have control of the largest Finnish American cooperative organization. Now more extreme measures were taken. Before midnight of November 25, a crowd of men forced their way into *Työmies* press and burned a part of the just-printed issue of the *Pyramid Builder* in the furnace and took the rest of it with them. The reason for this was that the number included a reply from the CCW to the attacks made on it by the Communist party.

All that winter and spring were spent in a battle of words, both sides making preparations for attending the annual meeting of the CCW to be held in Superior on April 21–23. On the evening of Sunday, April 20, a cooperative society program was presented at the labor society hall, at which two of the speakers were from Michigan. They were Katri Heikkinen from South Range and Charles Sillanpaa from Bruce Crossing.[73] It was said at the beginning of the official meeting the next morning that 222 representatives who were entitled to vote were there from 78 cooperatives in addition to "several hundred guests."

The following persons were delegates from Michigan cooperatives at this historic meeting: William Marttila from Drummond Island; Bert Aalto, Gust Lehtomaki, Sven Lindfors, and John Rukkila from Eben; Katri Heikkinen, William Hietala, and Arvid Jarvi from Hancock and its outlets; Fred Kaarlela, Uuno Sointu, Henry Parvianen, and Matt Saari from Herman; Oscar Laajala from Nisula; Matti Uusitalo and Oscar Hietikko from Pelkie; Adi Dyster from Ishpeming; Ilmer Immonen, Edward Jarviaho, John Marttila, John Rova, and John Wesanen from Mass; Bruno Henrickson and Gust Koivu from Newberry; Arthur Uusitalo from Palmer; Antti Aalto, Andrew Kainula, Oscar Niemi, Toivo Niemo, Arvo N. Rivers, John Seppala, Robert Saastamoinen, and Theodor Warmanen from Rock; Henry J. Iid, William Konno, Helmer Palo, and John Upponen from Rudyard; Matt Heikkinen, Hilda Kankaanpaa, August Rytilahti, and Charles Sillanpaa from Bruce Crossing; Charles M. Beltti, Charles Maki, Mike Maki, and Julius Sivula from Trenary; Eino Keranen, Otto Lahtinen, and Victor Mackey from Watton; Jalmar Lehto and Reino Salmi from Marquette.

Table 24: CCW Coooperatives by State, 1930

STATE	REPRESENTATIVES	VOTES	COOPERATIVES REPRESENTED	MEMBERSHIP
Minnesota	127	151	42	8,916
Michigan	53	78	17	4,330
Wisconsin	36	38	15	3,366
Other States	6	17	4	4,150
Totals	222	284	78	20,762

Table 24 gives a picture of the relative strength of the cooperatives in the states. Of the voting power at the meeting, Minnesota had 54 percent, Michigan 27 percent, Wisconsin 13 percent, and the other states 6 percent. But the relative voting strength of the states was secondary to the main issue, which was the question of whether the Finnish cooperative movement of the Midwest would remain politically neutral or begin to serve the revolutionary aims of the Communist Party of America. The Communist party was taking far-reaching measures. Long cablegrams were sent to the Central Cooperative Wholesale by the Comintern's cooperative organization in Moscow as well as by the central committee of the Communist party of Finland, then located in Moscow, giving detailed instructions and specific orders, the most important of which was the demand that Matti Tenhunen be made the political head of the CCW. The Comintern had sent Kullervo Manner from Moscow to be its representative in Superior.[74] The duty of the "leftist committee" was to attend to communist interests at the meeting. The majority of the delegates at the meeting were adamantly against all outside control. Matti Tenhunen, Oscar Corgan, and Jack Vainionpaa, who had openly supported the Communist party and worked for its advancement, were voted out of the board of the CCW by a vote of 167 to 89. In the ballots on other matters, the "leftist committee" received 30 to 68 votes out of a total of 284.

What percentage of delegates from Michigan were communistic is not clear. Only William Marttila, the delegate from Drummond, was obviously in favor of communism. He spoke on its behalf and served as secretary of the "leftist committee." Nevertheless, when the time came to fill the seven positions open on the CCW board, he was not even named as a candidate by the communists. The only candidate from Michigan was John Marttila of Mass. The communist candidates received from 34 to 68 votes, while the others received from 219 to 223 for the various positions. Otto Lahtinen of Watton was the only delegate from Michigan to be elected to the CCW board.

This thirteenth annual meeting of the CCW, which definitely halted the efforts of the Comintern and the Communist Party of America to gain control, still did not mean that the Finnish American cooperatives of the Midwest were completely neutral politically as the Rochdale Pioneers had been. The question was whether the extremists in the labor movement and the international leftists would become the sole authority in the cooperative movement or would the CCW be preserved as an organ of the entire labor movement. Even the majority among the victors saw in cooperatives an instrument that could be used in the class struggle. This is clearly indicated in the acceptance at the annual meeting of a resolution which reads as follows:

> The cooperative movement, despite its commercial character, is an important weapon among other organizations used in the class struggle, inciting class struggle especially against the middle class, as well as using the experience gained and the economic advantages received through this struggle to their own advantage and to the advantage of other organizations involved in the class struggle.

The thirteenth annual meeting of the CCW ended on Thursday, April 24, at 1:20 A.M. "We sang the 'International' and gave three cheers for cooperative unity." With these words, Secretary Toivo Merisalo ended his minutes.[75]

After their defeat in the annual meeting of the CCW, the communists held a secret meeting already on April 23, in which under the leadership of Kullervo Manner, representative from the Comintern, future action was discussed. Their decision was that the battle should be carried to, and made broader in scope, through the local cooperatives.[76] Following instructions, the communists, through this "enlarged leftist committee" were able to start quarrels and dissension. For example, a typical situation prevailed at the Watton store in 1930: "After that, the 'Third Era,' or the period of communist domination began. It caused some dissension among us, for in our group there were active members who believed in the early victory of communism, but the majority did not have faith in it, and so our store remained a 'Halonen store,' as it was called at the time."[77]

On the cooperative front in Michigan, the communists achieved their greatest success in Mass, Ironwood, and Eben, getting control of their stores. In these communities, the well-organized leftists, with their surprise tactics, got their own candidates on the board, although the majority of members of the cooperatives were in favor of political neutrality. The new board of the Eben Junction cooperative, to insure a majority for itself in the following meetings, sold or transferred about 175 shares to their own supporters, in many cases to persons who lived too far away to be regular customers, and refused to sell shares to those who were in favor of political neutrality. The chairman of the board, Sven Lindfors, who strongly "resisted the communists and promoted the Rochdale type of neutrality" was discharged although the act was against the rules.[78]

Using similar tactics, the communists in Mass added about three hundred new members and voters to their numbers. The Mass affair came up before the annual meeting of the CCW in 1931, where the Mass cooperative had a delegation of nineteen, which was proportionate to the membership they had increased through their scheming. The committee that examined their credentials cut the list down to fourteen.[79] Theodor Varmanen, who had once been dropped from membership, caused dissension in the Rock cooperative. In 1930 he was a delegate to the CCW annual meeting from the Rock Co-operative Company. On returning home he began to follow the orders of the "enlarged leftist committee" so forcefully that he was again dropped from membership.[80]

The communist attempts to gain control inspired the organization of cooperative clubs and guilds in connection with cooperative stores. Their purpose was to spread the idea of the cooperative movement and to defend the stores against the communists. In some communities, the wives of the store managers and the women employees were leaders of the guilds and clubs, but usually the leaders were men. Some of these clubs and guilds were troublesome to the managers, for they were inclined to interfere in their affairs. Between 1930 and 1940 there was at least one cooperative guild in every area served by a cooperative store.

The annual meetings of the CCW continued to be battlegrounds where the communists were very active. In 1931 they attempted to make Herman Aho and John Marttila of the Mass cooperative, which they controlled, presiding officers, but Aho received only thirty-two votes and Marttila fifty-one. They also attempted to get five of their men on the important Resolutions Committee, among them Emil Salo of the Ironwood store, which had also come into their hands. Political confusion is indicated by the fact that while the decision made by the board to drop the Työmies Society from CCW membership was accepted on the first day of the meeting, on the next day a donation of $200 from their annual profits was made for the support of the lecture courses of the Young Communist League.[81]

In the annual meeting of 1932, the communists had about 55 votes out of the total of 347. Their candidates for the chairmanship this year were delegates from the Mass Cooperative, Oskar Corgan and John Marttila. Mass attempted to make use of 21 votes and Eben 15 votes, but the meeting lowered them to 14 and 8. The only thing of any special importance that the communists did was to attempt to make the columns of *Työväen Osuustoimintalehti* available to them for "propaganda in favor of China and Russia," but their proposal was turned down by a vote of 159 to 37.[82]

Discouraged by their defeats three years in a row and also by the fiasco in Karelia, the communists did not show up at the annual meeting of the CCW in 1933 at all. However, they suggested by letter that a union between the Workers and Farmers Unity Alliance Wholesale, established by them, and the Central Cooperative Wholesale be effected. The CCW dictated strict terms. The communists must end their competitive wholesale business and close their cooperative stores; they must stop publishing libelous articles about the CCW and its member stores; they must also stop boycotting the CCW businesses. After they had lived up to these conditions for at least a year, the matter would be reconsidered.[83] At the next annual meeting, the delegates from Mass brought up the matter again, but the meeting confirmed the decision of the previous year just as it stood.[84] The idea of the "united front" was again brought up in 1935 at the annual meeting, and again the strict terms of 1933 were repeated, even though the communists had indicated their willingness to buy from the CCW.[85] Following the instructions of the party, the delegates from the Mass cooperative brought up the matter of the united front again at the annual meeting of 1936. But by this time, the CCW men's patience had come to an end. It was revealed that the communist cooperative stores had kept up their formal membership in the CCW, but at the same time they had been abstaining from buying. For this reason the CCW decided to refuse to negotiate with the Workers and Farmers Unity Alliance.[86] Thus ends this discussion of the part played by communism in the history of the Central Cooperative Wholesale. It proves that the great majority of even those Finnish laborers who had at first joined the socialist movement were at heart democratic and would not tolerate domination by extreme radicalism.[87] The activity of the Finnish American communists in the cooperative movement had followed the general "people's front" program, the effects of which were also being felt in the internal politics of a number of European states.

From 1935 to the End of the Independent Finnish American Cooperative Movement

After the conflict with communism had ended, a peaceful period of growth and progress, which continued for a quarter century, began in the Finnish American cooperative movement. Table 25 shows how the situation developed. Figures are given on CCW sales to member cooperatives in 1935, when the struggle against the communists was still disruptive; in 1939, after four peaceful years; and in 1958, or nineteen years later.

These figures throw light on the development of the Finnish American cooperative movement in the Midwest. Purchases from the cooperatives' own CCW year after year usually amounted to half the total purchases. The cooperative stores of Michigan were not able to keep up with this development completely. While their purchases from the CCW in 1935 were 21 percent of all the member businesses' purchases, in 1939 they were 18 percent, and in 1958, 16 percent. Of all the states, Minnesota became the strongest in cooperative activity. On the other hand, it is to be noted that about ten new stores had appeared on the scene. Those in Escanaba, Ishpeming, Newberry, and Negaunee displayed considerable strength. In addition, many cooperative stores had modernized their facilities.

Table 25: Growth of Michigan Finnish Cooperatives, 1935–58

MICHIGAN COOPERATIVES	PURCHASES FROM CCW 1935	1939	1958
Amasa Co-op. Society	$ 7,000	$ 12,000	$ 31,000
Farmer's Co-op. Ass'n, Herman	23,000	30,000	17,000
Farmers' Co-op. Trading Co., Hancock	85,000	93,000	119,000
Farmers' Co-op. Trading Co., Pelkie	38,000	70,000	199,000
Co-op. Oil Ass'n, Bruce Crossing	22,000	40,000	331,000
Northland Co-op. Oil Ass'n, Rock	12,000		
Rock Co-operative Co.	86,000	86,000	75,000
Ontonagon Co-op. Society	19,000	19,000	50,000
Republic Farmers' Co-op. Ass'n.	4,000	7,000	61,000
Rudyard Co-op. Co.	14,000	23,000	302,000
Settlers' Co-op. Trading Co., Bruce Crossing	63,000	81,000	84,000
Trenary Farmers' Co-op. Store	41,000	69,000	191,000
Wakefield Co-op. Ass'n	7,000	21,000	50,000
Watton Co-op. Store	14,000	17,000	93,000
Workers' Co-op. Soc., Marquette	6,000	11,000	67,000
National Co-op. Co., Ironwood	—	18,000	—
Newberry Co-op. Ass'n.	—	7,000	87,000
Norway Co-op. Ass'n.	—	7,000	—
Soo Co-op. Merc. Ass'n, Sault Ste. Marie	—	—	42,000
Chatham-Eben Cooperative Co.	—	—	42,000
Aura Farmers' Co-op. Ass'n.	—	—	42,000
Bay De Noc Co-op. Co., Escanaba	—	—	111,000
Ishpeming Cooperative Society	—	—	108,000
Negaunee Cooperative Services	—	—	70,000
Skanee Cooperative Ass'n	—	—	20,000
Total Purchases by Mich. Cooperatives	441,000	611,000	2,192,000
Total Purchases by Co-ops. outside Mich.	1,636,000	2,698,000	11,246,000
Total Purchases from CCW	$2,077,000	$3,309,000	$13,438,000

In bad times cooperatives showed themselves to be capable of great service to their members. One such instance was the establishment of the Copper Country Cooperative Enterprises in 1935. The Federal Emergency Relief Administration in Washington gave substantial financial aid, with the help of which the former streetcar barns and powerhouse in Hancock were made useable and new buildings were constructed. These buildings housed departments for the sale of farm machinery, oil, berries, and fish, as well as frozen-food lockers for rent, all organized on a cooperative basis. Only the oil and fish departments proved to be profitable and were still in existence in the 1960s, the fish business having been sold to Finnish fishermen of Lake Superior.[88]

The Finns put the concept of cooperative activity to work in dairy farming by establishing cooperative dairies in many communities. One of the largest was the Ontonagon Valley Co-Operative Creamery in Bruce Crossing. Its manager for a long time was Reino Suhonen. Another large cooperative dairy was the one in Marquette. The Copper Country Dairy in Dollar Bay became the largest of its kind. Its beginnings are worthy of a closer look.

The original impetus came from a housewife in whose home area in Finland cooperative creameries had been important aids to dairy farmers. When the Copper Country farmers of Traprock complained in 1937 that the price of 25 cents paid per pound of butter fat was not enough to support them, she told them of her experience with cooperative dairies in Finland. The dairy farmers became interested. The initial meeting was held in the Traprock school in the summer of 1937. Meeting after meeting was held, and in November of the following year the decision to start a cooperative dairy was made. A dairy which was opened for business in 1939 was built. At that time there were seventy members; after fourteen years the membership was over five hundred. During that period, over half a million dollars had been returned to members in dividends. In the 1960s the Dollar Bay cooperative dairy was still growing and developing. Eino Juntunen was manager for a long time.[89]

The first of the Finnish American movements to lose its independent character and to be absorbed into American life was the labor movement. At the beginning of the 1960s, leading Finnish churches followed, and at about the same time the same fate overtook the Finnish cooperative movement.

When good roads and rapid means of transportation became common, small businesses, both independent and cooperative, became unable to compete with the supermarkets established in their communities, and one by one they closed their doors or joined a larger store in a neighboring community. The CCW also began to feel the pressure, for its annual business of over $20 million was not enough to keep it in competition with the giant chain stores with outlets all over the continent. Vigorous efforts were made to stay in competition. One such effort was made through the *Cooperative Builder*, which from 1954 on was distributed every week to over 70,000 consumers, and through which an attempt was made to standardize prices even for weekend grocery sales.

The largest cooperative wholesale in the Midwest was the Midland Cooperatives, with headquarters in Minneapolis. The Central Cooperative Wholesale served 237 member stores, whereas the Midland Cooperatives served 550, and its annual sales rose to $50 million. The area served by the Midland included Minnesota, Wisconsin, the northern part of Iowa, and the eastern part of South Dakota. The two large organizations had had common distribution points for a long time. Unofficial discussions about a possible merger were carried on for years, until official consideration began at CCW district meetings in February 1963. The meetings were favorable to a merger and urged member cooperatives to instruct their delegates to vote for the merger at the CCW annual meeting in Duluth on March 18 and 19. The decision there was unanimously in favor of a merger.

The meetings of the Midland cooperatives were held in the beginning of April. Since they were in favor of the merger, the final vote was taken by mail. It was favorable, as was expected. The merger was finally completed when the new wholesale of the cooperative stores of the Midwest, whose official name was now Midland Cooperatives, Inc., held its first annual meeting in the Leamington Hotel in Minneapolis during December 5–6, 1963. Thus, the independent Finnish cooperative movement of the Middle West, with its pioneering, its struggles, and its period of vigorous growth, came to an end.[90]

15 Cultural and Educational Achievements

By their very nature, churches, temperance societies, cooperatives, labor organizations, and the Kaleva organization with their extensive publishing activity fostered the development of important cultural values. Because these groups and their activities have already been discussed, this chapter will deal with miscellaneous cultural and educational forces that have had no direct connection with any special group or movement. The oldest and most obvious of these are the Finnish-language newspapers.

Newspapers

Over the years, many foreign-language newspapers have been published in Michigan. The first of these were French papers, of which there were, between 1809 and 1919, thirty-three titles.[1] But German, Swedish, Italian, and Finnish immigrants were also interested in having newspapers of their own. The foreign-language newspapers in America suffered a severe blow in April 1917, when the United States entered the war against the Central Powers. Congress established the Committee on Public Information, and newspaperman George Creel became its head as civilian chairman. Under the direction of this committee, a pro-war propaganda campaign unique in the history of this country began, accompanied by an attitude of suspicion toward the vast field of foreign-language newspaper publishing in the country. Most of the newspapers ceased publication. Although censorship was strict, the Finnish newspapers of Michigan managed to continue in business without any major difficulties, for by this time they had behind them forty years of history in America, so that despite their language they were in spirit and in their view of the world pretty well Americanized.

The first Finnish-language newspaper in Finland was published in Turku in the fall of 1775 by Antti Lizelius, rector of Mynämäki. It was titled *Suomenkieliset Tieto-Sanomat* (Finnish language news). A hundred years and a few months later, Finnish American newspaper publishing began under somewhat unusual circumstances.

In the fall of 1875, H. Roernaes, the Norwegian pastor in Hancock, received a letter from a Finnish university student in New York, expressing a wish to come to the Copper Country to serve his countrymen in their intellectual endeavors. The letter-writer also informed the reader that he did not have money for his fare. Roernaes read the letter at a worship service of his Finnish-Swedish-Norwegian congregation. The Finns were immediately interested, thinking that now they would acquire a preacher who spoke their own language, and they collected the money needed. The student was Antti J. Muikku.

Muikku, the son of a carpenter, was born on March 22, 1846, in Liperi, from where the family moved to Joensuu. After his graduation from the lyceum at Jyväskylä, Muikku entered the University of Helsinki to study mathematics. His studies there ended because of a lack of funds. After working in several places, including the Pulkova Observatory near St. Petersburg, "broken in luck," as Akseli Rauanheimo described him, he drifted to America. He arrived in Hancock on a Saturday and was present at church services the following morning. Pastor Roernaes invited him to preach, or to greet the Finns who were present in large numbers on this occasion. Muikku made excuses, complaining of weariness after his long journey. He finally succeeded in overcoming his shyness and made a speech which has been preserved in the following form: "I left Finland and went to London, and from London I came to New York with the help of a Norwegian minister; from there I came here to Hancock, where I may possibly be of some service to my countrymen."

The newcomer was by no means a preacher or speaker of any kind. What Muikku had in mind was a newspaper to serve the growing Finnish population of the Copper Country. The first newspaper to be published in Hancock was the English-language *Hancock Times*, which was published between 1870 and 1872. It was followed in 1872 by the *Northwestern Mining Journal*. These papers had hardly any Finnish readers during this early period of immigration. Muikku spent the winter of 1875–76 soliciting funds and subscriptions. He got 300 subscribers. He named his weekly *Amerikan Suomalainen Lehti* (Finnish

American paper). The new newspaper came out on Fridays. It was small, consisting of four four-column pages 11½ by 17 inches in size. The price was two dollars a year. It was printed on a press owned by German-born E. P. Kibbee, which had the letters *ä* and *ö*, and at which a Finnish printer-apprentice, Fred Karinen, worked. The first issue came out on April 14, 1876. That date is considered the birthday of the Finnish American press.[2]

Muikku secceeded in making his paper many-sided and lively. Its political slant was Republican. But the unlucky editor was not able to keep his business on an even keel. Subscriptions did not increase in number because only a few of the immigrants appreciated the value of having a Finnish newspaper, and because Kortetniemi, leader of the Laestadians, forbade his congregation, to which most Finns belonged at this time, to subscribe to a secular paper. Muikku's greatest difficulty was caused by his inability to take care of the financial side of his business successfully. For one thing, Kibbee demanded payment for the previous issue before he would start work on a new one. The last number of the newspaper came out in July 1876 as an edition of only two pages.

Amerikan Suomalainen Lehti has disappeared almost completely. There may be only two copies left—an incomplete one in the Finnish National Library, and another, in fairly good condition, in the Finnish American Historical Archives at Suomi College. Muikku died the following winter on February 5 at the Frisk home on Quincy Hill. A monument was placed on his grave in the Hancock cemetery. On it was carved the following inscription: "A. J. Muikku. Died 1877. The founder of the Finnish American press. A memorial from his countrymen."[3]

Matti Fredd, a painter and decorator, became Muikku's successor in the newspaper business. Fredd was born in Vaasa on August 1, 1845. As an apprentice painter in Oulu he learned the Finnish language in addition to his mother tongue, which was Swedish. As a journeyman painter he traveled extensively as was customary in those days, going even as far as Turku, St. Petersburg, and some areas of Sweden. He received his master's papers in Raahe. He came to America in 1871 and started his own painting and decorating business in Hancock in 1876.

With the skill and dexterity that apparently ran in his family, Fredd made himself a printing press with the intention of publishing a newspaper. He named the paper *Swen Tuuwa.* The first issue came out in Houghton County on January 4, 1878. It was a small three-column paper. Its motto was "To you, Finn, I say just a few words." Disgusted with the slowness of setting type by hand, Fredd filled three-fifths of a column of his sample copy with the words "I don't care to jumble letters any more." This playful, free and independent style continued to be characteristic of the paper number after number. Fred Karinen became the typesetter, enabling the owner to devote himself entirely to his editorial duties. In October the paper was moved to Hancock, and at the beginning of the following year its name was changed to *Sankarin Maine* (Hero's record). Some opposition to Fredd's paper had developed. It was not lessened by his outspoken way of writing. Fredd called those who opposed it the "league." In the first issue of the paper as *Sankarin Maine*—it was now larger in size than it had been as *Swen Tuuwa*—he wrote as follows:

> Swen Tuuwa has died, but the hero's reputation lives.
> Swen was not long-lived, but he won the name of hero before his death.
> So it happened with *Swen Tuuwa* too.
> It was not possible to overthrow this bear by hand;
> Man, his fellow creature, always protects him from being shot.
> The league saw that attacks were in vain.
> The enemy turned and slowly went away.

The slogan now as "Long live *Sankarin Maine*, and may the people grow in honor." The content of *Sankarin Maine* was diversified and colorful, thus compensating to some extent for its poor diction. The editor's earnest purpose was to keep his readers up-to-date, especially on world happenings and on matters affecting the Finns of the Copper Country, as well as to goad them into thinking. The competition provided by a newly established Finnish newspaper in Calumet forced Fredd to stop publishing his paper in the spring of 1881 and to devote all his time to his painting and decorating business. This self-educated man who worked unselfishly for the advancement and betterment of his countrymen was also artistically inclined. As far as is known, an altar painting executed by him, depicting the Parable of the Sower, is the oldest Finnish American altar painting. This large picture was painted in 1878 for the Scandinavian church of Calumet. From there it was taken to the Norwegian church of Hancock and eventually to the Finnish-American Historical Archives at Suomi College.[4] The importance of the work of Fredd and Muikku as the founders of the Finnish American press has frequently been greatly underrated by more recent editors in their writings.

In addition to the Finnish newspapers in America, other

Finnish-language newspapers published outside Finland were *Haaparannan Lehti* in Sweden and *Inkeri* in St. Petersburg, Russia. Before these, the first newspaper published beyond the borders of Finland, *Pietarin Sanomat*, had appeared in St. Petersburg from 1870 to 1873.

Johan Takkinen, who was sent by the Lappish Congregation of the Firstborn to Calumet in 1877 to attend to Laestadian affairs in the Copper Country, was quite broad-minded about a secular paper. He was of the opinion that a newspaper which the Laestadians could read—Fredd's paper was not considered suitable—and which could serve as a medium for advertising church services was needed. In the spring of 1879, with Niilo Majhannu, David Castren, and August Nylund from Kiuruvesi, he organized the Amerikan Suomalainen Kirjapainoyhtiö (Finnish American Printing Company) in Calumet for the purpose of publishing a new newspaper. For editor they were able to get Alex Leinonen, who was born in Paltamo in 1846, attended school in Kajaani and Oulu, and worked as s surveyor until he came to America in 1870. He was working as a surveyor in Texas when he was called into newspaper work.

Leinonen had been a correspondent for Muikku's paper and gave the new paper the same, now familiar, name of *Amerikan Suomalainen Lehti.* The first number came out on July 4, 1879. Originally the paper was small, consisting of four pages of four columns each, but it eventually expanded to seven columns. The Finnish American Printing Company was unable to finance the project, so it became the property of the energetic and ambitious Leinonen. At its peak the paper came out as an issue of 800 copies, of which 300 were sent to Finland. At first, Leinonen was well disposed toward the Laestadians, but after the Suomi Synod was organized, he gave the synod his support. For about thirteen years he struggled with his paper, thus becoming worthy of being listed among the founders of the Finnish American press. In 1892 he sold his paper to Victor Burman, who, after raising the number of subscribers to three thousand, moved the paper to Hancock. In 1894 Burman moved the paper to Chicago, where it soon expired. Alex Leinonen, who for good reason has been called the first Finnish American newspaperman, died on November 23, 1902.[5]

The English-language newspaper in Calumet at that time was the *Calumet News*, which was started in 1881. The Swedes there had a newspaper titled *Posten*, the Slovenians had *Glasnik*, and the Italians had *Minatore Italiano.*[6] The Finns had dozens of news publications. Calumet was for a long time the most populous Finnish American community, a fact which contributed to its also being a leader in the world of Finnish American publishing for decades.

About the same time in 1879 that Alex Leinonen began to publish *Amerikan Suomalainen Lehti*, Helmer Grape from the Tornio River area of Finland started publishing an independent weekly called *Suometar*. In the intense and sometimes bitter competition among Finnish American newspapers for subscribers, *Suometar* survived for an exceptionally long time—twenty-four years altogether—although it had to struggle through many difficulties, including involvement in the church-related disputes caused by Eloheimo. Well-known newspaperman August Edwards bought the paper in 1903 and combined it with *Amerikan Sanomat* (American tidings), which he had been publishing in Ashtabula, Ohio, since 1897.[7]

In November 1889, Ino Ekman began to publish a weekly titled *Kansan Lehti* (People's paper) in Calumet. It expired after about a year but was revived to a short life under the editorship of D. Suoranen with the new name of *Uusi Kansan Lehti* (New people's paper). In 1890, Hannes Hela started a competing newspaper, *Kalevan Kaiku* (Echo of Kaleva), which was absorbed by *Amerikan Uutiset* (American news), which Fred Karinen brought to Calumet from Minneapolis in 1893. Kalle Haapakoski, a university student (born in Oulainen in 1867, died in Calumet in 1917), became the editor. He was an incisive writer whose caustic editorials molded the attitudes of the largest readership Finnish American newspapers had thus far had, especially against Suomi College and temperance societies.

At this time Ino Ekman also tried his luck at publishing a daily newspaper called *Päivän Uutiset* (Daily news), whose Saturday number was called *Viikon Uutiset* (Weekly news). The paper was started in 1891 and it apparently expired some time the same year. A paper of the same name, which lasted for only a few issues, was started by Fred Karinen and Kalle Haapakoski in 1898.

Päivälehti (Daily paper), established by Kalle Haapakoski, John H. Harpet, and Sanfrid Mustonen in the spring of 1901, became the most important Finnish-language newspaper in Calumet. Although Pine Street was already the home of many Finnish enterprises, including newspapers, stores, and churches, *Päivälehti* was first published in the Borgo Block on Fifth Street. Editorial work and typesetting were done upstairs and printing in the basement. Later a place was found for it too on Pine Street. *Päivälehti* was for a long time the most important Finnish-language newspaper in Michigan, and its influence reached far beyond the borders of the state. It had a succession of capable professional men as editors, including N. J. Ahlman, Severi Nyman, Into J. Teljo, and Aaro Jalkanen who was later the Finnish consul in Duluth.

Because of the high educational level of these men, the leftist press began to call the newspaper the "masters' paper."

Many printers and newspapermen, conservatives and radicals alike, received their early training working on *Päivälehti.* The paper had the courage to try innovations. For example, instead of using the titles Mr. and Mrs. it used the terms "Arvo" and "Arvotar" (masculine and feminine forms of "worthy"). Politically it was strictly Republican. Once, when it was in financial difficulties and in danger of liquidation through a public auction requested by a Calumet bank, the temperance people came to its rescue. The chairman of the "rescue committee" was Matti Manner of Hancock, the treasurer was Albin Lahikainen of South Range, and the secretary was Ed Komula of Chassell. The committee collected the necessary funds. As a result, *Päivälehti* was for a time under the control of temperance people. In the early years, especially while Ahlman was editor, the newspaper supported the labor movement, but abandoned it when the socialistic element became dominant in it. When J. L. Ollila was editor, *Päivälehti*, in keeping with its name, actually became a daily. In 1914 it was moved with its editor to Duluth, where it was published until 1948.[8]

The newspapers which sprang up among the Laestadians belong to a class of their own among the Finnish newspapers published in Calumet. Their most outstanding characteristic was their complete avoidance of church disputes and religious controversy. Their editors were just as likely as not to be members of the Suomi Synod instead of a Laestadian church.

Of the Laestadian papers, the first was *Valvoja* (Guardian), established in 1915 and edited until 1931 by John Turja and Into Johannes Teljo. Teljo was born in Uusikaupunki in 1876 and completed his studies for his master's degree in the University of Helsinki in 1902. The following year he came to America and took up newspaper work. Other editors of *Valvoja* were, at different times, Jussi Hinkkanen and Yrjo Sjoblom, as well as John Gustav Tuira from Oulu, who served through the 1920s and died in 1931.[9] In June 1931, Reino W. Suojanen, who was born in South Carver, Massachusetts, of a Jämijärvi family, became the editor-in-chief. He had begun his career in newspaper work in Fitchburg on *Pohjantähti* in 1924, but he accomplished his real life work in Calumet. In the beginning, Helmi Warren was his associate on *Valvoja.* In the fall of 1931, Emil Arvid Millen (formerly Haikola), who was born in Moose Lake, Minnesota, in 1891 became his associate. Their association continued for twenty-five years, to the end of 1956.

The Heidemanian Laestadians started a paper of their own titled *Opas* (Guide) in the spring of 1930. Victor Burman and Reino

Suojanen, members of the Suomi Synod, were selected to be the editors. When Suojanen moved over to the nearby *Valvoja*, he was succeeded by Kalle Ruuttila. After Burman and Ruuttila, the editor of the *Opas* was the Laestadian preacher of the Heideman church, Walter Torola, born in Haapajärvi in 1901.

With the passing away of the older generation and a decrease in the Finnish population of the Copper Country, it became evident that it was not possible to support two Laestadian newspapers in the same town, sponsored though they were by different factions of the same revival movement. In the summer of 1957, *Opas* of the Heideman Laestadians and *Valvoja* of the Mickelsen Laestadians were combined and became *Pohjolan Sanomat* (Northern tidings). Its name was the same as that of a paper published in Kemi, Finland. Millen of *Valvoja* and Torola of *Opas* became its editors. At the end of the same year, Niilo Mikael Lapinoja, a professional newspaperman who was born in Kalajoki in 1910, took over the editorship. In 1959 *Pohjolan Sanomat* became a weekly under the new name of *Amerikan Sanomat.* It ceased publication in June 1960. The end of Finnish newspaper publishing in Calumet had come.

In addition to newspapers, a number of religious publications to serve the Laestadian readership also appeared in Calumet. *Siionin Sanomat* (Tidings of Zion), a monthly edited by Henrik Koller between 1891 and 1896, was of comparatively short duration, as were *Lohduttaja* (Comforter) and *Kristillisten Lasten Kuukauslehti* (Christian children's monthly). A monthly titled *Rauhan Pasuuna* (Trumpet of peace) was probably a Finnish Methodist publication. *Naisten Lehti* will be discussed later.

Hancock, Calumet's rival in the early cultural activities of the Finns of the Copper Country, was far ahead and, through the publication of Muikku's and Fredd's newspapers, had the honor of being the pioneer in publishing. But when *Sankarin Maine* expired in 1881, Hancock was for a long time without a regular Finnish newspaper. This newspaperless period lasted until 1894, when Emil Hendrickson started *Kuparisaaren Sanomat* (Copper Country tidings). This paper, a weekly, was purchased by Victor Burman, who changed its name to *Amerikan Suomalainen* (Finnish American) and published it until 1899. Victor Mauritz Burman, born in 1865, came of an old sea-faring family of Raahe. He graduated from the Finnish lyceum of Oulu in 1887, studied law at the University of Helsinki, and worked as a clerk in the office of the Oulu provincial government until he came to America, where he went into newspaper work.

When *Amerikan Suomalainen* ceased publication in 1899,

Amerikan Suometar took its place the same year. The leftist newspaper *Työmies* was moved to Hancock from Worcester, Massachusetts, in 1904 and became its competitor and adversary. These papers have been discussed in connection with the church and the labor movement. In 1911, *Työmies* started a satirical bi-monthly called *Lapatossu* (Shoe), whose lively content appealed even to readers outside the labor movement. In the summer of 1914 it was moved with *Työmies* to Superior and was published there until 1921. Occasionally *Lapatossu* offended the moral sensibilities of readers by its articles and cartoons. Because of their publication of such offensive material, John D. Nummivuori, business manager of *Työmies*, and Jukka Salminen, editor of *Lapatossu*, spent several weeks in jail in Marquette in the spring of 1914.[10] The Työmies Publishing Company attempted to reach the general American public by publishing an English-language paper called the *Wage Slave*. The attempt failed because of lack of support.[11] The publications of the Suomi Synod and Suomi College have been discussed in connection with other subjects.

Of other papers published in Hancock, there was, first of all, the literary monthly, *Kansan Kuvalehti* (People's picture paper), which was published between 1901 and 1903. Its content included much material on contemporary history. It was started by N. J. Ahlman, Eetu Aaltio, and K. V. Arminen, who was an instructor in mathematics at Suomi College. Its level was probably too high for the immigrant generation, for subscriptions fell off rapidly and the publication expired within three years. A similar publication, which also suffered the same fate for the same reason, was a monthly titled *Koti-Home*. It was started in Duluth in 1922 and moved to Hancock in 1923, where it ceased publication after a short time. An additional reason for its demise was its bilingual character, which was indicated by its title. Bilingual publications seem never to have succeeded among Finnish Americans.

A monthly titled *Pelto ja Koti* (Field and home) was started in Hancock in 1912 to serve the Finnish farmers. It was moved to Superior, where it ceased publication in 1920. Its place in Hancock was taken by *Pellervo* started in 1913. However, it ceased publication the same year. The next publication of this type was a monthly titled *Aura* (Plow), published by the Suomi Synod's Book Concern. It appeared from 1914 to 1923, edited in its later years by K. H. Turvanen, who had graduated from an agricultural school. This specialized paper was the last Finnish agricultural publication in America.

Following Hancock and Calumet, the Finnish cultural centers of the Copper Country, Ishpeming appeared on the newspaper scene quite early. The Swedes already had a newspaper there, *Svenska Posten*, started in 1882. Ino Ekman, who had been publishing *Pohjantähti* in Ashtabula, Ohio, from 1886 to 1887, moved his paper to Ishpeming early in 1888. It came out twice a week as a five-column, eight-page publication. Although it had sales representatives all over the country from Massachusetts to Oregon, it did not remain in existence even to the next year.[12] In 1889 Fred Karinen began to publish a paper titled *Työmies* under the sponsorship of the Finnish National Temperance Brotherhood of Ishpeming. Karinen, however, would not submit to the demands of the leaders of the society, thus causing a parting of the ways. The society refused financial support and Karinen continued publishing the paper by himself.[13] In 1892, the Brotherhood began to publish its own paper, *Raittius Lehti* (Temperance paper), soon spelled as one word, *Raittiuslehti.* The paper was usually edited in Ishpeming but printed elsewhere. Karinen moved his paper to Minneapolis in 1892. There it merged with *Amerikan Uutiset* published by August Edwards.

Ironwood was the fourth Finnish center in the Upper Peninsula to attempt the publication of newspapers. The first of them was the weekly *Kalevala*, which had a unique editorial staff. The intellectual head of the paper was Pastor J. W. Eloheimo, the "bishop" of the Fenno-American Church, which he had established. One of his assistant editors was J. W. Lähde, who had had his elementary schooling in Finland. He had been ordained by the Augustana Synod and defrocked soon after because of drunkenness.[14] Another assistant editor was Iisakki Reinikka from Kurikka, whom Eloheimo had ordained. *Kalevala* was published from 1894 to 1895.

Over the years there have been at least four publications titled *Kansan Lehti* (People's paper). One of them was published in Ironwood in 1903–4, edited by Aku Paivio, one of the more gifted of Finnish American poets, who was later on the editorial staff of *Raivaaja* and still later published a leftist literary paper titled *Viesti* in Sudbury, Ontario.[15] The publications of the Finnish National Church in Ironwood have been discussed in connection with the history of the church.

In the Lower Peninsula there have been some short-lived newspaper enterprises in Kaleva and Detroit. The newspaper *Siirtolainen* played an important role in the origin and development of the farming community of Kaleva. It had been started in Astoria in 1891 as a weekly titled *Lannetar* (West), which was soon moved with its editors to Superior, Wisconsin. At the time of the move its name was changed to *Siirtolainen.* In 1894 the paper was moved to Brooklyn, New York, where it merged with *New Yorkin Lehti*, owned by immigrant agent G. A. Gronlund. Under the editorship of Akseli Jarnefelt, Antero Riippa, and

Jacob E. Saari, the *Siirtolainen* became the most widely read Finnish newspaper in America. In 1901 Saari and Riippa moved with their press to Kaleva. Following this event, Kaleva was for a short time one of the centers of Finnish American newspaper publishing. After a few years *Siirtolainen* was moved back to Superior.[16]

In 1926, a weekly titled *Detroitin Uutiset* (Detroit news) appeared in Detroit, edited and published by Jussi Hinkkanen, with Helmi Warren also on the staff. It ceased publication the same year. Early in November 1938 a small weekly titled *Finn-So News* was started in Detroit. It was intended to be a newspaper for second- and third-generation Finnish Americans. The editor and publisher was Bernhart Nippa, and the assistant editor was C. L. Nippa. The paper was strongly nationality-minded.[17] In connection with it, a nationalistic monthly, *Pine Street*, was also published for a short time, as was *Aurora News*, a continuation of *Finn-So News*. Both were edited by Bernhart Nippa.

On November 1, 1940, a "non-partisan Finnish-language weekly" began publication. It was a small four-column, usually four-page, newspaper titled *Detroitin Sanomat* (Detroit tidings). In addition to serving as the voice of the nationally minded Finns of Detroit, it gave abundant space to news from Finland. The owner and editor of the paper was Urho Kuusisto, born in the vicinity of the Pinjainen, or Billnäs, axe factory in the parish of Pohja. He worked as a typesetter on several newspapers in Finland. He came to Detroit in 1938. In 1939 he became a partner in the Ralph Baschal and Company printing shop, where *Detroitin Sanomia* was also published. When Kuusisto's partners were called into military service, the print shop had to be sold, and the Finns of Detroit were left without a newspaper of their own. The last number was published on July 9, 1942.[18]

Finnish American newspaper publishing has received its share of harsh criticism. The words of Aku Tela are among the most biting:

> It does not seem to have entered my editor's mind to make his paper nationality-minded. The ideal of nationality was not understood even by the editors, much less by the readers! The main content was about all kinds of villainy, each item worse than the preceding . . . and included the most vulgar and despicable calumny. . . . Thus the reputation of Finnish-American newspapermen is anything but enviable, for the worst schemers and adventurers have worked as such.[19]

Tela's criticism was unjustifiable, even at the time it was made, and it aroused bitterness in the ranks of Finnish American newspapermen, among whom there were many honest men who had the best interests of their nationality at heart. Oskari Tokoi, a former prime minister of Finland, who had had many years of experience in the editing of Finnish American newspapers, wrote thus:

> Work on a small, understaffed foreign newspaper was mentally and physically exhausting. It lasted from early morning to evening, and it consisted of the deadly monotony of writing news briefs, translating news dispatches, getting into printable form the reports of correspondents who only too often were lacking in writing ability, proof reading, and endlessly chatting with people who considered it their right to tell the editor what they thought about this and that, to complain about their troubles, and to ask advice. Even if an editor had once had enthusiasm and the desire to accomplish something worthwhile, a few years of editing a paper of this kind was enough to destroy all enthusiasm and interest.[20]

It is obvious, however, that in spite of the truth of Tokoi's words, the Finnish press in America, especially in Michigan where it had shrunk by 1964 to the publication of a single quarterly, *Suomi Opiston Viesti* (Suomi College message), had during the ninety years of its existence accomplished a unique and valuable cultural work among the Finnish immigrants.

Radio and Television

As the Finnish-language newspapers and periodical publications began to disappear from the scene in Michigan, Finnish radio broadcasts gradually took their place. The initiators of Finnish radio broadcasting were several pastors who, with the spiritual welfare of their widespread congregations in mind, extended the reach of their worship services through radio. Suomi College was the next to make use of radio. "It has almost become a habit to listen once a week to a program broadcast from the Calumet radio station by Suomi College," said Pastor Alfred Haapanen in a radio talk from Calumet on July 29, 1930.[21]

The veteran of regular news broadcasts in Finnish in the Copper Country was Reino W. Suojanen, who began broadcasting from Station WHDF, Calumet, in 1937. At first his programs were five-minute presentations sponsored by large flour mills, but during World War II they were expanded to half-hour programs six days a week, becoming associated at the same time with *Valvoja*, which Suojanen edited. The programs were financed by advertisements of Copper Country businesses. In 1957, "Radio Suojanen" moved to Hancock to the newly established Station WMPL. He made it a custom to interview Finns of various occupations. The Finns of the Copper Country began to call Suojanen "Wimpeli" after the call letters of the station. His interviews were called the Wimple "kestikievari," or Wimple Inn. Many guests from Finland stopped there to be interviewed. WMPL was probably the most Finnish radio station outside Finland, for of its three owners, two were Finns, the French-Italian president of the company was married to a Finn, and the employees were mostly Finns. Finnish-language radio news, especially during the war years from 1939 to 1945, was often both perturbing and exciting. It attracted neighbors to homes which had good radio receiving sets.[22]

Finnish news broadcasts from WHDF of Calumet were continued by Ralph Bekkala up to 1964. In 1947, Rudolph Kemppa, who was born in Toivola, Michigan, in 1909, began to broadcast from the Houghton radio station of WHDF. He also broadcast news on WMPL. Station WIKB of Iron River, Michigan, also had Finnish news broadcasts. Edith Aspholm began to air her program on September 18, 1958, continuing to do so every other Thursday to the late 1960s. Her programs were about cultural history and included lectures on subjects like Finnish immigration to America, Christmas in Finland, and Finnish Independence Day. The presentations were bilingual. They included a generous amount of Finnish music. They also served to promote the work of the Michigan Finnish History Society.[23]

In 1941–42, during the war, the Finns of Greater Boston participated in the multilanguage radio broadcasts which were sent to Finland as well as other countries.[24]

In 1962, Carl Pellonpaa and Eugene Sinervo started the Suomi Kutsuu (Finland Calling) television program on WLUC-TV of Marquette. The Suomi College Choir, visiting choruses and choirs from Finland, and numerous interviews have been presented on this Sunday morning program. Eugene Sinervo, Pirkko Venetjoki, Helen M. Keskitalo, and others have served as news broadcasters. Finland Calling is aired by one of the most powerful television stations in the Midwest, and the program is seen and heard in broad areas of Michigan, Wisconsin, and Ontario. This program celebrated thirty-seven years on the air in 1999.[25]

Printing Presses and Books

The beginnings of printing among the Finns in Michigan were as simple as they could possibly be. The first printing press was Matt

Fredd's homemade press, which was like the mangle of the old country, in which a wooden box filled with stones was pushed back and forth. In addition to *Swen Tuuwa* and *Sankarin Maine*, such unusual items as *Uusi Engeska ja Suomalainen Laakari Kirja Amerikan Siirtolaisille* (New English and Finnish medical book for immigrants to America), edited by Fredd, and *Lakkarikirja* (Pocket book), which was a small dictionary, were printed on this primitive press. Eight years after the end of Fredd's pioneer work, *Paimen-Sanomia* was started in Hancock with its own press, which later became the Finnish Lutheran Book Concern. This largest of Finnish American printing businesses has been discussed in connection with the history of the churches as the extensive activity of the Työmies Publishing Company has been discussed in connection with the labor movement.

There were several smaller printing and publishing businesses in Hancock at the beginning of the century. The *Kansan Kuvalehti* press, which was functioning between 1901 and 1903, was interested in poetry, publishing, among others, a collection of poems by Eetu Aaltio titled *Veräjillä Vierahilla* (At foreign gates) in 1901, as well as Ilmari Calamnius's *Nuoria Lauluja Vanhasta Säästöstä* (New songs from old collections) and Alex Halonen's *Kulkurin Kujilla* (On vagabond lanes) in 1902. The Finnish Bookstore, which opened in 1896 and soon afterward merged with the Finnish Lutheran Book Concern, carried mostly religious books and temperance literature. The Kotikirjaston Kirjapaino (Home Library Print Shop) at 732 Franklin Street published a few items in 1904. In the 1910s, *Pelto ja Koti* sponsored a small bookstore, and John G. Tuira ran a small printing business. In the 1920s, the enterprising J. H. Jasberg owned the Suomi Publishing Company, publishing books which, in the opinion of the Suomi Synod's Book Concern, were too worldly for a church-owned publishing house to handle, such as Jasberg's own widely distributed *Amerikoissa* (In America).

Although there were no large printing businesses in Calumet as there were in Hancock, there were some smaller printing and publishing enterprises. In addition to the newspaper presses, which very seldom published books, there was at the end of the century a small printing shop owned by J. E. Hendrickson and known in 1898 as the Hendrickson ja Eskola Suomalainen Kirjapaino. It was housed in the Temperance Hall.

The largest independent publishing business in Calumet in the first decade of the present century was Wilho Leikas and Company, whose press was on Pine Street, probably in the basement of the Finnish cooperative store, which had occupied the site for several generations. Leikas was a businessman. He ordered postcards, pictures of churches, and any other items that his traveling salesmen were able to sell, from Finland in wholesale lots. The same lack of guiding principles characterized his publishing activity. Although he was not a socialist, he printed and distributed many of Robert G. Ingersoll's anti-Christian writings as well as pamphlets by Gabriel Deville and other socialists, which appealed to large numbers of readers during this period of vigorous growth in the labor movement. Basically Leikas was of an accommodating nature. During the political struggles of the period he lost his health. His business closed around 1911.[26]

In the 1920s, J. A. Harpet owned a printing shop in Calumet. About the same time, the Laestadians had the Finnish Republican Printing Company, which published their songbooks and monthly church papers. The Rauha Publishing Association was its successor.

Literature was published in Calumet by several persons who had it printed on presses owned by others. In 1893, Kaarle Ala published Kristian G. Barth's history of the church, which covers the subject to the 1830s. A little later, Jaakko Suutala published Kalle Koski's exceptionally fine collection of poems. At the turn of the century, Johan Kieri and Oskar Lahti published religious tracts. At the beginning of the 1890s, the Kaleva Kirjapainoyhtiö (Kaleva Printing Company) was publishing Finnish translations of even comparatively lengthy novels. In Lake Linden there was for a short time the Ruutila Print Shop which published a small English-language weekly.

Next to the Copper Country, the most important center of Finnish-language publishing in the Upper Peninsula was Ironwood, where the leading publisher and printer was Otto Massinen. His printing business, which was known as the Suomalainen Painoyhtiö (Finnish Printing Company), was the publisher of the newspaper *Auttaja*[27] Small independent publishing businesses were owned there by William Maki, who had his own printing press, and later by Antti Hassel.[28]

In Ishpeming, *Työmies* press published a number of pamphlets, of which the best known was Eloheimo's *Julistus Siitä Yleis-Waltakunnasta*, on the topic of Finnish churches. As long as *Työmies* of Ishpeming was published, its press was also used for temperance society business.

The work of the Finnish-American Publishing Company of Kaleva in the Lower Peninsula was very extensive although it was short-lived, lasting from 1904 to 1910. Its presses turned out a steady stream of J. H. Harvey's Finnish translations of novels and other literature, including works of August Strindberg, Robert Louis Stevenson, Selma Lagerlof, Knut Hamsun, and Edmondo De Amicis, as well as the writings of lesser authors.

Libraries, Schools, and Cultural Societies

Finland has long been one of the most literate countries in the world. The strict Lutheran Church, which had control of the people's education, hundreds of years ago made literacy and knowledge of the catechism requirements for the right to partake of Communion and the privilege of marrying. In 1880, 97.6 percent of the population over ten years of age were literate. From 1900 on, statistics have used persons above the age of fifteen in figuring percentages. In 1930 the country was 99.1 percent literate. Literacy was accompanied by interest in reading. Almost every home had its own library, usually a glass-fronted bookcase in a corner, and towns had lending libraries. More books have been published per person in Finland than in any other country, and Helsinki has long been known as the city with the world's largest bookstore.

It was a rare Finnish immigrant who did not have a few books in the trunk that accompanied him to America. If nothing else, it at least contained the Bible or New Testament and a hymn book and a catechism. In the Finnish American Historical Archives there is collection of books published in 1880 or before and brought to America by the early immigrants.[29] Most of them are religious books, with editions of the Bible dating back to 1642 and 1776 heading the list. The religious literature published in Turku and Oulu to counterbalance the theology of the Enlightenment, often translated from German or English, is well represented, as are the works of Luther. But secular literature was also brought to America by the immigrants, beginning with such works as Christfrid Ganander's *Huoneja Koti-Aptheekista* (House and home apothecary) and the 1835 edition of *Kalevala*, and covering a variety of subjects up to accounts of the Russo-Turkish War. In 1965 there were 300 different titles in this collection.

From their very beginnings in America, Finnish American newspaper publishers sold books ordered from Finland, and some of them started regular bookstores. Many ministers also earned extra money by selling books ordered from Finland. But the most important suppliers of books to would-be readers were the libraries established by the various societies. The lending libraries of the dozens of temperance societies in Michigan especially were an indication of extensive educational activity, which was all the more valuable because the books in these libraries were usually ordered from the Suomen Kansanvalistusseura (People's Enlightenment Society) of Finland and had been carefully selected. An examination of these libraries has shown that the books were worn out by the readers so that replacement copies had to be ordered. The most popular works were books on Finnish history and novels. The labor organizations, which came later, also established libraries, usually restricting their literature to socialistic political writings. Churches, and especially their young people's groups, sometimes established libraries.[30]

Much valuable labor was donated for the care of these libraries. For example, Matti Reini was the librarian for the Valo Temperance Society in Ironwood for over thirty years. By 1950 these Finnish libraries were no longer being used much because of a lack of readers. The Suomi College library has Finnish books as well as textbooks and is open to the public. Finnish-language books have also been available over the years in the public libraries of many Upper Michigan communities. As late as the 1960s the Escanaba branch of the State Library asked for help in obtaining recent Finnish literature, indicating that older Finns, even from distant areas, came to borrow books from them. As a result of this request, the University of Turku sent a gift of two hundred works to the Escanaba branch.

Already in the first years of the 1880s, Kansanvalistusseura (People's Enlightenment Society), which had been established in Finland in 1874, had promoters in America. The teacher David Castren served as their representative in the Copper Country. Through his efforts Suomen Kansanvalistusseuran Haaraosasto (Branch of the People's Enlightenment Society) was organized. It came to be known as Calumetin Kansanvalistusseura. The reply of Dr. A. A. Granfelt, the secretary of the main society, dated July 2, 1883, to Castren's notification of the establishment of the branch society, ended with these words:

> On behalf of the committee of the People's Enlightenment Society we declare the Calumet organization to be a legitimate branch of the Society and hope that it will remain alive and active for a long time in the New World and that it will prove that Finnish men can demonstrate ability and integrity whenever they are needed for the promotion of a good cause.

The branch society had a good start and within two years it had its own hall, which became the home of educational activities among the Finns of Calumet. The membership fee was only 75 cents per year. It was sent to the head society, which in turn sent more than the money's worth of worthwhile literature to every member of the society. From 1883 to 1903, correspondence with the head society was handled by David Castren, Antti A. Pajari, J. H. Castren, C. J. Sorsen, U. Sodergren, and W. Liisanantti. Table 26 gives some idea of the activity of the branch society.

Table 26: Membership in People's Enlightenment Society, Calumet Branch, 1883–1912

1883	85	1903	41
1887	50	1905	51
1891	100	1907	53
1894	75	1910	34
1897	64	1912	14

After 1903, annual reports and membership fees were no longer sent regularly to Helsinki. The society, however, continued to function as a sort of link between the many local Finnish societies which held their meetings in the society hall. Table 27 lists the rent paid to the society by various organizations for meeting space in 1908.

Table 27: Rent Paid on People's Enlightenment Society Hall, Calumet, 1908

Hyvä Toivo Temperance Society	100
Saima Pesä L.O.M.M.	75
Sampo Maja (Lodge) K.O.T.M.M.	100
Suomen Ruotsalainen Apuyhdistys (Finnish-Swedish Aid Society)	30
Kaleva Sairastusja Loukkausapuyhdistys (Sickness and Accident Aid Society)	30
Tuulikin Tupa (Lodge)	60
Kalevan Ritarit (Knights of Kaleva)	100
Soittokunta Humu (Humu Band)	104
Voima Seura (Athletic Society)	90

By 1906 the People's Enlightenment Society Hall was being used so much that when time for repairs came it was enlarged. The project put the society into debt to such an extent that in 1910 the hall was sold to the Ahti Lodge of the Knights of Kaleva for $5,460, the total amount owed. Activity also became less as congregations, temperance societies, and labor organizations became more important as forms of group activity. The last meeting of Enlightenment Society members was held in 1912. On November 10, 1918, the board of directors indicated in its minutes that activity, which had been at a standstill for several years, could not be continued. A branch of the Enlightenment

Society had been established in Hancock in 1890 with a membership of about forty, but it was active only to 1893. O. W. Pasanen was a leader in it.[31]

Among the numerous Copper Country organizations, many of which expired early, one of the most prominent was Suomalainen Naisyhdistys (Finnish Women's Society) of Calumet, which was organized at the home of Serafina Ala on November 29, 1894, with twenty-four charter members. Meetings were held once a week, literature on subjects of interest to women was bought, night schools for the learning of English were started, and young girls were taught sewing. Correspondence was carried on with authoress Aleksandra Gripenberg, chairman of the Finnish Women's Society, whose rules and regulations were adapted for the Copper Country group. Maggie Watz, Serafiina Ala, Linda Mahlberg, Annie Nergord, and Dagmar Sillberg were among the first officers.[32] For the promotion of its ideals over wider areas, *Naisten Lehti* (Women's paper) was started, and it was published up to 1909. There is a difference of opinion about the date on which it was established.[33] The first editor was Hanna Jarnefelt, wife of Akseli Jarnefelt, of New York. Later, Linda Mahlberg was editor. The last editor was Augusta Lahti. Maggie Walz was the business manager and also its owner during the society's financially poor years. The publication was modeled after *Naisten Ääni* (Women's voice) of Helsinki. After 1909, the publication appeared in the Saturday issue of Päivälehti.

On June 12, 1895, the Minneapolis Finnish Women's Society was established as a branch of the Calumet society, and on October 6 of the same year a Finnish Women's Society was started in Hancock, Naema Lindbohm, Kristiina Waisanen, Hanna Sammeli, Annie Strolberg, and Ida Dyhr were among the first officers.[34] In Ishpeming a women's society was started in the spring of 1897. When the society started its public activities with a stage play on a Sunday in June during the time church services were being held, there was so much ill feeling that the organization ceased activity soon after.[35] The women's Toivo (Hope) Society organized in Laurium in 1908 was not of long duration, any more than were the other societies which had formed around the Calumet organization. The initiative of the versatile Maggie Walz resulted in the organization of the Calumet Valkonauha (White ribbon) as a branch of the World's Women's Temperance League. In 1910 Maggie Walz was sent as a delegate from Calumet to the world conference of the World's Women's Temperance League in Glasgow, Scotland. The first Finnish American women's society in the United States was the Naisyhdistys Pyrkijä in Brooklyn, organized in 1893. It was also the longest-lived, for it was still fully active toward the end of the 1960s.[36]

Because of their love of books and reading, the Finns were concerned about the education of their children. In 1873 David Castren, a public school teacher from Kemi, arrived in Calumet. Because of the availability of this capable teacher, an elementary school corresponding to the Finnish schools of the same level was started. Subjects taught were religion, Finnish, penmanship, arithmetic, geography, history, and singing. The parents were enthusiastic about the school, and Castren had difficulty in teaching the large number of children who attended. Local public school officials required that English should be taught. Castren of course was unable to teach English, and funds were not available for a second teacher. The children were sent to a local public school.

The Finns now arranged to hold Finnish school sessions on Saturdays and in the summertime when the public schools were closed. Persons assisting Castren in his teaching were, among others, Henry Knuutila, Pekka Vesterinen, J. J. Hoikka, and Kustaa Perala. The same kind of school arrangement was started in Republic in 1885 through the efforts of Pekka Vesterinen. These first children's schools developed later into the Finnish summer schools conducted for children by churches and temperance societies. They were of great importance in the cultural life of the Finnish immigrants.[37]

Another type of educational effort was adult education courses that were tried as an experiment in Calumet. Still another was the Finnish Literary Institute started in Ishpeming under the leadership of Jussi Hinkkanen in 1910. Projects of the latter in Ishpeming and South Range were short courses which included lectures on a variety of subjects from art to astronomy. Correspondence courses were also tried. With the assistance of his sister Alma, Jussi Hinkkanen also edited a bilingual periodical titled *Tiedon Henki—The Spirit of Knowledge*, four numbers of which were published before the Literary Institute, which had started with such high hopes, collapsed in 1911.[38] Somewhat later, Americanization classes were started. Immigrants were taught to read English and to use it in their everyday life. Their chief purpose was to prepare candidates seeking American citizenship for the simple examinations they would be required to take. Thousands of persons took advantage of these free evening schools. In the meantime, Suomi College had attained a dominant position in Finnish American education. Interest in music, drama, gymnastics, and sports was common among Finnish Americans in all the states, so that it is more logical to discuss it in a history of the whole country rather than in a history of a single state. At the beginning of the century, however, the Copper Country rose to such an important place in sports, gymnastics, and wrestling that it earned special mention beside the Finnish societies of Massachusetts and of Brooklyn, New York. Leading societies of the Copper Country were Reipas of Hancock, Ponnistus of Calumet, Visa of Painesdale, Vesa of Franklin, Kontys of Ironwood, and Huima of South Range. The women athletes' graceful performances and the pyramid shows of the men attracted large audiences. Special mention is made of the men gymnasts of the Huima society and their pyramid presentations in front of the Saima Hall, with Matti Miller often standing at the apex. Ponnistus of Covington was acclaimed even outside the state.

Even more important, although it was of short duration, was the interest in wrestling which began around 1910. Leaders in the activity were Kalle Lehto, Karl Wirtanen, and Gunnar Gronlund, all from Finland. For a time there was a wrestling school managed by Lehto in Painesdale. Big wrestling matches were held at the Opera House in Calumet, the Amphidrome in Houghton, and wherever large audiences could be accommodated. Sometimes even non-Finnish "world champions" were present to perform.[39]

Historical Societies

The Finns of Michigan have been originators of and pioneers in the establishment of historical societies. The Calumet Enlightenment Society established in 1883 had historical aims as did Amerikan Suomalainen Kirjallisuuden Seura (Finnish American Literary Society), whose bylaws were in N. J. Ahlman's handwriting.[40] The first publication of this society was T. Vallenius's *Amerikan Yhdysvaltojen Synty* (The birth of the United States of America).[41] The work of the Finnish American Literary Society, which had been started because of interest in history, did not last long. Another society, Snellman's Literary Society, accomplished even less.

After a hiatus of about fifteen years, there were again indications of interest in things historical in Hancock, when on May 13, 1919, "a meeting of citizens interested in church history" was held at Suomi College. Eight officials of the Suomi Synod were present on this occasion. A three-man committee was selected for drafting a constitution. The committee, which included Rafael Hartman, editor Fabian Tolonen, and Pastor Alfred Haapanen, presented a proposal already at a meeting held on May 21, at which fourteen Synod officials were present. The new organization was named Suomi-Synodin Kirkkohistoriallinen Seura (Suomi Synod Church History Society). The bylaws were approved at the same time. In the main, they followed the bylaws of the Church History Society of Finland which had been established in 1887, mentioning the establishment of archives, a book selection committee, a series of publications, etc. However, the duties which the society required of itself proved to be overwhelming. The last meeting of the society was held on December 23 of the same year.[42]

Thirty-four years later at the annual church conference held in Astoria in 1953, the matter was brought up again. The Synod Consistory was given the task of selecting a committee, the Suomi Synod History Committee, which would collect material for a history of the Synod and find someone to write it. The Consistory selected John Wargelin, Minnie Perttula-Maki, Henry Kangas, and David Halkola to the committee.[43] A history, titled *The Story of the Suomi Synod*, was written by Jacob W. Heikkinen, professor emeritus of New Testament at Gettysburg Seminary. It is a record not merely of the activity of clergy, congregations, and institutions but a story of the spiritual journey of the Finnish Evangelical Lutheran people in the United States.

Where societies and committees had failed early on, individuals had success. Viljami B. Rautanen, pastor of the Finnish Evangelical Lutheran Congregation in Calumet, published an extensive Finnish-American church history.[44] Salomon Ilmonen, over a period of thirty years, from 1908 to 1938, published a large number of works both short and long, among them *Amerikan Suomalaisten Historia* (History of the Finnish Americans) in three volumes and *Amerikan Suomalaisten Sivistyshistoria* (Cultural history of the Finnish Americans) in two volumes.[45] To finance his writing projects, Ilmonen established Amerikan Suomalainen Historiallinen Seura (Finnish American Historical Society) in Brooklyn, New York. Its headquarters were wherever Ilmonen, its secretary, was serving a pastorate, including Detroit, Los Angeles, and Fort Bragg. Many other persons continued the work Rautanen and Ilmonen had begun.

With his books and newspaper articles about the early history of the Finns in America, Ilmonen aroused interest in the celebration of the 300th anniversary of the Delaware Colony. Civic groups and officials took hold of the matter. The result was great celebrations in Chester, Pennsylvania, and elsewhere throughout the United States in areas populated by Finns, and even in Finland. The Delaware celebration did not end without leaving its mark. The interest of Finnish Americans in their past history remained alive. Here and there local Delaware committees kept on functioning, searching for new goals for activities related to the Finnish nationality.

Meetings started in connection with the Delaware festival continued in Crystal Falls. A number of persons who had been active in festival plans met at the farm home of Kalle and Ellen Nevaranta on June 4, 1938, to consider the possibility of preserving the memory of the Finnish pioneers of the area. Preliminary discussion had already taken place between interested individuals. At this meeting the following persons at least were present: Ivar Maki, Johanna Harmanmaa, Minnie Maki, and Hjalmar Makila from Crystal Falls; Elias Puotinen and John Koski from Amasa; Edith Aspholm and Charles and Maria Raatikainen from Iron River; Kalle Haavisto from Iron Mountain; and Ellen Nevaranta from Commonwealth, Wisconsin. Ivar Maki was elected chairman and John Koski, secretary. This small group organized the Iron County Historical Society. Ivar Maki was elected chairman of the board of directors, Hjalmar Makila, secretary, Johanna Harmanmaa, treasurer. Other members of the board were Elias Puotinen, Charles Raatikainen, Edith Aspholm, Ellen Nevaranta, and Kalle Haavisto.

Meetings were held in rapid succession. One of the first decisions made was to change the name of the society to the Finnish Historical Society of Hiawathaland, for in the minds of the members was the thought that the activity of the society might well be extended to include all the Upper Peninsula. The first practical act of the society was to print and distribute three thousand questionnaires in the Crystal Falls area. Finns were asked to fill them in carefully with details of their personal history. Only 8 percent were returned.[46]

Other activities of the society were more successful. Relief work was zealously carried on for Finland during the time of Russian oppression; Finnish films were shown; dances, outdoor festivals, coffee socials, and lectures were sponsored; delegates were sent to meetings of the Michigan Historical Society. The Crystal Falls society also hosted the Upper Peninsula conference of the Michigan society. Several branch societies were also established, the most important of them being one in Negaunee.

As funds accumulated over the years, the society began to consider putting up a fireproof building in Crystal Falls for a Finnish American archive. It was thought that a small cement block building could be constructed for a few thousand dollars. But an experienced archivist, who had been invited to a board meeting, pointed out that at least a thousand feet of shelves should be included in the plans, as well as a workroom with proper furnishings for researchers, and central heating. Furthermore, a trained archivist and an assistant should be hired. It was clear then that such a project could be properly handled only by an interested college or university. The matter was dropped, and the few materials that had been collected were turned over to the Finnish American Historical Archives in Hancock.

At the same meeting a proposal was made to raise a monument in memory of the Finnish pioneers. This was soon accomplished. On August 24, 1958, a fine granite monument was put up in front of the Crystal Falls City Hall and dedicated to the Finnish pioneers of the Upper Peninsula. It weighed sixteen tons and cost the Finnish Historical Society of Hiawathaland $7,000.[47] The unveiling of the monument gave impetus to the organization of the Michigan Finnish History Society and to the sponsoring of the writing of this history. The Finnish Historical Society of Hiawathaland was continuously interested in the project until 1967.

Another society of persons interested in the history of the Finns in Michigan is the Finnish American Historical Society of Michigan. The organizational meeting was held in Detroit at the home of Mr. and Mrs. William Murto in April 1945. In addition to the Murtos, the other persons present were Dr. George W. Sippola, Abel N. Karvonen, William Bilto, George Kallio, and Fanny Ojanpaa. Sippola was elected president; Bilto, secretary; and Kallio, treasurer. Bilto, an assistant professor at Wayne State University, died in 1947 and was succeeded by Alfred W. Wiitanen. Other persons who served as officers of the society were Andrew Brask, Lillian Meining, Noah Potti, William Pudas, and Antti Holm.

This Finnish historical society of Detroit has concentrated on Finnish activities in its own metropolis. It has planned programs for Finnish Independence Day and Kalevala Day. It has also participated in American Independence Day parades and in Dominion Day parades in Windsor, Ontario. Because of the proximity of colleges and universities, it has been able to obtain nationally known speakers. Government officials, including governors of the state, have also been available as speakers. The Detroit society has also taken part, from the very beginning, in the work of the Michigan Finnish History Society, with Dr. Sippola serving as their representative on the board. In a contest for the collection of funds for the publication of this history, Antti Holm, a member of the Detroit society, won third prize.

The Finnish American Historical Archives

The Finnish American Historical Archives at Suomi College in Hancock has become the center of interest as far as the history of the Finns in Michigan and in all the United States is concerned. J. O. Ikola, who as a writer was well known as Vaasan Jaakkoo (Jake of Vaasa), and who traveled in Michigan in the winter of 1948, wrote, in the dialect of South Ostrobothnia, a travelogue in which he gave a sorry picture of the archives.

> I came to Hancock with the idea of visiting Suomi College because I had heard that Finnish literature published in America and newspapers numbering in the hundreds had been carefully collected and were stored there. I planned to stay a week browsing in this treasure house of Finnish American history to acquire some knowledge of our countrymen's arrival in the country, their number, and the areas where they live, etc. Perhaps there would even be a collection of old photographs that would picture for posterity and the pioneer life of the older generation on Sundays and weekdays—their clearing of land, their homes, their tools, their clothing—and preserve their likenesses for future generations to see.
>
> I went there with high hopes, but I was sadly disappointed. The historical archives at Suomi College is nominally in the care of Kosti Arho, one of the instructors. He teaches Finnish language and literature; he is also the librarian of an 8,000-volume college library. . . . All this, in addition to his work in the seminary, takes up altogether too much of his time. There is no salary or allowance of any kind for the supervision of the historical archives. The archives itself is a small dark cubbyhole under an upstairs stairway, which is used for the storage of all kinds of miscellaneous rubbish. There were a few years' collections of tattered and dusty newspapers, and a couple of laundry baskets of trashy books mixed up helter-skelter. No catalog and no kind of organization!
>
> "There is no time nor anyone to do the work," sighed the weary instructor. . . . So it is when there is no one in charge. And no one in America works without pay. These Finnish Americans certainly help Finland, almost too much, but they do not realize or understand their own needs and how to take care of them. . . . There is no head or tail to this! It would require work, a man or two certainly, and operating funds.[48]

This picture of the archives as given by the visitor from Finland was to a certain extent a true one as far as the collection itself was concerned, but the "small dark cubbyhole" was not under a stairway but next to a lounge. Ikola's description was inaccurate because it was based on false impressions. Apparently it had not been pointed out to him that the larger part of the archives collection was housed in the general college library and the seminary library. It was true enough, though, that the materials were poorly catalogued.

Already in the first Suomi College bulletin it had been possible for President J. K. Nikander to write: "The library and the museum have received valuable contributions from interested persons. The editors of *Uusi Kotimaa* and *Siirtolainen* have donated books they have published, and surplus books from a certain lending library [Newport, N.H.] have recently been received."[49]

In his annual reports Nikander regularly exhorted friends of the college to remember the library with gifts of books. In this way considerable numbers of Finnish American publications were acquired. The first person to turn his attention to them was Pastor Ilmari Tammisto, an instructor in the seminary, who proposed to the college board in 1932 that this material be organized as an archives collection. The board decided in favor of the proposal and put Tammisto in charge. Space for the collection was lacking, however, and when Tammisto returned to Finland in 1936, the matter was shelved for the time being.

When Dr. Viljo K. Nikander was the president of Suomi College (1937–47), Nikander Hall was built. There was much more space for the library than there had been before. It was possible also to pay more attention to the archives. Dr. John I. Kolehmainen, a professor of history at Heidelberg College, who lectured at Suomi College during the 1945–46 school year, devoted a large part of his time to looking over the materials that had accumulated for the archives. His work in the archives resulted in the publication the following year of a 141-page work titled *The Finns in America: A Bibliographical Guide to Their History*. The Finnish American Historical Archives was given as its publisher, indicating a hopeful attitude toward the future of the archives. Despite this attitude of optimism toward the future, newspapers, books, and other archival materials were still kept wherever space could be found for them. In 1950 the collection was housed in a fairly large room on the top floor of Nikander Hall, which had been used at different times by the faculty and the seminary. Ellen Ryynanen, the librarian of the general college library, devoted some of her time to the archives, thus getting started the organization and cataloguing of the accumulated materials.

At a meeting held on February 8, 1954, Dr. Armas K. E. Holmio was named archivist by the board of directors of Suomi College. He was directed to make use of part-time help for clerical work and to purchase additional shelving. Lydia S. Holmio was his chief assistant for a long time. In 1965, when the archives area in Nikander Hall became inadequate, the collection was moved to the basement of the new Student Center, where three fireproof rooms were available, with about a thousand feet of shelving and a work area for the archivist. The Finnish

Library of Suomi College, a collection of books published in Finland, which numbered about 3,000 volumes of mostly historical works, was also stored there. The following figures give some idea of the growth of the Finnish American archives. In 1954 there were 1,000 catalogued items; in 1955, 2,000; in 1959, over 4,000; in 1961, 5,000; in 1966, 7,000; in 1968, 8,000; in 1970, 10,000; and in 1990, 20,000. There were also about 3,000 items waiting to be catalogued. The Dewey Decimal System of classification has been used, adapted to the special needs of the archives. A separate collection, the Suomi Synod Archives, is also stored there in nearly forty boxes which are estimated to contain about ten thousand items of historical value.

Other large collections acquired by the Finnish American Historical Archives are the libraries or archives of Suomalainen Kansallis-Raittius-Veljeys Seura (SKRV), Amerikan Suomalainen Historiallinen Seura (Finnish American Historical Society) of New York, and Suomalais-Amerikalais Yhdistys (Finnish American Association) and the Help Finland organization of Washington. Donors include many institutions, libraries, and businesses, such as the Book Concern of Hancock, Raivaaja of Fitchburg, Työmies Publishing Company of Superior, the Finnish Consulate in New York, the Finnish Historical Society of Hiawathaland, the universities of Helsinki and Turku, Harvard University, the libraries of the Jyväskylä Kasvatusopillinen Korkeakoulu, the South Ostrobothnian Maakuntaliitto, and Suomalaisen Kirjallisuuden Seura (Finnish Literature Society) of Finland. Most of the materials, however, have come in a steady flow from individuals who are deeply interested in preserving the history of the Finnish Americans for posterity.

More than once it has happened that some farmer has saved materials pertaining to Finnish American life and made notes on various aspects of it, only to have them destroyed as worthless after his death. An incident with ironic overtones occurred once when the archivist went to an old Finnish hall to look for materials of value to the Finnish American Historical Archives. In honor of his coming the hall had been tidied, and in the process invaluable records had been destroyed.

In addition to books and documents, the Archives has received financial support from individuals as well as organizations. The Knights and Ladies of Kaleva have been in the forefront with financial assistance. The biggest donations have been received from the Supreme Lodge of the Knights of Kaleva, Suomen Ruusu (Rose of Finland) and Hedelmä temperance societies of Cleveland and Warren, Ohio, respectively, and Suur-New Yorkin Suomalaisten Seurojen Keskustoimikunta (Central Organization of Finnish Societies of Greater New York). In some areas of the country it has been customary to donate the receipts from Finnish Independence Day programs to the Archives.

The largest amount of space in the Archives is taken up by newspapers and periodicals, which have been published continuously since the first Finnish newspaper appeared in America in 1876. In spite of this the newspaper collection is the Archives' weakest, comparatively speaking, for the number of Finnish newspapers that have been published in America is extremely large. Periodicals have been more successfully preserved. The second-largest collection consists of documents associated with the temperance movement. They include minutes and other records of eighty temperance societies nationwide. There is also an almost complete collection of Suomi Synod publications. Finnish American literature, including poetry, is very well represented, as are books about emigration and immigration published in Finland. Others of the more important collections include publications of the labor and cooperative movements and devotional literature. Another notable collection is the pioneer library of books brought to America by immigrants, starting with the Bible of 1642, the only copy in North America.

In the fall of 1959, Professor Jorma Vallinkoski, head librarian at the University of Helsinki, and Kaarlo Lausti, head librarian of the Helsinki Student Union library, visited the Archives. This visit resulted in a permanent relationship between the Finnish National Library and the Finnish American Historical Archives. The Archives also developed reciprocal relations with the libraries of Turku University and Helsinki University. There has also been some exchange of publications with other libraries.

Most of the materials in the Archives are about the Finns of Michigan and their history, because for generations Michigan has been the birthplace and center of many Finnish American activities, both religious and secular. Also, due to the location of the Archives in the state, materials about Michigan have always been more easily obtainable than materials from other states.

Several doctoral dissertations have been based on materials in the Archives, in addition to a number of lesser graduate studies.

Suomi College

The immigrant pastors who came to America from Finland in the early years were all graduates of the University of Helsinki. They were also familiar with the Swedish language. It was natural for them to make contact with their Swedish and Norwegian colleagues in America, who had behind them many years of experience in church work among their countrymen in the new homeland. The Finnish pastors based their plans for church activities on ideas they received from these experienced men. One of the things they observed was that the Swedes had established Augustana College in Rock Island in 1860, and started Gustavus Adolphus College in St. Peter, Minnesota, two years later. They also saw that both of these colleges had become centers of church work.

In 1890, the year in which the Suomi Synod was organized, the Synod Consistory chose a committee to look for a suitable place for a college and seminary, the need for which had been obvious to the founders of the Synod at its inception. New members were selected for this committee at every church convention. From 1890 to 1896 the committee inspected places offered and recommended in West Superior, Wisconsin, St. Paul, Minnesota, and Marquette, Michigan. Each of them was rejected because of a lack of local support. In the meantime, Nikander went to Augustana to learn about their operational procedures.

The problem of location was solved when unanimous agreement was reached on the idea that the future educational institution should be located where there was the highest concentration of Finnish immigrant population, namely the Copper Country. At the church convention held in Calumet in 1896 a site in Hancock was agreed on. In addition to the members of the Consistory, who served ex officio, and included Pastors J. K. Nikander, K. L. Tolonen, Johan Bäck, and Kaarlo Huotari, the following laymen were selected to the first board of directors of Suomi College: O. J. Larson, Victor Burman, Alex Leinonen, Jooseppi Riippa, J. H. Jasberg, August Pelto, and Andrew Johnson.

The board was divided into two sections. The Consistory, as one part, was to attend to questions concerning the church and religion, and the lay members, who were called the council, were to take care of business matters. Important general problems were to be considered and solved at combined meetings. The first meeting of the whole board was held on July 4. Far-reaching decisions were made at this meeting. Pastor Nikander was elected president of the college. He was also to serve as an instructor. Other instructors were Victor Burman and Jooseppi Riippa. The board did not go outside its own membership in its selection of teachers, except in the case of the English instructor. The president was to try to find one. The courses for the first year included religion, Finnish, English, arithmetic, geography, United States history, natural science, penmanship, drawing, bookkeeping, voice, band, and gymnastics. Finnish history was added a little later. The question of which language to use, English or Finnish, was solved by the decision to have English, United States history, and bookkeeping taught in English, singing and band in both languages, and all others in Finnish. In actual practice, however, English was used only in the teaching of United States history and English.

The worship service marking the opening of Suomi College was held in the Finnish Evangelical Lutheran church in Hancock on Tuesday, September 8, 1896. The church had been struck by lightning on the afternoon of August 8, immediately after Jooseppi Riippa had dismissed over a hundred children for whom he had been conducting a summer school. The tower was knocked down and the newly appointed Suomi College instructor was killed instantly. Victor Burman went to his funeral in Astoria, and Nikander was the only member of the faculty present at the dedicatory church services.

The opening hymn was the Psalm "Except the Lord Build the House." President Nikander used Proverbs 8 as his text. His sermon ended with the words: "Our college, once it has gotten started and has expanded its influence will be a mother that will give birth to smaller schools. . . . Our more mature students will give inspiring talks in their home communities, and they will conduct summer schools; thus it will be a blessing to our immigrants in many areas." This program, which was the disseminator of spiritual light as well as of secular knowledge among Finnish Americans, became a permanent part of the activity of the college.

On dedication day nine boys and two girls enrolled in the new school. The next morning Nikander started classwork in a rented Jacobsville sandstone building across from the Protestant Cemetery in West Hancock.[50] A long time later this building housed a large public sauna, and someone started the long-lived but erroneous story that Suomi College, like many an old-country Finn, had been born in a sauna. After the school had opened its doors, Burman returned, and C. J. Barr, teacher of Latin in the local high school, was hired to teach American history and English. Jaakob Holmlund, an organist-cantor from Finland, became the music teacher. The newly established school now had four instructors. In the spring semester the enrollment reached twenty-one. Seventeen took the examinations in the spring and passed to the next class.

Most of the students lived on the second floor of the school building where Nikander and J. H. Jasberg, the business manager, also lived. The classrooms, kitchen, and dining room were on the first floor. Strict order prevailed. A regular routine, specific in every detail, was followed: The rising hour was 5:40; before breakfast, everyone had to wash his face and hands, get dressed, comb his hair, brush his shoes, clean his room, and make his bed. Before lunch at twelve o'clock, hands and faces had to be washed again and hair combed; the same had to be done again at 5:40 before dinner. An evening prayer service took place at nine o'clock, and everyone had to be in bed by ten. Each student had to scrub the floor of his room every Saturday. In addition he had to take turns scrubbing the classroom floors. No one could leave the college without the president's permission. The tuition fee was $10 for the fall semester and $15 for the spring semester. Room and board cost $2 per week. When the number of students increased, the owners of the property put up an additional small building to accommodate the larger enrollment.

Early in 1898, dissension broke out in the Hancock congregation of the Synod and even found its way into the quiet confines of Suomi College. The result was that of the twenty-eight students in attendance at the time, six refused to submit to school regulations and left. Good order was more important to Nikander than the loss of one-fifth of this student body. By the third year of the school's existence (1898–99) the enrollment was thirty. Teachers, in addition to Pastor Nikander, were Pastor Robert Ylonen, born in Leivonmäki in 1867, John Kiiskila, who had just graduated from Valparaiso, and Jaakob Holmlund.

In the meantime the board, at the request of the Synod conference, had purchased three lots for the college in a good location on the main street of Hancock and requested an architect by the name of Pierce to prepare plans for a new building and supervise its construction. A decision was made to solicit funds for the building from non-Finns as well as Finns. Among Finns, the solicitation for funds centered mostly around Hancock, Calumet, and Marquette County. There was hesitation about venturing farther afield.

Work on the project was started in the summer of 1898 by Juhani Paavola, who leveled the ground with his team of horses. In October, the construction of the foundation was assigned to contractor William Scott of Hancock. By March 1899 work had progressed so far that Scott could be given the contract for the stonework, too. The cost of the foundation and the stonework was $6,557. The contract for the woodwork was given to Pajari and Ulseth of Calumet for $10,037.

The laying of the cornerstone took place on Tuesday, May 30, 1899. The third year's final examinations, which in those days were real interrogations, were completed in the morning, with twenty minutes alotted to each subject. Lunch was served at the Germania Hall. The cornerstone ceremony began after three o'clock. It was estimated that there were 2,000 people present, for railroads had made great reductions in fares for those who wished to attend the program, and the weather was fine. K. L. Tolonen, who was the president of the Suomi Synod at the time, officiated, saying: "I lay this cornerstone for the Suomi College and Theological Seminary building which is to be an institution of higher education for Finnish-American youth in the spirit of Evangelical Lutheranism. No other foundation can be laid than that which has already been laid, which is Jesus Christ."

After Tolonen had discussed the significance of Suomi College in a longer speech, a combined choir sang "Oi Terve Pohjola, Isäimme Onnela," after which A. J. Scott, the mayor of Hancock, gave a cordial speech in English. He spoke of the great progress made by the Finns of the area over a period of thirty years. His speech ended with the idea that Marquette was welcome to its normal school and prison, and Newberry to its mental hospital, for Hancock now had Suomi College, which was open to all young people of the area who wished to continue their education after completing their other schooling.[51]

Construction was held up for several months because the stonework contractor ran out of funds, but in January 1900, the middle of the fourth year of the school's existence, the building was completed. It was made of red sandstone from the Jacobsville quarries and was an ornament of Hancock in those days. The new building was dedicated on Sunday, January 21, 1900. Kustaa Sahlberg, immigrant pastor of the Seamen's Mission, gave the sermon at the festival worship service. In the absence of Tolonen, who was unable to attend, Nikander as vice president of the Synod dedicated the school. Then, on a cold, frosty day the instructors and students happily moved from the rented quarters to their new home.

The next year a large frame building was put up behind the college. It was used as a gymnasium, music room, and auditorium. In 1906 the newly established commercial department was housed in it. The building was torn down in 1940.

Nikander announced that he wished to resign from the presidency of the college in 1902. When Dr. Arthur Hjelt of Finland, an internationally known New Testament scholar who had a deep interest in young people, especially those of college age, visited Hancock in the summer of 1901, soon after Nikander's announcement, discussions were held with him about finding a new president. Hjelt suggested Matti Pesonen, and when Pesonen turned down the offer, he suggested Frans Evert Blomberg. When Blomberg also refused the presidency, Nikander agreed to continue in the office.[52]

The early curriculum of Suomi College was modeled after the Finnish "lyceum" of seven years, including grammar school and high school. In the spring of 1904 the first seventh-year class was graduated. Members were Alfred Haapanen, Heikki Haapanen, Salomon Ilmonen, Lydia Kangas, Pekka Keranen, Vintori Koivumaki, Matti Luttinen, Liisa Paavola, Vilhelmiina Perttula, and John Wargelin. In keeping with a Finnish custom, each graduate received a Finnish university student's white cap as a mark of his new status. The graduates ranged from twenty to thirty-five years in age, for in the difficult conditions of immigrant life, many had started their educations comparatively late.

In the fall of that year, a two-year theological seminary, which a student could enter on completing the seven-year course, was added. The crying need for pastors in the synod was the reason for this short training period. However, it was necessary to work exceptionally hard to complete the studies of those two years. The first generation of pastors from the Suomi Synod's own seminary completed their final examinations in the spring of 1906 and were ordained into the ministry at the annual church convention in Hancock on June 6. The new pastors were Alfred Haapanen, who was born in Karvia; Pekka Keranen, born in Puolanka; Salomon Ilmonen, born in Ilmajoki; Matti Luttinen, born in Piippola; and John Wargelin, born in Isokyrö.[53]

After the establishment of the seminary, the classes leading to enrollment in it were called the academic department. It corresponded to the American high school. (As late as the 1960s some high schools in the New England States were still called academies.)[54]

In 1910 Suomi College was ten years old. Opponents had prophesied a quick end, but it had survived and grown. The total number of students who had attended during the ten-year period was 243, of which 81 were from Hancock. The Copper Country, including Hancock, had contributed a total of 139 and other Michigan areas, 70. From other states from California to Massachusetts, 64 students had attended. Percentagewise, 73 percent were from Michigan and 27 percent from other areas, a ratio which has not changed much over the years.[55]

Even in the early years, the faculty of Suomi College and Seminary included many able men. Nikander was a classicist who moved easily from Latin to Greek and from Greek to Hebrew. K. A. Arminen kept the teaching of mathematics and related subjects at a high level, as did T. K. Wallenius the teaching of history, Finnish, and Finnish literature. L. W. Lund, a dentistry student, was equally capable in biology. Part-time instructors included Pastors Johan Bäck and Iisakki Katajamaa from neighboring communities; both had masters' degrees. The high academic level of the faculty is evidenced by the fact that when the president's administrative duties began to require more of his time, five different instructors were able, over a period of four years, to teach his Latin classes of different levels, and two seminary instructors were able to take on his Greek classes.

Over many years the debt incurred by the construction of Old Main, as the new building came to be called, was a heavy burden. Nikander, however, was unwavering in his belief that the school, which had been started through great effort, was headed in the right direction. The following story illustrates his attitude. One Sunday evening, when a certain farmer was driving him back home to Hancock from a meeting in South Range, he asked his driver to stop the horse by a big tree. Nikander stepped down from the vehicle and begged the farmer to do the same. Then, kneeling together at the foot of the tree, they prayed God to bless Suomi College. The problem of the debt was taken up at the annual church convention held in New Castle, Pennsylvania, in 1918. It was decided there that throughout the synod there should be a "Suomi College Week." Within two years the debt was paid.

Nikander died early in 1919, leaving Suomi College as his permanent memorial. The student body numbered 165 in the year he died. That figure was not surpassed until twenty-seven years later, in 1946, when his son, V. K. Nikander, was president of the college.

Up to 1920, Suomi College had three departments: the academy, the seminary, established in 1904, and the commercial department, started in 1906. The commercial department grew to such an extent that in some years it included 65 percent of the enrollment. More jobs were always available at the end of a school year to those who had completed their studies in the department than there were graduates to fill them. Music, which had always been an important part of the curriculum, came into its own in 1920 when a music department was established.

After J. K. Nikander's death, John Wargelin became the president of Suomi College and held the position up to 1927. The most important development during his presidency was the changing of the school to a junior college. It was a logical development. Although the seminary had changed from a two-year curriculum to a three-year curriculum within a few years of its establishment, experience had shown that students who went into the seminary directly from the academy were not able, in many cases, to attain the maturity for the ministry that the rapidly rising educational level of Finnish Americans was demanding of persons in positions of leadership. At this point the possibility of making the school a four-year college was considered, but that was financially impossible.

The junior college opened in the fall of 1923 with an enrollment of five students. There were 47 students in the academy and 42 in the commercial department. The beginning was difficult, for by 1926 the enrollment in the junior college was only eight. But the following year there were 36 students in the department, and a year later there were 70. Graduation from the junior college now became a requirement for enrollment in the seminary. The academy had been approved by the University of Michigan from 1920 on. The junior college also received their seal of approval.

After Dr. Wargelin left the presidency of Suomi College, Antti Lepisto was selected as his successor. Lepisto was born in Mäntyharju in 1883. He earned his bachelor of arts degree at the University of Chicago and was ordained in 1921. The most important occurrence during his term of office was the starting of a Bible school in connection with the college. Its purpose was to provide lay workers for congregations. The Bible school closed when Lepisto left his position in 1930 and Wargelin returned to the presidency.[56]

In the summer of 1930 a big campaign for the collection of money for capital as well as for a new building was started. The goal was $300,000, of which only $47,000 was obtained. The result, however, was that with the help of this money the college was able to survive the Great Depression of the early 1930s whereas other similar institutions had to close their doors. When Wargelin left in 1937, Dr. Viljo Nikander was called to take over the work which his father, J. K. Nikander, had begun.

Viljo Kustaa Nikander was born in Hancock on August 3, 1903. He completed his studies for the ministry in the Suomi Seminary in 1925 and earned his master's degree at the University of Chicago in 1928. In 1935 he completed his doctorate at Harvard University. The greatest accomplishment of his ten-year presidency was the acquisition of a new building, Nikander Hall, planned by architect Eliel Saarinen and his son-in-law, architect J. R. F. Swanson. It was planned to accommodate 150 students. It included a number of classrooms, a combination gymnasium-auditorium, a library, and a laboratory. The building with its furnishings cost $125,000, the greater part of which was obtained through collection campaigns directed by business manager Urho W. Tervo of the college, and Dr. O. H. Pankoke.

While Nikander was in office, World War II occurred. Young men went into military service and young women into war work. Student enrollment fell to 52, rising in 1946, after the end of the war, to

174, the largest enrollment up to this time. Nikander paid special attention to the qualifications of his teaching staff. The faculty often included as many as four persons with doctorates. As a rule, the seminary instructors had doctor's degrees.

When Nikander left Suomi College in 1947 to become a professor of philosophy at Wagner College, Suomi College entered a phase in which over a period of thirteen years, five persons served it as president, indicating the weakness of the board of directors. Presidents from 1947 to 1960 were as follows: Pastor Carl Tamminen from 1947 to 1949, Pastor Bernhard H. P. Hillila from 1949 to 1952, Pastor Edward J. Isaac from 1952 to 1954, David T. Halkola form 1954 to 1959, and Dr. Raymond Wargelin from 1959 to 1960.[57] The enrollment remained comparatively small, being under 100 in 1950–51. The financial situation also continued to grow worse. By 1959, debts had increased to $63,000, and credit was no longer obtainable. The president resigned and the board asked Raymond Wargelin, president of the synod, to take on the presidency of the college temporarily, until a new president could be found.[58]

Ralph J. Jalkanen, pastor of the Bethany Congregation in Ashtabula, Ohio, was now called to the presidency of Suomi College. Jalkanen was born in Hancock on August 8, 1918. His parents had come to the Copper Country from Sysmä, Finland. Jalkanen completed his studies for the ministry in the Suomi Seminary in 1943 and received the master's degree from Roosevelt University in 1955. Two of his first tasks as president of the college were to recruit more students and to obtain money for the school. He was so successful in both endeavors that at the time of the merger of Lutheran churches in 1962 Suomi College was free of debt and the enrollment had risen to 250.

The next step in the development of Suomi College was the inauguration of a building program. The Lutheran Church in America, into which the synod had merged, was in a position to allocate more funds for the college than the Suomi Synod had been able to supply. Copper Country businessmen collected large amounts of money, and the federal government in Washington began to provide aid for the building programs of institutions of higher education to satisfy the needs of the rapidly growing population. With funds available from these sources, Suomi College was able to build a new student center with dormitories for men and women, a dining room, and a coffee shop. In addition, construction was started in 1966 on a new library and laboratory building. Furthermore, two private homes had been purchased for use as dormitories, and the sixty-year-old Book Concern building had been acquired in 1965 and was being used for art and music and some commercial subjects. The college now had seven buildings. along with the increase in space there was also a rapid increase in enrollment so that in the fall of 1966 it passed the 400 mark.

Since Suomi College became a junior college in 1923, scores of persons have taught there. Of them, only a few longtime faculty members and some in special areas of service will be mentioned. Kosti Arho from Naantali, Finland, was the librarian and instructor in Finnish and Finnish history from 1922 to 1948. Ellen Ryynanen succeeded him as librarian, serving also as instructor in English. She was followed some years later by teacher-librarian Alma Van Slyke, a daughter of Victor Burman, one of the first women teachers at the college. Starting in 1940, Dr. John E. Anderson was an instructor in chemistry and related subjects for a long time, and starting in 1945, Pastor E. W. Feldscher taught German for many years. Dr. Armas Holmio served for twenty years as lecturer on the life of Christ, philosophy, and European history.

In the history of Suomi College the music and commercial departments, figuratively speaking, make up special chapters of their own. Waino A. Lehto was the head of the commercial department as well as its guiding spirit for over forty years. For the last few years of his term of service he also served as dean of the college. He was born in Worcester, Massachusetts, in 1894. He left Suomi College in 1964, a number of years after the usual age of retirement.

In 1922 Martti Nisonen, an orchestra conductor and composer from Pori, Finland, became the head of the music department of Suomi College. Under his direction the college choir and concerts reached a level of quality higher than before. When Nisonen died in the fall of 1946, Arthur J. Hill succeeded him. The choir then began to make annual spring concert tours, even to places as far away as California, New England, and Canada. At the same time, the choir became the most important advertising medium of the college. Time after time, its tours attracted students from communities not represented at the college before. In 1963, at the time of the Lutheran World Federation Conference in Helsinki, the Suomi College Choir visited Finland, appearing in various programs under the direction of Professor Hill. It also gave religious concerts at churches as far north as Oulu, as well as in Germany, Sweden, and Denmark.

For decades, the Theological Seminary lived a quiet life of its own, giving, however, a religious flavor to the whole college. Seminarians preached at the college chapel services as well as in Copper Country churches, often accompanied by groups of singers selected from the student body. They were the backbone of the Lutheran Student Association. They also conducted Bible study sessions. In the 1950s, after a bachelor's degree had become a requirement for admission to the seminary, the more advanced seminarians often served as part-time instructors in the junior college. Seminary instructors regularly taught the junior college classes in religion and philosophy. Over the years the seminary sponsored courses of lectures for pastors. These were attended not only by pastors of the Suomi Synod but also by ministers of other churches. Lecturers at these courses were nationally and internationally known American theologians. On several occasions theologians from Finland were among the lecturers.

In 1952 the seminary became partially autonomous, with a dean of its own. In 1955, when a layman was the president of Suomi College, the seminary was given additional autonomy. For example, its dean in person presented matters pertaining to the seminary to the board. The seminary was also given a separate budget. Dr. Walter Kukkonen was dean of the seminary from 1952 to 1955, and Dr. Armas K. E. Holmio from 1955 to 1958. After J. K. Nikander, the seminary instructors who taught the longest were Presidents John Wargelin and Viljo K. Nikander and Pastors Kalle Heikki Mannerkorpi, J. T. R. Hartman, Dr. Uuras Saarnivaara, Dr. Armas Holmio, and William S. Avery.

When four years of college became a requirement for admission to the seminary, the question of a merger with some larger Lutheran seminary came up. Such a merger would make available larger faculties and libraries to the seminarians than the Suomi Synod seminary could provide. The question was the cause of some controversy within the synod, with the older and younger elements in opposition to each other. The older people were mostly of the opinion that those concerned should quietly await the outcome of the discussions in progress about a possible merger of the synod with three other Lutheran churches, and then, when the Suomi Synod itself was past history, the question of moving the seminary elsewhere should be taken up. They appealed to the fact that the three other churches that were considering the merger were in no hurry to combine any of their institutions before the probable merger. When the matter came up before the congregations in the early part of 1958, the majority of the church members were of the opinion that the seminary should remain in Hancock for the time being. This was the unanimous opinion in Michigan, the synod's largest conference. But when the question came up before the synod convention in Detroit in June 1958, the younger people were in the majority, and the proposal that the seminary should be merged with the Chicago Lutheran Seminary in Maywood received 167 votes in its favor; votes in favor of staying in Hancock numbered 149. The merger was accomplished that fall. The board selected Dr. Walter J. Kukkonen and Pastor Karlo Keljo to teach at Maywood as representatives of the synod.

Over a period of fifty-four years, 119 men were ordained from the Suomi Seminary. By the spring of 1966, 34 of them had died, 11 had retired, and 74 were still active in the ministry.[59]

16 The Swedish Finns in Michigan

Broadly speaking, the people of Finland are Finnish, but because of the historical development of the nation, it is a bilingual country. The great majority of the people speak Finnish; a small minority speak Swedish. Serving as a sort of link between these two language groups there are many persons who speak both languages.

Among the hundreds of Finns who settled in the Delaware area, there were also some Swedish Finns. The Swedish-language passenger lists of the ships that brought the early immigrants to America and the colonial Swedish church records in which even the people of Savo have been provided with made-up foreign names, have frequently misled researchers and caused them to exaggerate the number of Swedish settlers, sometimes even to ignoring the Finns completely.[1]

The reasons for the Swedish Finns' settling in America during the later period of immigration were the same as those of the Finnish-speaking Finns. Seamen left their ships at American seaports; overcrowding at home forced many persons to seek a livelihood across the sea; the California Gold Rush attracted some; the desire to see the world motivated others. Numerous Swedish Finns of noble rank went to Russia, where foreigners and those speaking west European languages could expect to have more brilliant careers than they could find in the small country of their birth. They were often quickly Russianized. Excepting in the seventeenth and eighteenth centuries, the movement of Swedish Finns to Sweden was infrequent.[2] It was from the ranks of the common people that immigration to America occurred. Only a few educated persons came with them, although the percentage was higher among the Swedish Finns who came than among the Finnish Finns.

Between 1894 and 1913, a total of 39,578 persons emigrated from the Swedish-speaking rural parishes of Finland and 166,636 from the Finnish-speaking parishes. Because Swedish-speaking parishes often included a fairly large minority of Finnish-speaking Finns and the Finnish-speaking parishes did not usually include many Swedish-speaking Finns, the figures given cannot be considered absolutely accurate.

Pastor Carl J. Silfversten's estimate that one in four Finnish immigrants to America was a Swedish Finn is, in any case, an exaggeration. Taking into account the second-, and to some extent, possibly the third-generation Swedish Finns in America, he came to the conclusion that in 1930 there were at the most 76,000 Swedish Finns in this country.[3] Considering the smallness of the area in Finland from which they came—the south Ostrobothnian coastal parishes and the Åland Islands—the assumption that the figure was actually much smaller may be closer to the truth. The few immigrants from Nyland and the Turku Archipelago would not add much to the total. It is also to be noted that during the period of the heaviest emigration, government statistics did not indicate the language spoken by the emigrant. Of the immigrants to America from the Swedish-speaking parishes of Finland, a larger percentage returned home than of immigrants from the Finnish-speaking parishes. In any case, it is true that more Swedish Finns than Finnish Finns, in proportion to their representation in the total population of Finland, emigrated, and that consequently, rumors of a threat of a loss of population among the Swedish element in Finland were based on fact.[4]

In the eastern states, the Swedish Finns settled mostly in New York and in Worcester and Gardner, Massachusetts. There were smaller settlements in Quincy, Norwood, Springfield, and Fitchburg. There was also, for a time, a considerable settlement of Swedish Finns in Philadelphia. In the John Morton Building there were, among others, rooms named for Fredrika Bremer and Pietari Kalm.[5] The largest group of Swedish Finns to immigrate to Wisconsin settled in Superior; there was a smaller settlement in Ashland. In 1930 the number of Swedish Finns in Duluth was estimated to be 2,000. There was also a scattering of them in the iron range towns of Minnesota. Considerable numbers of them settled in the West: Butte, Montana; Telluride, Colorado; Bingham and Eureka, Utah; Seattle, Everett, Tacoma, Aberdeen, Hoquiam, Rochester, and Hartford, Washington; Portland, Astoria,

Marshfield, and North Bend, Oregon; San Francisco and Eureka, California.

Sakari Topelius said of the Ostrobothnian Swedes: "One sees them as craftsmen everywhere in cities and on country estates. They build ships and boats, houses and factories, more skillfully than anyone else."

The statement is true. But because they usually have been too few in number for group activities among themselves, they have joined Swedish congregations and organizations and, sometimes, Finnish groups. In Michigan, however, they have had a fairly large amount of independent activity, which may be divided into three types: congregations, temperance societies, and the Order of Runeberg.

Church Activity

Lutheran church activity among Swedish Finns in Michigan is thought to have begun as early as 1805, when worship services for them were held in Metropolitan. Pastor C. P. Edblom started a congregation there in 1895. It joined the Augustana Synod in 1902. Church activity at Dollar Bay, near Hancock, where Pastor J. K. Nikander preached in the early 1890s, became greater. His work was continued by another pastor of the Suomi Synod, Johannes Bäck. A congregation was organized and built a church of the Augustana Synod in 1902. The congregation included many Finns. In the 1950s and 1960s, the pastor of the Dollar Bay congregation was John F. Simonson, who also served Suomi College as an instructor in Bible literature and German.

Church work also made considerable progress in the Sion congregation of Ironwood, which was organized in 1908 and began its regular activities with services on Christmas morning. A church of their own was completed in 1912. Among the pastors of this congregation were Carl J. Silfversten, born in Närpiö in 1879, and Frans E. W. Kastman, born in Övermark in 1881, both of whom also served other Swedish-Finnish congregations at various times. The pastor of the Ironwood church also served a small congregation in Bessemer. In Brevort, in the eastern part of the Upper Peninsula, there was a small congregation made up mostly of people form Åland. It was served by Augustana pastors who lived in Newberry. In 1930, the total membership of the Metropolitan, Dollar Bay, Ironwood, Bessemer, and Brevort congregations was about 800. There were also large numbers of Swedish Finns in the congregations of the Augustana Synod in the Upper Peninsula. For example, 75 percent of the congregation at Crystal Falls were Swedish Finns; Escanaba, too, had a large number.

The Swedish Finns also had seventeen small Baptist congregations scattered about the United States. Five of them were in Michigan, namely in Dollar Bay, Felch, Gladstone, and Negaunee in the Upper Peninsula, and Roscommon, south of Grayling, in the Lower Peninsula. The total membership of these congregations in the 1930s was about 225.[6]

Temperance Societies

The Swedish Finnish temperance movement in America has already been discussed. Carl J. Silfversten, in his introduction to a short history of Swedish Finnish temperance societies, wrote as follows:

> American freedom included also the freedom to become intoxicated. . . . Swedish Finns were no exception to this rule. They have always aspired to be a little better than other people, and in that they have succeeded quite well. When others had their measures of liquor, the Swedish Finns also had theirs. Some drank in moderation, others, quite the contrary. But very few would leave their glasses untouched. . . . Before, the saloon business was considered as honorable as any other business. In most areas where Swedish Finns settled, there was always someone among them who would become a saloon keeper. Why not they, as well as others? The saloons were men's clubs, were they not, where the evils of the day were discussed in all seriousness. . . . So the years rolled on. The workingman became poorer and his family suffered; this was the rule. And the saloon keeper became rich, or so it was assumed, but this was an exception. However, a few persons began to think, and they thought as well as they knew how. They saw the saloons becoming a curse to the people and expressed their conviction publicly. Others awoke from the lethargy of habit and from the desire for liquor, stopped drinking, and became temperance men.[7]

Some Swedish Finns joined the Swedish branches of the Good Templars; others joined Finnish temperance societies. The first Swedish-Finnish temperance society was organized in Worcester on February 27, 1892. It was given the Finnish name Aavasaksa. It was active for twenty-two years, ceasing activity on January 3, 1914. The next temperance society to be organized was Vasa Stjärna (Star of Vaasa) in Escanaba, Michigan, in 1895. It joined the Good Templars but ended its activity the same year. In January 1897, Vasalåset (Lock of Vaasa) was organized in Whitingsville, Massachusetts; on April 11 of the same year, Sveaborg was started in Gardner; and on January 30 of the following year, Morgonstjärnan (Morning Star) in Ironwood. At this time there was a regular temperance revival among the Swedish Finns, which by 1910 had given birth to about fifty temperance societies, some of them, however, being of very short duration while others continued successful activity for a long time.[8]

Twenty Swedish Finnish societies joined the SKRV (the Finnish National Temperance Brotherhood). Their names are found in this present work in the chapter on the temperance movement. Of these societies, twelve were in Michigan but accurate information is available about only a few of them.

Victor Tornquist, Adolf Nyman, and Felix Henrickson were officers of the Morgonstjärnan in Ironwood. Soon after the society was organized, they made a "missionary trip" to Bessemer, with the result that the temperance society Nord was organized there among the Swedish Finns on April 24. It was no. 116 in the SKRV. Andrew Forslund was elected president and John Jacobson secretary.[9] At a meeting held on June 18, 1898, in the Kansan Koti (People's Home) in Negaunee, the Österbotten no. 118 was organized, twenty persons joining on that day. They had come from Swedish parishes of Ostrobothnia and gave the society the name of their home area. Martin Martinson was chosen president and Victor Nilson secretary.

In 1899, six Swedish-Finnish temperance societies joined the SKRV, all of them in Michigan. Among these were Liljan i Dalen (Lily of the Valley) of Amasa, Stjärnan i Hemmet (Star of Home) of Crystal Falls, Söner of Wasa (Sons of Vaasa) of Gladstone, and Klippan (Cliff) of Ludington.

In 1902 there were one hundred societies in the SKRV. Eighty-six of them were Finnish and fourteen Swedish Finnish. There was no difference of opinion between the two groups, but there was a language barrier, for only a very few members knew both Swedish and Finnish. The following paragraph is from the minutes of the 1902 annual meeting of the SKRV:

> A decision was made to ask the Swedish Finnish societies by circular letter if they would be interested in establishing a central organization of their own. The purpose of the Board of Directors was not to pressure them in any sense of the word to do so; they were simply of one mind in thinking that temperance work among them might thus be enlivened and acquire a different outlook. For this reason they hoped that even the annual meeting would not hinder, but rather help them whenever it should be right to do so.

The result of this suggestion was that representatives of the Swedish Finnish societies met in Crystal Falls on November 20 and 21 of that year. Advocates of a new central organization were Alex Pantti and Jacob Kaminen. The Svensk-Finska Nykterhets-Förbundet af Amerika (Swedish-Finnish Temperance League of America) was organized, to begin activity on January 1, 1903. At the time of its organization there were sixteen societies, with a total of over six hundred members, in the league. At that time, too, the hope was expressed that "brotherhood and a nationalistic spirit would prevail among them."[10]

Additional societies soon joined the Swedish-Finnish Temperance League. Just four days after the decision to form a league had been reached, the Syskonringen (Sisterhood) of Dollar Bay, which had been formed by the union of two previously established local societies, joined it. Other Michigan societies which also joined soon were the Lilja på Fjällen (Lily of the Mountain) of Felch, and the Hem av Enighet (Home of Unity) of Escanaba. In 1903, the Dalens Ros (Rose of the Valley) of Quinnesec, the Tärnan (Tern) of Ramsay, and the Wasa Älskling (Sweetheart of Vaasa) of Baraga were organized.

Because the Swedish Finnish population was so scattered, it was 1906 before a new temperance society, Lilla Hoppet (Little Hope) of Thompson, was organized in Michigan. Alpens Ros (Rhododendron) of Jessieville followed in 1908, and Frid i Hemmet (Peace of Home) of Hancock in 1909. In 1911 Swedish Finns organized Vänners Borg (Friends' Castle) in Manistique; in 1912, the Valborg in Munising; and in 1915 Ny Borg (New Castle) in Newberry.

Toward the end, there were eighty societies with a total membership of about 2,600 in the Swedish-Finnish Temperance League. The center of activity for the league was Michigan, where most of the annual meetings were held; for example, in Negaunee in 1903, in Ironwood in 1904, and in Escanaba in 1907. Because the societies were scattered across the country from the Atlantic to the Pacific, communication was difficult. This fact, plus the repeal of the prohibition law, caused the eventual cessation of temperance activity.[11]

The songbook used for a long time was *Sångbok för S.F.S.F. i Amerika*, the content of which was typical of the romantic Finnish nationalism of Runeberg and Topelius. Collan's "Savolaisen Laulu" (Song of one from Savo) was included in it in the Finnish language. As for socialism and communism, neither was at any time an important influence among the Swedish Finns of America.

The Order of Runeberg

Swedish Finns looking for security for the future at first joined either Finnish or Swedish illness and burial associations. They organized their own first insurance company of this kind, called the Imatra, in Worcester, Massachusetts, on May 2, 1889. It was followed in 1894 by the Finska Brödraföreningen Wasa of New York, and many others. In Michigan, similar companies were organized from 1898 on in Bessemer, Ironwood, and Calumet.

In actual practice it often happened that the same persons were officers in both the temperance societies and the insurance companies. Toward the end of World War I, the idea was born that a new organization should be set up that would inherit the purposes and tasks of the two above-mentioned organizations and absorb them both. The plan was supported in *Ledstjärnan*, a temperance publication, and in *Finska Amerikanaren*, a Swedish Finnish general newspaper.

Fears were expressed by members of the temperance societies that in practice the new organization might compromise their rule of total abstinence. Among the insurance people there was some hesitation about coming under the authority of temperance people. Both groups had their annual meetings in Waukegan, Illinois, in August 1920. The final outcome, after extended discussion, was a decision to unite. There were nine suggestions for a name for the new organization, but Orden av Runeberg won on the very first ballot. Thus the name of the great poet of Finland and all Scandinavia became the symbol of the highest aspirations of the Swedish Finns of America.

The purpose of the Runebergorden, as it was called, was made clear in the preamble to its constitution:

> The purpose of the Runebergorden is to gather together in brotherly harmony Swedish- or English-speaking men and women regardless of their political or religious views; to practice friendship, fellowship, and helpfulness; to foster temperance and cultural activities; to collect funds jointly to aid those who through illness or accident are unable to work; and in general to promote the welfare of our people who live in this country and support them in their efforts to get ahead.

The Order of Runeberg, which soon extended its activities to include the Swedish Finns of Canada, divided into the Eastern, Central, and Western districts. The total membership, which was 4,500 at the time the order was established, soon doubled, and their assets amounted to $100,000. Insurance money was paid at rates up to $10 per week for twenty weeks per year for one illness. The payment for funeral expenses was $125. In the first years, money taken in annually amounted to about $86,000, and money paid out, to $81,000.

During the time of the Russo-Finnish wars, the relief funds

collected by the Order of Runeberg for the members' former homeland were considerable. The president who served as head of the organization for the longest time was U. S. A. Heggblom of Detroit.

Other Activities

Among the Swedish Finns there was great interest in music and singing, a heritage form the music festivals of their home parishes in Finland. The center of musical activity in Michigan was Ironwood, where there were four choruses, and an orchestra called the Topelius Orkesteri. It may well be that the Swedish Finns were ahead of their Finnish countrymen musically in their own areas, but in sports and gymnastics the situation was exactly the opposite. Also, because of their widely scattered population, the Swedish Finns did not have as many libraries as the Finnish Finns.

In the publication of newspapers and periodicals the two language groups differed considerably. The Swedish Finns had at their disposal the wealth of publications put out by the Augustana Synod's publishing house, whereas the Finnish-speaking Finns had to depend on publications of their own. In spite of the availability of Swedish-language publications, the Swedish Finns produced independently a fairly large number of different kinds of newspapers and periodicals. The first of them, a Swedish and Finnish paper attempted by the Aavasaksa Temperance Society in the fall of 1896, died at its inception. The next attempt succeeded: *Finska Amerikanaren* was started in Worcester in January 1897. It was moved to Brooklyn after two years.

Proof of the Finnish nationalist point of view of *Finska Amerikanaren* is seen in the fact that during the time when Bobrikov was the tsar's governing representative in Finland, it was banned in that country. The paper also took a nationalistic stand on the events of 1918, thus losing a large number of leftist subscribers. Later, the paper was renamed *Norden.* Its seventieth anniversary was in 1966. After *Ledstjärnan*, which had become the voice of the Order of Runeberg in 1920, ceased publication, *Norden* took over its obligations, remaining in publication until 1982.

17 Finland and the Finns of Michigan

Kaisu-Mirjami Rydberg, whose father Riippa had been an editor of the newspaper *Toveri* in Astoria, wrote in her travelogue how Ragnar Ölander, secretary to the managing editor of the *Hufvudstadstbladet*, the leading Swedish-language newspaper in Finland, surprised his Finnish audience in Astoria with the purity of his Finnish and with his democratic behavior: "A Swedish gentleman—and he didn't let anyone help him with his coat; he wasn't proud."[1] This story reflects the persistent belief among the older immigrant generations that the Finnish people were divided into two classes: the poor and downtrodden and those favored by Fortune. The great majority of immigrants belonged to the former class.

In many a case, departure from the land of his birth was marked by tears and anguish for the emigrant.[2] The journey under primitive conditions on a ship from Oulu, Vaasa, Hanko, Helsinki, or Viipuri to England, and from there on a larger but equally disreputable ocean liner to America, often remained in the memory as a torturing nightmare. At his destination in some small mining town of Michigan, it might well be that life was even more difficult than the life he had struggled through in Finland. Melancholy and bitterness followed. When, in addition, knowledge of the English language, which would have made the earning of one's bread easier, was poor or entirely lacking, there was nothing to do but isolate oneself with others of one's own nationality.[3]

When to all this is added the accusatory spirit in which those who were left in Finland criticized those who emigrated, it is all the more remarkable and gratifying that such an authentic, healthy feeling for their nationality still continued to live in the hearts of the older Finnish immigrants. It centered around home and nature in the fatherland. An eighty-five-year-old sang thus to an eighty-year-old friend on the friend's birthday:

> Tree in the yard of my childhood home, my weeping birch,
> In my wanderings I'll always remember you with tear-wet eyes
> and cheeks.
>
> Tree in the yard of my childhood home, are you still there
> At the corner of the cabin where I was born, beside my
> mother's path to the well?
>
> Tree in the yard of my childhood home, do you remember a
> young boy?
> Do you remember the heart I carved in your outer bark?[4]

This feeling of the Finns for their nationality was associated with religious feeling. At church services of immigrants the words of the Hebrew patriot in Psalm 137 were often quoted: "If I forget thee, O Jerusalem, let my right hand forget her cunning. If I do not remember thee, let my tongue cleave to the roof of my mouth, if I prefer not Jerusalem above my chief joy." In his poem, "Eräs Farmari" (A certain farmer), Eetu Aaltio has his protagonist speak thus (free translation into prose):

> Why is it that longing fills my heart whenever the summer breeze stirs in the treetops? . . . Yes, I know the reason. It is because I cannot divide my love. As a child I played near my mother on my father's land. There I picked berries in the fields. I left my heart there, and that's where my thoughts return. Here, even Christmas is like any other day. Here, I have hayfields and meadows. I can hear the bells of my own cattle. . . . But a yearning fills my heart, even though fortune has favored me.[5]

The most precious treasure of the immigrant was his mother tongue. Up to 1900, Michigan Finns called the English language "lontoo" (London). They were able to get along without it in their totally Finnish communities. The Finns who went to school beyond the elementary grades in America and those who had learned English were called "high-toned Finns." To the immigrant, the Finnish language became a fortress to which he could withdraw from contact with the outside world:

In the Finnish language my mother sang
  While I lay in a cradle near by.
So now I, too, can express my feelings
  In the Finnish language.

I shall preserve my beautiful language;
  Like a treasure I shall cherish it.
Then, when I hear my Finland's wistful call,
  I shall really understand it.[6]

Political Activity

It was possible, however, to leave this fortress of isolation. For example, when Russian oppression began in Finland, a Finnish national guard was established in Ironwood, with the purpose of joining in the actual conflict against Russia whenever it should begin. The city armory was used for drilling. The commander of the guard was a man by the name of Ritari. The language used in the drills was Russian because Ritari had been a soldier of the Finnish guard in Finland and knew only the Russian vocabulary of military drill. Similar guards sprang up in several other communities. The Finnish Americans followed closely Finland's struggle for her rights as it was reported in newspapers.

The first mass action of the Michigan Finns in behalf of the Finnish cause occurred in Negaunee in the late winter of 1899. A public meeting held there was in favor of sending a letter signed by Finnish Americans to the president of the United States requesting that he take action against Russia's policy of oppression toward Finland. On April 10 in Calumet, a similar mass meeting selected a committee of three to prepare a similar communication. This committee, consisting of lawyer Oscar J. Larson, newspaper editor E. E. Takala, and Dr. Carl Sorsen, was also authorized to take the letter to Washington to be presented to President William McKinley.

The committee prepared a substantial twelve-page letter explaining the autonomy of Finland under Russia, with its own laws and institutions, and deploring the recent violations of Finland's rights as a political state. Early in June, Larson and Sorsen went to Washington; Takala was unable to accompany them. On the morning of Sunday, June 11, they were greeted by Senator McMillan from Michigan, who expressed pleasure at the fact that he was seeing them at such an opportune time, for that very afternoon he was going for a drive with President McKinley and would have a fine opportunity to talk with him about Finland and to deliver the Finnish American communication to him.[7] The result was that at the first peace conference held in The Hague, from May to July 1899, the U.S. delegate was instructed to bring up before the conference the problem of Finland. The discussion, however, was ended when Russia explained that the question was one of Russian internal policy and had no place in this conference, which had been called by Tsar Nicholas II for considering international matters. The vigor and ability of this committee from Calumet, however, were further demonstrated by the fact that it succeeded in bringing the matter before the legislature of Michigan, which on July 7, 1899, passed a resolution condemning the oppression of Finland by Russia. A practical result of the committee's activities was the publicity given to Finland by American newspapers, especially those of Michigan. Now the American newspapers, which had been accustomed to regarding the tsar of Russia as the very pillar of peace in Europe, began to look at things from other points of view and soon discovered that under pretensions of peace, crying injustice was being done to small nations through oppression and through ignoring their rights.

The Finnish National League of America

The political situation in Finland at this time was becoming more and more tense. The governor-general of Finland, Infantry General Nikolai Ivanovitsh Bobrikov, was given the task of creating the "closest relationship possible" between Finland and Russia. The ultimate aim was the Russification of Finland and the dissolution of the country as an autonomous political state. When Russian acts of oppression resulted in ever-increasing opposition, Bobrikov, in 1903, procured for himself full dictatorial powers, on the strength of which he banished many persons from Finland. Some were sent to Siberia; others were permitted to choose where they would go. Of the latter group, many came to the United States. Among them were newspapermen Severi Nuormaa (1865–1924) and Eero Erkko (1860–1927), founder and editor-in-chief of the newspaper *Päivälehti* and brother of the poet J. H. Erkko.[8] When Erkko arrived in America early in the summer of 1903, the Finns in New York and Brooklyn were without a newspaper, for *Siirtolainen* had moved to Kaleva, Michigan. Erkko started a printing business and a bookstore, and in the fall of the same year edited and published a literary Christmas album *Nuori Suomi* (Young Finland), which was a continuation of the albums he had published in Finland under the same title. A newspaper, *Amerikan Kaiku* (American echo), appeared the following year under his editorship and became in a short time and for a short while a leader among immigrant newspapers.

In his introduction to the first issue of *Nuori Suomi* Erkko wrote: "Conditions in Finland at the present time are dismal. Every mail from there brings new reasons for sorrow and despair." As the shadows deepened over his fatherland, however, Erkko was not inactive. Instead, in his publications, especially *Amerikan Kaiku*, he continued the struggle begun in Finland.

Erkko conceived a plan for a league that would join together the Finns of Finland and the nationalistic-minded Finns in America in a spirit of kinship and of love for the fatherland to help Finland in her struggle for freedom. He thought of Michigan as the home of the league, for there the Finns had the most powerful organizations. The organizational meeting was held in Ishpeming on August 4, 1904. Erkko considered the meeting so important from the viewpoint of Finnish nationalism that he brought with him from Brooklyn the editor-in-chief of *Svenska Amerikanaren*, Judge Edvard J. Antell, who was the acknowledged leader of the Swedish Finns in America.[9] In addition, he also brought Severi Nuormaa, the assistant editor of his own *Amerikan Kaiku.*[10] Victor H. Heini, a director of the Lutheran congregation, also attended.[11] John Ronnberg from Ashtabula was also present, as were C. Ahlskog, Johan Udell, J. Berg, and G. Blomgren from Chicago. There were ten delegates from Michigan: K. Brofelt and J. W. Dickley from Calumet; Dr. J. Jaakkola from Hancock; V. Malin from Marquette; Verner Nikander, J. J. Ventela, and A. Boulson from Negaunee; and Mikko Skytta, Jacob Kaminen, and Matti Lofberg from Ishpeming.[12] The meeting was characterized by a feeling of cheerful expectancy, for the mail from Finland was bringing better news, which was confirmed by the American newspapers. On the morning of the meeting, the newspapers reported that the Russian army was retreating toward Mukden, and that Japanese victories were causing discouragement among the Russian people and in their government. The organization of the Finnish National League of America was unanimously approved. A committee was selected to draw up bylaws and detailed rules and regulations. The second meeting of the Finnish National League, which was also its first annual meeting, was held on June 23–24, 1905, in Chicago. The bylaws were approved. The purpose of the league was

> to be, in spiritual as well as material ways, a bond between Finnish Americans, to awaken and keep alive in them feelings of patriotism and of love for the fatherland, each taking part as much as he can in

political activities. . . . The league is made up of local organizations which have been set up and are active in accordance with the principles given in the preceding clause.

Military defeats in the war against Japan brought about serious disturbances in Russia and a general strike in Finland which forced Nicholas II on November 4, 1905, to return to Finland her political rights. The exiles returned, among them Nuormaa and Erkko, the former to continue his political battle as the editor-in-chief of *Helsingin Sanomat* and later as editor of *Turun Sanomat*, and the latter as a member of the Diet, and from 1908 until his death, as editor-in-chief of *Helsingin Sanomat*. Erkko also served as a member in the first government of independent Finland. Soon after the return of these leaders to Finland, *Amerikan Kaiku* ceased publication, and the Finnish National League, whose directors were firstline citizens of Negaunee and Ishpeming, also ceased to be. There was apparently no room for a newcomer beside the church, the temperance societies, the labor organizations, and the Kaleva order.

In Calumet in November 1905, the Finns of Michigan celebrated Finland's political victory, with Oscar Larson as the main speaker. He expressed joy in the fact that Finland had won through a revolution "in which intellectual weapons, instead of spears and swords, were used." At the same time, among the Finns of Michigan as well as among Finns all over America, a political and Finnish national awakening had occurred. Along with it, another kind of nationalistic movement had also begun among the Finns of Michigan. Its purpose was to provide relief for the people of their famine-stricken fatherland.

Relief for Northern Finland, 1898 and 1902

Histories of Finland tell of numerous bad years, when crops failed. The resultant famines were accompanied by diseases and plagues. The people named the years for the afflictions which characterized them: the Great Cough Year, 1580; the Year of the Great Frost or the Straw Year, 1601–2; the Years of Many Deaths, 1695–97, the Autumn of the Plague, 1710. As has been pointed out in an earlier chapter, the severe famine of 1867–68 was among the causes of emigration.[13] Although 1892 and 1893 were also bad years, they produced no noticeable action among Finnish Americans.

The situation was different, however, in the fall of 1898, when the crops in northern areas of Finland were completely destroyed by frost. Finnish Americans set up numerous relief committees, whose contributions to the stricken areas, according to Ilmonen, amounted to 50,000 marks.[14] Finns in America were so moved by the situation in their former homeland that when a speaker at a meeting in Hancock, for example, showed his audience a sample of the pine-bark bread people were eating in the famine-stricken area, the listeners burst into tears.

The crop failure of 1902 was even more serious, extending as it did over all the northern part of Scandinavia. On November 10, the Finns of Hancock held a meeting at which an eleven-man Finnish American relief committee was selected. The following men were members of the committee: lawyer Oscar J. Larson, Pastors J. K. Nikander and Pekka Airaksinen; Dr. Carl Sorsen; druggist Uno Sodergren; editor N. J. Ahlman; and businessmen J. H. Jasberg, C. J. Wickstrom, Isak Nasi, Andrew Johnson, and August Pelto. This committee became the central agency for the organized collection of relief funds among the Finns of the United States and Canada. According to Dr. Konrad Relander, secretary of Finnish Emergency Relief, this committee sent over 203,000 marks to Finland.[15] The amount actually sent was considerably larger—at least $50,000 in American money—for, to speed things up, money was often sent directly to the church officials of the famine-stricken parishes.

The following story, illustrative of the situation in the areas where famine prevailed, has been preserved. A tenant farmer in Hyrynsalmi went to the church village to seek food. His wife and children stayed at home, where there was bread enough for only a couple of days. The farmer's search appeared to be hopeless, for in house as well as hut, there was a crying need for food. When the last bit of bread had been eaten at home, and the wife and children had become snowbound in their cottage, the husband's absence added to the hardships of the family. Eventually a horsedrawn sleigh from the parsonage arrived with the man and flour and other food. To help out in such situations, people who had come to the Copper Country from Hyrynsalmi collected money and sent it to Pastor Vayrynen of their home parish, asking him to buy food with it for those in greatest need.

The Finnish American Relief Committee undertook widespread activity by sending Dr. Carl Sorsen to speak on behalf of the Finns of northern Finland in New York, Chicago, Minneapolis, and elsewhere. The result was that in Chicago, for example, newspapers such as the *Daily News* and the Swedish *Skandinavien* took hold of the matter and arranged for collections which brought in tens of thousands of dollars. Dr. Louis Klopsch, editor of the New York publication the *Christian Herald* made a quick trip to the famine-stricken area to investigate. The result was that the *Christian Herald* made an appeal to the Protestant Christians of America, which raised $100,000 in money, large amounts of clothing, and a shipload of grain.

The famine in northern Finland forced thousands of people to emigrate. They came to America and Canada, where they already had relatives in better circumstances. Vihtori Peltonen, whose pen name was Johannes Linnankoski, published a booklet titled *Amerikkaan Siirtymisestä* (About moving to America) in which, without understanding this cause of departure from Finland, he condemned emigration as a betrayal of the fatherland. Many persons in Finland saw the ever-increasing emigration as a continuation of the national disaster of the years of famine. However, the relief work which had been initiated by the Finns of Michigan and which had become widespread under the leadership of their committee, received increasing recognition. An understanding of the positive aspects of emigration gradually developed in Finland, and a desire to get to know better the Finnish Americans and their way of life in their new homeland was born.

Visits and Return Visits to 1939

Over the decades, a large number of people from Finland have visited in Michigan and in other Finnish areas of America. Of these visitors only the most important will be mentioned—those who through lectures and travelogues made Michigan and the Finns of the state known in the old country.

In the forming of official and unofficial ties through personal contact, the church was of first importance because of the fact that the Suomi Synod was recognized in Finland and America as an offshoot of the Church of Finland, and because the National Church and the Laestadian or Apostolic Lutheran Church each had a close tie-in with corresponding revival movements in Finland. Three pastors—Matti Tarkkanen, Kaarlo Salovaara, and F. E. Blomberg—who had worked in America, proposed in the synodal meeting held in Savonlinna in 1907 that a "closer relationship should be established between the Finnish Evangelical Lutheran Church of Finland and the Suomi Synod of America." The matter was left for the bishops' conference which, however, was not able to act until Finland became an independent nation.

Already in the previous century, Aleksandra Gripenberg (1857–1913) and especially Konni Zilliacus (1855–1924) in their travelogues and the latter also in novels, had written about the Finns in America. They wrote in Swedish, but even in Finnish translation their works had no significance as bridges between the Finns of the old homeland and those of the new world. Not until after the turn of the century was a conscious effort made to bridge the gap between the two countries. Usually these early "bridge builders" traveled under their own sponsorship, although they did, at the same time, represent one aspect or another of church work.

In the spring of 1900, at the very threshold of the new century, Pastor Matti Tarkkanen, the secretary of the Seamen's Mission of Finland, visited Michigan and preached in churches of Marquette County and the Copper Country. Those who heard him remembered for a long time his allegation that of every one hundred married men who had come to America from Finland, an average of forty had neglected the families they had left behind.[16] That same year also saw the first known visit of a Finnish artist to America. The visitor was the composer Oskari Merikanto (1868–1924), well-known organist of St. John's Church in Helsinki. He gave organ concerts in many Finnish churches in America. Because of this he was nicknamed "Amerikanto" in Finland. The next visitor was Dr. Arthur Hjelt (1868–1931) whose activities in Hancock in the summer of 1901 have already been mentioned.[17] After his visit, Hjelt became an internationally known biblical scholar.

Another important visitor to Michigan was Vilho Reima, a teacher and a former president of the Koitto Temperance Society of Helsinki. He made two trips to America, one in 1906 and the other in 1910, lecturing mainly at temperance society meetings. On his first trip he visited the prison in Marquette, where all the twenty-one Finnish inmates were brought out to hear him. After his lecture he asked the men why they were there. Nineteen answered "Liquor did it." The warden spoke well of the men, saying that if people outside the prison behaved as well as the Finnish prisoners inside, the building would be mostly unoccupied. *Kansan Laulukirja* (People's songbook) edited by Reima and extensively used by Finnish immigrants, remains as a remembrance of his visits.[18] He also published two lively accounts of his visits to America.[19]

In the fall of 1912, authoress Aino Malmberg (1865–1933) made the first of her many lecture tours to America. She had taught English, and she had also been very active in the Finnish underground movement against Russia. From 1909 on, she lived in London, making lecture tours from there to America, and even to Australia, to explain Finland's struggle for her rights. She joined the British Labour party and, among other things, acted as interpreter for the future prime minister, MacDonald, at foreign congresses. When Aino Malmberg lectured in Upper Michigan, *Amerikan Suometar* suspected her of being a

Marxist. The editors apparently were not familiar with the Labour Party of England.[20]

A prominent Finnish churchman also visited Michigan in 1912. He was Jooseppi Mustakallio (1857–1923), director of the Finnish Missionary Society. K. L. Tolonen, a veteran of missionary work in Africa for the society, had brought about a close relationship between the Finnish society and the Suomi Synod. Before they started to work for the Suomi Synod in 1903, Samuli Heikki Rönkä (1863–1934) and his wife Ida (1874–1946), had also been missionaries in Africa, serving the Finnish Missionary Society. Another "African" was Albin Savola (1867–1934) in Ishpeming. He accepted a call to return to the Finnish Missionary Society in Finland, where he did some basic kinds of literary work. Mustakallio was present at farewell gatherings held by many Marquette County congregations to honor Savola.

In January 1911, through the initiative of the People's Enlightenment Society, plans were made for a great congress of emigrants to be held in Helsinki in the summer of 1912. The chairman of the planning committee was Eero Erkko, and the secretary was Vilho Reima. Members, among others, were Akseli Rauanheimo and Matti Helenius-Seppala. The purpose of the congress was to form an extensive organization of emigrants. However, there was disruptive discord in America. The SKRV could not agree on joint activities with other national-minded Finns, and the socialists condemned the whole business as a small bourgeois attempt to deceive the workingman. Nevertheless, about 750 Finnish Americans went to Helsinki on different ships and without organized leadership. They were sometimes met in England by persons from Finland. At their destination great celebrations were held. The best representation of Finnish Americans was from among the girls who worked as servants in New York. There were only a few Finns in the assemblage from Michigan and other Midwestern states. Aune Krohn's poem welcoming the visitors ended with these words:

Welcome, visitors from the West,
To renew old ties,
Ties with the land of your birth,
Ties with your fathers' God!

However, in comparison with the 750 who attended the emigrant congress in Helsinki, only two Finnish Americans attended the one held later in Lahti, and even they did not represent any special group or organization.

In the spring of 1913, Aarni Voipio, later a professor of practical theology at the University of Helsinki, visited America. He stayed a week or two in the Cooper Country, residing with an old friend, Pastor M. J. Kuusi, in the parsonage in South Range. Voipio's travelogue is exceptionally worthwhile reading.[21]

The next year saw the beginning of World War I, which eventually involved even the United States. During its last phases, a revolution began in Russia, which led Finland into the war for independence and to the genesis of Finland as an independent state. During this period of war, the Michigan Finns' contacts with their former homeland were very haphazard, often even nonexistent for long periods. On December 6, 1917, Finland declared itself an independent state and confirmed its independence in the winter and spring of 1918 through the heavy sacrifices which the war demanded.

Soon after the war had ended and Finland had reached a climactic point in her eight hundred-year, war-filled history by taking her place among the free nations of the world, lively interchange of visits with the Finns in America began. The first important visitor to come to America from Finland after the war was opera singer Ester Laitinen, who arrived in February 1920 for a yearlong visit. She pleased both the general American and the Finnish American audiences with her pleasant personality and her great artistic talent. At Lincoln Hall in Hancock she amazed her audience by singing in seven languages without using sheet music or any other aid.[22]

While Ester Laitinen was giving concerts in America, the Finnish Louhi Band from Monessen, Pennsylvania, was touring Finland. Directed by George Wahlstrom, the Louhi, a Janizary band, attracted much favorable attention with its fine performances all over Finland from Helsinki to Rovaniemi. Pastor F. Y. Joki accompanied the band as a lecturer. In Finland the band sold copies of *Tervehdys Suomelle* (A greeting to Finland), which had been edited by Yrjo Sjoblom and F. Y. Joki. It consisted of over one hundred pages and was richly illustrated. Hundreds of Finnish Americans joined the Louhi Band on this trip to Finland. There were, however, only a few persons from Michigan among them.

On the last day of the same year, Lauri Perala of Alavus, Agrarian member of Parliament, arrived in New York. He traveled in Finnish areas of America until March 1921. In North Dakota he met his brother, whom he had not seen since his early childhood. His longest visit was in the Copper Country, where J. H. Jasberg was his host. After a lecture in the Pelkie church, the usual discussion followed, led in this case by a woodsman who sharply criticized White Finland. In the first pew sat two small boys in ragged clothes. Perala felt sorry for the children and gave them the money which had been collected for him. He told them to buy themselves some clothes. The next morning the woodsman came to Perala to apologize for his behavior the previous evening and also to thank him for his gift to the children, who happened to be his sons.[23]

When Finland had attained independence, the church was able to act on the emigrant question. After delays caused by the wars, the bishops' conference held on October 18, 1920, passed a resolution to the effect that a representative of the church should go to America the following year to participate in the twenty-fifth anniversary celebration of Suomi College. Bishop Juho Rudolf Koskimies of Oulu was chosen to make the trip. He arrived in New York on April 13, 1921, and stayed in the United States for three months. He was in Michigan from May 8 to the end of the month, visiting eleven centrally located churches where people gathered from neighboring villages. He stayed in Ishpeming for four days and in Crystal Falls, Ironwood, and Hancock for three days each. He preached to the Swedes in Ishpeming, Newberry, Crystal Falls, Amasa, and Ironwood, as well as to the Laestadians in Calumet. The greater number of meetings at which he spoke were held for members of the Suomi Synod, although other Finns, often in large crowds, attended them to see and hear the bishop of Oulu. In Hancock he participated in a ceremony in which the president of the synod, Pastor Alvar Rautalahti, ordained Edward J. Isaac, Antti Lepisto, K. V. Mykkanen, and Wilho Ranta, who through the presence of the bishop became a part of the apostolic succession. The bishop spoke also at the unveiling of the monument erected to the memory of J. K. Nikander. From Michigan, Koskimies went to Minnesota, where he was present at the church convention in Ely. At this convention and in negotiations with the Consistory, important official relations between the Suomi Synod and the Church of Finland were started, such as the legal acceptance in Finland of certificates issued by Finnish American pastors, for example. Bishop Koskimies's highly successful visit was a powerful factor in the formation of a close bond between the old country and the Finnish Americans.[24]

Inspired by the success of the tour made by the Louhi Band of Pennsylvania, about forty businessmen and singers met in Hancock in August of 1920 to plan a trip to Finland for the next summer. A committee of which the following were members was selected: Emil Saastamoinen, Efraim Lohela, and Matti Mattson from Hancock; Matti Huhta from Kearsarge; John Lammi from Marquette; A. Raatikainen from Negaunee; Andrew Haapoja and Jussi Nisula from Ironwood; and Dr. J. Raihala from Virginia, Minnesota. A publishing committee was also selected to prepare a book titled *Liikemiesten ja Laulajain Suomimatka 1921* (Businessmen's and singers' trip to Finland) to be taken along.[25] The committee left the execution of the task to editor Fabian Tolonen. The book was published in the spring of 1921 in a large format and was lavishly illustrated. Well edited, it has become an important source book for students of the history of the Finnish Americans and their institutions. Composer K. W. Kilkka was the director of the chorus. He got together a small but powerful chorus of seventeen men. The chorus, accompanied by a large number of businessmen, was warmly received in Finland. It came to Finland as a counterbalance to the electrically charged atmosphere caused by the attempts of Sweden to gain control of the Åland Islands through political maneuvers.

In the summer of 1922, a chorus from Calumet called Suomen Sävel (Finnish Melody) left for the old homeland and, directed by Sanfrid Mustonen, gave concerts throughout Finland. Finnish American excursions to Finland increased to such size that steamship companies began to take them straight to Helsinki with their ocean liners. The *Andania* of the Cunard Line went there in the summer of 1926, and their *Lancastria* in 1927. The *Drottningholm* of the Swedish American Line also went there in 1927.

Akseli Gallen-Kallela (1865–1931), who, toward the end of the nineteenth century and in the first third of the twentieth century, was the greatest and most representative artist of Finland, spent some time in America from 1923 on, showing his works at great art centers. On February 12, 1924, he was in Hancock, where a public festival was planned in his honor. While listening to the program he sketched monograms of his initials and, after the festivities, gave them to those who requested his autograph. While visiting Suomi College in 1924, he painted an oil of a boat on the shoreline. The class of 1924 dedicated their yearbook (which featured his self-portrait) to him.

In the summer of 1925, Antti J. Pietila (1878–1932), a professor of dogmatics at the University of Helsinki, visited America, traveling to Finnish communities as far as the West Coast. Because of his fame as a scholar and his brilliance as a speaker, he drew large crowds of listeners. Although he was primarily a guest of the Suomi Synod, he found time to give speeches and lectures in temperance halls and Apostolic Lutheran churches. His extensive travelogue includes the most competent appraisal of Americanism in general and especially of American and Finnish American church life that has been written.[26]

Toward the end of that year, three Pietist leaders also visited America. They were Dr. Aukusti Oravala, Rector Vaino Malmivaara, and a merchant by the name of Kuoppala. Their chief purpose in coming was to visit the people who had come to America from central Ostrobothnia. Oravala wrote a charming book about the experiences they had and the impressions they received as they traveled among the Finns. His description, for example, of their visit in Nisula, where the immigrants, according to Oravala, had come from "Pettula" (Pine-Bark Land), which is the name he gave to Kainuu in Finland, is without an equal.[27] In 1926 Pastor Armas K. E. Holmio, a representative of the Finnish Missionary Society, traveled widely among the Finns of America.[28] So did Pastor K. V. Tamminen, a representative of the Lutheran Gospel Association of Finland, who was on his way to the association's mission field in Japan.[29] Disregarding many of the more or less private visits, mention may justifiably be made of the visit of the provost of Lapua, K. R. Kares, who came to America in the early summer of 1930 as the personal representative of Archbishop Gustaf Johansson (1844–1930). He participated in the church convention at Calumet and got back to Finland in time for the archbishop's funeral.

Not only did churchmen of Finland visit America, but Finnish American churchmen also made trips to Finland. Suomi Synod pastors traveled there widely on lecture tours at various times. Among them were J. K. Nikander, Viljami Rautanen, F. Y. Joki, John Wargelin, and Alfred Haapanen.

A visit of special significance was that of Dr. Rafael Engelbert to America in 1931–32. Sent by the Ministry of Education of Finland, he lectured on the history and culture of Finland at Suomi College during the fall semester. He also visited many of the Finnish communities of Michigan. In the winter and spring he was invited to speak at meetings of the Finlandia Society and other Finnish American organizations throughout the United States and Canada. A volume of nearly five hundred pages titled *Suomi ja Amerikan Suomalaiset* (Finland and the Finnish Americans) is a lasting memorial of Engelberg's visit.[30]

On December 11, 1937, the Helsinki University Chorus boarded a ship to America for a concert tour that had been planned for years. The director of this world-famous sixty-man chorus was Martti Turunen, who had inherited the position from the well-known Heikki Klemetti. In the first row of well-wishers who had come to see them off in a snowstorm stood the provost of Pälkäne, Kustaa Varmavuori, a former pastor to immigrants who had sung with the University Chorus fifty years before.[31] Another veteran singer was also there, namely Kalle Väänänen. In his powerful voice Väänänen called for silence and read a farewell message written in the meter of *Kalevala*. It concluded with the hope that the West would be dumbfounded by the power of the University Chorus's singing.

The tour, which took the chorus to the greatest music centers of the United States and Canada, was a series of triumphs. Songs like P. J. Hannikainen's "Terve, Suomeni Maa" (Hail, My Finland), Larin Kyösti's "Hiiden Orjien Laulu" (The Song of Satan's Slaves), V. A. Koskeniemi's "Nuijamiesten Marssi" (Peasants' March), Heikki Klemetti's "Oi, Kallis Suomenmaa" (O Beloved Finland), A. Oksanen's "Sotamarssi" (War March), as well as many others rang in the listeners' minds for weeks afterward. They also caused strong feelings of pride in their nationality among the Finns.

Having sung the "Pori March" under the dome of the Capitol in Washington, D.C., and a full concert before a capacity audience in Constitution Hall, and having visited a session of Congress which was interrupted for a speech to them upon their arrival in the gallery of the chamber, the Helsinki University Chorus went to Lower Michigan. Concerts were given in splendid Hill Auditorium in Ann Arbor, at Cranbrook, where Professor Eliel Saarinen, an architect, was their host, and in Detroit, where William Kyro had made the arrangements for a concert. The chorus visited the Ford Factory and the nearby museum in Dearborn where, in Thomas A. Edison's workshop, which has been of the greatest importance to mankind, they sang Horace's Latin ode "Integer vitae scelerisque purus," which is often sung at funerals of scientists.

After concerts in St. Louis and Chicago, the chorus came to Upper Michigan, arriving in Marquette on January 24. A short concert was given for high school students in the afternoon because the evening concert had been sold out. During the concert a snowstorm began. The singers had to wade through snowdrifts to get to the Northland Hotel, where they were staying. The storm broke power lines, and that evening members of the chorus stood at dark hotel windows watching a big fire that burned the buildings on a nearby street corner to the ground. The storm began to abate the following evening. Dressed in colorful mackinaws, a large crowd of people of the city came over the drifts on snowshoes to cheer up the singers, who by this time were feeling as though they were living in a prison compound.

Wednesday, January 26, "was critical, for we made at least ten attempts to go to Hancock where the next concert was to be." Under the leadership of Martti Nisonen and Sheriff John G. Salmi, the people of Hancock had worked for months preparing for the concert. All twelve lavishly illustrated pages of *Amerikan Suometar* of January 25 were devoted to the Helsinki University Chorus. In an attempt to get the singers to Hancock, twelve automobiles went to the station in Nestoria to meet them. But Marquette was for the time being surrounded by snowdrifts up to twenty feet high. The concert, which was to have been held at the Kerredge Theater, had to be canceled. The chorus eventually reached Duluth, somewhat delayed. This incident was the greatest disappointment experienced by the Finns of the Copper Country. Someone even wrote some verses describing the snowbound situation of the singers and the feelings of the frustrated would-be audience.[32]

The tour of the Helsinki University Chorus had been timed so that it would be at hand to open the 300th anniversary celebration of the Delaware Colony. This they did magnificently. The festive spirit among Finnish Americans was heightened by the undisputed victory of boxer Gunnar Bärlund of Helsinki over the famous Buddy Baer in Madison Square Garden on March 4.[33] The main festivities of the Delaware celebration were conducted in Pennsylvania, the early home of the immigrants. But celebrations were held in all Finnish communities. The Delaware Committee of Negaunee and surrounding areas, with August Raatikainen as chairman, Alli Hepola as secretary, and Erland Maki as treasurer, planned big celebrations in the Upper Peninsula, as did the Copper Country Delaware Committee with John Wargelin as chairman, Kosti Arho as secretary, and John G. Salmi as treasurer. John Wargelin was sent to Pennsylvania to represent the Finns of the Upper Peninsula. He was given only two minutes to deliver a speech at the Delaware Monument, for the committee for the main festival had assigned the greater part of the program time to leftist representatives.[34] The big celebration in Detroit was attended by Foreign Minister Rudolf Holsti, leader of the Delaware delegation from Finland, and his entourage. Members of this delegation who visited the Upper Peninsula were Dr. Sigfrid Sirenius, the writer Artturi Leinonen, and a member of Parliament, Westerinen.[35]

In the summer of 1939, the world-famous astronomer V. A. Heiskanen was in America on a fifty-day visit to lecture and to attend astronomy meetings. He also visited Finnish Americans whenever there was an opportunity to do so.[36] Professor Heiskanen was for some time the last of the more important visitors to America from Finland because of the outbreak of World War II in the fall of that year, the Russian attack on Finland, and the entry of the United States into the war as an immediate result of Japan's attack on Pearl Harbor on December 7, 1941. These events interrupted the normal life of Finns on both sides of the Atlantic.

Official Representation of Finland in Michigan

Before World War I, Russia had three consulates in the United States—in New York, Chicago, and San Francisco—where Finns were able to have contracts, credentials, and other official papers certified. Michigan was in the area of the Chicago consulate. There were also a number of honorary consuls who were not, however, of much help to the Finns, excepting Gustaf Wilson of Portland, Oregon, their fellow countryman, who served as an honorary vice consul from 1883 to 1905.[37]

After Finland had achieved independence, one of the most important matters to be taken care of was that of representation to foreign countries. The first minister to Washington from Finland, sent in 1920, was Armas Herman Saastamoinen, a businessman from Kuopio, who had previously been Finland's minister to Copenhagen.[38] Axel Solitander, an engineer, was the first Finnish consul general in New York, named to the position in 1919.[39] The creation of a network of consulates took a long time.

The first Finnish consulate in Michigan was the vice consulate set up in Calumet early in 1920. On March 24, 1920, Justice of the Peace Charles O. Jackola was named honorary vice consul. On December 12, 1924, he was promoted to the position of honorary consul, which he held less than a year, for he died on November 11, 1925. Jackola was born in Kemijärvi in 1872 and came to America as a ten-year-old. At the age of twenty, having studied accounting and law, he was elected justice of the peace, a position which he held until his death. He was one of the first musicians in the Copper Country. Rauanheimo speaks of him thus: "Charles O. Jackola is truly a typical justice of the peace. When one sees him at the judge's bench, one gets the impression that he can calm even the worst brawlers and ruffians. Even in outward appearance he is so calm that it seems neither fire nor earthquake could disturb him."[40]

The area covered by Jackola's consular activity was the entire Upper Peninsula. After his death the area was divided into two vice consulates. Houghton, Keweenaw, Baraga, Ontonagon, Gogebic, and Iron Counties belonged to the Hancock vice consulate. The eastern half of the peninsula was under the jurisdiction of the Marquette vice consulate. Dr. Henry Holm was named honorary vice consul for Hancock on April 6, 1926. Holm was born in Oulu on September 27, 1882, studied at the University of Helsinki, and moved to America in 1904 to avoid the illegal military service required by Russia. He received his medical degree in Chicago in 1908. He was, like his predecessor, one of the leading musicians of the Copper Country. His baritone solos attracted audiences from distant areas. He moved to California in 1933 and gave up his vice consulship on March 21, 1934.[41]

Holm's successor in the Hancock vice consulate was a businessman, Jacob Uitti, who was born in Jalasjärvi on July 24, 1878.[42] He was one of the leading Laestadians. He was manager of the Finnish Mutual Fire Insurance Company for many years. His consulship ended in 1942.

In the Marquette district, John Lammi was made vice consul on April 6, 1926. Born in Isokyrö on March 24, 1882, he had come to America in 1899. He, too, was a well-known singer.

On July 16, 1942, at the time of World War II, when America was an ally of Russia, Washington announced that the United States would sever consular ties with Finland and demanded that the Finnish consulates in America be closed before August 1. As a consequence of this dictum the vice consulates of Hancock and Marquette ceased activity.

On November 26, 1951, when the political situation was somewhat calmer again after the war, the foreign ministry of Finland set up two vice consulates in the Upper Peninsula again, one in Ishpeming and the other in Hancock, the areas of jurisdiction to be the same as they had been before the war, when the consulates were in Marquette and Hancock. In Ishpeming, Isaac A. Palomaki, manager of the Finnish Mutual Fire Insurance Company, who was born in Ishpeming on May 6, 1911, was named honorary vice consul. After his resignation on October 31, 1954, Eino A. Tenhunen, who was born in Richmond, Michigan, succeeded him, taking office on November 3, 1954. Tenhunen resigned on April 30, 1958. The new vice consul, named on April 9, 1959, was an insurance man, Wilho A. Partanen, who was born on June 14, 1923, in Keweenaw Bay, Michigan.

In Hancock, on reactivation of the consular office, Tauno Tervo was named vice consul on November 26, 1951. Tervo was born in South Range, Michigan, on September 5, 1906, a descendant of seafarers from Raahe, Finland. After completing his commercial studies at Suomi College he made insurance his vocation. In 1937 he purchased the late Frank James's insurance business in Hancock and developed it into the extensive Tervo Agency. Tervo held many positions of responsibility in his community and his church. During his term of service as vice consul, the activity of the consulate increased, sometimes including the entire Upper Peninsula. Tervo died on January 16, 1955.

On June 2, 1955, Eino Matthew Laitala, manager of the Finnish Lutheran Book Concern, was named to succeed Tervo. Laitala was born on July 29, 1902, in Ely, Minnesota, to parents who had come to America from Laihia. He graduated from Stout Institute. In 1964 the book concern became the property of Laitala and his two co-workers, Hilda Ruohoniemi and Norman Lassila. In 1961 the governor of Michigan named Laitala to the Conservation Commission. In 1965 he was chairman of the commission. Before this time, no Finnish American had ever been a chairman or even a member of such a commission. In addition to these positions, which required Laitala's participation in regular and extra meetings, and which obligated him to give talks throughout the state, he has at the same time held positions of responsibility in his church and community.

On December 12, 1924, a Finnish vice consulate was established in Detroit. Attorney Charles A. Bartanen was named to the office. He was born in Ylitornio on May 20, 1887, and came to Hancock with his parents in 1893. He graduated from the Detroit College of Law in 1922 and became an attorney in Detroit. Bartanen died on July 17, 1931. His successor in the vice consulate was lawyer George H. Heideman, who was born in Calumet on February 14, 1899, and received his Bachelor of Law degree from the University of Michigan in 1923. Heideman resigned on July 23, 1942, after consular ties were broken.

On November 18, 1951, after the war, a consulate was established in Detroit and Heideman was named consul. He resigned on July 1, 1955. Following Heideman's resignation, Harri Martti Virjo was made honorary vice consul on February 27, 1956, and promoted to consul on February 24, 1959. Virjo was born in Antrea on May 6, 1912, and graduated from the Viipuri Classical Lyceum. In 1937 he graduated as an economist from the Helsingin Kauppakorkeakoulu (Helsinki Business College). Virjo served for a number of years in the Finnish Army and was wounded in the wars. He attained the rank of lieutenant.[43]

The location of three Finnish consulates in Michigan and the visits of Finnish ministers from Washington and of consuls general from New York to Finnish celebrations in the state have greatly strengthened ties between the Finns of Michigan and their former homeland.

Help Finland 1939–50

The Finnish war for independence, which started in the first months of 1918, was officially ended on October 14, 1920, with the Treaty of Tarto (Dorpat), which became the foundation for relations between Russia and Finland. A large number of later agreements between the two countries were based on it. The most important of these were the nonaggression pact which was made in Helsinki on January 21, 1932, and the agreement made in Moscow on April 7, 1934, that the nonaggression pact should be in force until the last day of December 1945.

As war clouds gathered over Europe, Germany and the Soviet Union surprised the world by signing a ten-year nonaggression pact. According to secret minutes which were not revealed to the world until after the war, Finland was in the Soviet Union's sphere of interest. On September 1, 1939, Germany invaded Poland, two days later England and France declared war against Germany, and two weeks later the Russian army marched into Poland.

Finland exerted every effort to make her position secure through peaceful means. On the day that the news of Germany's invasion of Poland reached Helsinki, President Kyösti Kallio made a public declaration in which he stated that Finland would remain strictly neutral. On September 17 the Soviet Union informed the Finnish minister in Moscow that Russia would respect the neutrality of Finland. But on October 5 the Soviet Union demanded that Finland send a delegation to Moscow to discuss political matters. Former Prime Minister J. K. Paasikivi headed the delegation. One of the other members of the group was Foreign Minister J. K. Paasikivi headed the delegation. One of the other members of the group was Foreign Minister Vaino Tanner. Their instructions were to find out what Russia wanted without making any commitments other than to assure Russia of Finland's unconditional neutrality and her desire for peace. Ten thousand persons at the Helsinki station to see them off sang "A Mighty Fortress Is Our God" as the delegation left on the night train. Russia demanded military bases in Finland, the moving of the boundary line on the Isthmus of Karelia, some islands in the Gulf of Finland, and Hanko. The delegation started on the return trip on November 13. The Soviet Union rejected an offer of mediation by the United States.

On Sunday afternoon, November 26, 1939, seven cannon shells exploded in Mainila, a village of Karelia on the Soviet side of the border, killing and wounding several Russian soldiers. The shots came from the Russian side. The Finnish border guards saw the explosions. An angry exchange of notes between Moscow and Helsinki followed Russia's demanding that the Finnish army immediately withdraw 20–25 kilometers from the Russian border on the Isthmus of Karelia. The exchange of notes ceased when Molotov announced on November 29 that the Soviet Union was severing all diplomatic relations with Finland.[44] On Thursday morning, November 30, Russia started military action against Finland, attacking by land, sea, and air, and spreading death and destruction especially among civilians.

This attack had an electrifying effect on Finnish Americans.

What decades of work and struggle to build a new life in the new homeland had not accomplished was achieved in a twinkling by the destruction of life and property in the old homeland by Russian bombs. Finnish Americans forgot political and religious differences and began to work together to aid the land of their fathers in its unequal struggle to retain its freedom. Church members, socialists, temperance people, members of the Kaleva order, and persons who belonged to no organization joined forces. Only a thinning group of communists were on Russia's side and published their propaganda.

In the first rush of activity, meetings were held in homes, halls, or churches. Each person put his donation into the "conscience cup" on the coffee table. Typically, a general fund drive was planned for an area, to start the next day. Someone would offer to prepare contribution lists. The area was divided into districts for the solicitors and, after three or four days, the first meeting to report collections was held, often in connection with a program. Regular meetings were held, sometimes once a week, or in some places, twice a month. The solicitors went from door to door without bypassing non-Finns, for the matter was considered to be of universal importance. Contributions were small, but because thousands of persons gave what they could, the totals collected were often impressive. For example, in the small community of Trout Creek, ten persons collected $776.82 at the time of the Winter War. With the collections taken at meetings and the money earned through coffee socials, which amounted to $303.87, a total of $1,080.69 was sent to the consul general in New York to be sent to Finland.[45] Here and there it happened in a Finnish community that a woman who had worked all her life as a servant, saving her money for retirement, would bring a thousand dollars at a time for Finnish relief, thus depleting her bank account.

There was often a great deal of discussion about the purposes for which the funds should be sent. There were many needs: Red Cross, border protection, medical expenses, military equipment, the cost of sending volunteers, etc. The groups organized to take care of these needs had different names in different communities. One of the most popular and most appropriate names was "Lotta Svärd" after a famous female character in Runeberg's *Tales of Ensign Stål*, for women were usually the prime movers in these associations and committees.

Within a week or two of the beginning of the Soviet attack, in addition to the news of destructive bombings and of the heroic struggles of the defenders of Finland, there were also stories about the sufferings of civilians who were fleeing from the Russian avalanche in freezing winter weather, badly in need of clothing and food:

> All the sick, the women, and the children had to flee for their lives, so they were only about half clothed. Those who had clothes of some kind wandered westward along the autumn roads through heavy fog. I had the churches opened up and heated to provide rest and shelter for these refugees. Some of them, wrapped only in pieces of flannel, were taken to Savo by train. These people did not receive any clothing in the proper sense of the word until January.[46]

The Finnish American Relief Committee took immediate action. Extensive clothing drives were organized, and soon thousands of heavy boxes were on their way to the stricken country. In addition, innumerable individuals sent food and clothing to relatives and friends. Hundreds of churches and halls were headquarters for relief collections. In many areas American businesses were very generous. The clothing collected through public drives was usually sent to the consul general in New York. Money was also sometimes sent there, or to the Finnish legation in Washington. Sometimes it was sent directly to Finland. Funds and supplies intended for civilian relief were sent to Suomen Huolto (Finnish Relief), which President Risto Ryti established just before Christmas 1939 in compliance with the wishes of Herbert Hoover, former president of the United States.

Hoover had been made the head of the relief work being done throughout America for the benefit of Finland. A public drive began on December 20 in Madison Square Garden in New York where Hoover gave one of the most effective speeches that a non-Finn has ever given in behalf of Finland.[47] An American historian says that the relief organization headed by Hoover did its far-reaching work so well that there was hardly an American who "would not have danced, sewed, prayed, played bridge or bingo, banqueted, or simply showed his sympathy for Finland."[48] Funds collected by many local committees reached Finland by way of this channel. The most important groups who received aid through the Suomen Huolto organization were refugees, bomb victims, and families of fighting soldiers and of the wounded and fallen.[49]

The war ended on March 13, 1940. Suffering Finland had half a million homeless to care for, not one of whom wished to return to the parts Finland had lost to Russia. The uncertain peace, continually broken by the old enemy, lasted over fifteen months. Then, between July 22 and 26 of 1941, the Soviet air force bombed ten Finnish towns. On July 26, Finland began defensive action. This situation marked the beginning of a four-year struggle known as the Continuation War. Professor A. K. Cajander, the chairman of Suomen Huolto, sent a cablegram to the consul general in New York, who sent it on to all Finnish American relief organizations. It said in part:

> Without being to blame and against our will we are again at war. We have tried our utmost to remain at peace with our neighbor, but in vain. The constant unjust demands of the Soviet Union have finally culminated in open acts of war. Thus our fight for freedom continues in the same pattern as before: Humanity, culture, and justice against hostile communism and our enemy of nearly a thousand years.

Some of the Finnish relief organizations had ceased activity by this time. Now they went to work again with renewed zeal. It is impossible in this brief discussion to enumerate the accomplishments of all the Finnish relief groups in Michigan. A few examples will be given.

The Lotta Svärd organization of Hancock was started at the home of Professor Martti Nisonen of Suomi College and his wife, Martta, on Friday, December 29, 1939. Martta Nisonen was elected president; Mary B. Mickelsen, secretary; and Sirkka Saarnivaara, treasurer. This group was very active in its own right, but it also served as the central collection agency for many of the small Finnish communities of the Copper Country. By January 1, 1941, this Lotta Svärd and its twenty-four branches in small communities of the area had collected $5,836.90, of which $2,125.07 was sent to Finland as cash, and $3,647.66 was used to buy clothing and to pay the cost of sending it. There was $62.17 left in the treasury. In addition, many tons of used clothing were sent. By August 1942, according to minutes of the organization, $3,000 had been sent to the offices of the consul general and the Finnish legation, and seven tons of clothing directly to Finland. The last meeting with Martta Nisonen as chairman was held on August 5, 1942. At the next meeting, held on September 30 at Suomi College, speeches were given in her memory by Sylvia Nikander and Hilma Hamina. Martta Nisonen, who had worked hard to help her former homeland, had collapsed at her work on September 22. Alma Haapanen succeeded her as president of the Hancock Lotta Svärd.

The honor of having been first in providing aid to Finland belongs to the Ladies of Kaleva. On November 9, 1939, three weeks before the Russian attack on Finland, Annikki Lodge no. 3 of Brooklyn sent a circular letter to Kaleva lodges all over the country urging them to begin relief work for Finland without delay.[50] Especially in Michigan, the Ladies of Kaleva started Lotta Svärd groups in many communities and set up relief committees. Among the first in the state to get relief drives going were the Finns of Detroit, who, within four weeks after the outbreak of the war, sent about $4,000 to Hjalmar Procopé, the Finnish minister in Washington. They continued their relief activity at about the same pace for many years.[51]

Hoover's Finnish Relief ended its activities after it had collected \$3,500,000 for Finnish civilian relief. On December 12, 1944, Help Finland Inc. took its place. Its board of directors included the following persons from Michigan: Alma Haapanen, Yrjo Joki, Minnie Perttula-Maki, and John Wargelin. Members of the executive committee were Alfred Haapanen, Paul A. Heideman, Onni A. Koski, Abel Niemi, Fanny Ojanpaa, and Jacob Uitti. The honorary chairman of Help Finland was Herbert Hoover. The president was Dr. Viljo Nikander, the treasurer was Preston Davie, and the executive secretary, Esther L. Hietala. The office of the organization was in New York. In October 1945, Help Finland received \$46,107.85 from Michigan.

Already before Help Finland Inc. took over the relief work, some political activity had been undertaken. In the first part of April 1944 a delegation composed of President V. K. Nikander of Suomi College and Pastor Paul Heideman from Michigan, former Congressman Oscar J. Larson from Minnesota, and editor Henry Puranen from Massachusetts went to Washington, D.C., where they had a long discussion with Secretary of State Cordell Hull and his closest advisers about the situation in Finland. They left with him a comprehensive *pro memoria* which, in its seven sections, pointed out that Finland was a test case which would demonstrate whether Article II of the Atlantic Charter truly expressed a goal of the Allies in the war. The League of Nations had already condemned the Soviet Union's attack on Finland and dropped Russia from the league; for Finland to submit to the demands of Russia would mean national suicide; the only enemy of Finland's peace and political security was Russia.[52] On the return trip from Washington, Dr. Nikander stopped at New York for a conference with former President Hoover.

Oscar J. Larson and V. K. Nikander organized a small but effective political committee called the Save Finland Committee. In addition to other activities, this committee published Nikander's booklets *Is Finland Worth Saving?* which came out early in 1945, and *Are the Lights Going Out in Finland?* which appeared in October of that year. These booklets, which were distributed to members of Congress and to newspapers, explained the terms of the peace agreement which Finland, forsaken by her admirers, had been compelled to sign on September 29, 1944. They also discussed the treatment received in America by a former president of the League of Nations, Hjalmer Procopé, as well as other political actions of the day of concern to Finland. These matters were also discussed almost every day on Reino Suojanen's radio programs, in American and Canadian Finnish newspapers by a political writer who used the name Antti Jaakonpoika, and in the nationalistic press.

Finland's defeat in the uneven struggle created a general feeling of discouragement among Finnish Americans, in spite of which they still worked throughout the country at American Red Cross centers, and with inward pride, saw their sons' and daughters' names on the rolls of honor in schools or in front of town halls. A result of the activities of the Save Finland Committee and of the work of numerous individuals was that the feelings of discouragement disappeared. Soon after the war, Finland recovered her status as a nation popular with Americans. This was evident, for example, in the continued large amounts of relief funds which were donated by the National Lutheran Council and used to rebuild dozens of churches destroyed by the war, to re-establish Christian institutions, and to keep Finnish missions active in Africa, Palestine, Japan, and China. The sixty-five congregations of the Suomi Synod in Michigan played an important part in this work.

Visits and Return Visits after 1946

After World War II, which ended with the fall of Germany in May and the surrender of Japan in August 1945, about three years passed before millions of soldiers were at home again and international trade and travel returned to normal. Now began visits between Finland and Finnish Americans which increased year by year and have not yet, reached their peak. The church was again the first to establish ties. Dignitaries from Finland attended church conventions and Finnish celebrations in Michigan. For example, Ilmari Salomies visited once as bishop of Mikkeli and made a second visit as archbishop of Turku. Another important visitor was Eelis Gulin, bishop of Tampere, who made several visits. Still others were bishop of Mikkeli (later archbishop) Martti Simojoki, and bishop of Lapua Eero Lehtinen, not to mention numerous lesser churchmen.

Special interest was aroused in America by touring Finnish ballet and gymnastic teams which had won acclaim in the Olympics. They gave performances in such college towns of Michigan as Detroit, Ann Arbor, and Hancock. The colorful Jussi Chorus from Southern Ostrobothnia inspired memories of their youth in the hearts of the older generation, and the Helsinki University Chorus gave well-received concerts in Detroit, Hancock, Marquette, and Ironwood.

The most memorable visit of Finnish Americans to Finland was that of the Suomi College Choir in the summer of 1963. An invitation had come from the Bishops' Conference and the choir was the guest of the Church of Finland. Ralph Jalkanen, the president of Suomi College, was manager of the tour, and Professor Arthur Hill was the director of the fifty-member choir. The choir sang several times at the Fourth Lutheran World Conference, which was being held in Helsinki, and visited President Urho Kekkonen at his summer home in Kultaranta and Archbishop Ilmari Salomies in Turku.

The first concert by the choir was given in Lohja in the church of St. Lawrence, which had been built two hundred years before Columbus discovered America. Other church concerts were given in the following places: Hyvinkää, Turku, Eurajoki, Sääksmäki, Hattula, Lapua, Vaasa, Seinäjoki, Ilmajoki, Kauhajoki, Kokkola, Oulu, Rovaniemi, Kuusamo, Suomussalmi, Jyväskylä, Lahti, and Helsinki. In large parishes from which Finns had emigrated to America the singers, who were mostly third-generation Finnish Americans, often met relatives who marveled at the purity of their Finnish and the power of the singing with which they were greeting Finland from across the ocean.[53]

Architects Eliel and Eero Saarinen

It has been said that "the new Finnish culture has for some time appeared to be more imitative and adaptive than original." Music and architecture have been brilliant exceptions to this rule.

Jean Sibelius has won for Finland a permanent place in the world of music. Of the scores of other musicians of distinction the following are a sampling: Oskari Merikanto, Toivo Kuula, and Yrjo Kilponen, composers; Aino Ackté, Maikki Jarnefelt, Pia Ravenna, and Vaino Sola, singers; and Tauno Hannikainen, Heikki Klemetti, and Martti Turunen, directors of orchestras, bands, and choirs or choruses.

Eliel and Eero Saarinen are two of the few Finnish architects whose creations have affected architecture in areas outside Finland. Eliel Saarinen was born in Rantasalmi, the son of a provost, on August 20, 1873. He graduated as an architect from the Helsinki Polytechnic Institute in 1897. That same year, Saarinen, Armas Lindgren, and Herman Geselius set up an architecture firm whose first great triumphs were the Finnish Pavilion at the Paris Exposition of 1900 and the Pohjola Insurance Company Building and the Finnish National Museum in Helsinki. After the dissolution of the partnership, Saarinen designed the railroad station in Helsinki as well as other buildings.

Saarinen then began to concentrate on ever-increasing foreign demands. He earned lasting world fame by winning the second prize in the Chicago Tribune skyscraper contest. The decision of the board raised a storm in the world of architecture, for many leading experts considered Saarinen's design to be the best.[54] Louis H. Sullivan, one of America's greatest architects, said that the decision of the Chicago Tribune prize-awarding committee had "robbed the world of its most beautiful office building."[55]

A result of the contest was that Saarinen moved to America, where as the famous "skyscraper architect" he was offered many challenging projects. He settled down to live in Bloomfield Hills, Michigan, and participated in the expansion of the Cranbrook Academy of Arts. He won prize after prize in contests across the ocean as well as in America. He was invited to serve as a judge in architecture contests in Australia, Norway, and San Domingo. He is most deserving of credit for his contributions to the development of city planning, on which he concentrated during the last years of his life. He planned a monumental civic center for Detroit and a new arrangement of the Lake Front area of Chicago. He also prepared plans for Canberra, the capital of Australia, and for Suur-Helsinki (Greater Helsinki). Nikander Hall on the campus of Suomi College in Hancock was planned by Saarinen and his son-in-law J. R. F. Swanson and was dedicated in 1939.[56]

Eliel Saarinen, Michigan's most widely known and illustrious Finn, died on July 1, 1950. His son Eero continued in his footsteps, rising perhaps to even greater fame than his father. Eero Saarinen was born in Kirkkonummi, Finland, in 1910 and died in Ann Arbor in 1961. Like his father, he attained world fame by winning important contests. His designs include, among others, the $100 million General Motors Technical Center in Detroit, the United States Embassy in London (about which he had an exchange of words with the House of Commons), the Trans-World Airlines Terminal at Idlewild Airport in New York, the Art Gallery of the Smithsonian Institution in Washington, D.C., and the office building of the Bell Telephone Company in Holmdale, New Jersey. Both he and his father, each on his own, submitted plans to a contest for the Jefferson Memorial in St. Louis. Eero Saarinen's startling design won. He planned the memorial for a site on the Mississippi riverfront from where the Santa Fe and Oregon trails and other highways to the West had started. St. Louis thus acquired the gigantic Jefferson National Expansion Memorial, an arch of stainless steel 630-feet high symbolizing the city as the gateway through which tens of thousands of wagons and hundreds of thousands of pioneers had journeyed to conquer the Wild West for America and for civilization. Critics accused Saarinen of imitating the triumphal arches of the Roman emperors and Mussolini. Saarinen replied that he had gotten the idea for his design while twisting and turning a pipe cleaner. The judges adhered to their decision.[57] About two years after Saarinen's death, President John F. Kennedy named his widow, Aline Saarinen, to a committee whose duty it was to attend to the care of the facades of existing federal buildings and to the planning of new ones.[58]

Of the many Finnish architects of Michigan, John Kasurin is especially worthy of mention. Kasurin (Kasurinen in Finnish) was born in Siilinjärvi, the former Kasurila, in northern Savo on February 2, 1881, and died in Windsor, Ontario, on October 22, 1960. Kasurin had studied at technical schools in Helsinki and Stockholm and in Paris. He came to America in 1905. Having supervised the construction of Henry Ford's home in Dearborn, he settled permanently in Detroit. Many school buildings in Ann Arbor were planned by him, as were several churches and labor halls.

18 From What Parishes Did They Come?

The writer of a history of the Finns in America finds it impossible to give an absolutely reliable report on from where in Finland the Finnish people have come. Sources for such information are either lacking or inaccurate. Church records are usually the most dependable sources, but some churches kept no records. Where there are records, inaccuracies have come about in various ways: for example, a pastor educated in America and unfamiliar with the geography of Finland may have confused place names, writing Karstula for Karttula or Ähtävä for Ähtäri perhaps, or he may, through some misunderstanding, have written a parish name that does not even exist. He may have marked as born in Tornio all persons who came from the Tornio River Valley, or he may have considered all those born in Savo as coming from Kuopio. To the younger pastors, who had little or no knowledge of the Finnish language, Finland was sufficiently specific as a place of birth in their records. In addition to a lack of church records, and the errors in those that do exist, there is the problem caused by the fact that the great majority of Finns were not members of any church. Thus, necessary additional sources for the historian are newspapers, membership rosters of temperance societies, and memorial sketches in church calendars. But these sources are not always satisfactory either. For example, on a list of the eight hundred members of a certain temperance society, only forty had a birthplace indicated.

In the Upper Peninsula of Michigan, the Copper Country and the iron mining areas in the Marquette region—namely, Houghton, Keweenaw, Baraga, Ontonagon, Marquette, Dickinson, and Iron Counties—are one of the exceptions to the rule for several reasons. The records of Finnish churches in these areas were taken care of for a long time by ministers who had come from Finland; most of the records of temperance societies, of which there were many, are in the Finnish American Historical Archives; and the writers of these regions provided church calendars and newspapers with memorial tributes to the deceased.[1]

The great majority of Upper Peninsula Finns have lived for generations, longer than anywhere else, in these seven counties. A search through the aforementioned sources, eliminating repetitions as far as possible, gave a total of 11,065 birthplaces of persons who had come from Finland and lived in these counties. This total was divided almost equally between the Copper Country on the one hand and Marquette, Dickinson, and Iron Counties on the other. The number of those about whom accurate records are not available in documents is certainly much larger. Multiplication of the figures by two or three or four might result in a total closer to the actual truth but it is not justifiable because even that would not give an exact figure. The reason is that in the sources there is much more information about certain areas than about others—about Kainuu for example.

The division of Ostrobothnia into three parts—southern, central, and northern—is based on *Iso Tietosanakirja*, as are the boundaries of the historical provinces of Finland used in this chapter.

The count of Finns in the area known as Copper Island (Keweenaw County and the northern part of Houghton County) is included in the figures for the Copper Country. It has also been given separately under Copper Island because a large number of the Finns of the area are of the oldest generation of Finns in Michigan. It is also to be noted that Swedish Finns have not been included in these statistics.[2]

Table 28 also gives some idea of the dominance of south Ostrobothnia as a source of immigrants to America from Finland.[3] In addition, it shows that the Finns from Norway settled almost exclusively in Keweenaw County and in the northern part of Houghton County, and that Karjala, Uusimaa, and Finland proper have contributed comparatively little to immigration to America. The figures for Karjala and Uusimaa would be even smaller if it were possible to eliminate from this count all of those who came to America from other provinces but gave the port of embarkation, which was either Viipuri or Helsinki, as their place of origin. The point of embarkation was Hanko—where immigrant hotels were available—according to the Institute of Migration report of 1974.

Since the past century, the great Ostrobothnian center in Upper Michigan has been Ishpeming. As table 29 shows, people from

Table 28: Home Areas of Finns in the Upper Peninsula

HOME AREA	COPPER COUNTRY (KEWEENAW, HOUGHTON, BARAGA, ONTONAGON	COPPER ISLAND (KEWEENAW AND NORTH HOUGHTON)	MARQUETTE, DICKINSON, AND IRON	TOTALS FOR COPPER COUNTRY, MARQUETTE, ETC.
South Ostrobothnia	1,036	501	3,198	4,234
Central Ostrobothnia	1,139	766	662	1,801
North Ostrobothnia	643	525	229	872
Lapland and the Far North	544	490	134	678
Norway	192	185	12	204
Sweden	113	103	42	155
Kainuu	1,037	861	135	1,172
Satakunta	182	47	617	799
Häme	197	100	346	543
Savo	153	90	262	415
Karjala	77	31	58	135
Uusimaa	57	38	92	149
Finland Proper	6	5	22	28
Totals	5,376	3,742	5,809	11,185

Kuortane have overshelmingly outnumbers those from other areas, but Alahärmä, Kauhava, and Jalasjärvi have also been represented by hundreds of immigrants. Ylistaro, Kurikka, Lapua, Kauhajoki, Peräseinäjoki, Laihia, Kortesjärvi, and Ilmajoki have also been well represented. Over the years, the south Ostrobothnian Finns spread from Ishpeming to nearby cities and towns, particularly Negaunee and Marquette, where they are well represented. Negaunee is especially known as a center of Lappajärvi Finns.

For a long time Crystal Falls has also been a south Ostrobothnian center of Michigan. The preponderant element there has been Finns from Evijärvi, Alahärmä, Nurmo, and Kortesjärvi, but numerous families also came there from Ylistar Lapua, Kurikka, and Peräseinäjoki. From Crystal Falls, the south Ostrobothnian Finns spread to Amasa where families especially from Ylistaro, Ilmajoki, and Evijärvi, and their descendants, have lived for a long time. In Covington and surrounding areas, south Ostrobothnia is represented by Finns from Nurmo and Kauhajoki. Many persons from Laihia have lived in Trimountain and Paynesville.

Although most south Ostrobothnians have settled in the afore-

Table 29: Finnish Immigrants in the Upper Peninsula from Finnish-Speaking Parishes of South Ostrobothnia

HOME PARISH	COPPER COUNTRY (KEWEENAW, HOUGHTON, BARAGA, ONTONOGAN)	COPPER ISLAND (KEWEENAW AND NORTH HOUGHTON)	MARQUETTE, DICKINSON, AND IRON	TOTALS FOR COPPER COUNTRY, MARQUETTE, ETC.
Kuortane	41	15	369	410
Alahärmä	26	5	372	398
Jalasjärvi	38	10	305	343
Kauhava	35	10	230	265
Ylistaro	67	30	151	218
Lapua	72	30	130	202
Kauhajoki	71	35	115	186
Kurikka	19	8	147	166
Evijärvi	23	10	143	166
Nurmo	64	24	90	154
Laihia	80	58	73	153
Kortesjärvi	17	3	114	131
Isokyrö	53	25	74	127
Lappajärvi	44	12	76	120
Peräseinäjoki	6	2	112	118
Ilmajoki	21	15	93	114
Alavus	38	19	73	111
Vimpeli	68	50	21	89
Töysä	18	13	68	86
Alajärvi	48	33	38	86
Virrat	41	18	41	82
Isojoki	25	5	48	73
Seinäjoki	22	13	50	72
Vaasa	14	8	50	64
Vähäkyrö	43	33	20	63
Other parishes	42	17	195	237
Totals	1,036	501	3,198	4,234

mentioned larger south Ostrobothnian centers of Upper Michigan, there are also families originally from Alavus, Vimpeli, Virrat, and Vähäkyrö scattered in many different areas.

Table 30: Finnish Immigrants in the Upper Peninsula from Home Parishes in Central Ostrobothnia

HOME PARISH	COPPER COUNTRY	COPPER ISLAND	MARQUETTE, ETC.	TOTALS FOR COPPER COUNTRY, MARQUETTE, ETC.
Oulainen	120	97	40	160
Pyhäjärvi	105	68	30	135
Ylivieska	65	25	45	110
Nivala	90	58	8	98
Lohtaja	45	25	47	92
Veteli	41	25	36	77
Piippola	72	52	3	75
Toholampi	49	47	12	61
Pyhäjoki	25	18	34	59
Kalajoki	30	24	28	58
Reisjärvi	31	15	25	56
Haapajärvi	22	14	33	55
Sievi	26	23	29	55
Alavieska	31	25	22	53
Perho	17	10	36	53
Pulkkila	43	39	8	51
Kestilä	38	26	11	49
Merijärvi	20	12	28	48
Haapavesi	40	30	15	55
Other parishes	229	133	172	401
Totals	1,139	766	662	1,801

Immigrants from central Ostrobothnia (see table 30) settled in the Copper Country, especially in Keweenaw County and the northern part of Houghton County, in relatively larger numbers than immigrants from south Ostrobothnia. Because the communities of "Copper Island" are very close to one another and residents have frequently moved from one locality to another, depending on the availability of employment, it is difficult to give a more specific report on how many persons from a particular parish of Finland have lived or are living in a particular community.

The immigrants from north Ostrobothnia settled mostly in the same areas as those from central Ostrobothnia, namely, the Copper

Table 31: Finnish Immigrants in the Upper Peninsula from Home Parishes of North Ostrobothnia

HOME PARISH	COPPER COUNTRY	COPPER ISLAND	MARQUETTE, ETC.	TOTALS FOR COPPER COUNTRY, MARQUETTE, ETC.
Pudasjärvi	130	117	52	182
Oulu	126	113	50	176
Muhos	58	40	16	74
Kuusamo	60	47	8	68
Ii	46	41	15	61
Hailuoto	43	36	6	49
Utajärvi	30	27	16	46
Taivalkoski	24	20	18	42
Tyrnävä	33	25	4	37
Liminka	13	5	10	23
Other parishes	80	54	34	114
Totals	643	525	229	872

Country and, especially, the Copper Island area (see table 31). Oulu makes it difficult to form a clear picture of the situation in the same way as Viipuri and Helsinki did with regard to Karjala and Uusimaa, for there was prestige in claiming the chief city of northern Finland to be one's hometown.

Table 32 shows that in general the settlement in Michigan of immigrants from the far North and Lapland follows the pattern of distribution shown in the tables on central and north Ostrobothnia. Keweenaw County and the northern part of Houghton County were the favored areas. The first immigrants from the north of Finland had come there, and once established, the precedent was followed. Again it was hard to find out where immigrants from what parish had settled because Kemi, Tornio, and Tornionjoki were place-names used by many immigrants instead of the names of the parishes from which they actually came.[4]

In records of the sixteenth century, Kainuu was the name used for Ostrobothnia. In the old Finnish language "kainuu" meant low land and was thus a suitable name for Ostrobothnia. It was only later that the name Kainuu came to mean the lands beyond Kajaani. At times, such large numbers of persons left for America from these areas that

Table 32: Finnish Immigrants in the Upper Peninsula from Home Parishes in Lapland and the Far North

HOME PARISH	COPPER COUNTRY	COPPER ISLAND	MARQUETTE, ETC.	TOTALS FOR COPPER COUNTRY, MARQUETTE, ETC.
Alatornio	70	67	23	93
Tervola	84	80	13	97
Kemi	54	41	14	68
Kemijärvi	60	57	13	73
Karunki	60	50	1	61
Simo	27	22	22	49
Tornio	24	21	12	36
Tornionjoki	32	32	2	34
Ylitornio	24	20	10	34
Sodankylä	25	23	4	29
Rovaniemi	20	17	8	28
Turtola	20	18	4	24
Kittilä	18	17		18
Kuolajärvi	14	13	4	18
Muonio	10	8	4	14
Other parishes	2	4		2
Totals	544	490	134	678

percentagewise they were in some years among the parishes with the most immigrants to America. Only Vuolijoki is missing from the list of parishes of Kainuu in table 33. It did not become a separate parish until the early part of the present century. Immigrants from there were classified as being from Säräisniemi or Kajaani.

Most of the immigrants from Kainuu settled in the Copper Country, where the national environment reminded them of their ruggedly beautiful home area with its deep forests, hills, and lakes teeming with fish. Even the wolves and bears of northern Michigan were a part of the homelike scene. Some people from Kainuu also moved to Maine, especially to the South Paris and Harrison areas, where the natural surroundings, though less rugged, reminded them of Kainuu and the Copper Country. Over 80 percent of the people from Kainuu who came to Michigan settled in Keweenaw County and the northern part of Houghton County. A large number of people from Puolanka, for example, settled in Atlantic Mine and South Range. There were also large

Table 33: Finnish Immigrants in the Upper Peninsula from Home Parishes in Kainuu

HOME PARISH	COPPER COUNTRY	COPPER ISLAND	MARQUETTE, ETC.	TOTALS FOR COPPER COUNTRY, MARQUETTE, ETC.
Puolanka	375	320	14	389
Suomussalmi	205	175	77	282
Hyrynsalmi	120	84	1	121
Sotkamo	87	80	9	96
Paltamo	79	69	9	88
Ristijärvi	60	53	5	65
Säräisniemi	55	34	8	63
Kuhmoniemi	45	36	4	49
Kajaani	11	10	8	19
Totals	1,037	861	135	1,172

numbers of persons from Suomussalmi in these mining towns as well as in Ishpeming and Palmer. Immigrants from Hyrynsalmi settled in Painesdale and Trimountain as well as in Atlantic Mine.

There are seventy-five parishes in Satakunta. The sixty-three missing from the list in table 34 made no significant contribution to the Finnish population of the Upper Peninsula. The random sampling—probably the only possible procedure—used here to find these figures has revealed that there were twenty-two provinces from which no one came to America. Almost all the people who came from Karvia settled in Covington and Watton, from where some of them moved to Trout Creek. Immigrants from Merikarvia settled mostly in Crystal Falls, although some went to Ishpeming and Negaunee and surrounding areas. The immigrants from Siikainen did exactly the opposite. Most of them went to Ishpeming and Negaunee, and only a few settled in Crystal Falls. People from Ähtäri, Kankaanpää, and Soini settled mostly in and around Marquette.

Of the seventy-five parishes of Häme, only four, or one-nineteenth, were actively represented in immigration to Michigan (see table 35). Thirty-two parishes were not mentioned at all. The four leading parishes from which immigrants came to America are all on the northern borders of Häme, where the "America Fever" had spread from Ostrobothnia. Negaunee became the new home of people from Karstula, a small minority settling in Wakefield. People from Kivijärvi settled

Table 34: Finnish Immigrants in the Upper Peninsula from Home Parishes in Satakunta

HOME PARISH	COPPER COUNTRY	COPPER ISLAND	MARQUETTE, ETC.	TOTALS FOR COPPER COUNTRY, MARQUETTE, ETC.
Merikarvia	10	4	166	176
Siikainen	1		116	117
Karvia	47		39	86
Parkano	12		27	39
Kankaanpää	15	2	23	38
Ähtäri	1		32	33
Soini	11		19	30
Pori	4		22	26
Jämijärvi	3		18	21
Loimaa	11	8	7	18
Ikaalinen			15	15
Rauma	12	10	1	13
Other parishes	55	23	132	187
Totals	182	47	617	799

Table 35: Finnish Immigrants in the Upper Peninsula from Home Parishes in Häme

HOME PARISH	COPPER COUNTRY	COPPER ISLAND	MARQUETTE, ETC.	TOTALS FOR COPPER COUNTRY, MARQUETTE, ETC.
Karstula	25	16	150	175
Saarijärvi	26	20	53	79
Pihtipudas	41	36	11	52
Kivijärvi	22	7	22	44
Other parishes	83	21	110	193
Totals	197	100	346	543

largely in Negaunee and Baraga, and many persons from Saarijärvi settled in Ishpeming. Some people from Saarijärvi went to Munising.

As one moves eastward from Satakunta across central Finland, the number of immigrants to America diminishes rapidly the farther east one goes. Of the fifty-five parishes of Savo in the 1930s, there were thirty-six parishes that did not appear at all in the samplings taken for

Table 36: Finnish Immigrants in the Upper Peninsula from Home Parishes in Savo

HOME PARISH	COPPER COUNTRY	COPPER ISLAND	MARQUETTE, ETC.	TOTALS FOR COPPER COUNTRY, MARQUETTE, ETC.
Kiuruvesi	55	45	90	145
Kangasniemi	6	3	38	44
Pieksämäki	16	6	16	32
Mikkeli	14	4	14	28
Iisalmi	8	6	18	26
Pielavesi	10	7	12	22
Kuopio	5	1	10	15
Other parishes	39	18	64	103
Totals	153	90	262	415

this study (table 36). Here again, Kuopio, Mikkeli, and Iisalmi were important cities under which immigrants liked to be listed. Most of the people who came to Michigan from Kiuruvesi settled in Negaunee and Ishpeming. A large number also settled in Baltic and South Range. Negaunee appears to have attracted almost all the immigrants from Kangasniemi, whereas people from Pieksämäki were scattered quite evenly over the entire area.

There were so few people who came to Upper Michigan from the remaining provinces—Karelia, Uusimaa, and Finland proper—that they cannot be said to have become concentrated in any particular area. But wherever greater numbers of persons from a certain province or part of a province did settle, the situation was regularly of advantage to the Finnish nationality as a whole. "South Ostrobothnian socials," "Pyhäjoki coffee socials," "Karstula programs," or whatever, inspired other Finnish groups to participate in activities for the common good.

The older church records of the Hancock congregation of the Evangelical Lutheran Church in some instances give some indication of when the waves of immigration from certain parishes of Finland reached the Copper Country. For example, immigration from Puolanka and Suomussalmi was at its peak in the 1880s, decreasing in the next decade, and ceasing almost entirely by the turn of the century. Most immigrants from Hyrynsalmi came in the 1890s, and the largest numbers from Kiuruvesi, Paltamo, and Ristijärvi arrived between 1901 and 1910. Immigration from Laihia, Pudasjärvi, and Oulainen flowed in a small but steady stream over a period of three decades, from 1880 to 1910.

Notes

Foreword

1. John I. Kolehmainen, *The Finns in America: A Bibliographical Guide to Their History* (Hancock, 1947).

2. See Raymond W. Wargelin, "Armas Holmio," *Suomi-Konferenssin kirkollinen kalenteri vuodelle 1978* (Hancock, n.d.), 201–2.

3. Akseli Järnefelt, *Suomalaiset Amerikassa* (Helsinki, 1899).

4. V. Rautanen, *Amerikan suomalainen kirkko* (Hancock, 1911), 337.

5. J. K. Nikander, "Lyhyt silmäys kirkkokuntamme 25-vuotisen toimintaan," in J. K. Nikander, *Juhla-albumi Suomi-Synoodin 25-vuotisjuhlan muistoksi, 1890–1915* (Hancock, 1915), 51.

6. T. H. [Toivo Hiltunen], "Työmiehen kymmenvuotisen elämän vaiheet," *Työmies kymmenvuotias, 1903–1913: Juhlajulkaisu* (Hancock, 1913), 34.

7. F. J. Syrjälä, *Historia-aiheita amerikan suomalaisesta tyoväenliikkeestä* (Fitchburg, n.d.), 223.

8. Raymond W. Wargelin, "Salomon [*sic*] Ilmonen, Early Finnish-American Historian," *Siirtolaisuus* (Turku, Finland), no. 3 (1987): 2–11; "S. Ilmonen, Pioneer Finnish-American Historian," *Suomi Konferenssin kirkollinen kalenteri 1979* (New York Mills, Minn., n.d.), 155–69.

9. S. Ilmonen, *Amerikan suomalaisten sivistyshistoria: Johtavia aatteita, harrastuksia, yhteispyrintöjä ja tapahtumia siirtokansan keskuudessa*, 2 vols. (Hancock, 1930–31).

10. Ilmonen, *Amerikan suomalaisten sivistyshistoria*, vol. 1, chaps. 2, 6, 10, and vol. 2, chaps. 18–21.

11. Clemens Niemi, *Americanization of the Finnish People in Houghton County, Michigan* (Duluth, 1921), 41, 43.

12. John Wargelin, *The Americanization of the Finns* (Hancock, 1924), 17.

13. Eino Frederick Laakso, "The Significance of the Finns of Massachusetts" (Master's thesis, Clark University, 1931), 83–102.

14. Eugene Van Cleef, "The Response of Finnish Life to Its Geographic Environment" (Ph.D. diss., Clark University, 1926), 300–301. See also

idem, *Finland—The Republic Farthest North: The Response of Finnish Life to Its Geographic Environment* (Columbus, 1929), 201–2.

15. John I. Kolehmainen, "A History of the Finns in Western Reserve" (Ph.D. diss., Western Reserve University, 1937), 236–37.

16. *The Finns in America and Finland: A Bibliography of the Writings of John I. Kolehmainen, 1936–1937*, 3d ed. (New York Mills, Minn., 1988).

17. John I. Kolehmainen, *Sow the Golden Seed* (Fitchburg, Mass., 1955), vii; and John I. Kolehmainen and George W. Hill, *Haven in the Woods: The Story of the Finns in Wisconsin* (Madison, 1951), 150.

18. Walfrid John Jokinen, "The Finns in Minnesota: A Sociological Survey" (Master's thesis, University of Minnesota, 1953); idem, "The Finns in the United States: A Sociological Interpretation" (Ph.D. diss., Louisiana State University, 1955).

19. A. William Hoglund, *Finnish Immigrants in America, 1880–1920* (Madison, 1960).

20. Michael G. Karni, Matti E. Kaups, and Douglas J. Ollila Jr., eds., *The Finnish Experience in the Western Great Lakes Region: New Perspectives*, Migration Studies C3 (Vammala, Finland, 1975).

21. E. A. Pulli, "Historiamme valmistuu," *Siirtokansan kalenteri 1955* (Duluth, n.d.), 31–36.

22. Lauri Lemberg to Walfrid J. Jokinen, February 7, 1960, box 2, Walfrid J. Jokinen Papers, Immigration History Research Center, University of Minnesota.

23. Hans R. Wasastjerna, *Minnesotan suomalaisten historia* (Duluth, 1957).

24. "Michiganin suomalaisten historia," *Suomi Konferenssin kirkollinen kalenteri vuodelle 1968* (Hancock, n.d.), 152–54.

25. Armas K. E. Holmio, *Michiganin suomalaisten historia* (Hancock, 1967).

26. John I. Kolehmainen, *From Lake Erie's Shores to the Mahoning and Monongahela Valleys: A History of the Finns in Ohio, Western Pennsylvania and West Virginia* (New York Mills, Minn., 1977), vii.

27. Holmio, *Michiganin suomalaisten historia*, 587.

28. Ibid., 566.

Chapter 1

1. Interview with Helmi Warren, June 4, 1960.

2. Interview with John Wargelin, October 13, 1960.

3. Literally, place of origin; workshop.

4. Y. H. Toivonen, "M. A. Castrénen Kuolemasta Sata Vuotta," *Kansanvalistusseuran Kalenteri*, 1952, pp. 59, 79.

5. A. Oksanen (August Ahlquist), *Säkeniä* (Helsinki, 1881).

6. See *Oma Maa*, 1:553.

7. Dr. Juhani Paasivirta gives a good account of the knowledge

Americans had of Finland, and of Europe in general, in his *Suomen Kuva Yhdysvalloissa,* WSOY, 1962.

8. Evert Savola, *Suomesta Sointulaan,* 86.

9. Poem by Eloheimo about a tribe, *Raittiuden Ystaväin Kalenteri,* 1900, p. 26.

10. Evert Maattala, *Why Do I Want to Be a Finn?* (Hancock, Mich.: Finnish Lutheran Book Concern, 1915), 12.

11. John Lauttamus, *Amerilcan Tuuilahduksia,* 26. Lauttamus was born in Kauhava (Finland) in 1870, came to America in 1892, lived first in Calumet, and later moved to Minnesota.

12. *Koti-Home,* July 1922, p. 6.

13. Vettenhovi-Aspa, *Suomen Kultainen Kirja,* vol. 1 (Helsinki, 1915).

14. E. A. Louhi, *The Delaware Finns* (New York: Humanity Press, 1925).

15. *Työmies-Eteenpäin,* April 24, 1961.

16. *Työväen Osuustoimintalehti* (hereafter *TOL*), June 7, 1962.

17. *Siirtokansan Kalenteri,* 157–63.

18. *Kalevaissesa,* 37.

19. Noah Webster, *American Dictionary of the English Language* (1828); *Webster's New International Dictionary of the English Language* (Springfield, Mass.: G. and C. Merriam Co., 1948).

20. *Funk and Wagnalls New Practical Standard Dictionary of the English Language,* Britannica World Language Ed. (New York, 1956), 498.

21. *New Schaff-Herzog Encyclopedia* (New York and London: Funk and Wagnalls Co., 1909), 4: 313.

22. *New Practical Reference Library* (Chicago: Hancon-Roach-Fowler Co., 1918).

23. *World Book Encyclopedia* (Chicago: W. F. Quarrie and Co., 1919).

24. Edna Ferber, *Come and Get It* (Garden City, N.Y.: Doubleday, Doran and Co., 1935), 518, 94.

25. John Bartlow Martin, *Call It North Country* (New York: Alfred A. Knopf, 1944).

26. William L. Langer, *An Encyclopedia of World History, Ancient, Medieval, Modern,* rev. ed. (Boston: Houghton Mifflin Co., 1948), 181.

27. *New Funk and Wagnalls Encyclopedia* (New York, 1952), 14:4887.

28. Mongolian tribe, Japan, Finn. *Grand Forks Herald,* August 9, 1961.

29. Richard M. Dorson, *Bloodstoppers and Bearwalkers: Folk Traditions of the Upper Peninsula* (Cambridge: Harvard University Press, 1952), 123.

30. Domenico Comparetti's (1835–1927) work about the Finns was published in English in 1898, translated by Isabella M. Anderton, and titled *The Kalevala and the Traditional Poetry of the Finns.* John Abercromby's two-volume *The Pre- and Proto-Historic Finns* was published in London the same year.

31. *Siirtokansan Kalenteri* (Immigrant peoples calendar; hereafter *SK*), 1920, 126.

32. *American Suometar*, January 19, 1908. See also John I. Kolehmainen, "Suomalainen Rotu Punnittavana Yhdysvaltalaisessa Oikeudessa," *Siirtokansan Kalenteri 1949*, 39–45. See also Hans R. Wasastjerna, *Minnesotan Suomalaisten Historia*, 541–44.

33. *Kansanvalistusseuran Kalenteri* (hereafter cited as *KVK*) 1909, 177–85.

34. *Kalenteri Amerikassa Asuville Suomalaisille Siirtolaisille Vuodelle 1910* (New York: Finland Steamship Company Agency, 1910).

35. *Kansan Kuvalehti*, 1901:19. See also *Who's Who of Finnish Extraction in America.*

36. Larson is referring to William Zebina Ripley (1867–1941), a professor of economics at the Massachusetts Institute of Technology and Harvard, and to his work, *The Races of Europe*, published in 1900.

37. The word "Ugrian" comes from the old Russian word "ugra," which means "Hungarian."

38. Toivo Lehtisalo (1887–1962) was an eminent scholar in the Yurak-Samoyedic language.

39. This presentation of the Finno-Ugric family of languages, the primitive Finns, and their division into various peoples and tribes is based primarily on "Suomen Suku ja Suomen Kansa" by Paavo Ravila, which appears in *Suomen Historian Kasikirja*, vol. 1, ed. Arvi Korhonen. See also Kaarlo Hilden, *The Racial Composition of the Finnish Nation*, and R. E. Burnham, *Who Are the Finns?* "The last word of science" on the origin of the Finns is constantly being modified by new discoveries as research continues.

Chapter 2

1. From the works of Johnson and other Swedish historians, their concept of the Swedish character of the Delaware colony spread to other works. For example, Abdel Ross Wentz's *The Lutheran Church in American History* does not even mention the Finns.

2. *The Finns on the Delaware 1638–1655*, 79.

3. *Amerikan Ensimmäiset Suomalaiset* (Hancock, 1916); *Delawaren Suomalaiset* (Hämeenlinna, 1938).

4. A Finnish translation of the speech is in the Finnish American Historical Archives (hereafter cited as FAHA).

5. Ilmonen fixes the time of the Marttinen's coming to Delaware as 1642, or the third expedition, when the first of the larger groups of Finns arrived. *The Dictionary of American Biography* places it in 1654, or the tenth expedition.

6. In addition to the writings about Delaware listed above, see also Salomon Ilmonen, *John Morton, Amerikan Itsenäisyydenjulistuksen Allekirjoittaja* (Hancock, 1936); Ilmari Tammiste, *Suomalaisten osuus Uuden Ruotsin siirtokunnan perustamisessa. Esitelmä Suomen Yleisradiossa*, v. 1936; O. E. Djerf, *Ensimmäiset suomalaiset Amerikassa* (Ashtabula, 1905); and *Delaware-albumi*, published

by the Yhdysvaktojen Suomalainen Työväenjärjestö (New York, 1938). Akseli Järnefelt-Rayanheime portrays the life of the Delaware Finns in his novel *Uuteen Maailmaan* (Porvoo, 1921), English version: *Before William Penn* (Dorrance and Co., 1929).

7. *Tietosanakirja* (Finnish encyclopedia), 8:7ff.

8. Fitchburg, Raivsaja Printing Press, 1946.

9. Märta Edquist, *Lapin profeetta* (Porvoo, 1933).

10. *Tietosanakirja* 8:268r.

11. The most recent studies of immigrant settlements in Siberia and Amur have been made by D. Vaino Perala.

Chapter 3

1. See Gunnar Modeen, "Siirtolaisuus," *Iso Tietosanakirja*, 12:60.

2. To get an accurate picture, it would be necessary to figure out percentages of emigration, but there is no need for that in this connection.

3. Concerning Finnish navigation and the tar trade, see K. W. Hoppu, "Suomen Kauppalaivasto ja Laivanvarustus," *Oma Maa*, 5:361–77; and E. E. Kaila, *Pohjanmaa ja Meri 1600–1700 Luvuilla.*

4. Other works on emigration by Anna-Leena Toivonen include: "Etelä-Pohjanmaan Siirtolaisuuden Maakunnalliset Edellytykset," *Kytösavut* 4 (Vaasa, 1949); "Keskipohjalaista Siirtolaisuutta Vetelin Näkökulmasta," *Kyrönmaa* 9 (Vaasa, 1955); "Lapualta Suureen Länteen," *Kyrönmaa* 7 (Vaasa, 1950); "Vähänkyrön Läkkesepät ja Kyrönjokilaakson Siirtolaisuus," *Kytösavut* 6 (Vaasa, 1954); and "Ähtäri—Valtamerentakaisen Siirtolaisuuden ja Sisäisen Muutoliikkeen Vedenjakaja," *Kyrönmaa* 8 (Vaasa, 1951).

5. Aulis J. Alanen, *Ilmajoki Vuoden 1809 Jälkeen*, 90.

6. See Matti Aura, "Vahankyrön Kotiteollisuusoloista," *Suomen Teollisuushallituksen Tiedonantoja* 53 (Helsinki, 1911).

7. R. H. Oittinen, *Työväenkysymys ja Työväenliike Suomessa*, 40.

8. Ibid., 45.

9. For material about small tenant farmers, hired workers, and the landless, see ibid., 40–51.

10. Toivonen, *Etelä-Pohjanmaan Valtamerentakainen Siirtolaisuus*, 40 and table 1.

11. *Nuori Suomi IV* (Duluth, 1909), 27–34.

12. *Amerikan Suomalaisten Osoitekalenteri* (Ironwood, 1903), 100f.

13. *Runoja* (Calumet, 1896).

14. Toivonen, *Etelä-Pohjanmaan Valtamerentakainen Siirtolaisuus*, 62–67.

15. Ibid., 65.

16. See Agricola, *Kulkurina Amerikassa, Uutisraivaajana Canadassa*, 6.

17. *Sankarin Maine*, January 31, 1879.

18. *Suomalais-Englantilainen Sanakirja* (Finn-English dictionary) (Brooklyn, 1895), 555.

19. Quoted in Frederick Morley, *Report of the Commissioner of Immi-*

gration for the State of Michigan, for the Years 1881 and 1882, in *Michigan and Its Resources* (Lansing, 1883), 4.

20. Ibid., 5ff.

21. Rafael Engelberg, *Suomi ja Amerikan Suomalaiset*, 32f.

22. In addition to Toivonen's previously mentioned works there is "Sortovuosien Vaikutus Etelä-Pohjanmaan Siirtolaisuuteen," *Uusi Suomi*, February 25, 1956. Also published the same year in *Suomen Silta*, a Finland publication.

23. It was customary for young men to go voluntarily into the Finnish army. Especially popular were the battalion of guards and the naval guard called "Meriekipaashi." But when joining became compulsory, departure for America followed. Alanen, *Ilmajoki Vuoden 1809 Jälkeen*, 91.

24. George W. Sippola, "Biography of Alexander Larson," Manuscript.

25. For example, M. Santeri, *Elämää Ikuisessa Yössä* (Ironwood, 1911).

26. Interview with H. S., August 1962.

27. *Siirtolaisia*, trans. into Finnish by Juhani Aho (Porvoo, 1897), 4f.

Chapter 4

1. The writer has been told that in the 1830s or 1840s there was a Finnish name on a list of residents of Detroit. The document, however, has not been found.

2. Fredrika Bremer, *Homes of the New World*, trans. Maria Lowell, 3 vols. (London, 1853).

3. An old Michigan man who happened to be on the journey.

4. *Hemmen i den Nya verlden*, 2:230–34. Adrian Jaffe, "Fredrika Bremer's Visit to Michigan," *Michigan History* (June 1953): 152–54, gives excerpts from the English translation published in London.

5. C. A. Clausen, ed., *The Lady with the Pen: Elise Waerenskjold in Texas*, Norwegian-American Historical Association (Northfield, Minn., 1961).

Chapter 5

1. Ida C. Brown, "Michigan Men in the Civil War," Michigan Historical Collection, Bulletin no. 9, January 1959, Supplement, October 1960.

2. William B. Gates Jr., *Michigan Copper and Boston Dollars* (Cambridge: Harvard University Press, 1951), 15, 97.

3. T. C. Blegen, *Norwegian Migration to America* (Northfield, 1940), used the form Taftezon and says that he had a companion whose name was Henry F. Tefft.

4. Henry Moilanen, *Raittuis Kalenteri* (hereafter *RK*) 1961, 104f, writes that "the first Finn in Minnesota, Juho Valimaa," arrived in Minneapolis from Hietaniemi, Sweden, in 1861. In a letter to the author he tells of having

heard from relatives of Valimaa that he had visited in Michigan about the same time. Juuso Hirvonen, *Michiganin Kuparialue ja Suomalaiset Siirtolaiset*, 44f, says that G. F. Bergstad of Nurmijärvi, who had settled in Minneapolis, arrived in Hancock in the summer of 1858 and was "the first Finn in Hancock." This, however, is doubtful.

5. Alvah L. Sawyer, *A History of the Northern Peninsula of Michigan*, 1: 482f. See also *Hancock Centennial 1863–1963*, 12.

6. Ilmonen, *Amerikan Suomalaisten Historia*, 2: 67f.

7. Ibid, 70.

8. James Fisher, "Michigan's Cornish People," *Michigan History Magazine* (1945): 379.

9. *Sankarin Maine*, June 13, 1879, editorial.

10. R. L. Polk and Co., vol. 3, Houghton County 1899–1900.

11. There are thirteen books of the minutes of the Copper Country Bar Association.

12. Reminiscences of his cousin Edward Pyykkonen and Helmi Warren. See also Niilo Lapinoja, "Iso-Luvi Moilanen, Isoin Nyky-Suomalainen," *Amerikan Sanomat*, April 18, 1959. Also *Amerikan Uutiset*, July 12, 1963.

13. *Ohjeita Kansalaispaperin Hakijoille ja Sitä Koskevat Lait* (Hancock, 1909).

14. F. Clever Bald, *Michigan in Four Centuries* (New York, 1954), 278f, 348.

15. For example, *Amerikan Albumi 1904*.

16. New York Mills, *75 Years of Progress*, 17.

17. Advertisements in *Kansan Kuvalehden*, 1901–6, and information from Helmi Warren.

18. *RK*, 1899, 57–60.

19. Loukusa-Maija was another woman, sometimes confused with Keras-Mari. The latter died in 1943.

20. Reminiscences of Helmi Warren. See also Juho Rud. Koskimies, *Amerikan Matkalta*, 132. Also "Muistikuvia Kuparisaarelta," from papers left by V. Rautanen, published in *Uskonpuhdistuksen Muisto*, 1960, 16–18. A picture of Keras-Mari appeared in Ripley's *Believe It or Not*.

21. *Raittiuden Ystäväin Kalenteri*, 1900, 77f.

22. Interviews with Mrs. William Mackey and Pastor John F. Simonson, December 1964.

23. Notes in a letter from Ellen Ketola in FAHA. Also, interview with Jean Tomlinson, August 1963. See also the *Daily Mining Gazette*, January 9, 1965.

24. Memoir of Vihtori Kuusisto, *Paimen-Sanomia*, March 15, 1920.

25. *Meikäläisiä Merten Takana*, 14.

26. Information from Alfred Pelto, January 18, 1960.

27. *Kotikansaa*, 157f.

28. Viljo Heikkinen, "Nisula, Muistoja Entisilta Ajoilta," TOL, July 24, 1958. Also, Marianne Keranen, "August Nisula, Pioneer," manuscript, FAHA.

29. "Bohunk" comes from the first syllables of the words "Bohemian" and "Hungarian."

30. Manuscript, FAHA. For the fiftieth anniversary celebration of Herman, the *L'Anse Sentinel*, on June 20, 1951, published an extensive account of events in Herman based on stories by Mrs. Reino Taisto Dantes, Herman Keranen, Kusti Kontio, and other pioneers.

31. He had a three-hundred-acre farm there. He died in 1919.

32. Jacob Ruohonen, "Oskarin Suomalaisten Historia," a seventy-page manuscript, which includes hundreds of incidents in the lives of Oskar Finns. See also Angus Murdoch, *Boom Copper* (New York, 1943), 207f.

33. Ilmonen, *Amerikan Suomalaisen Raittiusliikkeen Historia*, 25.

34. *Paimen-Sanomia* (hereafter *PS*), October 19, 1903. See also *Amerikan Albumi*, x.

35. Notes in a letter from Walter H. Salmi in FAHA. See also Taisto Hayrinen, "Destination Toivola, 'Vale of Hope,'" *The Cooperative Builder*, May 18, 1944; Taisto Hayrinen, "Sähköistamistaistelu Pohj. Michiganin Metsäkylässä," *TOL*, April 27, 1948.

36. "Häväistyksen Päivät," *RK*, 1907, 158–70. The same article appears under the title "The Rockland Tragedy," in *SK*, 1961, 29–39, and in the *Industrialisti*, December 14, 1960.

37. Interview with Antti Maki in Nisula in the summer of 1960. Also letter from William Risto, December 19, 1960.

38. See *Köyhäliston Nuija* 2, 1908, 40. Also Elis Sulkanen, *Amerikan Suomalaisen Työväenliikkeen Historia* (Fitchburg, 1951), 125.

39. Ruben Ahlskog, "Saarnapaikka Rakentaa Kirkon," *Uskonpuhdistuksen Muisto*, 1959. Also information given by Ida K. Saari.

40. Interview with Anna Broemer, May 1962. Also letter from August Niska, February 1960.

41. Ilmonen, *Amerikan Suomalaisten Historia*, 2:165.

42. Notes of Karl Wirtanen.

43. K. J. Moilanen in the *Daily Mining Gazette*, August 26, 1961.

44. According to Suomi Synod church records, 38 percent of those who came in 1913–14 were from outside the Copper Country.

45. See the chapter on cooperatives.

46. *Our Hiawatha Land*, 84.

47. Statistics prepared by Pastor Leslie Niemi, in the *Daily Mining Gazette*, May 26, 1961, and in letter of August 1962.

48. William Kallio, notes dated January 15, 1960. See also Holmio, *Bethany Church 1900–1958*, (Hancock, 1958).

49. Robert Traver, *Small Town D.A.* (New York, 1954), chap. 22.

50. Martin, *Call It North Country*, 263–70.

Chapter 6

1. Alvah L. Sawyer, *A History of the Northern Peninsula of Michigan*, vol. 1.

2. Notes of Theodore Nyman.

3. Reminiscences of Helmi Warren.

4. *Ironwood Daily Globe*, Sept. 27–30, 1926. See also K. R., *Olenko Minä Veljeni Vartija?*

5. Information from Reino M. Hauta and Axel E. Tenlen.

6. Letter to FAHA, June 6, 1959.

Chapter 7

1. *SK*, 1920, 211f. Also, *Kansan Kuvalehti*, January 1903.

2. Martin, *Call It North Country*, 209.

3. *TOL*, February 16, 1961.

4. *RK*, 1908, 31–33.

5. *PS*, January 2, 1895.

6. "Negauneen Suomalaisan Kansan Kodin Perus-Säännöt."

7. Reminiscences of John Kujala. The song can be found on page 212 of the Finnish version of this present work.

8. Letter from Alexander Holm, January 9, 1960.

9. Sometimes the area near a mine was called a location.

10. Reminiscences of Matti Autio.

11. Information given by Alfred Miettunen, who came to Republic from Simo in 1883–84, and from Benjamin and Ruth Mykkanen. Also, article by Vihtori Laine in *PS*, 1920, 378–402. Also, *Kirkollinen Kalenteri* (hereafter *KK*), 1915, 102–205.

12. Information given by Frank O. Mackie and Ina K. Tuomela.

13. Letter from Matt Kivi, January 1960.

14. *SK*, 1932, 171f. Also *SK*, 1935, 135f.

15. Notes by Hjalmar Makila and Johanna Harmanmaa in FAHA. Also, Clemens Niemi, "Suomalaiset Crystal Fallsissa," *SK*, 1928, 103–7. See page 220 of the Finnish version of this present work for the "Crystal Falls Song."

16. An anonymous author's "Muistiinpanoja Stambaugh'n ja Iron Riverin Ympäristöltä," about 1930, in FAHA. Also information from Dr. Konstant Koski and Edith Aspholm.

Chapter 8

1. *Tie Vapauteen*, May 1931, 16–19.

2. *Pelto ja Koti*, 1916, 99f. Also, Francis Trombly, *The Story of Rock, 1873–1957*.

3. Taisto Hayrinen, "The Co-op Made Rock," *The Cooperative Builder*, October 22, 1953. Also, Mrs. Richard Campbell, "Horse and Buggy Era of Rural Mail Deliveries Recalled by Rock Veteran," *Escanaba Daily Press*, March 7, 1953.

4. Information about the Finns of Kipling and Stonington given by Arvid Mustonen, November 2, 1961.

5. *PS*, 1904, no. 45.

6. Interview with Ananias Lind in Watton and with Postmaster Peter Thelander and George Gray in Cooks in June 1961. See also Record of Deaths, Schoolcraft County. Also, J. J. Hoikka, "Metsistö Suom. Ew. Lut. Seurakunta," *KK*, 1907, 137–45. Also, Cooks news in *PS*, 1897–1906. Also, letter from Martha D. Wiljanen, June 25, 1961, and letter from Sandra Ylinen-Pantti, June 22, 1961.

7. Lewis C. Reimann, *Incredible Seney* (Ann Arbor, 1953) gives a good picture of the wildness of life in Seney in early days.

8. Dedication speech in *PS*, 1901, no. 25.

9. J. J. Hoikka, "Suomalainen Hautuumaa Pohjois-Michiganin Halkometsissä," *KK*, 1907, 146–49. Also, interview with Ananias Lind.

10. Leslie E. Niemi, "Fifty Years of Progress: A History of the Eben Finnish Evangelical Lutheran Church," manuscript, FAHA.

11. *Chatham Telephone Company 1951 Directory*.

12. Memoir of Victor Aho, 1962. Also, Lauri Ahlman, "Grand Maraisin Seurakunta," *KK*, 1924, 146–49. Also, *PS*, September 2, 1907, etc. Also, "Askel Raittiusseura, Grand Marais, Mich.," *RK*, 1904, 126–28.

13. Memoir of V. K. Kauramaki, and the 40th, 50th, and 60th anniversary publications of the Bethlehem congregation.

14. *Helsingistä Astoriaan* (Porvoo, 1927), 244f.

15. F. J. Syrjala, "Pimeydesta Suuria Valoja Kohden," *Kalenteri Amerikan Suomalaiselle Työväestölle*, 1918, 104.

16. Interviews with Father Collary, the Catholic chaplain at the state hospital, and with Pastor Evert Torkko, July 28, 1960. In addition to his regular congregation, Pastor Torkko attended to the spiritual needs of Finnish patients at the hospital.

17. Letter from Matti Maki, August 14, 1961.

18. *Työmies Eteenpain*, April 6, 1960.

19. Ilmonen, *Amerikan Suomalaisten Historia*, 3:140.

20. Frank A. Aaltonen was born in Hämeenlinna on September 23, 1884, and died in Brooklyn, N.Y., on February 24, 1958.

21. Jack Koivisto, "Sokerisaaren Suomalaisten Historiaa," manuscript, FAHA. Also, Joseph E. and Estelle L. Bayliss, *River of Destiny* (Detroit, 1955), 164–66.

22. *PS*, October 24, 1904.

23. *5th Anniversary of St. James' Lutheran Church*, 12

24. Toini Hill, "Drummondin Saaren Suomalaisten Historiaa," manuscript, FAHA; Lillian Bird, "A Finnish Community on Drummond Island," manuscript, FAHA; and interview with Kalle Holman, June 1960.

Chapter 9

1. Ilmonen, *Amerikan Suomalaisten Historia*, 3:143–50.

2. George Morski, "Railroad Race Located Kaleva," *Grand Rapids Press*, April 24, 1960.

3. Helen Lehto, "Kaleva, Michigan," manuscript which won the second prize in the Finnish American Historical Society (Detroit) contest; *KK*, 1924, 162–78; and *KK*, 1943, 49–56.

4. *PS*, May 27, 1912. See also *KK*, 1923, 79–81; Correspondence of the Suomi Synod Consistory; Letter from Lydia Ripatte, January 1960; Ilmonen, *Amerikan Suomalaisten Historia*, 146.

5. *PS*, October 24, 1894.

6. Ilmonen, *Amerikan Suomalaisten Historia*, 145.

7. Letter, June 1961.

8. *SK*, 1950, 184–86.

9. Ilmonen, *Amerikan Suomalaisten Historia*, 150f.

10. Notes of Alexander Hamlin in FAHA, in *Koiviston Viesti*, September 9, 1960, and in the archives of the Finnish American Historical Society in Detroit. See also *Michiganin Suomalainen*, 1961, 22.

11. *Finnish Album to Commemorate Detroit's 250th Birthday* (Detroit, 1951). See also the many articles about Finnish churches of Detroit in issues of *KK* (in Finnish). Also *Detroitin Suomalaisten Vuosikirjat*, 1931–36.

Chapter 10

1. He wrote his name thus in the minutes. The form "A. F. Fredrickson" is probably based on a misreading of this name as it appears in the minutes.

2. Theologisk Candidat fra Christiania Universitet i Norge og ordineret Evangelisk Luthersk Praest.

3. Skandinavisk Evangelisk Luthersk Kirkesamfund.

4. In a notation dated March 6, 1870, in the same book, Pastor Fridrichsen wrote: Den Norsk-Lutherske Menighed.

5. There is a difference of opinion as to the year these meetings were held. The English version of Uuras Saarnivaara, *The History of the Laestadian or Apostolic-Lutheran Movement in America*, 20, accepts 1870, based on apparently conclusive evidence.

6. The first explanation is given in writings on American Laestadianism by V. Rautanen, Juuso Hirvonen, and V. O. Jamsa, the latter by Henrik Koller. Saarnivaara makes no attempt to decide the matter.

7. Saarnivaara, *Amerikan Laestadiolaisuuden eli Apostolis-Luterilaisuuden Historia*, 48.

8. Minutes of church board meeting, October 6, 1889.

9. Andrew Mickelsen's father's brother married Hedvig Charlotta, daughter of Lars Levi Laestadius. They lived mostly in Cokato, Minnesota. Hedvig Charlotta had no children, so her death marked the end of the Laestadius strain in America.

10. Laestadians do not usually consider it right to include children in the membership count of the church. Their basic principle concerning mem-

bership is that only believers are true members. Membership fees, however, are accepted from other supporters of the church.

11. *Hymns and Songs of Zion*, 2d ed., 1962.

12. Ironwood, 1947. Other works by Saarnivaara on this subject are *Mikä On Totuus Amerikan Laestadiolaisesta Kristillisyydesta?* (Hancock, 1947); and *Vanhoillisuuden Hajaantumisen Historiaa Amerikassa ja Suomessa* (Rovaniemi, 1950). In Laestadian circles these books are considered controversial, but they do contain important historical source material.

13. *The New Postilla* (Hancock, 1960).

14. Reino Suojanen, "Heikki Koller. Pastori A. V. Tuukkanen Kertoo," *Valvoja*, July 14, 1936. Also interviews with Tuukkanen and Suojanen, March 1964.

15. Later, Backman was a rector in Ätsäri, Finland, returned to America, and was the pastor of the Astoria congregation for a short time in 1902. He died while rector of Hauho, Finland, in 1909. See Rautanen, *Amerikan Suomalainen Kirkko*, 35ff. Also *KK*, 1906, 42, and 1910, 207ff.

16. Henry Kangas, "Blades, Ears, and Corn. Suomi Synod 1890–1952," manuscript, FAHA, 51–53.

17. Letter to Nikander, who had asked for advice, August 10, 1889.

18. *PS*, 1889, 143.

19. Yrjö Koskinen discussed it in *Vartija*.

20. An imperial parish of the Church of Finland up to 1918 was one of the naming of whose rector was the right of the tsar-emperor. Up to 1809 such districts had been known as kings' parishes, and the right of appointment to them had rested with the king of Sweden-Finland.

21. Up to this point this survey of the early phases of the history of the Suomi Synod is based on the minutes of church conventions and of the Consistory, as well as, in certain parts, on the previously mentioned work by Rautanen and the manuscript by Kangas.

22. This survey of the period from 1896 to 1906 has been based on the minutes of the church conventions and the Consistory, and on J. K. Nikander's "Lyhyt Silmäys Kirkkokuntamme 25-Vuotiseen Toimintaan," *Juhla-Albumi Suomi-Synodin 25-Vuotis-Juhlan Muistoksi 1890–1915*, 11–51.

23. J. A. Karkkainen, "J. J. Hoikka," *Uskonpuhdistuksen Muisto*, 1917, 2ff. See also *KK*, 1918, 192ff.

24. *KK*, 1933, 22–25. Prof. Pietila wrote this exactly one month before his death on September 9, 1932. This lack of knowledge of the church was reflected in the fact that of the 292 lay representatives at the church convention in Virginia, Minnesota, in 1960, ninety were not subscribing to either of the church organs—*Amerikan Suometar* and *The Lutheran Counselor*. See also *Amerikan Suometar*, July 7, 1960.

25. Armas Holmio, "The Finnish Evangelical Lutheran Church in Japan," in Andrew Burgess, *Lutheran World Missions* (Minneapolis, 1954).

26. Minutes of the church conventions of 1900 and 1901.

27. Taisto John Niemi, "The Finnish Lutheran Book Concern 1900–

1950: A Historical and Developmental Study" (Ph.D. diss., University of Michigan, 1960). See also *Kirkkokuntamme Lehdistö ja Kustannustoimi* (Hancock, 1929); *Amerikan Suometar 1899–1919* (Hancock, 1919); and annual reports of the Suomi Synod and minutes of the meetings of the board of directors of the Book Concern.

28. Ironwood, 1926.

29. The exact wording of the agreement can be found in *Auttaja*, first number of 1963.

30. Information about the National Church has been obtained mostly from the works of J. E. Nopola: *Evankelis-Luterilainen Kansalliskirkko* (Ironwood, 1949); and *Our Threescore Years* (Ironwood, 1958). Information has also been obtained from the following publications: *Todistusten Joukko 1902–3; Amerikan Suom. Ev.-Lut. Kansalliskirkon 25-Vuotisjulkaisu 1898–1923* (Ironwood, 1923); annual reports and calendars of the National Church; reports on church conventions in *Auttaja.*

31. *Hengelliseltä Taistelutantereelta*, 1914, 42–48. See also Sippola, *Album to Commemorate Detroit's 250th Birthday*, 18. Also V. Rautanen, *Amerikan Suomalainen Kirkko*, 290–305. Also *PS*, 1898, 213 and August 8, 1901.

32. *PS*, December 18, 1902. A Methodist monthly, *Rauhan Airut*, was also published in 1902–3, in Ishpeming.

33. Information provided by A. V. Tuukkanen and others.

34. *PS*, April 1, 1891.

Chapter 11

1. Viljo Hytonen, *Yleinen Raittiusliikkeen Historia* and *Historiallinen Raittiuslukukirja.*

2. Hytonen, *Yleinen Raittiusliikkeen Historia.*

3. Wegelius's collection of sermons was titled *Se Pyhä Evangeliumillinen Walkeus Taiwallisessa Opisa ja Pyhäsä Elämäsä.* The excerpt given was taken from the edition published in Turku in 1836, which is now in the FAHA, and which Erik and Kaarle Leisto had purchased in the parish of Ii in 1881.

4. See Hytonen, *Yleinen Raittiusliikkeen Historia*, 189–97.

5. Ilmari Salomies, *Henrik Renqvist.*

6. Hytonen, *Yleinen Raittiusliikkeen Historia.* See also Granfelt, "Raittiusseurat Suomessa," *KVK*, 1886, 199–203. Also Eino Kuusi, "Maamme Raittiusliike," *Oma Maa* (Own earth), 2:755ff.

7. M. Toppari, "Mikä On Ollut Tarkoituksena?" *RK*, 1906, pp. 132–36.

8. *Siirtolaisen Opas*, published by the Suomen Merimieslähetysseura and the Suomi Synod, Helsinki, 1910.

9. Matthew Putkonen, *Kristillinen Siweyden Oppi Rakkaalle Suomen Kansalle, Etenki Talonpoikaselle* (Säädylle, Helsinki, 1865), 84.

10. R. H. Oittinen, *Työväenkysymys ja Työväenliike Suomessa*, 2d ed. (Helsinki, 1954), 82.

11. John H. Pitezel, *Lights and Shades of Missionary Life: Containing Travels, Sketches, Incidents, and Missionary Efforts, During Nine Years in the Region of Lake Superior* (Cincinnati, 1860).

12. John I. Kolehmainen, *Suomalaisten Siirtolaisuus Norjasta Amerikkaan* (Fitchburg, 1946).

13. Ilmonen, "Raittiusseura Pohjantähden Hancock 25-Vuotis Historia," *RK*, 1911, 132–56. According to another source, the hall was not completed until 1887.

14. Isak Sillberg, "Onnen Aika Seuran Synty ja Kehitys," *RK*, 1899, 38–40.

15. J. M. Eriksen, "Hyvä Toivo," *Yhteistyössä* (Hancock, 1908), 66–75.

16. V. W., pseud., in *Raittiuden Ystäväin Kalenteri*, 1900, 51–53.

17. It is given thus in the SKRV list of member societies. Ilmonen, on page 24 of his *Amerikan Suomalaisen Raittiusliikkeen Historia*, gives January 28 as the date.

18. SKRV roster of member societies.

19. Ilmonen, *Amerikan Suomalaisen Raittiusliikkeen Historia*, 25. The minutes Ilmonen used in 1912 have since disappeared.

20. SKRV roster of member societies.

21. Ilmonen, *Amerikan Suomalaisen Raittiusliikkeen Historia*, 26f.

22. Ibid., 30.

23. The discussion about the temperance society of Republic as the initiator of action is based on ibid, 36f. Ilmonen does not give his source. The minutes preserved by the Onnen Aika Society begin with November 4, 1888. The Aura Society made its decision to leave the Good Templars on January 22, 1888, that is, after the meeting held in Republic. See *Auran Historiikki*, 33.

24. The minutes of the Aamurusko Temperance Society from 1888 to 1933, as well as most of their other records and membership rosters, are in the FAHA.

25. The discussion about the activities of the SKRV is based almost entirely on the minutes and other records of the Brotherhood. All the SKRV records are housed in the FAHA.

26. The minutes are not in the SKRV collection.

27. Minutes have been saved beginning with 1892, as has the record of membership which was started in 1905.

28. Minutes began with July 21, 1889. The older minutes have been torn out.

29. SKRV membership roster. The page on which the decision was probably recorded has been cut out of the minutes.

30. According to the SKRV membership roster. The minutes of the SKRV board for this meeting are missing; there is a blank page where they should be.

31. *Kasikirja Suomalaiseen Raittius-Ystäwien Yhdistykseen Kuuluville Raittiusseuroille Amerikassa* (Red Jacket, 1890).

32. Ilmonen, *Sivistyshistoria* 1:44f.

33. For one society, no home area is given in the list.

34. Raittiuden Ystäväin Yhdistysen Kalenteri (hereafter *RYK*), 1900, 32–34.

35. Ibid., 63f.

36. Ibid., 77–79.

37. *RYK*, 1901, 39f.

38. The Tapio Society left the Brotherhood on September 30, 1896. On November 29, 1896, former members organized a temperance society called Totuuden Etsijä no. 91, in connection with the Brotherhood.

39. *RK*, 1898, 32f.

40. The minutes from 1908 to 1918 are in the FAHA.

41. *RL*, March 20, 1907. See also SKRV President's Annual Report, 115.

42. The minutes of the Vellamo Society in the FAHA cover the period from its beginnings to January 5, 1912.

43. SKRV President's Annual Report, 13.

44. *RK*, 1901, 99f. The minutes of the Toivola Society from 1891 to 1960 are in the FAHA.

45. From a history of the early days of the Toivola Society, which is in the FAHA. The author of the manuscript is not known.

46. The minutes of the Iltarusko Society from its organization to 1909 are in the FAHA.

47. The minutes of the Onnela Society from 1899 to 1900 are in the FAHA.

48. *RL*, March 20, 1896.

49. *RK*, 1903, 109f. The FAHA has the minutes of the Korven Kukka Society for 1901–4, 1910–32, and 1936–45, in addition to some account books.

50. Letters from John Wiljanen's daughter, Miss Martha D. Wiljanen, dated June 25, 1961 and July 13, 1961. See also *RL*, May 20, 1896, 1907, 142.

51. Obituary, *RK*, 1901.

52. In the SKRV roster there is a notation to the effect that this happened on August 16, 1898. The month and day may well be right but the year is incorrect, for people continued to join the society to the summer of 1899.

53. The FAHA has the quite carefully kept membership records of the Väinötär and the Elon Tähti from 1896 to 1903. The minutes have disappeared.

54. *RK*, 1906, 87ff. See also *Uusi Wartia Juhlajulkaisu*, 1907, 3f. The minutes have disappeared; the FAHA has only a small book which contains a record of membership fees.

55. *RK*, 1904, 151f. See also *RK*, 1915, 178f.

56. Annual Report of the President of the SKRV, 113f. The minutes for 1906–8 are in the FAHA. There is also a somewhat muddled record of membership fees.

57. The FAHA has minutes for 1912–14 and 1937.

58. The FAHA has minutes for 1906–17 and an account book for 1911–27. See *RL*, January 15, 1900.

59. Letter from Henry Moilanen, September 9, 1961.

60. *RL*, January 15, 1900. The FAHA has the minutes of the Yrittäjä Society up to October 19, 1902, and 1907–16, but the minutes of the organizational meeting are missing.

61. *RL*, January 15, 1900. See also *RK*, 1910, 164ff. The minutes have disappeared.

62. *RL*, January 15, 1900. Minutes cannot be found.

63. *RL*, March 15, 1900.

64. *RL*, November 1901.

65. The page on which the matter was apparently recorded has been removed from the annual report. This kind of mutilation occurs quite frequently in Finnish American historical sources.

66. *RK*, 1902, 128–30. The FAHA has the minutes of the Kyntäjä Society for 1900–1902, 1906–13, and 1917–18.

67. From the anniversary publication of the Copper Country Temperance League, 1913, 17. The FAHA has the minutes of the Auran Kukka for 1900–1904 and 1907–9.

68. *RL*, August 1901. The FAHA has the minutes of the Taimen Oksa for 1901–8.

69. All the records of the Pellervo Society have disappeared. See *RL*, January 1902, 12.

70. *Yhteistyössä*, 124f.

71. *RK*, 1906, 149ff.

72. The SKRV roster of member societies was not now kept up as carefully as in the earlier years. For example, days of the month are missing entirely for 1903. Some of them have been found in other sources, especially in calendars.

73. *RK*, 1906, 113ff.

74. *RK*, 1921, 164ff.

75. *Yhteistyössä*, 154–56.

76. See the discussion about Rockland in the chapter about Finns in the Copper Country. See also *Yhteistyössä*, 157f.

77. *Yhteistyössä*, 146–48. See also minutes and other records in the FAHA.

78. Minutes and other records in the FAHA.

79. Minutes for 1907–19 in the FAHA.

80. Minutes for 1907–10 in the FAHA. See also *RK*, 1912, 178.

81. Minutes for 1908–9 in the FAHA.

82. *Uusi Wartia*, 1907, 12f.

83. Interview with Kalle Nyman, July 1960.

84. *Uusi Wartia*, 1907, 13–17.

85. *RK*, 1914, 160–64.

86. *RK*, 1911, 167–72.

87. *Rauhankokous ja Pääpiirteitä Amerikan Suomalaisten Raittiustyön Historiasta* (Hancock, 1908).

88. *RK*, 1926, 137.

89. Ilmonen, *Amerikan Suomalaisen Raittiusliikkeen Historia*, 144.

90. *RK*, 1927, 28.

91. Exceptions were articles in the English language which occasionally appeared in the *Raittiuskalenteri*. Over the years the use of two languages even in other publications for Finnish Americans has never been much in favor, for neither the older nor the younger generation found them acceptable.

92. Heikki Karhu, for example, is one who complained about this in his annual report, *RK*, 1928, 49.

93. *RK*, 1931, 177.

94. There are figures on active societies only occasionally in the *RK*. Membership figures are no longer even mentioned.

95. *RK*, 1959, 61–65, and 1961, 88–93.

96. *RK*, 1922, 62–69; 1965, 87–90; 1959, 43–46.

97. *RK*, 1943, 89; 1958, 59–61. See also *Valoa*, 1961, 7; and reminiscences of Walter H. Salmi.

98. *RK*, 1943.

Chapter 12

1. R. H. Oittinen, *Työväenkysymys ja Työväenliike Suomessa*, 36–40.

2. Ibid., 67–106.

3. Eero W. Helin, "Piirteitä Kansallisseura Imatran 50-Vuotisesta Toiminnasta," in the anniversary publication *Imatran 50-Vuotisjuhla 1891–1941*.

4. Oittinen, *Työväenkysymys ja Työväenliike Suomessa*, 121.

5. *Kalenteri Amerikan Suomalaiselle Työväelle 1918*, 31.

6. *Työmies 10-Vuotias 1903–1913* (Hancock, 1913). See also *Työmies 20 Vuotta* (Superior, 1923); William Lahtinen, *50 Vuoden Varrelta* (Superior, 1953); and Elis Sulkanen, *Amerikan Suomalaisen Työväenliikkeen Historia* (Fitchburg, 1951).

7. *Vappu*, 1960, 18f.

8. Jussi Kuoppala, *Suomen Papisto ja Työväenkysymys Ennen Työväenliikkeen Syntymistä*.

9. Examples of books published by Työmies Publishing Company are translations from their original languages of works such as the following: Edward Bellamy, *Yhdenvertaisuus* (Equality), 1905; Allen E. Benson, *Mitä Sosialismi Todella On (The truth about socialism)*, trans. Aura Snell, 1914; A. Bogdanoff, *Lyhyt Taloustieteen Oppikirja* (Brief textbook of economics) 2d ed., trans. Leo Laukki, 1914; *Joukkoliike ja Vallankumous, Karl Kautskyn ja Anton Pannekookin Väittely Uudesta Taktiikasta* (Mass movements and revolution), trans. Yryo Sirola, 1912; Peter Krapotkin, *Taistelu Leivasta* (Conquest of bread), n.d.; *Luok-*

kataistelijan Asevarasto, 1913; Karl Marx and Friedrich Engels, *Kommunistinen Manifesti* (Communist manifesto), 2d ed., trans. Kaapo Murros, 1914; Walter Thomas Mills, *Yhteiskunnallinen Taloustiede* (Social science), trans. Eino V. Wartiainen, 1908; Kaapo Murros, *Suuret Haaveilijat*, 1905; *Oppikirja Sosialismissa* (Textbook of socialism), 1910; A. M. Simons, *Luokkataistelut Amerikassa* (Class struggle in America), 1908; Carl D. Thompson, *Sosialismin Rakentava Ohjelma* (Program of constructive socialism), trans. Toivo Hiltunen, 1909; *Tulevaisuutta Kohti: Sosiaalipoliittisia Esitelmiä* (Toward the future: Discourses on social policy), pub. in Finnish by N. R. af Ursin, 1905; and Clarence S. Darrow, *Silma Silmasta* (An eye for an eye), 1908. This sampling of works published in Hancock between 1905 and 1914, though not comprehensive by any means, gives some indication of the amount of socialistic literature published at this time, especially if we take into consideration the fact that *Raivaaja* of Fitchburg, *Toveri* of Astoria, and the Workingmen's College in Duluth were also publishing such literature.

10. *PS*, 1903, no. 9, 3.

11. "Sananen Sosialismista ja Sen Suhteesta Uskontoon," *RK*, 1907, 129–48. See also "Mihin Suuntaan Uudistustyö," *RK*, 1908, 44–53.

12. Hancock, 1913. In the *Paimen-Sanomia*, for example in no. 1 of 1906, Nikander sometimes published articles concerning the matter, taken from newspapers published in Finland.

13. Eighth ed., Superior, 1919; Hancock, 1913.

14. Minutes of the meeting, 42–61, 77f., 119–21, 123f.

15. An example of this kind of funeral sermon appears in Santeri M.'s novel *Elämää Ikuisessa Yössä*, 87ff. The narrative is about an iron mining town in Michigan.

16. *Vastaus Vapaa-Ajattelija Robert Ingersollille*, 1904; and *Kristillisiä Ajanksysymyksiä*, 1905.

17. Karl Kautsky, *Kristinuskon Alkuperä* (Origin of Christianity), trans. J. K. Kari (Superior, 1918). See also Bouck White, *Natsaretin Kirvesmies* (Carpenter of Nazareth), trans. Kalle Tähtelä (Fitchburg, 1905); and J. H. Crooker, *Uskonto-Opillisia Periaatteita* (Principles of religious doctrine) (Fitchburg, 1910). A. B. Sarlin's translation *Miten Jesus Kuoli* (How Jesus died) (Hancock, 1911) also belongs in this group.

18. See book lists of the Book Concern for these years.

19. An article in *Työmies-Eteenpäin* dated April 28, 1961, discusses the two last-mentioned reasons.

20. Elis Sulkanen, *Amerikan Suomalaisen Työväenliikkeen Historia*, 132.

21. Interview with two former miners.

22. Henry Kangas, "Blades, Ears, and Corn," 162f.

23. No. 53, January 21, 1914.

24. See Laukki's account of the meeting held at Hendrickson's home in *Suomalaisen Sosialistijärjestön Keskipiirin Kokouksen Pöytäkirja*, 1912, 212.

25. *Miners' Bulletin*, nos. 1–66. See also scattered issues of *Työmies*

and *Truth* published at the time of the strike; *Amerikan Suometar*, and *Lakkotutkimus*, 1913.

26. Bylaws of the league and minutes of April 9, 1914, to September 12, 1915.

27. *Kalenteri Amerikan Suomalaiselle Työväestölle 1918*, 33.

28. Emil Leino and John Lind, "Historiaa Bessemerin Työväenyhdistyksen ja Sosialistiosaston Toiminnasta," manuscript, FAHA.

29. Sulkanen, *Amerikan Suomalaisen Työväenliikkeen Historia*, 426–31, 436–44.

30. Some of the minutes and account books of the Munising socialist organization are in the FAHA.

31. *Kalenteri Amerikan Suomalaiselle Työväelle*, 1919, 18f.

32. See W. N. Reivo, "Syndikalistiemme Revisionistisuus," *Vappu*, 1918, 33–95.

33. In addition to newspapers: Kaarlo Valli, *Liekeissä* (Astoria, 1923); Magnus Raeus, *Yli Kuoleman Kenttien* (Worcester); Laurie Luoto, *Valkoisen Leijonan Metsästäjät* (Superior, 1926); Henkipatto, *Suuri Rikos* (Superior, 1921); *Kalenteri Amerikan Suomalaiselle Työväelle, 1919* (Fitchburg, 1918); Otto V. Kuusinen and Yrjo Sirola, *Suomen Työväen Tulikoe* (Superior, 1923). A complete listing would be much longer. Special publications overflowed with reports on matters pertaining to the civil war in Finland.

34. J. Edgar Hoover, *Masters of Deceit* (New York, 1961), 48–55.

35. Sulkanen, *Amerikan Suomalaisen Työväenliikkeen Historia*, 269ff. See also *Pöytäkirja Yhdysvaltain Suomalaisen Työväenjärjestön Perustavasta Edustajakokouksesta Chicagossa, January 24–27, 1927.*

36. There is an account of this in the chapter about cooperatives.

37. V. Molotov, *Neuvostoliitto Käännekohdassa: Työväen Tasavalta Sosialismia Rakentamassa* (Worcester, 1930).

38. 15 West 126th Street.

39. Yrjo Sirola was an exception. He suffered a stroke and died in the Kremlin hospital.

40. Interview with the commander of a Finnish regiment.

41. G. N. Kuprijanov, "Karjalais-Suomalainen Sosialistinen Neuvostotasavalta Neuvostovallen 30 Vuoden Aikana," *Punalippu*, Petroskoi: Karjalais-Suomalaisen SNT:n Valtion Kustannusliike, 3–16. In the same way, Finnish American Communist literature remained silent on the outcome of the Karelian venture. To a certain extent, Eemeli Rautiainen's *Neuvostomaata Rakentamassa: Amerikan Suomalaiset Sosialistisessa Rakennustyössä Neuvosto-Karjalassa* (Petroskoi, 1933), was an exception. But in addition to factual information, the content is mostly an expression of praise for the Soviet Union and of hostility toward Finland and America, especially toward those who had returned to America from Karelia.

42. Especially the following: John R. Leino, "Punaisen Sumun Maa," published in the *Raivaaja* from November 1948 to January 1949; Eemeli Parras, "Kalevalan Laulumailta," in the *Punatähti* of 1936, 34f., tells about Parras's visit

to Uhtua but does not mention his Finnish American friends; John Hamlin, *Työmiehenä Venäjällä*, 2d ed. (Porvoo, 1934); *S.T. Järjestön Neljäs Edustajakokous Brooklynissa 27–28 Päivinä Marraskuuta 1932*; "Finns Return to United States after Effort to Colonize Karelia," *Milwaukee Journal*, April 27, 1941; David Johnson, "Why I Left 'Paradise' and Came Back Home," *Detroit News*, June 17, 1962; *Havaintoja Matkalta Karjalaan ja Siellä Oloajalta* (Fitchburg, 1934); August Lehmus, *Suomalaiset Kommunistit Itä-Karjalassa* (Hämeenlinna, 1959); Arvo Tuominen, *Kremlin Kellot*, 6th ed. (Helsinki, 1957); and idem, *Sirpin ja Vasaran Tie*, 2d ed. (Helsinki, 1956).

43. A more detailed account appears in the chapter on cooperatives.

44. Sulkanen, *Amerikan Suomalaisen Työväenliikkeen Historia*, 333.

Chapter 13

1. Interview on May 20, 1963, with John Maki, oldest of the Kaleva Knights in 1960 and a personal friend of Stone. He says that these were Stone's guiding ideas. Although in some publications the temperance question is given as the chief reason for the birth of the Kaleva organization, it is an error.

2. See Ilmonen, *Amerikan Suomalaisten Sivistyshistoria*, 1:104ff.; and *Kalevaisten 50-Vuotisjuhlajulkaisu*, 9–20.

3. Information given by members of the Nyyrikki Lodge. See also *Kalevainen*, 1913, 26; 1918, 27; 1940, 61; 1942, 28f.; 1950, 60; and 1951, 56, 59.

4. Information given by a committee selected by the Etelätär Lodge. See also *Kalevainen*, 1948, 44f. and 1955, 26f.

5. *Kalevainen*, 1951, 59.

6. One of his last acts as a Knight of Kaleva was to provide information for this present work with Albert Turunen, having been commissioned to o by his lodge.

7. Information given by the Osmo Lodge of Knights and the Kyllikki Lodge of Ladies. There is more information about the Ironwood Kalevainens in the *Kalevainen* of 1929, 1933, 1935, 1942, 1944, and in almost every number since 1949. See also *Kalevan Naisten Historian Ääriviivoja*, 45–49, 109f., 127f.

8. The statement in the *Kalevainen* of 1950, 66, that the Sotka Lodge was organized on March 5, 1907, is erroneous. On that day the Y.E.V.J. and Y.H. signed the charter of the Sotka Lodge.

9. *Kalevan Naisten Historian Ääriviivoja*, 26–30, 118f. See also *Kalevainen*, 1913, 15, 51; 1935, 29; 1940, 32f.; 1944, 38; 1950, 66; 1951, 61f.; 1953, 52.

10. *Kalevan Naisten Historian Ääriviivoja*, 11f.; See also *Kalevaisten 50-Vuotisjuhlajulkaisu*, 73; *Kalevainen*, 1935, 48, and 1963, 82f.

11. Information given by the Taatto Lodge of Knights and the Sammotar Lodge of Ladies. See also *Kalevainen*, 1933, 44f., 49; 1935, 47; 1937, 23; 1945, 75; 1951, 60; 1953, 41; 1961, 14f. and 57; 1963, 66, and *Kalevan Naisten Historian Ääriviivoja*, 70f., 107, and 148–50.

12. *Kalevan Naisten Historian Ääriviivoja*, 63 and 96.

13. Information provided by Alli Hepola, Victor Makela, and Sakari Lukkarinen, authorized by the Allitar Lodge of Ladies and the Ahtolainen Lodge of Knights. See also *Kalevaisten 50-Vuotisjuhlajulkaisu*, 92f. Also *Kalevan Naisten Historian Aariviivoja*, 12f., 114–16. Also *Kalevainen*, 1916, 21, 55; 1935, 32; 1939, 21–24; 1944, 43; and almost every number from 1950 on. Also *Siirtokansan Kalenteri*, 1963, 125f.

14. *Kalevan Naisten Historian Ääriviivoja*, 57f. See also *Kalevainen*, 1928, 33 and 1930, 39.

15. Information sent by Amanda Siro, authorized by the Laaksotar Lodge. See also *Kalevaisten 50-Vuotisjuhlajulkaisu*, 76. Also *Kalevan Naisten Historian Ääriviivoja*, 55f. and the *Kalevainen*, 1933, 42; 1935, 27; 1939, 37; 1944, 35; 1948, 43; 1951, 47f.; 1959, 47; 1963, 68.

16. *Kalevan Naisten Historian Ääriviivoja*, 19, says that the founder of the Auratar Lodge of Ladies was Saara Rayha. In the history of the Auratar Lodge in the FAHA, which ends with 1951, the founder is given as Saara Royha. If this name refers to Sara Royhy, a member of the Annikki Lodge of Brooklyn, who traveled in America in 1914–17 lecturing at Kaleva meetings and elsewhere, the information is incorrect. In her travelogue *Muistelmia 1135 Vuorokauden Matkoilta* she says she visited in Detroit for the first time after the Aura and Auratar Lodges had already been established, 172f.

17. Information provided by Andrew I. Brask and Etta A. Suksi, authorized by the Aura and Auratar Lodges. See also *Kalevainen*, 1931, 20; 1934, 27; 1938, 45, 51; and almost every number since then. Also *Detroitin Albumi*, 1951, 14.

18. Information provided by Ida Korhonen and John Maki, authorized by the Kanerva and Elias Lodges. See also *Kalevan Naisten Historian Ääriviivoja*, 31f. and the *Kalevainen*, 1936, 31f.; 1938, 30; 1943, 50; 1947, 49; 1954, 46; and almost all numbers following.

19. Information sent by John J. Pölky, authorized by the Virokannas Lodge. See also *Kalevan Naisten Historian Ääriviivoja* and the *Kalevainen*, 1943, 46; 1947, 44; 1954, 45f.

20. *Kalevan Naisten Historian Ääriviivoja*, 119.

21. *Kalevainen*, 1928, 2.

22. *Kalevan Naisten Historian Ääriviivoja*, 22.

23. *Kalevainen*, 1947, 9.

24. *Kalevainen*, 1950, 45.

25. *Historia K.H.Y. Majan Kokouksessa Ironwoodissa, Elok. 17–21 p:nä, 1914*, paragraphs 21, 22, 58.

26. *Kalevainen*, 1935, 13–15.

27. *Kalevainen*, 1936, 20f.

28. *Kalevainen*, 1939, 24–26.

29. Information provided by Toivo Pelto. See also Herman Maki's article in the *Kalevainen* of 1940, 50–52.

30. *Articles of Incorporation and By-Laws of the Upper Peninsula Kaleva Pirtti.*

31. *Kalevainen*, 1943, 41; 1944, 18f.; 1953, 40; 1960, 17f.

32. See Alice H. Osman, "The Effect of a Kaleva Summer Camp," *Kalevainen*, 1956, 17f.

33. Report by Aino M. Uksila, secretary of a Louhetar Lodge committee, in the *Kalevainen*, 1936, 9–12.

34. *Kalevainen*, 1940, 32f.

35. Memoir of Matti Erkkila, "Ääni Vuosikymmenien Takaa," *Kalevainen*, 1963, 6–9.

36. S. C. Olin, *Finlandia: The Racial Composition, the Language, and a Brief History of the Finnish People* (Hancock: Book Concern, 1957).

37. *Kalevainen*, 1918, 13–17. The editor of this number was the druggist Werner Nikander, who asks in his preface that the reader "accept with broad-minded tolerance what is good and reject what is objectionable." When *Kalevainen* was no longer available to the theosophists, they began to use certain Finnish newspapers as their organs of propaganda. The editors of the papers opened their columns to the theosophists, sometimes purposely but more often in ignorance of the real nature of their writings.

38. *Liikemiesten ja Laulajain Suomimatka*, 1921, 63.

39. G. A. Aho and J. E. Nopola, *Evankelis-Luterilainen Kansalliskirkko*, 374f.

40. Santeri M., *Elämää Ikuisessa Yössä*, 2d ed. (Ironwood: Otto Massisen Kirjapaino ja Kustannusliike, 1911).

41. *Kalevainen*, 1921, 6. See also John A. Harpet, "Kalevainen ja Kalevaisten Järjestö," *Kalevainen*, 1923, 4. Also "Neljänkymmenen Vuoden Takaa," *Kalevainen*, 1955, 44.

42. *Kalevainen*, 1928, 12–15; 1956, 7f. See also *Siirtokansan Kalenteri*, 1925, 203–6 and 1951, 155f.

43. John Lauttamus was born in Kauhava in 1870, arrived in America in 1892, and first lived in Calumet. From 1906 on, his home was in Cloquet, Minnesota. He was by trade a blacksmith and belonged to the local temperance society as well as to the Vainamoinen Lodge of the Knights of Kaleva. His lively collection of stories *Amerikan Tuulahduksia* was published in 1922 by WSOY.

44. *Parliamentary Law and Rules of Order.* Compiled in the American language by Uriah Smith. A patented work. Adapted and translated into Finnish by John Stone, Duluth, 1906.

Chapter 14

1. Esko Aaltonen, *Kuluttajat Yhteistyössä* (Helsinki, 1953), 7–22.

2. Ibid, 52–75. See also V. S. Alanne, *Kuluttajaosuustoiminnan Perusteet* (Superior, 1937), 7–14; Leo R. Ward, *United for Freedom* (Milwaukee, 1945), 9–42; and Henry H. Bakken, *Cooperation to the Finnish* (Madison, Wis., 1939), 29–33.

3. *Kansallinen Elämäkerrasto*, 2:194ff.

4. Esko Aaltonen, *Consumer Cooperation in Finland* (Helsinki, 1954), 35–104.

5. *Historik Öfver Svensk-Finnarne i Worcester, Mass., 1880–1929*, 8, in which it is said that this business was "ett ko-operativt handelsaktiebolag."

6. Hans R. Wasastjerna, *Minnesotan Suomalaisten Historia*, 178.

7. F. Tolonen, "Amerikan Suomalaisten Liike-Elämästä," *Liikemiesten ja Laulajain Suomimatka 1921*, 99–106.

8. Savele Syrjala, *The Story of a Cooperative* (Boston, 1947), 14. Angus Murdock, *Boom Copper*, 154, tells about a meat and grocery store started in Tamarack in 1890, which the mining company financed and which succeeded so well that the *Saturday Evening Post* published an article about it, calling it a cooperative store. However, it was not a cooperative in the true sense of the word.

9. Bertram B. Fowler, *Consumer Cooperation in America* (New York, 1936), 261.

10. *TOL*, September 29, 1953.

11. *Cooperative Builder*, October 1, 1953.

12. *United Co-operative Society of Fitchburg: Annual Report 1959*. See also *United Co-operative Society of Maynard. Fifty Years of Progress.*

13. Information given by Eino E. Kankaan in October 1961.

14. Examples selected from tables for 1913 in *Lakkotutkimus*, 30–32.

15. V. S. Alanne, *Rockin Osuuskunta, Rock Co-operative Company* (Minneapolis, n.d.), *25-Vuotias, 1913–1938.*

16. Interview with manager Alexandar Laitala, September 6, 1961.

17. Jacob Vainionpaa in *Pelto ja Koti* (Form and home). He also says that the business was established immediately after the strike, not while it was going on. Organizational meetings may have been held already in 1913.

18. Alanne, *Rockin Osuuskunta*, 58.

19. *Pelto ja Koti*, 1917, 98, 165.

20. *Pelto ja Koti*, 1914, 275.

21. *Pelto ja Koti*, 1917, 149, 286.

22. Ibid., 336f.

23. *Pelto ja Koti*, 1916, 146f.

24. *Pelto ja Koti*, 1914, 280 (advertisement).

25. Walter H. Salmi in the *Cooperative Builder*, August 18, 1955.

26. *Pelto ja Koti*, 1917, 300.

27. *Pelto ja Koti*, 1916, minutes of the meeting, 381f.

28. At least in June 1917 the Paynesville cooperative was not a branch of the Hancock cooperative.

29. *Pelto ja Koti*, 1918, 40, 257.

30. Walter H. Salmi's notes.

31. *Pelto ja Koti*, 1917, 150.

32. Information obtained by William Kallio, Watton, Michigan.

33. *Pelto ja Koti*, 1917, 165. See also *SK*, 1946, 123f. The Konnos had been married in Kauhajoki in 1910 and came to Chatham from Finland in 1912.

34. *Pelto ja Koti*, 1917, 148, 300.

35. *Pelto ja Koti*, 1914, 66

36. *Pelto ja Koti*, 1916, 242–54.

37. *Pelto ja Koti*, 292–94.

38. *Pelto ja Koti*, 254, 294.

39. *Pelto ja Koti*, 1917, 219.

40. The invitation appeared in the August 1 issue, which was printed and distributed two weeks before the official date of publication.

41. Minutes of the meeting in *Pelto ja Koti*, 1917, 304–6. Also interview with Walter H. Salmi, August 20, 1961.

42. *The Central Cooperative Wholesale Story*, 4.

43. In this connection it is interesting to note that in Finland, the original home of cooperatives, centralization developed until in 1952, for example, there were on the average 1,800 members and 14 outlets for every cooperative store. In Sweden in the same year, corresponding figures were 1,400 members and 12 outlets for every cooperative. *TOL*, February 12, 1952.

44. The statistics have been taken from *Tili ja Liikekertomus Tilivuodelta 1919*, prepared by the manager of the CCW.

45. About the early days of the Marquette Workers Co-op. Society.

46. *Pelto ja Koti*, 1917, 164.

47. Undated newspaper clipping.

48. A radio talk about cooperatives by Victor Peltonen over WIKB, Iron River, on March 3, 1960.

49. *Pelto ja Koti*, 1918, 90, 340. Also Peltonen's radio talk. Also letter from Edith Aspholm, December 2, 1961.

50. Reminiscences of Charles T. Dantes in the FAHA, about the early days in Herman.

51. For example, the Herman news published in the *Pelto ja Koti*, 1920.

52. *Pelto ja Koti*, 1917, 148; 1920, 91.

53. Alanne, *Rockin Osuuskunta 25-Vuotias*, 26.

54. *Pelto ja Koti*, 1918, 317.

55. *Keskusosuuskunnan Vuosikirja 1926*.

56. Information provided by William Kallio, January 1, 1961. Also V. Mackey, "Ääriviivoja Wattonin Osuuskaupan 25 v:n Taipaleelta," *TOL*, August 7, 1951.

57. Information provided by Walter H. Salmi.

58. Alanne, *Rockin Osuuskunta 25-Vuotias*, 59. See also *Who's Who of Finnish Extraction in America*, 133. Rivers moved to Maynard, Mass., in 1932 to become general manager of the United Coop. Society. Under his managership the Maynard cooperative became a million-dollar business. Sales in 1959 were $1,780,000.

59. *Pelto ja Koti*, 1918, 427f.

60. *The Cooperative Pyramid Builder*, July 1926, 22.

61. Later he was also elected to the board of the Cooperative League of America.

62. The figures are from closed accounts in the care of Walter H. Salmi and from annual reports of the CCW.

63. Taisto Hayrinen, *He Kohtasivat Bruce Crossingissa*, 9.

64. *Pelto ja Koti*, 1920, 95.

65. Hayrinen, *Ha Kohtasivat Bruce Crossingissa*, 10.

66. Annual report of CCW for 1930, 78.

67. *Pelto ja Koti*, 1918, 236f.

68. Statistics from annual report of CCW for 1930.

69. Table based on statement on pages 52–57 of annual report of CCW for 1930.

70. *Tili-ja Liikekertomas Vuodelta 1919*, 9.

71. Minutes of meetings of the SSO (Finnish Socialist Organization). William Marttila presents a collection of resolutions of the cooperative movement in his *Osuustoiminta ja Sen Merkitys Luokkataistelussa* (Superior, 1930), 34–38.

72. There is a photographic reproduction of the last part of each of these letters in *Keskusosuuskunnan Tiedonantaja* of December 31, 1929. The first letter is signed by Max Bedacht, Wm. Z. Foster, and H. Puro. These letters appear in their entirety in the annual report of the CCW for 1930, pages 11 and 13, and in William Marttila's *Osuustoiminta ja Sen Merkitys Luokkataistelussa*, 88–91.

73. *TOL*, April 22, 1930, 8.

74. Manner traveled under an assumed name and stayed at hotels awaiting developments. Other persons have been suggested as having been the representative, but those who have followed the situation closely are sure that the representative of the Comintern was Manner. Kullervo Manner was the speaker of the Finnish Diet in 1917, and fled to Russia after the Finnish War for Independence.

75. The description of the meeting is based on the minutes which appear in the annual report of the CCW for 1930, pages 6–20. See also report in *TOL* and *Työmies*. See also George Halonen, *Tsistelu Osuustoimintarintamalla;* William Marttila, *Osuustoiminta ja Sen Merkitys Luokkataistelussa;* and E. Sulkanen, *Amerikan Suomalaisen Työväenliikkeen Historia*, 296–304.

76. Halonen, *Taistela Osuustoimintarintamalla*, 71f.

77. V. Mackey, *Ääriviivoja Wattonin Osuuskaupan 25 v:n Taipaleelta*. See also *TOL*, August 7, 1951.

78. Alanne, *Rockin Osuuskunta 25-Vuotias*, 56.

79. Annual report of the CCW for 1931, 8f.

80. Alanne, *Rockin Osuuskunta*, 55.

81. Minutes of the meeting in the annual report of the CCW for 1931, 5–18.

82. Minutes of the meeting, annual report for 1932, 5–15.

83. Minutes of the meeting, annual report for 1933, 14.

84. *CCW Year Book 1934*, 11f.

85. *CCW Year Book 1935*, 11. Also *Työmies*, February 16, 1935.

86. *CCW Year Book 1936*, 8.

87. In Finland the socialist cooperative people had separated from the rest and established an organization based on their own principles, the Kulutusosuuskuntien Keskusliitto (K.K.) already in 1916, and in the following year they established a business organization called the Osuustukkukauppa (O.T.K.)

88. Walter H. Salmi's notes.

89. Erick Kendal, "Nykyaikainen Osuusmeijeri Ylä-Michiganin Kuparialueella," *TOL*, April 20, 1954.

90. In this report on developments in the cooperative movement after 1935 and about its union with Midland, the annual reports of the CCW, reports in *TOL*, and the last part of Erick Kendal's manuscript "Michiganin Suomalaiset Keskusosuuskuntaa Perustamassa," which is in the FAHA, have been used as source material.

Chapter 15

1. Georges J. Joyaux, "The French Press in Michigan," *Michigan History*, 153, 155–65.

2. This date is given in secondary sources forty years later. Since the sixth number, a copy of which is in the FAHA, came out on June 2, the first number must have come out at the end of April, or the paper was published at irregular intervals.

3. This gravestone is now in the FAHA. Muikku's remains were taken from the old cemetery in Hancock to Lake View Cemetery in 1915. There, a new, larger gravestone was set up the following year. See J. A. Karkkainen, "Amerikan Ensimmäisen Suomalaisen Sanomalehtimiehen Muiston Kunnioittaminen," *Suomi-Opiston Joululehti*, 1916, 27f. See also Juuso Hirvonen, *Michiganin Kuparialue ja Suomalaiset Siirtolaiset*, 68–73. See also Ilmonen, *Amerikan Suomalaisten Sivistyshistoria*, 1:21f. See also "Amerikan Ensimmäinen Suomalainen Sanomalehti," *Suomi Opiston Joululehti*," 1954, 21–23.

4. Information received from Matti Fredd's son Victor Fredd. Victor Fredd has presented the FAHA with an almost complete collection of the papers published by his father. The altar painting mentioned is also in the Archives. See *Kansan Kuvalehti*, 1903, 61. See also Rolf Winter, "Amerikan Suomalainen Lehti ja Sen Seuraajia," *Amerikan Suometar*, November 1954.

5. Hirvonen, *Michiganin Kuparialue ja Suomalaiset Siirtolaiset*, 86–88. See also Fabian Tolonen, *Muutamia Historiatietoja Amerikan Suomalaisista Sanomalehdistä: Amerikan Suometar 1899–1919* (Hancock, 1919), 80–83. See also *PS*, November 20 and 27 and December 4, 1902; *Kansan Kuvalehti*, December 1902, and *KK*, 1904, 215–17.

6. Alvah L. Sawyer, *A History of the Northern Peninsula of Michigan* (Chicago, 1911), 1:487.

7. Information about the history of the *Suometar* is contradictory. See Hirvonen, *Michiganin Kuparialue ja Suomalaiset Siirtolaiset*, 88; Ilmonen, *Amerikan Suomalaisten Sivistyshistoria*, 19; and Tolonen, *Muutamia Historiatie-*

toja Amerikan Suomalaisista Sanomalehdistä, 85. The above explanation is based mostly on John I. Kolehmainen's studies. The Finnish American press would be worthy of an intensive critical study which could be done in the National Library of Finland and in the Finnish American Historical Archives, where sources are available.

8. Erland V. Lansdale, "Muistelmia Päivälehden Alkuajoilta," *SK*, 1950, 163–69. To keep the record straight it is well to mention a paper titled *Wainola* which K. Korte attempted to publish in the Red Jacket area of Calumet in 1892.

9. Yrjo Sjoblom, "Valvojan Toimittajana 43 Vuotta Sitten," *Michiganin Suomalainen*, 1962, 3–6.

10. Jukka Salminen, "Ristikkojen Takana," *Vappu*, 1914, 167–76.

11. *Vappu*, 1960, 19.

12. *Pohjantähti* of Ishpeming is not mentioned by Hirvonen, Tolonen, or Kolehmainen. The FAHA has only no. 40, dated June 25.

13. For the relationship between Karinen and the SKRV see last paragraph of section on SKRV in chapter about temperance societies in this work.

14. On page 25 of *New York Mills, 75 Years of Progress* (New York Mills, 1960), there are some peculiar biographical details about Lähde.

15. Kolehmainen, *Sow the Golden Seed* (Fitchburg, 1955), 86f.

16. Tolonen, *Muutamia Historiatietoja Amerikan Suomalaisista Sanomalehdistä*, 86f.

17. The last number in the FAHA is dated December 19, 1940.

18. Letter from Kuusisto dated February 12, 1960. There is a complete collection of *Detroitin Uutisia* in the FAHA. Almost all the Finnish newspapers published in Michigan are listed in John I. Kolehmainen's "Finnish Newspapers and Periodicals in Michigan," *Michigan History*, 1940, 119–27; and idem, *The Finns in America: A Bibliographical Guide to Their History*.

19. *Kansanwalistus-Seuran Kalenteri*, 1894, 166.

20. Oskari Tokoi, *Sisu*, 233.

21. *Uskonpuhdistus Muisto*, 130, 10f.

22. Reino Suojanen's notes.

23. Edith Aspholm's extensive history in the FAHA.

24. Armas K. E. Holmio, *Radiosaarnoja Suomeen Sotavuosina 1941–1942* (Hancock, 1946).

25. Helen M. Keskitalo's story about the beginnings of the Suomi Kutsuu (Finland Calling) program, which is in the FAHA.

26. Interview with Walter H. Salmi in September of 1963. Salmi was an agent for the business. See Wasastjerna, *Minnesota Suomalaisten Historia*, 267. See also Sulkanen, *Amerikan Suomalaisen Työväenliikkeen Historia*, 338. The FAHA has a large collection of materials published by Leikas.

27. See the discussion about the National Church in this work. Otto Massinen died in Cleveland on November 16, 1928.

28. William Maki edited and published the *Amerikan Suomalaisten*

Osoitekalenteri Vuodelle 1903, which is an important source for the study of the history of the Finns in the Upper Peninsula of Michigan.

29. Lack of space has made it impossible to collect more recent materials of this kind.

30. It is unfortunate that a complete library belonging to a temperance society or labor organization has not been preserved.

31. Kuusi (A. A. Granfelt), "Kansanwalistus-Seura Amerikassa," *KVK*, 1904, 175–79. See also *Kansanwalistus-Seuran Wuosikertomus*, 1903, 37f. See also Ilmonen, *Amerikan Suomalaisten Sivistyshistoria*, 28f. See also *Kansan Kuvalehti*, 1903, 37f. See also Juuso Hirvonen, *Michiganin Kuparialue ja Suomalaiset Siirtolaiset*, 91–96, and letter dated August 8, 1960, from Kosti Huuhka, director of the Kansanvalistusseura. It may be well to mention here that in New York Mills, Minnesota, the Amerikan Suomalainen Kansanvalistusseura (Finnish American Enlightenment Society) was established in 1887, but it was completely independent of Suomen Kansanvalistusseura. It published a few calendars and other items but expired within a few years.

32. *Calumetin Suomalaisen Nais-Yhdistyksen Kalenteri 1896.*

33. Hirvonen gives 1895 as the date, and Kolehmainen gives 1897. The volume for 1909 in the FAHA is labeled volume 10. Accordingly, the first year of publication must have been 1900, unless there was a temporary cessation of publication. In 1898 an attempt was made in San Francisco to publish a women's paper called *Amerikan Suometar*. *Naisten Viiri* of New York and Superior was published by the labor movement from 1936 to 1978; *Toveritar* appeared in Astoria from 1911 to 1930, and *Työläisnainen* in Superior from 1930 to 1936.

34. *Calumetin Suomalaisen Nais-Yhdistyksen Kalenteri 1896.*

35. *PS*, 1897, 189.

36. *Naisyhdistys Pyrkijän 60 Vuosijuhla 1935*. See also *The Finnish-American Blue-White Book 1966.*

37. Ilmonen, *Amerikan Suomalaisten Sivistyshistoria*, 25f. See also Saarnivaara, *Amerikan Laestadiolaisuuden Historia*, 41f.

38. *Mikä on The Finnish Literary Institute*, Ispeming, 1910. Professor J. J. Mikkola of Helsinki is listed among the 11 members of the teaching staff.

39. J. L. Ollila, "Hajanaisia Piirteitä Voimistelu-ja Urheiluharrastuksista Amerikan Suomalaisten Keskuudessa," *Liikemiesten ja Laulajain Suomi-Matka 1921*, 130--37. Also interview with Karl Wirtanen.

40. *Nuori Suomi*, 4:180.

41. Hancock, 1904.

42. Minutes in the FAHA.

43. *Suomi-Synod Yearbook*, 1945, 21, and 1962, 60f.

44. Rautanen was born in Helsinki on May 24, 1882, and died in Cleveland, Ohio, on March 13, 1960. Over a period of decades he wrote innumerable timely newspaper articles which he signed V. R.

45. Ilmonen was born in Ilmajoki on February 14, 1871, and died in Fort Bragg, California, on March 7, 1940.

46. It is a well-known fact that Finnish Americans in general are uncommunicative about their affairs.

47. From notes about the meetings of the society in the FAHA. See also Hjalmar Makila, "Finnish Archives of Hiawathaland," *RK*, 1950, 70f., and Henry Ollila, "Hiawatha-Alueen Suomalainen Historiaseura," *Michiganin Suomalainen*, 1961, 12.

48. *Vaasan Jaakkoo Rapakon Takana 1947–1948*, 263f. Jaakko Oskari Ikola, editor-in-chief of *Vaasa* from 1924 and member of the Finnish Diet from 1927 to 1930, was born in 1887 and died in 1960.

49. *Suomi-Opiston Luettelo Lukuvuonna 1897–1898*, 15.

50. *PS*, 1896, 277, 289–91.

51. *PS*, 1899, 186f.

52. Blomberg was not "a former missionary to seamen" as *Suomi-Opiston Albumi 1896–1906*, 78, states; he went to Brooklyn as a pastor to seamen after he refused the call to Hancock. He served Finnish congregations in Brooklyn, New York, and Jersey City from 1903 to 1906.

53. On page 17 of the *Fiftieth Anniversary Publication of Suomi College and Theological Seminary 1896–1946*, there is a statement to the effect that Vihtori Koivumaki and Jacob Mantta were also ordained at this time. Mantta was ordained in 1908 and Koivumaki in 1909.

54. In the Finnish school system, six years of secondary school corresponds to the American high school, and an "ylioppilas," or undergraduate, is comparable to a student who has completed a two-year junior college course in America.

55. In the 1965–66 school year, 63 percent of the students were from Michigan and 37 percent from other states.

56. *Suomi-Raamattukoulu: Kertomus Lukuvuosilta 1927–1930.* Antti Lepisto died in Duluth on March 2, 1954.

57. Carl Johannes Tamminen was born in Piikkiö in 1900, completed his studies for the ministry in the Suomi Seminary in 1927, and died November 7, 1958. Bernard Hugo Paul Hillila was born in Gwinn, Michigan, in 1919, completed his studies for the ministry at the Suomi Seminary in 1941, received the master's degree from Western Reserve University in 1945 and his doctorate in education from Columbia University in 1955. He taught at Valparaiso University from 1968–84. Edward John Isaac was born in Boston, Massachusetts, on October 7, 1896, received his A. B. degree from Tufts College in 1919, and graduated from the Philadelphia Lutheran Theological Seminary in 1921. He died on July 28, 1954. David Taito Halkola was born in Seattle in 1923 and received his master's degree from Western Reserve University in 1947.

58. Minutes of the Consistory, December 10, 1959.

59. Annual reports of Suomi College and Theological Seminary for the years from 1902 to 1964. See also annual reports of the president of the Suomi Synod from 1894 to 1962 and the Suomi-Opiston Jahlajulkaisut, 1894–1962.

Chapter 16

1. For example, Amandus Johnson, *Swedish Settlements on the Delaware, 1638–1664* (1911; Baltimore, 1969). See also Carl J. Silfversten, *Finlandssvenskarna in Amerika* (Duluth, 1931).

2. L. A. Puntila, *Ruotsalaisuus Suomessa*, 14.

3. Ibid., 77–83.

4. KVTK, 1919, 47.

5. Silfversten, *Finlandssvenskarna in Amerika*, 96.

6. Ibid. See also *Hälsning från Amerika* (Brooklyn, n.d.), 97–138.

7. Silfversten, *Finlandssvenskarna in Amerika*, 300ff.

8. Ibid., 303ff.

9. RL, April and May 1898.

10. Annual reports of the president of the SKRV, in FAHA.

11. *Minnesskrift 1902–1917. Svensk-Finska Nykters-förbundet av Amerika* (Chicago, 1917). See also *Svensk-Finska Nykterhets-Förbundet af Amerika i Ord och Bild*, 1908 (Chicago, 1908).

Chapter 17

1. *Katselin Amerikkaa* (Helsinki, 1946).

2. Kaarle Aukusti Järvi, "Siirtolaisten Lähtö," *KVK*, 1895, 91–99, gives an apt description of the feelings of emigrants on the ship *Norra Finland* when it left for England from the outer harbor of Oulu.

3. Juhani Paasivirta, a university man from Helsinki who visited America, saw in just this isolation an explanation for the extremist ideas which controlled large numbers of political and religious thinkers who were basically dissatisfied Finnish Americans.

4. Charles Raatikainen, for Arthur Uusitalo's birthday, in Crystal Falls.

5. *Veräjillä Vierahilla* (Hancock, 1901), 70–72.

6. Anni M. Pennanen, *Airut*, 1917, 17.

7. *Amerikan Suometar* (hereafter cited as *AS*), June 15, 1899. See also Ilmonen, *Amerikan Suomalaisten Sivistyshistoria*, 1:89f.

8. *KVK*, 1904, 206.

9. Edvard Johannes Antell was born in Viipuri in 1852, completed his studies in law at the University of Helsinki, died in Brooklyn in 1926. He was editor of *Finska Amerikanaren* from 1897 to 1924. His father, Samuel Henrik Antell, was governor of Viipuri, Finland and later became a senator.

10. Nuormaa was a newspaperman, writer, and poet, who in his youth had been interested in studying the Finno-Ugric languages. In his political activities he was strictly anti-Russian.

11. Victor H. Heini was born in Askainen in 1862. In Brooklyn he owned a carpentry business and often held positions of trust in his church.

12. Brofelt was also a newspaperman exiled from Finland.

13. See chapter 3.
14. Ilmonen, *Amerikan Suomalaisten Sivistyshistoria*, 93.
15. Later he was known as Reijo Waara.
16. *PS*, May 10, 1900.
17. See chapter 15. See also *PS*, November 20, 1902. It includes Hjelt's travel sketch, reprinted from *Teologinen Aikakauskirja*, 1902, 338ff.
18. Hancock, 1907. Second printing, Ishpeming, 1909 and third printing, Ishpeming, 1917. The book eventually became the official songbook of temperance societies.
19. *Amerikan Mailta* (Helsinki, 1907). See also *Muistelmia siirtolaistemme vaelluksista ja elämästä* (Helsinki, 1937).
20. *AS*, December 18, 1912. Of Aino Malmberg's works we shall mention only *Maailmaa kierrellessä* (Helsinki, 1922) and *Suomi Austraaliassa* (Helsinki, 1929). See also *Kansallinen Elämäkerrasto.*
21. *Nuorten parissa Uudessa Maailmassa* (Helsinki, 1914).
22. From concert programs and newspaper clippings in the FAHA.
23. Lauri Perälä, *64 päivää siirtokansan keskuudessa* (Vaasa, 1921).
24. *Report of Bishop J. R. Koskimies to the Ninth General Church Convention on His Visit to Finnish American Congregations as a Representative of the Church of Finland* (Turku, 1923). See also Juho Rud. Koskimies, *Amerikan matkalta* (Porvoo, 1925). As an appendix to the book there is a list of pastors of the Church of Finland who have served in America.
25. Hancock, 1921.
26. *Helsingistä Astoriaan* (Porvoo, 1927).
27. *Kotikansaa* (Porvoo, 1926).
28. *Kolmekymmentätuhatta kilometriä Amerikassa* (Turku, 1928).
29. *Valtamerten takana* I and II (Helsinki, 1926).
30. Helsinki, 1944.
31. Varmavuori died in the year of the Helsinki University Chorus tour to America, on May 18, 1938.
32. *YL Amerikassa* (Helsinki, 1939). See also *American Tour of the Helsinki University Chorus* (Helsinki, 1937).
33. E. A. Pulli, *Pilvenpiirtäjäin varjossa* (Helsinki, 1938).
34. The minutes of the Delaware Committee of Negaunee and surrounding areas, as well as their correspondence and financial records, are in the FAHA. See also the small publication put out by the same committee and titled *Delaware Tercentenary*, and letter from Wargelin to August Raatikainen.
35. Artturi Leinonen, *Atlanttia ja Amerikkaa katselemassa* (Porvoo, 1938).
36. *Kävin tähtilipun maaassa* (Helsinki, 1946).
37. Gustaf Wilson, former name Hemmi, was born in Oulu on June 2, 1827. He left his vocation of seaman and went to the California gold fields in 1850. After serving in the United States Army and taking part in Indian wars he settled in Portland as a merchant. He was made a Russian honorary vice consul in 1883, remaining in this office until his death on September 21, 1905.

38. From the very beginning Saastamoinen participated in the independence movement and in the war for independence. He died while serving as the Finnish minister to London in 1932.

39. *SK*, 1920, 88–91.

40. Järnefelt-Rauanheimo, *Meikäläisiä merten takana*, 64.

41. The earlier statement in this work to the effect that Holm moved to California in 1931 is based on Ilmonen's notes and is apparently erroneous. According to the Finnish Ministry of Foreign Affairs' roster of consuls the move was made in 1933.

42. According to Werner Nikander's *Amerikan suomalaisia*, Jacob Uitti was born in 1876.

43. According to information from Finland's Ministry of Foreign Affairs about consular representation in Michigan. See also *Foreign Consular Offices in the United States*, 1943 and 1959, Department of State Publications 4979 and 6813.

44. *The Development of Finnish-Soviet Relations During the Autumn of 1939 in the Light of Official Documents* (Helsinki: Ministry for Foreign Affairs of Finland, 1940).

45. Account books and correspondence in the FAHA. The minutes about relief activity during the Winter War have not been saved in all communities. During the Continuation War activity was more regular.

46. Eino Sormunen, bishop of Kuopio, who was himself a child of the border region, made this statement to the Duke of Södermanland, who was the director of Swedish relief to Finland.

47. A Finnish translation of this speech was published in *Työssä Suomen Hyväksi. Muisto-albumi Suomen Avustustoiminnasta Uuden Englannin Valtioissa 1939–1941* (Fitchburg, 1941).

48. Robert Sobel, *The Origins of Interventionism: The United States and the Russo-Finnish War* (New York, 1960).

49. *Suomen Huollon Työ: Kertomus Toiminnasta 15 Päivään Toukokuuta 1941* (Helsinki, 1941).

50. *Kalevan Naisten Historian Ääriviivoja*, 134f.

51. The minutes of the Finnish Relief organizations and committees of Hancock, Crystal Falls, Toivola, and Wakefield, and other places are in the FAHA, contained in fourteen cartons.

52. The *Pro Memoria* was published in its entirety in the *Daily Mining Gazette* of April 12.

53. R. J. Jalkanen, "Näkemyksiä Suomi-Opiston Kuoron Suomi-Retkueelta," *KK*, 1964, 39–49.

54. See *The Architectural Forum*, February 1923, 41–44; *The Architectural Record*, February 1923, 151–57; and *The Western Architect*, January 1923, 7f.

55. *The Architectural Record*, February 1923, 157.

56. Kyösti Ålander, "Eliel Saarinen," *KVK*, 1951, 187–89. See also *Kansallinen Elämäkerrasto*, 5:2–4; Urho Toivola, *Aurinkoista Amerikkaa* (Porvoo, 1932), 145–48.

57. *New York Herald Tribune*, September 2, 1961. See also the *Detroit News*, September 2, 1961. The *Detroit Free Press* of March 16, 1959, gives an amusing account of the telephone call by which the prize-awarding board announced the winner. The elder Mrs. Saarinen took the call and invited the younger Saarinens to a champagne celebration of her husband's victory. The telegram which arrived the next morning made it clear that the winner was the younger Mr. Saarinen, whereupon a second celebration became necessary.

58. Aline Saarinen is a graduate of Vassar and was on the staff of the *New York Times* as an art critic.

Chapter 18

1. Similar "islets of information" about Finnish immigrants in America, from which the researcher can learn much, exist also in Massachusetts, Maine, Ohio, and northern Minnesota.

2. The reason for this omission was the difficulty in finding information as well as the fact that as far as these seven countries are concerned, there would have been a small increase only in the number of south Ostrobothnians in Iron County.

3. See Anna-Leena Toivonen, *Etelä-Pohjanmaan Valtamerentakainen Siirtolaisuus*, table 1 at end of book.

4. Pekka Savolainen and Erkki Kokkonen's study titled "Siirtolaisuus Lapin Alueelta, vv. 1808–1930 Seurakuntien Kirkonkirjojen Mukaan" in *Historiallinen Arkisto*, 1959, 596–621, Helsinki, 1964, describes in an interesting way the problems experienced in studying emigration from Lapland.

Index

Titles in the Great Lakes Books Series

Freshwater Fury: Yarns and Reminiscences of the Greatest Storm in Inland Navigation, by Frank Barcus, 1986 (reprint)

Call It North Country: The Story of Upper Michigan, by John Bartlow Martin, 1986 (reprint)

The Land of the Crooked Tree, by U. P. Hedrick, 1986 (reprint)

Michigan Place Names, by Walter Romig, 1986 (reprint)

Luke Karamazov, by Conrad Hilberry, 1987

The Late, Great Lakes: An Environmental History, by William Ashworth, 1987 (reprint)

Great Pages of Michigan History from the Detroit Free Press, 1987

Waiting for the Morning Train: An American Boyhood, by Bruce Catton, 1987 (reprint)

Michigan Voices: Our State's History in the Words of the People Who Lived It, compiled and edited by Joe Grimm, 1987

Danny and the Boys, Being Some Legends of Hungry Hollow, by Robert Traver, 1987 (reprint)

Hanging On, or How to Get through a Depression and Enjoy Life, by Edmund G. Love, 1987 (reprint)

The Situation in Flushing, by Edmund G. Love, 1987 (reprint)

A Small Bequest, by Edmund G. Love, 1987 (reprint)

The Saginaw Paul Bunyan, by James Stevens, 1987 (reprint)

The Ambassador Bridge: A Monument to Progress, by Philip P. Mason, 1988

Let the Drum Beat: A History of the Detroit Light Guard, by Stanley D. Solvick, 1988

An Afternoon in Waterloo Park, by Gerald Dumas, 1988 (reprint)

Contemporary Michigan Poetry: Poems from the Third Coast, edited by Michael Delp, Conrad Hilberry, and Herbert Scott, 1988

Over the Graves of Horses, by Michael Delp, 1988

Wolf in Sheep's Clothing: The Search for a Child Killer, by Tommy McIntyre, 1988

Copper-Toed Boots, by Marguerite de Angeli, 1989 (reprint)

Detroit Images: Photographs of the Renaissance City, edited by John J. Bukowczyk and Douglas Aikenhead, with Peter Slavcheff, 1989

Hangdog Reef: Poems Sailing the Great Lakes, by Stephen Tudor, 1989

Detroit: City of Race and Class Violence, revised edition, by B. J. Widick, 1989

Deep Woods Frontier: A History of Logging in Northern Michigan, by Theodore J. Karamanski, 1989

Orvie, The Dictator of Dearborn, by David L. Good, 1989

Seasons of Grace: A History of the Catholic Archdiocese of Detroit, by Leslie Woodcock Tentler, 1990

The Pottery of John Foster: Form and Meaning, by Gordon and Elizabeth Orear, 1990

The Diary of Bishop Frederic Baraga: First Bishop of Marquette, Michigan, edited by Regis M. Walling and Rev. N. Daniel Rupp, 1990

Walnut Pickles and Watermelon Cake: A Century of Michigan Cooking, by Larry B. Massie and Priscilla Massie, 1990

The Making of Michigan, 1820–1860: A Pioneer Anthology, edited by Justin L. Kestenbaum, 1990

America's Favorite Homes: A Guide to Popular Early Twentieth-Century Homes, by Robert Schweitzer and Michael W. R. Davis, 1990

Beyond the Model T: The Other Ventures of Henry Ford, by Ford R. Bryan, 1990

Life after the Line, by Josie Kearns, 1990

Michigan Lumbertowns: Lumbermen and Laborers in Saginaw, Bay City, and Muskegon, 1870–1905, by Jeremy W. Kilar, 1990

Detroit Kids Catalog: The Hometown Tourist, by Ellyce Field, 1990

Waiting for the News, by Leo Litwak, 1990 (reprint)

Detroit Perspectives, edited by Wilma Wood Henrickson, 1991

Life on the Great Lakes: A Wheelsman's Story, by Fred W. Dutton, edited by William Donohue Ellis, 1991

Copper Country Journal: The Diary of Schoolmaster Henry Hobart, 1863–1864, by Henry Hobart, edited by Philip P. Mason, 1991

John Jacob Astor: Business and Finance in the Early Republic, by John Denis Haeger, 1991

Survival and Regeneration: Detroit's American Indian Community, by Edmund J. Danziger Jr., 1991

Steamboats and Sailors of the Great Lakes, by Mark L. Thompson, 1991

Cobb Would Have Caught It: The Golden Age of Baseball in Detroit, by Richard Bak, 1991

Michigan in Literature, by Clarence Andrews, 1992

Under the Influence of Water: Poems, Essays, and Stories, by Michael Delp, 1992

The Country Kitchen, by Della T. Lutes, 1992 (reprint)

The Making of a Mining District: Keweenaw Native Copper 1500–1870, by David J. Krause, 1992

Kids Catalog of Michigan Adventures, by Ellyce Field, 1993

Henry's Lieutenants, by Ford R. Bryan, 1993

Historic Highway Bridges of Michigan, by Charles K. Hyde, 1993

Lake Erie and Lake St. Clair Handbook, by Stanley J. Bolsenga and Charles E. Herndendorf, 1993

Queen of the Lakes, by Mark Thompson, 1994

Iron Fleet: The Great Lakes in World War II, by George J. Joachim, 1994

Turkey Stearnes and the Detroit Stars: The Negro Leagues in Detroit, 1919–1933, by Richard Bak, 1994

Pontiac and the Indian Uprising, by Howard H. Peckham, 1994 (reprint)

Charting the Inland Seas: A History of the U.S. Lake Survey, by Arthur M. Woodford, 1994 (reprint)

Ojibwa Narratives of Charles and Charlotte Kawbawgam and Jacques LePique, 1893–1895. Recorded with Notes by Homer H. Kidder, edited by Arthur P. Bourgeois, 1994, co-published with the Marquette County Historical Society

Strangers and Sojourners: A History of Michigan's Keweenaw Peninsula, by Arthur W. Thurner, 1994

Win Some, Lose Some: G. Mennen Williams and the New Democrats, by Helen Washburn Berthelot, 1995

Sarkis, by Gordon and Elizabeth Orear, 1995

The Northern Lights: Lighthouses of the Upper Great Lakes, by Charles K. Hyde, 1995 (reprint)

Kids Catalog of Michigan Adventures, second edition, by Ellyce Field, 1995

Rumrunning and the Roaring Twenties: Prohibition on the Michigan-Ontario Waterway, by Philip P. Mason, 1995

In the Wilderness with the Red Indians, by E. R. Baierlein, translated by Anita Z. Boldt, edited by Harold W. Moll, 1996

Elmwood Endures: History of a Detroit Cemetery, by Michael Franck, 1996

Master of Precision: Henry M. Leland, by Mrs. Wilfred C. Leland with Minnie Dubbs Millbrook, 1996 (reprint)

Haul-Out: New and Selected Poems, by Stephen Tudor, 1996

Kids Catalog of Michigan Adventures, third edition, by Ellyce Field, 1997

Beyond the Model T: The Other Ventures of Henry Ford, revised edition, by Ford R. Bryan, 1997

Young Henry Ford: A Picture History of the First Forty Years, by Sidney Olson, 1997 (reprint)

The Coast of Nowhere: Meditations on Rivers, Lakes and Streams, by Michael Delp, 1997

From Saginaw Valley to Tin Pan Alley: Saginaw's Contribution to American Popular Music, 1890–1955, by R. Grant Smith, 1998

The Long Winter Ends, by Newton G. Thomas, 1998 (reprint)

Bridging the River of Hatred: The Pioneering Efforts of Detroit Police Commissioner George Edwards, by Mary M. Stolberg, 1998

Toast of the Town: The Life and Times of Sunnie Wilson, by Sunnie Wilson with John Cohassey, 1998

These Men Have Seen Hard Service: The First Michigan Sharpshooters in the Civil War, by Raymond J. Herek, 1998

A Place for Summer: One Hundred Years at Michigan and Trumbull, by Richard Bak, 1998

Early Midwestern Travel Narratives: An Annotated Bibliography, 1634–1850, by Robert R. Hubach, 1998 (reprint)

All-American Anarchist: Joseph A. Labadie and the Labor Movement, by Carlotta R. Anderson, 1998

Michigan in the Novel, 1816–1996: An Annotated Bibliography, by Robert Beasecker, 1998

"Time by Moments Steals Away": The 1848 Journal of Ruth Douglass, by Robert L. Root Jr., 1998

The Detroit Tigers: A Pictorial Celebration of the Greatest Players and Moments in Tigers' History, updated edition, by William M. Anderson, 1999

Father Abraham's Children: Michigan Episodes in the Civil War, by Frank B. Woodford, 1999 (reprint)

Letter from Washington, 1863–1865, by Lois Bryan Adams, edited and with an introduction by Evelyn Leasher, 1999

Wonderful Power: The Story of Ancient Copper Working in the Lake Superior Basin, by Susan R. Martin, 1999

A Sailor's Logbook: A Season aboard Great Lakes Freighters, by Mark L. Thompson, 1999

Huron: The Seasons of a Great Lake, by Napier Shelton, 1999

Tin Stackers: The History of the Pittsburgh Steamship Company, by Al Miller, 1999

Art in Detroit Public Places, revised edition, text by Dennis Nawrocki, photographs by David Clements, 1999

Brewed in Detroit: Breweries and Beers Since 1830, by Peter H. Blum, 1999

Detroit Kids Catalog: A Family Guide for the 21st Century, by Ellyce Field, 2000

"Expanding the Frontiers of Civil Rights": Michigan, 1948–1968, by Sidney Fine, 2000

Graveyard of the Lakes, by Mark L. Thompson, 2000

Enterprising Images: The Goodridge Brothers, African American Photographers, 1847–1922, by John Vincent Jezierski, 2000

New Poems from the Third Coast: Contemporary Michigan Poetry, edited by Michael Delp, Conrad Hilberry, and Josie Kearns, 2000

Arab Detroit: From Margin to Mainstream, edited by Nabeel Abraham and Andrew Shryock, 2000

The Sandstone Architecture of the Lake Superior Region, by Kathryn Bishop Eckert, 2000

Looking Beyond Race: The Life of Otis Milton Smith, by Otis Milton Smith and Mary M. Stolberg, 2000

Mail by the Pail, by Colin Bergel, illustrated by Mark Koenig, 2000

Great Lakes Journey: A New Look at America's Freshwater Coast, by William Ashworth, 2000

A Life in the Balance: The Memoirs of Stanley J. Winkelman, by Stanley J. Winkelman, 2000

Schooner Passage: Sailing Ships and the Lake Michigan Frontier, by Theodore J. Karamanski, 2000

The Outdoor Museum: The Magic of Michigan's Marshall M. Fredericks, by Marcy Heller Fisher, illustrated by Christine Collins Woomer, 2001

Detroit In Its World Setting: A Three Hundred Year Chronology, 1701–2001, edited by David Lee Poremba, 2001

Frontier Metropolis: Picturing Early Detroit, 1701–1838, by Brian Leigh Dunnigan, 2001

Michigan Remembered: Photographs from the Farm Security Administration and the Office of War Information, 1936–1943, edited by Constance B. Schulz, with Introductory Essays by Constance B. Schulz and William H. Mulligan, Jr., 2001

This is Detroit, 1701–2001, by Arthur M. Woodford, 2001

History of the Finns in Michigan, by Armas K. E. Holmio, translated by Ellen M. Ryynanen, 2001